Valor across the Lone Star

VALOR ACROSS THE LONE STAR

The Congressional Medal of Honor in Frontier Texas

—✦—

BY CHARLES M. NEAL JR.

Texas State Historical Association
Austin

Library of Congress Cataloging-in-Publication Data
Neal, Charles M.
    Valor across the Lone Star : the Congressional Medal of Honor in frontier Texas / by Charles M. Neal Jr.
        p. cm.
    Includes bibliographical references and index.
    ISBN 0-87611-184-3 (hardcover : alk. paper)
    1. Medal of Honor—Biography. 2. Texas—History, Military—19th century. 3. Texas—Biography. I. Title.
        UB433 .N43 2002
        355.1'342—dc21

                                                                        2002009714
5   4   3   2   1   02   03   04   05   06

    Published by the Texas State Historical Association in cooperation with the Center for Studies in Texas History at the University of Texas at Austin. Publication of this book is partially supported by a grant from the Summerfield G. Roberts Foundation, Dallas.

    ∞ The paper used in this book meets the minimum requirements of the American National Standard for Permanence of Paper for Printed Library Materials, z39.48—1984.

    Book design by Holly Zumwalt Taylor. Dustjacket design by David Timmons.

Frontispiece: Cpl. John W. Comfort, 1875. One of Mackenzie's enlisted scouts, Comfort was a Civil War combat veteran with the Twenty-ninth Pennsylvania Infantry, surviving the vicious hand-to-hand struggles at Chancellorsville, Gettysburg, Chickamauga, and Lookout Mountain at Chattanooga. After the Civil War he served in the First U.S. Artillery before enlisting in the Fourth U.S. Cavalry. On November 5, 1874, several miles southeast of Laguna Tahoka, he was specially cited for gallantry "in running down and killing an Indian at a long distance from his command," for which he was awarded the Medal of Honor. At the Battle of Wounded Knee on December 29, 1890, he was recommended for a second Medal of Honor, but it was denied. *Photograph courtesy the National Archives.*

Dedication

This book is especially dedicated to Sgt. Charles M. Neal Sr., my late father and formerly of the First U.S. Cavalry; and to my mother, Ophelia R. Neal. Without their constant encouragement this book would never have been possible.

To Wilbur George Allen, who just prior to his passing made me promise to "see this thing through," and to Frances Allen and my beloved wife, Judy, the original "Old Army Widows." To my lovely daughters, Karen and Terri, and to my colleagues at Aldine Junior High, and coworkers at Continental Airlines, who all with patience and understanding tolerated my preoccupation with the past and . . .

To the sixty-seven interesting and unusual men about whom this book is written, whose lives became such a big part of mine for almost thirty years.

Table of Contents

—— ✦ ——

Acknowledgments

I n this twenty-five-year quest, many people along the way have given of
themselves to help make this dream come true. Some went above and
beyond the call of duty, especially my right and left arms, Wilbur George
Allen and Raymond Collins. My compatriots with the Medal of Honor Historical
Society, especially Rudy Friedrich, John Lelle, James Kenney, Charles
Chambers, Ed Murphy, and Ben Cranefield Jr., who often took to the streets and
boonies to search out my various leads. Lt. Col. David Perrine, who tracked
down the two granddaughters of Peter Roth in a small Bavarian village in
Germany; John M. Carroll, who like myself felt very strongly that these men
were due their just recognition; and James D. Walker, who recognized the sheer
frustration and perplexity on my face among the narrow aisles of the National
Archives and quickly pointed me to that little blue book on the Medal of Honor
that exposed all of the file numbers. This, more than anything else, spawned the
accumulation of information. Elmer O. Parker and Elaine Everly of the Old
Military Records Section of the National Archives kept the information flowing
over the years with their lengthy correspondence, which most surely taxed their
valuable time. The assistance of Jack Loftin, the best little ol' local historian in
Texas, on battle sites was immeasurable. There were most certainly others and
their contributions have not gone unnoticed. They are listed below in alphabetical order. If I neglected to mention anyone due a degree of credit, it was not
intentional, but due to a declining memory on my part.

Dr. Manuel Alcala of the Mexican National Archives; D. C. Allard, U.S. Navy
Historical Center; Arizona Department of Health Services, Office of Vital Records;
Lt. Col. Lillian E. Baker, Fort Sam Houston Information Office; Bernard A. Bernier
Jr., Library of Congress; Marie B. Berry, San Antonio Public Library; Martha B.
Blaine, Oklahoma Historical Society; Kathleen Bonds, clerk of Napa County,
California; Roger D. Bridges, Illinois State Historical Library; Marie T. Capps, U.S.
Military Academy Library; Carol J. Carefoot, Texas State Archives; George S.

Acknowledgments

Chalou, National Archives; Fred G. Clark, U.S. Bureau of Customs; J. J. Cox, U.S. Veteran's Administration; Richard J. Cox, Maryland Historical Society; William R. Creech, National Archives; David Crossman, University of Wyoming; Dwight A. Curtiss, U.S. Soldier's Home; John D. Cushing, Massachusetts Historical Society; Virginia Daiker, Library of Congress; Sam Daniel, Library of Congress; Eugene D. Decker, Kansas Historical Society; Donald L. De Witt, Arizona Historical Society; John A. Dwyer, National Archives; Mark Eckhoff, National Archives; Peter A. Evans, California Historical Society; Sara Erwin, Gilcrease Institute; Robert E. Feeney, Massachusetts Adjutant General's Office; William Felker, The Free Library of Philadelphia; Miss Y. T. Feng, Boston Public Library; Dale E. Floyd, National Archives; Alys H. Freeze, Denver Public Library; Lea La Friniere, Missoula, Montana; Jan Gattis, University of Oklahoma Library; Anthony G. Girolanis, Cook County, Illinois Clerk's Office; Emma Goldman, Brackettville, Texas; Mrs. Noel V. Gordon, Detroit Public Library; David B. Gracy, Texas State Archives; Rose K. Greenberg, National Archives; Gene M. Gressley, University of Wyoming; Gail R. Guidry, Missouri Historical Society; Paul Guzzi, Massachusetts Division of Vital Statistics; Mr. and Mrs. W. S. Halcomb of San Antonio, Texas; Gladys Hansen, San Francisco Public Library; Virginia R. Hawley, Western Reserve Historical Society; Paul T. Heffron, Library of Congress; Marian G. Holt, District of Columbia Public Library; Edgar M. Howell, Smithsonian Institution; Lynn M. Jimenez, Stanford University Library; Larry Jochims, Kansas State Historical Society; Marie E. Keene, Gilcrease Institute; John M. Kinney, Texas State Archives; Susan Kingery, Arizona Historical Society; Robert W. Karuskopf, National Archives; Claire R. Kuehn, Panhandle-Plains Historical Museum; Gary F. Kurutz, Huntington Library; Robert H. Land, Library of Congress; Carolyn B. LeaMond, Cincinnati Historical Society; R. D. Leandri, U.S. Veteran's Administration; William H. Lear, National Archives; Barbara Ledbetter, Fort Belknap Archives; Roland E. Lex, San Francisco National Cemetery; C. Lindner, Free Public Library of Philadelphia; Mary Leen, The Bostonian Society; Herbert Leventhal, U.S. Military Academy Archives; William G. Lewis, National Archives; William E. Lind, National Archives; Rella Looney, Oklahoma Historical Society; J. Ignacio R. Mane, Mexican National Archives; Gail Marciano, New York Historical Society; The Registry of Vital Records and Statistics of the Massachusetts Department of Public Health; Agnes MacDonald of Eugene, Oregon; Harriet McLoone, Huntington Library; Richard S. Maxwell, National Archives; Harriet C. Meloy, Helena, Montana; Gene Moore, San Francisco Public Library; Irean Moran, University of California–Berkeley Library; Gary L. Morgan, National Archives; Michael P. Musick, National Archives; R. Mersinger and Thelma Martin, National

Personnel Records Center–St. Louis; Rex E. Neal, Eugene, Oregon; Mark L. Nelson, Essex Institute; Timothy K. Nenninger, National Archives; S. P. Nesmith; Institute of Texan Cultures; New York Department of Health–Bureau of Vital Records; Arthur L. Loivas, Museum of New Mexico; Don Pace, Safford, Arizona; Patricia J. Palmer, Stanford University Library; Laura Peacock, Jacksboro, Texas; Helen S. Perry, Department of the Army–Cemetery Division; Gerry Phillips, National Archives; Mary S. Pratt, Los Angeles Public Library; Jean Preston, Henry E. Huntington Library; Kenneth W. Rapp, U.S. Military Academy Archives; Delia H. Richlen, *The Missoulian* newspaper; H. Saas, Buffalo and Erie County Historical Society; Amelia Sainz, clerk, Graham County Superior Court; Edward Salt, Valley Forge Freedom Foundation; Mary Sanders, Western Publications; Edward G. Sanford, Boston Public Library; Charles A. Shaugnessy, National Archives; Lt. Col. Claus R. Simpson; Alice L. Sharp, State Historical Society of Colorado; Frank H. Skelly, Columbia, Missouri; John J. Slonaker, U.S. Army Military History Research Center; Diane Spitler, Atlantic City Free Public Library; Richard J. Sommers, U.S. Army Military History Research Center; Bernice C. Sprenger, Detroit Public Library; Bruno Szymusiak, Springfield, Illinois; Texas Department of Health–Division of Vital Records; Sara Timby, Stanford University Library; Ida Chapman Toller, Seiling, Oklahoma; M. R. Topple, British Military Attaché's Office; Mrs. Jimmie A. Vonde, Mountainair, New Mexico; Ernest Wallace, Texas Tech University; Donald L. Wardle, U.S. Veteran's Administration; Laverne H. Watson, South Carolina Confederate Museum; Arthur Weaner, Adams County, Pennsylvania Historical Society; Carol Williams, Texas and Southwestern Cattle Raiser's Foundation; Jay Williar, California Historical Society; David R. Winkles, Oklahoma Historical Society; June Witt, University of Oklahoma; and George Younkin, Fort Worth Federal Records Center.

A great amount of gratitude goes to Lucinda Post, Barbara Adams, Diane Day, Ann Stewart, and Darsie Gillum, who over the past decade so competently edited and typed my crudely typed pages. My final debt of gratitude goes to Holly Z. Taylor, associate editor of the Texas State Historical Association, who so astutely honed this work into its final form.

CHARLES M. NEAL JR.   *Porter, Texas*
February 2002

Valor across the Lone Star

Foreword

The Medal of Honor is the highest award for valor in action against an enemy force that can be bestowed upon an individual serving in the armed services of the United States. As a general rule, the Medal of Honor is awarded for a deed of personal bravery or self-sacrifice above and beyond the call of duty by a member of the armed forces of the United States in action against an enemy of the United States. Often presented by the president of the United States in the name of Congress, it is frequently called the Congressional Medal of Honor. Today the chief feature of the medal is a five-pointed star in the center of which appears the head of the heroic Minerva, symbol of wisdom and righteous war. Surrounding this central feature are the words "United States of America." An open laurel wreath, enameled in green, encircles the star, and the oak leaves at the bases of the prongs are also coated in green to give them prominence. The medal is suspended by a blue silk ribbon, with thirteen white stars representing the original states. The ribbon is attached to an eagle supported upon a horizontal bar, which is attached to two points of the star and on which appears the word "valor."

Although a formal system of recognizing acts of individual gallantry dates back to the American Revolution, it was not until the Civil War that a medal for rewarding bravery received wide-scale recognition. On March 25, 1863, Secretary of War Edwin Stanton awarded the first medals to survivors of the "Great Locomotive Chase." Twenty brave men in blue received the Medal of Honor for heroism on the bloody field of Antietam. Nineteen medals were awarded for gallantry at Fredericksburg and fifty-eight medals were eventually presented as a result of four days of bloodshed and heroism at Gettysburg. One hundred and twenty medals were awarded for bravery at Vicksburg, ninety-six alone on May

22, 1863, the highest one-day total in the medal's entire history. Two weeks after Gettysburg and Vicksburg, the first African American, a former slave named William Harvey Carney of the Fifty-fourth Massachusetts, received the Medal of Honor for the gallant assault on Battery Wagner, South Carolina. Ninety-eight Americans, including ninety sailors and eight Marines, received the Medal of Honor as a result of heroism at Mobile Bay in August 1864. Later in the war, fifty-two soldiers in the Union army received Medals of Honor at Petersburg. In fact, the Civil War saw the first and only female to receive the medal. Rather than consider her request for a commission in the army, President Andrew Johnson ordered New York-born Dr. Mary Edwards Walker, a flamboyant and controversial civilian acting assistant surgeon, who zealously and untiringly administered to the Union sick and wounded, both in the fields and in hospitals at First Bull Run, Chattanooga, Chickamauga, Atlanta, and the furious fighting during Gen. Ulysses S. Grant's 1864 Virginia campaign, be given the Medal of Honor. Although the medal was ruled unwarranted in 1917, it was restored in 1977.

Today, when most Texans think of the Medal of Honor, they think of a fair-featured, baby-faced boy from Central Texas named Audie Leon Murphy, who during World War II became the most decorated combat soldier in United States history. One of twelve children, Murphy saw action in North Africa, Italy, France, and Germany. On a battlefield in France on January 26, 1945, he killed or wounded about fifty German soldiers and stopped an onslaught of enemy tanks, for which he was awarded the Medal of Honor. Appearing in forty-five motion pictures, thirty-nine of which he was the star, Murphy went on to achieve unprecedented celebrity status.

In fact, fifty-seven men who were born in the Lone Star State have received the Medal of Honor. Certainly one of the most interesting was Pvt. David Bennes Barkley-Cantu, one of three Texans to be so honored for heroism during World War I. Disguising his Mexican heritage to enlist in the United States Army, Barkley was assigned to the Eighty-ninth Infantry Division at Souilly, France, where he was given the dangerous task of infiltrating German lines. Barkley and another soldier completed their mission but Barkley developed cramps while swimming across the Meuse River and drowned on November 9, 1918, just two days before the armistice ended the war.

Other noted Texans who received the Medal of Honor include Pvt. Herman C. Wallace of the Seventy-sixth Infantry Division, who stepped on a concealed antipersonnel mine near Prumzurley, Germany, in February 1945. Upon hearing the characteristic noise indicating that the mine had been activated, Wallace placed his second foot on the mine. Although he was killed when the charge detonated, Wallace's heroism was credited with saving the lives of two of his comrades. There was also Sgt. Cleto Rodriguez, who with a comrade led an attack near Manila in the Philippines, also in February 1945, killing more than eighty Japanese soldiers.

Texans are also likely to remember Maj. Horace S. Carswell Jr., a Fort Worth native and graduate of Texas Christian University, who while flying a B-24 during a night mission in the South China Sea in an attack on a Japanese convoy in October 1944 had two engines knocked out and a third damaged, the hydraulic system damaged, and a fuel tank punctured. Carswell ordered the crew to bail out, and with the copilot badly wounded and his parachute too badly damaged to use, crash landed the aircraft, killing the copilot and himself. Carswell was posthumously awarded the Medal of Honor in 1946; Carswell Air Force Base at Fort Worth honors his memory.

Another Texan and Medal of Honor recipient was Sgt. Roy P. Benavidez from Cuero, who distinguished himself by a series of daring and valorous actions in May 1968 near Loc Ninh, Vietnam. As part of a twelve-man Special Forces Reconnaissance Team, Benavidez was sent by helicopter into a dense jungle in a daring evacuation attempt. Under heavy enemy fire and severely wounded in the leg, head, abdomen, and with grenade fragments in his back, Benavidez carried and dragged a number of wounded men to a waiting aircraft.

In *Valor across the Lone Star,* Charles M. Neal Jr. takes us back to another time and another era, the Texas frontier of the Indian Wars, as he recalls the exceptional heroism of other recipients of the Medal of Honor. These men of honor were not native Texans but individuals from a largely immigrant army, men from distant Sweden such as Frederick Bergendahl, or young men from Ireland named John Connor, William McCabe, William McNamara, and John Mitchell. There was also Swiss-born Ernest Veuve and Gregory Mahoney from South Wales. Also American-born Robert G. Carter from distant Maine, and William DeArmond from Ohio, John Harrington of Michigan, Missouri-born Edwin Phoenix, George W. Smith from New York state, and Emanuel Stance from the Louisiana piney woods, as well as New Jersey-born William "Billy" Wilson, and a young Hoosier named Allen Walker. There were also the Seminole-Negroes Adam and Isaac Payne, whose descendants reside at Brackettville today. All were men of exceptional courage. Equally admirable in Neal's narrative are the Native Americans, who in defense of their land and way of life also fought with unprecedented heroism.

Neal first became interested in the army in Texas from stories he heard his father relate of having served at Fort Clark in the First Cavalry Division of the last mounted cavalry regiment, the Fifth Cavalry, in the mid-1930s under Cols. George Patton and Jonathan Wainwright. During trips to Brackettville and the Texas border in the 1950s, Neal became fascinated with Col. Ranald S. Mackenzie, Lt. John Lapham Bullis, and the Seminole-Negro Indian scouts. He would later write a thesis entitled "America's Nineteenth Century Cambodia: The R. S. Mackenzie Raid on Remolino, Mexico." In the process, Neal learned that Mackenzie had recommended two troopers who were in the raid for the Medal of Honor, one of whom died of his wounds and another who had an arm amputated. The medals were denied, Neal concluded, because of the sensitive geopolitics of the incident, since Mackenzie had no written orders that permitted the raid. While uncovering details of the raid on Remolino, Neal also learned that Mackenzie was reliant on a spy in Mexico named William McCabe, who brought to light the fact that the Mexican army on two occasions had crossed into Texas in pursuit of hostile Indians. Documents of the Mexican incursions were used to quash Mexican diplomatic outrage over the controversial incursion into Mexico. As Neal ably writes, McCabe later enlisted in the United States Army and was awarded the Medal of Honor for gallantry in action near Tule Canyon in 1874. In 1881 he was sent into Mexico as a spy by Col. William R. Shafter and lost to history.

Neal became determined to tell the complete story of McCabe and other Medal of Honor recipients. After spending several summers at the National Archives delving into rich and exciting primary sources, Neal recalls having literally done a dance in the Central Search Room when an archivist delivered Mackenzie's letterbooks, which had been gathering dust for decades. An Air Force veteran and classroom teacher in United States and Texas history for many years, Neal should be congratulated for the admirable depth and breath of his research. In *Valor across the Lone Star* he gives us a vivid and realistic sense of bravery on the raw and untamed Texas frontier, a frontier that seemed to stretch endlessly from the frigid snow-swept high plains of the Panhandle to the burning deserts and impenetrable brush country of the Mexican border.

Neal provides great detail and understanding to the story of conflict and heroism in Texas in the last half of the nineteenth century. He has produced an excellent survey of some very brave and exemplary men. *Valor across the Lone Star*, a result of diligent and painstaking research, is certain to delight a wide variety of readers. This readable and engaging volume, solid and thorough throughout, makes an important contribution to our understanding of the Texas military frontier.

JERRY THOMPSON   *Texas A&M International University*

Will C. Barnes, a California native and 1881 Apache campaign Medal of Honor recipient, later an official of the U.S. Forest Service, contributed greatly to the heritage of Texas by working tirelessly to save the Texas Longhorn cattle breed from extinction. *Photograph courtesy the Arizona Historical Society, Tucson.*

Introduction

Since the inception of the distinct Army and Navy Congressional Medals of Honor in 1861, and their new 1956 companion, the Air Force Congressional Medal of Honor, they have become the most exclusive, coveted, and respected awards for military heroism in the world. From among the 48 million men and women who have served in the military and naval services of the United States since 1861, only 3,458 individuals have merited this award. One in five of these select few sacrificed their lives in earning the award.

Most Americans can readily associate Medal of Honor deeds with such storied locations as Iwo Jima, Normandy, Pork Chop Hill, or Khe Sanh. Few, however, would associate it with such places as Eagle Nest Crossing, Beals Creek, Laguna Tahoka, or Galveston Bay. These were also the scenes of desperate conflicts during which valorous deeds of gallantry were performed, and for which Medals of Honor were awarded. These places are not located across vast oceans on distant continents, but are here in the United States, specifically, in Texas. The deeds performed in these places were no less valiant or purposeful. These deeds after all, preserved the united in the United States of America. They pacified our borders and brought order to chaos in the American West. Just like the deeds of the modern era, these intrepid deeds often were essential in determining the outcome of a conflict. These conspicuous deeds too were performed above and beyond the call of duty and at the risk of life.

From among the total of all Medals of Honor awarded, surprisingly, more than half were awarded for gallant deeds performed within forty of the American states. Texas itself was the scene of two Civil War actions, seventeen Indian Wars actions, and one Mexican border action during which sixty-seven men

1

earned the award of either the Army or Navy Congressional Medal of Honor. Their valorous deeds encompassed a time span of American history from 1861 to 1891. These deeds were performed across the varied geographical expanse of the Lone Star State from the Gulf Coast to the canyons and plains of the Panhandle, and finally to the chaparral brushlands of South Texas.

In 1973, when work on this book began in earnest, the author, along with thousands of other military historians and medal collectors, eagerly awaited release of the U.S. Senate Committee on Veteran's Affairs publication, "Medal of Honor Recipients, 1863–1973." A product of several years of research by the Congressional Research Service of the Library of Congress, it was a massive 1,231 page compilation, the most extensive source ever on the topic. Unfortunately, it was rife with errors and omissions. Even its official listing of awards accredited to Texas was grossly in error and flawed in its criteria. It was severely deficient in the area of Civil War and Indian Wars reference sources. It contained biographical references only for the most storied of Indian War recipients; all others, including fifty-eight in-Texas recipients, were simply classified as "lost to history." The deed citations for forty-seven in-Texas Indian Wars recipients prior to 1874 still stated only "gallantry in action," with no clues or references to the specific details. It lacked documentary sources on the actions themselves, the award referral process, and the incumbent presentation ceremonies. Four in-Texas recipients, killed in action performing their deeds, were not even listed as posthumous awardees. The necessity to rectify these shortcomings, errors, and omissions became the genesis of this publication. In its final form it is thusly the first macro-examination of the Congressional Medal of Honor, its recipients, and their relationships to a single American state. The nineteen chapters herein describe those twenty engagements during which sixty-seven men performed their Medal of Honor deeds. There is a brief biography for each recipient, unfortunately incomplete for twelve of these men, who disappeared into obscurity after their discharge from the army. The appendix includes a compilation of statistics on the Medal of Honor, its recipients, and their relationships to Texas. It also includes a listing of Texan recipients updated through 2002. The bibliography lists extensive resources about the 1869–1875 Indian Wars campaigns in Texas and Medal of Honor history.

The research necessary to compile this publication exposed many unique revelations about Medal of Honor history related to Texas with almost every passing day. Early research divulged that San Antonio was, for thirty years, the scene of the first-ever Civil War deeds for which Army Medals of Honor were awarded. These deeds in April 1861 by Cpl. John C. Hesse and Sgt. Joseph K. Wilson were eventually revoked by a Medal of Honor Review Board in 1917,

Cornelius C. Smith, an 1891 recipient, left, was the grandson of John W. Smith, a courier who carried William B. Travis's plea for help from the Alamo. *Photograph courtesy the National Archives.* John C. Hesse, right, was the earliest Civil War recipient of the Medal of Honor, but a 1917 review board removed the award since his deed was not performed in combat. *Photograph courtesy the Library of Congress.*

as their deeds had not been performed in actual armed conflict with an enemy. Sgt. Milton M. Holland, a runaway slave born in Austin, fought for the Union during the Civil War and in 1864 became the first Texan to be awarded the Medal of Honor. The Medal of Honor awarded to Sgt. Denis Ryan of Company I, Sixth U.S. Cavalry, is officially credited to have occurred in Indian Territory (Oklahoma). The engagement during which Ryan earned his medal occurred on December 2, 1874, and was a running battle, which actually occurred mostly in Texas, but carried over into Oklahoma. I chose not to contest the decision of nineteenth-century military officials.

Even two recipients who did not earn their medals in Texas and were not born in Texas were found to have interesting connections to the Lone Star State's heritage. Will C. Barnes, an 1881 recipient during the Apache campaigns in Arizona, worked tirelessly to rescue the Texas Longhorn cattle breed from near extinction later in life as an official of the U.S. Forest Service. Cornelius C. Smith, an 1891 recipient from California, had a Lone Star-studded family tree. His grandfather, John W. Smith, was a courier, who carried William B. Travis's last plea for help from the besieged Alamo garrison.

Along the way research also divulged why some gallant individuals were denied the award. John B. Charleton made the mistake of releasing several deserters he had captured near San Antonio in 1874, and with their release also went any chance for a favorable recommendation from his commanding officer, Col. R. S. Mackenzie. Pvts. Peter Corrigan and William Pair became the victims of 1873 geopolitics. While performing their acts of gallantry one lost his life and the other an arm during a secret raid into Mexico, one purportedly not sanctioned by their government. A public awarding of the Medal of Honor to the two may well have created an international furor. Sgt. Otto Strupp of the Sixth U.S.

3

Cavalry lost his command's horses to Indians in 1870 near Wichita Falls and then drove his men on foot in a twelve-mile pursuit of the Indians. After catching up with them, he led his men in a spirited surprise attack, which resulted in the recapture of most of his horses and most of those belonging to the Indians. Losing the horses in the first place, however, meant losing out on a Medal of Honor. Col. James Oakes, a model soldier, who gave many years of loyal service on the Texas frontier, lost his 1909 appeal for a Medal of Honor, despite the performance of a most creditable deed in 1850. Unfortunately, he had outlived the witnesses, whose accounts and affidavits about the deed were required.

Even inanimate objects, among them ships with Texas names, contributed to the story. Seaman Hugh Mullin of Illinois jumped overboard from the USS *Texas* to save a fellow sailor at Hampton Roads, Virginia, in 1899, enabling him to receive an in-line-of-profession Navy Medal of Honor. Capt. Albert H. Rooks of Washington state earned his Navy Medal of Honor while in command of the USS *Houston* during World War II.

Places in Texas named to memorialize various recipients also became a part of the research. The Headquarters Building at Kelly Air Force Base at San Antonio has borne the name of Neel E. Kearby, a World War II air combat recipient, since 1973. Airmen at Webb Air Force Base at Big Spring ate their meals in a dining hall named for Capt. Stephen L. Bennett, a Texas-born Vietnam recipient. Many National Guardsmen have trained at Camp Barkley in Taylor County, named for World War I recipient David B. Barkley. Students at Texas A&M University stroll through Eli Whiteley Memorial Medal of Honor Park, and young grade-school students attend classes in Edinburg at Alfredo Gonzalez Elementary School, both named in honor of Texan recipients. Many World War II veterans received their training at Camp Howze, Mathis Field, and Carswell Field; all memorialized the names of Texan recipients. Today veterans receive medical care at the Audie L. Murphy VA Medical Center at San Antonio, and people in Houston drive down Marcario Garcia Drive, both daily reminders of two gallant Texas heroes of World War II. These are but a few of the honors that commemorate the Medal of Honor and its illustrious recipients in the Lone Star State.

Since President Theodore Roosevelt's Executive Order of September 20, 1905, ceremonies awarding the Medal of Honor have been made with formal and impressive ceremony, with the recipient being ordered to Washington, D.C., for presentation by the president. This has not always been the practice and in some instances was impractical. Presentation ceremonies are known to have taken place in Texas, both before and after 1905. The first receipt of a Medal of Honor in Texas occurred on October 1, 1863. On that date Sgt. John Mackie acknowledged receipt of his Navy Medal of Honor from on board the USS *Seminole*, then anchored several miles off Sabine Pass. He was the first U.S. Marine to receive the Navy Medal of Honor. In addition to four posthumous award ceremonies to next of kin cited in Appendix D, and the Indian Wars-era ceremonies described in the appropriate chapters herein, there were two ceremonies in Texas for living recipients. In April 1945 Sgt. Hulon Whittington of Bastrop, Louisiana, received his Army Medal of Honor from Maj. Gen. John P. Lucas in a ceremony at Brooke Army Hospital at San Antonio. Originally scheduled to receive the medal from President Truman at the White House, Whittington was judged to be too badly wounded to make the trip. The most recent presentation ceremony to a living recipient occurred on December 6, 1966, when Marine Corps Sgt. Robert E. O'Malley was presented his Navy Medal of Honor by President Lyndon Johnson at the LBJ Ranch at Stonewall.

While some recipients earned or were awarded their medals in Texas, there were others who parted company with their prized medal in Texas. Leonidas S. Lytle and Solon D. Neal both lost or had stolen their original 1862-design medals in San Antonio in 1893 and 1898. These two retired sergeants curiously were joined with the highest of all ranks in being among those who lost a valuable medal on the streets of San Antonio. Zachary Taylor, who became our nation's twelfth president, while a general at San Antonio in 1848 lost a solid gold medal Congress had awarded him. It was found on February 24, 1915, by construction workers excavating for the foundation of the Majestic Theatre in downtown San Antonio.

There were other more tragic aspects about the story of the Medal of Honor in Texas, and these too became a part of the story. On a cold night in December 1873, Pvt. Franklin M. McDonnold, an 1872 recipient, deserted from Fort Griffin into obscurity. Research into his deed and background were fraught with mystery and possible fraud. Pvt. Adam Payne, an 1874 recipient, was shot and killed by a deputy sheriff in 1877. Research revealed that the deputy sheriff who fired the fatal shot was none other than 1870 recipient Claron A. Windus. This is the only known instance of the death of one recipient at the hand of another. On March 8, 1934, a spirited polo game at Fort Sam Houston turned tragic. Gordon Johnston, a Philippine Insurrection recipient, was jostled by several opposing players, fell from his horse, and died several days later from his injuries.

Even the searches for the recipient's final resting places, usually a somber endeavor, provided several fascinating experiences. Most memorable was the search performed by Lt. Col. David P. Perrine, who at the request of the author launched a search for the gravesite of former Pvt. Peter Roth in Rottenmunster,

Germany, in 1972. Perrine, the great-great-grandson of a Sixth U.S. Cavalry officer of the 1870s, was led to Roth's grave by Roth's elderly granddaughters, who clearly remembered sitting excitedly on his lap as children while he related stories of his fights with the Indians in North America.

Shortly after I made the final compilation of all the data I had collected over the years, I became aware of a myriad of medallic and Medal of Honor statistics gleamed from my own sources and those of other interested researchers. Was I aware that the Mexican Legion of Honor, Mexico's premier award for military gallantry, was created in January 1836 as an incentive for recruiting volunteers into General Santa Anna's campaign against Texas revolutionaries? Did I know that almost half of the Indian Wars posthumous awards went to soldiers killed in action in Texas? Did I know that Texas A&M had provided at least seven Medal of Honor recipients, more than any other school outside of the military academies? Did I know that the Seminole-Negro Indian Scout Cemetery at Brackettville had the highest per capita Medal of Honor interments of any private cemetery? Was I aware that San Antonio National Cemetery held that same distinction for national cemeteries? Did I know that almost 20 percent of all World War II Army Air Corps recipients were Texan, and that 13 percent of all World War II air combat Medal of Honor awards went to Texans?

These chapters, biographies, and bits of information about the Medal of Honor and its relationships to Texas weave an intriguing mosaic, which hopefully is as enjoyable to read as it was to research and write. The mosaic is not complete and likely it never will be, but we have at least created a beginning.

Map of Engagements in Frontier Texas

Map of Engagements in Frontier Texas

* Numbers correspond to chapter numbers.

1. *Attack on the CSS* Royal Yacht (Galveston County)

    At Galveston Bay entrance, one and three quarters of a mile south from Bolivar Lighthouse.

2. *A Wild Reconnaissance on Matagorda Peninsula* (Matagorda County)

    Between ten and twelve miles down the peninsula from the mouth of Caney Creek.

3. *Repulsing the Tribes in Comancheria* (Lubbock/Crosby County)

    Lubbock County, September 15–16, 1869: Seven miles east of Lubbock on Farm/Ranch Road 835. Crosby County, October 28, 1869: Seventeen miles northwest of Spur and two miles west of Farm/Ranch Road 836 on the plain above Blanco Canyon.

4. *Sergeant Stance to the Rescue* (Menard County)

    Fourteen miles north of Fort McKavett on Farm/Ranch Road 2873 near Del Vanado Ranch and P&H Oil Field.

5. *Surrounded at the Little Wichita* (Archer County)

    Four miles south of the State Highway 25 crossing of the North Fork of the Little Wichita River on the bluff above the road, three miles southeast of Lake Kickapoo Dam.

6. *Skirmish at Bluff Creek* (Archer County)

    Seven miles north of Archer City on State Highway 79, and two miles to the west along Bluff Creek.

7. *Ambushed in Congrejo Canyon* (Crosby County)

    Nine miles north of Crosbyton on Farm/Ranch Road 651, and one mile to the west.

8. *Striking the Comancheros on Beals Creek* (Mitchell County)

    Fifteen miles south of Colorado City on State Highway 208 and five miles west to the juncture of Beals Creek and the Colorado River.

9. *Ambush at Salt Creek* (Young County)

    Eight miles northwest of Graham on U.S. Highway 380 at the crossing of Salt Creek on the north end of Lake Graham.

10. *Battle of the North Fork of the Red River* (Gray County)

    Two miles east and north of Lefors at the juncture of Farm/Ranch Roads 1321 and 1474.

11. *Besieged on the Upper Washita* (Hemphill County)

    Sixteen miles southeast of Canadian on State Highway 33 and four miles south to Lyman Train historical marker.

12. *The Buffalo Wallow Fight* (Hemphill County)

    Seventeen miles south-southeast of Canadian to Farm/Ranch Road 277 and east five miles then south one mile to Buffalo Wallow monument.

13. *For Habitual Courage Near Quitaque Peak* (Motley/Floyd Counties)

    Five miles west-southwest of Flomot.

14. *Repulsing the Cheyenne at Tule Canyon* (Briscoe/Swisher Counties)

    Ten miles west-northwest of Silverton.

15. *Gallantry on the High Plains* (Lynn County)

    November 3, 1874 (Veuve): Six miles south-southwest of New Home at northeast tip of Double Lake. November 5, 1874 (Comfort): Four miles south of Wilson at northeast tip of Tahoka Lake.

8

16. *Baldwin's Battlewagons to the Rescue* (Gray County)
    Thirteen miles south of Pampa on State Highway 70 and one mile east.
17. *Pursuit and Close Combat on the High Plains* (Dawson County)
    Eight miles east of Lamesa on Farm/Ranch Road 827.
18. *Outgunned at Eagle Nest Crossing* (Val Verde County)
    Six miles west of Comstock on U.S. Highway 90 at Pecos River High Bridge.
19. *Gallantry among the Chaparral* (Jim Hogg County)
    Twelve miles north of Guerra on Farm/Ranch Road 649.

George H. Bell, circa 1900. His valorous deeds of November 7–8, 1861, in Galveston Bay merited for him the fifth Navy Medal of Honor of the Civil War. *Photograph courtesy the National Archives.*

CHAPTER 1

Attack on the CSS Royal Yacht

November 7–8, 1861

— ★ —

Coxwain George H. Bell

On April 15, 1861, and in the several days following the surrender of Fort Sumter, South Carolina, President Abraham Lincoln issued a number of proclamations concerning the defense of the Union. His call for 75,000 temporary volunteers to defend the Union was quickly fulfilled. Another of his proclamations called for the Union Navy's blockade of the Southern Confederacy, which proved to be a much more time-consuming objective. The suppression of the Confederacy's marine trade in exchange for articles of war became the U.S. Navy's top priority. The success or failure of the blockade would do more to determine the outcome of the war than any other single act. The Gulf of Mexico presented many unique problems to the Union Navy in enforcing the blockade. Spanish Cuba, just seventy-five miles from Florida, as well as the British Bahamas and French-controlled Mexico, offered convenient and safe havens for blockade-running ships. The shallow waters of most ports along the Gulf Coast severely limited the movements of most of the Union Navy's vessels. Southern rivers emptying into the Gulf often formed a myriad of channels at their mouths. Shallow lagoons and bayous dotted the coast and offered innumerable sanctuaries for Confederate vessels and blockade runners. Texas, though far from the main land battle areas, was a veritable storehouse for the Confederacy. Its high production of cotton and its border with Mexico made it a high priority for the naval blockade.

The Gulf Blockading Squadron under the command of Flag Officer William W. McKean had the difficult task of effectively controlling all marine commerce along the 1,500–mile coastline of the Gulf of Mexico. Patrolling and enforcing the blockade from the Florida Keys to Brownsville, Texas, stretched the squadron far beyond its normal capabilities.

Blockade duty along the Texas Gulf Coast definitely meant patrolling off Galveston Bay. More than half of all Texas marine commerce passed through Galveston and the Confederates had expended considerable efforts to make it secure. Almost every available piece of heavy and medium-range artillery available to Texas state officials had been removed to Galveston to strengthen its harbor defenses. Two heavy eight-inch Dahlgren gun batteries were placed at Bolivar Point. Three eight-inch howitzers, two thirty-pounder rifled guns, and two ten-inch mortars at Fort Point guarded the entrance to the harbor. Fort Jackson on the northeastern tip of Pelican Spit protected the inner harbor with two eight-inch seacoast howitzers and one ten-inch mortar. Inside the harbor was an array of heavily armed gunboats capable of inflicting severe losses on any force able to make it between the guns of the forts.[1]

Confronting this array of forts and vessels on November 5, 1861, were two Union blockading vessels, the USS *Sam Houston* and the USS *Santee*. On the morning of November 5, 1861, these two vessels were anchored about seven miles outside of the harbor entrance. Capt. Henry Eagle, commanding the *Santee*, and Lt. James E. Jouett both scanned the eastern and southern horizons in search of any approaching sails or plumes of smoke.[2] The two officers eventually trained their marine telescopes upon the vessels within the harbor. The Confederate gunboat, *General Rusk*, could be seen at anchor just off the tip of Pelican Spit and the schooner, *Royal Yacht*, lay about three-quarters of a mile south of the Bolivar Lighthouse. The *Royal Yacht* was a four-masted schooner, well outfitted and reputed to be the fastest schooner along the Texas coast. If the *Royal Yacht* did come out and attempt to run the blockade she would be assisted, no doubt, by the *General Rusk*. The *General Rusk*, a formidable foe, was a huge 750-ton steamer, well armed and reasonably fast. The destruction or capture of the *Rusk* would have been a tremendous psychological victory for the Union since the Confederates had used the *General Rusk* on April 17, 1861, to capture United States troops aboard the USS *Star of the West*. The incident, which occurred in Matagorda Bay, was the first large-scale capture of Union troops by Confederate forces.[3]

It would be a difficult and dangerous task, but a great embarrassment to the Confederacy if the *General Rusk* or *Royal Yacht* could be captured or destroyed within heavily defended Galveston Bay. Nevertheless, Eagle believed that a boarding party of at least two launches could accomplish the mission. Lieutenant

USS *Santee*. Its last combat actions of the Civil War were along the Texas coast, after which it became a U.S. Naval Academy training ship. Every naval officer who attended the Naval Academy between 1867 and 1912 trained on its deck. *Photograph courtesy the National Archives.*

Jouett concurred that such a mission could be executed and he volunteered to organize and lead such an expedition. During his evening watch duty of November 5, Jouett met with a hastily organized staff of volunteers who had agreed to help him prepare for the mission. Present at the meeting were Lt. John G. Mitchell, Lt. Bayse Westcott, Gunner's Mate William Carter, Master's Mate Charles W. Adams, Master's Mate Henry S. Lambert, and Coxwain George H. Bell. The mission was outlined to this planning staff and each man was delegated his area of responsibility.[4]

It was decided that the expedition would be comprised only of three launches; two launches would penetrate into the harbor while a third launch would remain at the harbor mouth as a signal and guide boat. Mitchell was in charge of enrolling and selecting the volunteers for the boarding crews. Westcott was in charge of preparing the launches, and Gunner's Mate Carter obtained and prepared all of the armaments and combustibles necessary for the expedition. Jouett, Master's Mate Adams, and Coxswain Bell worked out the navigational details. Bell was assigned as the pilot to bring the captured vessel out of the bay.[5]

At 8 A.M. on November 6 Jouett and Eagle mustered the volunteer enlisted personnel for inspection and outlined the preparations and details of the expedition. Immediately after dismissal the men assumed their various duties with their assigned crews. Westcott and his crew caulked and stowed the equipment in the boats. Carter worked with the ship's carpenter to install a twelve-pound howitzer on a swivel at the front of the first launch. Below deck in the captain's anteroom, Jouett, Adams, and Bell scanned the nautical charts for Galveston Bay. They had

13

to consider the time, winds, and tides needed for the best approaches in and out of the harbor. It was also up to Bell to memorize the locations and depths of the channels and bars. At 1 P.M. the expedition's crew was mustered for small arms practice. By 4 P.M. all but a few minor details were completed and the men settled down to eat and rest. As the crew lounged about the deck playing cards, writing letters, and just relaxing, they heard music from a band concert onshore.[6]

All day Thursday, November 7, was spent completing last-minute preparations. Signals were verified in drills, assignments reviewed, weapons cleaned and checked out, equipment stowed, and personal matters taken care of. At 5:30 P.M. the raiding crew was mustered for a final inspection. When everything was ready the men were given their evening meal and the chance to get a few hours of sleep. At 10 P.M. the men were awakened and the three launches were lowered into the water shortly afterward. By 10:30 P.M. all three launches were in the water, their crews were mustered, and the men began to embark into the small bobbing launches.

The primary objective of the mission was for the first and second launches to penetrate into the harbor, board, and attempt to bring out or burn the *General Rusk*. If for whatever reason this could not be accomplished with total surprise, then they would attempt to bring out or burn their secondary target, the *Royal Yacht*. The third launch, commanded by Master's Mate Lambert, would remain just outside of the harbor at the bay entrance buoy beacon.[7]

The *Santee* was still anchored about seven miles off the mouth of the harbor when the three launches cast off at 11:40 P.M. and slipped quickly out of sight into the darkness. The oars of each launch were wrapped in burlap to muffle the dips of the oars in the water. Each launch had a sixteen-man rowing crew plus two gunners, the coxswain, and the launch commander. Slight opposing winds from the southwest made rowing through the two-foot swells difficult. Jouett, Carter, Bell, and sixteen sailors were in the first launch. Mitchell, Adams, and eighteen sailors and marines followed closely in the second launch.

At approximately 1 A.M. both launches passed the *Royal Yacht* about an eighth of a mile to their right. Just inside the bay Jouett noticed the dim lamps outlining a new addition to the harbor defenses, the Confederate steamer *Colonel Stell*, which was anchored just inside Bolivar Point about a quarter of a mile to their right.[8] After almost two hours of the men's arduous rowing, both of the launches were within two hundred yards of their primary target, the *General Rusk*, when the crew of the first launch heard a faint grinding noise. They had grounded on Pelican Spit. Before a warning could be uttered, the second launch rammed into the first launch's stern, shattering several oars and creating a noisy commotion. The noise attracted the attention of sentries aboard the *General Rusk* and from a sentry outpost on the northern tip of Pelican Spit. The Confederate sentries' cries of "Who goes there?" went unanswered. A second and third round of challenges went unanswered before the sentries opened fire in the direction of the noise. Jouett ordered his men not to return the fire.[9]

Realizing that the crew aboard the *General Rusk* was now at general quarters and that the idea of total surprise was now defunct, Jouett ordered his men to turn the boats about and to pull for the *Royal Yacht*, the secondary target. The firing from the Confederate sentries ceased abruptly as the two Union launches escaped silently into the darkness. The winds and tides were now in favor of the two launches, which moved sleekly to the northeast toward the mouth of the bay.

Capt. Leon Smith, commanding the *General Rusk*, had called his crew to general quarters at the outset of the sentries' firing and kept his crew at their stations for more than an hour. When no further noise was heard he ordered his men to lie down with their arms and sleep.[10] While Smith's crew slept, the Union sailors continued pulling toward the *Royal Yacht*. Their rowing became more deliberate and unified and the two launches moved abreast of one another. When they were about five hundred yards from the *Royal Yacht*, Jouett restated his orders, "Second launch, board on the starboard bow, first launch on the starboard beam."[11]

The lone Confederate sentry aboard the *Royal Yacht*, having heard the firing to the southwest an hour earlier, peered vigilantly across the bay. He discerned the presence of the Union launches when they were within two hundred yards of the *Royal Yacht*. He challenged them with "Boat ahoy," but was met with only silence. Jouett then urged his oarsmen, "Give way strong men," and turned to Carter to issue the order, "Ready with the gun Mr. Carter." The sentry offered his challenge again and Jouett urged his men, "Give way strong boys!" When the launches were within fifty yards of the *Royal Yacht*, Carter was ordered to fire the howitzer but the primer apparently had become damp and the gun failed to fire. Carter immediately set about repriming the gun just as the second launch veered to the right toward the *Royal Yacht*'s bow. The first launch was within twenty-five yards of the schooner when Jouett gave the order, "Trail oars, stand by to board." The first launch coasted to within thirty feet of the schooner's side before Carter succeeded in firing the howitzer. The shot struck the schooner just below the water line at the mid-beam. The recoil forced the first launch to come almost to a complete stop just before it made contact with the schooner.[12]

Carter at the bow, alone, managed to board the schooner. The sentry had sounded the alarm and the Confederate crew, having heard the howitzer, began pouring from the hatchways. As soon as Carter hit the deck he ran into a withering fire. He had dropped behind one of the schooner's deck posts, but was wounded in the right arm almost immediately and was able to offer only limited resistance. The Confederates rushed to the railing and fired on both launches with pistols and shotguns. The second launch was last seen approaching the starboard bow near the foremast, but the first launch had drifted toward the stern and was dangerously exposed. Seaman Henry Garcia was killed instantly and fell backward among his fellow seamen, which caused a panic. Within seconds Gunner's Mate Edward Conway and Seamen Francis Brown, Hugh McGregg, and Charles Hawkins were seriously wounded, causing a state of sheer pandemonium among the crew, most of whom abandoned their posts and sought cover in the bottom of the launch.[13] Realizing that the entire crew would be wiped out if they did not gain the cover of the schooner's side, George Bell quickly jumped to the bow of the launch. Their only chance for survival at this point was to get a grapnel hook over the railing of the schooner and secure the launch along and under the counter. Grabbing a grapnel and line, Bell stood up amid the hail of gunfire and swung the hook over his head. As he released the grapnel, a rifle ball struck him in the upper back area. Jouett rushed to the front of the launch just in time to catch Bell's slumping body. As Jouett lowered the gravely wounded sailor to the bottom of the launch, he gasped out, "Oh, Mr. Jouett. They are killing us from the other boat."[14]

For whatever reason, instead of following the order to board on the starboard bow, the second boat had taken a position on the schooner's port beam on the opposite side of the schooner. The first launch was caught in a murderous crossfire from friend and foe alike, which threatened to wipe out the entire crew. Jouett screamed out, "Cease fire!" but his cry was drowned out by the noise of the firing. Only the four aft oarsmen in the first launch had not taken cover in the bottom of the boat. Jouett urged them to pull for the side of the schooner. He grabbed the grapnel line and with an almost impossible leap he gained the railing of the schooner and bounded onto the deck. While wielding his pistol in one hand he pulled the launch alongside and called out to the launch crew, "Now is your time! Come on aboard!"[15] All but George Bell refused to surrender their cover in the launch. Bell, though gasping heavily from his throat wound, made a futile attempt to climb aboard before he fell back into the launch. Jouett turned and began to run forward to assist Carter when a Confederate crewmen jumped from a dark hatchway and thrust a boarding pike into Jouett's right side. The shock of the sudden attack and the intense pain of the wound forced Jouett to drop his pistol. The Confederate sailor tried to push

Jouett overboard but in the struggle the shaft of the pike shattered on the corner of a hatchway. Jouett struggled with the Confederate sailor, eventually removed the blade from his side, and managed to strike his adversary over the head with it, rendering the Confederate unconscious.[16]

Several men in the first launch, including George Bell, began to fire their pistols toward the Confederates along the railing. Slight and sporadic firing from the second launch also helped drive the Confederate crew away from the side and toward the forward cabin area. Carter and Jouett, although wounded, were still the only Union crewmen on the deck. Jouett, unable to find his pistol in the darkness, called out to Carter, who rushed to Jouett's side. Carter had two pistols and together the two fired their pistols in the direction of the forward cabin area and the Confederate sailors concentrated there.

After several minutes Carter and Jouett forced the Confederate crewmen to flee from the deck and take refuge in the forward cabin hatchway. Jouett, intent on destroying the schooner, quickly began preparing to set the *Royal Yacht* on fire. Despite his near collapse from loss of blood, Jouett began to pile combustibles around the schooner's twelve-pound pivot gun on the forward deck and frantically tried to ignite the combustibles twice. He knew the firing had alerted the Confederate defenses and that they would have to accomplish their duties quickly if they were to be successful.

A single signal rocket fired from the *General Rusk* lit up the sky and confirmed Jouett's worst fears; it would be just a few minutes before the whole Confederate defenses came to life. The alarm had been sounded and the *Rusk* and *Stell* were both at general quarters, rapidly preparing to get under way. Single rockets from the artillery batteries from Fort Point and Fort Jackson arched through the sky and illuminated the bay entrance.

Several of the sailors and marines from both of the launches had finally made it onto the schooner's deck and joined Carter and Jouett in the forward cabin area. Jouett, after a third attempt to ignite the combustibles around the pivot gun, had lost consciousness briefly and struck his head on the gun. He finally abandoned the idea of burning the gun mount and decided that capturing the Confederate crew was the key to the mission's success. Running, at times staggering, he joined Carter, who was still standing guard over the forward cabin hatchway. Jouett ordered the Confederate crewmen to come up on deck but they refused. He then ordered several of the Union sailors to go down and drive the Confederates on deck, but, to his surprise, none of the men were willing to enter the hatchway. Angrily, he took his pistol in hand and hurtled through the hatchway. Inside the interior door he could see ten of the Confederate sailors crouched against the far wall of the cabin. Jouett pointed his pistol at them and shouted for them to go onto the deck. Two of the Confederates were part of the way up the ladder when someone shouted, "Santee," the pre-determined code word for retreat on this mission. Jouett pulled the two Confederates from the ladder, pushed them back into the cabin, and made them sit down. He rushed on deck and found that all of his crew except Carter had fled to the launch and were preparing to push off from the schooner.[17] Jouett shouted to Carter to hold the Confederates down in the hatch and hurried toward the stern. Bell was arguing and resisting the effort to push off from the schooner when Jouett jumped into the launch, drew his cutlass, and forced the able-bodied members of the crew back onto the schooner. The second launch was not even within sight and Jouett no longer counted it in the mission.[18]

Jouett and the crew members rejoined Carter at the forward cabin hatchway. Jouett again descended into the hatchway and had given the order for the Confederates to go onto the deck when he again heard someone shout the retreat signal. He could hear his men stampeding across the deck and again he was forced to leave his prisoners behind. He managed to climb back up the ladder to regain the deck, but was too exhausted to pursue his crew. Only Carter remained at his post. Jouett begged Carter to try and drive the crew back. Carter ran to the stern of the schooner and found the launch already fifty yards away. He cried out to them, "Go back cowards! Go back and tell your shipmates that you deserted your officers. Mr. Jouett and myself will bring this vessel out alone." On the launch, the wounded Bell rose, pistol in hand, and forced his fellow crewmembers to return the launch to the schooner's side.[19]

Carter returned to Jouett, who was now near total collapse, then bounded down the ladder and forced ten of the Confederate crewmen on deck. Thomas Chubb, captain of the schooner, and two other men refused to come on deck. Jouett angrily ordered these men to come up on deck, but they continued to refuse. Jouett then warned them that if they did not come up immediately he would throw a loaded shell into the cabin. The Confederates still would not yield, so Jouett wrapped rags around a solid cannon shot, set the rags on fire, and threw the flaming shot into the forward cabin. Within seconds the three recalcitrant Confederates were Jouett's prisoners. Under Carter's direction, the sailors and marines quickly planted combustibles around the schooner's gun mount, magazine, and lower superstructure. Jouett had the schooner's colors lowered and took possession of them.[20]

At 3:15 A.M., as the Confederate prisoners were being herded into the first launch, the fires aboard the *Royal Yacht* began to spread quickly. Less than a quarter of a mile away, the lanterns and the glare of the open boiler doors on the *Rusk* could be seen clearly as it approached rapidly from the west-southwest. The first launch pushed off from the side of the *Royal Yacht* around 3:20 A.M. There were thirteen Confederate prisoners, six wounded Union sailors and marines, and Henry Garcia's body in the bottom of the launch.[21] Along with Carter and Jouett there were only eight men capable of manning the oars. George Bell, despite his grave condition, courageously moved to his position at the steering tiller. Jouett gave him a star to steer by and commanded the oarsmen to, "Give way strong, men." Carter moved to the front and took his position beside the howitzer, while Jouett moved throughout the launch to supply the wounded with water.[22]

The fires that had reached the sails of the *Royal Yacht* illuminated the area around the schooner for several hundred yards. The *Rusk* could be seen rounding the bow of the schooner. The same demoralized spirit that the sailors and marines had exhibited earlier appeared again in the crowded launch. One of the young sailors shouted, "My God, here comes the steamers! They'll run us down!" Similar panic was displayed among some of the other men before Jouett rose, pistol in hand, and shouted, "Silence! The first man that opens his mouth, I'll blow his brains out! Make up your minds to capture that steamer if it attacks us for I'll never surrender a man of you. No Rebel prison for me and while I live we'll fight or go to the bottom!" Except for the straining and labored breathing of the oarsmen, silence fell over the boat as it glided through the darkness toward the *Santee*. The lookouts aboard the *Rusk* apparently had not yet spotted the Union launch, which was about two hundred yards northeast of the burning schooner.[23]

The *Rusk* came to a dead stop just off the port bow of the *Royal Yacht* and began lowering several of her launches into the water. At about 3:50 A.M. George Bell steered the first launch as close as possible to the breakers along the eastern shoreline of Bolivar Peninsula. To make matters worse, the launch began to take water. The signal lights that Captain Eagle and Master's Mate Lambert had promised were nowhere to be seen. After three hours of rowing, Lieutenant Jouett became desperate and began to fire his pistol at intervals in the hope that their fellow shipmates would come to their aid. Not until daylight did they discover the *Santee*, and at 6:15 A.M. the first launch finally made it back.[24]

Jouett, Carter, and Bell were all in a state of near collapse and had to be carried below deck to sick bay for medical care, where the ship's doctor, Thomas M. Potter, treated all eight of the men wounded in the mission.[25] Carter was the least seriously wounded of the eight and required only minor treatment for a flesh wound in his right arm. Jouett had lost a large amount of blood from the wound on his right arm and chest, which required surgery. George Bell had performed his duties bravely despite a severe gunshot wound in the back between his shoulder blades. He had lost a large amount of blood from his back wound and from a contusion in his thyroid cartilage. His breathing had become dangerously labored and he was coughing up blood. Eight days later Potter performed surgery to remove a large-caliber ball that was lodged in Bell's throat.[26]

Amazingly, George Bell recovered quickly from his wounds. On July 10, 1863, some twenty months after his gallantry in Galveston Bay, the United States Navy officially conferred the Navy Medal of Honor upon him. Lieutenant Jouett had credited George H. Bell's cool professionalism and gallant actions, despite his severe wounds, as being instrumental to the success of the expedition. His citation under General Order no. 17 stated:

> Served as pilot of the USS *Santee* when that vessel was engaged in cutting out the Rebel armed schooner, *Royal Yacht*, from Galveston Bay, November 7, 1861, and evinced more coolness in passing the four forts and the Rebel steamer, *General Rusk* than was ever before witnessed by his commanding officer.[27]
>
> Although severely wounded in the encounter, he displayed extraordinary courage under the most painful and trying circumstances.

It was sixteen months later, on November 26, 1864, before Bell received his medal. On that date, Adm. David Porter personally presented the Navy Medal of Honor to George Bell in a ceremony aboard the USS *Mohican* anchored in Hampton Roads, Virginia.[28]

George Bell continued to serve with distinction in the U.S. Navy for three more years after his tour aboard the *Santee*. He also served aboard the *North Carolina*, *Western World*, *Ohio*, and *Brooklyn* during his later service with the Gulf and Atlantic Blockading Squadrons. He participated in numerous actions against Confederate blockade runners and was especially active in engagements at Fort Pickens in Pensacola Bay; Fort Polaski, Georgia; Forts Morgan and Gaines in Mobile Bay; and at Fort Fisher, North Carolina. During his brief but action-filled tenure with the U.S. Navy, George Bell placed his name on the long list of distinguished heroes of the United States Naval service. Bell's actions in Galveston Bay, Texas, above and beyond the call of duty and at the risk of his own life, earned for him the fifth Navy Medal of Honor.[29]

CHAPTER 2

A Wild Reconnaissance
on Matagorda Peninsula

December 29, 1863

Col. Frank S. Hesseltine

Despite several strategic Union military victories in the East during mid-1863, the Union Army and Navy suffered several debilitating setbacks in their attempts to isolate Texas from the rest of the Confederacy. The Union's initial attempts in 1863 at Mansfield, Louisiana, and Sabine Pass, Texas, failed and Texas continued to be a virtually unhindered supply pipeline for the Confederacy. Its lengthy border and extensive commerce with French-controlled Mexico greatly alarmed President Lincoln, who expressed "the importance of re-establishing the national authority in western Texas as soon as possible."[1]

Gen. Nathan Banks, commander of the Union Army forces in the Western Gulf region, had opposed the earlier attempts at Mansfield and Sabine Pass in favor of an invasion of Texas at some point along the Texas middle Gulf Coast. In October and November Banks had demonstrated the veracity of his strategy by successfully seizing Aransas Pass and Fort Esperanza on Matagorda Island. Esperanza was then used as a staging base to launch probing intrusions onto the mainland. The initial objective was to locate the soft spots in the Confederate defenses, which required the dispatch of numerous probing reconnaissance operations.

Maj. Gen. C. C. Washburn, who was in command of Texas Gulf Coast operations, began to carry out General Banks's orders in late December. The orders were to "scout actively all the country in your front and press your scouts in the

Francis S. Hesseltine, circa 1890. He led the Medal of Honor Legion's membership in the efforts to retain their original 1862-style medals after a design change in 1897, and opposed the War Department's insistence that the new-design medals be issued only upon exchange of the original. Hesseltine was the first recipient to be issued the 1897-style medal without submitting his original. *Courtesy of the Burton Collections, Detroit Public Library.*

direction of Caney Creek and make demonstrations with a view to amuse and confuse the enemy."[2] One of the first demonstrations intended to amuse and confuse the enemy was a reconnaissance down Matagorda Peninsula to test Confederate strength in the vicinity. A secondary objective was to capture a Confederate picket detachment stationed on the peninsula. These Confederate pickets were mounted irregular exempts under the command of Capt. William Henderson; their spying on Union ship movements along the middle Texas Gulf coast had rendered many Union naval efforts ineffective. Washburn wanted desperately to have these Confederates either captured or driven from the peninsula.[3]

Early on the morning of December 28, General Washburn requested that Gen. T. G. Ransom select a one hundred-man detachment to execute the reconnaissance. Ransom selected four companies of the Thirteenth Maine Volunteer Infantry for the mission. Col. Frank S. Hesseltine, commanding the Thirteenth Maine, immediately questioned the wisdom of the order, believing that ordering the landing of one hundred men on a narrow peninsula in proximity to a known large concentration of enemy forces in order to amuse and confuse was akin to insanity. Ransom explained that he too questioned the wisdom of the order, but the instructions had to be carried out. Hesseltine then claimed the right, "if one hundred of his men were to be sent on such a wild expedition to command them in person." Ransom granted his request and consoled him somewhat with word that he would accompany them aboard the *Granite City* to coordinate naval support.[4]

During the afternoon of December 28, 1863, Colonel Hesseltine assembled the commanding officers of the selected companies. They included: Lt. John Ham, Company C; Lt. Robbins Grover, Company H; Lt. Augustus Myrick, Company D; and Lt. John Felton, Company K. Each was instructed to select twenty-five soldiers from their respective companies. They were to see that ammunition and rations were issued and have the men assembled at the pier by eight o'clock that night.

Shortly before midnight all preparations were completed and Capt. Charles W. Lamson, commander of the *Granite City*, gave the order to get under way. Ten minutes after departing, the *Granite City* was joined by the heavily armed gunboat the USS *Sciota*, which was to serve as escort until the troops were embarked. The two ships cruised in convoy slowly along the coast so as to arrive at the planned landing site at the first light. The sixty-mile distance from Fort Esperanza on Matagorda Island took the better part of six hours. While the troops slept, General Ransom, Colonel Hesseltine, and Captain Lamson conferred about communication signals. At night, fires would be used to delineate their position, one on each flank and a third to mark their main position. Semaphore flags would be used in daylight.[5]

A little past 6 A.M. on December 29 the *Granite City* dropped anchor at a point known as Smith's Landing, some seven miles south of the mouth of Caney Creek. The *Granite City*'s boats began conveying the troops ashore at about 7 A.M. in a foggy mist. By the time the last of the troops reached shore the waves had increased to more than four feet and winds were gusting to forty miles an hour. The landing point was near a weathered old clapboard house tucked between two high sand dunes. The inhabitants of the house turned out to be an elderly couple, who claimed to have lost two sons to the war and only wanted to be left alone.[6] A search of the house turned up two boarding pikes, which apparently had washed ashore from the wreck of the USS *Hatteras*. Hesseltine next dispatched Lieutenant Ham and ten men from Company C to scout several miles northward along the beach and establish a perimeter for early warning. The weather worsened with every passing minute and Hesseltine began to worry about the safety and comfort of the men and the chances for the mission's success. The situation deteriorated gravely as they were on a narrow peninsula of open sand dunes and exposed to bitterly cold winds that cut them off from their transports. The physical suffering from the elements, however, may have been the least of their worries, as there remained the risk of being overrun by one of the Confederate cavalry units known to be in the area. Hesseltine formed the men into a skirmish line that extended across the peninsula and ordered the advance southward.[7]

Unknown to Hesseltine, the landing had been observed by a Confederate lookout post south of the breastworks at the mouth of Caney Creek. The very moment Hesseltine had ordered the expedition's southward movement, mounted couriers were spreading word of the troops' landing. One courier carried news of the federal troop landing to Col. Augustus C. Buchel, commanding the Second Brigade of the First Texas Cavalry. Buchel was camped at Cedar Lake, twelve miles north of the federal landing point. A second courier also relayed word of the landing to Second Division Headquarters at the McNeel Plantation near Brazoria. Offshore, the *Granite City* slowly moved abreast of the troops as they moved down the peninsula. The *Sciota* had turned about and was steaming up the coast to conduct a reconnaissance of the Confederate gun emplacements at the mouth of the San Bernard River.[8]

Around 9 A.M. the most advanced company, led by Lt. Robbins Grover, began to encounter scattered rifle fire from the Confederate pickets. From the amount of firing it appeared that this mounted picket detachment numbered only around ten men. After scattered volleys the Confederates remounted their horses and fell back a short distance. For more than an hour they repeated this tactic several times, clearly intending to delay the Federal movement as long as possible. Shortly before noon Ham and his detachment returned from their scout up the peninsula with the somewhat consoling message that no Confederate troops were observed in the immediate area north of the landing point. Hesseltine led the advance and continued the expedition's movement down the peninsula, harried sporadically by the Confederate pickets.

By 2 P.M. Hesseltine's command, hindered by numerous marshy bayous and isolated sniping from the Confederates, had only advanced seven miles down the peninsula. At 2:15 Hesseltine was startled by the discordant blaring of the *Granite City*'s steam whistle. Raising his marine telescope, he turned to view the ship just as the Parrott gun on the forward deck fired. The shell burst on the beach to their rear about half a mile away. They quickly realized what Captain Lamson was attempting to communicate—by focusing his telescope upon the farthest horizon of the peninsula Hesseltine was able to discern a large column of mounted men about a mile away, which was rapidly snaking its way down the peninsula. Ham and his company were ordered to remain in place as a rear guard while Hesseltine double-timed the other three companies down the beach in search of a suitable location to fortify. After a quarter of a mile he halted the troops at a jutting sand dune near the Gulf side flanked by marshy inlets on two sides and the men began working feverishly to construct a defensible breastwork from driftwood.[9]

While Hesseltine's troops hauled wood and dug emplacements in the sand, the *Granite City* had turned about and drew abreast of the oncoming Confederate cavalry. Buchel, who was commanding the Confederate force, had been alerted to the Federal troop landing shortly before 9 A.M. He had originally believed the landing to be an attempt to capture the newly constructed artillery breastworks at the mouth of Caney Creek. Upon his arrival there, he was informed by the lookout at a small sub-post that the Federals had proceeded down the peninsula. Several minutes later Lt. Col. R. R. Brown's cavalry brigade from Brazoria arrived on the scene. The total Confederate strength at this point was almost six hundred mounted troops. Buchel decided that Brown's force should remain near the breastworks in the event that the movement down the peninsula was a ploy to draw them away.[10]

By noon Buchel and his force were moving down the peninsula in pursuit of the Federals. Two hours and six miles into the pursuit, they spotted the Union gunboat offshore. Buchel moved his force to the western shore of the peninsula to hide their approach, but an alert sailor on board the *Granite City* observed the movement and sounded the alarm. Lamson turned the ship about and maneuvered her into position to use the starboard side guns. At 2:30 P.M. the guns aboard the *Granite City* began lobbing solid rifle and spherical case shot at the Confederate cavalry column. Buchel's force forged ahead despite a feverish barrage. The heavy seas prevented the gunners aboard the ship from achieving much accuracy, but their persistence eventually slowed the Confederate advance and gave the Union troops more time to entrench themselves.

The rear guard under Lieutenant Ham began to come under scattered firing from the advance elements of the Confederate cavalry shortly after 2:30 P.M. Hesseltine, having observed a number of the more bold Confederates advancing at a gallop on the western shoreline, ordered the bugler to sound recall. Ham's small detachment was concentrated near the east shore, where high sand dunes obscured the Confederates from his sight. Thus hidden, the Confederates advanced quickly along the west beach. When Hesseltine realized that Ham's retreat was not progressing fast enough he quickly collected a small detachment and led the men on a run toward the advancing Confederates. After a quarter-mile sprint, Ham's exhausted detachment was dangerously strung out along the beach. With only muzzle-loading weapons, a man who stopped to fire and reload quickly found himself outdistanced by his comrades. Hesseltine's detachment moved to a point about five hundred yards in front of the nearest Confederate cavalry and formed a skirmish line. Just as the last of Ham's detachment stumbled into the safety of the line, Hesseltine directed a volley into the approaching Confederates. Buchel, a Prussian and former officer in the Turkish army, was a stickler for uniformity. Hesseltine and his Pine State charges could see now the results of Buchel's influence on uniformity. Each Confederate mount bore a rider attired in undyed gray cotton pants with contrasting leather jackets, cowhide boots, and high black felt hats adorned with a single silver star. Several of these riders were seen to slump in the saddle during the first volley. The return fire was mainly sporadic and ineffective pistol fire. The continued naval gunfire and the troops' proximity to the Confederates created an untenable situation and both sides broke off and retreated. For the moment, Hesseltine's force had won. While the Confederates backtracked a short distance, Hesseltine led his men back down the beach to the "project," which now was beginning to resemble a genuinely defensible position.[11]

The supporting fire from the *Granite City* continued to hold back the Confederate cavalry, but the heavy seas coupled with a misting rain rendered it less effective. Buchel had regrouped his force and formulated a plan of attack. After fifteen minutes the Confederates resumed their advance. Buchel had divided his force into three groups; one detachment for each shoreline and a dismounted force to move among the sand dunes. One mounted force would move forward while the other remained stationary. When the advance mounted force halted, the other would rapidly ride forward and halt. In this staggered movement the Confederate force quickly narrowed the distance to less than a quarter of a mile. The boggy marsh on the Gulf side front of the breastwork slowed the Confederate advance on the right by forcing them to dismount and advance on foot. Hesseltine's selection of the site had proven to be a most redeeming decision. The Confederates, all but those on the west shoreline, were now dismounted and had formed into multiple skirmish lines. By 3:30 Confederate rifle fire began to hit the sand and wood emplacement. The naval fire support had decreased to the point of a single shot every few minutes, the narrow two hundred-yard distance between the lines making it as dangerous to the Union troops as to the Confederates. Hesseltine knew that when they were occupied to the front that the Confederate cavalry was going to make a mad dash on their left and surround them. As bullets hailed around him, Hesseltine ran from one position to another, imploring the men to hunker down and patiently continue to hold their fire. By now, the cavalry on the left had emerged from behind the sand dunes, so close that the stars on their hats were easily visible. Within seconds of emerging from behind the sand dunes they initiated a mad dash along the west beach. Hesseltine, having anticipated this action, ordered his men to open fire. The volley raked the exposed Confederate ranks and at least two Confederate cavalrymen reeled as if hit. Buchel yelled out for a retreat and the remainder of the force turned about. The Union soldiers erupted into cheers and jeers at the retreating soldiers; the second round of the encounter had also gone in favor of Hesseltine and the Thirteenth Maine.[12]

As night fell, Hesseltine, as instructed, ordered fires built on each flank to mark their position for the gunners on the *Granite City*. To counter any other flanking actions along the west shore, Hesseltine ordered a small emplacement constructed to guard that approach. After this incumbent activity the Union troops settled into a pensive, quiet stance among the cold, damp sands of Matagorda Peninsula. Each man now experimented within his own excavation how to achieve the greatest amount of comfort from a single blanket. New England ingenuity was stretched to its limits that night on the Texas Gulf Coast.

At 8:20 that evening, the *Sciota*, which had returned from her reconnaissance, anchored alongside the *Granite City*. Within an hour, the *Granite City* was steaming south toward Cavallo Pass. Lamson and his crew had completely expended their powder and ammunition supplies in supporting the infantry. Intending to obtain more supplies, she steamed toward the USS *Monongahela*, USS *Estrella*, and USS *Penobscot*, which were anchored off Cavallo Pass on blockade duty. After the offshore activity had ceased, an eerie silence fell as the wave crescendo subsided with the tidal activity. Except for strategically placed sentries, most of the Union infantrymen enjoyed an anxious sleep.

The night was restful only until 11:45, when the Confederates attempted a small flanking movement, once again along the west beach. Fortunately, the Union pickets gave an earlier warning. After firing their warning shots, they sprinted for the safety of the breastworks. During those brief seconds, Hesseltine dispatched the flank guards and waited for the Confederates to appear. Suddenly, the sand dunes to their front lit up with muzzle flashes. Over the next thirty minutes a fierce firefight ensued. Shortly after midnight the *Sciota* finally had enough steam to get under way. For what seemed like an eternity, Hesseltine's command endured a tremendous fusillade of musket fire from the sand dunes to their front. At 12:15 A.M. the *Sciota* was able to maneuver close enough to unleash her eleven-inch guns on the Confederate positions. Under fire from Hesseltine's infantry and the *Sciota*, the Confederates withdrew into the darkness and silence once again fell over the sands of Matagorda Peninsula. The solitude was broken only by the surf and the moans of several wounded soldiers. All were minor wounds and none proved to be incapacitating.[13]

If Frank Hesseltine dreamed during the early hours of December 30, he certainly awoke to a nightmare. During the early morning hours a heavy dense fog had set in, limiting visibility to about one-eighth of a mile. The fear of Buchel's cavalry emerging en masse from the fog was chilling. Unless the fog lifted soon, whatever actions the Confederates took would be free from the *Sciota*'s interference. Sentries were doubled and posted out several hundred yards for earlier warning. While Hesseltine pondered the calamity of the heavy fog, others reveled in its benefits. Ten miles up the coast at Hawkins Landing on Caney Creek, the CSS *John F. Carr* was a beehive of activity. Capt. S. K. Roberts, commanding the *Carr*, had received a request from Buchel late on the evening of December 29. Buchel had requested naval fire support and a troop transport landing behind the Federals to protect the picket detachment on Matagorda Peninsula.[14]

By 10 A.M. on December 30 the *John F. Carr*, with fifty-seven sharpshooters and six field artillery pieces aboard, was snaking its way slowly down Caney Creek. With only a thirty-inch draft, the *Carr* could easily navigate the shallow channel at Carancahua Bend and enter East Matagorda Bay. By 10:30 A.M. the fog had burned off enough to allow quarter-of-a-mile visibility. As soon as Captain Roberts gained the deeper waters of the bay, the throttles on the *Carr* were pushed forward to full open and both stacks belched forth their telltale columns of black smoke. After thirty minutes under full steam the *Carr* was throttled back as the Federals' position was located just above Edelbach Flats.[15]

Hesseltine had just complemented Felton on his job in constructing the breastworks when the twenty-pound Parrott rifle on the *Carr*'s forward deck erupted. An instant later the impact literally disintegrated a nearby dune and the entire breastwork was showered with sand. The *Carr* slowed almost to a crawl in the water and seconds later all three light artillery pieces on the port side unleashed shrapnel shot. Everybody hit the sand as pieces of metal shot and loose splintered wood pieces flew overhead. As the *Carr* began a loop to the north and west, her gun crews began reloading for a second volley. Hesseltine, in light of the impending second barrage from the *Carr*, shouted to his officers to leave him several men from each company and take the others and evacuate them from the breastworks. He directed Grover to have them crawl out to the east until obscured by the high sand dunes on the east beach. Remaining behind with his small entourage, Hesseltine fully intended for the Confederates to believe that the breastworks were still fully occupied. The signal fires had to be built up to compensate for the lingering fog. Casting his eyes toward the *Carr*, Hesseltine could see the loop almost completed, while a quick glance to the right exposed a black pillar of smoke rising from the *Sciota*, which was finally getting under way. Seconds later the *Carr* unleashed her second volley. This time, however, she came to a dead stop in the water and the Confederate gunners maintained a constant barrage. The hidden retreat had proven to be more effective than anticipated. The *Sciota*, too, began to unleash its total armaments. She had drawn directly abreast of the signal fires and with high elevation settings was attempting to lob shells over the breast-works at the *Carr*. The heavy waves thwarted her efforts and some of her shells began falling dangerously close to the breastworks. Hesseltine ordered his nine assistants to evacuate the works and join the others. Despite the intense shelling, he continued for the next ten minutes to run about gathering driftwood and piling it on the signal fires. Only after the fires were raging did he recover his gear and join the others.

The *Carr* continued to shell the works for another fifteen minutes and in doing so retarded Buchel's force, which was poised to make an assault. The *Carr*'s firing eventually obliterated the works and, when no white flag was forth-coming, she moved in closer to discover it was vacant. Roberts now endeavored to carry out the second part of his mission.[16]

At 3:30 P.M. Roberts steered the *Carr* southwestward down East Matagorda Bay about three hundred yards offshore from the west beach of the peninsula. In addition to supporting Buchel's cavalry, he had been assigned the secondary task of retrieving Henderson's picket detachment to prevent the men from being captured. By 4:30 P.M. he had been joined by the CSS *Cora* and had dropped anchor in the shallow waters near Hog Island.[17] Shortly afterward he began to launch his small boats. Roberts's original plan was altered when the *Cora* brought in forty-three volunteers from Matagorda City. Instead of recovering the pickets, the volunteers, led by Capt. E. S. Rugeley, were disembarked in order to set up an ambush. By 6 P.M., just before reaching shore, the Confeder-ate force was startled by the sudden appearance of five Union vessels just off-shore from the opposite beach. The re-supplied *Granite City* along with the *Penobscot*, *Estrella*, and *Monongahela* had arrived to assist the *Sciota*. Within minutes, the *Sciota* and *Estrella* opened fire upon the still-anchored *Carr*. Roberts quickly lifted anchor and cast off, desperately attempting to evade the barrage from the *Estrella* and *Sciota*'s six twenty-pound Parrott rifles and how-itzers. By sunset the wave heights had increased to six feet and the temperature had plummeted. Rugeley's young volunteers turned their small rowboats about and rowed southwest.[18]

After evacuating the breastworks Hesseltine's command had continued to march down the peninsula. Upon rejoining them Hesseltine had divided the men into two separate detachments, either one able to fall back on the support of the other in the case of attack from either direction. After advancing about twelve miles down the peninsula, shortly after sundown a fire was observed to their front about a quarter of a mile away. Upon reconnoitering the fire,

Hesseltine found a distraught man attempting to extinguish the flames with a shovel. The flames were the remains of the man's house, which had been set on fire by the Confederate pickets because the man had previously rendered assistance to a Federal cavalry detachment.[19] The fresh water this man's well provided was the first water the men had enjoyed since leaving the breast-works. After filling their canteens, Hesseltine and his command resumed their march. By 11 P.M. the men could go no farther and Hesseltine allowed them to build fires, which brought little relief from the piercing cold night air. The glare of one of the fires exposed a house hidden among the dunes. The inhabi-tants, two women and two infants, grudgingly allowed the troops to enter. Most of the troops crowded into the house and enjoyed the relative comfort of a blazing fire in the large fireplace. The water in the canteens, filled only an hour earlier, was frozen solid.[20]

At 9 A.M. the next day Hesseltine and his men were startled by naval gunfire down the peninsula. The *Carr*, in attempting to evade the *Estrella*'s barrage in the heavy seas the night before, had run aground. Upon discovering her beached, the *Estrella* and *Sciota* had moved in to complete her destruction. Hesseltine quickly assembled the command and resumed the march down the peninsula. Six hours later the troops were back aboard the *Sciota*. The ordeal of confusing and amusing the enemy was finally over. General Ransom personally greeted each man with a handshake as they boarded the ship. Sailors manning the rigging greeted them with cheers, which were heartily returned for the valiant efforts of those on board. Capt. George H. Perkins ordered the issue of double rations that night. Slightly before midnight the *Sciota* came to anchor just inside Matagorda Bay. Comfortably housed inside the cabins, the men gave thanks and rejoiced in welcoming in a new year, 1864.[21]

In his written report to General Ransom the next day, Frank Hesseltine unselfishly and proudly wrote that, "On the march, the sick and exhausted sol-diers had been nobly aided by their comrades so that not a man, musket or equip-ment was left to the enemy."[22] His report continued with liberal praise for his Navy comrades, adding:

> Captain Perkins, of the *U.S.S. Sciota* excited my admiration by the daring man-ner in which he exposed his ship through the night in the surf till it broke all about him, that he might, close to us, lend the moral support of his XI-inch guns and howitzers, and by his gallantry in bringing us off during the gale.[23]

He added for Captain Lamson, of the *Granite City*, that "great credit is due for his exertion to retard and drive back the enemy. By the loss he inflicted upon them it is clear but for the heavy sea he would have freed us from any exertion."[24] He summarized his expedition of amusing and confusing the enemy as not altogether valueless as it had resulted in the destruction of one Confederate gunboat. It had secured information concerning enemy forces in the area, and added many new and important details to the maps of the area.

Ransom included his comments on the affair when he forwarded the report to the army chief of staff. At Fort Esperanza on January 3, he wrote:

> I have the honor to transmit herewith the official report of Lieutenant-Colonel Hesseltine, Thirteenth Maine Infantry, of his expedition up the peninsula and in doing so I feel that it is due to Colonel Hesseltine that I should recommend him for his conduct as well as that of his brave officers and men as deserving of the highest praise.[25]

In that same endorsement, Ransom, in his own personal comment on the reconnaissance, alluded that its success had proven Colonel Hesseltine "an officer of rare courage and judgment."[26] At division headquarters, Maj. Gen. C. C. Washburn added a commendation on January 6, 1864, commenting, "The conduct of Colonel Hesseltine and his men is deserving of great praise."[27]

Shortly after his daring episode of amusing and confusing the Confederates on Matagorda Peninsula, Hesseltine was reassigned to court martial duty at New Orleans. In mid-1864 he returned to Maine, where he raised a new corps of troops for the Thirteenth Maine Infantry. Over the next year and a half he served with his regiment in the Washington, D.C., perimeter defenses. During the winter of 1864 he served under Gen. P. H. Sheridan in the Shenandoah Valley campaign. On July 6, 1865, he ended his brief military career at Augusta, Maine. During the mustering-out ceremony for his beloved Thirteenth Maine Infantry, he rode a souvenir from the Texas Gulf Coast campaign. Zip, a beautiful chestnut stallion, was captured from Confederate forces at Aransas Pass in November 1863 and had borne Hesseltine throughout his service at Washington, D.C., and in the Shenandoah Valley. The horse was kept on the family farm in Maine, where for many years it was a fond symbol of his harrowing experiences on the Texas Gulf Coast beaches.[28]

After resuming his law studies, Hesseltine successfully passed the Maine State Bar exams in late 1865 and became an attorney. His first job, ironically, was as a registrar of bankruptcy court in Savannah, Georgia. During one of his earliest cases, he met a young woman who was attempting to reconcile her family's estate. The woman turned out to have been a prominent resident of Matagorda, Texas. From her, Hesseltine learned of the aborted ambush plans of

December 30 by Henderson and Rugeley's command, which were thwarted by the fateful weather change. He also learned that twenty-two young Confederate soldiers had been lost that night by drowning and exposure when their small boats were swamped by the heavy waves. Despite his judgment and conspicuous acts of gallantry, it appeared that fate had intervened to preserve the success of his reconnaissance of Matagorda Peninsula.

A year earlier in Georgia, another twist of fate had befallen Hesseltine. His beloved and respected former commanding officer, Gen. Thomas Ransom, had died from the infection of an old wound. It was he who had argued in favor of a Texas Gulf Coast invasion instead of a thrust up the Red River. It was also he who had recommended Hesseltine as deserving of the highest praise. If that highest praise were ever to be construed or conveyed into a Medal of Honor award, it most certainly would have come as a result of Ransom's efforts. His confidence and admiration for Hesseltine's services had been unwavering.

After a successful law career and the intervention of thirty years, Hesseltine became very active in the affairs of the Loyal Legion, an organization comprised of former Union Army and Navy officers. The various Loyal Legion chapters, known as Commanderies, conducted excellent analysis and narratives of Civil War campaigns and strategies. The publication in the late 1880s of both Abraham Lincoln's Civil War papers and the compiled records of the rebellion generated a great deal of interest about overall strategy and various campaigns that had been virtually ignored previously by the dominant eastern press. One of those that had been ignored was the South Texas Gulf Coast campaign of 1863–1864. The delicate nature of Lincoln's correspondence in dealing with French-controlled Mexico had raised many questions about the general staff's approach toward intervention in Texas. Hesseltine, as one of the few remaining survivors of the South Texas Gulf Coast campaign, was asked to prepare and present a paper upon the subject. Attending the presentation at the Boston Commandery in December 1894 was Massachusetts Congressman William Everett, who was very impressed with the presentation, especially with the personal narrative of the December 28–31, 1863, reconnaissance of Matagorda Peninsula. Everett felt that Hesseltine's timely advance and attack on the Confederate cavalry to protect Ham's retreat and his remaining behind in the breastworks despite intense naval gunfire merited more than great praise. Additional commendatory comments by former Navy Capt. George H. Perkins, also a Boston Commandery member, convinced Everett that Hesseltine should petition the War Department for a Medal of Honor. On February 20, 1895, Everett submitted Hesseltine's application and copies of the commendatory reports from Generals Ransom and Washburn. On February 25, 1895, Secretary of War Daniel S. Lamont ordered that the Medal of Honor be granted to Frank S. Hesseltine. The medal was engraved and issued on March 2, 1895. It was sent to his residence at Melrose, Massachusetts, and there is no evidence of a formal award ceremony.[29]

George E. Albee, circa 1895. He joked that his gallant deeds in 1869 in Texas against the Comanches and Kiowas were in part retribution for the 1669 burning by Indians of his ancestor Benjamin Albee's gristmill in Connecticut. *Photograph courtesy the Library of Congress.*

CHAPTER 3

Repulsing The Tribes in Comancheria

September 16 , 1869

——— ⭐ ———

1st Lt. George E. Albee

O n March 4, 1869, Ulysses S. Grant became the eighteenth president of
the United States. Determined to root out the corruption and inefficien-
cy of the Department of the Interior, Grant dismissed many entrenched
civil servants from the Indian Bureau and replaced them with religious leaders,
who he felt were beyond corruption. The Society of Friends, or the Quakers,
long had been involved in Indian betterment programs and were the most willing. Many were appointed to influential positions within the Indian Bureau,
where they implemented their benevolent peace policy, the basis of which was
that kind treatment of the Indians coupled with the basic civilizing tenets of the
Medicine Lodge Treaty would eventually convert the Indians away from their
warlike culture. Almost immediately there were policy conflicts between the
Quakers and army officials. Despite army protests, the Quakers ordered the
release of Satanta, Mow-wi, and Lone Wolf.

Satanta and Lone Wolf, having bragged to the previous Indian Bureau officials
about their heinous crimes in Texas, had been tracked down and captured by the
army. Conferences were held with the various tribes during which the Quakers
fervently espoused forgiveness to the Indians for past evil deeds. The Quakers
further angered army officials by instituting a liberal policy of issuing passes to
the tribes for off-reservation hunting privileges. The policy was perfectly legal

under the Medicine Lodge Treaty but its extreme application had grave ramifications. By late summer more than half of the Kiowas, Comanches, and their affiliated bands were absent from the reservation.[1] Almost immediately reports of Indian attacks began to pour in from Texas frontier counties.

After two treaties, numerous peace conferences, several reasonably successful military campaigns, and a new benevolent humanitarian-based Indian policy, the frontier areas of Colorado, Kansas, and Texas in 1869 were no safer than they had been a decade earlier. It was unmistakably clear that if the frontier areas along the southern High Plains were to be rendered safe for settlement, then the Texas Panhandle sanctuary of the warring tribes and their Comanchero allies would have to be wrested from their control. The Comancheros were mostly New Mexicans from near Albuquerque who traded goods to the Indians in return for stolen Texas livestock. This material support allowed the Indians to continue raiding.

Gen. Joseph J. Reynolds, commander of the Fifth Military District, which included Texas and Louisiana, was heavily involved in the politics and implementation of Reconstruction policies. He had little time for Indian affairs and the pacification of the frontier. In early 1869 he turned responsibility for frontier pacification over to Col. Ranald S. Mackenzie. Mackenzie, a twenty-nine-year-old New Yorker, had graduated first in the West Point class of 1862. He compiled a brilliant combat record as one of the young wonder generals of the Civil War. At the war's end Gen. Ulysses S. Grant had labeled him "the most promising young officer of the Army."[2] During the two years Mackenzie was under his command, Reynolds became convinced that only Mackenzie's brilliant organizational skills and concepts of strategy, along with his aggressive nature, could bring an end to the turmoil on the Texas frontier. Mackenzie was given free rein and he quickly formulated plans for tactical operations on the southern High Plains.

Under the Military Reconstruction Acts, Texas had been divided into subdistricts to facilitate localized operations, which resulted in a strictly reactive stance on the army's part. Troops available only within these subdistricts had been dispatched in response to Indian raids. Mackenzie quickly realized the futility of this approach. One of his recommendations was to periodically combine troops from these subdistricts and send military expeditions to seek out the off-reservation tribes. Before this could be done, intelligence data about the southern High Plains had to be acquired. Mackenzie set about organizing a complex system of spies and informants. Former Indian captives were interviewed to obtain additional information. The tribes on the reservations were queried for information about the haunts and movements of the off-reservation bands, whom they referred to as the Quohadas or runaways. The U.S. Army officially classified these bands as "hostiles." Scouting patrols were dispatched further and further north and west to explore for and map the fresh water sources so necessary for large-scale operations in an arid climate. Post commanders at the frontier outposts were encouraged to recruit intelligent and energetic civilian guides who had a thorough knowledge of their local regions. Mackenzie added further incentive by promising the scouts and guides rewards of captured livestock when they found Indian encampments. Mackenzie also sought and obtained authorization for additional Indian scouts in Texas. Mackenzie often worked into the early morning hours, diligently applying his brilliant mathematical skills to formulate the immense logistics necessary to maintain large bodies of troops in the field for extended periods of time. The formulas for per-day hay and corn consumption for Civil War operations had to be reformulated for the arid west. The physical effects of men and animals consuming alkaline-saturated water had to be studied and army surgeons had to plan diets to counter those effects. Land navigation techniques on a boundless plain with few known points of reference had to be refined and passed on to the officers. Sextants and the latest astronomical almanacs had to be ordered. The details seemed endless, but by August 1869 Mackenzie was ready for his first thrust into the southern High Plains.

Despite all of Mackenzie's meticulous planning, the ultimate success of those plans depended greatly on the officers and men actually involved in field operations. Each had to be willing to energetically pursue the Indians and to boldly confront them in combat. By the end of August the officers and men expected to perform these deeds were headed toward Fort Concho, the designated base of operations. Mackenzie's plan was to first send forth a one hundred-man reconnaissance patrol to determine if information that had been obtained from an informant was true. Capt. Henry Carroll was to command this patrol assisted by Capts. Edward M. Heyl and George C. Gamble and Lt. Eugene Dimmick.[3]

Shortly after noon on September 4, 1869, Captain Carroll and his fifty-man detachment of Companies F and M, Ninth United States Cavalry, arrived at Fort Concho. Upon his arrival Carroll reported immediately to the post commander's office. He expected to see Col. Edward Hatch but found Captain Gamble serving as the acting post commander due to Hatch's extended leave of absence. Lieutenant Dimmick had been assigned as the post treasurer and was heavily involved with contractors in the post's construction projects.

Though Captain Carroll's immediate verbal response to the total lack of an officer to command Company B went unrecorded, Captain Gamble quickly calmed him down. Gamble believed he knew an infantry officer on the post who might be willing to command the company for the duration of the patrol. An orderly was sent to find 1st Lt. George E. Albee. Albee, a twenty-four-year-old New Hampshire native, eagerly accepted Carroll's offer and orders were drawn up assigning Albee to command the forty troopers from Companies B and E, Ninth United States Cavalry. Lieutenant Albee immediately located the two ranking non-commissioned officers of those two companies, informed them of the change, and instructed them to finalize preparations for their departure on September 5.

Shortly before sunrise on September 5 Captain Carroll led the 103-man column as it marched northward from Fort Concho along the west bank of the North Fork of the Concho River. Because of extremely warm temperatures, sometimes in excess of one hundred degrees, Carroll rested the troops for several hours during the heat of the day and resumed the march during the late afternoon. By September 8 the command had progressed more than fifty-five miles and was encamped near the mouth of Dobson Creek. They had not seen any signs of Indians. Shortly before noon on September 12 the command passed east of Gunsight Peaks. Carroll halted the march two hours later on a good vantage point overlooking the upper Colorado River basin. Twelve miles to the northeast Muchaque Peak could easily be seen rising starkly to five hundred feet above the surrounding terrain. The informant, a New Mexican, had mentioned Muchaque Peak as the site of one of the prominent Comanchero trading rendezvous bases. With only two hours of sunlight remaining, Carroll decided to encamp for the night and enter the area early the next morning.[4]

The command rose at 4 A.M. on September 13 and by sunrise had arrived at the south bank of the Colorado River. Within minutes a smoke signal was seen to the northeast and moments later a second smoke signal was seen to the north emanating from a jutting point on the escarpment. The command realized that the Indians were aware of their presence. Just after crossing the Colorado the command discovered a trail of five pony tracks leading northwest. Carroll believed these tracks were a ploy meant to draw the troops away from Muchaque and decided to disregard them for the moment. He divided the command into two groups and sent one to approach the suspected encampment from the southeast and the other to approach from the south. Lieutenant Albee's detachment entered the area at the designated time only to find old evidence of a large Indian presence. Carroll decided to camp there and allow the men to eat and rest while the guide, Frank Jones, attempted to pick up any fresh trails.[5]

As the smoke signals had come from the north and northwest Carroll decided to resume the march on September 14 in that direction. Shortly after entering the canyon at the head of the Colorado River, Carroll learned that neither the Mexican informant nor the guide were familiar with the terrain to the northwest but he decided to push on despite this revelation. By sundown the command had emerged from the canyon onto the flat high plains. For the first time the U.S Army had penetrated into the southern High Plains sanctuary of the Comanches, Kiowas, and their allies. The command finally went into camp shortly before sundown at or near Saleh Lake.[6]

At daybreak on September 15 the members of the command were amazed to find a network of well-traveled trails converging and diverging from the lake. Carroll decided to follow the trail leading northeast toward the location where the second smoke signal had been seen the day before. Less than an hour into the march, as they neared Laguna Quatro, they discovered five fresh pony tracks converging onto the trail from the southeast. The command moved along the trail for another twelve miles before striking another trail of eleven ponies northwest of Double Lakes and also converging from the southeast. The command followed the trail throughout the afternoon and easily advanced another twenty miles before reaching the middle portion of Yellowhouse Canyon, where they camped on the North Fork of the Double Mountain Fork of the Brazos River. While the soldiers set up camp five Indians appeared on the northern ridgeline, made a loud demonstration, and raised their weapons high to invite combat. Even after forty miles in the saddle Lieutenant Albee and Captain Heyl could not resist the challenge and flew to their mounts. Along with a handful of similarly eager troopers, the band of eleven men sped across the riverbed and up the incline amid the loud boisterous banter of the others. Both Heyl and Albee had Civil War and frontier combat experience and knew what an ambush was. They had read about Capt. William Fetterman in Wyoming, who had led his eighty troopers over a ridgeline into a Sioux ambush three years earlier. Neither Fetterman nor any of his eighty troopers survived. Heyl had already been wounded twice in Indian combat. Albee, still chafing under the stigma of his Civil War regiment's official censure for cowardice, was not about to stop and he cleared the ridgeline first. Two hundred yards away were five Indians, who instantly unleashed a volley from muzzle-loading carbines and pistols. Albee, luckily the recipient of a poorly aimed volley, charged toward them with his pistol blazing. When the Indians saw the other troops they turned about and fled. Heyl and his band of troopers emerged from the canyon on the right and joined the chase. The Indians quickly scattered. Within seconds Albee found himself out of sight of the others and several hundred yards behind a single Indian. Albee continued his pursuit for several miles before he terminated the chase and he met Heyl and the others back at the canyon rim. They too had found their mounts second best in their races with the Indian ponies. Once back at the campsite they learned that Carroll, having found freshwater springs, had decided to move the camp to a place near pools below these springs six miles further up the canyon.[7]

Just as Albee and Heyl and their accompanying troopers reached the new campsite around 5 P.M., the northern ridgeline was again filled with a line of mounted warriors with upraised rifles, lances, and pistols. Their increased numbers caused Captain Carroll to take a more prudent approach to the challenge. Albee and Heyl were again willing to engage the Indians and were assigned the available troopers from Companies E and F. Heyl was instructed to focus on the Indians to his front while Albee led his men up the canyon and attempted to gain the rear. Heyl and his troopers gained the ridgeline and found the Indians arrayed in a single line several hundred yards away. In the meantime, Albee galloped up the canyon and turned into a sub-canyon. The plan was for Heyl to occupy and stall the Indians. His troops had advanced to within five hundred yards of the Indian line before the Indians opened fire. Several troopers' horses were wounded and Heyl had no alternative than to return fire. Just as Heyl's troops unleashed their first volley the Indians turned and fled northeastward. Albee's detachment emerged out of the sub-canyon and onto the level plain just as the last of the Indians passed. Both detachments fell in behind them in pursuit. They continued the chase for several miles and exchanged sporadic gunfire before darkness forced Heyl to halt the pursuit. Albee, who was on the extreme left of the line, either out of stubborn doggedness or temporary deafness, continued on into the darkness. On a hunch he turned westward, deviating from the path the fleeing Indians had taken. The hunch paid off after several miles when he gained a slight rise and discovered an Indian village less than a mile away. After staking out his horse he made his way on foot to within a quarter of a mile from the village, where he was able to discern at least one hundred lodges and teepees. It was at least three hours after sunset before he returned to the camp in Yellowhouse Canyon. Albee's return relieved Carroll's anxiety and he was elated about the discovery of the village. Since Albee was certain that he had not been discovered and since most of the command's horses were severely worn by the day's marches and pursuits, Carroll deemed it better to wait until the next morning before attacking the village. A number of Albee and Heyl's troopers found their clothing pierced with ball and arrow points, which created a great deal of anxiety among the other troops, most of whom had never before fired their weapons in action against Indians.[8]

The company cooks were up at 5 A.M. on September 16. An hour later the command was eating breakfast and packing up gear when a sentry suddenly yelled, "Indians!" and pointed to the southwestern ridgeline. There, arrayed in full war regalia, was one warrior carrying a red flag. Another appeared and another until finally eleven warriors were counted. They raised their weapons high in challenge just as they had the previous evening.

Albee and Frank Jones, the civilian guide, as well as another trooper, had been the earliest risers and by the time most of the others had lined up for breakfast they were already saddling their mounts and stowing their gear. Albee, as he had done twice the previous day, requested permission to attack, which Carroll granted. Albee, Jones, and the lone trooper quickly galloped up the incline toward the Indians. Just as they had the evening before, the Indians unleashed an inaccurate volley and then turned and fled. Unlike the previous day, Albee and the others were on fresh mounts and began to gain on the Indians. Just as they had the previous day, the Indians fled and then scattered. Albee fell in behind three warriors while Jones and the trooper sped after the flag bearer and his group. After less than a mile of pursuit the three Indians ahead of Albee turned to face their pursuer and unleashed a flurry of arrows, all of which missed their mark. Albee returned fire with his pistol. One shot struck one of the Indians in the leg, passed through his leg, and killed the Indian's pony. As the wounded warrior fell to the ground one of the others went to his aid. The third attempted to shield the others but Albee's pistol fire sent him fleeing. The other mounted warrior bolted away with his wounded comrade in tow. The click of the hammer on a used primer forced Albee to rein up just behind the fleeing Indians. After inserting a new cylinder into his pistol, Albee turned about and galloped after the others. He met them shortly afterward, having again been bested in their race with the lighter Indian ponies.[9]

Upon returning to the campsite the command was found saddled and ready to move out. After Albee had finished relating the results of his foray, Carroll informed him that since his mount was already winded he was placing him in charge of the pack train guard. Albee reluctantly remained behind while the command moved to attack the village he had discovered the previous evening. Just as the command began its movement up the canyon, a long line of Indians again appeared on the northern ridgeline. Heyl's detachment was sent to confront and occupy the Indians while Carroll rode toward their flank. Once on the level plain a running battle ensued for more than eight miles in which at least five Indians were seen to fall, while an estimated twenty-five were wounded. Only four troopers were wounded, none seriously. The attack was broken off when the command's horses became winded and the troops became too dangerously scattered. After regrouping, the command resumed the march on the village, which according to Albee was less than two miles away. The final approach into the village was accomplished by the convergence of four detachments. They found the village abandoned, apparently only hours before, since cooking fires were still smoldering. The village was searched thoroughly but nothing of immense value was found. Lt. Ira J. Culver did find a curious artifact in the center of the village. Apparently a crude signpost, two sticks had been tied together at right angles. The longer stick had been stuck into the ground and the shorter stick was pointing in the direction taken by the departing Indians. Below the stick was a strip of rawhide about two feet long, the smooth side of which contained a crudely drawn picture of a soldier. The vertical stick had several cloth streamers attached at the top, no doubt meant to attract the attention of any of the band who might still be out. One pair of children's moccasins was also found, indicating that this band had their families with them.[10]

Carroll realized that the command was now absolutely lost as far as the guides were concerned. They were short of rations and ammunition so he decided to guide the command directly east to intercept the road between Fort Griffin and Fort Concho. During this movement they were forced to ignore four fresh trails made by an estimated six or seven hundred Indians. These bands of Indians had with them loose stock estimated at three thousand head. During the return march the command also discovered that the water of the northernmost fork of the Brazos River was not brackish and the area was ideally suited to use as a base of operations. On the evening of October 7 the command arrived back at Fort Concho. The patrol had been very successful. They had traversed almost seven hundred miles of the Texas South High Plains, an area never penetrated before by a U.S. Army command in active field operations. The command had inflicted summary damage upon the off-reservation Indians and, most importantly, they had confirmed the location of a freshwater stream suitable for use as a permanent supply base.

Mackenzie was elated at the results and was anxious to initiate the follow-up expedition. After he learned from Captain Carroll that the guides were unfamiliar with the area, Mackenzie began a frantic search to locate someone from the Carroll expedition who would be willing to accompany the second expedition. Mackenzie's search led him to Albee's quarters, where Albee succumbed to Mackenzie's pleas and agreed to accompany the second expedition. He jokingly reminded Mackenzie of his New England ancestor, Benjamin Albee, whose gristmill had been burned in 1669 by Indians, claiming that after two hundred years it was about time to even the score. Capt. John M. Bacon, who was to command the Ninth Cavalry troops, immediately had orders drawn up assigning Albee as temporary commander of the twenty-five troopers of Company L, Ninth Cavalry.[11]

On October 10, 1869, Albee, with Sgts. Ezra Taylor and George Mason at his side, followed Mackenzie and Bacon out of Fort Concho along the road to Fort Griffin. By October 18 the Bacon expedition had arrived at the old abandoned Fort Phantom Hill, where they were joined by a detachment of the Fourth Cavalry and eleven Tonkawa Indian scouts commanded by Lt. Peter M. Boehm. Early in the morning of October 20, Sergeant Simone led the Tonkawa scouts westward from Phantom Hill. Over the next four days the expedition snaked its way along the Clear Fork of the Brazos River to a point ten miles west of the Double Mountains. Albee reassured Mackenzie, who was becoming extremely anxious, that the Fresh Water Fork of the Brazos was less than twenty miles to the northwest. After less than two hours into the day's march on October 25 the command struck the mouth of Duck Creek. Over the next two days Mackenzie conducted a survey of the surrounding terrain. The conical shaped peak, later named Soldier Mound, was of special interest to him, as it would afford an excellent view of the surrounding terrain for miles. Several nearby springs of reasonably good water would provide enough for the establishment of an infantry encampment. After moving westward for twelve miles he came to the rippling waters of the Fresh Water Fork of the Brazos River. The water was superior in quality to any yet encountered and was in such quantities that Mackenzie became convinced that it would be an excellent location for a base of operations.[12] The white subsurface rock strata of the canyon wall would become the basis of its official naming on army maps. The stream upon which they camped that night became known as the White River. The canyon name somehow was translated to Spanish and was known thereafter as Blanco Canyon. It was an idyllic oasis among the surrounding flat and arid terrain. There was no doubt as to why the area held extensive proof of a large, previous, and recent Indian presence. The question still remained as to who would ultimately control the area—the Indians or the army.

During the early morning hours of October 28 several squads of troops were dispatched to reconnoiter the surrounding terrain. By noon all of the squads had returned to the camp. The entire command was strung out along the White River enjoying their noon meal when the cry of "Indians!" rang out from several sentry posts. Albee instantly scanned the nearby northern ridgeline for familiar faces. The scenario was somewhat familiar, but within seconds approximately three hundred warriors were arrayed along the ridgeline. Once arrayed they broke into a loud banter and raised their weapons in a challenging manner just as they had previously. Unlike before, however, the warriors rode over the precipice in a headlong rush toward the command. Albee quickly realized their intent was to stampede the command's horses and he and a handful of troopers were soon mounted. While the others clamored to get organized, Albee's detachment bolted toward the middle of the onrushing line of Indians. Albee, well in advance of the others, was soon among the Indians, where his close-range pistol fire emptied several saddles. The Indians quickly turned and fled back up the incline and onto the flat plains. Though their initial intent to stampede the command's horses had failed, they retreated only a short distance before they turned and prepared to again meet the soldiers in combat.[13]

Once Bacon had organized the command they joined Albee's detachment and the entire command sped off after the Indians. Once upon the level plain the command formed into a single rank and advanced toward the Indians. When they were within four hundred yards of the Indians Bacon ordered a charge into the Indians' line. At two hundred yards the order was given to open fire. A number of the Indians and their ponies fell in this first volley and the remainder turned and fled. Over the next four hours the troopers pursued the Indians for seven miles.[14] As in most clashes with bodies of Indians the skirmishing became very scattered. Albee was conspicuously daring in several hand-to-hand encounters during this skirmishing and was lauded for his conduct in the reports of fellow officers. Several times during the fighting it became necessary to sound recall, but, once reorganized, the troops again charged into the milling Indians. At Mackenzie's suggestion, small detachments of troopers were dispatched to inquire into the condition of fallen Indians, in hopes of obtaining wounded prisoners. Albee led one of these small groups, which was viciously attacked by hordes of Indian women, who had secreted themselves in nearby ravines. Unwilling to shoot women armed only with knives and sticks, the command was unable to capture or recover a single Indian casualty although at least forty had been seen falling from their mounts. Bacon decided to terminate the chase when the Indians began to set the grass on fire. As the command's horses were severely worn down Bacon decided to encamp where they were. Despite the cold night air he was unwilling to invite further attack and issued orders against campfires.[15]

At sunrise on October 29 the command woke to find twenty-five warriors hovering on the northern horizon. The command was quickly mounted and charged after the Indians. The troops' first volley dropped several more Indians and their ponies. Unlike in the earlier clash, the command's horses were fresh and they were able to gain ground on the Indians. Albee's detachment, on the extreme right end of the attacking line, was able to enter the Indian ranks as they veered away from the advancing center of the command's line. Albee and his detachment once again found themselves involved in a close encounter that evolved into numerous hand-to-hand clashes. Arrows flew in every direction as pistols and rifles, once emptied, were used as clubs. The Indians resorted to their final arsenal, lances, and inflicted several minor wounds upon a number of Albee's detachment before the main body of troops entered the skirmish. Once again the Indians fled in panic from the cavalry troopers and Tonkawa Indian scouts. The command was halted, regrouped, and ordered to resume pursuit. The Indians, now distinctly recognized by the Tonkawa scouts as Kiowas and Comanches, fled to the northwest. The chase continued over the next several hours for about seven miles. The Indian trail turned westward and eventually southwestward.

Shortly before noon the Tonkawas, suspecting close proximity to the Kiowas and Comanches, excitedly broke into a gallop. Bacon restrained them upon the command's arrival at the eastern rim of Blanco Canyon. Using his telescope, Bacon was able to discern a small Indian village in a sub-canyon on the west side. Several companies were dispatched around the head of the canyon to cover escape routes from the village. The Tonkawas led the remainder of the command over the canyon rim toward the village, which was about two miles away. The Tonkawas, led by Sergeant Simone, entered the village just as the Indians hurried to their mounts. Tonkawa Scouts Henry and Anderson brazenly charged into them. Anderson received an arrow wound from one of the mounted warriors. Enraged over Anderson's injury, Henry bolted toward the perpetrator and used the butt of his carbine to deliver a lethal blow to the head of the Indian who had wounded Anderson.[16] In the meantime, Albee's detachment on the right had cut off and encircled a small group of women and children who were attempting to escape. The other troops from the Ninth Cavalry companies swarmed into the village and within minutes dismounted to ferret out any remaining Indians. The two companies dispatched to cover the escape routes set about rounding up the loose stock, which had stampeded when the shooting started.

Short on ammunition and with severely worn mounts, Bacon decided to terminate the expedition and camp there for the night before returning to Fort Concho. During the interrogation of the prisoners it was learned that several other Indian camps were within ten miles of this village. The captives disclosed that most of the village inhabitants had returned to the reservation to obtain their annuity goods. The captives further revealed that annuity goods were also issued for those bands that did not go in and would be brought to them when the others returned from the reservation. The captives also verified suspicions about the existence of the Comanchero trade system based in New Mexico, confirming that citizens from the west frequently came to their camps to trade goods for the stolen livestock.[17]

Early in the morning of October 30 the command began its trek back to Fort Concho. Before departing, they set the village on fire, hoping that the plumes of smoke would send a message and that the devastation would indicate that the Indians' sanctuary on the southern High Plains was no longer safe. During the return march the command discovered an extensive wagon trail network, signs of substantial Indian camps, and months-old cattle trails leading toward the Red River. The tired and haggard command arrived back at Fort Concho on November 14.

Both the Carroll and Bacon expeditions had been profoundly successful due in great part to the gallant services of Lieutenant Albee. His immediate response to menacing Comanches and Kiowas on September 15 prevented the possible stampede of the command's horses, thus assuring the continued success of the expedition. His discovery of the village on the evening of September 15 during a dangerous solo reconnaissance added valuable information about the Quohadas. His voluntary attack upon a numerically superior band of Indians on the morning of September 16 inflicted the first known casualties by the U.S. Army upon Indians on the southern High Plains of Texas. His willingness to guide the Bacon expedition with his recently acquired knowledge of the terrain contributed greatly to its success. His actions in repulsing the attack upon the mostly immobile command on October 28 and again during the extensive actions of that afternoon as well as his quick and decisive movement on October 29 resulted in the successful capture of seven prisoners. The captives eventually were used as ransom to gain the release of Tonkawa and white captives held by the warring tribes, setting into motion a common procedure used throughout the remaining years of the Plains Indian Wars. The discovery of a freshwater fork on the Brazos River enabled Mackenzie to establish a base of operations deep inside the Indians' sanctuary. Troops operating from this base eventually successfully wrested control of the South High Plains from the hostile Indians and their allies, the Comancheros.[18]

Lieutenant Albee's significant contributions to the outcome and results of both expeditions went without just reward for almost a quarter of a century. In 1888, anticipating proposed federal legislation, the War Department began a compilation of documentation on gallant acts U.S. Army personnel had performed since the end of the Civil War. This documentation was to be used in the certification and award of brevet rank, Certificates of Merit, and Medals of Honor, primarily for gallant acts performed during post–Civil War Indian campaigns. The documentation was to be reviewed by a board of active duty-officers and their decisions would be the basis for granting the various awards.[19]

In early July 1893, while in Washington, D.C., on business affairs as an inspector of artillery ammunition for Winchester Repeating Arms Company, Albee stayed at his usual haunt, the Army and Navy Club, where he had a chance encounter with an old friend, Henry W. Lawton, at the time a lieutenant colonel in the army inspector general's office. They reminisced about their services in Texas under Colonel Mackenzie when both were lieutenants. Albee recalled his hair-raising accounts about the 1869 Carroll and Bacon expeditions. His foolhardy attacks upon the Indians with only a handful of men in the afternoon and evening of September 15, along with his solo reconnaissance and discovery of the village the next day, made Lawton recall long-ago friendships as the names of Mackenzie, Carroll, Bacon, Heyl, Boehm, and Tonkawa Henry all brought back cherished memories. Albee also recalled repulsing the attack upon the command at noon on October 28 and the captures made the next day in the attack on the village. Lawton, intensely involved in the legal examination of the meritorious service board's decisions, suggested to Albee that he might be able to receive a Medal of Honor for one of these actions. Lawton was familiar with the medal application process and knew that eyewitness accounts were extremely important to the process. Lawton informed Albee that Henry Carroll, John M. Bacon, and William R. Shafter were all still alive. Although uncertain of Carroll's duty station at the moment, Lawton was in contact with Colonels Shafter and Bacon. Bacon was the inspector general for the military Department of the Columbia at Vancouver Barracks, while Shafter was commanding the First Infantry at Angel Island, California. After providing Albee with Bacon's address, Lawton requested that Albee write a resumé of his actions, including the dates and names of other officers involved in the actions. On July 27, 1893, Lawton wrote to Bacon and suggested that if he made the application perhaps Albee could be awarded a Medal of Honor. The ever-precise Lawton even included a copy of Bacon's original report commending Albee's actions and a suggested application letter format. On August 2, 1893, Bacon submitted the application form along with a copy of the original report and commendation dated December 16, 1869. Shafter, former commander of the Twenty-fourth Infantry, had access to the regimental archives and submitted copies of all reports commending Albee. In his letter transmitting the reports he added:

> As the senior surviving officer of that regiment on duty with it at that time to request that in consideration of the fact that to the present time, no official recognition has been accorded this officer, that he be now awarded a Medal of Honor for conspicuous gallantry in action with hostile Indians on the Brazos River, in 1869.[20]

On December 15 Bacon cemented the process by writing in a letter to the adjutant general:

> I have the honor to state that I was an eyewitness to the conspicuous gallantry exhibited by this officer during the engagement. At the onset of the engagement my camp was charged by Indians in numbers largely superior to my own, when Lieutenant Albee promptly moved out with a small detachment, and by his good management and example held the Indians in check until the command could saddle up and re-inforce him. During the engagement which followed, lasting from 2 PM until night, Lieutenant Albee commanded his company of the 9th Cavalry in a most satisfactory manner, and was specially noted by all for his superb courage and coolness under fire. His entire conduct on the occasion was so marked for personal courage that I commended him for it in a report made soon after to the late Brigadier-General R. S. Mackenzie, then commanding the sub-District of Pecos, Department of Texas.[21]

On January 12, 1894, Col. John M. Schofield, after evaluating the submitted documentation, submitted the formal recommendation to award Albee the Medal of Honor to the Secretary of War. Six days later, Secretary of War Daniel S. Lamont ordered the medal for George E. Albee and on January 30, 1894, Asst. Adj. Gen. H. C. Corbin forwarded the Medal of Honor to Albee at his office at the Winchester Arms Company at New Haven, Connecticut. In a footnote to the accompanying letter, Corbin, a former fellow officer with Albee in the Twenty-fourth Infantry, added "My congratulations over and over again."[22]

A quarter of a century had passed since George Emerson Albee had rode and fought upon the High Plains of Texas. Though he possessed his nation's highest award for gallantry, his greatest satisfaction came in knowing that his actions had in a small way helped transform the vast region into one of the most productive agricultural areas in the world. The heritage of the region is thus entwined with the sacrifices of the U.S. Army and men like George Albee, who dared to go above and beyond the call of duty.

Fort McKavett Texas
July 24th 1870

To the
Adjutant General
United States Army
Washington D.C.

General,
I have the honor to acknowledge the receipt of a Communication of July 9th 1870 from the Adjutant General's Office, enclosing Medal of Honor. I will cherish the gift as a thing of priceless value and endeavor by my future conduct to merit the high honor conferred upon me.
I have the honor to be
very respectfully
your obedient Servant
Emanuel Stance
Sergeant F Co, 9th Cavly

Sgt. Emanuel Stance's letter acknowledging receipt of his Medal of Honor. Though likely composed by his company commander or a clerk as was the practice during the Indian Wars, Stance's signature indicates a degree of literacy uncommon for the enlisted soldiers of the period. *Courtesy the National Archives.*

Chapter 4

Sergeant Stance to the Rescue

May 20–21, 1870

★

Sgt. Emanuel Stance

Because of increased Indian raiding activity upon Central Texas between 1866 and 1868, the U.S. Army decided in March 1869 to regarrison Fort McKavett. The post, abandoned seven years earlier at the outset of the Civil War, was the only strategically located post in Central Texas suitable for continuous habitation.[1]

By August 1869 the post was manned by two companies of the Ninth U.S. Cavalry and several companies of the Twenty-fourth U.S. Infantry, which were assigned there to stem the rising incidence of crime along the central Texas frontier. At least 114 murders in 1868 had been attributed to Indian raiding bands.[2] By the latter part of 1869 and early 1870, Indian raids had declined dramatically, no doubt as a result of successful U.S. Army expeditions into West Texas. These expeditions during the spring and fall of 1869 had inflicted severe losses upon hostile Apache, Kiowa, and Comanche bands and severely depleted their horse herds.[3] Spring was expected to bring the usual onslaught of numerous small raiding bands intent upon replenishing their herds. The key to rendering these raiding bands less mobile was to prevent them from accumulating herds. It was a simple strategy, but it was extremely difficult to put into practice, especially by small cavalry commands in reactive military operations.

Raiding bands needed to cover wide areas to acquire the required number of horses. The established settlements in Central Texas along the San Saba, Llano, and Colorado Rivers had always yielded good horses in large numbers. The El Paso Mail and Adams & Wickes Freight Line way stations were usually manned by only one or two station agents. They also kept sizable herds of livestock and Indian raiders considered them prime targets.

It was late March 1870 before the raiding bands began to fan out from their sanctuaries. Clay, Parker, and Montague Counties in North Texas were the first to feel the wrath of the marauding bands. Way stations west of San Angelo were the next to feel the raiders' sting. Reports of stolen stock and Indian sightings slowly began to come in from the settlements further to the south and east. One small cluster of scattered settlements in the path of these marauding bands was in southeastern Mason and northwestern Gillespie Counties. Loyal Valley, Cherry Springs, and Squaw Creek were comprised of around twenty families, mostly German immigrants.[4]

Shortly after sunrise on Sunday, May 16, a twelve-man Apache raiding band moving south splashed across the Llano River about seven miles southwest of Mason.[5] Several hours later they were camped in a ravine on the west end of Mosely Mountain near the small settlement of Loyal Valley. Carnoviste, the chief and leader of the band, instructed six of his men to raid the farms and ranches to the east and to rejoin him with their prizes. Carnoviste led the other six men southwest toward the juncture of Squaw and Beaver Creeks. This band traveled only about four miles before they reached the Phillip Buchmeier farm, where a rock fence enclosed the house, a field of knee-high spring wheat, and four children.[6]

Minutes later the six Apaches had crept to within a few yards of the children and quickly rushed in. After a brief struggle the two boys, Willie and Herman Lehmann, Buchmeier's stepsons, were seized and bound astride Indian ponies. Caroline fled amid a flurry of arrows and fainted a short distance away in the wheat field. Auguste, an infant, was hidden from the Apaches' view and she was overlooked. By the time Caroline regained consciousness and made it to the house to sound the alarm, the Apaches, with her two brothers as captives, were racing northward. As Carnoviste's band fled northward to the rendezvous point they were joined by the other band, who had stolen a herd of horses. The raiders fled and did not stop until they arrived at the Llano River at sunset, some twelve miles from the Buchmeier farm.[7]

Phillip Buchmeier immediately rode to Loyal Valley to sound the alarm and met other local ranchers who also had reported confrontations with Indian raiders. A rider was immediately dispatched to Mason, the nearest settlement. Word of the raid reached Fort McKavett via a dispatch rider from Menard on the evening of May 19. The Indian raiders were then camped just southwest of what is now the town of Eden. After making raids on several local ranches they again resumed their trek northwest with the latest supplement to their herd, which brought the total number of stolen horses to around twenty-five. Capt. Henry Carroll, who was temporarily in command of Fort McKavett, determined after listening to the exhausted dispatch rider from Menard that the raiding party would probably try to escape to the west. Whether their flight was to the southwest or northwest would be determined by the tribe involved, which was undetermined at the time. Most of the trails of previous Indian raiders had either led to the north toward the Kiowa–Comanche Reservation in the Indian Territory or toward the Rio Grande and Mexico. In order to intercept or pick up the Indians' trail, Captain Carroll decided to send out two scouting patrols. Shortly after evening stable call, Lt. John L. Bullis and Sgt. Emanuel Stance were summoned to the post headquarters, where Carroll instructed Bullis to take ten enlisted troopers from Company F, Ninth Cavalry, with five days of rations to scout south and west from the post in the country between the Llano and South Concho Rivers. Stance was instructed to also take nine troopers from Company F and to scout to the north and east along Kickapoo Creek from its source, the Kickapoo Springs, to its junction with the Concho River. Carroll's orders further stated that, "Both . . . parties will endeavor to the utmost to intercept the Indians that stole the children of Phillip Buchmeier of Loyal Valley on 16th Instant."[8]

At first light the next morning the designated troopers prepared to depart. After a quick breakfast of coffee and pancakes, the men saddled their mounts and drew their arms, ammunition, and rations. The road that wound its way north from the post was part of the upper San Antonio to El Paso mail route. The way station at Kickapoo Springs, twenty-five miles to the north, was one of the more active stations along the route. Kickapoo Springs was also a way station for the Adams & Wickes Freight Line and a sizable herd was kept there for the freight and mail team changes. The location had proven to be a magnet for trouble over the past two years; Indians had raided the station at least five times since 1868.[9] Sergeant Stance knew that if the Indian raiders were anywhere in the area, they would not be able to resist it. Stance's patrol left the post about 7:30 A.M. and splashed across the San Saba River on the way north. Sergeant Stance stopped the advance occasionally at prominent points along the way and scanned the surrounding terrain with a marine telescope. A herd of cattle or horses being driven would create a telltale dust cloud that could be seen for miles. By noon the patrol had arrived at Nine-Mile Waterhole, where they rested and enjoyed a brief dinner. Unknown to the troops, Carnoviste's band had observed them and taken evasive measures. Instead of driving their captured herd parallel to the road they were moving behind a broken ridgeline a quarter of a mile east of the road. Stance and his men resumed their march shortly after 1 P.M.[10]

The patrol had marched about five miles farther north when Stance suddenly raised his hand to halt the detachment. He used his telescope to scan the terrain to the east. Between a break in the ridgeline he observed a band of Indians driving a herd of horses and immediately informed the men of his discovery. The men were quickly ordered into a skirmish line with a few new recruits designated to pursue and round up the loose stock. They advanced at a trot until they rounded the cleft of the ridgeline and the Indians spotted them. The Indians began to yell as Stance ordered his troops to charge into the rear of the Indians about three hundred yards away. The first volley from the troops scattered the Indians and stampeded their herd. At this point several other Indians emerged from over a rise to the northeast, less than fifty yards from Stance's position. The second volley from the Spencer carbines sent all but several of these Indians back over the rise in pandemonium. Stance reined to the right and charged into them with his pistol blazing. One Indian, who wore a black vest and was mounted on a black stallion, reeled as if hit, and now all turned to escape Stance's onslaught. The fighting became scattered as individual troopers fired at and chased individual Indians. After less than five minutes of skirmishing the Indians were in total disarray and fled in confusion to the northeast. Stance ordered the bugler to sound recall and within minutes all of the men were present and accounted for. Instead of dispatching the men to pursue the Indians, Stance had them round up the loose stock. Stance did not know that his pistol fire had mortally wounded one of the Indians, who fell dead from his mount once he was over the rise.[11]

On the other side of the rise the Apaches were in headlong flight. The two captive Lehmann boys had been left under guard while the other Indians had charged over the rise to participate in the fighting. The two boys had watched as the Apaches quickly came galloping back over the rise, minus the one warrior, and were hastily hoisted up behind two of the fleeing Apaches. They had ridden about fifty yards when Willie fell from the back of the horse he was on. The Apache either did not notice the boy's fall or was in too much of a hurry to care. Willie took advantage of the opportunity and quickly hid in some nearby bushes.[12]

Several hundred yards away Stance and his men drove the captured herd onto the wagon road. The detachment formed a moving corral and resumed the march toward Kickapoo Springs. Stance personally assumed the advanced scouting position to guard against ambush. Less than thirty minutes later, four or five miles south of Kickapoo Springs, the Stance patrol encountered a wagon moving southward. The teamster, E. Maczen, a merchant from Fredericksburg, was returning home after making a delivery to Fort Concho. Sergeant Stance warned him about the Indians and encouraged him to return to Kickapoo Springs, which Maczen agreed to do. The patrol arrived at the Kickapoo Springs way station just before sundown and camped there for the night. A government supply train with a small infantry guard, which was returning to Fort McKavett from Fort Concho, also was camped at the springs. Immediately after his arrival Stance informed Mr. Flannagan, the way station agent, that Indians were in the area and that he should secure his livestock.[13]

By the time he retired for the night Stance had decided that it would be best to terminate the patrol and return to Fort McKavett with the captured herd. The safety of the government train and its small escort had to be considered. The next morning at sunrise the government train and Maczen headed onto the road toward Fort McKavett with Stance and his men following an hour later. By nine that morning the patrol had traveled ten miles and arrived at the junction of the bypass road from Menardville. Stance noticed that Maczen had turned on the bypass road so he halted the patrol for a brief rest and rode to a nearby prominent elevation, where he drew out his telescope and searched to the southeast along the bypass road, hoping for a glimpse of Maczen's wagon. Noting nothing on the bypass road, Stance turned the telescope onto the Fort McKavett Road, where almost two miles away he could see the government train and its small escort snaking up a rise. Just as he was about to lower the telescope he noticed a rise of dust and obscure movement among the trees on the left side of the road. A closer look with the telescope brought into view a band of around twenty Indians about a mile away, who were moving south-ward parallel to the road. They were apparently intent upon capturing a small trailing herd of assorted livestock that several of the accompanying infantry-men were driving.[14]

Stance quickly roused his men and told them what he had observed. Mounting up, the troopers dashed up the road with two privates driving the cap-tured herd behind them. After half a mile Stance slowed them to a trot to allow the driven herd to catch up. Stance believed his force would appear much larger with the driven herd immediately to the rear. They continued at a trot until the Indians discovered them and began a noisy demonstration, whereupon Stance ordered a charge upon the Indians. The Indians attempted to make a stand, but according to Stance, "I set the Spencers to talking and whistling about their ears so lively that they broke in confusion and fled to the hills." In their haste to get away the Indians were forced to leave behind five more horses, which were added to Sergeant Stance's growing herd.[15]

After regrouping the entourage into a moving square with the livestock in the middle, the patrol resumed its route toward Fort McKavett. The determined Indians made several desultory forays on the convoy's left flank over the next seven miles with little effect. They seemed intent upon at least stampeding and recapturing some of the horses but Sergeant Stance and his troops were just as intent upon holding them. Stance held his troops in check despite the Indian forays. By the time the convoy arrived at Nine-Mile Waterhole, the Indians had become an intolerable nuisance. According to Stance, "I turned my little command loose on them at this place and after a few volleys they left us to continue my march in peace."[16] The little convoy reached Fort McKavett intact at 2 P.M. on May 21, an arrival that created more than the normal uproar. Captain Carroll was elated about the patrol's success. The cool and efficient manner in which Stance had conducted his small force won him Carroll's immediate praise. Stance had demonstrated through tactful management that a small cavalry force could recapture stolen stock from Indians and hold them while performing tactical movements, a problem that had plagued many of the army's most able Indian fighters.

The success of this one patrol would not be realized for weeks and even years afterward. Stance's patrol had successfully recaptured fifteen horses that the Indians had stolen from local ranchers. The aggressive attack by Stance and his men was responsible for the escape of Willie Lehmann, who, after falling off the back of a fleeing Apache's horse, had hidden in some bushes and remained there overnight, fearing that the Indians would return and find him. On the morning of May 21 Willie found the wagon road but then saw three mounted Indians coming along the road. Fearing that they were hunting for him, Willie once again hid in some bushes and remained there throughout the day and night. On the morning of May 22 he was picked up by a teamster bound for San Angelo and was left for safekeeping at the Kickapoo Springs way station. Stance's prompt warnings to Mr. Flannagan, the station agent at Kickapoo Springs, and Mr. Maczen, the Fredericksburg merchant, may have prevented further property loss and may have saved these men's lives.[17]

Sergeant Stance's bravery in leading both of the attacks against the Indians and his efficient management in preventing any casualties within his small force would not go without reward. On the morning of May 26, 1870, Lt. B. M. Custer, the post adjutant, delivered Stance's completed report of the scout to Captain Carroll. Carroll added an endorsement to the report before he forwarded it to Col. R. S. Mackenzie, commander of the Sub-District of the Pecos. Carroll's endorsement cited Sergeant Stance's habitual gallantry as the reason for bringing him to the attention of higher authority. Carroll wrote:

The gallantry displayed by the Sergeant and his party as well as good judgment used on both occasions deserves much praise. As this is the fourth and fifth encounter that Sergeant Stance has had with Indians within the past two years, on all of which occasions he has been mentioned for good behavior by his immediate Commanding Officer, it is a pleasure to commend him to higher authority.[18]

Mackenzie forwarded the report and endorsement to Fifth Military District Headquarters at Austin, where Gen. Joseph J. Reynolds read the report and endorsements and made the formal request for the award of the Army Medal of Honor to Sergeant Stance. On June 28, 1870, the documents were received at the adjutant general's office in Washington, D.C., where Gen. W. T. Sherman approved the recommendation. The order for the medal's issue and engraving was issued on July 5, 1870.[19]

On July 9, 1870, a letter of commendation from General Sherman and a small package containing the Medal of Honor were sent by registered mail to Fort McKavett. On July 24, Stance was summoned to the post headquarters building, where in Mackenzie's presence Captain Carroll presented Stance the letter and package.[20] Later that day Stance wrote the letter regulations required to acknowledge receipt of official correspondence from the adjutant general's office. Stance wrote:

> General:
> I have the honor to acknowledge receipt of a communication of July 9, 1870 from the Adjutant General's Office enclosing a Medal of Honor. I will cherish the gift as a thing of priceless value and endeavor by my future conduct to merit the high honor conferred upon me.
> Sergeant Emanuel Stance
> "F" Company, 9th Cavalry[21]

Emanuel Stance continued to serve on the Texas frontier for seven more years. He participated in numerous other engagements against Indians, Mexican bandits, Comancheros, and other belligerents in West Texas but his actions of May 20–21, 1870, would forever place his name among heroes of the western frontier. The small bronze star that he wore with pride was the first awarded to an African American for gallantry in action during the Indian Wars.

John Kirk, circa 1900. This tough sergeant-major had to literally conduct basic marksmanship train-ing to his new recruits, all the while under constant fire from the Kiowas and Comanches. *Photograph courtesy Robert G. Crist, Camp Hill, Pennsylvania.*

CHAPTER 5

Surrounded at the Little Wichita

July 12, 1870

—— ⭐ ——

Cpl. John Connor	Farrier Samuel Porter
Sgt. George H. Eldridge	Cpl. Charles E. Smith
Cpl. John J. Given	Sgt. Alonzo Stokes
Sgt. Thomas Kerrigan	Cpl. James C. Watson
Sgt. John Kirk	Bugler Claron A. Windus
Sgt. John May	Sgt. William Winterbottom
Pvt. Solon D. Neal	

T he U.S. Army's successful campaigns in late 1869 had achieved what the federal planners had desired. They had forced the hostile Quohada Comanche and Kiowa, minus their vast herds and trappings, onto their designated reservations and into the hands of the Indian Bureau. Almost immediately these new arrivals balked at being represented by the less militant resident bands, whom they regarded as lesser warriors, traitors, and cowards. Among the Southern Plains Indian culture the size of a chief's horse herd and the number of scalps on a war lance registered his status and influence. The Quohada chiefs had lost those, which could only be regained by intense raiding activity. The less militant resident bands, led for the most part by the chief Kicking Bird, were unwilling to surrender their power. They became determined to convince the Quohadas that they were not lesser warriors or cowards and vowed to match the Quohadas, herd for herd and scalp for scalp.[1]

Despite a bitterly cold January and February the bands from both factions struck hard into the nearby North Texas settlements. Parker and Montague Counties were especially hard hit, even before the end of February. By May the North Texas frontier counties were saturated with large, well-armed, and brazen bands who were vying to outperform one another. The U.S. Army's escorts and patrols were not immune, as evidenced by the May 30 attack upon Lt. I. W. Walter's twenty-man cavalry escort to a geological survey team. Walter lost one soldier and the survey team lost two of its members. The next day the Indian raiders killed a stagecoach driver eighteen miles west of Fort Richardson. As reports of these and other outrages were relayed to the reservation agents, the Indian Bureau, not unexpectedly, rose to the Indians' defense.[2]

On June 15, Col. Benjamin Grierson, post commander at Fort Sill near the Kiowa–Comanche Reservation, received a letter from Lawrie Tatum, the reservation's U.S. Indian Agent. According to Tatum, the soldiers were violating the Medicine Lodge Treaty by escorting cattle herds across reservation lands. Tatum further added, "I consider it liable to bring on difficulties with the Indians of this reservation."[3] The army had provided escorts to cattle herds for several months. Until 1867 the Chisholm Trail and its various segments ran east of the 98th Meridian. After 1868 herders had gradually shifted their trails across the Indian Territory to the west to avoid more populous areas and to connect to the closer railhead at Dodge City, Kansas. The herders had tempered the concerns of other tribes, such as the Chickasaw and Wichita, by giving them cattle as a sort of transit fee. The situation had not created problems until the arrival of the Quohada Comanches and Kiowas.

Grierson acted promptly and denied further escorts for the herders. On June 18 he informed Col. James Oakes, post commander at Fort Richardson, of Tatum's concerns. Oakes immediately made the suspension of herd escorts public by publishing an order in the *Weatherford Times*. By June 20 the Indians had been informed that cattle herders would no longer be allowed to cross the reservation with an army escort. By sunset on June 22 three cowboys lay dead along the Chisholm Trail segment south and east of the Kiowa–Comanche reservation.[4]

Just over two weeks later, on July 6, an Indian raiding band attacked a stagecoach sixteen miles west of Fort Richardson. The driver and two passengers narrowly escaped and immediately reported the incident to Colonel Oakes, who quickly dispatched Lt. James H. Sands and a cavalry detachment to recover the mail. Later that day Oakes dispatched a fully outfitted cavalry detachment of fifty-eight men under the command of Capt. Curwin B. McLellan. They were to trail and overtake the Indians, hopefully before they could cross the Red River.[5]

McLellan was one of the few experienced Indian-fighting officers in the Sixth U.S. Cavalry. He had served more than ten years as an enlisted man on the Texas frontier before the Civil War with the Third U.S. Infantry and Second U.S. Cavalry. Although most of the enlisted men in his command were young and inexperienced there were some hardened Civil War veterans sprinkled among the ranks. First Sgt. John Kirk of Company L had endured three years of rugged Civil War service with the Ninth and Twentieth Pennsylvania Cavalry regiments. Sgt. William Winterbottom of Company A had seven years of continuous cavalry service and he still bore the scars of wounds he had received at Campti, Louisiana, with the Third Rhode Island Cavalry. First Sgt. Alonzo Stokes of Company H had five years experience with the Sixth Cavalry, and Civil War service with the Tenth Ohio Light Artillery. The exploits of the veteran core of the command continued down through the ranks. Cpl. James C. Watson, one of the few survivors of the 183rd Pennsylvania Infantry's fourteen assaults against the 53rd Georgia Infantry's trenches at Cold Harbor, Virginia, in 1864, rode in the forward rank of Company L. There were also other eager but less seasoned troopers in the patrol, such as Pvt. Solon D. Neal of Company L. Too young for Civil War service, Neal had four years of cavalry experience and had been relieved of his duty as post librarian to complete the patrol's roster.[6]

By 3 P.M. on July 10 McLellan's command had trailed the Indians to the headwaters region of the Middle Fork of the Little Wichita River in present-day Archer County. Earlier in the day a bullwhip that was believed to have belonged to the stagecoach driver was found, providing evidence that the Indians were very near. Despite a drizzling rain, the guide, James B. Dosher, led the command north and then west. By sundown the command was camped on a high bluff on the south side of the North Fork of the Little Wichita. The river was impassable, which forced the command to remain in camp all day on July 11 to dry out their clothing and bedding and to care for the horses. Shortly before noon an incident heightened fears about a nearby Indian presence when a small herd of domestic cattle was seen running just outside the campsite. They were at least forty miles from the nearest ranch, and Dosher casually remarked to McLellan that "there was somebody after them cattle, or they would not have been running."[7] Kicking Bird and his band of around a hundred warriors were indeed just several miles away, their flight to the north also stalled by the rain-swollen river. White Horse and his raiding band of sixty to one hundred Kiowas were just a few miles away to the northeast, but on the north bank of the river. The band, in flight after attacking settlements near Victoria Peak, was also looking for a safe crossing point.[8]

A heavy downpour around 3 A.M. on July 12 forestalled McLellan's idea of an early river crossing. By 10 A.M. he decided to mount the command anyway and attempt to find a safe crossing point. White Horse's band had successfully forded the river at the old Radziminski Crossing earlier that morning and had found Kicking Bird's camp. White Horse had also discovered McLellan's encampment and two of his men rode southward along the river's edge with two of Kicking Bird's men to point out the crossing point. The two opposing sides were on an inevitable collision course.

James B. Dosher, affectionately referred to as "Jim" by the troops, was an excellent guide and an experienced frontiersman who as a former Texas Ranger had scouted the area many times. He and Private Neal were about a mile ahead of the main command advancing to the northwest along the bluffline overlooking the river. Sgt. George H. Eldridge, the left flank point-man, was about half a mile to the west advancing abreast of Dosher and Neal. The main body of the troops followed in two files of seventeen troopers each from Companies H and L. Captain McLellan, Surgeon George W. Hatch and Capt. Charles H. Campbell rode at the front of the two files. Five hundred yards behind the two files, a twenty-man rear guard was with the pack mules that carried the command's supplies and baggage. These men were from Companies A and K under the command of Lt. H. P. Perrine. Sgt. William Gallagher and several troopers were in charge of the eight pack mules.[9]

Dosher and Neal had proceeded about four miles along the bluff when Dosher spotted the four Indians about a quarter of a mile to their right. Neal was sent to notify McLellan while Dosher rode to his left to a small rise where he could better see the troops, then motioned with his hat for McLellan to move the troops away from the bluffline and bring them forward, which McLellan did. At this point the Indians discovered Dosher. They made no offensive moves but yelled out some whoops and galloped northwest around a large, flat-topped hill and disappeared from sight.[10]

The command had advanced to meet Dosher when a large body of horsemen was sighted approaching from the west, about a thousand yards away. McLellan believed these horsemen were a patrol under Maj. G. A. Gordon operating from Fort Griffin. A quick look with his marine telescope discerned that it was not Gordon but Indians, a great many of them. McLellan ordered the command into a single-rank formation. Lieutenant Perrine with the rear guard and Sergeant Gallagher's pack mule detachment were ordered to remain stationary. Bugler Claron Windus sounded the advance and the troops moved slowly forward with their Spencer carbines ready. Nothing had yet been heard from Sergeant Eldridge, the flanking trailer. The troops, still in single-rank formation, continued in a slow advance until approximately five hundred yards separated them from the Indians. McLellan halted the command at this point and began to confer with Dosher, "Well, Dosher, do you reckon they are going to fight?" Dosher retorted, "If you will wait a few minutes, you'll see."[11]

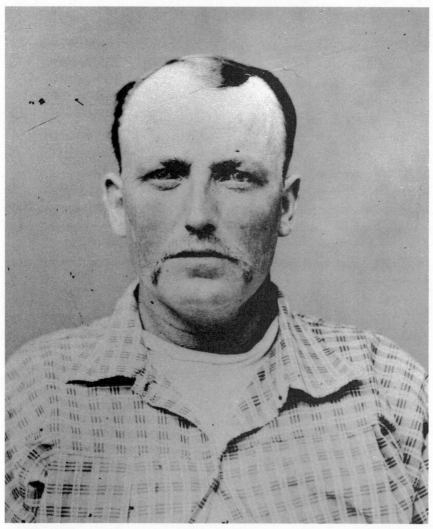

George H. Eldridge, 1900. His brazen attack on a band of Kiowa and Comanches attempting to capture the pack mules with his command's ammunition supplies prevented a military disaster at the Little Wichita River on July 12, 1870, and saved many lives. *Photograph courtesy the Arizona Historical Society, Tucson.*

The troops waited and minutes later two bands of Indians nearly the same size as the one in front of them merged with the main body of Indians. Small bands of mounted Indians also appeared on both flanks, all conducting loud demonstrations. McLellan's command was now confronted on three sides by what appeared to be about 250 mounted Indians. McLellan ordered the men to dismount and prepare to fight on foot. The seriousness of the situation permeated the command as McLellan barked out orders for the formation and management of firing squads. Every fourth man was detailed to hold and control four horses. While this was going on about fifteen Indians charged from the west toward the rear guard and pack mule detachment and all hell broke loose.

Sergeant Eldridge, who had not been seen since early that morning, emerged suddenly from a nearby thicket and rode pell-mell into the right rear portion of the charging Indian band. Two Kiowas went down from his nearly point-blank pistol fire. Continuing along the entire length of the attacking force, Eldridge screamed like a demon, all the while firing and swinging his pistol at the Indians. The Indians, panic-stricken by this brazen attack, broke off their assault. Eldridge, for the moment, had defeated the initial Indian attempt to isolate or capture the pack train. He joined the rear guard amid the cheers of his fellow troopers.[12]

While the command's attention had been diverted by the actions in the rear, the main body of Indians in front had slowly advanced. Sporadic firing by the Indians commenced when they were two hundred yards from the troops. Surgeon Hatch became the first casualty when he suffered a grazing bullet wound to his left foot; the same bullet killed his horse. The Indians' firing intensified as they drew to within 150 yards of the command, whereupon McLellan ordered the troops to commence rapid firing. The thundering roar of twenty-four Spencer carbines echoed across the valley of the Little Wichita. Several Indians and ponies went down and the Indian ranks broke. The Indians quickly began their circling maneuver, remaining about 150 yards out from the command. Once the circle was complete, the Indians reduced their firing for fear of hitting one another on the opposite sides of the ring.[13]

McLellan took advantage of the decreased Indian fire and motioned for the rear guard and pack train to join the main command. Except for Lieutenant Perrine; Sergeants Eldridge, Winterbottom, and Gallagher; and Corporals Given and Connor, the rear guard was comprised largely of inexperienced raw recruits. Perrine assumed the lead position at the left front of the pack train, with Winterbottom and Connor each managing a ten-man file alongside the pack mules. Inside the files, Gallagher and several troopers controlled the eight pack mules that were carrying the command's extra ammunition, foodstuffs, medical supplies, and extra clothing.[14]

An estimated fifteen Indians were concentrated between the command and the rear guard. Aware that the main command's troops would have to be careful not to shoot in the direction of the rear guard, the Indians launched their second attack. McLellan had formed the main command into a defensive square about fifty yards wide with the horses in the middle. Company H formed the south perimeter, with 1st Sgt. Alonzo Stokes in charge. The western flank was manned by Company L, led by Sgt. John Kirk. The northern side of the square was made up of men from Companies D and K and McLellan personally commanded this group. Capt. C. H. Campbell led the troopers of Company A, which manned the eastern perimeter. McLellan ordered all firing halted at this point unless large bands appeared in direct frontal attacks.[15]

Lieutenant Perrine, commanding the rear guard, ordered all pistols drawn and directed the men to advance at the gallop. Several troopers yelled excitedly as they spurred their mounts into the fray. Sporadic firing accompanied the rear guard's dash for the safety of the defensive square. Indian war whoops mingled with the shouts of the troops. Pvt. George Blum became the rear guard's first casualty when he fell from a short-range pistol shot to the head fired by a Kiowa who rode in close to him from the side. As Blum fell from his horse, Sergeant Gallagher fired two quick shots, wounding the Indian who had shot Blum and killing the Indian's horse. The rear guard was within one hundred yards of the main command but several men straggled behind. Sergeant Winterbottom, in charge of the file on the right of the pack mules, reined in briefly to assist several of these stragglers but he was overtaken and attacked by two Indians. He whirled and killed the closest Indian with one pistol shot. Winterbottom then incurred a serious bullet wound to his left side and an instant later his horse fell dead from a rifle shot to the head. Others in the rear guard, unaware of Winterbottom's predicament, rode on. Perrine's horse was killed under him as Perrine was firing his weapon. Sergeant Gallagher received a grazing flesh wound to his left arm and ribs and lost his hold on the reins of one of the pack mules. Sergeant Kirk, who was in charge of the southwest side of the defensive square, called for covering fire to drive the Indians away from Perrine and Winterbottom. Kirk then sprinted the fifty yards or so to the side of the badly wounded sergeant. Perrine, though dazed by the hard fall he had taken, found the strength to get up and limped toward the main command. Corporal Given saw Kirk run past him and realized that someone else was in trouble. Given turned his horse about and galloped to Perrine's side. Given fired his Colt .44 with deadly accuracy and drove back a party of nearby Kiowas as he successfully escorted Perrine to the defensive square. Sergeant Kirk, amid a hail of arrows and bullets and despite several forays by individual Indians, managed to lift Winterbottom over his shoulder and began a labored run for the main command. He soon found Corporal Given at his side, providing a shield from the hostile fire.[16]

Cpl. John Connor was the last man in the rear guard to reach the perimeter of the square. He noticed Kirk's predicament, reined his horse about, and bolted for the endangered men. Firing his Spencer carbine at the approaching Indians, he drove them back then reined up on the other side of Corporal Given and together they accompanied Kirk and Winterbottom to safety. Just as Connor neared the perimeter he suffered a grazing wound to his forehead. As he faltered, near collapse, another rifle ball struck and killed his horse, pinning Connor to the ground. Sgt. Thomas Kerrigan and Cpl. Charles E. Smith rushed the short distance to his side and extricated Connor from under the horse. Corporal Smith then lifted Connor over his shoulder and brought him to safety despite a fusillade of Indian bullets and arrows.[17]

The Indians circled the command, shrieking, whooping, and firing randomly. From time to time individual warriors broke off from the circling band and made forays inside the circle. One such incursion early in the fighting involved a young Indian adorned with buffalo horns and a large badge of feathers who rode at breakneck speed about fifty yards from the perimeter, yelling and taunting the troops. Dosher, who had been kneeling and firing from the southeast edge of the defensive square, soon tired of this young warrior's antics. Steadying himself and his rifle on a large rock, Dosher waited for him to ride into his sights. The young man, riding low on the opposite side of his horse with just his head protruding above the saddle, ran level with Dosher's rifle sight. Dosher squeezed off a shot that struck him in the head and the fallen warrior's horse ran into the soldiers' ranks, where it was promptly captured. Other warriors then charged en masse, attempting to retrieve the fallen man, but troops fired at them and wounded at least two. That group retreated out of range and another group on the opposite side charged to distract the soldiers. When this attack of fifty Indians on the southwest side erupted into a close-range firefight, several Indians raced in and quickly retrieved the badly wounded warrior.[18]

Almost half an hour had passed since the fighting began and, according to McLellan, "the only chance of escape from annihilation was a carefully guarded retreat to some more defensible position." The noise of the battle was deafening and smoke obscured visibility. McLellan approached Dosher to discuss what should be done. After a few minutes of ear-to-mouth conversation, Dosher pointed out a young recruit whose gun was elevated so much that he was overshooting on each shot. Dosher told him, "If all your men are shooting like that one, we had better get out of here." McLellan then dashed along the lines, shouting out orders and instructions. He returned to Dosher and remarked, "Lead out and we will follow."[19]

The former Texas Ranger reloaded his two Colt revolvers and, leading his mule, he directed the command back along its earlier path. Company H, led by Captain Campbell with Sergeants Stokes and Kerrigan maintaining the ranks, followed about twenty yards behind Dosher. McLellan ordered volley firing at the Indians, who attempted to block their retreat, an effort that left three Indian ponies riderless within seconds. Before they scattered, Dosher got close enough to the Indians before they broke ranks that the smoke from their muzzles came almost halfway to him. Luckily, not one member of the command was injured in the breakout. The entire command, except for the most seriously wounded, were now dismounted, with the stock being herded into the center of the moving square of soldiers. The most severely wounded were lashed to their saddles atop the most gentle animals. In this arrangement, the retreat progressed along the crest of the rolling prairie.[20]

Kicking Bird, the Kiowa chief, demonstrated his tactical prowess by dividing his warriors into two lines on the right and left of the command's line of retreat. He ordered staggered attacks, first from the left and then from the right, with one side attacking as the other withdrew. The livestock inside the square became increasingly difficult to manage because of the constant firing and movements. A number of the command's horses were wounded and five had been killed. Pvt. Peter Conroy of Company L suffered a severe cut on the left shoulder when one of the horses kicked him. Despite being lashed astride horses, Sergeants Winterbottom and Gallagher, along with Corporal Connor, helped as best they could to control the herd of frightened animals. All three continued to shoot at the Indians whenever they rushed nearby positions. Sergeant Stokes, mindful of a stampede among the stock and possible panic by the new recruits, rendered excellent service in managing his men and animals despite his position under constant fire.[21]

Several minutes after the command achieved its breakout from the encirclement, its path of retreat neared the point where Private Blum had fallen. Corporal Given was deeply shaken over the loss of his friend. The two had been close for more than a year. Given watched intently for any movement from Blum's body. Volley firing on any Indian or group of Indians who approached the body had so far kept them from taking his scalp. Given refused to stand by and leave Blum behind, especially if there might be a spark of life left. He went to McLellan and requested permission to try and retrieve his friend. McLellan gave him permission to make the attempt as soon as the command came within a hundred yards of the body. Given then went to Dosher and told him of his intentions. He gave Dosher his picture and that of his sisters

Kicking Bird (Tene-Angpote), the Kiowa chief who led the Indians at the battle of the Little Wichita River, is pictured just weeks after the battle. The army blouse he is wearing is likely that of Capt. Charles H. Campbell, which was lost when the Indians captured the pack mule carrying the officer's spare clothing. *Photograph courtesy the Smithsonian Institution National Anthropological Archives.*

and sweetheart and asked him to care for them until they returned to the fort. Several minutes later Given sprinted to the side of his fallen friend. The troopers on the left side of the square commenced rapid firing to drive the Indians back on that side. Given made it to Blum's side, which was within twenty-five yards of the bluff line overlooking the North Fork of the Little Wichita River. Quickly cradling Private Blum's head, Given felt for any signs of life. The rapid firing on the east side of the square had thus far been successful in keeping the Indians away from Given. Kicking Bird seized an opportunity and led a small party over the edge of the bluff at a point two hundred yards north of Given. The Indians then attacked the square on the north and west sides. As they attacked, Kicking Bird galloped up and over the rim of the bluff line and drove his war lance into Given's back. Given died instantly and panic raced through the ranks of the young recruits. Only by the gallant and efficient example of Sergeants Kirk and May was the eastern perimeter stabilized. Sergeant May instructed his young charges to sight their targets and lower their gun elevations for better accuracy.[22]

The retreat continued slowly in a southeasterly direction, maintaining the crest or high ground as much as possible. The Indians followed and continued sporadic firing from every available place of concealment. The main Indian resistance came from occasional charges and snipers from elevations along the path of retreat. By 1:30 P.M., almost three hours after initial contact with the Indians, the retreat had covered nearly four miles. Rolling prairie gave way to a quarter-mile-long slope toward the Middle Fork of the Little Wichita River. McLellan, who was leading the advancing defensive square, scanned the terrain with his telescope; the Indians were visible, concentrated among the trees and brush near the banks of the river.[23]

The skies had cleared around 9 A.M. and the temperature had risen to near ninety degrees by 2 P.M. The men and animals were thirsty but the Indians appeared intent on preventing the command from reaching the water. During the command's descent, Indian snipers fired from nearby mesquite thickets. Several warriors directed their fire at Dosher as he led the way down the slope. Their firing made the sand and rocks at his feet spray up, startling his mule so much that it had to be taken into the square with the other animals.[24]

McLellan ordered Captain Campbell to lead a detachment from Company H to drive the Indians away from the nearby thickets and secure a crossing point at the river. Two detachments of five men in file formation charged toward the right and left while the front of the defensive square poured rapid fire into the trees along the river where Indians could be seen. Sergeants Stokes and

Kerrigan, along with Corporal Smith, led the charge into the trees with pistols blazing. The main command ceased fire when the two files closed into the trees and fighting erupted at close range. Pvt. Albert Ford was knocked from his horse with a gunshot wound to the left shoulder just as he entered the stand of trees. Pvt. Robert Steward suffered a shattered right forearm while firing his weapon. Sergeants Kerrigan and Stokes immediately came to the aid of these disabled troopers. They placed themselves between the Indians and the wounded troopers and maintained a constant fire at the nearby Indians, which drove them from the tree line.[25]

When the Indians on the west bank of the river retreated, McLellan wasted no time in ordering the main body of the command to quicken its pace toward the river. Campbell's small force, now dismounted and fighting on foot, pushed on across the river, which forced the Indians to withdraw. While the forward part of the main command waded into the water, the Indians fired from all directions. "The bullets fell into the water like hail," Dosher later remarked. Pvt. Gustav Smith suffered a gunshot wound to his left leg as he waded into the river, a superficial wound caused by a bullet ricocheting off the water.[26]

The dense brush and trees along the river's edge provided welcome shade and cover. The Indians, however, now had the commanding elevations to their front and rear and a tremendous volley of rifle fire and metal-tipped arrows rained down on the soldiers. Small groups of Indian snipers filtered into the dense brush along the riverbank, both upstream and downstream from their position. The snipers and the fusillade from both ridgelines began to take a toll. Pvts. Benjamin Amey and Samuel Wagoner suffered shoulder wounds within minutes of one another.[27]

Large groups of Indians were concentrated upstream and downstream and the command was again threatened with encirclement. This time, however, the Indians had the advantage of high ground on two sides. After just fifteen minutes, McLellan decided their position was rapidly becoming untenable and he ordered the command to reform. By 4 P.M. the command had moved up the incline toward the ridgeline between the Middle and South Forks of the Little Wichita River. Dosher led the way with the troopers of Company H behind him. The command quickly gained the southeast ridge and the rolling prairie beyond to continue its defensive retreat. The Indian resistance weakened as only small bands appeared on the flanks to harass them with the main body of Indians still hovering in the rear, remaining out of range of the increasing accuracy of Companies K and D. A little after 4:30 P.M., some two miles southeast of the river crossing, the command neared a fifty-foot high, flat-topped hill along the

Claron A. Windus, circa 1880, who fought with gallantry in July 1870 against Kicking Bird's force on the Little Wichita River. In 1877, as a deputy sheriff in Kinney County, he shot and killed Medal of Honor recipient Adam Payne, who was attempting to evade arrest on a murder warrant. *Photograph courtesy Claude W. Dooley, Marble Falls, Texas.*

line of march. The Indians had placed a number of snipers atop this hill, who fired down into the command as it came into range. A small detachment of volunteers from Company L was instructed to clear the hill of snipers. Sergeants Kirk and May, Corporals Watson and Porter, and Private Neal collected and

71

loaded extra pistols from the wounded. Mounted on the command's best horses, they dashed toward the hill with supporting fire from Company H and charged straight for the Indian ponies at the bottom of the hill. The Indians hurried down the hill and made it to their ponies just a few seconds before the troopers. Two of the Indians fell to close-range pistol fire while the other two escaped to safety in nearby mesquite thickets. The main body of Indians seemed confused, for they offered no assistance to their comrades, and May, Kirk, Watson, and Neal held the high ground until the command had safely passed. Half an hour later, when the command had reached the South Fork, the main body of Indians was seen in the distance riding away to the northwest.[28]

During the next six hours, the command made brief stops but steadily put distance between it and the Indians. Around 10 P.M. the command crossed the West Fork of the Trinity River and struck an arm of prairie running southwest. They followed this stretch of prairie for two hours, then followed another segment leading to the east until they saw a campfire in the distance. McLellan halted the command and he, Dosher, and Windus approached cautiously to see if they had run into another group of Indians. The three advanced to within seventy-five yards of the campfire when shots rang out. Dosher yelled, "We're soldiers from Fort Richardson!" and the shooting ceased immediately. The campfire belonged to a party of about twenty local cattle drovers who were camped there with a sizable herd. The battered command camped with the cowboys that night and the cowboys, fearing that the Indians might reappear, started toward Belknap with their herds early the next morning. The command was still about fifty miles from Fort Richardson and the wounded desperately needed medical care.[29]

Early on July 13, Dosher, Eldridge, and Windus volunteered to ride ahead to Fort Richardson and bring back a relief party. Three hours later, the picket guards were attacked by a band of nearly forty Indians. Fearful that they might be the advance of a larger force, McLellan ordered the command to mount up. He then set fire to the unnecessary and untransportable property. After marching southeast for two hours, the command struck the Fort Belknap Road at a point thirty-two miles west of Fort Richardson. After two more hours of marching they arrived at Rock Creek Station, where they rested for three hours. Less than an hour after resuming their march, the command met up with Dosher, who was heading a relief party. The command camped at Indian Hill that night and resumed its march early the morning of July 14. By noon the soldiers arrived back at Fort Richardson.[30]

The battle of the Little Wichita River, as the engagement became known, was the most serious encounter between hostile Indians and the U.S. Army in

Sgt. Solon D. Neal's Medal of Honor headstone at the San Antonio National Cemetery. His former residence on Wyoming Street in San Antonio was razed to make way for the construction of the Hemisfair Tower, seen in the background. *Photograph courtesy Charles M. Neal Jr. Collection.*

Texas during the post–Civil War era. The Indians were far better armed than any previously encountered and were not encumbered by camp equipment or families. Captain McLellan's command, though outnumbered five to one, dealt the warring tribes a severe blow, killing at least fifteen and wounding a larger number. It could not be called an outright victory, but it did prevent this large raiding party from inflicting further damage upon the Texas frontier.[31]

McLellan filed his report on the engagement with the post adjutant on July 16, 1870. He made special mention of thirteen enlisted men who made themselves conspicuous through acts of bravery during the engagement. These men

73

were 1st Sgt. Alonzo Stokes, Sgt. Thomas Kerrigan, and Cpls. Charles E. Smith and John Connor of Company H; 1st Sgt. John Kirk, Sgt. John May, Cpl. James C. Watson, Bugler Claron A. Windus, Farrier Samuel Porter, and Pvt. Solon D. Neal of Company L; Sgt. William Winterbottom of Company A; Sgt. George H. Eldridge of Company C; and Cpl. John J. Given of Company K.[32]

On July 17, 1870, Colonel Oakes, commander of the Sixth Cavalry and the post of Fort Richardson, affixed an endorsement to McLellan's report. He added, "the gallantry and good conduct of the officers and men and the dispositions made by the officer in command were deserving of a more decided success. A more obstinate attack, and resistance could not have been made without resulting in total annihilation of the command and everyone engaged is deserving of the highest commendation of praise."[33] This endorsement, along with McLellan's report, was forwarded to the Department of Texas headquarters at Austin for review by Col. J. J. Reynolds, the department commander. Reynolds forwarded the documents to the Adjutant General's Office in Washington, D.C., on August 4. It appears that E. D. Townsend, the adjutant general, strongly recommended to Secretary of War W. W. Belknap that Medals of Honor be conferred upon the men McLellan had specifically cited for gallantry. On August 28 Belknap concurred and officially directed that Medals of Honor be conferred upon the thirteen listed men. John Potts, chief clerk at the War Department, then ordered the medals and sent them to the M. W. Galt & Brothers Company for engraving. On September 7 Townsend forwarded the engraved medals to Colonel Reynolds in Austin.[34] Reynolds recognized the recipients in General Order no. 59 on September 26. A copy of the general order with an accompanying letter of transmittal from the adjutant general was enclosed with each medal, and these were forwarded to Colonel Oakes at Fort Richardson. The torrid pace of scouting patrols and the constant dispersal of the regiment's companies made it virtually impossible to hold a dress parade ceremony to accommodate members of five companies. Oakes apparently conducted semi-formal presentation ceremonies to eleven of the recipients on scattered dates between October 13 and 22, likely in the post adjutant's office.[35]

On a cool, sunny Sunday, October 23, 1870, Cpl. John Connor, just days after he was released from the post hospital, stood beside the post adjutant, Lt. Sumner Bodfish, as the post garrison stood in inspection formation. Minutes later Connor was directed front and center to a point facing Colonel Oakes. Connor, near death just weeks before and still sporting sterile gauze around his forehead, stood erect as Colonel Oakes pinned the Medal of Honor to his dress tunic.[36] After the close of the ceremony the first man to greet him was the friend who had carried him to safety, Cpl. Charles E. Smith.

During the few weeks after the engagement, several scouting patrols were dispatched to the battle site, ostensibly to bury the remains of Corporal Given and Private Blum, which were never found. On September 30, Corporal Given's Medal of Honor was forwarded to the Treasury Department for disbursal to his next of kin. As of March 18, 1872, the medal was still in the possession of Charles F. Herring, the chief clerk of the second auditor's office. There is no evidence of a final disposition to the next of kin.[37]

James B. Dosher, 1890. His service in the Mexican War and as a frontier Texas Ranger and Confederate cavalryman were only preludes to his record of gallantry as a U.S. Army scout. He is the only person to have worn the badge of a Texas Ranger and to be awarded the Congressional Medal of Honor. *Photograph courtesy Tina Mathis Wyatt, Abilene, Texas.*

CHAPTER 6

Skirmish at Bluff Creek

October 5, 1870

———— ✪ ————

Sgt. Michael Welch	Pvt. James Smythe (Anderson)
Cpl. Samuel Bowden	Pvt. Benjamin Wilson
Cpl. Daniel Keating	Guide James B. Dosher

T he militant non-treaty bands of the Kiowa, Comanche, and Southern Cheyenne tribes hurting under losses from successive expeditions at the hands of the U.S. Army during 1868 and 1869 eventually began to drift onto their designated reservations in early 1870. Their arrival, however, completely overwhelmed the newly arrived Quaker administrators, who were unable to cope with the problems created by the influences of the militants upon the resident bands.

Maj. George W. Schofield wrote to Gen. P. H. Sheridan in February 1870 warning of impending problems on the Kiowa–Comanche Reservation. Schofield commanded a battalion of the Tenth U.S. Cavalry at nearby Fort Sill, but could not initiate actions upon the reservation without the Indian Bureau's permission. In desperation, Lawrie Tatum, the Quaker agent, had finally requested that Schofield arrest some of the Indians. Eager to assist Tatum but apprehensive about the legality of the request, Schofield asked Indian Bureau Superintendent Enoch Hoag for permission. A precise, forcefully injected military presence likely would have suppressed the problems, but in April Hoag denied Tatum and Schofield the authority to act.[1]

Schofield and his troops were just a few miles away, but they could only watch as the situation on the reservation deteriorated.[2] By late May the situation had become so dangerous that most of the Quakers, fearing for their lives, had fled to Iowa, Pennsylvania, and New England. Only Tatum and a few others remained. Tatum did the only thing he could short of overt physical action; on June 18 he began sending out written warnings of impending raids emanating from his reservation.[3]

Affairs were no better at the Cheyenne–Arapaho Reservation, where Lt. Col. A. D. Nelson reported a near-chaotic atmosphere on September 23. In one incident a white security guard had struggled with three Arapaho men who were attempting to steal lumber. One chief, Little Raven, supported the guard's efforts, but Quaker agents, in order to calm the militants, forced the guard to pay $103 to the thieves. The Quaker agents also issued rations to the militant Cheyenne in violation of the expressed orders of E. S. Parker, the commissioner of Indian Affairs. The recalcitrant Cheyenne promptly left the reservation, openly announcing that they were on the warpath. They took with them several previously peaceful bands of Cheyenne and Arapaho.[4]

In mid-September the hostile Kiowa and Comanche also left their reservation after forcibly taking extra rations, also having coerced previously peaceful bands to join them. By the last week of September these groups were poised to strike the Texas frontier. The well-intentioned Quakers simply could not contend with the warrior societies of the Plains Indian culture, which looked upon kindness from an adversary as a weakness.

The Kiowa and Cheyenne moved west and then south, crossing the Red River at Doan's Crossing in present-day Wilbarger County. The other force, comprised mainly of Comanche and some affiliated bands, moved south, then east, and crossed the Red River at Red River Station in Montague County. This party, shortly after crossing the river, split into five separate bands, each numbering around twenty, which fanned out into Montague, Clay, and Cooke Counties.

One of these small bands was a group of eighteen Wichita tribesmen led by an aged chief, Keesh Kosh of the Keechi tribe. By the third week of September this band had struck farms near the town of Montague and had penetrated even deeper to eastern Jack County, just twelve miles east of Fort Richardson. After raiding and pillaging the Stroud and Reilly ranches they began their rapid escape to the northwest.[5]

Word of this and other Indian depredations reached the military authorities at Forts Griffin and Richardson. Col. James Oakes, commander of the Sixth U.S. Cavalry at Fort Richardson, organized three scouting patrols to pursue and, hopefully, intercept the Reilly ranch raiders before they could cross the Red River. In the mid-morning of September 25 a courier was dispatched to the sub-post of Camp Wichita twenty-five miles to the northwest. Capt. T. C. Tupper, posted there with sixty-nine troopers, was ordered to move out immediately and scout the area between the Little Wichita and Wichita Rivers.[6] Capt. Daniel Madden and thirty troopers were to move directly north from Fort Richardson on September 29; their primary objective was to pick up the trail of the Indians who had raided the Stroud and Reilly ranches. Their area of operations would be to the east of Captain Tupper's area of operations. The first patrol dispatched was that of Capt. William A. Rafferty, which operated to the south and west of the other two patrols. His area of operations was the upper Salt Creek basin of Young County, an area raiding Indian bands historically had used as a path of escape.[7]

At noon muster on September 25 Captain Rafferty read Special Order no. 197 to Company M. Informing his sixty-nine men that the final scouting rotation complement for the month was due up, he called off the names of the twenty-two men in that complement. They, along with five Tonkawa Indian scouts and post guide James B. Dosher, were to scout the area of the headwaters of the West Fork of the Trinity River. Plans were for them to return via Salt Creek, scouting the area between unless a trail was found. In such case the trail was to be followed and the Indians captured if possible.[8]

Rafferty's patrol, which included Army Surgeon H. J. Terrell, with Jim Dosher in the lead, moved out the main gate of Fort Richardson and headed west shortly before sunrise on the morning of September 26. During the first day the patrol scoured the many creeks across the Fort Belknap road for signs of Indian trails. None were found and the command went into camp along Cameron Creek, two miles north of Fish Pond Mountain, after marching sixteen miles. Over the next four days the command moved forty miles in a circular path northwestward, southward, and then eastward. By September 30 the command was back on the Fort Belknap Road just a few miles west from where they had departed from it. They had encountered large herds of grazing buffalo along the march and found one abandoned horse but had not located one sign of an Indian presence. On the morning of October 2 the soldiers questioned the workers at the Ledbetter Salt Works, who reported no signs of a recent Indian presence in the area. After consulting with Dosher, Rafferty decided that the next most probable area to investigate would be the Trinity River crossing at the mouth of Brushy Creek, some twenty miles to the northeast. They would first move west along the Belknap Road and then move northeastward up Brushy Creek to the crossing.[9]

On October 4 Dosher, as was his usual practice, left camp before sunrise to have the best opportunity to spot any Indian spies. He had ridden two miles southeast to the Brushy Creek Crossing when he found a fresh trail that had obviously been made during the night. Dosher quickly rode to inform Rafferty of his finding. After a brief study of the field map Dosher was confident that they could overtake the Indians on the prairie lands north of the West Fork of the Trinity, south of the Little Wichita. The command quickly remounted and initiated a rapid advance north. The march continued at a rapid gait for more than three hours, with brief periods of dismounting to walk, water, and graze the mounts. By mid-morning the command arrived at the stretch of prairie Dosher had designated but the Indians were nowhere in sight. Dosher persisted, however, and scout details were dispatched along each flank. The advance continued for five more hours before the men were allowed to stop and refresh themselves and their mounts from the waters of Onion Creek. The Tonkawa scouts were sent to attempt to find the trail. At 7:30 that evening they rejoined the command and reported that they had failed to locate any signs. Rafferty decided to camp for the night at the juncture of Onion Creek and the Little Wichita River, about two hundred yards from the Van Dorn Crossing.[10]

The command had been in the saddle for more than twelve hours and had covered about fifty miles during the day's ride. All except Dosher were disheartened. Dosher continued to insist that the Indians were nearby. Rafferty, attempting to console Dosher, casually commented, "Well, Dosher, I want us to get them fellas." Rafferty planned to allow the troops to build camp fires to prepare their meals, but Dosher interceded, saying, "Captain, I thought you said you wanted to get them fellas." "I do," Rafferty retorted. Dosher impertinently suggested that Rafferty should not build any fires unless he did so in a nearby deep ditch, "so if the Indians are near, they won't discover us." The campfires were eventually built in the ditch as Dosher suggested. Rafferty went a step further and constructed a wall of poles and blankets to block the glare of the fires. If the Indians were nearby they would have to come very close to discover the command. That night Dosher also recommended that the command leave camp the next morning at least an hour before sunrise. If they waited until sunrise, the Indian lookouts would already be in place and would discover the command's approach.[11]

An hour before sunrise on October 5 Dosher and Tonkawa scout Johnson had already commenced searching for the trail. The rest of the command followed about half a mile behind. After crossing the Little Wichita River at the old Radziminski Crossing, the command was still about four hundred yards behind the scouts and all were proceeding in a northwesterly direction. Just before Dosher and Johnson began to ascend to the prairie land on the north side of the river, they found a very fresh trail from a single shod horse, tracks that had apparently been made earlier that morning, for the heavy dew had been disturbed. After following the tracks for another mile they came upon a freshly killed beef cow and realized that the Indians were close at hand. The command had moved about five miles since crossing the river and a short distance to the left were a number of small chalk hills. Sgt. Michael Welch and Pvt. James

Anderson had been detailed as flankers and were several hundred yards to the left along the bank of Bluff Creek.[12]

Dosher and Johnson were within three hundred yards of a small hill to their immediate front when they noticed a campfire with several Indians sitting around it eating breakfast, their horses tethered just a few yards away. Johnson excitedly jumped off his mule and began to switch his saddle onto his lead horse. Dosher raised his arm and motioned for Rafferty to bring the troops forward. When Johnson threw his saddle onto his horse he gave out a yell and the Indians, having heard him, began to run for their horses. The troopers, in ranks of fours, charged toward the Indians with Rafferty in the lead. Keesh-Kosh, the band's leader, had mounted his horse and reeled about to fire when Dosher's first rifle shot hit him in the shoulder. He dropped his shotgun and fell from his horse. The first rank of troopers had quickly advanced into the fray and were now within pistol range. One young Indian, who had returned to aid the wounded Keesh-Kosh, had just raised his pistol toward Dosher when Corporal Bowden killed him with a single pistol shot. Keesh-Kosh, having fallen to his knees, was about to raise his weapon toward Bowden when Corporal Keating fired a single shot, which killed the aged chief. Bowden, Keating, and Pvt. Benjamin Wilson charged after the main body of Indians, who were attempting to drive their herd to safety. A running skirmish ensued for about a quarter of a mile during which Bowden, Keating, and Wilson engaged the Keechi herders in close hand-to-hand fighting, at one point seizing the reins of the led horses from the grasp of one herder and driving the others away.[13]

After wounding Keesh-Kosh, Dosher had turned his attention toward a mounted Indian on a nearby rise who was firing down into the mass of troopers and Indian scouts. Dosher charged up the rise toward the mounted Indian but his horse was hit twice and fell dead, throwing the wily scout violently to the ground. Sergeant Welch, seeing that the incapacitated scout was in danger, rushed in with his pistol blazing. They saw the Indian slump in his saddle, but he then turned about and bolted into the mesquite woodlands. Welch took Dosher up behind him and carried him back down the hill to the Indian campsite, where Rafferty and Surgeon Terrell were examining the camp trappings.[14]

The Indians had scattered in all directions and, except for the distant firing of Bowden and Wilson in pursuit of the Indian herd, a hush had fallen over the immediate scene. The bugler had just began to blow the first notes of "recall" when one of the troopers shouted that he saw a mounted Indian riding along the creek's edge about five hundred yards to the north. Anderson and Keating, who were driving the captured herd back toward the camp, had the best angle to cut him off and they both bolted to block his way. Anderson, on the right, spurred

81

his horse into a gallop toward the fleeing Indian and within seconds was beside the young Indian and his pony. He grabbed the rein from the startled Indian and leveled his pistol at him, intending to elicit his surrender. The young man instead jumped from his pony and made a desperate leap into some nearby dense brush and vines. Anderson reined his horse to a halt and dove into the bushes behind the fleeing Indian. Rafferty, who had arrived at the scene, yelled for Private Anderson to abort his efforts just as he was about to make the capture. Rafferty apparently wanted this Indian to survive and carry a warning to other Indians who might contemplate raiding into Texas.[15]

The troopers' horses were so worn out that pursuing the Indians any further would have been fruitless. The search among the Indian camp had turned up a number of interesting items. A silver peace medal with a bust of President Martin Van Buren was found around the neck of the dead chief, Keesh-Kosh. The medal's engraving indicated that it had been presented to him in 1839. Four documents were also found on his body. Two of them were dated in 1866; one served as a pass to allow buffalo hunting off the reservation and the other served as a solicitation for gifts. The third document, dated April 7, 1869, recognized Keesh-Kosh as chief of the Keechies by the voice of the tribe. The final document, dated April 18, 1870, had been signed by U.S. Indian Agent Lawrie Tatum. It again certified Keesh-Kosh as the chief of the Keechies and recommended him as "a reliable man." Several pistols, a loaded shotgun with brass tacks decorating the stock, and an assortment of bedding and women's and children's clothing also were found. The latter items were proof that this particular band had indeed been involved with recent raids. These items were later found to have been taken during the plundering of the Henry Riley ranch twelve miles east of Jacksboro. After collecting and taking inventory of the captured items and burying the two dead Indians, Rafferty mounted the command and headed back to Fort Richardson, where the command arrived at noon on October 7. The items they had captured and the information gleaned from those items helped the army prove that the Department of Interior's Office of Indian Affairs had condoned and even encouraged the absence of Indian bands from their reservation.[16]

On October 10 Captain Rafferty submitted his official report of the scout and engagement to Col. James Oakes. In it he specifically mentioned that much credit be given to the zeal and energy Dosher displayed on the march and during the fight. Rafferty also mentioned five enlisted men of Company M, Sixth U.S. Cavalry, who had rendered themselves conspicuous by good conduct and gallantry during the pursuit and fight.[17] On October 12, 1870, Colonel Oakes enclosed an endorsement commending Rafferty and his men, including the guide Dosher, to the favorable consideration and notice of the department commander.[18]

This endorsement, along with Rafferty's report, was forwarded to Department of Texas headquarters at San Antonio. On October 24 Col. J. J. Reynolds, the departmental commander, made the initial recommendation that the men be presented with Medals of Honor, which was forwarded to the adjutant general's office for review.[19] Reynolds had recommended that Sgt. Michael Welch, Cpl. Samuel Bowden, Cpl. Daniel Keating, Pvt. James Anderson, and Pvt. Benjamin Wilson be awarded Medals of Honor. He further recommended that a medal be granted to the guide, Dosher, if the law would sanction it. This recommendation was received by the adjutant general's office on November 7, 1870, and after an endorsement by Gen. W. T. Sherman the order for the medals was forwarded to the engraver.[20] On November 19 the six medals were transmitted, along with congratulatory letters to the recipients at Fort Richardson. Records indicate that there was no single award ceremony for this group of recipients. It appears that each recipient was simply presented his Medal of Honor by the post adjutant on scattered dates between January 1 and January 17, 1871.[21]

In 1917 the Medal of Honor awarded to James B. Dosher was revoked by an Army Medal of Honor Review Board as he was judged to have served in a civilian capacity.[22] On June 12, 1989, due to the efforts of William G. Cody, grandson of William F. "Buffalo Bill" Cody, the five medals awarded to army scouts employed by the U.S. Army Quartermaster Department, including those awarded to Dosher and Cody, were reinstated by a Department of the Army Board for Correction of Military Records. The reinstatement was based upon the well-documented combat services the scouts had rendered in the field, which the board judged were experiences in common with those of the soldiers. The board also concluded that contracts the scouts signed with the Quartermaster Department were as legally binding and substantially the same as a soldier's enlistment contract. Another point was that two civilian surgeons had been granted medals and that the services of a scout were just as military in nature, if not more so, than those of a surgeon. A fourth deciding factor was that Indian scouts, who performed basically the same function as the white scouts, had not been removed from the Medal of Honor Roll.[23]

On December 4, 1991, in a ceremony at the University of North Texas at Denton, Lt. Gen. Horace G. Taylor rectified the review board's decision and presented a new-style Medal of Honor to Mrs. Velma Reed, a great-granddaughter of James B. Dosher. Reed transferred custody of the medal to the Texas Parks and Wildlife Department, which placed the medal on permanent display at Fort Richardson State Historical Park in Jacksboro.[24]

Robert G. Carter, circa 1870. He was forced to retire early from his beloved Fourth U.S. Cavalry as a result of the injuries incurred at Congrejo Canyon. Carter used his fifty-year writing career to trumpet the regiment's accompishments on the Texas frontier. *Photograph courtesy the National Archives.*

Ambushed in Congrejo Canyon

October 10, 1871

———— ★ ————

Lt. Robert G. Carter

The problem of Indian raids emanating from the Kiowa–Comanche and Cheyenne–Arapaho Reservations in the Indian Territory had worsened so much by the spring of 1871 that Gen. W. T. Sherman decided to personally investigate the situation. By the middle of May 1871 Sherman had traversed more than five hundred miles on his tour of the military posts along the Rio Grande and Central Texas frontiers. On May 18, after examining affairs at Fort Griffin, Sherman's small party was moving east along the old Butterfield Stage Road toward his final Texas stop at Fort Richardson. He had heard many angry and tearful pleas from victims of Indian attacks but he personally had yet to see one Indian warrior. Shortly after noon Sherman's party passed near Cox Mountain, the halfway point to Fort Richardson. By 8 P.M. he was at Fort Richardson meeting with yet another delegation of frontier Texans who were complaining about the dangers of Indian raids. He went to sleep that night believing that there was credence to the claims of East Texas Republicans, who charged that claims of Indian depredations were concocted and exaggerated in order to have federal troops transferred from East Texas to the western frontier to accelerate Democratic Party control.[1]

At 4 A.M. the next morning Colonel Mackenzie woke Sherman and took him to the post hospital, where a teamster, Thomas Brazeal, was being treated for wounds received in an Indian attack. Sherman learned from Brazeal that the attack had occurred near Cox Mountain just before 2 P.M. the previous day.

Sherman realized very quickly that through some quirk of fate he and his small escort could have been the victims instead of Brazeal and his eleven fellow teamsters and quickly became a believer in the frontier Texans' claims. Sherman dispatched Mackenzie and a detachment of troops to the scene to investigate the affair and pursue the attackers' trail. Sherman and Gen. R. B. Marcy then started for Fort Sill near the Kiowa–Comanche Reservation, confident that they would soon see Mackenzie there.

Sherman and Marcy arrived at Fort Sill on May 23. Colonel Grierson and his staff greeted them and over the next few days conducted Sherman on a tour of the post and the outlying facilities. On the nearby Kiowa–Comanche Reservation Lawrie Tatum received a report from an interpreter, Horace Jones, who had overheard conversations among the Indians concerning the raid on the wagon train near Cox Mountain in Texas. When Tatum summoned Kiowa chief Satanta to his office and inquired about the attack, he was startled to hear Satanta boast about his role in the affair. Satanta also implicated several other chiefs. Tatum sent word to Grierson, who in turn informed Sherman. Sherman sent word to Tatum to have Satanta and the chiefs he had implicated meet him at the fort. Sherman eventually lured the Indians to the porch of Colonel Grierson's quarters, where the army had jurisdiction. Sherman then coaxed them to repeat their confessions and, at Tatum's urging, arrested the three chiefs.[2] Mackenzie arrived two weeks later and confirmed that the raiders' trail had indeed led to the Kiowa reservation. Mackenzie returned the three chiefs to Texas for trial, where two eventually were found guilty in the Thirteenth District Court at Jacksboro and were sentenced to die by hanging. Pressure from Superintendent Enoch Hoag and others concerned that the executions would precipitate a general Indian war eventually obtained commutation of the sentences to life imprisonment.[3]

Army officials who wanted to maintain pressure on the Indians in order to drive them onto the reservations immediately authorized two expeditions for that purpose. If the first campaign had been successful there would have been no need for a second. The first expedition, however, turned out to be a debacle. Lasting from August 2 to September 13, the joint Mackenzie–Grierson expedition of more than one thousand troops snaked its way more than five hundred miles through the Indian Territory and into the Texas Panhandle. It was punctuated by logistical and jurisdictional disputes compounded by an unusually hot, dry summer. Mackenzie gained valuable information about the terrain but the experience deterred him from ever conducting a campaign in the heat of the summer again. Since only two abandoned Indian camps were found, Mackenzie initiated preparations for the second follow-up campaign upon his return. This time he planned to scout solely within Texas to avoid jurisdictional disputes and intrigues with Colonel Grierson.

One of the chief aides who assisted Mackenzie with the myriad of details necessary for the fall campaign was an aggressive recent West Point graduate, Lt. Robert G. Carter. Despite being with the regiment a little less than a year he had become one of Mackenzie's most favored officers. Like most young "shavetail" lieutenants he was very demanding of the men under him but realized quickly it was necessary to be flexible in the execution of rules and regulations. Although strict, Carter's persona quickly gave way to humor and mirth and because of this he became the target of many of the officers' pranks and jests. The other officers delighted in seeing Carter's straight-laced veneer cracked by a smile or laugh.

By October 1 the command was fully rehabilitated and logistical arrangements were in place to commence the campaign. The staging base was to be old Camp Cooper, five miles north of Fort Griffin. The entire six hundred-man complement of eight companies of the Fourth U.S. Cavalry, two companies of the supporting Eleventh U.S. Infantry, and the Tonkawa Indian scout detachment had been in place since September 25. On the morning of September 30 Lieutenant Carter and a small detachment were dispatched to scout for a suitable wagon route west of the Clear Fork of the Brazos River. Shortly after Carter and the detachment returned on October 3 the order was given to mount up.[4]

As per his usual routine, Mackenzie dispatched Captain Boehm and the Tonkawa scouts to lead out and cover the flanks. The objective of the expedition was to hunt down, engage, and induce the hostile Quohada bands under Mow-wi (Handshaking) and Para-o-coom (He Bear) to go onto the reservation and cease their raids upon the Texas frontier. At the behest of Lawrie Tatum, Mackenzie was also to attempt to recover two captives, Clinton and Jeff Smith, who had been captured near Boerne, Texas, in 1869 and were believed to be held by Mow-wi. By October 7, the command had arrived at the base camp site near present-day Spur. Mackenzie was eager to begin active field operations so he dispatched the Tonkawa scouts on the night of October 7 to reconnoiter the area for any sign of the Indians. Dispatching scouting parties in the darkness became one of Mackenzie's standard operating procedures. After the Tonkawas had failed to return within twenty-four hours Mackenzie became extremely concerned and anxious. Remembering that one of the large villages discovered in October 1869 was directly northwest of Soldier Mound, he led the entire cavalry command out of camp at 8 P.M. on October 8.[5]

By sunrise on October 9 the command was advancing rapidly up Blanco Canyon along the White River. After ten miles the command came upon the setting

Mackenzie had described. The river had been appropriately named, as its shallow flow raced over the rocks to create white rapids. One deep arroyo from the west exposed a twenty-feet-high waterfall. Several hundred yards upstream water cascaded over several ten-feet-high rock ledges to form Silver Falls. Mackenzie stopped the command for breakfast and, while the troops rested after eating, Capt. E. M. Heyl was dispatched to reconnoiter the area for the missing Tonkawa scouting detachment. Heyl had recently transferred to the Fourth Cavalry from the Ninth Cavalry and was familiar with the area as he had scouted it with Capt. Henry Carroll's expedition in September 1869. Shortly after 2:30 P.M. the Tonkawa scouts finally returned to the main command, reporting that they had observed four Indians on the east canyon rim. The "Tonks" had caught them spying on Heyl's detachment as they moved upriver. When discovered, the Indians fled into a series of deep ravines and easily outran the scouts' already fatigued mounts. Johnson did report that a fresh trail had been discovered leading toward the location of the village captured in 1869. By 3:30 P.M. the column was moving rapidly upstream. After proceeding about two miles, a rifle shot was heard toward the rear of the command, which caused a great deal of confusion and the advance was halted to determine the source of the shot. An anxious young trooper in one of the rear companies had accidentally discharged his Spencer carbine. After this delay Mackenzie decided to halt the advance and camp for the night. The campsite was selected in a three-quarters-of-a-mile-long sub-canyon on the east side of the river, two and a half miles south of the mouth of Crawfish Creek. The location was not particularly popular among the officers since the southeast approach from the main canyon was obscured by a series of foothills. A muddy, sandy creek bed ran through the center of the camp, which was bordered on the north by fifty-feet-high cliffs. The decisive factor in the site selection was likely the excellent stand of timber that lay several hundred yards north.[6]

By midnight the entire command was bedded down. Sentry posts had been established around the encampment and at distant strategic points. Inside the cordon the horses had been staked out within rope enclosures and further confined by rope tethers ten feet in length, secured by ten-inch metal picket pins driven into the ground. Lieutenant Carter, serving as guard mount officer, completed his first inspection round of the sentry outposts and staked out his still-saddled mount. He lay down to take a brief rest before his next tour but soon heard a yell, followed by a gunshot, from the down-river sentry post. Seconds later loud yells and several rifle shots were heard in the direction of Captain Mauck's campsite on the southeast quadrant. Carter realized that the camp was under attack and frantically grabbed for his picket pin in the darkness, only to see it jerked out of the ground and whirled beyond his reach. He sprinted after his stampeded mount, which was bucking and kicking his way toward F Company's herd. Luckily the pin became entangled in the side line ropes and Carter was able to get a hold of the picket rope. He spent several minutes trying to calm and control the horse before he could finally mount. During these brief moments pandemonium swirled about him. Panic-stricken horses ran blindly to and fro while picket pins flew dangerously through the darkness. Soldiers in various states of dress and decorum ran after their mounts, no doubt contemplating the one hundred-mile walk back to Fort Griffin should their frenzied efforts result in failure. Cursing and yelling intermingled with the boisterous yells of the Indians as the invaders dashed pell-mell through the camp. Officers barking out their orders added their cacophony to the mass bedlam. As the minutes passed the disorder gradually subsided but wild firing from the sentry posts made it extremely dangerous to venture beyond the immediate area of the campsite.[7]

By 5 A.M. the situation had been stabilized. After ascertaining their losses, details from each company with those horses available were dispatched to round up any loose stock. At the first opportunity Carter ventured out to check on the distant sentry posts. The nearest post, which was manned by Company F troopers, had been stampeded over. Shortly after crossing the river Carter discovered the westbound trail of the command's stampeded herd trailing off to the west. At the westernmost sentry post near the western bluff his inquiry about the direction taken by the stampeded herd was confirmed. After recrossing the river he visited with the sentries atop a small knoll one mile north of the camp. While querying the men about their observations a shot was heard from up the valley and Carter set off to investigate. After a ride of almost a mile he encountered two small detachments of troops just above the mouth of Crawfish Creek. While conferring with Captain Heyl and Lt. W. C. Hemphill about the source of the shot heard earlier, Carter mentioned his discovery of the tracks leading northwest. As he turned to point out the location of his discovery, about a dozen Indians driving a small horse herd could be seen rounding the south rim of Congrejo Canyon's mouth.[8]

The sun was just beginning its ascent over the horizon as the troops bolted after the Indians. The chase continued in the gray darkness of the canyon for about a mile before the troops could close the distance enough to fire at the Indians with their pistols. Seconds afterward the Indians abandoned the herd and rode into a ravine. Hemphill and several troopers peeled off to round up the horses the Indians had abandoned. Heyl, Carter, and ten troopers reined up at the ravine and listened for the sounds of the fleeing Indians who, within seconds, emerged out of the ravine about two hundred yards to their left and bolted across the canyon floor. The two officers spurred their mounts into the ravine and up the bank onto the prairie beyond. The others hesitated but within minutes they were close behind the two officers. The chase continued to the northwest toward a high twin-faced butte, whose jutting white rock face was now illuminated at its summit by the creeping sunlight. Just as the troops rounded a slight rise at the base of the butte on its southwest side, they again spotted the Indians. They were about a quarter of a mile away, their numbers having increased considerably; some could be seen changing to fresh mounts. The severity of their predicament spread a pall of shock among the troops. They had ridden about four miles since leaving the camp and their mounts were severely winded. The Indians, certain that they now had the soldiers at a disadvantage, charged toward them amid loud war whoops. Heyl, the senior and most veteran officer, was the first to efface the shock and speak, nervously exclaiming, "Heavens, but we are in a nest! Just look at the Indians!"[9] Everyone wheeled about and began to retreat. Carter, on the most debilitated horse among the officers, knew that he and most of the other men could not outdistance the Indians. The deep ravine they had crossed minutes earlier was still about an eighth of a mile away and it was the only semblance of defensible cover on the canyon floor. Carter, with his horse gasping loudly and swaying from exhaustion, rode up beside Heyl. Shouting out that his mount and those of several others were in critical condition he expressed his desire to dismount the men and make a defensive stand. Several seconds passed before Heyl reined up on his spirited black stallion and shouted out, "Yes, that is right! Deploy out on the run men, and give them your carbines!"[10] An instant later a dust cloud enveloped the troopers as they reined up and dismounted. Two troopers were deployed as horse holders while the remainder deployed in two separate squads in skirmish lines. Heyl and seven of the men deployed about a hundred yards to the right. Carter and five other troopers remained in place to defend the left flank. Heyl's squad opened fire on the Indians at three hundred yards. The Indians fanned out when Carter's squad commenced firing. Several ponies went down and the Indians quickly checked their advance.

When they saw the Indians halt their approach, both detachments began to slowly retreat toward the ravine, now just two hundred yards to their rear. The six-to-eight-foot depth and ten-foot width of the ravine to Carter's left created an obstacle for the Indians. The part of the ravine Heyl's squad was approaching was shallow and had rounded sides. Carter ordered Sgt. Benjamin Jenkins and Pvt. Andrew Melvill to concentrate on any Indian or groups of Indians who slowed and appeared intent upon crossing or entering the ravine. Their success in killing several ponies over a five-minute span also alerted the troops that sizable numbers of Indian women were participating in the affair. After the initial volley from the troops the warriors had halted their advance and massed around their fallen comrades. The women contributed to the fight by leading spare horses to those who needed them, performing their chores amid their own eerie shrieking and wailing. The women themselves added a whole new dimension to the affair, since their presence clearly indicated the presence of a village from which increased numbers of warriors might emerge to join the battle. The troopers may have recalled the stories about Maj. Joel Elliott's troops on the Washita River in 1868, when female Indians had mutilated the fallen soldiers so badly that they could not be identified by their fellow troopers.[11]

The Indians had quickly resumed their advance but had been checked effectively by Jenkins and Melvill on the far left. They now initiated their circling tactic directly to Heyl's front. The increased sunlight and their closer approach enabled the troops to observe their adversaries more closely. Most of the Indians were bare-chested with colorful blankets wrapped around their waists and those prominent as leaders wore long colorful war bonnets. Most were profusely painted with spots and stripes and this practice, also duplicated on their mounts, clearly identified them as the Quohada Comanches.[12]

In addition to Jenkins and Melvill, Carter's squad included Pvts. William F. Downey, John Foley, and Leander Gregg. All but Gregg were veteran troopers whose previous conduct assured Carter that they would not easily yield ground to the Comanches. Heyl's detachment, on the other hand, was comprised entirely of new recruits recently assigned to Company K. One advantage was that their mounts tended to be stronger, not yet debilitated by extensive scouting and field service. Both detachments continued to fire single shots sporadically as they slowly fell back toward the ravine. Both squads were within yards of the ravine, but the ultimate hope was that the main command would hear the firing and come to their rescue. An extensive bow in the ravine started two hundred yards to Carter's left and wound around their rear to a location somewhat to the right rear of Heyl's position, which placed Heyl and his squad in closer proximity to its hoped-for refuge and cover. Heyl and his squad, therefore, arrived at the edge of the ravine while Carter and his men were still some fifty yards from its edge. Heyl quickly realized that the ravine's shallowness at their contact point offered little protection.[13]

The Indians' circling tactic, with the adversary enveloped within the ring, was one of the most common modes of attack the Plains tribes used. The circle the Quohada Comanches formed was approximately an eighth of a mile in diameter and just to the left front of Heyl's position. The tactic, though appearing theatrical

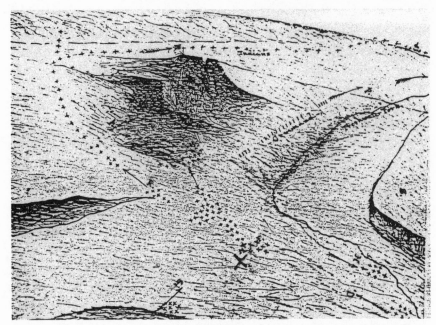

Sketched map of Blanco Canyon by Robert G. Carter, circa 1921, entitled "The Battle of Blanco Canyon." *Courtesy Ernest Wallace and the Crosby County Pioneer Museum.*

in nature, actually served several cultural and strategic functions within the Plains Indians' mode of warfare. Battle to most of the Plains tribes was a rite of maturity for young men. Young men participating in the circle could perform feats of horsemanship and bravado during combat in plain view of their comrades, with advancement to warrior status based on the degree of bravado they exhibited. These demonstrations often became highly distracting to their adversaries and this was no doubt one of the elements in the overall strategy. Each Indian could fire or launch weapons from the same point in the circle, thus enabling them to maintain a constant barrage. The circle's diameter could easily be shortened to create an even more intense barrage. The circle could be conducted in either direction but was most commonly performed in a counterclockwise movement with each Indian firing pistols, rifles, or bows from the lower left quadrant of the circle. The Comanches apparently achieved effective execution of the circle, for Heyl's position soon became untenable. Without a shouted command or warning Heyl's squad suddenly mounted up and bolted off to the southeast. One of Carter's men yelled out, "Lieutenant, look over there quick, they are running out."[14]

Despite yells, threats, and curses, Heyl's retreat continued unabated. Carter and his squad now became the sole focus of the attacking Comanches, whose success in driving away one group of soldiers resulted in celebration. While the Comanches held their brief celebration, Carter and his squad gained the edge of the ravine. Now devoid of their support from the right the ravine no longer offered a viable defensive position. A simple stampede of Indian ponies down the ravine coupled with coordinated attacks from the sides would offer them little chance for a substantive defense. Carter and his men could not remain where they were and become encircled, which would mean certain death. Once they crossed the ravine the decision process was surrendered to the Indians. One heavyset, powerfully built Indian mounted on a black stallion assumed the lead and initiated an advance toward Carter's squad, which had remounted after the ravine crossing. The Indian advance began slowly but when they were within about two hundred yards the Indian raised his pistol and, amid blood-curdling yells, initiated a massive frontal charge. Carter ordered his men to unlock their magazines and unleash rapid fire into the Indians' ranks. Seconds after the chief had raised his pistol and shouted out commands, the rear ranks of the Indians unleashed a salvo of arrows, which arched into the troopers. Surprisingly, only three of these arrows found their mark, hitting none of the men but wounding three of the horses. The Indians followed with a pistol volley and Pvt. Bill Downey sustained a wound to his right hand. Downey had just fired his carbine, but was unable to move the lever to eject the spent cartridge with his injured hand. As the Indians neared the far edge of the ravine Downey's efforts became frantic. Carter yelled for him to use his knife to pry the cartridge out. After several seconds of desperate efforts Downey succeeded in doing so and immediately chambered another cartridge. One Comanche, noticing Downey's predicament, had jumped the ravine and was just a few yards away. Just as the Indian raised his weapon to fire, Downey heard the chamber on his carbine close and he squeezed off a shot, which struck the Comanche squarely in the chest and he fell backward.[15]

Now that the troops were at least fifty yards from the ravine, the Indians swelled in and over its depths. As the great mass of them gained the prairie between the troops and the ravine Carter decided that this was the most opportune time to make a dash for safety. He shouted, "Now men, unlock your magazine, bunch your shots, pump it into them and make a dash for your lives. It is all we can do."[16] Their volley raked the Indian ranks and several ponies fell. The troopers turned about and began their dash for safety. The Indians spent several minutes rebounding from the confusion the volley wrought before they dashed after the troops. Parra-o-coom, the Comanche chief on the black stallion, led the pursuit. He was without question the most volatile and aggressive chief among all of the Quohada. Astride his ornately decorated stallion he quickly closed the distance, urging the others forward as he waved his pistol high. Several hundred yards into the chase, Private Gregg, the trailing trooper on the right, yelled to Carter that his horse was giving out. Carter turned to see Gregg's gray pony swaying in total exhaustion. Parra-o-coom also saw Gregg's failing mount and honed in on the young soldier. Carter, on the opposite side of the squad and about fifty feet away, reined up to slow down and moved to assist Gregg. He drew his Smith & Wesson pistol and attempted to maneuver into position for a clear shot. His first shot missed; the chief then assumed a position behind Gregg and used him as a shield. As Carter maneuvered for another shot, Private Melvill, just to his front, was struck in the right arm by a pistol shot. Carter was forced to aid Melvill, who was struggling to maintain a grip on his reins and pistol. Meanwhile, Gregg was desperately working the lever to chamber a round. Either the magazine was empty or a cartridge was jammed in the chamber, for several attempts proved futile.[147] Carter yelled for Gregg to use his pistol and Gregg finally threw his carbine down in frustration. Just as Gregg lowered his hand to his holster, Parra-o-coom raised his pistol, fired, and Gregg fell, killed instantly from a shot to the back of his head. Parra-o-coom gave out a triumphant yell as Gregg's body hit the ground, a yell that was answered in kind by a discordant yell emanating from a source off to the squad's left. Carter, fully expecting death at the hands of another band of Indians, reined up only to be confronted by Texas, the fierce yet cherubic wife of Sergeant Johnson of the Tonkawa scouts. Their rescue was at hand. First over the rise, Texas was fantastically arrayed in all her finery and was as anxious to engage the Quohadas as any man present. Carter turned to see Parra-o-coom and the other Quohadas turn about and retreat toward the twin-faced butte.[18]

Close behind Texas was the main body of Tonkawa scouts with Captain Boehm in the lead. Boehm had turned Heyl, Hemphill, and their squads around and with the Tonkawas their force numbered around forty. There was no time for recriminations as Boehm forcefully took command, saying only to Carter, "Bob let's push them now. Mackenzie is in our rear."[19] They formed a single skirmish line and initiated a slow advance. The Indians could be seen massing at the base of the butte where Heyl and Carter's squads had first encountered them. As the skirmish line came to Gregg's body the soldiers halted briefly to ascertain his condition. The twenty-one-year-old native of Belmont, Ohio, lay in a pool of blood, his light brown hair blowing in the breeze. All in Carter's squad knew the outcome of the examination but the confirmation that Gregg was dead fortified their resolve. As the line resumed its advance the Tonkawas broke into their

"Johnson," Tonkawa chief of scouts for Ranald S. Mackenzie, in a carte de visite taken at Fort Griffin, Texas, circa 1872–1874 by photographer H. S. Shuster. Johnson was often accompanied by his wife, "Texas," who headed the Tonkawa scout detachment that rode to the rescue of Lieutenant Carter's small force in Congrejo Canyon. *Courtesy the Lawrence T. Jones Collection, Austin.*

loud, shrill war cries. Within minutes the entire skirmish line was emitting its own chorus of yells and epithets. Comanche sharpshooters were seen along the distant cliff line while Comanche women shuttled fresh horses to those needing them on the canyon floor. All were noisily yelling and wailing and the concerted noises from the Indians echoed eerily off the canyon walls. As the line of troops traversed the ravine and moved a short distance beyond they began to come under scattered sniper fire from the butte and nearby cliffline. This firing became more dangerous, especially to those on the left of the line, where Carter and his squad were positioned. Anxious to initiate the action, Carter volunteered to take his squad and clear the snipers from the butte. Boehm, realizing that their path of advance toward the main body of mounted Indians would place the line in greater danger, granted the permission. Carter assumed the advance, followed closely by Jenkins, Foley, and several other troopers. Carter spurred his mount and charged up a zigzagging pathway as bullets ricocheted around him. Wielding his pistol, Carter drove several snipers from their positions in nearby ravines. As he came to a jutting boulder in the pathway he attempted to swerve but his horse suffered a wound in the left foreleg and faltered, pinning Carter's left leg between the rock and his horse. He tumbled from the saddle but held on to the saddle pommel and was dragged to the summit in a semi-conscious state. Several of the squad members came to his assistance when they reached the summit. Below them the troops had erupted into spirited cheers as Mackenzie and the main command arrived on the scene. Fortunately for Carter, Mackenzie's approach in the distance had prompted the Indians to abandon their positions around the summit only minutes before. They could be seen fleeing across the shelf land and arroyos of the escarpment leading up to the plains of the Llano Estacado. Boehm's force engaged them with volley firing; the booms of the carbines echoed across the canyon floor. Members of Carter's squad assisted him to the canyon floor along a less treacherous return route.[20]

Shortly before 8 A.M. the staccato notes of assembly reverberated across the canyon. Fifteen minutes later the entire command was assembled at the base of the butte. By 8:45 Mackenzie was conducting a simple and somber memorial service at Gregg's graveside. After the service, rocks were gently placed over Gregg's grave to prevent wolves from disturbing his remains.[21] Lt. C. A. Varnou was given charge of Gregg's personal effects and it was almost a month later that Gregg's parents in Ohio received them via registered mail with an accompanying "We regret to inform you . . ." letter. Shortly after the service Mackenzie dispatched the Tonkawas to search for the main Indian encampment while the main command camped there to await their return. During this brief lull, Asst. Army

Surgeon Rufus Choate was summoned to examine the wounds of the injured. Choate's diagnosis about Carter's leg was that he had likely sustained a serious fracture. His leg was so swollen that the boot had to be cut off for the leg to be examined. A single laceration had bled profusely but was clotting sufficiently enough to be bandaged. At 2:30 P.M. and moments after having a makeshift splint applied, Carter limped in response to the bugler's sounding of "Boots and Saddles." Mackenzie confronted Carter as he labored to mount up. He made Carter aware that he wanted him along on the operation but recommended that for his own safety and well being it would be best if he escorted the dismounted troopers back to the supply camp. Carter became mildly indignant over Mackenzie's perception of his unfitness to perform and asked if returning to the supply camp was an order. Mackenzie, himself the possessor of several battle scars, replied, "No lieutenant . . . it is not an order, but I repeat, I am considering your comfort and safety." Carter brushed his empathy aside, replying, "Then sir, it is left to me, I go forward with the command."[22]

Over the next six days Carter endured his pain on a one hundred-mile pursuit of the Indians. At a point near the present-day Muleshoe National Wildlife Refuge severe sleet and snow thwarted the command's mission. The command had narrowed the distance between themselves and the Indians to less than two miles before the storm forced them to turn back. On October 15, as the command again descended back into Blanco Canyon near its head, Captain Boehm's detachment killed two Indians. During this brief skirmish Mackenzie sustained an arrow wound in his right leg and another trooper received a gunshot wound. At various times on the return to Fort Richardson, the swelling and pain in Carter's leg forced him to ride in the ambulance with Mackenzie, allowing them to further cement their friendship.[23]

Carter served faithfully under Mackenzie for only two more years. Two weeks after his return to Richardson, Carter captured ten deserters amid a bitterly cold storm. His recapture of them after a one hundred-mile pursuit and the subsequent dismantling of a network that aided army deserters forever embellished Mackenzie's admiration and confidence in Carter. During Mackenzie's secret punitive raid into Mexico in May 1873 Carter served as his loyal aide and confidant. Carter's quick action to save the life of Capt. Clarence Mauck from assassination by one of the Kickapoo prisoners further elevated his standing with Mackenzie and the regiment's officer corps. Carter's pride in and admiration for the officers and men of the Fourth U.S. Cavalry was no less profound.

In September 1873, after suffering from recurrent problems with his left leg, the post surgeon at Fort Clark ordered Carter off active duty and suggested that he attempt to obtain medical treatment for the irregular and damaged veins in his leg. Carter loved the army and was extremely proud of his accomplishments during his tenure on the Texas frontier. His Civil War service and his West Point training had prepared him well, but now all of this was in jeopardy. After his near-death experience and injuries of October 1871 he found himself under increasing and insistent pressure from his wife to leave the army and pursue a commercial career. After being advised against corrective surgery in October 1873, Carter was granted a certificate of disability and placed on convalescent leave. During this extensive leave of absence, from December 1873 until March 30, 1876, he resided variously at Bradford and Newtonville, Massachusetts. In his appearance before an Army Retirement Board in October 1875 he declined to elect for the recommended experimental surgery and was placed on the retired list of the army, effective June 28, 1876.[24]

Though his active-duty military career had apparently come to an end, Carter waged a personal battle of sorts on behalf of Mackenzie and the Fourth U.S. Cavalry for the next sixty years. On March 22, 1875, he wrote to the adjutant general's office and requested copies of all orders and circulars issued from 1873 and 1874 and up to date. During 1874–1875, through these documents and from correspondence with Captain Boehm, he became cognizant of the fact that the Fourth Cavalry under Mackenzie had delivered the most crucial blows to the Indians during the 1874 Indian Territory and 1876 Powder River campaigns. Despite these and later successes against the Utes and Apaches, the newspapers featured copious articles about the exploits of Miles, Custer, Crook, Carr, Price, and their commands. Carter was aware of Mackenzie's antipathy toward newspaper reporters. He had expressly forbidden them from accompanying his commands, while Miles, Crook, and most of the others had actively courted them. If the deeds of Mackenzie and the Fourth Cavalry were to be preserved and recorded for posterity, then Carter decided it was up to him.[25]

After a brief commercial career and seven years in teaching, Carter's financial independence allowed him to pursue the goal of a literary career. Many of his early literary creations were based upon his extensive diary entries from his Civil War and Texas frontier experiences. After Mackenzie's untimely death in 1889 there was an extensive decline in Carter's literary output. A year before that an Indian Wars-era Meritorious Service Board had convened to accept recommendations for a pending brevet scheme, Medals of Honor, and Certificates of Merit. Now, without the requisite impact of a commander's recommendation, the deserving members of the old Fourth Cavalry again found themselves at a disadvantage. Carter alone had the time and resources to act on behalf of his former comrades, which he did with his usual energy, personally searching out and copying the requisite reports. He spent countless hours in the Pension Bureau, locating lost comrades whose eyewitness accounts were crucial to the award process. Most of the documentation for Indian War brevets and Civil War post facto Medal of Honor awards granted to his former comrades were as a result of his efforts. His connections within the inspector general's office through his old friends, Henry W. Lawton and Edward M. Heyl, enabled him to navigate the maze of required forms and procedures.

Carter's efforts did not go without reciprocal efforts from his comrades. On December 13, 1893, Peter M. Boehm, then retired and living in Chicago, submitted the first of many supportive letters recommending Carter himself for a Medal of Honor. Subsequent supporting letters from W. A. Wilcox, Henry W. Lawton, Sgt. Joseph Sudsburger, and C. A. Varnou greatly strengthened his case. He submitted his application and supporting documentation on November 6, 1897, and on February 27, 1900, the secretary of war endorsed the adjutant general's recommendation to formally confer the Medal of Honor upon Robert G. Carter for his actions of October 10, 1871.[26]

Thirty-five years after receiving the Medal of Honor and sixty-four years after performing his deed of bravery, Robert G. Carter published his book *On the Border with Mackenzie; or Winning West Texas from the Comanches.* During the last ten years of his life and during the major writing and organization of the book, he was severely impaired with arthritis and was clinically blind in one eye. Without his dogged determination there would be a five-year void in the history of West Texas. There would be no accounts of the deeds and sacrifices of many deserving individuals who took dangerous steps in the process of pacifying West Texas. Though he was not actually present during the pivotal 1874 campaign and despite his questionable use of accounts by fellow officers, the people of Texas, especially, owe Robert G. Carter and his beloved Fourth U.S. Cavalry an immense debt of gratitude.

Carter received the first copy of his book at Christmas 1935. Although all of his beloved comrades had passed on to final muster, he had doggedly continued to raise their guidon with his pen. His long life had provided him with many productive and comforting memories. His life had spanned the long chasm of time between the horse and the airplane. The Llano Estacado region of Texas, which was once a remote, desolate, somber setting for a simple soldier's funeral, had become one of the most productive agricultural areas in the world. Just three weeks before Robert G. Carter's death on January 4, 1936, the U.S. Cavalry Association published its December 1935 edition of the *U.S. Cavalry Journal*, in which appeared the first review of *On the Border with Mackenzie*. In one final irony, the review was written by Col. Jonathan M. Wainwright at Fort Clark, Texas, in the very same office Carter had occupied as Col. R. S. Mackenzie's adjutant sixty-two years earlier. Wainwright closed his review, describing *On the Border with Mackenzie* as "an interesting account of the life experiences of a gallant young cavalry officer whose name today on the retired list carries with it the citation: Medal of Honor, . . . and two brevets."[27] Just six years later Wainwright himself was recommended for the Medal of Honor for his heroic defense of a small island named Corregidor.

CHAPTER 8

Striking the Comancheros
on Beals Creek

March 28, 1872

Sgt. William Wilson

S ince the early days of the Texas Republic in the 1830s and 1840s and continuing after statehood despite the presence of a sizable portion of the U.S. Army, Texas frontier settlers suffered at the hands of marauding Indian bands. On the infrequent occasions when the army or citizen groups caught up to the Indians, they were found to be well outfitted with store-bought clothing, camp equipment such as metal pots and pans, and abundant supplies of guns and ammunition. It was obvious that these Indian raiders were trading with some commercial source either to the south, north, or west of the frontier. It was common knowledge that many of these Indian bands received safe haven in Mexico and on the federal reservations in present-day Oklahoma. Several tribes, especially the Kickapoo, Mescalero, Lipan, and Mimbres Apaches, long had been trading with Mexican citizens who traded in stolen Texas livestock. Countless scouting patrols of Texas Rangers and U.S. Army troops had trailed Indian bands to the Mexican border and to the boundaries of the Indian Territory reservations, but federal laws forbade further pursuit. In many instances these patrols also found that the Indians fled neither south across the Rio Grande nor north across the Red River, but rather to the northwest toward New Mexico Territory. Although New Mexico had become American territory after 1850, both civil and military efforts to suppress the unlawful activities there had met with as little success as those on the Texas frontier.[1]

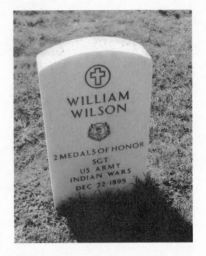

Sgt. William "Billy" Wilson's headstone in San Francisco National Cemetery. Wilson's deed of gallantry in 1872 enabled the destruction of the illicit Comanchero trade in Texas livestock and enhanced the late nineteenth-century growth of the West Texas cattle industry. *Photograph courtesy Charles Chambers, Houston.*

In 1867 the War Department built three new military posts along the outer fringes of the northwest Texas frontier. Forts Richardson, Concho, and Griffin were primarily meant to be bases for operations into lands heretofore controlled by the hostile tribes. Of these three new posts, Fort Concho appeared to be in the most ideal location to intercept westbound stolen herds. It was established in November 1867 near the juncture of the north and middle forks of the Concho River, directly in the path of escape so many of the westbound raiding bands used. In the past, many of these bands had veered north of the Pecos River to escape the scouting patrols sent out from Fort Stockton. This avenue of escape north of the Pecos and south of the upper reaches of the Colorado River was through a vast arid region thought to be totally devoid of surface water and unfamiliar to both state and federal authorities. Fort Concho was to serve as the base for operations into this region.

As the frontier became resettled after the Civil War, the degree of depredations increased steadily. Northern demand for Texas beef added new impetus for the expansion of the Texas livestock industry. This demand for meat and hides in the legitimate markets also meant increased activity among illicit livestock traders. Counties northwest of San Antonio were being especially hard hit by Indian raiding bands. Twenty-seven settlers were reported murdered and nine others abducted between 1866 and 1871 in seven counties from Bexar County northwestward to Coleman County.[2] In that same area, more than eleven thousand head of livestock valued at a quarter of a million dollars had been stolen by Indian raiding bands.[3]

The few Texas Rangers, citizens, and army troops who had gazed upon the immense buffalo herds of northwest Texas knew full well that the Indians had little personal need for the great quantities of livestock obtained by their raids. On several occasions between 1867 and 1871, army commands in both New Mexico and Texas had struck joint New Mexican–Indian encampments including sizable herds of stolen livestock.[4] The fleeing Indians and their compatriots left behind sacks of flour, corn, coffee, and other goods in large quantities. The New Mexicans who had brought these goods to trade for the stolen Texas livestock became known as Comancheros.[5] Exactly how long this Comanchero trade system had existed is open to speculation. New Mexicans likely had hunted the buffalo on the southern High Plains for more than a century. Shortly after the Civil War, federal Indian Commission officials granted legal permits allowing New Mexicans to trade with the Plains tribes. The issue of the trade of arms and ammunition by New Mexicans to the Plains Indians first brought the trade permits into question. During mid-1865, one of the federal peace commissioners, while negotiating guidelines for the Little Arkansas Treaty with the various southern Plains tribes, learned of the arms-for-cattle trade from the Indians themselves. This commissioner, Jesse H. Leavenworth, informed A. B. Norton, the newly appointed superintendent of Indian affairs in New Mexico, of the practice. Leavenworth firmly believed that the trade was an inducement to steal stock and children in Texas. Norton immediately suspended all outstanding trade permits but his further efforts to suppress the trade became stymied by the factional politics of the United States War and Interior Departments and a variety of other factors.[6]

By 1869, when the United States Army made its first forceful penetration onto the Texas High Plains, evidence of vast herds of domestic livestock were clearly apparent, including an extensive trail system. While most of these trails were aligned to migratory buffalo, there were other trails distinctly made by vast herds of domestic livestock and large two-wheeled Mexican-style carts. Trade bases or rendezvous points were discovered at strategic water sources. Some, like those at Quitaque and Las Lenguas, had crude rock habitations and irrigation systems indicating more than just transient occupation.

Although never substantiated, it is believed that the Comanchero system may have had operatives working along the Texas frontier in its own information-gathering system, which was especially active near military posts. Ostensibly, the primary function was to scout out locations of the best and most sizable herds. Whether they reported on army patrol activity or occasionally reported misinformation is pure speculation. In September 1869, when Capt. Henry Carroll's expedition first penetrated onto the Texas Southern High Plains, the Comancheros clearly had an early warning system in place. After traversing the divide between the Concho and Colorado Rivers, Carroll reported that smoke signals constantly appeared to his front.[7] James R. Cloud, for several years one of the civilian guides at Fort Concho and a local rancher, developed such suspicions toward Marshall Cato, a black bartender in nearby San Angelo.[8] Cloud's suspicions arose as a result of Cato's extensive absences in the company of his Indian wife prior to and following Indian raids in the vicinity. His large purchases of ammunition and other goods had prompted local citizens to pay closer attention to his activities. Informed by someone that his activities were under scrutiny, Cato moved to the settlement near Fort Griffin. It was reported that United States troops killed him in a Comanche encampment shortly after extensive raids were perpetrated upon several local ranches.[9] Maj. John P. Hatch, a commander at Fort Concho for a number of years, developed suspicions toward a former West Point classmate who, after being suspended from the academy, had pursued his road to wealth through a series of illicit endeavors across the West. He was reportedly killed and identified by army officers in an Indian camp on the North Fork of the Red River in September 1872.[10]

Another element in the Comanchero trade system was the use of captives taken by those tribes involved in the trade. The Kiowas and Comanches, in particular, would often select adolescent males for capture who could then be used as spies. These young men often would be forced, under the threat of harm to themselves or their family, to locate the most opportune herds. As they were able to speak the language, they could move easily in and around the settlements without raising a great deal of suspicion. Captives who proved uncooperative were ransomed off by various intermediaries. Texas frontier history is rife with accounts of Indian raids where white males were seen as active and willing accomplices, which led to a great deal of early confusion about who was actually perpetrating most of the frontier depredations. Some, most notably the Quaker Indian agents, were unwilling to admit the Indians' guilt and blamed the raids on whites dressed as Indians, a claim that became even stronger when several whites dressed in Indian attire were killed during clashes with frontier settlers.[11]

If the Comanchero trade system was to be dismantled, stringent efforts needed to be made in New Mexico. Most of the territory's major newspapers had editorialized for years against the evils of the trade. There had been several successful interceptions of Comancheros driving large herds westward. These captures in eastern New Mexico by United States troops could have been instrumental in ending the trade but they came to naught. In spite of the fact that the captured herders could not provide legal proof that they owned the livestock in their possession, they escaped prosecution. New Mexican juries were reluctant to return guilty judgments; too many New Mexicans were profiting from the trade. The sale of horses and beef cattle to the United States Army Quartermaster Department purchasing agents in New Mexico yielded a poor farmer much more revenue than a year of hardscrabble farming. The system was not only a vicious circle, but an extremely profitable one, and it became clear that the cycle would have to be broken somewhere other than in New Mexico.

After 1867 the U.S. Army in Texas slowly began to penetrate and map the areas northwest of Forts Concho and Griffin. The army's area of operations was expanded as each freshwater source was discovered and mapped. Sufficient water sources at strategic points were vital for large-scale command operations into the lands dominated by hostile Indians. Until enough of these sources could be located and accurately mapped, only small unit operations were practical. If any of these small units happened onto a concentration of Comancheros and their Indian allies, the outcome was likely to be a military disaster.

By March 1872 the problem of depredations, especially the theft of livestock, had risen to devastating proportions. Shortly after sunrise on March 27, 1872, an oft-repeated scenario began to unfold: The sleepy soldiers at Fort Concho were woken by two cowboys from the nearby Five Mile Ranch, who reported the theft of some horses and mules during the night. Maj. John P. Hatch, commander at Fort Concho, detailed a cavalry detachment to investigate and attempt to overtake the guilty parties. Sgt. William Wilson and Gabriel Monroe, the post guide, along with twelve enlisted troopers from Company I, Fourth Cavalry, left the post shortly after eight that morning. By 10 A.M. Sergeant Wilson's detachment had reached the Five Mile Ranch. The raid on the ranch's corrals appeared to be the work of a small band of raiders estimated to be fifteen in number. They had absconded with nineteen horses and five mules.[12]

After resting and feeding their horses, the detachment started trailing the raiding band. The tracks led to the northwest, but after fifteen miles the tracks turned in a northerly direction at a point near present-day Water Valley. By 3 P.M. the detachment had advanced about twenty miles from the Five Mile Ranch. The trail was still fresh and distinct but Wilson was forced to rest the men and water the horses at Sumac Springs. Wilson and Monroe rode to the top of Battle Peak, a prominent elevation, to scan the terrain for the presence of the raiding band and the telltale dust cloud of a driven herd of livestock. Shortly after 4 P.M. Wilson and Monroe returned to the campsite at Sumac Springs, remounted the detachment, and resumed the march. The soil was getting thinner as the detachment neared the rim of the Colorado River valley, yet Monroe was having little trouble following the trail. As soon as the troops reached the canyon rim, darkness rendered further tracking impossible and Wilson ordered the men into camp for the night.[13]

The detachment started on the trail again the next morning just before sunrise but within an hour Monroe had lost the trail in the exposed bedrock of the valley rim. After several minutes of consultation, Wilson decided that their best chance of regaining the trail lay in splitting the detachment and tracking both sides of the river. Monroe and two troopers continued along the rim of the valley in a northwesterly direction. Wilson and the remaining ten troopers found a break in the rim of the valley and made their way down to the river's edge. Two troopers crossed to the north side of the river and commenced a slow concerted movement up the river. Movement along the south bank of the river was very rough and slow. Many narrow ravines, rock falls, and the proximity of the cliff line to the river created opportune ambush sites. The troops had proceeded about ten miles along the river with no signs of the Indian trail when Wilson decided to set up camp, eat, and rest the horses. After the horses had been unsaddled and staked out to graze, small fires were started, and the men were allowed to have their first cooked food in more than twenty-four hours.[14]

Wilson and his troops had been encamped for a little over an hour and had just finished their meal when Monroe and two troopers came galloping into camp. Monroe informed them that he had located the thieves' camp about two miles away on a creek feeding into the Colorado from the west. Monroe disclosed that the raiders were definitely not Indians. He believed they were either Mexicans or perhaps those New Mexicans who traded with the Indians. The troops saddled their mounts and, after a few minutes of consultation, Monroe and Wilson decided that the advance should be made along the south bank of the river. This route would enable the troops to approach unseen until they reached the end of the cliff line at the mouth of the creek. The command slowly approached along well-traveled trails until they rounded the jutting cliff line and made a turn to the left. Wilson then quickened the pace and kept the troops in a single-file formation. The command continued its approach along the south bank of Beals Creek for several hundred yards. Just as they rode over a slight rise, the troopers observed one man swimming in a small pool of the creek about two hundred yards away. He was the first to spot the oncoming troops and he began shouting the alarm as he hurried up the bank.[15]

Wilson ordered the men into a rank formation as they came under scattered firing from the men in an oak grove on the north bank of the creek. Wilson began barking out orders. Monroe, one corporal, and six troopers were ordered to charge to the left and cut the milling herd away from the grove of trees to their front. The six troopers on the right were to follow Wilson and they would attempt to gain the low ridge behind the Comancheros and, in the process, cut them off from their mounts and surround them. Wilson and his six-man rank charged across the creek under scattered firing. One group of three Comancheros was seen running up a small ravine toward the top of the hill. Wilson ordered his men to take cover in a small depression and direct their fire toward those men in the oak grove to their left about two hundred yards away. While Wilson's six men engaged the Comancheros, Monroe and his seven men raced toward the captured herd and began driving them away. Sergeant Wilson, still mounted, concentrated his efforts on the three Comancheros who had ran to the north up a small rise and had disappeared over this rise at the head of the ravine. Wilson charged up the ravine after them. Just as he gained the crest of the rise he could see that the three were attempting to mount their horses. Two of them were mounted and were waiting for the third, who was having trouble getting on his horse. The Comancheros opened fire on Wilson who was, at that point, less than seventy-five yards away. Charging pell-mell down the slight incline toward the Comancheros, Wilson swayed methodically in the saddle and opened fire with his Colt revolver. His first shot killed a heavy-set Comanchero and caused the third Comanchero's horse to take flight. When but twenty yards away, Wilson's second shot found its mark and a second dead Comanchero tumbled from his mount. The third Comanchero now attempted to mount the second dead Comanchero's horse, but he was quickly overtaken by Sergeant Wilson, who reined his horse to a stop between the Comanchero and the nearby horse. The third Comanchero found himself staring down the barrel of Sergeant Wilson's Colt pistol and he quickly threw up his arms in the universal sign of surrender. Wilson dismounted and searched the man for any concealed weapons. As he bound his prisoner's hands behind his back, he could see the other troops chasing the other Comancheros into the brush.[16]

After securing the herd with a couple of troopers, Monroe and five of his men had joined in the attack on those Comancheros hidden in the oak grove. Two concerted volleys from the eleven Sharps carbines sent the twelve Comancheros fleeing, at least three of whom were wounded. Wilson herded his prisoner down the hill to the oak grove where Monroe and the other troops were congregated. Wilson ordered three men to establish a perimeter to the north in case the Comancheros decided to return and the remainder of the detachment began collecting the equipment the Comancheros had abandoned.[17]

Just over an hour after this brief skirmish had begun, the recaptured herd was being driven southeast toward Fort Concho. The abandoned Comanchero saddles and equipment were burned and the single plume of black smoke signaled to the fleeing Comancheros that the beginning of the end to their illicit trade was at hand. At about 2:30 P.M. Wilson mounted the remainder of the detachment and began a forced march toward Fort Concho following the trail of Monroe and the other troopers, who were driving the recaptured herd. After a brief stop at Star Spring to water and rest the horses, the command continued on to a night camp at Sumac Spring. Early the next morning, the command resumed its march and arrived back at Fort Concho around 8 A.M. on March 29. The patrol had covered a total of 125 miles. The entire detachment had conducted themselves well in the face of a desperate and determined enemy and had inflicted what was to become the most severe blow yet dealt to the Comanchero trade.

The prisoner Sergeant Wilson captured, identified as Apalonio Ortiz, was placed in the post stockade and Wilson was requested to complete his report on the incident.[18] Major Hatch was elated at the results of the pursuit and engagement. The prisoner turned out to be a twenty-nine-year-old farm laborer from the small village of La Cuesta near Las Vegas, New Mexico.[19] Under interrogation over a two-week period, he divulged the complete operational details of the Comanchero trade. He provided the name of his employer and the wages he was to receive and also related his operations up until the day of his capture. He divulged what had hardly been credited, that there were at least two good wagon roads across the Staked Plains with adequate permanent water and grass and that all of the stolen Texas cattle were driven over them to New Mexico. In addition, he named the major Comanchero leaders, the merchants who supplied them, the modes of transport they used, travel time and distances between water sources, the layout and locations of the rendezvous points, and the names of the chiefs and tribes involved in the trade. This information was not only used by the army in tactical operations, but much of it was turned over to civil authorities in Texas and New Mexico to use in the prosecution of those involved.[20]

In his original report to the Department of Texas commander, Gen. C. C. Augur, on March 30, Major Hatch wrote glowingly about Sergeant Wilson, stating, "He is an intelligent and energetic non commissioned officer and entitled to full credit for the successful result of his scout."[21] General Augur was so pleased with the results of Sergeant Wilson's brave conduct that he recognized him specially in General Order no. 6, issued April 6, 1872, from departmental headquarters at San Antonio. On April 17 General Augur forwarded the reports and an endorsement to the Military Division of the Missouri Headquarters adding, "The attention of the War Department is respectfully invited to the creditable conduct of Sergeant Wilson in the affair reported upon."[22] Wilson's report and the endorsements from Generals Augur and Sheridan were forwarded to the War Department. The secretary of war, upon Gen. W. T. Sherman's recommendation, formally granted the Medal of Honor to Sergeant Wilson on April 27, 1872.[23]

The medal was sent to Department of Texas Headquarters at San Antonio to forward to Wilson's proper duty station. On June 13 General Augur entrusted the medal and a personal letter of commendation to Lt. William Hoffman of the Eleventh U.S. Infantry.[24] Hoffman carried the medal and Augur's letter to Sergeant Wilson's duty station with the R. S. Mackenzie expedition headquarters at the camp on the Fresh Water Fork of the Brazos River. Shortly after 3 P.M. on July 21, 1872, the staccato bugle notes of assembly reverberated up Blanco Canyon in what is now Crosby County. The two hundred-plus men of Companies A, D, F, I and L, Fourth U.S. Cavalry, hurried into dismounted company inspection formation. A thirty-seven-star United States flag fluttered briskly in a warm breeze beside a brilliant royal blue and yellow Fourth Cavalry regimental banner. Smaller red and white swallowtail company guidons, now unfurled, added their minute fluttering sounds to the commotion. The orders "Dress right" and "Front" bellowed by a myriad of sergeants resonated along the canyon walls. Within a few minutes the sounds ceased as abruptly as they had begun and Blanco Canyon was silent except for an isolated neighing horse or coughing trooper. Lt. John A. McKinney, the expedition adjutant, ordered the massed formation to attention as Colonel Mackenzie and the other senior regimental officers took their place at the front facing the massed formation. Mackenzie, after a few words about the need and purpose of the expedition, ordered Sgt. William Wilson to come "Front and center." Sergeant Wilson smartly paced himself to the front of the formation where he came to attention and exchanged salutes with Mackenzie. Mackenzie, acting upon the written request of General Augur, read Department of Texas General Order no. 6. He then stepped forward and presented the Medal of Honor to Sergeant Wilson. After exchanging salutes again, Wilson did an about face and briskly returned to the ranks.[25]

William Wilson continued serving with distinction in the Fourth Cavalry until 1895, but the deed he performed on Beals Creek on March 28, 1872, unquestionably was the zenith of his military accomplishments. The significance of his deed in suppressing the Comanchero trade can not only be measured by the countless number of lives saved, but also by its singular contribution to the heritage of Texas. The vibrant growth of the Texas livestock industry after 1872 was in no small part due to William Wilson's gallantry in action against that band of Comanchero cattle thieves. The very essence of the image of Texas, the cowboy and the ranching industry, is thus entwined with the gallantry of Sgt. William "Billy" Wilson.

The enlisted men's huts at Fort Griffin, Texas. On a cold December night in 1873 a young infantry corporal left one of these huts and disappeared into obscurity. His desertion created one of the most puzzling controversies in Medal of Honor history. *Photograph courtesy Charles M. Neal Jr. Collection.*

CHAPTER 9

Ambush at Salt Creek

August 3, 1872

—— ★ ——

Pvt. Franklin M. McDonnold

U ntil the mid-1880s most passengers, light freight, and mail transported in the American West was conveyed via horse- or mule-drawn coaches. The private firms throughout the West that served the various route segments operated for the most part across arid, sparsely populated, and undeveloped regions. The segments of those routes that traversed the domains of hostile Indian tribes often incurred the wrath of those tribes.

The three primary routes across the western frontier of Texas were eventually served by the firm of Sawyer, Risher, and Hall, known commonly as the San Antonio–El Paso Overland Mail Company. This firm's route segments suffered the wrath of Kickapoo and Apache tribes as well as desperadoes who used the Mexican border as a sanctuary in the route segment between San Antonio and El Paso. Along its northern and northwestern segments the hostile Kiowa, Comanche, and Cheyenne used the Indian Territory as their sanctuary. Because of these factors the San Antonio–El Paso Overland Mail Company and the other freighting concerns operating along the same routes incurred abnormally excessive losses.[1]

During the span from 1866 through the spring of 1872 there were at least sixty-nine attacks upon freight trains, way stations, and coaches. In the course of these attacks at least forty-four employees and customers had lost their lives, and thousands of livestock either had been stolen, killed, or injured.[2] The worst of these attacks occurred in April 1872 at Howard's Well. A combined band of Kiowas, New Mexican Comancheros, and Mexican bandits struck a freight train encampment, killing thirteen and wounding four.[3] Among the contents stolen from the wagons was a shipment of U.S. Army pistols and ammunition. This incident intensified the already heated relations between the army and officials of the San Antonio–El Paso Overland Mail Company. A series of ill-fated events over the years had provoked accusations between the two parties. The army accused the company and some of its employees of misusing army property and of collusion with the desperadoes attacking the coaches. Company officials retaliated with charges that the army often delayed their coaches with late deliveries of their mail packets, that the army had falsely arrested their employees, and that the army had provided timid military escorts who often neglected their duties.[4]

The events of June and July 1872 only exacerbated the situation. The eighteen North Texas frontier counties west of Fort Worth had been ravaged by numerous well-armed raiding bands of Kiowas and Comanches. Fourteen frontier Texans had lost their lives during those months.[5] Two mail coaches and one way station had been attacked, resulting in one El Paso Mail Company employee being wounded. Numerous livestock were killed or injured.[6]

The attraction of a stage coach or freight wagon delivering to the Indians the items they desired was too irresistible. The Indians only had to wait at a preselected site, launch an ambush, and overwhelm the two men atop the coach, usually by shooting one of the lead horses or mules. Once the attack was concluded the Indians had all they needed for a successful escape—spare horses or mules complements of the stage company and, thanks to the U.S. Postal Service, they had excellent water storage devices in the leather and canvas mail packets. The key to the successful defense of a stagecoach lay in the absolute alertness of the driver and his escort and how quickly and accurately each could wield his weapons. These factors had punctuated the few successes in repelling stagecoach attacks ever since the military escort program began. Far too many young army escorts regarded stage escort duty as a mundane forty-eight-hour duty of traveling to a distant post via the coach and returning on the opposite-bound coach the next day.

One of these scenarios began to unfold in the early morning hours of August 3, just across from the courthouse on the northeast quadrant of the town square at the El Paso Mail office in Jacksboro.[7] Just outside a four-horse team was hitched to a Concord-style coach. The coach, its team, and a sizable shipment of U.S. Mail were to be driven westward to the station at Fort Griffin, where similarly outfitted coaches would continue westward. The driver on this run was Peter M. Collins, a tall, lanky, twenty-four-year-old formerly from Westchester County,

A Concord-style coach of the San Antonio–El Paso Overland Mail Company stops at the Concho Mail Station in Benficklin, Texas, in 1878. This is the same kind of stagecoach driven and defended by Peter Collins and Franklin McDonnold in an attack on the Salt Grass Prairie in 1872. *Photograph courtesy West Texas Collection, Angelo State University, San Angelo, Texas.*

New York. He had served a five-year stint in the Fourth Cavalry and had been discharged a year earlier.[8] On this run, just one of many he had already made along the route to Fort Griffin, there were no passengers but there was a heavier than usual mail load. By 6 A.M. the mail had been stowed and Collins cracked his whip to guide the team onto the road to Fort Richardson. Within a few minutes he slowed the team to greet the lone sentry at the eastern edge of the parade ground. The coach raced past the still-darkened barracks and Collins reined the team to a stop in front of the post adjutant's office. Shortly after one sharp whistle in the darkness, the assigned military guard strode out of the building and down the flagstone walkway. Collins greeted the guard as he swung into the seat beside him, recognizing him as a brief acquaintance from Fort Griffin. The guard, Pvt. Franklin M. McDonnold, twenty-two years old and formerly from Bowling Green, Kentucky, had been in the army for just over a year.[9] Collins guided the team westward, trailing a cloud of red dust.

Pete Collins only wielded his whip to urge the four-horse team up the myriad of small dry arroyos and creek banks that dotted this portion of the route. By 9 A.M. they had arrived at Ham Spring Station. Collins and McDonnold ate a quick breakfast while the team was watered and fed. An hour later Collins was once again driving the coach westward. The road became relatively smooth along this segment and the team, invigorated, responded well to Collins's urgings. McDonnold intently scanned the horizon in every direction as they descended the gradual incline of the eastern rim of the Salt Creek Valley, an area that had been plagued with Indian raids since the beginning of settlement. Just two

113

months earlier a surveying crew had been attacked twenty-five miles north of Fort Belknap. The Abel Lee family was all but wiped out on June 9 at a point between Fort Belknap and Fort Griffin. Almost one month later, on July 6, Benjamin Peebles, a ranch hand on the McDonald Ranch on Kings Creek, was murdered in front of his co-workers.[10]

Collins and McDonnold reached Rock Creek Station by 2 P.M. While the men enjoyed their dinner, a new team of horses was hitched to the coach and around 2:30 Collins guided the coach back onto the road at a run. The coach was traversing the most dangerous segment of the northern route of the El Paso Overland Mail. As the coach rocked along Collins reminded McDonnold to scan every ridgeline, every elevation, and every tree for Indians. They were nearing Cox Mountain off to their left, which marked the eastern edge of the blood-soaked Salt Creek Prairie, and Collins could relate firsthand to many of the tragedies of the area. Almost two years before he had been among the contingent of troops sent from Fort Griffin to try and intercept the Indians who had killed Frank Taylor, the stage driver on this very same route. Both men became quiet and somber as they passed the site of the Warren Train massacre of the previous year. The charred remains of one of the ten freight wagons was still there, flanked by seven small wooden crosses—a stark reminder to be vigilant. The road gradually descended to the sparsely timbered prairie lands to the west. Collins reined up the team as it splashed into the clear trickling waters of Flint Creek. It was a little after 3 P.M., but the temperature still hovered in the low nineties and the men and horses refreshed themselves with the cool water.[11]

Fort Belknap, their planned overnight station stop, was still fifteen miles west so Collins popped the whip over the team's ears. The horses pulled vigorously up the incline and onto the slightly rolling prairie land. For two more hours the coach rocked along and over the prairie before Collins reined up the team in the gravel bed of Salt Creek. Collins allowed the team to drink for only a few minutes before he once again wielded his whip. The refreshed team showed a burst of vigor as the horses pulled up the bank and onto the rolling prairie. Indian Mound, one of several conical-shaped elevations in the area, was off to their right about half a mile away.

Precisely what transpired over the next hour is uncertain, but apparently McDonnold heard the faint thumps of horses just before he noticed a swelling dust cloud off to the right. Suddenly a band of eight or ten Indians emerged out of a wooded ravine several hundred yards away. They began yelling their war whoops as they charged directly toward the coach, and McDonnold opened fire on them with his Springfield rifle.[12] The Indians broke into two bands, half of them trailing behind the coach, while the others ran parallel to the road about one hundred yards away. Collins frantically lashed out with the bullwhip. McDonnold, aware that he couldn't fire in two different directions from a moving coach, urged Collins to turn the team into a stand of trees off to their left.[13]

The thicket of trees was about two hundred yards away and as Collins hauled back on the reins to turn the team to the left one of the lead horses was killed. The rest of the team stumbled and floundered and the coach swerved and slowly rolled onto its side in a cloud of dust.[14] Both Collins and McDonnold jumped clear. The Indians on the side dashed in for the kill but were met with a hail of rifle fire from McDonnold, who had rolled along the ground and came up firing. Collins retrieved his Sharps carbine from the coach after a frantic search. McDonnold, now apparently in a rage, did not wait for the dust to clear, but ran through it to confront the Indians at point-blank range. The Indians trailing from the rear entered into the still-swirling dust and ran into McDonnold's fire. The attackers on the verge of success were forced back and retreated to begin their usual encircling movement. The leader of the group was mounted on a white horse and McDonnold began to concentrate his firing at him.[15]

While McDonnold kept the Indians at bay Collins examined the overturned coach for damage. The Indians remained about one hundred yards away. As the Indians circled the besieged coach, McDonnold took deliberate aim at the Indian on the white horse with each squeeze of his trigger until he hit his target. The Indians halted and turned to retrieve their fallen leader. Apparently during this brief lull Collins and McDonnold consulted with one another about what to do. Both finally agreed that they had to get the coach upright and make it into the nearby tree line. The coach was, after all, their only source of cover at this point. The mail could not just be abandoned. Both also likely had an aversion to walking and fighting the seven miles to the next way station at Belknap. While the Indians still hovered over their fallen chief, Collins and McDonnold began executing their plan to get the coach upright. Collins unharnessed the dead horse while McDonnold double looped a rope to the upper railing on the coach. Collins tied up the loose reins from the dead horse and removed the lines from the harness of the other lead horse. Within a few minutes Collins had positioned the untethered horse while McDonnold looped one end of a rope through the harness on one side and Collins looped the rope through the harness on the other side.[16]

By the time Collins backed off and popped his bullwhip over the backside of the tethered horse, the Indians recovered from the shock and lamentations over their fallen leader and remounted. While Collins urged the horse forward with repeated tugs on the harness, McDonnold ran to the far side of the coach and gave one slow, deliberate shove. The coach slowly tilted upright onto its wheels. The Indians once again charged across the prairie toward the coach, McDonnold once again opened fire on them, and again they broke off into two bands. One band took a position across the road to appear to block that direction as an avenue of escape. Several other Indians hovered to the rear. Within minutes Collins had secured the harnesses and was again in the driver's seat. He called for McDonnold to join him, and after firing several shots at both bands, McDonnold climbed onto the seat beside Collins, who set the whip to popping. The coach lurched forward toward the nearby tree line. The Indians to the front made a mad dash to cut the wagon off from the tree line, but McDonnold's rapid firing scattered them in every direction. Arriving at the tree line just yards ahead of the Indians, McDonnold jumped to the ground and resumed his rapid firing into the Indians' ranks. McDonnold shot two Indian ponies, causing their riders to suffer treacherous falls. Collins, after securing the team and coach among the trees, joined McDonnold in firing at the Indians. Under fire from the two determined coach defenders, the Indians decided that the wounding of one chief and four ponies was all they were willing to risk and they sped off to the north. While waiting to see if the Indians would return, Collins rechecked the coach. He untied the line to the trailing horse and reattached him to the reins. When the Indians did not return after half an hour, the two decided they should make a dash for Fort Belknap, still some nine miles to the west.[17] Shortly before sundown the well-lathered three-horse team labored into Fort Belknap with a coach well decorated with bullet holes and occupied by two exhausted but relieved riders. The arrival of the coach and its riders created a great deal of excitement and news of the encounter quickly spread beyond Fort Belknap.

After a night of uneasy sleep, Collins and McDonnold resumed their south-westward journey at sunrise. After a brief stop and change of teams at Franz's Station the coach finally pulled up at the Clear Fork Station shortly after 3 P.M. The sight of a bullet-marked stagecoach was not a rarity on the Texas frontier, but the ability of a driver and guard to describe the attack was. The uproar brought Col. William H. Wood, the post commander, to the way station. After listening to their account, Wood requested that both men report to his office the next morning.

On August 5 Collins and McDonnold related the details of the incident to Colonel Wood and Wood incorporated the account into a post order, which was forwarded to Department of Texas Headquarters at San Antonio.[18] Gen. C. C.

Augur was elated about Collins and McDonnold's successful defense of the coach and the mail. Mail contracts had been embroiled in Texas Reconstruction politics and Indian and bandit attacks had rendered the mail routes dangerous and inefficient. The U.S. Army, as protector of the mail routes, was under a great deal of pressure to suppress these attacks. The army's performance against the fast-striking and far-ranging Indian raiders had been much less than stellar. Collins and McDonnold's successful defense of the mail coach was one of the few positive outcomes and Augur was eager to publicize this rare success.[19]

Augur incorporated an extract of the Fort Griffin post order citing Collins and McDonnold into Department of Texas General Order no. 17 on August 20, 1872.[20] This commendatory order was forwarded to Washington for the attention of the War Department. On August 31, in a conference between the Secretary of War and Adj. Gen. E. D. Townsend, the decision was made to "give McDonnold a Medal of Honor."[21] The Medal of Honor along with an accompanying letter of transmittal was forwarded to Private McDonnold on September 8. He acknowledged receipt of the Medal of Honor from Fort Griffin in a letter to the adjutant general's office on November 7, 1872. He made no mention of a formal award ceremony.[22]

In the cold darkness of December 4, 1873, Cpl. Franklin M. McDonnold deserted from the United States Army at Fort Griffin. He was not apprehended by authorities nor did he ever apply for a pardon. He simply disappeared into obscurity. His desertion created one of the most perplexing mysteries involving a Medal of Honor recipient. The solution to this mystery may or may not absolve him of complicity in a conspiracy that may possibly have resulted in the only known fraudulent award of the Medal of Honor. We do not even know if Franklin M. McDonnold was his true name or an alias created to hide his enlistment.

Secondary sources supplement and corroborate the official primary sources on the stagecoach attack. Only two sources were found that related a story of an attack upon a stagecoach circa 1872 in the locale of Fort Griffin that resulted in the award of a medal for bravery. One of these sources by John Creaton, "An Autobiography, 1856–1932," was found in the Center for American History at the University of Texas at Austin. Creaton's account from pages eight and nine of his typescript autobiography related his version of a stagecoach attack and is as follows:

> The stage ran daily from Dallas to Fort Concho. Week days it was a two mule buckboard with room for one passenger if he wanted to go that way and Sunday was the four horse Concord stage. A military guard always went with the coach. One Sunday it left and had for a guard a bandsman whose time had expired and reenlisted and was given a furlough, as he only wanted to go to Fort Concho

they made him the escort. When they got near Fort Phantom Hill seven Indians ambushed them. They killed one of the lead horses and that caused the coach to overturn. The Bandsman had a Springfield rifle and he and the driver got behind the overturned coach and fought the Indians. There was one on a white horse which the soldiers finally killed and the rest withdrew. The soldiers were given the Congressional Medal for this fight.

Creaton's account contains a few discrepancies but it mostly corroborates the official sources. The other source located was a typescript entitled "Jim Greathouse, or Whiskey Jim," found within the Frank Collinson Collections at the Panhandle-Plains Historical Museum Archives at Canyon, Texas. It was this source that raised the aura of suspicion that there may have been a staged attack on a mail coach that resulted in a fraudulent award of a Medal of Honor. According to Collinson,

> One evening in the fall of '75 here came Collins whipping his team of three horses, which were about all played out; there should have been four. The hack was shot full of holes, but the mail all O.K. Collins' story was that after he had changed horses at King's Creek in west Young County, three stage robbers had tried to hold him up. He was well armed, and had been carrying on a running fight with them for over a mile, when one of his lead horses was shot. That stopped him. He got off the stage and gave them such an exhibition of shooting that they pulled out, but they had shot the hack all to pieces. He quickly cut the dead horse lose, hooked up the other like a spike turn and started for Griffin on a dead run. The hold-ups showed up once more, but he kept coming and made it to Fort Griffin where he was the hero. Griffin celebrated their fighting stage driver. The commander at Fort Griffin sent two guards with him the next trip or two. There was the horse lying dead to show where the fight had come off. The Griffin Commander reported this to Washington and recommended that they honor the stage driver, Collins, with a medal, which in the course of a few months they did. The commander pinned on the medal for bravery. Steve Collins was the man, but Steve also like to drink and on one trip he got an extra jag on. Some of the men had always thought the story was just a little "fishy," so they poured whiskey into Collins. Finally Collins could not hold the story any longer and told how it happened.
>
> He had shot the horse himself; shot the holes in the hack; had thrown out a few express boxes when he crossed the Clear Fork and had come in on the run. The story got to the Fort and the Post Office, and they reported to Washington. Collins sent the bravery medal to the commander and pulled out for the buffalo range. He later went to New Mexico. I never heard of him after he left Texas.

The Collinson account as told by Collins contains many discrepancies, the most glowing of which are his single-handed defense of the stagecoach and his attribution of the attack to robbers, not Indians. Each sentence in both accounts was analyzed extensively. The Collinson account, obviously because of its serious implications, underwent a more stringent examination and research. An attempt was made to either invalidate or corroborate each statement from available official sources. Of the twenty-seven statements in the Collinson account, eighteen were found to deviate from the official scenario and could not be reconciled by official records. Only four proved factually accurate, clearly corroborated by official records. Four of the statements were not relevant to the official scenario and one could not be reconciled by any available records. One statement appeared to offer a quick resolution to the controversy, Collinson's purported statement that "the story got to the Post Office and they reported to Washington and Collins sent the bravery medal to the commander and pulled out for the buffalo range." Extensive searches were conducted of indexes and registers of letters received for Fort Griffin, the Eleventh U.S. Infantry, the Department of Texas, and the Adjutant General's Office for 1873 through 1880. There was no entry from Peter (Steven) Collins, Franklin M. McDonnold, nor anyone else, even anonymously, returning a postal medal or Medal of Honor. This initial fruitless search only rendered Collins's other statements even more suspect.

Another aspect of the incident that would have established the likelihood of the official scenario was in proving that there had been an Indian presence in the area near Salt Creek. Official records indicate that in the three-month span from July to September 1872 at least nine settlers were murdered by Indians within a thirty-mile radius of the Salt Creek crossing on the Fort Richardson–Fort Griffin Road. The post returns and tabular statements of scouts and patrols for the third quarter of 1872 for Fort Richardson alone indicated two detachments operating westward during the week of August 8, both of which were dispatched in response to citizen reports of Indian attacks several days previous. The span of May through August 1872 proved to have been one of the worst periods ever for Indian raids in North Central Texas. The area, without equivocation, was saturated with depredating Indian bands. Mail coaches with military escorts from Company H, Eleventh Infantry had already repulsed attacks by Indians on July 14, 19, and 23 near the mail route crossing on the Colorado and San Saba Rivers. The most commonly used pathway from the West and Central Texas settlements to the reservations in the Indian Territory was directly north from Salt Creek. The freshwater sources of the headwaters of the West Fork of the Trinity River and thence the Little Wichita River offered consistently spaced water sources. Observation possibilities from the prominent conical peaks along the route made it ideal. The area contained the closest concentration of white settlement to the Kiowa–Comanche Reservation and was not referred to as "the blood-soaked Salt Creek Prairie" without reason. The author believes the same band that attacked the mail coach near the San Saba River on July 23 attempted to capture the stagecoach and its animal team at Salt Creek thirteen days later but were repulsed by Collins and McDonnold's actions. Depending upon terrain and conditions, the usual rate of travel per day for a horse was around fifteen miles. After thirteen days of travel at that rate these Indian raiders would have been precisely at the Salt Creek crossing of the Fort Richardson–Fort Griffin Road.

Another point of fact in placing certain Indian bands in the area came not from army sources, but from Indian Affairs peace commissioners who, as of July 28, 1872, had scheduled negotiations with the most recalcitrant bands who refused to abide by the stipulations of the Medicine Lodge Treaty. These negotiations were to be held at the old abandoned military post of Camp Radziminski in the Indian Territory, just eighty miles north of Salt Creek. Members of the Kiowa band led by Chief White Horse straggled in late over the next two weeks. Members of the Peace Commission reported that the late-arriving bands were extremely arrogant and bragged about their raids in Texas and that several of these Indians sported fresh gunshot wounds.[23]

The aforementioned facts establish to a high degree of certainty the occurrence of the recognized official scenario. The character and experiences of those involved in the official scenario and those who wrote versions of it must also be considered in the equation. The desertion of Franklin McDonnold and his possible rationale is crucial to a valid assessment. It occurred at least two years before Collins purportedly made his drunken confession to Collinson so it seems unlikely, but not improbable, that he did it out of fear of impending discovery of his part in the fraud. A close examination of the desertion problems of the Eleventh Infantry, however, makes his act seem less suspicious. This regiment incurred desertion rates almost twice that of the U.S. Army as a whole during the two decades following the Civil War. The arduous regimen and dangers of duty at Fort Griffin coupled with the lawless state of affairs outside of the post were likely the primary factors contributing to the post's high desertion rate, and of those regiments posted there.[24]

The character and experiences of those who provided the information in the two accounts purporting to relate to the Collins–McDonnold episode must also be taken into account. Peter M. Collins, the other man on the stagecoach seat on

August 3, 1872, bears his share of the examination. He was born in Westchester County, New York, in 1844. Prior to the Civil War he worked as a porter at or near Ossing, New York. On September 28, 1863, his first known enlistment was with Company H of the 158th New York Volunteer Infantry under the alias of George P. Taylor. He next enlisted in the regular army under his true name on September 26, 1866, and came to Texas with Company H of the Fourth U.S. Cavalry and spent most of his enlistment at Fort Griffin, where he was discharged as a private on September 26, 1871. He immediately obtained employment as a teamster on the Fort Smith segment of Ben Ficklin's San Antonio–El Paso Mail Company line. He left this employment circa 1876 to hunt buffalo on the High Plains. By 1890 he was residing near Fort Stanton, New Mexico.[25]

Frank Collinson, to whom Peter Collins purportedly made his drunken confession, was just sixteen years old when he first came to Texas in 1872. At the time of the Collins–McDonnold incident on Salt Creek he was employed on a ranch near San Antonio. As a newly arrived English immigrant from a moderately affluent family he was, in frontier lingo, a greenhorn—naïve and susceptible to a good old-fashioned leg-pulling. It was three years later before he met Collins in 1875. After a career of financing buffalo hunters and managing large ranches in northwest Texas he began a literary career at the age of sixty-six in 1922. His published stories based upon his frontier experiences were quite flowery and were based solely upon his remembrances.[26]

John Creaton was also sixteen years old as of August 3, 1872. He was from a local ranching family near Fort Griffin and was working as a clerk at the Fort Griffin post sutler's store on that day in August 1872. He later went on to a distinguished career as the longtime sheriff of Maverick County at Eagle Pass, Texas. His autobiography, written approximately at the same time as Collinson's literary career, was fact-filled, detail-oriented, and extremely accurate.[27]

During 1916–1917 a special Army Medal of Honor Review Board compiled and examined all documentation for Medal of Honor awards granted up to May 1916. This board, comprised entirely of Civil War- and Indian Wars-era general officers with a battery of clerks at its disposal, evaluated each award for its compliance to new award criteria. Each recipient was assigned a case number. On October 28, 1916, they examined case number 2356, the file for Pvt. Franklin M. McDonnold. After the examination he was officially certified as eligible for enrollment upon the official Army and Navy Medal of Honor Roll. The minutes of the review board do not indicate an awareness or consideration of his desertion, nor is there mention of his medal being returned. The battery of clerks available to the board could have readily accessed such information.[28]

After two decades of research, a wealth of information about the vital aspects of this episode was accumulated. This information formed patterns about aspects of the episode no singular document precisely or declaratively has addressed. The conclusions of the author based upon this compiled information follow:

1. Franklin M. McDonnold was the only soldier ever awarded a Medal of Honor for defense of a stagecoach.

2. The purported Collins confession as Collinson remembered it never mentioned or implicated Franklin M. McDonnold in the staged episode.

3. Collins's purported confession was the result of persistent behavior by his fellow hunters to elicit an obligatory confession to them, who already felt his experience to be less than truthful. He likely confessed only to satiate his tormentors and to save himself from further imbibery. The author strongly believes that Collins told his tormentors what they wanted to hear but in so doing he consciously turned the tables on them by spinning a yarn to pull their legs and inadvertently brought the August 3, 1872, incident into question. Collinson only compounded the issue by believing that a person's credibility increases with a corresponding increase in the intake of alcohol.

4. It is also quite conceivable that Collins, in the fall of 1875 and while on a solo trip, did stage an attack in order to get a post office medal. He may have done this out of envy or jealousy over McDonnold's receipt of the Medal of Honor for the August 3, 1872, incident.

5. The third party involved in the Salt Creek incident, the Indians, without doubt were in close proximity to Salt Creek on August 3, 1872. In the three weeks previous these bands had demonstrated a propensity and disposition to attack stagecoaches. The author believes that one of these bands, while moving northward to the sanctuary of the reservation, came across the stagecoach manned by Collins and McDonnold on August 3, 1872, near Salt Creek in present-day Young County, Texas. The author believes that Collins and McDonnold repulsed the Indians' attack as outlined in Department of Texas General Order no. 17, issued on August 20, 1872, by Gen. Christopher C. Augur.[29]

6. The John Creaton account unquestionably was about the Collins–McDonnold incident but it also incorporated details from several similar stagecoach attacks, both before and after 1872. Creaton and his family's close personal relationships with the officer corps at Fort Griffin would have provided him with information and extra insight into something so controversial as a staged stagecoach attack and a fraudulent medal award.

7. The author believes that Franklin M. McDonnold used only a variant of his surname upon enlistment. The author further believes that his was an underage

enlistment. After examinination of numerous documents and census records on numerous McDonnolds and their variant spellings the author believes that Franklin M. may have been a resident of Cooke County, Texas.[30]

8. The Medal of Honor Review Board of 1916–1917 with its battery of clerks and with access to the official records chose not to remove Franklin M. McDonnold from eligibility on the Army and Navy Medal of Honor Roll. After years of research the author concurs with that decision and believes it was a legitimately awarded Medal of Honor.

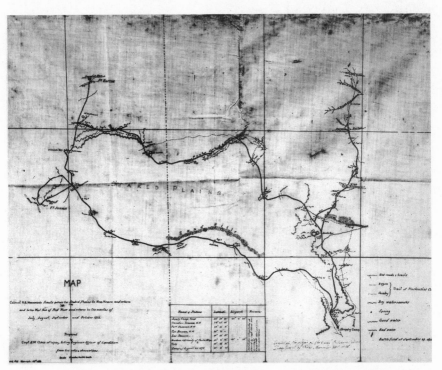

John W. Clous's map of the 1872 Ranald S. Mackenzie Staked Plains Expedition. The expedition encompassed a march of almost one thousand miles across the hostile and arid terrain of northwest Texas and eastern New Mexico for fifty-eight days. It is a testament to the stamina of the men of the Twenty-fourth U.S. Infantry and Fourth U.S. Cavalry and is a lasting credit to the grit and determination of the Indian Wars-era U.S. Army. *Courtesy the National Archives.*

CHAPTER 10

The Battle of the North Fork of the Red River

September 29, 1872

Pvt. Edward Branagan	Cpl. William O'Neill
Sgt. William Foster	Blacksmith James N. Pratt
Farrier David Larkin	Pvt. William Rankin
Cpl. Henry A. McMaster	Sgt. William Wilson
Sgt. William McNamara	

Despite relatively successful military actions against hostile Indian encampments in 1869 and 1871, the Texas frontier was no safer in early 1872 than it had been four years earlier. Col. R. S. Mackenzie, unlike many of the influential officers in the post–Civil War U.S. Army, was genuinely sensitive to the plight of frontier Texans. He had seen the mutilated and burned bodies of victims for three years and had become openly critical of federal Indian policy and northern insensitivity to the plight of frontier settlers. He expressed this in a memorandum to his superiors in 1872, stating:

> The parties committing depredations in Texas east of the Guadalupe River are, first the Kiowas and Comanches of the Fort Sill reservation as a body, together with parties from the affiliated bands and from the Cheyenne and Arapahos. Secondly, parties of Comanche (the Qua-hada and Coo-che-tek-kos bands) who live on the heads of the rivers on the eastern edge of the plains and rarely visit the agency. Thirdly, Apaches from the Guadalupe Mountains and Fort Stanton reservation who are now at peace with the Comanches and frequently live with them on the plains. Fourth, the citizens of New Mexico living

on the Pecos between Puerto un Luna and Las Vegas as a body, with of course some few exceptions and having accessions from other parts of the territory.

In order to give peace to the Texas frontier it would be necessary to take the arms and horses from the Kiowa and Comanche Indians, and the operations necessary to accomplish such result would incidentally secure the suspension and probably stop the outrages of the other parties. The Comanches and Kiowas will not give up their arms and horses without going to war to a man and they will not give up organized murders, rape and robberies so long as they keep them.

The condition of affairs on the frontier is such that no very great period of time can elapse without serious measures being taken to prevent the horrible outrages now of frequent occurrence.

There is probably no such thing as an innocent Indian among the Kiowa or Comanche tribes and there are certain classes of acts peculiarly wrong. For example those committed on certain white women captured and the burning alive of wounded men. It is my belief that the individual Indians who have committed these outrages are in many instances perfectly well known. To give a few names, "White Horse" a leading young man of the Kiowas I believe was engaged in carrying off two families and in the outrages perpetrated on the women, one case occurring in 1870 and one during the past summer. "Big Bow" a leading Kiowa Chief was engaged I believe in the murder of certain teamster's at Howard's Well last spring. Very many Kiowas and Comanches, among them "Satanta" and "Big Tree," but many others who are known and have not been punished in the murder etc. in 1871, of the teamsters of Mr. Warren, one man being burned.

Now, there is just the same wrong both legal and moral in burning a man alive in Texas, as there is in Massachusetts. The same inequity in a dozen wretches raping the wife or daughter of some unfortunate frontier Texan that there would be in a similiar outrage committed in the city of New York. The legal and moral obligation incumbent on the government is the same, yet no one supposes that such transactions could be allowed when the authors were known to go unpunished or without attempt at punishment if committed in New England or Illinois.[1]

On June 4, 1872, in a report on the recent conditions of the frontier sent to the Department of Texas commander, Gen. C. C. Augur, Mackenzie had stated that, "the outrages committed by Indians have been more frequent than I have ever known them."[2] He was without doubt alluding to, among others, the massacre of the Anastacio Gonzales wagon train at Howard's Well in Crockett County on April 20. During this surprise attack fifty Kiowa, Mexican bandits, and New Mexican Comancheros seized a shipment of the latest model U.S. Army small arms and thousands of rounds of ammunition.[3] The Department of Texas command staff,

David Larkin, circa 1897. This photo from Beyer and Keydel, *Deeds of Valor*, II, 167, portrays the brave young Irish American trooper whose valor despite heavy fire from concealed warriors prevented the breach of the perimeter and greatly contributed to the outcome of the engagement on the North Fork of the Red River. *Courtesy the Burton Collections, Detroit Public Library.*

chafing over the negligence of not providing an escort for the arms shipment, quickly came up with the necessary logistics and manpower Mackenzie requested. On May 31 Augur sent out Special Order no. 102, which formally granted Mackenzie everything he had requested for his Staked Plains expedition.

By the early part of July Mackenzie had assembled his force of more than four hundred cavalry and infantry at the main supply base at Blanco Canyon on the White River. Once the logistics and reconnaissance functions had been completed, Mackenzie decided to move first against the Comancheros of eastern New Mexico. On the morning of July 28 the command, consisting of five companies of the Fourth Cavalry and one company of the Twenty-fourth Infantry, moved westward out of Blanco Canyon. Beside Mackenzie was the captured Comanchero agent, Apalonio Ortiz, who assured Mackenzie that his information was indeed "la verdad." Col. John W. Clous and his infantry detachment were to carefully measure the distances and map the terrain along the command's path.[4] They were, after all, marching into a portion of the North American continent where the U.S. Army had never before conducted tactical operations. Over the next thirty-six days, amid dust and torrential rains, the command traversed the desolate plains of northwest Texas and eastern New Mexico. They sent the Comancheros of eastern New Mexico fleeing and proved to them that they no longer had a sanctuary to which they could flee after committing crimes upon the Texas frontier. The mapping Clous and his men performed made certain that the U.S. Army would never wander blindly across the plains and canyonlands of northwest Texas.

The entire command, tired and haggard, was back at the Blanco Canyon supply base by September 3. During the entire 640-mile trek the command had not encountered one single Kiowa, Comanche, Cheyenne, or Apache. The only significant trails discovered had been obliterated by the late August rains, and disappointment and despair permeated the command. Mackenzie knew that somewhere in the vast expanse of the High Plains were the well-armed hostile bands of White Horse, Beaver, Black Duck, Horseback, Black Beard, Bull Bear, Big Bow, and Mow-wi. He was determined to make one more sweep of the plains.

After the command's return to the supply base, much time was spent resting and recuperating the troops and their mounts. Assistant Army Surgeons Rufus Choate, Ira J. Culver, and Thomas B. Davis tended to the troops' daily medical needs. Teams of farriers led by Maj. Alfred E. Latimer and Lt. John A. McKinney reconditioned the command's horses and mules. All the horses were exercised daily, reshod, and fed with extra grain and hay forage. The field kitchen produced fresh bread daily and with fresh beef daily as well the spirits of the men began to improve. Mackenzie instituted target practice, both mounted and dismounted, in the mornings after water call. Private shooting matches, horse races, foot races, card games, and buffalo hunts were the order of the day later in the afternoon.[5]

While the troops relaxed, the kerosene lamps in Mackenzie's tent burned late into the night. Along with Colonels Shafter and Clous and Captains Davis and Mauck the group pored over all the data on the various trails found during the reconnaissance forays. If Col. J. J. Gregg's command, operating out of Fort Bascom, New Mexico, had effectively scouted the Canadian River Valley as promised, then the Indians likely would be forced southward. Since incoming supply trains from Forts Griffin and Concho had reported no large Indian movements across their trails, the Indians had to be to the north. The new guide, Canueto Garcia, who had been hired during the command's trek through New Mexico, felt the best chance of finding the Indians lay in scouting the headwaters of the North Fork of the Red River. These factors cemented the decision to move to the north.[6]

On Saturday morning, September 21, with Companies A, D, F, I, and L, Fourth U.S. Cavalry, nine Tonkawa scouts and a sixteen-wagon train, escorted by Company E, Twenty-fourth U.S. Infantry, Mackenzie again took to the plains. By September 28, after seven days of fruitless searching, the entire command camped on the Salt Fork of the Red River near present-day Clarendon.

In the predawn hours of September 29, Capt. Wirt Davis, Lt. Peter M. Boehm, and nine of the Tonkawa scouts left the camp heading northeast. Mackenzie was adamant that all scouting and spy contingents leave camp in the dark so Indian spies did not observe their movements. Mackenzie and the remainder of the command departed the campsite several hours later, following the trail the scout detachment left. The scouting detachment under Captain Davis and Lieutenant Boehm, guided by Tonkawa scout McCord, had taken up a line of march toward the upper part of the South Branch of McClellan Creek. Just before noon the scouting detachment arrived at a small lake in a grove of cotton-wood trees on the South Branch of McClellan Creek.[7]

Earlier that morning, Kai-wotche, a lesser chief of the Cooch-cho-teth-ka band of Comanches, and two young Indians had collected wild grapes from the many vines along the banks of the creek.[8] The scouting detachment had come within half a mile before the three Comanches saw them. Mounting up quickly, the Indians rode rapidly downstream along the north bank behind trees and tall grass to avoid detection. When Captain Davis and his scouting detachment arrived at the creek, the Comanches were hastily spurring their mounts downstream and then northward. The scouting detachment halted to rest and water their horses and to allow the main command to catch up. As Davis and McCord wandered along the bank of the creek, they noticed the fresh trail of two horses and one mule as well as recently disturbed grapevines and fresh scattered grapes on the ground.[9]

Mackenzie and the remainder of the command arrived less than an hour later. After a brief discussion between Mackenzie and Davis, they decided to have the Tonkawas lead out and follow the discovered trail with the main command following at a short distance. The Tonkawas rode briskly for almost three hours, at first to the east and then in almost a straight northerly direction. At 3 P.M. the main command was within a mile and a half of the North Fork of the Red River when they met Sergeant McCord and his scouts. McCord excitedly reported that the Indians for whom they had been searching for so long had been discovered in a pleasant valley about three miles to the north.

After a thirty-minute ride, the entire command was halted behind a rise over-looking the river valley. Mackenzie reconnoitered the distant village with his tele-scope and quickly assigned each of the company commanders their tactical objec-tives. Junior officers circulated among their companies making sure that extra ammunition was placed in blouse pockets.[10] Bridles, halters, and saddles were tightened and secured and the troops formed a single column. Mackenzie led the still-dismounted command across the river and halted on the north bank. Mackenzie mounted the command and the troops advanced toward the seemingly still village. In the beginning the advance was over an undulating prairie that sloped gently toward the village. The village, four miles long, extended northward from the north bank of the river. The approach was made at a moderate gait until the command cleared the last rise overlooking the village, about a thousand yards from the nearest portion of the village. Indian herders on the south bank could be seen herding a large group of horses toward the riverbed. Now aware that the village was aroused, Mackenzie gave the order to form into an echelon, or staggered-V formation.[11] Mackenzie, along with Captain Clous and Surgeon Rufus Choate, rode to the left of Company A, which was the lead company at the head of the formation. Captain Davis and Company F were to the left and just behind the lead company. Immediately to their left on the outside was Capt. John Lee's Company D. On the right wing and just beside the lead company was Lt. Charles L. Hudson's Company I followed on the far right by Lt. Lewis Warrington's Company L.[12]

When within about a quarter of a mile of the nearest portion of the village, Mackenzie ordered the bugler to sound the charge, the prearranged signal for each commander to lead his company toward its assigned tactical objective. Capt. John Lee's company quickly veered to the left toward the herd of horses being driven toward the main body of the village. Their tactical objective was to prevent the herd on the south side of the river from being driven into the main village. Lee's company splashed across the shallow rivulet near the north bank and met the Indian herd and herders in mid-riverbed. Seconds after opening fire, the herders abandoned the horses and the troopers turned the animals back toward the south bank. Within minutes, Lee's company had secured the Indian herd and attained the first tactical objective of the engagement.[13]

Company D's turn to the left made Capt. Wirt Davis's Company F the lead company on the left wing. When the Indians at the lower end of the village found themselves cut off from their mounts by Company D's actions, they took up positions in considerable numbers along and under the banks of Cabin Creek, which flowed through the main body of the village. Davis, Lieutenant Boehm, and the forty-two troopers of Company F had been assigned the task of securing the lower quadrant of the village. An instant after the bugler began to sound the "charge," Davis yelled out, "Right front into line," an order that changed the company into a formation of five ranks of eight troopers abreast.[14] Each of the non-commissioned officers found themselves at the end of each rank. Sgt. John B. Charleton was in charge of the first rank and was positioned on the extreme right. Sgt. John Kelly was in charge of the second rank and was positioned on the extreme left. The other ranks, led by Sgts. William McNamara, William Foster, and James Lane, along with the following ranks led by Cpls. Joseph Erwing, Hugh A. Moore, William Miller, and John A. Brooks, eventually merged into a single charging line that extended about a quarter of a mile. When this charging line closed into the lower part of the village strung out for a quarter of a mile above Cabin Creek's mouth, they ran directly into the Indians' fire.[15]

Pvt. William Rankin, a daring veteran trooper and perhaps the finest horseman in the command, was on the extreme right and a short distance in advance of the charging line. Having noted a small band of Comanches attempting to control and mount a small number of horses, he charged into their midst with his Smith & Wesson .44 blazing.[16] Just as Rankin neared a small ridge thickly covered with high grass, a large number of Indians raised in line and gave the troops a volley.[17] Rankin fell from his horse with a severe stomach wound, the first casualty of the engagement. Just seconds behind Rankin, Pvt. John Dorcas fell dead with a gunshot wound to the throat. Pvt. John Kelly was the next to fall, also with a gunshot wound to the throat. Private Beals reeled about with an arrow wound in the thigh. Charleton immediately abandoned his mount, and with carbine and canteen in hand, ran to Rankin's side. After examining Rankin's wound, he removed his own blouse and placed it under Rankin's head. Charleton then rolled over and opened fire on the nearby Indians and later claimed to be certain that he had killed the Indian who shot Kelly and Dorcas. At this point, the rank of troopers just behind Charleton's, having dismounted, entered the fray and rendered valuable service. Most conspicuous among them was Pvt. Edward Branagan, whose dauntless conduct in driving the Indians from the grassy rise and in helping remove the wounded proved invaluable. Along with his fellow squad members, Branagan stabilized that portion of the village and enabled the other squads to seal off the right flank.[18]

When the right wing of Company F's charging line had veered to the right, the other half of the company under Lieutenant Boehm had veered to the left toward the mouth of the creek to outflank the Comanches and prevent their escape. The first four troopers to reach the mouth of the creek were led by Sgt. James Lane. Farrier David Larkin was in the advance, followed closely by Pvts. Henry Hennier and Thomas C. Poland. One Comanche suddenly rose from some nearby bushes and began unleashing a hail of arrows. Larkin charged toward him and used his pistol to kill the Comanche, after which the other Indians stampeded upstream. Luckily Larkin had escaped injury but his horse was disabled with an arrow wound in the right foreleg. At this point Davis issued the order to "Prepare to fight on foot," which was relayed along the line. Within seconds the entire company had dismounted and every fourth trooper took control of four horses and removed them to the rear. Skirmish lines were quickly formed and soon thirty-two Sharps carbines raked the tree line along the lower part of Cabin Creek. The Indians fled over the bank and up the creek and entrenched themselves along a crescent-shaped pool of the creek several yards upstream. Sgts. William McNamara and William Foster, both battle-hardened veterans of the Civil War, rendered excellent service during this phase of the battle. They quickly dispersed the men into squads and led them into the most intense action of the battle. A severe fifteen-minute firefight ensued in which nineteen Indians were killed, at least one of whom drowned when he jumped into the pool in an effort to escape the raking volleys.[19]

After Captains Lee and Davis led their companies to the left and lower portions of the village, Lewis Warrington guided his Company L to the right toward the upper portion of the village at the head of Cabin Creek. Warrington dispatched one squad to cross the creek bed and intercept a band of Indians seen driving a herd of horses northward. The creek bed proved to be extremely damp and muddy and several troopers had difficulty controlling their mounts in the wet sand and mud. Once the squad crossed, Corporal Wilson regrouped them and they sped after the Indian herd. The remainder of the company dismounted and took positions along the east side of a ravine into which many Indians had fled. Shortly after commencing his movement up the ravine, Warrington noticed that sizable numbers of Indians were already escaping at the ravine's head. Once the company reached the head of the ravine, Warrington noticed that firing toward a branch ravine would endanger the members of Company A, who were pushing through the middle portion of the village some five hundred yards below them. Warrington then noticed a sizable number of Indians taking cover in small sand hills about eight hundred yards west of his position. Since they would be in an excellent position to fire both on his company and that of Company A, he decided to move his company across the ravine, remount, and attack the sand hills. Warrington led the attack on the snipers in the sand hills and drove them from their positions. These Comanches fled with Warrington and his company in hot pursuit. A running fight ensued for two miles before the troops could close within rifle range. Warrington quickly ordered a halt and the troops formed a compact skirmish arrangement. The quickly formed line unleashed rapid volley firing, sending a number of Indian ponies down in a hail of lead. One Comanche was seen to fall from his horse after riding a short distance. The company remounted and headed back toward the main camp at a gallop. As the troopers came over a rise, they ran headlong into a mounted warrior fleeing the main village. He attempted to halt and wheel about but scattered pistol firing killed both him and his horse. Upon arriving back at the village, Warrington again dispersed his troops along the western side of the previously secured ravine. Before this was completed, a runner from Colonel Mackenzie arrived with verbal orders to remount the company and pursue a body of Indians who were fleeing to the west. Warrington remounted the company and led them westward once again. Within minutes they overtook a band of warriors and their families. Upon the company's approach, the entire band scattered into the woods. The company dismounted and moved through the woods in skirmish formation. Three women were ferreted out of the brush and taken prisoner. Several squads were mounted and sent to skirt the woods. They returned after less than fifteen minutes with a sizable herd recovered from the fleeing warriors. Upon returning to where the guard detachment had been left, the entire company dismounted and formed a square inside of which the prisoners and captured stock were placed. Just as this square began its movement, a runner arrived with the order to return to the main village area. Just as Warrington acknowledged the order, an Indian sprang out of some nearby bushes. Privates Horst and Hyland fired their pistols and the Comanche fell dead. The company, in the moving square formation, returned to the lower end of the village as instructed.[20]

Lt. William A. Thompson and the thirty-eight troopers of Company A had been assigned the tactical objective of securing the middle portion of the village. While the other companies had veered off to the right and left, Thompson had led his company straight into the middle of the village. Intense firing from a grassy alluvial terrace on the left immediately wounded three horses and forced Thompson to issue orders to dismount and fight on foot. Once the horses were removed to the rear, the troopers quickly formed skirmish lines. Before the assault could commence, Capt. A. E. Latimer notified Thompson to remount the company and move them to a point two hundred yards further up the village. The order was executed in less than five minutes despite continuous sniping fire from the Indian positions, in great part due to the forceful and energetic efforts of Cpl. Henry A. McMaster. Once at the newly designated assault point, the various squads were dispersed throughout the village. Corporal McMaster's squad drew the unenviable task of moving down along the creek to block the Indians fleeing upstream from Company F's movements. Downstream, frantic cries of "casualties!" could clearly be heard over the din of gunfire, war whoops, and the screams of fleeing Indian women and children. The repeated volleys of Company F, coupled with those of Company L on the extreme right and Indian snipers in sand hills to the right front, seemed to all be directed toward McMaster's squad. Bark torn away by errant bullets flew through the air while limbs and leaves fell like rain. McMaster had been in a similar situation in the peach orchard at the battle of Cedar Creek, Virginia, in 1864. He had carried out his orders then and today was no different. Far in advance of his other squad members, he moved down the east bank of the creek. Just as he reached a bend in the creek, several Comanches appeared. McMaster rushed toward the Indians with his carbine blazing; his firing caused the Comanches to flee, panic-stricken, back around the creek bend where, in desperation, they flung themselves into one of the creek's pools, which was about thirty feet long. Within several minutes the Indian firing was almost completely suppressed and Company A was ordered to remount and round up the loose horses, which were running wildly among the Indian lodges and cavalry mounts.[21]

The last company in the echelon formation to veer toward its tactical objective was Company I under the temporary command of Lt. Charles L. Hudson.[22] His company's objective was to secure the northernmost part of the village at the head of Cabin Creek. Second, the troopers were to rapidly move in an arch from the northeast to the southwest, enveloping and closing off the Indian's avenue of escape to the west. The company quickly attained its first objective as it charged into the northernmost lodges and found them abandoned. After a quick search to ascertain that all of the inhabitants had indeed fled, Hudson reformed the company into a compact column of fours. Small bands of Indians and a number of single fleeing Indians could be seen running to the west. Most were leading or herding a sizable number of horses. Hudson led the column across the creek bank, intending to complete the enveloping maneuver and capture the fleeing Indians and their herds. The upper part of Cabin Creek at this point near the valley rim was fed by water seeps underlying the deep sedimentary alluvium and was extremely boggy, but did not appear so on the surface. Halfway across the bed, which was perhaps fifty yards wide, the horses began to sink deep into the muck and movement became extremely difficult. The energetic Hudson, so intent upon executing the important phase of envelopment, struggled with his mount to within ten yards of the west bank, about twenty yards ahead of the nearest trailing trooper. His last desperate urgings to his mount only resulted in its miring itself permanently, and the horse's desperate struggle ejected Hudson into the muck. Several Comanches then emerged from a nearby clump of cane and willow trees and ran toward the exposed and virtually helpless young officer. Blacksmith James Pratt, one of the nearest trailing troopers, handled his mount superbly while firing at the advancing Comanches and managed to get to Hudson's side to hoist him out of the muck and behind him on his mount. Pratt dismounted and led his mount and the somewhat dazed officer to the safety of the east bank. Colonel Mackenzie personally observed the incident and realized that the enveloping movement would not be executed quickly enough to prevent a breakout of the Comanches along that line.[23]

Sgt. William Wilson, detailed as an aide to Mackenzie's staff, was ordered to take command of the company and seal off the avenue of escape.[24] Wilson was not just a forceful and respected non-commissioned officer but was also a highly skilled equestrian. He quickly regrouped the company on the east bank and led the men a short distance downstream to an easier crossing point. Once onto the west bank, Indian snipers among a stand of cane and willow trees became the first obstacle to overcome. The snipers, having seen the troopers rapidly approaching, had already commenced their retreat and could be seen running toward a tree line to the west. The big prize was a sizable herd of ponies being driven westward and Sergeant Wilson turned the company toward the herd. Wilson and Cpl. William O'Neill and their squads were far in advance of the rest of the company. Their opportune position on the extreme left of the line narrowed the distance to just yards when the Comanches turned to the southwest. Wielding their pistols with expert efficiency, the soldiers engaged the herders in hand-to-hand combat. The Indian herders were soon fleeing and the herd belonged to Company I. Once the herd was turned, the company formed a moving corral and began moving back toward the main village. At this point Lieutenant Hudson rejoined the company. One of the troopers, dispatched to round up loose stock nearby, informed Hudson of the presence of a body of Indians in the dense woods off to their right. Leaving a guard over the captured herd, Hudson dismounted the remainder of the company and moved the troopers through the woods in a skirmish line. The troops' first volley sent the Comanches fleeing into the hills beyond. The troops then remounted and sped southwest after the Indians. The chase continued for several miles before Hudson halted the pursuit. During the pursuit Hudson had noticed a small, detached village on the south side of the Red River. Observing a sizable herd still grazing around it, he decided it was imperative that at least the herd be captured. The approach into the village was made in a mounted single rank and, except for a few parting shots from pistols, rifles, and arrows by the fleeing Indians, there was no serious resistance. Squads were dispatched to round up the horses, several hundred in number. Continuing south and eastward, the company completed its enveloping arch as instructed. By the time Hudson and his troopers reached Captain Lee's staging area for the livestock, the fighting had ended.[25]

Colonel Clous and his infantry troopers had thoroughly cleared out the village and collected documents and artifacts from the lodges. Once their search was completed, kerosene was splashed over each of the 262 lodges that comprised the village and ignited. Burial details had already started collecting the bodies of the twenty-three Comanches killed in the engagement for mass burial.[26] Among the nineteen killed around the crescent-shaped pool was found the severely wounded body of Corporal McMaster. The ambulance, now in a slow measured gait, carried McMaster toward the field hospital set up by Surgeon Rufus Choate near the crossing point of the Red River. Choate, his skills honed in some of the finest medical institutions of the East, labored under canvas and kerosene lanterns to help his patients. The Tonkawa scouts, long embittered enemies of the Comanches and Kiowas, began to savagely stab and scalp the Indian corpses. Colonel Mackenzie intervened to stop them and became involved in a brief scuffle with the Tonkawa scout Henry. After a few tense moments, the Tonkawas were restrained and the Indians' bodies were placed in the common grave and covered.[27]

Clous's company had already established a campsite about two miles east of the Indian village. Squads of cavalry troopers secured the captured herd of more than a thousand head of livestock. Boehm and the Tonkawas were detailed to move and secure the herd in a depression about a mile east of Clous's camp. Lts. Henry W. Lawton and Mathew Leiper along with Sgt. William Foster, Pvt. Nathan Osmer, and two squads from Company F began to count, interrogate and assemble the 124 captured women, children, and elders into groups.[28] Apalonio Ortiz recognized the majority of the prisoners as Comanches who had been present at the Comanchero rendezvous at Muchaque the previous winter. Among the prisoners were seven Mexican women and one teenage boy. The boy, Francisco Nieto, had been captured in November 1870 during an attack on a Mexican cart train between Fort Duncan and old Fort Inge.[29]

Before the troops had set the village on fire, both Mackenzie and Clous had insisted on a thorough search of all lodge contents. In several of the prominent lodges the troops found bags and articles belonging to the U.S. Mail.[30] José Carrion, one of the civilian teamsters in Clous's command, identified one saddled mule and forty-two other mules as those belonging to his former wagon master, Anastacio Gonzales.[31] The Comanches and Kiowas of this village were thus implicated in the Comanchero trade and in several recent depredations committed in Texas.

Shortly after 10:30 P.M. gunfire from the direction of the Tonkawa camp awoke the main command. The firing continued on and off for thirty minutes before order was restored. The next morning Mackenzie learned that one of his greatest fears had materialized. The Indians had succeeded in stampeding and recapturing almost their entire herd and most of the animals belonging to the Tonkawa scouts. Much to Mackenzie's chagrin, the troops treated the recapture somewhat lightheartedly. The Tonkawas, guide Henry Strong, and Lieutenant Boehm all appeared at the main temporary camp on foot the next morning with their saddles piled high on mules. Sgt. John B. Charleton later recalled that when they came in, "we gave them the grand laugh."[32]

During the day of September 30 the command moved southward eighteen miles and camped on the South Branch of McClellan Creek. During the early morning hours of October 1 the Indians again attempted to stampede the command's herd. Though not as successful as before, they did manage to seize a few more horses and mules. Though harried several times by waning numbers of Indians, the command arrived back at the main supply camp on October 8. The troops were tired and haggard, but at the same time they were proud of their accomplishments. They had marched for more than fifty days across almost one thousand miles of terrain, most of which the U.S. Army had never traversed before. The mapping Clous and Hoffman accomplished would make certain that the army never ventured blindly onto the Staked Plains. Their mere presence in eastern New Mexico prompted civil and military officials to take steps to suppress the illicit Comanchero cattle trade. They had severely chastised one of the worst bands of hostile Indians in the southwest and had been able to implicate them as participants in the Comanchero trade and in a variety of crimes committed on the Texas frontier. Their single most important accomplishment was the restoration of Texan faith and confidence in the federal military presence on the West Texas frontier.

At mid-morning on October 9 Lt. John A. McKinney, the expedition adjutant, distributed to each company commander a copy of a circular Colonel Mackenzie had issued earlier that morning. The third paragraph of this circular was a request:

> They will also hand in a report of the part taken in the engagement of the 29th ultimo by their companies by 10 o'clock A.M. tomorrow, giving details of men and horses killed or lost or wounded in the engagement and during the entire scout. They will include in their report the names of any men who by their actions they consider worthy of special mention.[33]

By October 11 all of the company commander's reports, including that of Captain Clous, had been turned in to Lieutenant McKinney. Mackenzie penned his report on the engagement the next day. In his report to Gen. C. C. Augur, Department of Texas commander, he wrote:

> I wish to bring the names of the following enlisted men to the favorable consideration of the Department Commander, of A Company, Corporal Henry A. McMaster, of F Company, 1st Sergeant McNamara, Sergeant William Foster, Farrier David Larkin and Privates William Rankin and Edward Branagan, of I Company, Sergeant William Wilson, Corporal William O'Neil, and Blacksmith James Pratt.[34]

General Augur heartily endorsed Mackenzie's recommendations and forwarded the list to Lt. Gen. Philip Sheridan, commander of the Division of the Missouri. On November 4, Sheridan, in a letter to General of the Army W. T. Sherman, recommended "the named soldiers be rewarded for their good conduct by medals such as are now in the hands of the War Department for distribution for gallant conduct." Sherman concurred with Sheridan's recommendation and submitted the list to the Secretary of War on November 15, recommending that Medals of Honor be conferred by general order on the men specially named. General Order no. 99 of November 19, 1872, officially conferred the Army Medal of Honor upon the nine soldiers. The medals were engraved and sent from the adjutant general's office in Washington, D.C., on November 21 to Department of Texas Headquarters at San Antonio, where they were forwarded to the proper military posts.[35]

Lt. Col. G. P. Buell, post commander at Fort Griffin, Texas, received a small package containing five of the medals on Christmas Day. Two days later, Buell personally presented the Medal of Honor during the evening dress parade to Sgt. William McNamara, Sgt. William Foster, Farrier David Larkin, Pvt. Edward Branagan, and Pvt. William Rankin.[36] A motley assemblage of Tonkawa Indians, white buffalo hunters, and local citizens gazed curiously at the ceremony while herds of shaggy-haired buffalo grazed nearby. Cpl. Henry A. McMaster, who had died from his wounds on the morning of November 11, lay in the nearby post cemetery. As was the practice, his medal had been sent to the second auditor's office of the Treasury Department for forwarding to his family in Maine.[37] The three remaining medals arrived at Fort Concho, Texas, on December 26, 1872, where 1st Lt. George G. Lott of the Eleventh U.S. Infantry, post adjutant, carried out the presentation on December 29 in a ceremony described by a correspondent for the *Army and Navy Journal*. The account is unique and quite rare:

> Quite an interesting occurrence took place at this post yesterday evening, when in the presence of the whole command on dress parade, medals of honor were presented to First Sergeant Wilson, Corporal Pratt, and Blacksmith Brannigan, all of Company I, Fourth Cavalry, for bravery displayed in the fight with Comanche Indians last September, on the North Fork of Red River, under General Mackenzie's command. The men having been ordered to the front by the post adjutant, the three men advanced to within a few paces of him, when each in his turn was handed a medal, and from their appearance as they faced about to return to the ranks, it was evident they felt proud of the mark of distinction conferred upon them. Fame is as dear to the soldier of a republic as of an empire, even to a

soldier of the most ordinary intelligence in the ranks, and the awarding of these medals to men who have proved their courage above their fellows is but right and proper, and must without doubt, be an incentive to good conduct, and a most powerful adjunct in elevating the tone of the enlisted men in the Army.[38]

The difficult sacrifices that each man made in earning the Medal of Honor would yield much good, long after their passage from the Texas frontier. Because of the army's severe chastisement of the warring off-reservation bands of Kai-watche, Patch-o-ko-naily (Beaver) and Parra-o-coom (Bull Bear), other bands became inclined to pursue the road to peace. The cost in lives among both settler and Indian was immeasurable. The captured Indian women and children were eventually exchanged for captives the Indians held. This policy, conceived jointly by General Augur and Lawrie Tatum, practically eliminated the Comanche and Kiowa practice of taking captives and exchanging them only upon the payment of a ransom. As a result, many Texan and Mexican families were reunited with lost loved ones.[39]

The state of Texas was also quick to demonstrate its appreciation to the troops. On January 16, 1873, Sen. A. J. Fountain of El Paso and Rep. J. H. Brown of Dallas introduced a "Joint Resolution of thanks to General Mackenzie and Command for their heroic conduct in their brilliant victory over the hostile Indians on our northwestern frontier." The greatest tribute to the warriors in blue came, however, from their former adversaries, the captured Kiowa and Comanche women and children. The soldiers' treatment of them was so kind that elderly Kiowas still spoke glowingly of their treatment more than fifty years later when Col. W. S. Nye interviewed them in the 1930s, a monument to the often-maligned character of the Indian-fighting U.S. Army.[40]

Sgt. George Kitchen, 1910. When the horse of a fellow trooper was killed under him, Kitchen turned about and rode into a charging mass of Indians to rescue the fallen trooper. *Photograph courtesy Joseph J. Cody, San Antonio, Texas.*

CHAPTER 11

Besieged on the Upper Washita

September 9–12, 1874

Sgt. Frederick S. Schwabe (Hay)	Sgt. William Koelpin
Cpl. John James	Sgt. John Mitchell
Cpl. John J. H. Kelly	Cpl. William W. Morris
Cpl. Thomas Kelly	Sgt. Frederick S. Neilon (Singleton)
Sgt. George K. Kitchen	Sgt. Joseph J. Pennsyl
Cpl. John W. Knox	Cpl. Edward C. Sharpless

On August 31, 1874, Gen. Nelson A. Miles and his Indian Territory expedition force of 625 men were camped on Battle Creek, about twenty miles southwest of present-day Clarendon.[1] Just one day earlier, they had made the first serious contact with the off-reservation hostile Plains Indian tribes. Despite only suffering two wounded, the Miles column had inflicted at least eleven casualties on the various hostile bands of Arapaho and Southern Cheyenne. The troops and scouts had pursued the Indians for five days and in the process had exhausted their food and water. Furious that his supplies had not been promptly forwarded, Miles decided on September 1 to dispatch Capt. Wyllys Lyman with a train of empty wagons and an escort detachment back along the trail.[2]

Lyman took thirty-six empty wagons and thirty-eight men from Company I, Fifth Infantry, and left the base camp at 2 P.M. on September 1. Heading almost due north, the train arrived at the Second Battalion cavalry encampment on McClellan Creek at about 10 P.M. The next morning at 5:30 the Lyman train was once again on the wagon trail, now moving in a northeasterly direction. Lt. Frank West, Sixth Cavalry, and twenty troopers had joined the train as a mounted escort. All day on September 3 and 4 the train maintained a rapid pace and by 9 A.M. on September 5 they were just south of the Canadian River near its juncture with Oasis Creek. They had expected to meet the supply train from Camp Supply here, but it was not there. West and five men rode ahead to check on the train.[3]

Some forty-three miles northeast, Capt. C. W. Hotsenpiller and twenty-nine men of Company E, Nineteenth Infantry, and a mounted detachment of ten troopers of Company K, Sixth Cavalry, were camped with the Camp Supply train near Wolf Creek. Among the contingent were six cavalry troopers and one infantryman, all traveling to rejoin their companies with the Miles column. Three of them were returning from furloughs, but not so for Sgts. George K. Kitchen and Josiah Pennsyl or Cpls. William W. Morris and Edward C. Sharpless, who had been busy over the past few weeks making last-minute adjustments to Sixth Cavalry logistics and were enjoying a brief respite of inactivity.

By early morning on September 6, Lyman's train was camped on Commission Creek. Though the members of the Lyman train had seen several small Indian trails traversing the wagon road, there was no general alarm about the Indians. When a courier from Lieutenant West arrived at noon announcing the arrival of the Camp Supply train at about noon the next day, there was a great sense of relief. The courier brought no word of significant sightings or signs of a large Indian presence. Thinking it was safe, a party of three of the teamsters from Lyman's train decided to do some buffalo hunting. Despite the troops' presence, a band of Indians attacked the three teamsters, who were only a few hundred yards from camp. One young teamster, twenty-four-year-old Arthur W. Moore, was killed. By the time the troopers could reach him, the Indians had already scalped Moore and shot him sixteen times.[4]

Shortly before noon on September 7, Lieutenant West arrived with the Camp Supply train. The teamsters and soldiers immediately began transferring the stores into Lyman's wagons. Before they finished, a brief thunderstorm erupted into sheets of rain. Despite the rain, the transfer was completed and by 3 P.M. the Lyman train was headed out to the southwest in a slow drizzling rain. Lyman halted the march after seventeen miles and made camp on Oasis Creek just above its juncture with the Canadian River. At first light on September 8, Lyman and wagonmaster Jack Callahan found the Canadian River had risen slightly and deemed it too dangerous to try to traverse down the muddy embankment. While still camped there that night, Lt. Frank D. Baldwin and three civilian scouts came into the camp, bringing with them a captured white boy who had lived among the Indians for fifteen years. Baldwin also brought the disturbing news of a large Indian presence to the west along the wagon trail.[5]

The Lyman train members awoke at 6 A.M. on September 9. After a light breakfast, the train forded the Canadian River with some difficulty. An hour later, just as the train neared the head of Grape Creek, they discovered the first sign of a large Indian presence. A large trail of unshod ponies and travois poles was found traversing the trail from the east and trailing off to the west. By 8 A.M. the train was within eight hundred yards of traversing the divide between the Canadian and Washita Rivers when several mounted Indians were observed on the surrounding ridgelines. In response, Lyman formed the train into two parallel lines about twenty yards apart. In this configuration, the first and last wagon of each line could be moved in between the lines to form an egg-shaped defensive corral. Large bodies of Indians appeared atop sand hills off to the right. Lyman halted the train and Callahan gave strict orders for his teamsters to keep the wagon intervals as close as possible. The teamsters themselves would have to cut loose any disabled mules as no soldiers could be spared. Lyman deployed the infantry troops into their defensive configuration. Fifteen infantrymen were dispersed on each side in skirmish lines some twenty-five yards from the wagons. The Indians began firing from long range at both sides of the train. The seven dismounted cavalry troopers and the remaining eight infantrymen took positions at the front and rear of the train. The troops deployed at the front formed two diagonal lines resembling the barb of an arrow. West took his thirteen mounted men and deployed in advance of the forward skirmishers.[6]

It was essential to maintain the high ground and the train veered off the trail to the left in order to do so. West and his troopers found it necessary to charge and drive away concentrations of Indians from nearby elevations. With the bugler sounding the notes of "charge," one detachment set off toward the Indians on a nearby elevation. As they made their way over the crest of a hill, Corporal Sharpless and a fellow trooper found themselves confronting a large body of concealed Indians. They also discovered that they were alone. They had heard the bugler sound the "charge" but they had failed to hear the bugle command for "recall" shortly afterward. The two hurried back down the hill to the train, where one of their fellow troopers, anxious to know how the Indians were armed, asked if they had heard any bullets. Sharpless quickly replied, "I only heard one, but I passed two on the way down."[7] This would be the last lighthearted moment for the members of the train as the numbers of Indians on the surrounding ridgelines increased until there were around four hundred of them.[8]

The largest concentrations of Indians appeared to be in front of the train's path. Lyman felt that these Indians could not be allowed to impede the train's movement and again ordered West to charge and drive these Indians from their positions. West and his troopers mounted up and charged toward the Indians in the front of the train's path. They had advanced about a thousand yards before coming into pistol range of their adversaries. Sgt. John Mitchell, in charge of the right front infantry skirmishers, rendered gallant and outstanding service at this point. Seeing a number of mounted Indians attempting to outflank West's detachment along a lower ridge and from the right rear, Mitchell sprinted forward to a dangerously exposed position, where he delivered a deadly rapid fire with his Springfield .45-caliber rifle, which dropped two Indian ponies and sent the other Indians fleeing for safety. West's detachment continued its movement and drove the Indians from the southern ridgeline. West now found his tiny command in a virtual hornet's nest as he spotted an extremely large body of mounted Indians approaching from the west. He realized that there would be too many Indians for the train's small command to handle. The exact circumstances of what occurred next are left to speculation, but West apparently requested two volunteers to make a dash for the Miles command on Sweetwater Creek. Cpls. Edward Sharpless and William Morris assumed the hazardous task. After quickly collecting extra ammunition from the other troopers, West gave them brief directions to the cavalry encampment on Sweetwater Creek. The large body of Indians seen earlier was only a quarter of a mile away. Morris and Sharpless bolted down the incline toward the Washita River about a quarter of a mile to the south. A band of around twenty Indians broke off from the large mass of Indians approaching from the west and began chasing the two troopers. West ordered a parting volley fired at this pursuing band and then ordered a retreat to the train.[9]

Around noon the train was halted at some water holes on the prairie, where at Callahan's suggestion the mules were watered while the kegs and canteens were partially filled. By 2 P.M. the train was within about a mile and a half of the Washita River. The Indians had taken up positions behind some prominent sand hills and West and his troopers were again dispatched to try and clear the way for the train. As before, the Indians fled at the first volley from the troopers' Colt .45-caliber pistols. Unlike before, however, the number of mounted Indians hovering nearby was overwhelming. The large body of Indians seen previously approaching from the west had, for the most part, not entered directly into the attack on the train. West, upon gaining the ridge overlooking the Washita valley, observed several hundred milling, mounted Indians and ordered

THE UNITED STATES OF AMERICA

TO ALL WHO SHALL SEE THESE PRESENTS, GREETING:
THIS IS TO CERTIFY THAT
THE PRESIDENT OF THE UNITED STATES OF AMERICA
PURSUANT TO ACT OF CONGRESS APPROVED MARCH 3.1863,
HAS AWARDED IN THE NAME OF CONGRESS TO

Corp. Edward C. Sharpless, Co. H, 6th U.S. Cav.

THE CONGRESSIONAL MEDAL OF HONOR
FOR
MOST DISTINGUISHED GALLANTRY IN ACTION

at Upper Washita, Tex. September 9-11, 1874. While carrying dispatches he was attacked by 125 hostile Indians, whom he (and a comrade) fought throughout the day.

GIVEN UNDER MY HAND AT THE CITY OF WASHINGTON
THIS *fourteenth* DAY OF *November* .1927.

RECORDED IN THE OFFICE OF
THE ADJUTANT GENERAL

Dwight F. Davis
SECRETARY OF WAR

MAJOR GENERAL
THE ADJUTANT GENERAL

A copy of the Medal of Honor certificate for Edward C. Sharpless. Once the recipient obtained this certificate he was entitled to an increase in his military pension. *Courtesy the National Archives.*

a withdrawal to the train. The observing Indians charged in pursuit of the tiny cavalry command. The Indians closed in from three sides and a fourth band of Indians charged in from the northwest and concentrated themselves between the cavalry and the wagons.[10] With pistols drawn, the little command charged through the milling mass. When they were but two hundred yards from the forward skirmishers, Pvt. John W. Burkitt's horse was killed under him, violently throwing the veteran trooper to the ground. Sgt. George K. Kitchen turned about and, while wielding his pistol at the milling Indians, picked up the shaken Burkitt and, despite intense Indian fire, carried him into the safety of the wagon corral.[11] Once again Sergeant Mitchell and his right front skirmishers delivered well-directed fire into the nearest Indians and rendered several Indian ponies riderless. Upon arriving back at the train, the cavalrymen dismounted and began to herd their horses into the corral inside the wagons. Seeing the large body of Indians behind West, Lyman ordered the train into a defensive park, convinced that the train could no longer safely advance in light of the increased number of Indians and the intense firing.[12]

Before the last two wagons at the rear of the train could be driven into place, the Indians simultaneously launched two assaults on the train. The Indians who had chased the cavalry made a frontal assault upon the right front portion of skirmishers. Sergeant Mitchell and his five skirmishers poured volley after volley into the Indian ranks.[13] Lt. Granville Lewis and Sgt. William DeArmond along with only three other skirmishers formed the small rear guard. The wagons were still moving slightly for final adjustments into the egg-shaped formation and had just cleared a ravine when another band of around seventy Indians charged the right rear portion of the train. Sergeant DeArmond, seeing that the corral was not yet completed, quickly led his three skirmishers toward the charging Indians and fired at them furiously with his Springfield rifle. DeArmond and the skirmishers continued their rapid fire until the Indians, then only forty yards away, veered to the right. The Indians' firing intensified further and the cattle inside the still-uncompleted wagon corral stampeded, which added to the confusion. The Indians attacking the rear quickly regrouped and with reinforcements commenced another charge, this time toward the left rear of the train.[14] DeArmond, Lewis, and the other men shifted to meet this new assault and soon came under a severe crossfire. Despite the bullets searing the air and striking the sand around him, DeArmond furiously worked his Springfield to good effect and broke up the leading rank of Indians. While firing from a kneeling position, DeArmond fell with a severe head wound. The other three skirmishers—young, inexperienced recruits—panicked and began to falter under the intense fire. Lewis urged them back but was struck down by a rifle shot to the left knee and was wholly disabled.[15]

Captain Lyman, still mounted near the right skirmishers, noticed Lieutenant Lewis's predicament and yelled for Sgt. Frederick Hay to take charge of the rear guard. Hay and Corporals Knox, James, and Kelly sprinted to relieve the beleaguered rear guard and delivered a rapid fire into the Indian ranks, killing and wounding several Indians. Corporals Knox and James and Pvt. T. Kelly dashed into the tumult to retrieve DeArmond and Lewis and carried them into the cover of the wagon corral. The right side skirmishers poured a fusillade of lead into the Indian ranks and within a few minutes the Indians were retreating. The main attack on the train's rear guard had been thwarted, at least for the moment. Pvt. Patrick M. Canna was detailed to care for Lieutenant Lewis, who was suffering terribly from a shattered kneecap. DeArmond had already died from his head wound and his body was wrapped in canvas and placed into one of the wagons.[16]

The Indians performed horsemanship demonstrations during their encircling movement. Standing atop their ponies and riding backward and hanging from one side of their pony to fire under the pony's neck were just a few of the antics that continued over the next several hours. Long-range sniping along with the individual horsemanship displays rendered the areas outside of the wagon corral very hazardous. The bullets from unseen Indian marksmen began to strike the wagon train.[17] Shortly before darkness set in all the train members, soldiers and teamsters alike, started digging trenches. The train on the right front and rear was protected by a series of pits close to the wagons and forage sacks and boxes were used to fortify some of these. Four detached, enclosed little works, one of which commanded nearly the whole vicinity, were made on the left and one on the right at various short distances at points that seemed appropriate and were occupied by small parties. The unarmed teamsters were used to supply the various trenches and just before sunset one teamster, James McCoy, was seriously wounded while carrying ammunition to the front trenches.[18]

Daytime temperatures had hovered near one hundred degrees almost every day since the Miles column had departed from Fort Dodge on August 14. The first week of September had brought only a brief respite from these high temperatures, and the members of the Lyman train suffered desperately from thirst. The train's two hundred head of mules, horses, and cows had consumed the water they had obtained earlier in the day. Lieutenant West recalled a pool of water some four hundred yards ahead of the train's position and requested volunteers to go for water. Sgts. Josiah Pennsyl and William Koelpin and Corporals Knox and James quickly responded. Sergeant Pennsyl led the party into the darkness, with each man carrying at least six canteens. The foray was successful and uneventful and within the hour the party returned with partially filled canteens, all that the shallow pool would provide in the darkness. The night was uneventful thereafter except for the brief, but somber, burial ceremony for Sergeant DeArmond, which was held inside the wagon corral.[19]

At dawn on September 10 the Indians resumed their long-range sniping and the troops sporadically returned fire during the day. The result of this long-range firing, whether intentional or not, exacted a toll on the livestock in the corral, where at least twelve mules were killed during the day. The Indians, by now recognized as Kiowas and Comanches, had also dug trenches for protection during the previous night. Some of these trenches, especially on the east and west ridgelines, were as close as two hundred yards from the train. The majority of the Indian trenches were on the more distant ridgelines at least four hundred yards from the wagons. The Indians once again resumed their demonstrations on horseback an hour or two before sunset until at least two Indians were shot and fell from their ponies, which prompted a fusillade from the Indian trenches. The trenches at the train's front, occupied by the armed teamsters and cavalry troops, again drew the brunt of the Indian firing. Despite this intense fire, Sgt. Frederick Neilon ran from pit to pit dispensing ammunition and was severely wounded in the left leg during one of these resupply forays near the left front trenches. Despite his painful wound Neilon continued to hobble from trench to trench to deliver the ammunition. Once he regained his own trench, he declined medical care and continued to fire and encourage the others around him. Around 10 P.M. the Indians approached closer and verbally harangued the members of the wagon train. Lyman described the language later as "more forcible than complimentary and announcing that they had heap Comanches and Kiowas." He further added, "the replies of my men were even superior in Doric strength, however."[20]

Lyman knew that the three wounded men could not survive much longer without proper medical care. He circulated through the trenches requesting volunteers to attempt to get through to Camp Supply. Among the several volunteers was the small, wiry William F. Schmalsle. Lyman felt Schmalsle's small stature was a valuable asset and when he stepped forward, confident in his ability to make it through the cordon of Indians, Lyman knew he had his man.[21]

While Lyman was busy writing out his dispatch to Col. W. H. Lewis, commander at Camp Supply, a group of teamsters and troops made an unauthorized attempt to get water from the same water hole as the night before. Sergeant Kitchen later recounted:

> Several details tried to reach the water, but the Indians had placed a strong guard around it and their fire was too well directed to allow for our men getting near. They would permit us to get within 50 yards of the hole in fancied security before opening fire on us, and then poured their fire in a way which balked every effort of ours to reach the spot. In the meantime, a desultory fire was kept up by them from all sides of us.[22]

Around midnight, while sporadic firing continued on the south end of the train, young Bill Schmalsle made his dash into the darkness from the north end of the train. The bright moon overhead was translucent behind a thin veil of clouds. Shortly after Schmalsle had disappeared from sight, the men gathered at the north end of the train heard a clamor of pony hooves and Indian yelps and they feared the worst. Despite being chased several miles, Schmalsle had eluded his pursuers. Once through the cordon of Indians he rode into a herd of buffalo, where his horse stepped in a prairie dog hole and fell with him. When he got to his feet, his horse stampeded with the buffalo, leaving him afoot. He commenced walking until daylight, when he hid. He later recounted that he saw two Indians at about 10 A.M. When night came he took up the road again and continued until 9 A.M. on September 12, when he reached the hay camp about twenty miles south of Camp Supply. A rider was sent at once to Camp Supply with Lyman's dispatch.[23]

Back at the besieged train, the Indians resumed their firing shortly after sunrise on September 11. Pvt. Daniel Buck received a grazing wound to his head while serving at the left rear pits. Minutes later, Assistant Wagonmaster James L. Stanford was wounded while carrying ammunition to the forward outer pits.[24] Once again the Kiowa and Comanche Indians resumed their spectacular displays of horsemanship, which continued for a brief time until two more of their number were killed. The day was intensely hot and the stench of the dead livestock carcasses and waste was becoming unbearable. The thirst of the men became even more severe and many became desperate. The agonized groans of teamster James McCoy ended that afternoon when he died. Shortly before sundown McCoy was buried in a simple ceremony alongside Sergeant DeArmond. Mules were used to tamp the dirt over their graves to mask the location from the Indians. After the burial ceremony, several of the men began to rummage through the provisions in the wagons in search of anything that might satiate their desperate thirst. One of the men, while searching the boxes in one wagon, discovered some cases of canned tomatoes. Aware that most of the contents were juice, the men cut open the cans. Teamster John Long later remarked that the juice from the opened cans "was the best drink I ever had."[25]

Several men at the pits under the charge of Sergeant Kitchen found a barrel of vinegar and some bags of sugar. They attempted to make the vinegar more palatable by mixing it with the sugar. Sergeant Kitchen later remarked:

> One of the ten men whom I had in my rifle pits, drank in spite of my efforts to prevent any excess, so much of this drink that he became delirious and very violent. We had to tie him hand and foot to keep him inside the pit; he frothed at the mouth, bit and fought, and exhibited every token of insanity. It was two days before he recovered from the effects.[26]

Sergeant Mitchell, in a conversation with Sergeant Kitchen later that night, asked, "How much longer can we stand this?" Kitchen thought perhaps the best plan would be to abandon the wagons and fight their way to the river. Mitchell quipped, "We should fire the train to keep the Indians from getting it and fight our way off by its light." This conversation only punctuated the desperation that gripped the train's members.[27]

At approximately the same time that the bedraggled Bill Schmalsle was walking into the hay camp near Camp Supply, Lyman noticed numerous scattered bands of Indians moving southwestward away from the train. Light firing from small bands of Indians continued for several hours after sunrise. The need for water was critical and Lyman felt the need exceeded the imminent dangers posed by declining numbers of Indians. West and his men were ordered to mount up and clear the ridgeline beyond the pools of water. Sergeant Mitchell led a supporting detachment of fifteen infantry skirmishers, who formed a circle around the water pools. Teamsters led teams of mules in harnesses to the pools after the water kegs and canteens had been replenished. Shortly after this was accomplished a violent storm set in and drenched the area. The rain continued all day and made the wagon corral a miserable quagmire. All day scattered bands of Indians were seen in the distance moving both northward and southward.[28]

Lyman, despite the declining numbers of Indians, still felt it best not to chance moving the train and remained in place all day on September 13. Shortly after 10:30 P.M., Billy Schmalsle's voice boomed from the darkness. Accompanied by five other scouts, he brought word of the approach of a relief detachment from Camp Supply. The harrowing experience appeared to be finally coming to an end. Lt. Henry P. Kingsbury and a hastily assembled detachment of fifty-one soldiers and scouts and seven civilian employees arrived at 2:30 A.M. on September 14. Along with this detachment was an ambulance and a local assisting physician, A. I. Gray. Despite a thirty-eight-hour, eighty-eight-mile ride in torrential rain, Gray began immediately to care for the wounded.[29]

At 9 A.M. on September 14 Lyman assembled the train and resumed the drive toward Miles's column. Less than two hours later and shortly after reaching the north bank of the Washita River, they found a body of soldiers camped on the south bank. This body of troops was Capt. Adna Chaffee and Company I, Sixth Cavalry. Chaffee had with him an ambulance and three other wounded men, survivors of another clash with the same Indians who had attacked the train. After conferring with Doctor Gray, Chaffee and Lyman felt that it would be best to remain camped there for the time being and couriers were sent to notify Miles of the train's location.[30] At approximately 3 P.M. bugles sounded on the southern horizon announcing the approach of Miles and the main body of troops. Almost half an hour later General Miles rode into Chaffee's camp flanked by Corporals Sharpless and Morris. The two had a harrowing tale to relate to their fellow troopers. Unable to outrun the lighter Indian ponies, the two had holed up on a rise that gave them a vantage point in all directions, where they had picked off their pursuers at will all day long until the Indians broke off the engagement and returned to the main body. They then escaped under the cover of darkness and made their way to Major Compton's encampment on Sweetwater Creek.[31]

On September 25, 1874, Lyman filed his official report on the incident with the Indian Territory expedition adjutant, Lt. G. W. Baird. In this report Lyman commended the excellent service of Sgts. John Mitchell, Frank Singleton, William DeArmond, Frederick S. Hay, William Koelpin, George K. Kitchen, and Josiah Pennsyl, as well as Cpls. John J. H. Kelly, John W. Knox, John James, Thomas Kelly, William W. Morris, and Edward C. Sharpless. On March 21, 1875, Miles filed his official report of the Indian Territory expedition and made the initial recommendation for award of the Medal of Honor. Gens. P. H. Sheridan and W. T. Sherman both endorsed his recommendations and Secretary of War W. W. Belknap ordered the medals issued and engraved on April 23, 1875.[32]

The medals for the seven Fifth Infantry recipients were sent to the commanding general of the Department of the Missouri at Fort Leavenworth, Kansas, on May 15, 1875. The medals for the five Sixth Cavalry recipients were sent to Department of Arizona headquarters at Prescott, Arizona, on May 18, 1875. The medal for Sgt. George K. Kitchen was forwarded to and received at his new duty station, Fort Dodge, Kansas, on October 30, 1875.[33]

On a warm, bright July 28, 1875, seven Fifth U.S. Infantry soldiers smartly marched single file to the front of the entire garrison assembled in dress parade formation at Fort Leavenworth. They halted sharply at the designated point and performed a right face movement under the orders of the post adjutant. Lt. George W. Baird stepped forward and loudly addressed the gathering, "It is my pleasure to announce to you today General Order no. 20 issued this morning by the Commanding General, Nelson A. Miles." The recipients' names in the order of rank and seniority were announced to the garrison and Baird read the content of the order:

> Medals of Honor have been awarded to the enlisted men therein named and it is now the pleasing duty of the Colonel Commanding to bestow these tokens of the approval of Congress and the highest military authorities upon soldiers who can so worthily wear them. The Commanding Officer is glad also while making this public recognition of their service, to men who yet live to enjoy the deserved honor, to be able to inform them that a like token of recognition and

approval has been recommended and granted for their comrade, Sergeant
DeArmond, which lies dead on the field of honor.

At the completion of the reading, Miles stepped forward to address Sgt. John
Mitchell. After exchanging salutes, Miles retrieved a medal from Lieutenant
Baird and stepped forward to pin the Medal of Honor upon the left breast pocket
of Sergeant Mitchell's blouse. Once the medal was in place, Miles presented
Mitchell with a personal letter of congratulations and once again exchanged a
salute. This same procedure was repeated for each of the recipients over the next
ten minutes. After an "About face!" order, the recipients were joined by Miles
and Baird as well as the post adjutant and post commander. The command "Pass
in review!" was followed by an outpouring of other orders and within minutes
the order "Eyes right!" echoed across the parade ground. Thus ended one of the
largest and most formal Medal of Honor presentation ceremonies of the Indian
War period.[34]

Several days later, Mrs. Julia A. DeArmond was summoned to the Fort
Leavenworth post headquarters building, where she was presented with her husband's Medal of Honor. The exact circumstances of the presentation of the Medal
of Honor to Sergeant Pennsyl, Corporal Morris, and Corporal Sharpless is not
known. Sergeant Neilon (Singleton) was discharged on a disability on May 6,
1875, as a result of his leg wound and his medal was sent to him via registered
mail to his residence in Boston, Massachusetts.[35]

Several weeks before the award ceremony at Fort Leavenworth, the last of
the Comanche, Kiowa, Arapaho, and Southern Cheyenne had surrendered and
been disarmed. Within three years, the scene of the Lyman wagon train battle
would be almost devoid of the immense buffalo herds that had grazed upon it
for eons. Many of the Indians who had taken part in the battle shortly found
themselves imprisoned at Fort Marion, Florida. Most were eventually returned
to their families in the Indian Territory. For these Indians, the difficulties, dangers, excitement, and sacrifices of the Lyman train battle would become somber
memories when compared to the complexities of changing from their nomadic
hunting culture to the ways of the white culture. Both soldier and Indian alike
had to face up eventually to the monumental changes of the late nineteenth and
early twentieth centuries.

The place where each had cheated death remains much the same now as it
was in 1874. Today, roads, power and telephone poles, windbreak lines of trees,
and an occasional ranch house and oil pump are all that alter the terrain from
how it appeared in 1874. The battle site has been used for grazing and remains

untouched by the plow. The land still belongs to the same family that settled it in the 1880s. Today only a state historical marker on nearby State Highway 33 alerts passing motorists to what occurred there so many years ago. The remains of Sgt. William DeArmond, James McCoy, and an unknown number of Indian warriors still lie somewhere under that hallowed ground.

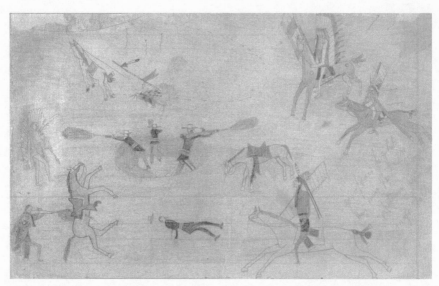

This ledger drawing is possibly Arapaho, Kiowa, or from the Kiowa–Comanche Wichita Agency, circa 1875–1895. It is believed to be a depiction of the buffalo wallow fight of September 12, 1874, a popular tale among the Kiowa. *Courtesy the Texas Memorial Museum, Austin, no. 1988-21.*

CHAPTER 12

The Buffalo Wallow Fight

September 12, 1874

——— ✭ ———

Scout Amos Chapman	Pvt. Peter P. Roth
Scout William Dixon	Pvt. George W. Smith
Pvt. John Harrington	Sgt. Zachariah T. Woodall

After almost a year and a half of planning during 1873 and the early months of 1874, the U.S. Army's most comprehensive campaign against the hostile Southern Plains Indian tribes was well under way by the early days of September 1874. The five-pronged attack aimed primarily at the Texas and Oklahoma panhandle areas was intended to force the defiant Comanche, Kiowa, Cheyenne, and Arapaho bands back onto their designated reservations in the Indian Territory. All members of those tribes not formally enrolled and residing on their designated reservation lands by July 20, 1874, were to be considered hostile and would be hunted down by the army. Indian couriers bearing those warnings were sent out to all bands then known to be roaming the vast expanse of the southern Great Plains, especially those bands that inhabited the Staked Plains of northwest Texas. By the deadline only a few bands had entered the reservations.

The northern prong of the expedition to take the field against the Indians was the command led by Gen. N. A. Miles. This 625-man column began its movement southward from Fort Dodge, Kansas, on August 14, 1874. The western prong of 224 troops under Maj. William R. Price of the Eighth U.S. Cavalry left Fort Bascom, New Mexico, on August 28, 1874. The plan was for the Miles and Price columns to drive the hostile tribes southward into the other three prongs.

155

From the south, Col. R. S. Mackenzie led a 642-man column north from Fort Concho, Texas, on August 23, 1874. Two other smaller commands were part of the master plan: one led by Col. John W. Davidson from Fort Sill, Indian Territory, was to move westward, and another, led by Col. George P. Buell, was to move northwestward from Fort Griffin, Texas.[1]

By September 11 Price's command had moved more than two hundred miles eastward to a point on Red Deer Creek in present-day Hemphill County, Texas. Because of supply difficulties, the Mackenzie column had been forced to remain at its main supply base in Blanco Canyon near present-day Spur, Texas, since September 11. One day earlier at Fort Sill, Davidson and his 610-man force had begun their movement up the Washita River. Buell's small column had moved northwest from Fort Griffin as planned and by September 9 the troops were camped on the upper tributaries of the Wichita River in present-day Knox County.[2]

The Miles column made the first serious contact with the Indians on August 30 near the mouth of Palo Duro Canyon in southeast Armstrong County. The Delaware Indian and white civilian scout detachments in advance of the main body of the column were ambushed by a large war party of Cheyenne warriors. Only after an assault by a combined force of artillery, infantry, cavalry, and scouts were the attacking Cheyenne routed and sent fleeing to the southwest toward the mouth of Tule Canyon. Critically short of supplies, Miles was forced to halt the pursuit and retrace his trail until his supply trains arrived from Camp Supply.[3]

By September 10 Miles had withdrawn his command to an encampment along the south fork of McClellan Creek in present-day Gray County. The men and animals of the command had earned a well-deserved rest. The water, despite the severe drought conditions of the time, was moderately good in quality. The numerous large cottonwood trees along the banks offered the men a brief respite from the unrelenting heat. At about 1 P.M. Indians attacked two soldiers near the camp. Lt. J. S. Payne recounted the attack, which took place between the cavalry battalion encampments:

> Whilst a number of officers were seated upon the top of a knoll, someone had
> called attention to two soldiers who were just leaving camp, mounted, en route
> up the valley, and the remark had just been made that it was dangerous for so
> small a party to leave the command, when a body of mounted men suddenly
> appeared upon a high hill, further up the stream. They disappeared almost
> instantly and whilst we were discussing the question whether they were Indians
> or a hunting party of soldiers, our attention was again attracted to the two sol-
> diers before mentioned, who had now proceeded to a point some five hundred
> yards from camp. The point of a bluff ran quite close to the creek at the spot the

two soldiers then were, the valley narrowing to a hundred yards or less. Just as the leading man was about to turn the spur of the bluff, an Indian, mounted on a gray pony and yet unseen by the two soldiers, was coming at full speed around the point. He was followed at short distances by several others. There was no time to give warning. In a moment the leading warrior was around the bluff and raising his rifle he fired upon the lead trooper breaking the latter's right arm. The brave's lance was instantly in rest and rushing upon his helpless foe, he ran him through, hurled him from his horse and dismounting, tore away the bleeding scalp of his victim and flaunting it in the command's faces, mounted and was gone. The other soldier had only his revolver, which he emptied with the effect to keep the other savages at bay. Pursuit was made of course, but so weary were our animals it was unavailing and poor Petitjohn was unavenged.[4]

The death of Pvt. James H. Pettyjohn spread a pall of sorrow, frustration, and anxiety over the encampment.

General Miles was even angrier that his supplies had not arrived. At his evening staff meeting shortly after the simple and somber funeral ceremony for Pettyjohn, Miles decided to send a party of couriers to the supply base, Camp Supply, which had been designated as the primary supply base for both the Fort Dodge and Fort Bascom columns, was about 125 miles northeast of their present position. The couriers were not only supposed to carry dispatches to Camp Supply, but also, should they meet the train en route, they were to direct the train to the new encampment.

Miles had at his disposal two civilian scouts who were thoroughly familiar with the panhandle regions of both Texas and the Indian Territory and he summoned them to his tent. The two men, Amos Chapman and William (Billy) Dixon, arrived at the general's tent around 5 P.M. Dixon later recalled that "When General Miles handed us the dispatches, he told us that we could have all the soldiers we thought necessary."[5] After a brief discussion, the three decided that a smaller party stood less a chance of discovery in the Indian-infested countryside. Lts. Edmund Hentig and William M. Wallace and Capts. Adna R. Chaffee and William A. Rafferty selected a single enlisted trooper from each of their companies to accompany the scouts. A runner was sent to notify each of the selected troopers; after drawing their rations and field complement of two hundred rounds of ammunition they were to assemble at the general's campsite. Chapman and Dixon, clad in buckskin trousers ornamented with fringes and dark flannel shirts, stood around the campfire drinking coffee as they anxiously awaited the soldiers who were to accompany them on this dangerous assignment. The first soldier to arrive was Sgt. Zachariah T. Woodall, a twenty-four-

Amos Chapman. Gen. Nelson A. Miles referred to Chapman as "one of the bravest of the brave men I have ever known." *Photograph courtesy Ida Chapman Toller and Wayne Montgomery.*

year-old native of Alexandria, Virginia. He was a superb horseman and an expert rifle marksman. Within several minutes Pvts. John Harrington and Peter Roth rode up to the tent. The last man to arrive was Pvt. George W. Smith, a four-year army veteran from Greenpoint, New York. James Pettyjohn, who had been killed only a few hours earlier, had been his bunkmate at Fort Lyon, Colorado, and Smith was still upset over the loss of his friend.

At a little past 6 P.M. the two civilian scouts and the four soldiers started up the east bank of the creek headed due northeast. The couriers traveled for most of the first night, periodically walking and riding the horses. By the time they camped on Sweetwater Creek just prior to sunrise on the morning of September 11, they had placed thirty-two miles between themselves and the Miles encampment. During the day they secreted themselves in a secluded arroyo and took turns on guard while the others slept. At sundown on September 11 the couriers mounted and resumed their trek to the northeast, ever alert for the slightest movement on the horizons. The party was still about twenty miles south of the Washita River according to collective estimates, and a good night's ride would enable them to gain the Washita before sunrise. By midnight they had reached the upper branches of Gageby Creek, where they rested for several hours. Around 3:30 A.M. on September 12 they remounted and resumed their ride to the northeast. Around 6 A.M. the detachment neared the last ridgeline overlooking the Washita Valley. The relief the men yearned for suddenly turned into sheer disbelief. Directly before them, less than a quarter of a mile away, rode a large body of mounted Indians. The Indians apparently saw them in the same instant, for small bands quickly broke off to the right and left. The couriers soon found

William "Billy" Dixon, circa 1900. He was presented his Medal of Honor on Christmas Eve 1874 at Nelson A. Miles' encampment on Carson Creek in Hutchinson County. Dixon would later establish a ranch on the site. *Courtesy the National Archives.*

themselves surrounded and cut off from any possible avenues of escape. The two civilian scouts, wily veterans of the plains, knew that their only chance for survival lay in making a defensive stand. Their horses were already fatigued after the long ride and any attempt at a running escape or running fight would have been futile, resulting in each man being overrun and quickly killed.[6]

In between the couriers and Indians was a ravine about twenty yards across that ran down to their right toward Gageby Creek. This was the only nearby cover and the logical place for them to seek cover. They rode into this ravine and quickly dismounted. Smith was placed in charge of the horses at the head of the ravine. They immediately opened fire on the Indians but their firing at the Indians, now recognized by Chapman and Dixon as Kiowas and Comanches, was sporadic. The Indians began to make concerted forays in small groups to test the detachment's strength. Severe close-range firing resulted and the couriers killed several Indians and their ponies. The fighting continued in this manner, on and off, for more than an hour before the Indians withdrew. A lull developed as the Kiowas and Comanches could be seen milling in groups far out of range from the couriers' rifles. They appeared to be arguing among themselves, perhaps in heated discussions about what would be the best strategy. After half an hour of inactivity on the Indians' part, a band of around twenty-five men came riding pell-mell over a rise and charged headlong at the head of the ravine. Private Smith was the first to

Pvt. Peter Roth. circa 1900 at Rottenmunster, Germany. In 1973 his elderly granddaughters could still vividly recall sitting on his lap as he recalled stories of his adventures against the Indians in North America. *Photograph courtesy Lt. Col. David P. Perrine.*

engage the assaulting band. With his pistol in one hand and the horse reins in the other, the former drugstore clerk made a valiant effort to fend off the attack. He held his ground briefly, but after expending his last pistol shot, he received a close-range gunshot wound to his left arm, which caused him to lose his grip on the horse reins. The horses stampeded down through the ravine and the Indians captured all but one of them. Realizing now that the ravine was an untenable position, the couriers concurred that it was imperative that they move to higher ground or face annihilation. They quickly organized themselves into a skirmish line and moved out of the ravine, backtracking toward the high ground to their left about three hundred yards away. The lone horse not captured by the Indians followed. One young brave brazenly attempted to seize that horse but he fell victim to Sergeant Woodall's marksmanship. This horse, which was Billy Dixon's, was eventually captured by the Indians; the saddlebags contained his most treasured mementos, photographs of his deceased family members.[7]

The skirmish line the couriers formed wavered as they moved across the sandy incline. As each man kneeled to take better aim at a particular Indian, he fell behind. Stopping to reload the pistols and rifles also caused several of the men to become fragmented from one another. Private Harrington later recalled, "Whenever we attempted to secure a knoll or other vantage ground, the Indians

160

would be ahead of us in such numbers as to make us change our direction."[8] Though it was obvious that the Indians could easily have made a frontal assault and stampeded them, the Indians apparently feared the couriers' marksmanship. Unwilling to incur the necessary casualties at the time, the Indians toyed with them and waited for the right moment. Billy Dixon purposely began to take calculated rifle shots at the medicine man, who was the only mounted Indian and the one leading and encouraging most of the Indian assaults. Harrington recounted later:

> The medicine man decorated with buffalo horns and an immense headdress of eagles feathers reaching to his horse's tail, looking like the devil himself, tried to force them to charge over us. The medicine man . . . kept riding around us all the time getting bolder and firing his pistol when he came in range·

Amos Chapman recognized him from the Fort Sill reservation and shouted, "not to mind him, for he couldn't hit anything." The old medicine man did come up to within twenty yards of the couriers at one point before Billy Dixon finally killed his horse under him, throwing him roughly to the ground. The couriers now felt encouraged and aggressively moved toward a small knoll about two hundred yards away.[9]

Smith, despite his arm wound, continued to deliver pistol fire from his position on the northern end of the skirmish line. As the skirmish line moved away from the ravine and up the incline away from Gageby Creek, the Indians were able to use their encircling tactic more effectively. Shortly after the Indians completed their first circle, the couriers, at Dixon's urging, suddenly charged at the Indians between them and the knoll and ran pell-mell through the circle of Indians. The breakthrough was successful in part due to the fact that the Indians feared that firing from parts of the circle would hit their companions on the other side. Once through the circle, the couriers continued their run for the knoll, which was still about a hundred yards away. The Kiowas were shocked at this brazen move and resumed their showmanship on horseback. According to Sergeant Woodall:

> At this stage we were eye witness to some of the most magnificent feats of horsemanship that could not be equaled by any like number of men in the world, rising readily from the stirrups while the horses were in rapid motion and standing erect on the backs of their animals while they delivered their fire and then instantly dropping, as if shot, into their stirrups, swinging themselves rapidly under their bellies, in which position they could easily aim and fire. These tactics were continued by them for some time. There was one spot on the prairie where the grass stood over five feet tall. Toward this place the Indians would ride as fast as their ponies could go, and I noticed every time any of the

men fired at an Indian near this place, the latter would drop as if hit, while their ponies would continue on until finally caught by some of the squaws. Fully 20 of them dropped in this manner, leading us to believe that they were all hit. Nothing more was seen of them for about an hour during which our attention was engaged in an opposite direction by another party of Indians, who repeatedly charged us, eventually forcing us from our position. In moving to higher ground, we approached the bunch of tall grass, before referred to, near which we had seen so many Indians drop. We got within 50 yards when a line of Indians suddenly sprang up, presenting as good a skirmish line as any body of soldiers could form, and poured murderous fire on the party.

Smith was the first to fall with a bullet wound in his back. The others, seeing Smith fall, ran faster toward the knoll with bullets searing the earth and air all around them. Woodall was less than fifty yards from the knoll when he was the next to be hit. A grazing wound in the groin sent him sprawling to the ground, but he righted himself and stumbled forward, firing as he went.[10]

Billy Dixon was the first member of the courier detachment to reach the knoll, on top of which was a buffalo wallow. He shouted for the others to join him. Private Roth was the second man to gain the refuge of the wallow, followed closely by the limping Woodall. Private Harrington was about twenty yards away from the wallow when he was struck in the hip by a rifle ball. In desperation, he limped and crawled into the safety of the wallow. While Woodall and Dixon drove the Indians back with their deadly accurate marksmanship, Harrington and Roth dug with their hands and knives to deepen the wallow. Only Smith and Chapman had not reached the meager refuge. Chapman was still about a hundred yards away, sitting on the ground, wielding his pistol to keep the Indians at bay. Dixon and the others yelled for Chapman to come and join them. Chapman replied that he could not walk; he had suffered a severe gunshot wound to the right ankle. Dixon decided to attempt to help Chapman. He tried three times and found his way blocked by mounted bands of Kiowas each time. On his fourth attempt, the others in the wallow opened up rapid firing on the blocking Indians and relieved a couple of ponies of their burdens, a fusillade that enabled Dixon to reach Chapman. Chapman managed, with Dixon's help, to stand up long enough to enable Dixon to hoist him up piggyback style. Dixon then trudged up the slight rise and into the wallow under a hail of protective firing. Once inside the wallow, the seriousness of Chapman's wound was evident—a rifle ball had shattered his right foot at the ankle joint and his foot dangled limply.[11]

The sun was now almost directly overhead and the fight had gone on for three hours. Despite the heat, thirst, and the pain of their wounds, the band of couriers remained stoic and continued to dig and fortify their position. The security of the wallow strengthened their determination. They had inflicted at least four casualties on the Indians so far and had managed to hold them at bay, despite twenty-five-to-one odds, for more than three hours. Every time an Indian had ventured near Smith's fallen body he had met a hail of gunfire from the wallow. The Kiowas had not yet taken a scalp and they could be seen having animated discussions in groups far out of the range of the wallow defenders' rifles. The Indian groups must have been discussing strategy for they soon launched a new series of assaults. Once again they resumed their usual circling movements and their exhibitions of horsemanship. When they had drawn attention to one side of the circle, groups from the opposite side of the circle would rush toward the wallow. On at least two occasions, the Indians were within a few yards of the wallow before they were driven back at pistol range. At least half a dozen Indians fell during these attacks.[12]

By 3 P.M. the detachment was dangerously low on ammunition. The four cavalry troopers had each carried sixty rounds in their bandoliers while the scouts had limited themselves to forty rounds apiece on their person. The balance of their two hundred-round allowance had been lost in the saddlebags on the stampeded horses. Each man was now probably down to around twenty rounds, enough possibly to stave off one or two more Indian assaults.

Once again the Indians withdrew in small groups to the prominent points around them. The sun that had blistered down upon them for the past seven hours disappeared behind a rolling bank of gray clouds. The winds, almost non-existent minutes before, began to swirl and dust swelled about the buffalo wallow. The tumbleweeds, so common to this part of the Great Plains, jumped and tumbled along, lodging against the most meager of obstacles in their path. The winds began to cool the beleaguered wallow defenders while lightning leaped from the swelling clouds off to the northwest and thunder could be heard in the distance. While the men in the wallow discussed the ramifications of the impending change in the weather, the winds increased. These breezes swirled dust around and over Smith's body, leading someone to suggest they had seen him move. The attention brought by this twist in the weather prompted Woodall to glare intently at Smith's body, where his bandoliers of ammunition stood out as a dark slash of hope. Woodall began to wonder about Smith's bandoliers, which were still full as he had been shot early in the fight. Roth volunteered to go and retrieve Smith's bandolier. Just as he bolted from the wallow a slow pelting rain began to fall. The twenty-four-year-old native of Beffendorf, Germany, sprinted to Smith's body. A cloudburst of rain almost obscured his actions, but he soon returned to the wallow empty handed. Slumping down on the side of the wallow, he announced to the others that Smith was still alive. All had assumed that Smith was dead. Almost five hours had passed since he had been shot and not seeing any movement, all had presumed he had died instantly from the close-range gunshot wound. Billy Dixon was the first to break the atmosphere in the wallow and he told Roth that he would need help bringing Smith to safety. Roth agreed to accompany Dixon. While the three other wallow defenders trained their rifles on the Indians, Dixon and Roth ran to Smith's side. The two lifted Smith's limp body up between them and held his arms in place around their necks. In this manner they carried and partially dragged Smith into the wallow.[13]

Once inside the wallow Smith's penitent comrades quickly examined his wounds. The bullet had entered his back on the right side between the shoulder blade and the spine. The wound was so large that it exposed the right lung. As Roth gingerly wiped the dirt from Smith's face, Dixon stuffed a silk handkerchief into the gaping hole in Smith's back. Smith's presence in the wallow was a breath of fresh air to the others. Their guilty feelings about not tending to his welfare earlier were drowned out by his gallant, weak words of encouragement. Despite the severity of his wounds, Smith sternly urged his comrades to prop him upright so he could help in the fighting. After several brief probing forays by mounted warriors around 4:30 P.M., Smith began to shiver from the cold dampness, causing him severe suffering from his wounds. When he no longer had the strength to sit erect and hold a pistol, he threatened to take his own life unless the others promised to use his prone body as a shield on the wallow's edge.[14]

A cold rain again began falling about an hour before sunset and the Kiowas who, among all Plains Indian tribes, despised rain, were seen moving off to the southwest. By sunset the wallow had filled with several inches of rainwater and further added to the forlorn group's misery. Dixon and Roth began to collect the large bushy tumbleweeds from the immediate area around the wallow.[15] These round wiry tumbleweeds made good substitutes for mattresses and, when piled into the wallow, they provided a cushion between the cold rainwater and mud in the bottom of the wallow. Smith was laid on one of these "prairie mattresses," which greatly reduced his suffering. Dixon set about cleaning the rifles and pistols while the others remained on alert.[16]

Around 8 P.M. the men began to ponder their fate if the Kiowas returned in the morning. All felt that someone should go and seek help, but a brief debate broke out about who should go. Roth and Dixon were the only ones not incapacitated by wounds. Both readily volunteered, but Dixon argued that he knew the countryside better and stood a better chance of finding the trail in the darkness. The others objected, for despite his familiarity with the countryside Dixon was an excellent marksman and his presence at the wallow was highly desirable under the circumstances. The majority prevailed and, after receiving some brief directions from Dixon and Chapman, Roth struck out on foot into the darkness around 9 P.M. Smith's condition had worsened and he suffered acutely from his wounds. His ever-weakening pleas to the others to shoot him and end his painful suffering fostered an aura of despair and helplessness. Finally around 10 P.M. sleep brought Smith a welcome respite from his suffering.[17]

Roth returned to the wallow in disgust shortly past midnight. He had been unable to find the wagon trail to Camp Supply after almost three hours of searching. After several minutes of silence Roth inquired about Smith's condition. Dixon reached over to feel for breath but felt only cold flesh; death had finally relieved Smith of his suffering. Shortly after sunrise a pelting rain again began to fall. Another consultation was held among the wallow defenders and the decision was finally made that Dixon would attempt to find the wagon trail. Despite the increased danger of travel in daylight, Dixon unselfishly left behind all but four of his remaining cartridges.[18]

Dixon left the wallow at a run, promising the men he would get help as quickly as possible. He started off in a straight northerly direction, hoping to strike the wagon trail south of the Washita River. He had made his way about a quarter of a mile when he ran across the trail from Camp Supply. The rain had stopped and the visibility was excellent. Ever alert for the slightest sign of movement, Dixon moved swiftly along the trail for another quarter of a mile. Just as he struck the ridgeline overlooking the Washita River, he noticed a large body of mounted riders about two miles off to his left on the western horizon. Unable to discern immediately whether they were troops or Indians, he moved off the trail and hid in some nearby tall bushes. After almost twenty minutes of suspense he could finally see the four-abreast column in their distinctive blue uniforms. Unable to restrain his joy, he ran back onto the trail and fired his rifle once to attract their attention. Within a few minutes Dixon was surrounded by curious and smiling troopers of the Eighth Cavalry commanded by Maj. W. R. Price. After listening to Dixon's brief description of the engagement and the location of the wallow, Price dispatched six soldiers to ride ahead and locate the wallow.[19]

The men in the wallow heard the shot Dixon fired and thought that the Indians had killed him and were now coming for them. As soon as the six troopers came within rifle range, Chapman, thinking they were Indians, opened fire on them. Luckily, only the horse ridden by a Sergeant Steiger was wounded in the face. Dixon quickly ran up on a nearby hill and began yelling and waving his arms to let them know that he was all right. The firing ceased. Surgeon McLean (or McLain), Private Florel, and Pvt. Smith F. Foster advanced to investigate. Private Foster later recounted the scene: "Chapman lay on the bank at the wallow and a dead soldier was lying in the pit with a pale red handkerchief over his face. The pit was nearly square, not round."[20]

McLean began to examine Chapman's ankle and Chapman inquired, "How long will it take to get well?" McLean replied, "Oh a long time if it does not have to be amputated."[21] Chapman became very somber and embittered, realizing for the first time the severity of his wound. McLean and two of the troopers treated the wounds of the wallow defenders as best they could. As the Price column had exhausted its own supplies, all they could provide the men in the wallow was some dried buffalo meat. Lt. Alfred H. Rogers and his Company C were dispatched to notify General Miles of the courier detachment's condition and location and to get an ambulance to their relief as quickly as possible. Price was unable to assist the men in the wallow any further. The rifles and pistols of his command were of different caliber from those of the wallow defenders and he was unable to leave any ammunition. Desperately short of supplies himself and in search of his own incoming supply wagons, Price abandoned the men in the wallow and rode off to the east at the head of his command. Miles later severely criticized and officially censured him for this decision.[22]

During the daylight hours of September 13 the men in the wallow feared that the Indians might return to continue the attack. A cold constant rain fell throughout the day and only added to the men's disgust and despair. Darkness and the thought of another long night shivering in the cold only added to the despair. Rogers and his men found Miles near Sweetwater Creek around 3 P.M. on September 13. Miles ordered Capt. Adna Chaffee and his company to proceed with an ambulance to relieve the wallow defenders. Around 10 P.M. on September 14 the men in the wallow heard the faint sounds of a bugle in the distance. Relief had come at last. The elated men fired into the air to signal their location. After about fifteen minutes the weary defenders were greeted by the friendly faces of Captain Chaffee and his troopers. Their long ordeal was finally over; their bravery, camaraderie, and determination had enabled them to survive against twenty-five-to-one odds. Woodall, Chapman, and Harrington were placed in the ambulance. Roth and Dixon helped members of the relief party wrap Private Smith's body in a blanket and place it at the bottom of the wallow. By the light of hand-held torches, the remains of Pvt. George W. Smith were covered forever by the earth of the Texas Panhandle. Chaffee set up a camp on nearby Threemile Creek and treated the survivors to their first hot food and drink since they had left the McClellan Creek encampment.[23]

The next morning at daybreak Chaffee moved the survivors to a campsite near the wagon trail crossing on the Washita River. Within an hour Capt. Wyllys Lyman, in command of a recently besieged supply train, arrived at the north bank of the Washita River crossing. After a brief consultation between Lyman, Chaffee, and Surgeon Gray, the decision was made to camp there while Gray treated the wounded. Couriers were sent to notify Miles of the train's location and the advance portion of the Miles command arrived later that afternoon. After the subsidence of the Washita River, the supply wagons were unloaded and an immediate start was made with the wounded toward Camp Supply. The wounded were taken to the post hospital after they arrived at Camp Supply on September 18. Army Surgeon Peter A. Cleary, Drs. W. E. Sabine and A. I. Gray, and hospital steward Seymour Kitching began to tend the wounded. Amos Chapman's right foot was amputated on September 20. Woodall and Harrington recovered from their wounds quickly and spent the next several weeks recuperating the command's broken-down horses.[24]

News of the fight at the tiny buffalo wallow spread rapidly across the country. Within weeks, stories of the epic event had appeared in most of the nation's newspapers. General Miles, more than any one person, was responsible for publicizing the event. On September 24 he submitted a report about the fight at the buffalo wallow to the adjutant general's office in Washington, D.C., in which he recommended the participants for special recognition, stating:

> I deem it but a duty to brave men and faithful soldiers to bring to the notice of the highest military authority an instance of indomitable courage, skill and true heroism on the part of a detachment from this command with the request that the actors be rewarded and their faithfulness and bravery recognized by pensions, medals of honor or in such way as may be deemed most fitting. The simple recital of their deeds and the mention of the odds against which they fought; how the wounded defended the dying, and the dying aided the wounded by exposure to fresh wounds after the power of action was gone, these alone present a scene of cool courage, heroism, and self sacrifice, which duty as well as inclination prompt us to recognize, but which we cannot fitly honor.[25]

Secretary of War William Belknap concurred with the recommendation and endorsed it on November 4, officially granting the Medal of Honor to all six men. The medals were forwarded to the engraver and then returned to the adjutant general's office for distribution to the proper duty stations.[26] The six Medals of Honor for the buffalo wallow defenders were sent to Miles at his encampment on Carson Creek in present-day Hutchinson County. During the evening retreat ceremony that Christmas Eve, General Miles's slight New England accent resounded across the Canadian River Valley as he read his personal presentation statement aloud:

> I take pleasure in presenting to you a Medal of Honor as a recognition by the government of your skill, courage and determined fortitude, displayed in an engagement with five others on the twelfth of September 1874, against hostile Indians, in overwhelming numbers. This mark of honor, I trust will be long worn by you and though it in a small degree compensates for the hardships endured, yet it is a lasting emblem of distinguished services well earned in a noble cause. It will ever recall the fact to you and yours, of having materially aided in clearing this fair country of ruthless savages, and freeing it for all time to civil settlement. This must be an ever increasing gratification to you. This badge of honor is most worthily bestowed.[27]

General Miles then stepped forward and pinned the Medal of Honor to Billy Dixon's overcoat.[28]

Exactly one month later on January 24, 1875, in camp near Fort Sill, Indian Territory, 1st Lt. G. W. Baird read General Order no. 28 to a dress parade of troops:

> The Commanding Officer takes pleasure in announcing to the troops of this expedition that his recommendation that the distinguished heroism displayed on the twelfth of September 1874, by Sergeant Z. T. Woodall of Company I, Privates John Harrington, Company H and Peter Roth, Company A, Sixth Cavalry, and Scouts Amos Chapman and William Dixon be recognized, has been approved by the highest military authority and that the Congress has bestowed upon each of these men a Medal of Honor. It is now his pleasing duty to bestow upon men who can worthily wear them, these tokens of the recognition and approval of their Government.[29]

General Miles then stepped forward to face Sergeant Woodall and Private Roth, who were standing in a line facing the troops, who were massed in parade formation. As he pinned the Medal of Honor to each of the men's left breast pocket he also shook the hand of each and presented him with a personal letter of congratulations. During his return trip to Fort Dodge, Kansas, Miles stopped briefly at Camp Supply on February 8, 1875, just long enough to present the Medal of Honor to Amos Chapman.[30] Pvt. John Harrington's medal was forwarded to his duty station of Fort Lyon, Colorado, where he acknowledged its receipt on March 29, 1875.[31] The Medal of Honor awarded to Pvt. George W. Smith was forwarded to the second auditor's office of the Department of Treasury for disposition to his next of kin. On September 8, 1875, the medal was sent to the postmaster of Greenpoint, New York, for special delivery to Smith's father, Mr. Charles G. Smith.[32]

None of the participants of this epic event in frontier history ever returned to the scene of the buffalo wallow fight. Billy Dixon, who remained an army scout at nearby Fort Elliott until 1883, admitted prior to his death in 1913 that his own procrastination and the remoteness of the spot had prevented him from revisiting the scene.[33] Private Smith's remains were never removed from the buffalo wallow site despite his father's appeal to General Miles in December 1874.[34] Through the efforts of the Panhandle-Plains Historical Society in 1925, the Buffalo Wallow Battleground site was formally dedicated.[35] A red granite monument inscribed with the six names was placed at the site on September 12, 1925. The inscription on the monument best summarizes what occurred on that tiny mound of earth fifty-one years earlier, "Stand silent! Heroes here have been, who cleared the way for other men."[36] Even today, the location is in a remote, sparsely populated area. Those who do visit the site eighteen miles southeast of Canadian, Texas, gaze upon a countryside much changed from those fateful days in September 1874. Today windblock lines of trees separate fields of wheat and corn. Oil pumps dot grazing lands populated by white-faced Hereford cattle where hundreds of thousands of buffalo once grazed.

In 1916 the United States Army decided to compile an official Army Medal of Honor Roll based upon a new set of eligibility requirements. The objective of a select board of general officers, including Miles, was to review and validate all United States Army Medal of Honor awards. They were to strike from the roll those Medal of Honor awards not complying with the new criterion. One of the new criteria created by Section 122 of the National Defense Act of 1916 mandated that the medal only be awarded to officers and enlisted men of the United States Army. The board judged scouts Amos Chapman and William Dixon to be neither. Despite General Miles's protests, Chapman and Dixon and three other Army scouts were removed from the official United States Army Medal of Honor Roll effective February 15, 1917. They were not required to turn in their medals but wearing them was made a misdemeanor criminal offense. Miles wrote a scathing criticism into the board minutes stating the decision to be "a flagrant act of injustice, unworthy of the government in whose defense these men risked their lives."[37]

Seventy-two years passed before the U.S. Army corrected its flagrant act of injustice. On June 12, 1989, a United States Army Board for Correction of Military Records voted to restore Amos Chapman, William Dixon, and three other former army scouts to the U.S. Army Medal of Honor Roll.[38]

Adam Payne's Medal of Honor headstone in the Seminole-Negro Indian Scout Cemetery at Brackettville, Texas. Described by fellow tribal members as "a bad man who wore horns on his head," Payne was shot and killed by Kinney County Deputy Sheriff Claron A. Windus, also a Medal of Honor recipient, while resisting arrest. *Photograph courtesy Charles M. Neal Jr. Collection.*

CHAPTER 13

FOR HABITUAL COURAGE NEAR QUITAQUE PEAK

September 20, 1874

Pvt. Adam Payne

B y noon on September 19, 1874, Col. Ranald S. Mackenzie was convinced that all preparations were complete and it was time for his southern column of the 1874 Indian Territory expedition to commence active field operations. At an afternoon officer briefing Capt. Peter M. Boehm, commander of the scouting detachment, divulged the findings of several reconnaissance forays into the surrounding country. Boehm believed these findings indicated a high probability of an Indian presence in the area of the headwaters of the Tongue and Pease Rivers, some thirty miles to the north. Mackenzie, accordingly, ordered that a small scouting party be dispatched at sunset to investigate. The main column would begin its advance at 5 A.M. on September 20 and would follow the scouting party's tracks.

Mackenzie's scouting or reconnaissance detachment at this point consisted of thirty-eight members, of which the largest contingent was the group of twenty-one Seminole-Negro scouts.[1] Another contingent, comprised of seven members, was the group of Tonkawa Indian scouts, while the remaining numbers were filled out by civilian guides, enlisted scouts and at least one Lipan Apache. Boehm requested that Sergeant Johnson select three of his Tonkawa scouts for the assignment, and a like request for two Seminole-Negro scouts was made to Sgt. John Kibbets. Kibbets selected Cpl. George Washington and Pvt. Adam Payne.[2]

Of those selected Payne was by far the least experienced; he had served only ten months in the scouts and often was perplexed by army regulations and uniformity. Despite his inexperience he had quickly gained a reputation for his audacity.[3] At least six feet tall and weighing almost two hundred pounds, Payne was unquestionably the most imposing figure among the entire command. His rejection of army uniformity was expressed in his practice of wearing a leather headpiece adorned with buffalo horns, which only further enhanced his formidable appearance.[4]

Shortly after 5 P.M. Kibbetts issued Washington and Payne their allotments of sixty rounds each of ammunition and reminded each that this was a scouting patrol, not a pursuit patrol and that they were to find the Indians, not fight them. It was a concise statement of basic West Point teachings; a scouting patrol's timely use of its marine telescopes and spare horses was supposed to enable them to circumvent a clash with the enemy. Just before sundown on September 19 the five scouts, each with one spare horse, left the cavalry encampment at Silver Falls, traveling east by northeast.[5] By scouting along the edge of the escarpment they would be able to scan the lower elevations many miles to the east. Even a small campfire could be seen for miles in the clear night air. The headwaters of the Pease and Wichita Rivers were fed by a series of springs of good quality and Tonkawa John Williams (also known as Willums) felt that the area would be the most opportune locale to reconnoiter. After ascending the eastern incline of Blanco Canyon, the five turned to the northeast and began searching for signs of Indians along the escarpment. As was the practice, they rode for two miles and then walked for the third mile. The reconnaissance proceeded in this manner for about fifteen miles. Near midnight they turned slightly to the northeast and descended the escarpment. Shortly before sunrise they arrived at the southeast base of Quitaque Peak, where they decided to camp. Within minutes their small campfire glowed against the wall of Quitaque's red and gray sedimentary layers. After a light breakfast the men rested, following the usual routine of each man standing one hour of watch duty while the other four slept.[6]

Payne had the last watch and was wakened around 10 A.M. He saw only small clouds of dust, whipped up by the small whirlwinds so common to the High Plains and sub-escarpment areas of northwest Texas. Close scrutiny of these clouds did not discern any continuous ones that might indicate a herd of horses being driven or lodge poles being dragged along. By the end of Payne's watch, several of the other scouts had wakened. After conferring among themselves and upon John Williams' urging, it was decided that they would move southeast toward Roaring Springs, then veer back to the west and pick up the trail of the main command. Just as the four other scouts began to gather up their blankets and camp equipment, a party of around ten Indians driving a herd of approximately forty horses appeared over a rise from the northeast about five hundred yards away.[7] At the same time, several smaller groups of Indians appeared from the southeast and south, much closer. The Indians began to whoop and holler their war cries. Although the precise sequence of events is unclear, apparently the nearest small band from the south quickly made a dash for the scouts' hobbled spare horses, which were grazing along Brushy Creek. Payne apparently ran toward the primary mounts, which were already saddled and individually tethered to a single rope line. Drawing his pistol on the run, he opened fire on the closest group of Indians and one shot killed the horse from under one of the Indians. Payne arrived at his mount seconds ahead of the onrushing Indians and grabbed the reins just as the other four horses were stampeded beyond his grasp. Once mounted, Payne bolted toward the other scouts, who were frantically trying to unhobble and mount their led horses. He reined up between the scouts and nearby milling Indians while they unhobbled their horses and mounted up bareback. The five scouts mounted and bolted to the southwest in hopes of reaching the safety of the main command. Payne wielded his pistol as he led the way through the scattered morass of Indians and horses. Once they were into the clear, the other scouts, unencumbered by the weight of saddles, rifles, saddlebags, and blanket rolls, began to outdistance Payne. Most of the Indians had been engaged in rounding up and herding the stock, but a group of around seven Indians seemed intent upon chasing the scouts. Payne was about one hundred yards behind Corporal Washington, who luckily had caught up with his own saddled primary mount.[8]

Washington had to come to a complete stop before he could dismount and then mount his primary horse. Realizing that Washington might be overtaken by the Indians, Payne reined up and turned to face the pursuing Indians. Unsheathing his carbine, he leveled it at the onrushing Indians and opened on them at one hundred yards. One Indian pony went down in a heap and threw its rider to the ground, halting the band. At that point one of the Indians drew out what appeared to be an old Lehman rifle and fired at Payne's horse, killing it. Payne jumped off his horse to the side, uninjured, but found himself alone against the Indians. Washington had successfully transferred to his other mount and was unaware of Payne's predicament. Payne quickly unharnessed his saddle and equipment and piled it atop his dead horse for extra cover. He was determined to put up a fight and began to grapple through his saddlebag for his extra ammunition, cramming it into his hip and breast pockets. The Indians had been hovering about their fallen friend but then began a rush toward the single embattled scout. Payne opened up with his Sharps carbine when the onrushing Indians got within fifty yards of his position. His feverish firing scattered and slowed some of the more wavering Indians. The more determined Indians continued to fight with pistols and arrows. When they were within twenty-five yards Payne aimed at the Indian who was leading the charge and fired. The Indian fell backward from his horse and the others quickly turned about. The riderless horse ran straight toward Payne, who took advantage of the opportunity and seized the horse. Before the Indians realized what was happening, Payne had thrown his saddle atop the horse and secured the saddle harness. He quickly mounted and bolted off to the southwest, with the Indians in pursuit. The other scouts could be seen as they neared the ridge of the escarpment, about half a mile away. The Indians, about three hundred yards away, broke off into two bands, one to the left and one to the right. The chase progressed up the gradual incline along the eastern rim of the Caprock Escarpment. Payne reined up at opportune sites and fired at the pursuing Indians. The Indians for the most part hovered out of range, hoping that one or the other of their bands would be able to outflank this scout and cut off his escape route.[9]

Just as quickly as Payne resumed his flight, the Indians resumed and intensified their efforts. As Payne neared the more pronounced incline of the escarpment rim, the lighter Indian ponies gradually began to close on him. He drew up at the rim of the escarpment and again turned on his pursuers, where he saw that there were at least seven or eight determined Indians still ascending the incline below him. One band of persistent Indians on his right seemed the most imminent threat since they were snaking up an arroyo, which afforded them the opportunity to gain the flat plains quicker than the others. Payne fired on them until a last frantic search among his pockets for remaining cartridges proved fruitless. Stowing his carbine, he turned his mount about and began a wild ride for the main command. As the Indians gained the rim of the escarpment each began whooping and hollering, confident that on the flat plains their light ponies would overtake the scout. Payne, for his part, liberally applied the quirt to his mount, hoping that his horse would hold out for just a few more miles.[10]

The main column had started out from the cavalry camp in Blanco Canyon at 6:15 that morning. By noon, when the scouts were attacked, the main column had set up a campsite at a small shallow lake approximately seventeen miles north-northeast from their main camp at Silver Falls. The Fourth Cavalry regimental quartermaster, Henry Lawton, had established the camp in order to feed the troops and horses. About 2:30 P.M., just as the troops were finishing their meal, one of the sentries shouted, "Mounted rider coming in from the northeast!" A short time later a second rider, and then a third and fourth one appeared over

Tonkawa Indian Scout John William, also known as Willums, circa 1898. His life no doubt was saved by Pvt. Adam Payne's gallant actions. Williams was the first to reach the safety of the main column. *Photograph courtesy Western History Collections, University of Oklahoma.*

the same rise to the northeast. The first rider, Tonkawa scout John Williams, shouted excitedly, "Comanche, Comanche, he gotta my saddle and my pony; come quick." The two other Tonkawa scouts arrived next, followed several minutes later by Corporal Washington. As John Williams continued to excitedly relate the chain of events, Payne emerged from over the rise with several Indians in close pursuit. The pursuing Indians drew up at the sight of the command and, just as quickly as they had appeared, passed out of sight.[11]

Mackenzie was elated that contact had finally been made with the elusive Indians. He was even more elated about the conduct of Private Payne, which no doubt had saved the lives of the other four scouts. Payne's boldness and good judgment in preventing the loss of his and Corporal Washington's horse, equipment, and arms, would not go without recognition. Much to Mackenzie's chagrin, the Indians now had three additional Sharps carbines and at least ninety rounds of ammunition the other scouts had left behind. A pursuit detachment was quickly mounted and sent in search of the attacking Indians. Upon arriving at the scene of the initial attack at Quitaque Peak, it was noted that the Indians had split up. A small trail of around three horses led off to the north while the driven herd and the main body of around twenty Indians trailed off to the south. Upon the arrival of the main cavalry command, Mackenzie conferred with Payne and the other scouts. After ascertaining that the Indians and their herd were being driven in a north-northwesterly direction, Mackenzie formulated his plan. The herd and larger body of Indians fleeing to the south were likely a ruse intended to draw them away from the main Indian camps. The three tracks leading north were likely the couriers sent to notify the main camp of the army's presence and location. Mackenzie, as a result of the actions and information gathered at Quitaque, decided to deploy a battalion to the south to attempt to overtake the southward fleeing band. At the head of the main body of his command, he turned the troops northward, where he felt certain the main Indian camps would be found.[12]

Pvt. Adam Payne served with continued merit and valor throughout the remainder of the campaign. He was one of the several far-ranging scouts who located the main Indian encampment in Palo Duro Canyon on the evening of September 27. He again demonstrated his ferocious nature in combat near Double Lake on November 3, and again on November 6 near Laguna Tahoka. Adam Payne was relieved of his scouting duties with the Mackenzie column on December 2, 1874, and was discharged from the army at Fort Clark on February 19, 1875.[13]

On January 7, 1875, Mackenzie submitted his report on the campaign to the Department of Texas Headquarters. In this report he cited eight men from his command as deserving of medals for gallantry. Only one of those eight, Adam Payne, was accorded a separate statement of praise by Mackenzie who wrote, "Seminole Negro Adam Payne for habitual courage. This man has, I believe, more cool daring than any scout I have ever known."[14] This report, with a concurring endorsement by Gen. C. C. Augur, commander of the Department of Texas, was forwarded to the adjutant general's office in Washington, D.C. On February 2, 1875, Adj. Gen. E. D. Townsend sent a reply to General Augur stating:

> In referring to your endorsement of the 8th ultimo, forwarding a report from Colonel R. S. Mackenzie, 4th Cavalry, relative to the meritorious conduct of officers and men of his command during Indian engagements last fall and suggesting that Medals of Honor be awarded to certain enlisted men named therein; I have the honor to inform you that it is the ruling of the War Department that Medals of Honor can be awarded for special and distinguished service in Indian warfare involving some acts of conspicuous bravery or service above the ordinary duty of a soldier, and the Secretary of War therefore desires that the particular acts of gallantry be stated in each case.[15]

This request was forwarded to Mackenzie at Fort Sill, IndianTerritory, and on August 31, 1875, he replied directly to General Townsend. In the last paragraph of his reply, Mackenzie stated in regard to Private Payne, "Seminole-Negro Adam Paine [sic], for gallantry on September 20th, when attacked by a largely superior party of Indians. This man is a scout of great courage."[16] On October 19, 1875, General Townsend received Mackenzie's reply. The secretary of war immediately ordered the medal awards to be conferred and Townsend sent them to be engraved. Private Payne's Medal of Honor was sent to Colonel Mackenzie at Fort Sill on October 29, 1875. Mackenzie forwarded the medal to the commanding officer at Fort Clark on November 7. Adam Payne, having been discharged from the scouting detachment on February 19, 1875, did not reenlist. He was not residing at the Seminole-Negro village near Fort Clark but was employed as a teamster at Brownsville, Texas. The exact circumstance of his receipt of the medal is not known.[17]

Col. Ranald S. Mackenzie. His use of a special force of enlisted troopers, his secret deals with the Comancheros and the Kiowa chief Kicking Bird, and his extensive use of a spy network within Mexico might lead one to believe that he was a twentieth-century military officer. *Photograph courtesy the National Archives.*

CHAPTER 14

Repulsing The Cheyenne
at Tule Canyon

September 27, 1874

--- ⭑ ---

Pvt. William McCabe   Cpl. Edwin Phoenix
Pvt. Gregory Mahoney

D espite incessant rains over the previous two days, Col. R. S. Mackenzie had doggedly led the main southern column of the 1874 Indian Territory expedition northward from its supply camp on the Fresh Water Fork of the Brazos River. By the evening of September 22 the command was camped on Little Cottonwood Creek in present-day southeastern Briscoe County, where shortly after 5 A.M. on September 23 the guard mount officer awoke Colonel Mackenzie as instructed. Mackenzie instructed him to bring the guide known as Johnson to his tent. Johnson was actually a New Mexican, known only to Mackenzie and a select few by his real name, Francisco Tefoya. Tefoya had claimed he could find the sites of the main winter Indian encampments and Lt. Henry W. Lawton enrolled him as a guide at Fort Concho. Upon "Johnson's" arrival at his tent, Mackenzie informed him that it was time for him to do what he had said he could do when he was hired—find the Indians. An hour later Tefoya rode westward into the darkness with one spare horse and a lot of hope for success riding on his shoulders.[1]

By 9 A.M. the main command was on the march. The heavy rains over the previous three days had rendered the clay soils into a quagmire and the command was forced to encamp early, after covering only nine miles. At 6 A.M. on

179

September 25, after gaining the level terrain of the High Plains, Mackenzie decided to disperse the scouting contingent on reconnaissance forays. Henry Strong, one of the civilian guides, was dispatched to the north and east along the escarpment. The enlisted scouts and the Seminole-Negro scouts were dispatched to the west and north with instructions to attempt to locate the two-horse trail Tefoya had left. Mackenzie and the main command continued their slow trek to the north-northwest and arrived at Tule Canyon, where they encamped in the late afternoon.[2]

The scout detachment had moved due west of the head of Tule Canyon as instructed and was advancing straight northward. At noon they came to a topographical rarity for the area, a small red hill flanked on the west by a large playa lake. While the detachment stopped there for a brief rest, Sgt. John B. Charleton observed from atop the hill what he first thought was a herd of buffalo off to the north. An alerted Lieutenant Albee observed the moving form on the horizon through his telescope and quickly exclaimed, "They are Indians, Sergeant, and they are going to attack us. Get your men ready for action."[3] Within minutes the scouts had formed a defensive square with the horses and handlers in the middle. Within ten minutes the Indians had completely encircled the square. The scouts opened fire and successfully broke through the cordon of circling Indians. A moving battle occurred over the next seven hours as the detachment retreated slowly along their own tracks. Shortly before 7 P.M. they arrived at the north rim of Tule Canyon, just above the main command's campsite. The Indians, upon seeing the large troop encampment, turned about and within minutes they were out of sight. The scouts had not sustained any losses but they had killed or wounded at least two of the attacking Kiowas and had disabled a sizable number of their horses. An hour after they had begun their retreat they struck an extremely large trail heading eastward, which Albee estimated to have been made by no less than fifteen hundred horses.[4] Strong, having returned from his solo scout to the east, related that he had observed three Indians and a driven herd of around one hundred horses heading north. Francisco Tefoya had also returned and reported trails in the west that led northeast.[5]

Mackenzie was convinced that the main Indian encampment had to be near and to the northeast. He turned his attention toward deceiving the Indians and to keeping the command's horses secure. If the main encampment were nearby the Indians, in desperation, would have only one tactical strategy in mind—to stampede the command's horses in order to stop the troops' movements. Mackenzie felt it best to divide the command and force the Indians to have to attack two separate campsites and decided to move the Second Battalion to another location.

The alternate site, selected during the morning's march, provided a good view of the First Battalion's campsite and had more than adequate grass for grazing the animals. As the Second Battalion moved out of the canyon and onto the plains the soldiers benefited from a bright autumn moon. One officer later wrote "the long column moved almost silently across the grassy plains, the hoofbeats deadened by the wet grass and softened clay soil, not a word being spoken, expecting every minute to come upon their foe."[6] At 10:30 P.M. the battalion went into bivouac in a series of ravines between upper Tule Canyon and Rock Creek Draw. All possible precautions were carried out to prevent a possible night attack to stampede the horses. Guard outposts were established in a circle around the site and the horses were staked out and hobbled with troopers sleeping close to the herds. The night passed without incident and the men received their first rest in sixteen hours.[7]

Before sunrise on September 26 Mackenzie again dispatched Francisco Tefoya to search for the main Indian camp. Shortly after sunrise a courier was dispatched to Captain Lawton with orders to get the supply train up as soon as possible. The Second Battalion remained in camp all day, allowing both men and animals a much-needed rest. At about 8 A.M. a mixed band of Quohada Comanches under Black Horse and several Kiowas under Big Bow were chasing buffalo on the plains near the head of Tule Canyon. Francisco Tefoya almost ran headlong into them and escaped by hiding his tracks among the buffalo herd. The Indians, while searching for Tefoya, discovered Mackenzie's camp near Rock Creek Draw. Tefoya reported his encounter to Mackenzie at noon.[8]

Shortly after sundown McLaughlin, as instructed, broke camp at Tule Spring and moved the First Battalion five miles to the southeast near a series of ravines on the east side of Rock Creek Draw. At 5 P.M. the Second Battalion had also moved to find more adequate grass and water and was camped less than a mile away in Rock Creek Draw. When McLaughlin left the campsite at Tule Spring he had instructed seven troopers to remain behind to tend the campfires until well after dark and then rejoin them at the new campsite. This was meant to be a ruse to confuse the Indians but it was subverted by a bright September moon. As these seven troopers made their way toward the new campsite, a band of around twenty Indians trailed them. The troopers exchanged shots with the Indians when it appeared they might get between them and the other commands. Henry, one of the Tonkawa scouts who was acting as a flanker for the First Battalion during its move out of Tule Canyon, also exchanged shots with the Indians and narrowly escaped an ambush. These incidents made the entire column certain that they were going to be visited by the Indians that night.[9]

181

Mackenzie scattered the companies in a circle around a saucer-shaped depression in which the horses were placed. Each horse was picketed on a one-inch rope, thirty feet long, with the picket stake driven fifteen inches into the ground. In addition, each horse was cross-lined, where a rope was looped around a foreleg and a similar loop was placed around the hind leg on the opposite side. As a final measure of security both forefeet were hobbled, or tied together with a two-foot length of rope. The horse could only move a few inches at a time, just enough to graze. If the animal attempted to run it would fall on its side.[10] An extensive system of guard posts around the perimeter was established before sundown. The men were ordered to sleep with their carbines and with their boots on so they would be able to react to any attack instantly. The various companies were dispersed in sleeping parties of from twelve to twenty men around the herd. Men from each of these parties manned the various guard outposts at intervals throughout the night. The guard outposts, from four to five hundred yards outside the command, were in ravines or other such features that allowed the men to observe the area with little chance of being seen by the Indians.[11]

At 9 P.M. the guard outposts had just undergone their second shift change. Pvt. Ernest Veuve of Company A nestled down at the head of a small ravine on the southwest side of the Second Battalion camp while Pvt. J. A. Magruder of Company F was on duty at the head of a ravine on the southwest edge of the First Battalion campsite. Pvt. Moses Goodwin of Company H was situated beside a small mesa-like rock formation on the northeast side of the Second Battalion campsite. His post was near the mouth of the ravine that separated the battalion campsites. Shortly after 10 P.M. the Indians launched a concerted attack. Private Veuve encountered a large band of around thirty or forty Cheyenne as they rode pell-mell toward his outpost. Unseen by the Indians until they were almost upon him, Veuve raised up and opened fire. The lead Indian's horse went down and the others turned about. Within seconds Cpl. Edwin Phoenix and several other troopers joined Veuve and together they unleashed a hail of fire at the shadowy figures on the southern horizon. Private Goodwin, hearing galloping ponies, yelled out the challenge and commenced firing when he received no reply. When Private Magruder opened fire the bedlam was complete. Muzzle flashes from Springfield carbines lit up the perimeters of the two camps.[12]

The Indians, thwarted in their initial attempt to stampede the horses, began their encircling tactic and fired sporadically throughout the night. The main body of Indians placed themselves upon the high ground just west of the Second Battalion and fired into the camp until well past midnight. Despite more than three hours of incoming fire from the Indians, only two of the command's horses

Lt. John A. McKinney, Col. Ranald S. Mackenzie's trusted adjutant. McKinney transcribed and submitted all Medal of Honor correspondence for the Fourth Cavalry from 1872 to 1875. The details of Mackenzie's secret pacts died with him on November 26, 1876, when he was killed by the Northern Cheyenne near the Powder River in Wyoming. The hardened Mackenzie wept uncontrollably when McKinney's body was brought into camp. *Photograph courtesy the National Archives.*

were wounded. One of these belonged to Lt. William A. Thompson, who was holding the animal at the time the bullet struck. Indians continued riding back and forth well past midnight. At times the Indians would shout curses in English at the soldiers. Some of the troopers' replies were equally uncomplimentary but for the most part the taunts were ignored and the troopers attempted to sleep, knowing that a big fight would soon occur. Around midnight, during a lull in the firing, Wagonmaster James O'Neal led a ten-wagon train into the south end of the First Battalion campsite with a much-needed supply of forage and ammunition. The Indians, intent upon their efforts to stampede the horses, did not notice the train's approach. The soft ground so muffled the sounds of the wagons that the Indians, who were galloping about and at times were involved in conversations about their future actions, did not hear them approach. By 2:30 A.M. the infantry troopers had established their camp and the scene was calm.[13]

At sunrise on September 27 the Indians resumed their long-range fire into both battalion campsites. Some of the Indians had worked their way up ravines to points within one hundred yards of some of the company positions on the north side of the encampments. Their fire became especially intense and threatening and within minutes the battalion trumpeters were arousing those bleary-eyed troopers who had not yet risen with their boots on ready for action. Officers raced about shouting, "Stand to your horses!" Pvt. John Comfort proceeded with reckless abandon to a nearby point on a ridge and fired rapidly down upon the Indians in the ravines. Henry Strong soon joined Comfort and together they fired upon the nearby Indians and suppressed their return fire. The firing was so intense that the Indians mounted and fled northward into the depths of Tule Canyon. Colonel Mackenzie, fearing any additional injury to the command, decided to dispatch troops to drive the remaining Indians away from the encampments. He ordered Captain Boehm to mount his troops and drive the Indians from the area. Boehm was given specific orders to proceed no more than two miles in doing so. The company herd guard, consisting of six troopers, eagerly sprang into action. Their horses, having been left saddled for just such a contingency, allowed them to be the first to mount and move out after the Indians. Captain Boehm and the remainder of the scouting detachment and Capt. Theodore Wint and his Company L were instructed to protect the flanks.[14]

Cpl. Edwin Phoenix, as corporal of the guard, led the five other troopers out of Rock Creek Draw and onto the flat plains to the southwest. Although an estimated 250 Kiowa, Comanche, Cheyenne, and Arapaho hovered around the command, a band of around a dozen Cheyenne appeared to be the most menacing. They all appeared to have firearms and they moved to intercept the Company E guard's advance. Corporal Phoenix and Pvt. Gregory Mahoney outpaced the other four troopers until they were almost two hundred yards in the lead. A hail of Cheyenne rifle and pistol fire zinged past but the two determined troopers continued their advance and opened fire with their Colt .45 pistols at fifty yards. Several Indian ponies went down, throwing their riders. Several more of the warriors were seen to reel as though wounded and they fled to the southwest. Within seconds Phoenix and Mahoney were among the remaining Cheyenne. Their now-empty pistols became handy clubs and a desperate hand-to-hand struggle ensued for several minutes before the Cheyenne turned and fled. Lieutenant Hatfield and the main body of Company E charged past in pursuit of the fleeing Indians.[15]

Boehm and the scouting detachment, in order to cover the right flank for Hatfield, had ridden down into Tule Canyon. As they proceeded up Tule Creek they came upon a grassy knoll where four Cheyenne sat holding their horses. The Indians quickly bolted to remount when they saw the approaching scouts. One of the Seminole scouts shot the horse from under one Indian and as the Indian ran across the canyon floor Tonkawa Charley ran him down and shot him.[16] Pvt. William McCabe and two Tonkawa scouts immediately chased two of the mounted Indians who were fleeing up the north incline of upper Tule Canyon. Tonkawa Henry dismounted and from a kneeling position aimed at one of the fleeing Indians. His first shot killed the horse of one Indian and threw him roughly to the ground. Henry quickly remounted and rode up to the dazed Indian. Before he could dismount, the Indian sprang to his feet and pulled Henry from his mount. Henry fumbled for his pistol, which was covered by the folds of a blanket worn around his waist. The Cheyenne began to beat Henry about the head with his bow while Henry fumbled to find his pistol. One of the scouts came to Henry's rescue and killed the Cheyenne with a single pistol shot.[17]

Private McCabe, while chasing the last of the four Indians, had emerged alone from Tule Canyon and was doggedly pursuing the Indian across the plains. McCabe passed isolated, startled, fleeing Indians whose horses had collapsed. After a mile this Indian, aware that he could not shake his pursuer, turned to confront him. He leveled his lance and charged as McCabe closed to within twenty yards. McCabe parried the first thrust of the lance and killed the Indian with a single shot. As Tonkawa Henry had begun his pursuit of the large, heavyset Cheyenne the third Indian had run up the incline a short distance. He suddenly turned and opened fire with his pistol upon Captain Boehm. Sergeant Charleton then shot the Indian once at twenty-five yards with his pistol. This Indian, immense in stature, only turned more defiant. Charleton emptied his pistol, striking the Indian at least five times, yet he remained standing. In the meantime this

Indian was still firing, not at Charleton, but at Captain Boehm, who was unable to return fire since his horse had become unmanageable. Charleton, in desperation, drew his Springfield carbine and with his third shot finally killed his determined foe.[18] Guide Henry Strong heard the firing and turned up a ravine toward the sounds. As he proceeded up the ravine, an Indian in full war regalia, painted white with red spots from head to toe, jumped down from a ledge into his path. This Indian attempted to seize the horse reins; Strong responded by killing him with a single shot from his carbine.[19]

By 7 A.M. the main body of the Indians had formed a line along the southwestern horizon. Lieutenant Hatfield and the main body of E Company in the center, bounded on the left by L Company and the remainder of the scout detachment on the right, continued their advance toward the Indian line. The Indians' strategy was not to confront but to draw the command away from the main Indian encampment. As the troops approached to within several hundred yards of the Indians they turned and fled to the southwest. On the northeast end of the line one Indian circled on his horse to taunt the troops. Henry Strong quickly tired of the Indian's antics and galloped between him and the main body of Indians and charged. After a quarter-mile chase Strong shot the Indian from his horse.[20] Captain Boehm then formed the troops into three compact columns of fours and chased the Indians. About one hundred and fifty yards behind the Indians they could easily see the Indians turning and firing. Lt. Charles Hatfield described the scene:

> Painted and strung with sleigh bells in full regalia, with everything to impress the imagination, it was highly spectacular. . . . Their gorgeous head dresses, otter skin scabbards, with bows and arrows, and occasional decorated spears held aloft as guidons and rifles held in their hands, were plainly visible.[21]

After pursuing the Indians for almost three miles Boehm called an end to the chase when he saw the Indians in the distance changing en masse to spare fresh horses from a cached herd. By the time Boehm and the troops arrived back at the Rock Creek Draw campsite, breakfast was waiting for them. The first offensive actions by the First Southern Column had cost the Indians at least six dead and several wounded at the cost of only three horses wounded within the command.

At 3 P.M. Mackenzie mounted the command and spent the next thirteen hours ordering a series of countermarches and quickly abandoned encampments to confuse the Indian spies. These ruses were successful and the command surprised the main Indian encampment in Palo Duro Canyon at 5:30 A.M. on September 28. The troopers' actions at Tule Canyon contributed to the preservation of the command's mobility and enhanced the success at Palo Duro Canyon. In the seven-hour engagement at Palo Duro Canyon more than four-teen hundred Indian horses were captured. Three Indians were confirmed killed and a much larger number were wounded; while the command incurred only one trooper wounded. Cpl. Edwin Phoenix, Pvts. Wiliam McCabe, Ernest Veuve, Gregory Mahoney, and John W. Comfort were foremost among those who demonstrated bravery during the action. McCabe, Veuve, and Comfort were in the advance over the rim and onto the canyon floor. McCabe was in the advance along the zigzagging trail into the canyon and was among the first to engage the Indian sentry near the canyon floor. Private Comfort further dis-tinguished himself by volunteering to make dangerous reconnaissance forays into sub-canyons to ascertain Indian concentrations. Corporal Phoenix and Private Mahoney further distinguished themselves by extricating Lt. Charles Callahan from a dangerously exposed position after his horse was killed under him, pinning him to the ground.[22]

By 1 P.M. the entire command had withdrawn from the canyon floor. Almost two hours were spent collecting the stock and organizing the command into a mov-ing square formation with the stock in the middle. Below them, the smoke from the burning lodges had completely obscured the canyon floor. For the next nine hours the captured herd of 1,424 ponies, colts, and mules were driven inside the moving corral toward the wagon train encampment at Tule Canyon. By 1:30 A.M. on September 29 most of the men had their first food and sleep in more than twenty-four hours. After only five and a half hours of sleep the troops were awakened. Mackenzie was ready to institute the final step in suppressing the Indian problem on the Texas frontier. Each company commander was ordered to select fit horses from the captured herd to replace those lost from their companies during the cam-paign. He next allowed the civilian guides and several Seminole-Negro scouts to select a total of sixty-five animals as a reward for their hazardous duty. Capt. J. B. Parke, Tenth U. S. Infantry, commander of the infantry battalion, was then ordered to shoot the remaining 1,046 colts, ponies, and mules, which proved to be a telling blow to the warring tribes of the South Plains. Dismounted, the Plains tribes were but a shadow of their once formidable mobile raiding capability.[23]

On January 7, 1875, Mackenzie filed his report on the troops' performance dur-ing the campaign. In one paragraph of this report he wrote, "The following enlisted men of the Fourth Cavalry are deserving in my opinion of Medals for gallantry, . . . of Company E, Corporal Phoenix and Privates McCabe and Mahoney."[24] On February 2, Adj. Gen. E. D. Townsend replied to Gen. C. C. Augur, commander of the Department of Texas, stating:

I have the honor to inform you that it is the ruling of the [War] Department that Medals of Honor can be awarded for special and distinguished service in Indian warfare, involving some act of conspicuous bravery or service above the ordinary duty of a soldier, the Secretary of War therefore desires that the particular acts of gallantry be stated in each case.[25]

This reply was forwarded to Mackenzie, who was stationed at Fort Sill, Indian Territory, on April 28, 1875. On August 31, 1875, Mackenzie replied directly to the adjutant general, stating:

I have the honor to designate the men of the Fourth Cavalry who particularly distinguished themselves during my late campaign against hostile Indians, with the particular act of gallantry of each, and to whom Medals of Honor were suggested to be awarded, as follows: Corporal Edwin Phoenix, Private William McCabe and Gregory Mahoney, Company E, were in the advance of the attack by Captain Boehm's company on a very large party of Cheyennes, and were strongly recommended by Captain Boehm for gallantry, September 27th.[26]

This reply was received by the adjutant general's office on September 24, 1875, and was immediately referred to the office of the secretary of war for official endorsement of the awards. On October 13, 1875, the secretary of war endorsed the awards and returned the endorsement to the Adjutant General's Office, stating, "Respectfully referred to the Adjutant General who will cause Medals of Honor to be properly engraved and transmitted to the Soldiers, the Farrier, and the Seminole Negro Scout named in the communication of Colonel Mackenzie of August 31, 1875."[27] On October 19, 1875, the adjutant general compiled and sent the official listing, stating, "I have respectfully to request that 'Medals of Honor' be engraved for the following men: Corporal Edwin Phoenix, Co. E, 4th U.S. Cavalry, Private William McCabe, Co. E, 4th U.S. Cavalry, Private Gregory Mahoney, Co. E, 4th U.S. Cavalry."[28] After engraving, the medals were sent to each recipient via registered mail. Cpl. Edwin Phoenix had been discharged from the Fourth Cavalry and had reenlisted in the Third U. S. Infantry. He received his Medal of Honor from Capt. Charles Hobart at Holly Springs, Mississippi, on November 5, 1875.[29] Pvt. Gregory Mahoney's Medal of Honor was sent to him at Fort Elliott, Texas, where he acknowledged its receipt on January 28, 1876.[30] Pvt. William McCabe had been discharged from the army for a disability on May 30, 1875, and was serving as a civilian guide for the U. S. Army Quartermaster Department at Fort Brown, Texas, where he acknowledged receipt of his Medal of Honor on January 28, 1876.[31]

Only four short years after the actions at Tule and Palo Duro Canyons the buffalo were virtually exterminated from the Southern Great Plains. By that time the canyons and plains of Northwest Texas had become home to some of the largest and most productive cattle ranches in the world. The cowboy culture became forever a part of the heritage of the Lone Star State. This heritage was significantly engendered by the heroic and energetic actions of young United States Army troopers like Edwin Phoenix, William McCabe, and Gregory Mahoney.

Cpl. John W. Comfort, circa 1877. As part of the Fourth U.S. Cavalry Comfort participated in engagements at the Big Bend of the Brazos River, Red Hill, Palo Duro Canyon, and Laguna Tahoka. He was cited for gallantry in action after an engagement near Laguna Tahoka on November 5, 1874. *Photograph courtesy the National Archives.*

CHAPTER 15

Gallantry on the High Plains

November 3 and 5, 1874

Pvt. John W. Comfort   Pvt. Ernest Veuve

By the first week of October 1874 the United States Army's strategy of using five columns of troops to converge, drive, and harass the hostile Southern Plains tribes was beginning to elicit the desired results. Col. Nelson A. Miles enthusiastically confirmed the expedition's results when he reported:

> This command is driving large numbers of Indians in the direction of the Cheyenne Agency where I believe they will surrender if not to these forces, they are traveling rapidly in their endeavor to escape our forces. The expedition is operating in four columns with gratifying success.[1]

The success of the strategy could definitely be seen upon the various tribal reservations in the Indian Territory. Trails from the west were flooded with large numbers of Indians eager to be free from the constant pursuit of the troops. Near Fort Sill, notorious, recalcitrant chiefs such as Satanta, White Horse, Big Tree, White Wolf, and Tabananica had succumbed to the harassment and surrendered themselves and their bands.[2] Further north at the Cheyenne–Arapaho Agency only a few sub-chiefs and their bands had surrendered. They reported that only small bands under Big Horse and Big Horn had decided to come in and would arrive in a few days. Interpreters quickly set about interrogating prisoners for information about the bands still remaining out. The tribe with the largest number of members still out appeared to be the Cheyenne.[3] At Palo Duro Canyon they had occupied the most distant camps and had escaped with most of their horses and supplies. Among the Cheyenne still out were the bands of Stone Calf,

Gray Beard, Cloud Chief, Medicine Water, Medicine Arrow, Heap of Birds, White Horse, and Howling Wolf. These bands comprised an estimated 1,000 members, including approximately 350 warriors.[4] Next largest of the Indian groups still off the reservation were the Quohadas, the mixed bands of Comanches, Kiowas and Kiowa–Apaches who had never registered on any reservation. Among them were the bands under Black Horse, Wild Horse, Isatai, Otterbelt, and Quanah. Their bands numbered an estimated six hundred members including an estimated one hundred warriors. Also thought to be living with the Quohadas was the Kiowa band of Big Bow. None of the Indians interrogated knew of this band's exact whereabouts, but it was believed to be among the canyons on the eastern edge of the plains or on the lagunas of the South Plains. Big Bow had an estimated twenty-five warriors with him. Still another band refusing to surrender were the Ay-Chat or Cold Weather Kiowas. Their membership numbered an estimated 250, among them 70 warriors led by Lone Wolf, Poor Buffalo, Maman-ti, To-hausen, and Red Otter. Somehow all of these bands had evaded the columns of troops and the scouting detachments sent to search for them. Somewhere in the vastness of Northwest Texas these recalcitrant bands remained as potentially dangerous adversaries who would have to be located, captured, or driven into the reservations for the expedition to be considered successful. The primary objective of the expedition's second sweep was to find these elusive bands.[5]

After destroying the combined Kiowa, Comanche, and Cheyenne winter encampment in Palo Duro Canyon the main southern column under Col. R. S. Mackenzie backtracked to consolidate, rest, and re-supply. The areas around Palo Duro needed to be thoroughly reconnoitered to determine the direction of the Indians' flight. By October 5, in spite of severe weather, the command had advanced north and then east to a point ten miles east of the head of Mulberry Creek Canyon. On the morning of October 6 Mackenzie decided not to resume the march as the command had struggled through mud the entire previous day. At 3 P.M., however, he decided to mount the command, except for the supply wagons, and move northeast. Throughout the late afternoon the horses, often sinking knee-deep into the mud, had to be led by their dismounted riders. Mackenzie finally halted the command at 8 P.M. near a playa lake at the head of Mulberry Creek Canyon. During the five-hour march the command had covered only ten miles of terrain.[6]

At daybreak on October 7 a mild wet norther struck just as the command was preparing to break camp. Mackenzie's decision to go ahead with the march drew a great deal of disfavor from both the officers and enlisted men, who questioned why he was pushing the command to the point of severe debilitation. After two hours, about five miles into the march, the command came upon six Mexican ox carts loaded with dried meat. The fifteen men with the cart train claimed to be buffalo hunters. Mackenzie angrily launched into a tirade, telling them that he suspected they had traded arms and ammunition to the Indians. His outburst ended with the order that they were all under arrest, and were placed in chains under armed guards.[7] Many of the officers and enlisted men sympathized with the Mexicans as just a few hours before they had been on the receiving end of Mackenzie's angry tirades. After interrogating each of the prisoners Mackenzie finally culled two, José P. Tafoya and Theodore Valdez, from the others and induced the two to serve as guides with the promise to release the others. Mackenzie agreed to pay Valdez and Tafoya fifty dollars a month, the usual pay for quartermaster department guides.[8] Mackenzie, apparently, without the knowledge of anyone else in the command, had successfully pulled off a secret deal that he had made almost a year earlier with Valdez and Tafoya.[9] Both had been involved in the trade for years and knew the plains like the back of their hands and since Valdez had spent much time among the Quohadas he knew all of their haunts.[10]

At 5 A.M. on October 8 several parties of scouts left camp to follow trails discovered the previous evening and to reconnoiter the surrounding country. A scouting party comprised of Lieutenant Thompson, Henry Strong, and several Tonkawa Indian scouts headed southeast. After an hour spent skirting the ravines on the western edge of Mulberry Canyon, Strong observed three heads peering over the edge of a nearby ravine, but when they arrived at the ravine to investigate no one could be seen. In the canyon below them they saw a single ox-drawn cart, but when they reached the cart they found only a teenage boy, who claimed he was there to dispense government clothing to the Indians. Colonel Mackenzie was summoned to the scene. While encamped there, three New Mexicans rode into the camp and said they were with the boy and the ox cart, but claimed they were only there to hunt buffalo. Mackenzie became incensed at the disparity between the two stories and ordered the wagon burned. Just as he had the previous day he launched into a verbal tirade and warned the three to stay off the plains. The three New Mexicans and two burros were released and they hastily set forth for New Mexico.[11]

Anxious to recuperate and revamp the command in order to commence the second sweep operations, Mackenzie decided to return to the main supply base in Blanco Canyon. During the fifteen-day return march he dispatched several reconnaissance teams to investigate the locations of suspected Indian haunts provided by the New Mexicans. One of Mackenzie's first orders upon arriving at the main base was to instruct each company commander to cull from his ranks any unserviceable mounts and troopers of questionable physical stamina. As a result it was found that the seven cavalry companies could mount only 181 able-bodied troopers on an equal number of questionably able mounts. With this in mind Mackenzie decided to reinstate and increase the size of the enlisted scout detachment, which would enable larger areas of terrain to be scouted and prevent unnecessary movements by the main command. Each of the seven men selected for the detachment were selected from a large pool of volunteers and were paid an extra fifty dollars a month for the rigorous and dangerous demands placed upon them. Detached from their assigned companies, the enlisted scouts became the responsibility of Captain Boehm and Lieutenant Thompson and served along with the Seminole-Negro and Tonkawa Indian scouts and the civilian guide contingent.

By October 25 the detachment's composition was finalized and included: Sgt. John B. Charleton and Pvts. William McCabe, John W. Comfort, William Rankin, Frank Fitzgerald, Richard Mansfield, and Robert Shiels. The eldest of the group was William Rankin, whose two decades of service in the U.S. Army included Civil War combat in some of the most daring and dangerous cavalry engagements of the conflict. His pre- and post–Civil War service in Indian campaigns had rendered him an excellent tracker. When most of his fellow detachment members were still children he had been trailing Satanta and his band through the foothills of southeastern Colorado. He was without question the best mule packer in the regiment, an extremely critical skill in highly mobile detachments.[12]

Richard "Dick" Mansfield at age thirty-one was the second oldest of the group. The Ireland-born Mansfield was the quiet, aggressive type, who had gained a reputation as a walking commissary depot and whose excellent butcher skills could render a buffalo carcass into a week's supply of fillets in minutes. The detachment depended on his skills for quick sustenance while away from the main supply camp. At times Lieutenant Thompson would also detach additional men from his Company A to accompany the detachment. One such trooper so assigned for the second sweep was Pvt. Ernest Veuve. Dependable, brave and intelligent, Veuve was also proficient in Spanish, and on this scout his skills as an expert farrier would be critical. He was to be in charge of caring for the needs of the detachment's livestock. The most intriguing member of the detachment was William McCabe. A longtime resident of Mexico, he had labored for years in the silver mines of Chihuahua. During the French occupation of Mexico he had served as a scout for the Mexican Loyalist forces of Gen. Ignacio Zaragosa.

194

Mackenzie was so impressed with McCabe's skills that he allowed him to enlist and be assigned to the regiment without undergoing basic training. McCabe's intrepid attack upon a large band of Cheyenne warriors at Tule Canyon in September had proven he was fearless in action. His fluency in Spanish had proven to be an invaluable asset to Mackenzie in his dealings with the New Mexican Comancheros.[13]

Pvt. Robert Shiels of Wayne, Ohio, like so many farmers of the era, found himself displaced by market upheaval. His short, stocky stature in no way detracted from his tenaciousness and intelligence. Capt. Eugene B. Beaumont was so impressed with Shiels's abilities that he promoted him to sergeant in the unusual span of two years. The reduction of sergeant slots under army reorganization in 1873 had placed Shiels back into the private soldier ranks.[14]

The unquestioned possessor of the most unmitigated gall and audacity was Pvt. John W. Comfort. Philadelphia-born and reared, Comfort had gone against his family's wishes in 1862 to enlist and fight during the Civil War. He rose quickly to the rank of corporal with the Twenty-ninth Pennsylvania Infantry. He had personally led his squad into the killing fields at Chancellorsville and at Gettysburg he had deftly handled his men to repel part of Jeb Stuart's brigade at Rock Creek. Later, at the battle of Chattanooga, he led his squad in a race to the top of Lookout Mountain amid often bitter hand-to-hand fighting. His promotion to sergeant only intensified his efforts. Gallant conduct at Resaca, Pine Log Creek, and Atlanta brought Comfort and his company to the attention of Gen. W. T. Sherman, who was so impressed with the unit's performance that he selected Comfort's company as one of the pathfinder units in his march to the sea at Savannah. After the war Comfort reenlisted in the regular army and served a three-year enlistment with the First United States Artillery. The boredom of Reconstruction duty sent him into the early stages of alcoholism and his drinking habits often led him into serious trouble as he became insubordinate, often mutinous, and difficult to control. He left the First Artillery amid such difficulties and his condition got no better at his civilian job as a streetcar conductor in Philadelphia. Disenchanted, he reenlisted in the Fourth Cavalry in April 1870. He was where he wanted to be—wherever there might be action. He had participated in two campaigns onto the Staked Plains and knew the terrain as well as anyone in the regiment.[15]

Pvt. Frank Fitzgerald from Chicago had an obscure background. It was believed that his expertise in firearms was gained through civilian employment at the St. Louis Arsenal. Post-war reductions in the civilian workforce had forced him to cast his fate with the army. Pvt. Edward J. O'Brien was the odd man in the detachment. Born into an upper-middle-class family in Poughkeepsie, New York, he had been educated as an engineer. His desire to serve as a scout was likely a quest for adventure and excitement. His abilities to draw maps and to quickly construct wooden frames for makeshift shelters, wash basins, and other camping necessities made him a valuable asset to the detachment.[16] The young-ster of the detachment was also its only non-commissioned officer. Sgt. John B. Charleton, a Bowling Green, Virginia, native, had left home to satisfy his wan-derlust in the west. He had served under Sgt. John W. Comfort in the First United States Artillery from 1865 to 1868. Energetic, intelligent, and aggressive, Charleton was the detachment's unquestioned leader.[17]

During the mid-morning hours of October 25 the scouts who were sent out from Cottonwood Springs on October 21 began to return to the supply camp. By late afternoon the last of the scouts had returned. By sundown Francisco Tafoya, Tonkawa Sergeant Johnson, Seminole-Negro Sgt. John Ward, and the civilian guide, Henry Strong, had conferred and reported to Lieutenant Thompson about their sightings. The two larger groups of scouts had been dispatched into the Muchaque and Quitaque Peak areas. Small trails leading off to the southwest had been reported in the Quitaque Peak area. The group scouting the Muchaque Peak area had reported no fresh Indian signs. Guide Henry Strong had drawn the most difficult and dangerous assignment—he made a solo scout into the area of the playa lakes west of Palo Duro Canyon. He, too, returned with news of no major encampments but he had observed numerous small trails crossing his line of travel, all moving to the southwest. The scouts dispatched directly west had also observed numerous small trails. After listening to Thompson's summary of the scouting reports, Mackenzie decided that the most opportune area for the second sweep would be to the west onto the plains located above the headwaters of the Double Mountain Fork of the Brazos.[18] Uncertainty about the size of possible Indian concentrations forced Mackenzie to alter his previous plan and retain Companies F and K for the second sweep. The highly debilitated condition of Captain Boehm's company dictated that it be left behind as previously planned.[19]

At 5:45 P.M. on October 30 Mackenzie led his nearly two hundred-man column out of the cavalry camp in a southwesterly direction following the trail of the scouting detachment. After thirteen miles the command made a turn to the west and ascended onto the plains near midnight.[20] Temperatures plummeted over the next two hours and by 3 A.M. the command was struggling through a blinding snowstorm. Shortly before sunrise the command took shelter in Plum Creek arroyo and remained there throughout the daylight hours.[21] The command resumed its advance at sundown after the sleet and snow had stopped falling. After moving northwest for three miles they reached the mouth of Rescate Canyon. By midnight the command had traversed the canyon mouth and had turned northwest along Rescate Canyon's western rim. After twelve miles the entire command arrived at Buffalo Springs and went into camp shortly before sunrise.[22]

November 1 was muster day, the day each month when roll calls for personnel accountability were required. With this in mind Mackenzie kept the command encamped for the day. After covering fifty miles in sixteen hours of riding amid harshly cold temperatures, the troops welcomed the rest. Unfortunately for the scouting detachment, Thompson was the first to submit his completed muster rolls. The scouts knew that any time Mackenzie made camp long enough to unsaddle and graze the horses, he also dispatched the scouts to reconnoiter the surrounding area. With this in mind Thompson had his men saddle their mounts so they would be ready to move out on a short notice. Their preparations were justified, for within an hour of receiving Thompson's muster rolls, Mackenzie ordered the scout detachment to mount up. Thompson and the enlisted scout detachment rode up the west canyon rim toward the north. After several miles Thompson split the detachment into two groups. He and several of the men rode down into the canyon, crossed the river, and continued their northward movement searching out the side canyons and arroyos on the north side of the canyon. Henry Strong and the second group continued along the south rim of the canyon. After about eight miles Thompson's group observed several mounted Indians riding into the mouth of a side canyon. Thompson, along with Rankin, McCabe, and Mansfield, charged into the canyon and into the Indians' small camp. The Indians had fled to the head of the sub-canyon and galloped off to the northwest. Strong's group, having observed the incident from the far rim, broke into a gallop in an attempt to intercept the Indians near the head of Rescate. According to Strong, they were late and were forced to chase after the fleeing Indians. Four of the Indians lagged behind and Strong gained on them. Dismounting, he drew out his sporting rifle and opened fire, killing two of the men while a woman and another man managed to outdistance his rifle's range and escape over a rise to the west. The detachment returned to the Indian camp and found several items indicating that the band apparently had just returned from a raid into the settlements. The detachment returned to the Buffalo Spring campsite just before sundown. Mackenzie, now certain that there was an Indian presence in the area, decided to resume the march along the tracks of this fleeing band.[23]

At 9 A.M. on November 2 the command marched west out of Rescate Canyon and onto the plains. Several hours into the march the command's collective suspicions were verified—single Indian videttes could be seen to the right on the distant horizon. Mackenzie knew that their appearance was meant to draw the command away from their camps; he did not accommodate them and turned the command toward the playa lakes to the southwest. The scouting detachment was dispatched at a trot to force the Indian spies to constantly move and change their positions. They maintained their changing positions only along the north and western horizons. Mackenzie had seen this cat-and-mouse routine before and was determined to play the game to the hilt. Shortly after sunset and after having traveled west and southwestward twenty-seven miles the command went into camp. Sentry outposts were set up at unusually far distances to guard against stampede attempts. At Mackenzie's direction the camp was to be a cold camp, with no fires allowed.[24]

Shortly after midnight on November 3 the command was wakened and thirty minutes later the troopers were moving southwestward at a trot. Theodore Valdez now proved his worth by guiding the advance scouting detachment across the treeless plains in the darkness. Just at sunrise the command arrived at the north end of Laguna Rica as planned. The surrounding area had abundant grass but only a single small seep provided fresh water, wholly insufficient for the needs of the command. The water in Laguna Rica, like most playa lakes of the region, was brackish and highly alkaloid in content and was unfit for human consumption. The abundant grass was also an indication that sizable numbers of Indians and their herds had not frequented the site. Both men and animals needed a rest so the command went into camp for breakfast and rest.[25]

By 8 A.M. Dick Mansfield and Henry Strong had bacon frying and coffee boiling. The atmosphere around the enlisted scouts' campfire was quite jovial. Their joy over eating for the first time in twelve hours was short-lived as they were in the saddle again by 10 A.M. The enlisted scouts had been dispatched eastward, while the Tonkawas, Seminole-Negroes, and the New Mexican guides were dispatched to the southeast toward Laguna Quatro. Moving intermittently at a trot, the enlisted scouts quickly traveled nine miles and arrived at the north end of Laguna Sombiga (Mound Lake) shortly after noon.[26] By the time the main command arrived on the scene the enlisted scouts had been resting for more than two hours. After informing Mackenzie that no Indian signs had been located north of the line of march, the enlisted scouts again resumed their march eastward. Mackenzie and the main command followed at a leisurely pace so as to maintain close proximity to the other scouting parties, which were at or near Laguna Quatro. After nine miles of difficult riding through a sandy, chin oak-studded terrain, Charleton's group arrived at the southern tip of the southernmost of the Double Lakes.[27]

Mackenzie and the remainder of the command arrived shortly before 4 P.M. Though there was sufficient water, the site had no wood, insufficient grass, and was badly exposed to the cold winds. Mackenzie wanted a better campsite if possible and requested that several parties of scouts reconnoiter the area for a more suitable locale. Henry Strong and Privates Comfort and Veuve were dispatched to reconnoiter northeastward along the western shore of Double Lake. Shortly after starting out the three ran into the wagon ruts left by the 1872 expedition's supply wagons, a trail that led northwestward between the two lakes. Just as the trio neared the southern tip of the northernmost lake a fresh trail of twenty-eight shod and unshod horses intersected the wagon trail from the southeast. Comfort turned back to inform Mackenzie of the discovery. Strong and Veuve loaded their weapons and stuffed extra cartridges into their overcoat pockets as they galloped off to follow the tracks. After less than a mile the tracks veered to the northeast. After three miles they came to a running freshwater stream that flowed southward into the lake. When they stopped to water their mounts Strong unsheathed his marine telescope and scanned the lower terrain to the east and northeast. One mile to the northeast he observed several plumes of smoke. Remounting, the two rode over a rise and discovered to their surprise a sizable horse herd below them to the left in a small, shallow, valley-like depression.[28] They also saw the main command approaching rapidly less than half a mile to their rear. Strong and Veuve unsheathed their carbines and began their advance on the now-visible village, which was on the south side of a small playa lake. Slowing to a trot to allow the main command to catch up, the two were able to approach within one hundred yards of the still unsuspecting village. When they were within twenty-five yards of the closest and most prominent lodge, three Indian men suddenly jumped up. Apparently aroused by the massive pounding noise of the main command's hoof beats on the exposed gypsum bedrock, they began running toward the far end of the village. Strong quickly shot the trailing Indian and the other two hastened their flight. Strong spurred his mount toward the second Indian while Veuve, having dismounted, chased after the third. Just as Strong passed near the third Indian, the Indian drew a pistol and raised it to fire at Strong. Veuve, just a few feet behind, dove into the Indian and knocked him to the ground. The two struggled on the ground briefly before Veuve killed him with a pistol shot. Strong continued to pursue his adversary and killed the Indian near the entryway to a lodge.[29]

Mackenzie, at the head of the main command, entered the village a few minutes afterward. The command's approach from the west had caught the Indians completely off guard. The three Indians killed in the brief encounter were the only able-bodied males in the village. The quick envelopment of the village had resulted in the complete surprise and capture of the other village inhabitants. Nineteen women and children were eventually ferreted out from the various lodges.[30] As it was near sundown Mackenzie decided to camp at the village site for the night. During that evening the captives were extensively interrogated, from which it was learned that the other male inhabitants of the village were out looking for the soldiers. Mackenzie's night marches and cold camps, so cursed by the troops, had confounded the Indians. These Indians had also been expecting a band of Cheyenne from the west to join them. The camp of these Indians as best could be determined belonged to the Quohada Comanche band headed by the sub-chief, Patch-o-ko-naiky, translated as Beaver.[31] Among the captives was an elderly white woman who had been held by the Indians since she was a child. She had been captured near San Antonio and remembered little of her past. Another of the captives was an elderly Mexican woman whom Henry Strong recognized as having been among those captured on the North Fork of the Red River in 1872. While interrogating her it was learned that the other males from the village were with the Cheyenne. They also learned that the Kiowa-Apaches had left a month earlier for the mountains west of the Pecos River and that the Quohadas under Mow-wi had left for the reservation. If this information was correct then the Indians indeed were in severe disarray. Mackenzie was elated about the information. The count of the horses discovered during the approach to the village was 144, which were divided among the scouts.[32]

The command remained in the village until noon on November 5. After burying the three dead Indians and allowing everyone a hot meal, the scouts were dispatched to lead out to the east. By 11 A.M. Thompson and the enlisted scouts, along with Henry Strong, were in the saddle riding eastward. Mackenzie and the main command followed with the captured herd and the prisoners in tow. After eight miles the enlisted scouts selected a campsite near the southwestern edge of Lake Tahoka. Tahoka was a Comanche word for fresh water but the scouts soon learned that this did not apply to the lake waters, which were found to be extremely brackish and bitter. Informed earlier by the New Mexicans of the general location of three freshwater springs on the northwest side of the lake, the scouts quickly remounted and rode off along the west shore of the lake. After two and a half miles the detachment came to a small Indian encampment that had been abandoned in great haste apparently just minutes earlier. About two hundred yards away five Indians were seen running down the incline toward a gully.[33] Although the precise details of what transpired over the next half hour are unclear it appears that Private Comfort assumed an extremely aggressive

The Sgt. Ernest Veuve Building at the U.S. Army Reserve Training Center at Fort Missoula, Montana, was dedicated to the memory of Indian Wars veteran Ernest Veuve in 1972. *Photograph courtesy Wilbur George Allen.*

stance in engaging these Indians. The Indians disappeared into the ravine where they had hidden their own mounts and a herd of horses. Three of the Indians were mounted by the time the scouts arrived at the gully. The scouts opened fire as they charged over the rise. A fourth Indian had just mounted but the firing from the scouts stampeded the horse from the grasp of the fifth. He ran to catch up with the others as they bolted up the ravine to the northwest but fell under a hail of pistol fire. The Indians' route of escape enabled several of the enlisted scouts, including Private Comfort, to intercept the Indians from the side. Comfort, realizing the value of the small herd of horses the Indians were driving, became determined to cut them away. Brazenly charging into their midst, he opened fire with his pistol and within minutes had successfully turned the herd away from the Indians, who fled, lucky to escape with their lives. As Comfort had charged in among the fleeing Indians and turned the herd back, his attention was directed toward one Indian who appeared to be directing the others. Comfort spurred his mount toward this Indian, who turned about and bolted back down the incline toward the southeast. This Indian was evidently intent upon escaping into the broken terrain along the escarpment ten miles to the southeast. Not aware of the destruction of the nearby village he may also have wanted to divert the scouts in the opposite direction. On a lighter and fresher mount, he obviously felt that he could outdistance the scouts. While the other scouts became involved with the other Indians and their scattered herd, Comfort focused on the Indian to his front. As Comfort's mount settled into a steady gallop Comfort must have wondered about the Indian's intentions. By now more than a mile separated him from his fellow scouts, who were moving in the opposite direction after the other Indians and their scattered herd.[34]

Sergeant Charleton, having known Comfort personally for almost a decade, later would allay Comfort's ferocity in combat to, "something in Comfort's past which made him seek death rather than shun it."[35] Despite the fact that his military career had been punctuated with incidents of drunken insubordination, Comfort was, above all, a soldier, duty-bound to accomplish his assignments. Whatever his motivations in continuing the chase, Comfort quickly realized that he would never be able to overtake the lighter and fresher Indian pony. His mount was slowing and the distance between him and the fleeing Indian had slowly widened to more than two hundred yards. The fleet Indian pony was fast, but not as fast as a Sharps-propelled .50-caliber slug. Pulling up on the reins, Comfort drew his mount to a halt and in an instant he was kneeling on the ground unleashing rapid fire at the fleeing Indian. The Indian pony went down quickly and threw its rider to the ground. The Indian scrambled to his feet and began running across the plain. Comfort sprinted after him, with the chase continuing for another quarter of a mile before the Indian became convinced that he could not elude his pursuer and turned to meet him. Comfort, with his Sharps carbine leveled, advanced to within yards of his adversary. Confident that this Indian would be able to provide valuable information, Comfort moved to the side and waved the barrel of his gun toward their previous path. To a warrior, capture was a devastating humiliation. Enraged, the Indian drew out a knife and lunged at Comfort, who ended the confrontation by killing the Indian with a single shot from his carbine.[36] By the time Comfort returned to the scene of the original clash the main command had arrived. Comfort came in leading his horse, which was piled high with accoutrements taken from the dead Indian and his pony. These items, along with articles found at the abandoned Indian camp, and the captured herd of twenty-seven branded horses, proved without a doubt that these Comanches had just returned from a raid into the Texas frontier settlements. Mackenzie was elated at the results of the action.[37]

At the campaign's end Mackenzie submitted a report of his column's activities. As a part of that report dated January 7, 1875, Mackenzie designated eight enlisted troopers, among them Veuve and Comfort, who, in his opinion, distinguished themselves during the campaign and who deserved Medals of Honor.[38]

On February 2, 1875, the War Department replied to the Department of Texas commander and requested that Mackenzie submit another report in which the particular acts of gallantry were stated in each case. On August 31, 1875, while stationed at Fort Sill, Indian Territory, Mackenzie penned a reply in which he stated the particular act of gallantry for each recommended recipient.[39] The citation submitted for Pvt. Ernest Veuve stated, "for the very gallant manner in which he faced a desperate Indian, November 3." Beyond mention of Comfort's gallant deed in "running down and killing an Indian on the Staked Plains with no other soldier within a long distance of him, November 5," he further added, "This man is a very distinguished soldier for personal gallantry." In closing, Mackenzie summarized, "that those mentioned have come either under my own notice or have been brought in a marked way to my knowledge."[40] On October 13, 1875, the secretary of war officially conferred award of the medals by requesting that the adjutant general's office have the Medals of Honor properly engraved and transmitted to the eight men Colonel Mackenzie had designated.[41] The adjutant general forwarded the official listing of the recipient's names and units to the chief clerk of the war department on October 19. The medals were engraved and mailed to the recipient's duty stations on October 29, 1875.[42]

Private Veuve's Medal of Honor was forwarded to his duty station at Holly Springs, Mississippi. According to Private Veuve's letter acknowledging his receipt of the medal, it was presented to him on November 5, 1875, by his commanding officer, Capt. Charles Hobart.[43] This letter and the station and regimental records make no mention of a formal award ceremony. Captain Hobart likely presented it to him in the adjutant's office in the presence of those clerks and officers present. The Medal of Honor awarded to Pvt. John W. Comfort was received at Fort Sill on or around December 15, 1875, and was then forwarded to his temporary duty station at Cantonment on the Sweetwater in the Texas Panhandle. He received it on or around January 28, 1876, and post and regimental records make no mention of a formal ceremony.[44]

Frank D. Baldwin, one of only five men to be awarded two Congressional Medals of Honor by the Army. The first was for a Civil War deed and the second was for his wagon attack on Gray Beard's Cheyenne encampment in present-day Gray County, Texas. *Photograph courtesy the Library of Congress.*

CHAPTER 16

Baldwin's Battlewagons to the Rescue

November 8, 1874

Lt. Frank D. Baldwin

T he sun was only two hours above the eastern horizon on September 11, 1874, but it had already caused beads of sweat to form on John German's forehead. As the Fannin County, Georgia, native walked along the old stage trail near the Smokey Hill River in northwestern Kansas his steps were more sprightly than they had been in almost a decade. He was now less than a month away from completing a nine-year-long dream of moving his family to Denver, Colorado. German and his family had left their home and kin near Morgantown, Georgia, on April 10, 1870. Over the next four years the family moved progressively westward, stopping long enough to work to finance the next segment of the journey.[1]

John German led the way as he had since leaving Georgia, walking about fifty yards ahead of the family's ox-drawn wagon. Atop the wagon seat were his wife, Lydia, and his oldest daughter, Rebecca, who wielded the light whip above the oxen occasionally to prod their labored movement. Lydia, John's wife of twenty-one years, had raised seven children, each of whom could be depended upon to pull their weight in responsibilities. Even now the youngest of the brood, Sophia, Julia, and Adelaide, rested in the back of the wagon after having helped their mother prepare breakfast and repack the wagon. Eighteen-year-old Stephen and his younger sister Catherine were tending the family's small livestock herd, which was drinking from the trickling waters of the Smokey Hill River.[2]

Stephen and Catherine suddenly heard the snapping of twigs and the sound of horses. A band of Indians emerged yelling and whooping from the timber and dashed up the incline. Stephen was the first to see them and he screamed out the alarm, "Indians, Indians!" The Indians were a raiding band of Cheyenne led by Kicking Horse, who apparently had been waiting in ambush.[3] Stephen and Catherine broke into a run. John German heard his son's alarm and started running toward the wagon. His dream of building a new life in Denver ended seconds later when a Cheyenne warrior shot him in the back. Lydia jumped screaming from the wagon and ran toward John only to be intercepted by a large, heavyset, mounted warrior. He grabbed her by the hair and she pleaded to him, "Oh, let me get to father!"[4] She was shot point-blank in the chest and fell with her arms outstretched toward John. Rebecca, enraged, grabbed a hand ax and jumped from the wagon and attacked the heavyset, mounted warrior until another Indian shot and killed her. Stephen was chased down and riddled with arrows. Catherine was wounded in the thigh by an arrow, then seized by another Cheyenne, who jerked the arrow out and kicked her repeatedly before throwing her on his horse. As they rode up to the wagon Catherine reeled in shock and horror as she saw her mother, father, and sister's bodies being scalped and mutilated. Other Indians swarmed over the wagon in a frenzy. Joanna, Sophia, Julia, and Addie were pulled screaming from the wagon. They were all crying with terror, which only evinced roars of laughter from the Cheyenne. The girls' bonnets were jerked off to expose their hair. Joanna, a sweet-natured, pudgy fifteen-year-old with long, flowing blonde hair was pulled aside. As the others were herded away they heard a rifle shot and turned to see their sister dying on the ground. Several Indians fought to claim her scalp but after a short argument Joanna's scalp was reserved for the Indian who had shot her. After killing the oxen and burning the wagon, several minutes more were spent distributing the hostages and booty. The attack had lasted only about fifteen minutes. After a few more minutes of mutilating the deceased and pillaging, the jubilant Cheyenne galloped south amid cries and whoops of victory.[5]

As the blood of the German family slowly seeped into the Kansas soil, other tragic scenes were unfolding at approximately the same time. Some two hundred miles south near the Washita River in Texas, a young teamster, James McCoy, was gasping his last breath of life. Wounded two days before in a fight with hostile Kiowa and Comanche warriors, he at least had the consolation of comfort and care from friends in his losing struggle to survive his wounds. Sixty miles to the southwest, Pvt. James H. Pettyjohn was set upon by a band of Kiowa warriors while he was looking for a lost journal. He, too, was killed and mutilated, but unlike the German family he was at least accorded a dignified burial surrounded by friends.

Private Pettyjohn's funeral had only compounded the despair of the soldiers of the northern column of the Indian Territory expedition. They had been sent by their government to enforce the dictum of a treaty and to force hostile Plains Indian tribes onto their designated reservations. Many within the United States Army now felt that their government was grossly negligent in its commitment to support their efforts. It was doubly galling to believe, with reasonable suspicion, that Private Pettyjohn's death and those of other recent victims of Indian depredations were likely inflicted by firearms and ammunition that government-licensed traders had sold to the Indians. For Colonel Miles it was even more embittering to see his troops in a near state of starvation, while fleeing bands of Indians were able to abandon vast quantities of foodstuffs to the elements. The cavalry troops sent after Pettyjohn's killers returned after less than an hour of pursuit. Though on the chase within minutes of the killing, the poor condition of their horses forced them to abandon the chase even when they still had the culprits in sight. The troopers' despair about the Pettyjohn incident had elicited serious doubts about the expedition. The army general staff, however, was determined to stay the course. They firmly believed from previous experiences that the Plains tribes could not sustain their mobility during the winter. This belief was based upon sound, well-known animal science that freezing temperatures destroyed the nutrient value of grass. Without these nutrients the Indian ponies would eventually weaken to the point of rendering their riders immobile, which would force the Indians into winter encampments that would become the primary targets for the pursuing army columns. The success of this strategy was solely incumbent upon the ability of the Quartermaster Department to provide enough forage to maintain the strength of the cavalry horses. The troops in the field believed that the inadequate forage shipments coupled with the torrid pace of movements would break down their mounts long before the Indian ponies weakened. The killing of Private Pettyjohn and the short-lived and unsuccessful pursuit of his killers had only reinforced their doubts.[6]

Frosty temperatures in early October began an early assault on the prairie grasses. By the beginning of November the once dark green, undulating waves of grasses of the Texas Panhandle enabled the tan-coated antelope and deer to blend well into the prairie. While the Indians sought out the remaining vestiges of green pastures in the lower elevations, the Quartermaster Department was struggling to refine the expedition's logistics system. Mackenzie, Miles, and Buell's late sum-mer anger about late and inadequate forage shipments began to elicit results by mid-October. Immense quantities of supplies and forage arrived via railroad at Fort Dodge, Kansas, and Atoka, Indian Territory. Steady streams of supply wagon trains snaked their way to designated depots at Camp Supply, Fort Richardson, and Fort Griffin. The full power of the federal government was final-ly being unleashed upon the hostile Plains tribes. The Quaker Peace Policy exper-iment had proven to be a dismal failure; the Indian Territory expedition's goal was to whip the southern Plains tribes into submission.

On their second sweep the converging columns further narrowed the area of Indian movement so the frequency of contacts increased, especially after the first week of October. On October 9 Col. G. P. Buell's column struck a large Kiowa encampment on the Salt Fork of the Red River, which sent the inhabitants fleeing northward. Four days later, a Navajo Indian scout detachment with the W. R. Price column struck a band of hostile Indians on Gageby Creek. Capt. Adna Chaffee's Company I of the Sixth United States Cavalry struck a Comanche village on the Washita River on October 17 and drove the Comanches eastward. Almost two weeks later near Elk Creek in Indian Territory those same fleeing Comanches ran headlong into Maj. G. W. Schofield's Ninth United States Cavalry detachment. More than three hundred members of Tabananica, Red Food, Little Crow, and White Wolf's Comanche bands were forced to capitulate. This large-scale surren-der was the first of many to follow over the next four months.[7]

The army's strategy was slowly proving to be well founded although there were still some obstacles, particularly the weather. Heavy rains in early September had severely limited mobile command movements. Overcast skies had obscured the signal rocket firings so the various columns were unaware of the other columns' whereabouts for almost two weeks. Flooding streams in an area devoid of bridges and rock bed fords had severely undermined the logistics system. The deep, waxy soils of the Texas Panhandle mired the heavily laden supply wagons and made movement virtually impossible during wet weather.

One week into the second sweep of the Texas Panhandle the converging columns had boxed most of the hostile Indians into a 160-square mile area between the Canadian River and the Prairie Dog Town Fork of the Red River. Despite the constant dispersal of numerous scouting parties, some Indians had managed to slip through the cordon of troopers. The final sweeps in the winter months would seek these small bands, but the large bands within the boxed-in area were the primary concern. By early November more rain and flooding had rendered resupply efforts ineffectual. The Miles column, by far the largest of the five columns, also required the longest supply line. Supplies for this column were shipped by rail to Fort Dodge, Kansas. From there, long trains of mule-drawn wagons brought the supplies to the staging base at Camp Supply in the Indian Territory. Wagon trains from Camp Supply distributed the needed supplies to several semi-permanent encampments within the main area of operations. One supply encampment for the Miles column was on the Washita River near the mouth of Dad's Creek. On November 4 Miles was camped at a large playa lake some eighty miles southwest of this supply camp. Short on supplies and grain forage, Miles decided to dispatch an empty train to the encampment. This train required an escort, for even empty supply trains were inviting targets to the Indians. Miles selected two companies from those available. From the three available Sixth Cavalry companies, Lt. Gilbert E. Overton's Company D was selected as the mounted escort. Company D, Fifth United States Infantry, then commanded by 2nd Lt. Hobart K. Bailey, was designated as the infantry escort.[8] Miles also wanted this resupply train to serve a scouting function and assigned eight civilian scouts to accompany the escort detachment. Satisfied that two Gatling guns were sufficient to defend the main body column, Miles decided to send a field howitzer to bolster defenses at the supply encampment. As the column was also short on medical supplies, a civilian contract surgeon, Junius L. Powell, accompanied the train.[9]

Miles gave command of this multipurpose detachment to 1st Lt. Frank D. Baldwin, one of his most trusted officers. Baldwin was a Civil War veteran and had seven years of frontier military service. His appointment as chief of scouts for the Miles column had thrust him into the most active position among the entire expedition. By mid-October he already had participated in five engagements. At 1 P.M. on November 4 Baldwin led the twenty-three-wagon train and its escort eastward from the Miles campsite.[10] On Friday November 6, just after crossing the Salt Fork, the scouts discovered a trail of more than one hundred Indian ponies coming from the northeast and trailing off to the southwest. Baldwin was unaware that this trail had been made by a large, well-armed band, which hours before had mauled Lt. H. J. Farnsworth's Eighth United States Cavalry detachment on McClellan Creek. Despite being harried for three months, the Indians had proven that they were still formidable foes.[11]

Just before sunset on November 7 the command went into camp in a dense grove of cottonwoods on the South Fork of McClellan Creek. At 7 P.M. scouts A. J. Martin and J. C. Frederick arrived with dispatches from Miles, who indicated that he had decided to move up Baldwin's trail, but the dispatch still left Baldwin confused about the main column's exact location. Concerned about a scouting detail sent out earlier he decided to illuminate his location with signal rockets. Shortly after the second rocket Miles acknowledged with two rockets of his own. Baldwin then knew that Miles was almost directly south, about fifteen miles away. The scouting detail, having seen the rocket firings, returned to camp an hour later.[12]

At 6:40 A.M. on Sunday November 8 scouts A. J. Martin and Thompson McFadden were dispatched to deliver Baldwin's report of his operations to Miles. As per the usual daily routine the other civilian scouts had left earlier to scout along the command's line of travel. At 7 A.M. Baldwin led the train and escort northeast across the South Fork of McClellan Creek. The train had progressed about two miles when scout William Schmalsle galloped toward them from the northwest and reported that an Indian camp lay in that direction. Baldwin wanted to determine the exact size and location of the Indian camp and rode off with Schmalsle to reconnoiter the Indian position. Baldwin and Schmalsle skirted the south rim of the canyon through which the North Fork of McClellan Creek flowed and after four miles they came to a jutting point on the canyon rim, from which Baldwin was able to scan the camp with his marine telescope. About two miles away more than six hundred ponies were grazing and just beyond the ponies Baldwin counted more than one hundred shelters and teepees. Schmalsle also viewed the camp with the telescope and noted that the most prominent teepees were not adorned with colorful symbols, as were those of the Kiowa and Comanche. He concluded that they were most likely Cheyenne, possibly Gray Beard's band, which was all Baldwin needed to hear. The two mounted their horses and galloped back to the train, where Baldwin ordered Schmalsle to ride and inform Miles of the discovery. Just as Schmalsle mounted his second horse of the morning, Baldwin added another message, "Tell General Miles that Gray Beard's camp had been located and would be attacked at once."[13]

As Schmalsle galloped southward, Baldwin decided to employ a unique strategy. He ordered the infantry into the empty wagons and the command began its approach toward the Indian camp. They moved two miles before gaining the level plain above the Indian camp. Once upon the plain, the command turned northwest and thirty minutes later halted directly above the lower end of the village. The village, still quiet and undisturbed, was about fifteen hundred yards away. Lieutenant Baldwin knew that to wait any longer would increase the risk of discovery, which up to now was the only factor in their favor. If he left a guard with the wagon train, as was standard operational procedure, he would reduce the attacking force to a dangerously small number. It would be suicidal to attack a village this size with fewer than fifty troops. Since there was no hope of immediate reinforcement he began to implement a unique departure from the usual tactics. The train would not be left behind; instead, it became part of the attack force. The wagonmaster and the teamsters were informed of the decision and not one balked. The wagons were formed into two files, with the horse-drawn mountain howitzer in the middle. The five men assigned as the artillery detachment were ordered to cover the rear gap between the wagons. The lead wagons were drawn up parallel to Lieutenant Baily's company on the right and Overton's cavalry company on the left. Baldwin knew that the attack force would have to penetrate the village as quickly as possible in case there were white captives in the village. Baldwin knew that captives Clara Blinn and her infant child had been executed at the first sound of gunfire at the outset of Custer's attack on the Cheyenne on the Washita River in 1868. He had also heard the story from Fifth United States Cavalry troopers about the attack on a Cheyenne village at Summit Springs, Colorado, in 1869, when the charging cavalry troopers watched in horror as a Cheyenne warrior stabbed a white captive to death in plain view of the troops.[14]

Shortly after 8:30 A.M. Baldwin ordered his attack force over the rim of the canyon. The initial approach was across rough and broken terrain. The infantry skirmish line was forced to string themselves out almost to the northern canyon rim. When the command reached the crest of a low ridge, half a mile from the Indian camp, loud yelling could be heard in the village. Baldwin ordered the bugler, Pvt. Adam Funk, to blow the charge. Lieutenant Overton's company and three scouts rushed forward on the left, firing their pistols and yelling to stampede the Indians' herd. The wagons with the infantry skirmishers on their right broke into a headlong rush. As the train rushed past, the artillery detachment followed closely on their heels until they halted at the crest of a rise. Baldwin ordered Sgt. Charles Reinstine's crew to halt on the crest and prepare for action. Three hundred yards below the village were a number of ravines toward which a large number of warriors were advancing. The Indians began to fire sporadically on the advancing line of infantry and Baldwin ordered Sergeant Reinstine's crew to begin lobbing shells toward these ravines. Seconds after the second shell fell among the ravines the Indians were seen fleeing en masse. Within five minutes Baldwin rushed into the village at the head of the charging line. The village's occupants were fleeing up the incline toward the northwestern bluff line. It had taken only twenty minutes after the charge was sounded to carry the village. The Cheyenne warriors, once their families were safely on the open plain, made angry demonstrations along the bluff. The Indians formed a long battle line and began to fire down into the canyon, Baldwin again ordered Reinstine's crew to prepare for action. As the Indians' firing began to fall among the command, Baldwin gave Reinstine the order to open fire. The first shot raked the lip of the bluff. After an adjustment to the howitzer elevation a second canister shot was fired. Two Indians and their mounts went down immediately and the line turned about and disappeared beyond the bluff line. Baldwin ordered Reinstine and crew to remain at the ready should the Indians make another appearance.[15]

While the artillery crew kept the Indians at bay, Baldwin and the rest of the command began a thorough lodge-by-lodge search of the village, paying particular attention to articles that might tie the inhabitants to specific criminal acts. Scalplocks, mail pouches, engraved personal items, clothing, and captives often were presented to Indian agents who had repeatedly denied that their tribe was involved in such activities. Only a few minutes into the soldiers' search, a single mounted Indian appeared several hundred yards away and searched among several detached lodges for something. He came to one collapsed lodge, where buffalo robes and blankets were scattered about in piles, then drew out his pistol and fired into a pile of robes. Before this Indian could fire another shot, one of the infantry sharpshooters shot him. Baldwin and a throng of troopers ran to the scene to investigate. When they arrived near the piles of robes and blankets they noticed movement under one robe. They lifted the robe cautiously and revealed a dirty, emaciated, little white girl; it was Julia German. The shocked soldiers were greeted with a simple inquiry: "Be you-uns soldiers?" One soldier, just a few feet away, pulled back the flap on a still-intact lodge and found Addie German gingerly placing sticks on a small fire, too weak to react to the turmoil around her.[16] Once the two girls were placed on a wagon bed gate, the older one, Julia, remarked, "We're so glad, we heard sisters praying all the time that God would send the soldiers to deliver them."[17] Baldwin overheard and inquired about the sisters. When Baldwin learned that the two elder sisters, Sophia and Catherine, had been in the village at the outset of the attack, he completely changed his plans. Surgeon Powell and a few of the teamsters and troopers were detailed to remain behind in the village to control the herd and care for the girls.[18]

Not wishing to allow the Indians to simply melt away into the vast plains, especially if there was a chance to recover the other two girls, Baldwin decided to renew the attack. The command was reformed and the infantrymen were dispersed within several wagons. Baldwin, at the head of the command, led them up the incline and onto the plain beyond, where about a quarter of a mile away more than one hundred warriors were drawn up in a battle line. Sergeant Reinstine and crew were again ordered into action. Once set up they opened fire with canister rounds and sent several more warriors and their mounts down immediately. This brief barrage was followed by an all-out charge toward the Indian line. Baldwin led the scouts and Overton's company into the Indian line, outdistancing the train by several hundred yards. For several minutes the mounted command engaged the Indians at close range, even to the point of hand-to-hand combat. After several minutes the train arrived on the scene. The infantrymen were out of the wagons in an instant and, under Lieutenant Baily's guidance, they attempted a rapid encirclement maneuver. Before this could be accomplished the Indians wheeled about and retreated to the northwest. Once again Baldwin reformed the command and the chase resumed. for another mile before the exhausted condition of the horses and mule teams forced it to be halted at a large playa lake. While the main body of the command remained at the lake to rest and water the stock, Baldwin and several scouts rode northward to reconnoiter the area. Upon his return Baldwin reported that a band of around eighty mounted warriors was seen off to the northeast about two miles away, moving southward. As Baldwin's mount was severely worn from the reconnoitering foray he dispatched Lieutenant Overton to take his company and intercept the band.[19]

Overton advanced toward the Indians for more than two miles. When the Indians discovered them, Overton formed his company into a skirmish line and advanced toward the Indians at a trot. Just prior to his charge into the milling mass of Indians, Overton ordered the carbines stowed and pistols drawn. The charge scattered the Indians into several fleeing bands. During this brief close-range clash at least one Cheyenne warrior was shot from his horse at point-blank range.[20] One of the fleeing bands began a looping movement to the south toward Overton's rear. Overton, observing this movement, dispatched a courier to notify Baldwin of his predicament. Upon the courier's arrival and report Baldwin quickly led the command out to Overton's relief. The two forces met about half a mile east of the large playa lake. Baldwin observed the Indian band that had been looping behind Overton break off and ride southward. He chose to ignore them, confidant that Miles was moving up his trail and would likely make contact with the band should it attempt to reenter the village. He also knew that it was likely a ploy meant to divide the command into smaller, more vulnerable groups or were being used as decoys to draw them away from the main body. His hunch paid off as within minutes of a northward turn he could see a large mass of Indians to his left. Reinstine and crew were once again ordered to prepare for action. The

213

infantry was formed into skirmish lines with Overton's still-exhausted company assigned to the flanks. The command had advanced about a quarter of a mile when the order to open fire was given. The thunderous roar of the howitzer and sixty rifles completely dispersed the Indians. Only the mounted warriors maintained a line as small groups of Indians moved north and northwest. The warriors formed a line on a terrace about a quarter of a mile to the northeast and once again Baldwin led his reassembled command up the incline toward the Indian line. When within five hundred yards of the Indian positions the infantrymen again jumped out of the wagons, quickly formed a skirmish line, and upon command the entire force delivered a volley into the Indians, who wheeled about and fled with Baldwin's force in rapid pursuit. Much to Baldwin's chagrin the Indians eventually widened their lead to more than two miles. They were clearly visible and would have been within reach had the cavalry horses been serviceable. Baldwin now felt the same anger as Miles over the failure of the logistics system to provide adequate forage supplies. Later that day he expressed his frustration in his diary:

> If I only had well mounted company of cavalry it would be but a short run to go right into their families, for they can be clearly seen not more than 2 1/2 miles distant and my success would be most complete, but the cursed crime of neglect to furnish this expedition with grain shows itself.[21]

The chase continued into the heavy breaks of the upper reaches of the North Fork of the Red River. The effort was gallant but futile as the Indians again turned about and fled toward the northern horizon. Once again the command was halted at another small playa lake and allowed to rest. Undaunted, Baldwin and two scouts continued for two more miles before the mounted warriors' trail split up again. When Baldwin returned to the lake, Maj. C. E. Compton and the lead contingent from the Miles column were waiting for him. Compton had received Baldwin's report of the last sighting of the Indians and led Company H of the Sixth Cavalry north in pursuit. He returned two hours later with totally worn-down horses. After a brief rest the entire command began a labored trek back toward the Indian village. Shortly before sunset Baldwin's weary battle wagon command encountered Miles camped at the large playa lake two miles north of the village. Upon their arrival Baldwin found the German girls' appearances much changed from eight hours earlier. Pvt. George "Scotty" Russell somehow had been delegated to care for the needs of the girls.[22] Russell had bathed and fed them and gingerly smoothed their hair with a currycomb. Surgeons Powell and Waters had concluded a thorough physical exam of the two emaciated girls.

Adelaide (Addie), right, and Julia German, who were taken as captives by the Cheyenne and res-
cued by Frank Baldwin and his troops. *Photograph courtesy the Western History Collections,
University of Oklahoma.*

Their primary debilitation appeared to be severe malnutrition. One of the civilian teamsters summed up the feelings of all those present when he remarked in a trembling voice, "I have driven my mules over these plains for three months, but I will stay forever or until we get them other girls." Frank Baldwin's energetic and bold actions that day assured that the teamster's vow would be realized quickly. His lightning-fast attack and dogged pursuit of the Cheyenne had forced them to abandon all their camp equipment and winter supplies. They had lost everything of value except for Sophia and Catherine German, but the captive girls assured the tribe's safety, for Stone Calf, the Cheyenne chief holding them, wisely used them to obtain safe passage and as ransom in exchange for desperately needed supplies.[23]

Miles assumed guardianship over the German girls after the superintendent of the Indian Office refused. The girls were sent to Fort Leavenworth, where they were eventually turned over to an aunt, Mrs. Patrick Corney.[24] Sophia and Catherine were turned over to Cheyenne agency officials in late February 1875 and were retained at the agency, where they identified the major perpetrators of the attack upon their family and of subsequent cruelties performed on them during their captivity.[25] Sophia and Catherine were finally reunited with their younger sisters in May 1875. Miles obtained government assistance for them by petitioning Congress to divert a portion of Cheyenne annuity funds for their support. All four went on to receive a public school education; Julia and Addie eventually earned teaching degrees. All four went on to marry and live productive lives. Catherine, cognizant and appreciative of Frank Baldwin's contribution to their freedom, years later presented him with a written account of their ordeal. After reading about the horrible cruelties perpetrated upon the girls, the comfort of knowing that his actions had relieved them from that misery was Baldwin's only reward for two decades.[26]

In 1880 Baldwin became one of a number of American army and naval officers dispatched to Europe to study military organization and observe maneuvers. The bare American uniforms made those wearing them appear deficient and deedless when compared to the medal-arrayed uniforms of their European counterparts. The experience made the Americans even more self-conscious when some of the European nations conferred honorary medals upon some of the visiting Americans, which caused a great deal of embarrassment, fostered resentment, and launched controversy. In 1884 the War Department attempted to quell the controversy when it issued orders that only Civil War corps badges, marksmanship badges, and the Medal of Honor could be worn on uniforms on occasions of ceremony. In 1889 the War Department initiated an effort to officially identify those officers and enlisted men deserving of recognition for gallant and meritorious acts and began to compile a report on meritorious services performed by active-duty army personnel since the end of the Civil War. This report was to be used in sanctioning the award of brevets, Certificates of Merit, and Medals of Honor.[27]

On January 17, 1890, in compliance with the War Department's order, General Miles, in his capacity as commander of the Department of Arizona, submitted that department's compiled report on meritorious service. In that report submitted to the adjutant general's office was the recommendation to award a Medal of Honor to Frank D. Baldwin for "gallantry at McClellan Creek, Texas, for recapturing two white girls, November 8, 1874; and for a successful attack on Sitting Bull's Camp, Redwater River, Montana, December 18, 1876." Later in 1890 and early 1891 events occurred that eventually led to Frank Baldwin receiving recognition for his Civil War exploits. On November 28, 1890, he was transferred and reunited with General Miles at Division of the Missouri headquarters at Chicago. Another key event was the silver encampment of the Grand Army of the Republic at Detroit in August 1891, where Baldwin was reunited with former comrades of the Nineteenth Michigan Volunteer Infantry. Reminiscing about various incidents and comrades became fundamental topics of conversation. John Coburn, an attorney from Indianapolis, mentioned an October 5, 1863, conversation with Col. A. C. Gilbert regarding Gilbert's intent to recommend Baldwin for a Medal of Honor for his actions that day in defending a railroad bridge over the Stone River. Gilbert had been killed in action several days later, before he could act upon the recommendation. Coburn, the former brigade commander, became firmly bound to complete Gilbert's endeavor and solicited fourteen letters describing Baldwin's actions from former officers and enlisted men. Along with his own personal recommendation, Coburn submitted these accounts to the Secretary of War on November 6, 1891.[28] Despite the overwhelming evidence of Baldwin's gallantry, the Secretary of War ruled that his conduct was "no more than your duty."[29] Upon learning of the adverse ruling General Miles personally intervened. He apparently sensed that an exploit in which Baldwin had been wounded, captured, and later released by Confederate Gen. Joseph Wheeler might not have set well with the War Department. Miles elicited details of another of Baldwin's Civil War exploits: at the battle of Peachtree Creek, Georgia, on July 20, 1864, in which Baldwin had led his company in a counter charge under intense fire against Confederate emplacements. Ahead of the advancing line of troops he dashed into the Confederate line and captured two commissioned officers and the guidon of a Georgia regiment. General Miles submitted the required

217

documentation and eyewitness accounts to the Secretary of War and on December 3, 1891, the Medal of Honor was officially conferred upon Frank D. Baldwin. Whether the rapidity of the award was due to the influence of a major general as opposed to that of a mere volunteer colonel is open to speculation. The War Department may also have preferred that its Medal of Honor recipients be captors instead of captives.[30]

An announcement of the award appeared in a December 1891 edition of a Chicago newspaper. On February 18, 1892, Baldwin's former scout, William F. Schmalsle, having read the article, wrote from Miles City, Montana, to congratulate him on the award. Schmalsle further added, "I think you ought to had one long ago for getting those little German girls."[31] Baldwin showed the letter to Miles, who greatly admired Schmalsle for his daring exploits during the 1874 campaign. The idea for renewing efforts on his earlier recommendation for a second Medal of Honor was thus born. Miles was no doubt determined that members of his staff would never again face the embarrassment of their European experiences in the 1880s. In the meantime, Miles, never one to bypass an opportunity for pomp and ceremony, rented the dining and conference hall of the Pullman Building in downtown Chicago. At a banquet on or around August 30, 1892, Miles personally pinned the Medal of Honor to Baldwin's blouse. Minutes before Miles had read the official citation, adding a great deal of flowery praise in behalf of Baldwin's valuable services to the Union. After the ceremony a newspaper reporter interviewed the somewhat embarrassed and reserved Baldwin. The reporter's article in the newspaper a few days later was apparently even more flowery and disconcerting to Frank. His wife, Alice, ever supportive of his career, remarked, "They can't lay it on too thick to suit me."[32]

On March 26, 1894, just prior to assuming command of the Department of the East, Miles initiated the Medal of Honor application process for twelve officers on his staff. The applications submitted were exclusively for Indian War deeds of gallantry and first on the list was Frank D. Baldwin.[33] Unable to locate the original reports, the adjutant general's office disapproved the application on July 25. Miles renewed the process on October 30, enclosing an impressive personal letter of citation about Baldwin's deed in recapturing the German girls with his small command. On November 27, 1894, the adjutant general's office approved issue of the medal. On December 18 President Grover Cleveland completed the process by directing that the award be granted to Baldwin.[34] When Baldwin was notified that he was to receive a second Medal of Honor, the letter, by ironic coincidence, was sent to the Kiowa–Comanche Reservation headquarters at Anadarko, Oklahoma. Just two months earlier Baldwin had been assigned to duty at Anadarko as the acting Indian Agent. Just as he had gallantly battled against the Indians two decades earlier, Baldwin now used his administrative skills to help better the lives of his former adversaries. In both endeavors he brought credit and acclaim, not only upon himself, but also upon the uniform that he wore proudly for another decade. There was no record of a formal ceremony for his second Medal of Honor.[35]

Lewis Warrington III's Medal of Honor headstone in San Antonio National Cemetery. Lewis Warrington III, the grandson of War of 1812 naval hero Commodore Lewis Warrington, became the only officer Medal of Honor reicpient during the Indian Wars to receive his award at the time of the deed, and not retroactively, as were all others. *Photograph courtesy Charles Chambers, Houston.*

CHAPTER 17

Pursuit and Close Combat
on the High Plains

December 8, 1874

Pvt. Frederick H. Bergendahl   Lt. Lewis Warrington

Pvt. John F. O'Sullivan

B y the first week of November 1874 most of the hostile Southern Plains tribes were stampeding toward their various reservations, anxious to surrender. Still managing to evade the various pursuing army columns were the Kiowa bands under Maman-ti, Red Otter, To-hausen, and Poor Buffalo. The Quohada Comanches also had proven elusive. Their bands, led by Isa-tai, Black Horse and Mona, comprised one hundred mounted warriors. The Southern Cheyenne bands of Medicine Water, Kicking Horse, Gray Beard, Medicine Arrow, Sand Hill, Red Moon, and Stone Calf also remained out. Together, these bands included at least 350 warriors, still a formidable force to be reckoned with. Gen. P. H. Sheridan, overall campaign commander from the Wichita Agency near Fort Sill, received daily reports of the surrenders. These reports from agents, officers, and interpreters provided an encouraging picture of the campaign. After evaluating the reports from the first sweep operation, Sheridan reported to Gen. W. T. Sherman that there was every indication that the campaign would finish the Indian War on the South Plains before the onset of winter. The reason he offered was that since the Indians had "no opportunity to kill game to get food for their families, no land on which to graze their stock, and no sense of safety for their lives, they would now surrender unconditionally and thus there existed the fair prospect of a close to the Army's labors before long."[1]

The third sweep of the campaign would have to be adequately supplied if it was to be successful. Late fall, especially November, was one of the busiest times for the Plains tribes, for it was when they decided upon a site for their permanent winter encampment and busied themselves with preparations for the winter. Hunting and raiding bands were extremely active and these movements were expected to expose them to discovery. The army strategists counted upon the Indians' trails to lead them to their ultimate objectives, the large winter encampments.

By November 8 Colonel Mackenzie had returned to his supply camp on the Fresh Water Fork of the Brazos River at the end of his second sweep. His efforts and those of his command had inflicted a measure of damage upon several small bands of Quohadas, but had failed to rein in sizable numbers of the Indians or locate a major winter encampment as anticipated. The exceptional quality of the livestock Mackenzie's command captured on November 3 enabled him to replenish the debilitated command's stock with the fresh captured stock. During the first and second sweeps the command had been forced to either abandon or shoot forty-four animals. The New Mexican guides, the Tonkawa, and Seminole-Negro scouts were afforded first choice among the captured herd, as Mackenzie had promised, to reward them for their hazardous and strenuous duties. Lieutenants Lawton and Thompson had second choice in order to replace worn-out teams for the supply trains and replacement mounts for the enlisted scouts. Those left over were distributed to the companies on an as-needed basis and others were purchased by some of the officers as spare personal mounts. Teams of farriers set about reshodding the horses that needed it. Adequate supply shipments, now getting through for the first time during the campaign, allowed the command's animals to partake of their fully allotted daily corn rations. Preparations for the third sweep were on schedule and going as anticipated. Once ready, the command needed to be pointed in the right direction and it was hoped that information obtained from the prisoners captured on November 3 would provide that direction.

Unusual efforts had been exerted in caring for the prisoners. They had been issued extra blankets for protection against the cold nights and extra cooking utensils and foodstuffs for their own meal preparation. Early on the morning of November 9, Lieutenants Leiper and Lawton, along with Sergeants Rankin and Foster, began their second interrogations of the captives. Though the interrogations were disappointing, Mackenzie knew that only his scouting patrols would ultimately determine the final line of march.[2]

By November 11 the command's men and animals were well into their rehabilitation. Lieutenant Albee and a ten-wagon train were dispatched to Fort Griffin for even more supplies and forage. As the bulk of the Seminole-Negro scouts were within weeks of terminating their enlistments, Mackenzie also decided to send them along to Griffin. Albee carried with him dispatches that Mackenzie wished to be telegraphed to Col. J. H. Taylor requesting the latest information on the movements of the other columns and any intelligence on the whereabouts of the Indians. In these dispatches, Mackenzie expressed his intent to begin the third sweep of the plains on November 16.[3] Over the next eight days the command endured hail, sleet, and a series of cold rainstorms; all believed they had experienced the last capricious swing of High Plains weather on November 18 with a freezing rainstorm. Upon arising at sunrise on November 19, the entire command thought itself suddenly and miraculously transposed to an Arctic region.[4] Everything was covered in a heavy sheet of ice and topped with a light blanket of snow. Despite the diligence of the herd guards, at least one horse had frozen to death on the picket line.[5] Several of the men on sentry duty that night had also suffered debilitating frostbite to their hands and feet and Surgeon Daniel J. Caldwell labored throughout the day treating the afflicted extremities. Toward late afternoon Caldwell had to perform another of his many functions, as the column's meteorological observer. He took hourly readings with a sling barometer. The numbers indicated increasing pressure, which meant clearing, but colder, weather was in the future. The news boosted Mackenzie's spirits. Caldwell's predictions proved accurate and at sunrise on November 20 the brilliant, clear, blue sky framed scores of ducks and geese flying south.[6]

At sunrise on November 22 "Boots and Saddles" resounded across the encampment announcing that the third sweep was under way. By 10 A.M. the command was making its way up Blanco Canyon and by November 24 they had progressed twenty-four miles to a temporary base camp between Mount Blanco and the mouth of Congrejo Canyon. From here Mackenzie dispatched three scouting parties to search out the areas around Salado Lake, Palo Duro, and Quitaque. At 6:45 A.M. on December 4, after a week in camp awaiting the scouts' return, Mackenzie led the command out of Blanco Canyon and onto the plains. Theodore Valdez, José Tafoya, and the Seminole-Negroes had made a significant discovery—they had found a series of trails between Casa Maria and Laguna Salado leading off to the lagunas west of Muchaque.[7] The command's general direction of movement was southwest. Despite incessant rains and gale-like winds, Mackenzie finally halted the march at 9 P.M. at a large playa lake three miles northeast of Laguna Tahoka. Shortly after sundown the rain turned into sleet and added significantly to the misery index. During the night, Capt. Theodore J. Wint, Lt. Lewis Warrington, and Lt. W. T. Duggan, and their company, who were the last to encamp in the most exposed position, had ten animals die from exposure. Buffalo chips, usually the primary source for kindling fires on the treeless plains, were too wet to ignite and the men spent a miserable night wrapped in their blankets in the mud. On December 5 at the camp near Laguna Tahoka the previously cut-down roots of mesquite trees provided only enough fire tender for a few precious minutes of relief from the bitter cold. Because of new findings by the scouts earlier in the day the line of march was changed to the southeast and at noon on December 6 the command went into bivouac near several lakes west of Ojo Blanco Springs. The good cover, wood, and water afforded the troops their first comfortable night's sleep in seventy-two hours.[8]

At mid-morning on December 7 one of the scouting parties encountered and killed a single Indian near the head of Indian Canyon. By noon on December 8 the command was camped in Indian Canyon on the Colorado River just opposite the mouth of Wet Tobacco Creek. The profusion of good timber and grass, as well as good shelter from the bitter winds, enabled the troops to enjoy a leisurely meal and some welcome rest. Shortly before 3 P.M. Capt. Theodore Wint and Lts. Lewis Warrington and W. T. Duggan warmed themselves around a small campfire with cups of coffee in their hands. Wint had just inspected the company's bivouac area and the mule herd while Duggan had returned from supervising corn rationing to the company's horses. Warrington, as guard mount officer, had responsibility for manning and inspecting the outlying sentry posts. He had completed his midday rounds an hour earlier and was enjoying a brief respite. As a shivering Duggan crowded closer to the fire, Warrington reminded him for the umpteenth time that his own eagerness to volunteer for cavalry duty had created his present misery. But for that, he could be back in the creature comforts of the main supply base.[9] Around 3:30 their banter was suddenly interrupted by a noisy commotion at Mackenzie's tent. A runner from the sentry post on an elevation northeast of camp had observed a body of Indians south of the camp moving northward along the west bank of the river. Lieutenant Warrington rode immediately to Mackenzie's tent. Ten troopers from Company I had been detailed as the herd guard and were standing by with their horses already saddled. Mackenzie ordered Warrington to take the guard and move out after the Indians.[10]

The sentries had first observed the Indians with the field telescope when they were about half a mile below the mouth of Wet Tobacco Creek. From the higher elevation of the north bank, Warrington observed the Indians veering to the northwest around the south rim of Wet Tobacco Canyon's mouth. Splashing across the shallow waters of the Colorado at a moderate gallop, Warrington led his ten troopers to the right of a rise that ran parallel and on the north side of the creek.[11] The chase continued for three miles before the rise flattened to the point that the Indians could see their pursuers. The troops at this point were about half a mile behind and a little to the right of the Indians. Both groups broke into a full gallop. After two miles of pursuit one of the Indians was forced to abandon his mount. He ran in among the small herd his comrades were driving and his companions slowed their movement to enable him to seize a mount. When within two hundred yards, Warrington drew up and opened fire at this still-unmounted Indian, who was frantically trying to seize a pony. With each roar of the .50-caliber Sharps carbine, the Indian herd bolted beyond the young man's grasp. In desperation he ran into a nearby ravine; Warrington stowed his carbine and followed. As he neared the ravine, the Indian began to scramble up the ravine. His efforts were futile in the mud and Warrington holstered his pistol and pulled his picket rope from the saddle pommel. His first throw of the looped rope lassoed the Indian and, with a single jerk, the young man was incapacitated on the ground and Warrington's leveled pistol convinced him that further struggle was futile. Once he had the Indian securely bound, Warrington turned him over to a nearby trooper whose horse was worn out. Seven other dismounted troopers leading exhausted mounts were strung out for some distance back along their path.[12]

Only two troopers, Pvts. John O'Sullivan and Frederick Bergendahl, had been able and willing to continue the pursuit. Warrington quickly rejoined them and after another half-mile run closed on the Indians at the head of the canyon. The Indians had halted at the precipice of the canyon head, apparently finding it difficult to get the herd and their own mounts up the muddy bank. As Warrington and the two determined troopers drew nearer, the Indians dismounted to fight. Privates Bergendahl and O'Sullivan superbly handled their mounts as they climbed the incline on the right and drew to within fifty yards of the Indians before they opened fire with their pistols. One Indian fell wounded and the other two at his side dragged him slipping and sliding onto the level plain. The remaining Indians had managed to force their horses onto the plain and hold them in place. While Bergendahl, Warrington, and O'Sullivan floundered and struggled to gain the edge of the cliff line, the

Indians continued to fire down upon them. As the troopers neared the cliff's edge the Indians hastily hoisted their wounded comrade onto his horse and bolted across the level plain. By the time Warrington and the two troopers gained the level plain, the Indians had traversed more than an eighth of a mile across the flat plain. Warrington realized that the success of the pursuit depended upon animal stamina. Mackenzie had repeatedly touted the superiority of grain-fed mounts in winter operations and with this in mind, the troopers followed at a leisurely trot. After three miles another Indian pony collapsed in exhaustion and its rider took to his feet. He desperately attempted to stay up with the others but, after less than a mile, he turned to face his dogged pursuers. Before he could raise his bow to unleash his first arrow, Bergendahl shot him and the Indian fell to his knees. Private O'Sullivan shot the Indian again as he struggled to draw another arrow from his quiver. O'Sullivan was barely eighteen years old and this was likely the first Indian he had killed in a close-range confrontation.[13]

The three soldiers doggedly continued the pursuit for another mile before the remaining two able-bodied Indians abandoned their mounts and began sprinting across the plain. Bergendahl and O'Sullivan, having pushed their mounts to the end of their endurance, dismounted and sprinted after the Indian on the left. Mackenzie wanted information, not dead bodies, and they would attempt to appease him. Warrington, on his large reddish-brown stallion, quickly overtook the powerfully built Indian on the right. Just yards behind his adversary, he saw him ready his bow and reach for an arrow. Just as the Indian stopped to turn and let the arrow fly, Warrington fired his pistol and struck the Indian in the chest. A large breastplate of animal bones, commonly worn by most Plains warriors, apparently abated the effect of the bullet for the Indian raised his bow to shoot as Warrington dismounted. From a distance of about a hundred yards, Bergendahl performed an astounding display of marksmanship with his Sharps carbine. His shot completely shattered the bow and rendered it a useless piece of cedar and buffalo sinew.[14] Infuriated, the warrior threw the arrow in spear fashion, narrowly missing Warrington's head just as he planted his boots on the ground. Further enraged that this arrow had missed its mark, the Indian drew out a knife and charged toward the young officer. Still somewhat off-balance from dismounting, Warrington used his carbine to parry the blows. Warrington, though exhausted himself, managed to shove the Indian back far enough to level his carbine. He pulled the trigger only to hear the sickening sound of the firing pin on an empty chamber—he had forgotten to reload and his horse was crowding him and obscuring him from Bergendahl and O'Sullivan's vision. Wielding his carbine in his left hand, Warrington again parried the warrior's stabbing blows while desperately groping for the cartridges in his right coat pocket. The cartridges, to his dismay, had fallen through the torn pocket lining and were beyond his grasp. He frantically shoved the Indian back, ripped the pocket lining, and seized a single cartridge. He parried a stabbing blow and shoved his determined foe backward. As Warrington fumbled to load the cartridge, the Indian again lunged forward, but this time he grabbed onto the saddle pommel on Warrington's horse. Exhausted and on one knee, Warrington finally chambered the cartridge and pulled the trigger, killing the Indian. After catching up to his horse, Warrington rounded up the other troopers' horses and led them to Bergendahl and O'Sullivan, who had found themselves second best in a footrace with the other Indian. The horse bearing the Indian that had been wounded earlier was seen sauntering over the horizon, its rider slumped over and motionless. Together they rounded up the nine horses the Indians had abandoned and began their trek back to the main command.[15]

During their return, a band of Indians bolted out of a ravine on their left and hurried across the plains.[16] As the horses were still winded and they only had a few rounds of ammunition remaining, Warrington decided against an encounter with them and continued his march back to the encampment, where they arrived just before 9 P.M.[17] The command was in the process of breaking camp and the three were not even allowed time for rest or food. Information apparently elicited from the prisoner captured earlier had prompted Mackenzie to initiate a movement toward Laguna Sabinas. The command remained on the march for the next fourteen hours.[18] They arrived at Laguna Sabinas shortly before noon on December 9. They found only crude stick trellises, evidence that the location had been used extensively for drying buffalo meat strips. A lone Indian thought to be a woman sat silently on her mount on the distant western horizon. She remained there a considerable time without moving or uttering a sound, constantly under the eye of a marine telescope. She was perhaps a decoy, but may have been a mother or wife awaiting the return of her loved one. Mackenzie became convinced at this point that the Indians still out were on their way to the reservations or were seeking refuge either along the Pecos River or in the Guadalupe Mountains.[19]

Over the next nine days the command trudged through intermittent rain, sleet, and snow for 130 miles before finally arriving back at the main supply camp.[20] After a warm meal and a restful night's sleep, the command awoke on the morning of December 19 to a snow-covered landscape. During the early morning hours, in spite of the snowstorm, Mackenzie had left to return to Fort Griffin and his eventual destination, the departmental headquarters at San Antonio. At mid-morning, Lt. John A. McKinney passed word by several orderlies that he would deliver important pronouncements at the adjutant's tent in ten minutes. At the prescribed time McKinney emerged from his tent and announced loudly to the assemblage that it was his pleasure to announce to you at this time that, "Special Order Number 37, issued at these headquarters earlier this morning by Colonel Mackenzie has formally ended this campaign."[21] After the jubilant cheering subsided, he went on to announce the various new home post assignments for the various companies of the command; most of these assignments were not met with unanimous jubilation. McKinney also reminded Lieutenant Warrington that upon Mackenzie's request he was to submit a detailed account of his affair with the Indians on December 8.

Later that evening Lew Warrington penned his report in the adjutant's tent and it was included with Mackenzie's official report and itinerary of the third sweep and was submitted to the Department of Texas headquarters on January 7, 1875. Mackenzie, in his initial cursory report on the expedition written at Fort Griffin on Christmas Eve reporting on the various clashes with the Indians, remarked that the two killed and the one captured on December 8 many miles from the command were "under circumstances which reflect the greatest credit on Mr. Warrington."[22] In a cover letter accompanying his January 7, 1875, report, an entire paragraph was dedicated to Warrington, O'Sullivan, and Bergendahl's actions of December 8, 1874. Of these actions, Mackenzie remarked, "Lieutenant Warrington deserves some reward for very gallant conduct on December 8th. Private Bergendahl, Regimental Band and on this expedition as a private with his former company at his own request, and Private O'Sullivan, Company I, deserve consideration for gallantry on December 8th."[23] In a separate letter that Mackenzie also penned on January 7, 1875, he addressed the commendable conduct of officers and enlisted men who were brought to his attention or about whom he had personal knowledge. He wrote of Warrington "as particularly deserving credit for his actions of September 28th and December 8th."[24] In that same letter, Mackenzie mentioned Privates O'Sullivan and Bergendahl along with six other enlisted men as "deserving of medals for gallantry."[25]

The unusual intensity of the 1873–1875 Indian campaigns created a flood of recommendations for the Medal of Honor unseen since 1863–1865. Apparently the adjutant general of the army, Edward D. Townsend, and Secretary of War W. W. Belknap became concerned that the recommendations by field commanders did not include sufficient specific details of the acts of gallantry. Some of the commendatory reports, including Mackenzie's of January 7, 1875, failed to even include the basic information required for engraving if granted. On February 2, 1875, the adjutant general wrote to General Augur and requested that he elicit from Mackenzie an additional report in which, the particular acts of gallantry be stated in each case. Warrington's report and Mackenzie's compiled campaign report had been submitted through channels, first to Department of Texas headquarters on January 7 and to Missouri Division headquarters on January 21. In spite of the fact that both Augur and Missouri Division Commander P. H. Sheridan, were personally acquainted with the Warrington family and had reviewed the documents, neither inserted an endorsement recommending him for a Medal of Honor. It appears that Colonel Townsend, after reviewing Mackenzie's December 24, 1874, and January 7, 1875, reports and their mention of Warrington's gallantry, became the genesis for Warrington's Medal of Honor award. There would have been a number of legal issues involved in his being awarded a Medal of Honor and these issues most certainly were scrutinized over the following four months. Warrington's very detailed account of December 19, 1874, most certainly exceeded the new criteria that specific acts of gallantry be stated in each case. A second issue may have been that Warrington was an officer and no officer had yet been recommended for a Medal of Honor in Indian warfare. The original Medal of Honor statute of July 12, 1862, which had dictated awards only to enlisted men and non-commissioned officers, had been amended on March 13, 1863, to include commissioned officers. In his report of December 19, Warrington had not recommended himself for a Medal of Honor so he could not be disqualified on that basis. His commanding officer, Colonel Mackenzie, had not specifically suggested that he be awarded a Medal of Honor, stating only that, "he deserved some reward which would reflect the greatest credit on Mr. Warrington." The deciding factor was likely that Warrington had but one year in his present rank of first lieutenant and special legislation would have been necessary for his promotion.[26]

In light of these circumstances and in clear consideration of Mackenzie's recommendation of a reward to reflect the greatest credit on Warrington, on March 27, 1875, Townsend forwarded his recommendation to Secretary of War William W. Belknap, who directed that the medal be awarded. After engraving, the medal was returned to the adjutant general's office, where on April 12, 1875, it was sent via registered mail to Warrington's duty station at Fort Sill, Indian Territory. There is no record of a formal award ceremony and the circumstances of its receipt by Lieutenant Warrington are unknown.[27]

Recommendations for medals for Privates O'Sullivan and Bergendahl became stalled by the specific acts controversy. Six months after receiving the adjutant general's request for a more detailed report to include, "the specific acts of gallantry in each case," Mackenzie replied in kind. On August 31, 1875, he wrote of O'Sullivan's and Bergendahl's gallantry and suggested that Medals of Honor be awarded to them, "for gallantry in a long chase on the Staked Plains after a party of Indians on December 8th."[28] After review and endorsement by General Sherman at army headquarters at St. Louis, the report was forwarded to the adjutant general, where it was received on September 24, 1875. After ascertaining the correct spellings of names from the regimental rolls, the adjutant general forwarded the certified list to the secretary of war for official endorsement on October 13, 1875. The medals were ordered, issued, and engraved and on October 19, 1875, were sent by registered mail to the recipients' appropriate duty stations. Pvt. John O'Sullivan had been discharged from the army on March 22, 1875 and his Medal of Honor was forwarded to his residence at the Fifth Avenue Hotel in New York City. He acknowledged its receipt there on November 18, 1875. Pvt. Frederick H. Bergendahl was stationed at Fort Sill where, on or around October 29, 1875, he is believed to have received his medal. There was no mention nor record of a formal award ceremony.[29]

Gen. P. H. Sheridan, commander of the Division of the Missouri, who oversaw all military operations in the trans–Mississippi West against hostile Indian tribes between 1867 and 1883, wrote in his 1874 annual report to the secretary of war that, in his opinion, the 1874 Indian Territory Expedition "was not only comprehensive but also was the most successful of any Indian campaign in the country since its settlement by the whites and much credit is due the officers and men engaged in it."[30] Sheridan had been the primary proponent of winter campaigns as the ultimate strategy in suppressing the hostile Plains tribes and he had witnessed his strategy's ultimate execution. He was fortunate to have a field commander such as R. S. Mackenzie and determined officers and enlisted troopers like Lt. Lewis Warrington and Pvts. John O'Sullivan and Frederick Bergendahl. It has been said that the job of any military force is to kill and break things in order to elicit peace when all other efforts have failed. The endurance and determination of these three men in performing their assigned duties against superior numbers, in spite of bitter winter conditions, accomplished just that. The southern Great Plains frontier, once the sanctuary of violence-prone raiders and their supporting illicit traders, was gradually transformed into a vast productive agricultural region. The gallantry of the U.S.

Army on the western American frontier was one of the first steps in that transformation and reflects great credit upon the character, service, and sacrifices of these men.

Seminole-Negro Scouts, Fort Clark, Texas, circa 1890. Medal of Honor recipient John Ward is the man on the left on the front row. *Photograph courtesy the Autry Museum of Western Heritage, Los Angeles. In memory of Sharon Johnson.*

CHAPTER 18

Outgunned at Eagle Nest Crossing

April 25, 1875

— ☆ —

Pvt. Pompey Factor   Sgt. John Ward
Trumpter Isaac Payne

On April 21, 1875, U.S. Indian Agent J. M. Hayworth reported that, "possibly only 35 Comanches and 180 Essaqueta Apaches'" were still not registered or accounted for by informants.[1] The reports by agents at the Cheyenne Agency were just as positive and all affirmed the success of the army's Indian Territory expedition. The success of the expedition could be measured in part by the relative tranquillity of the western frontier Texas counties in the early part of 1875. Reports of Indian attacks declined by one half. There was a 60 percent decline in frontier killings by Indians since 1873.[2] One of the few incidents reported was on April 5, 1875, when word was received at Fort Clark from Capt. John W. French, commander of Fort Duncan, that Indians had attacked a stagecoach on the San Antonio Road near Bell's Ranch in Maverick County. The trail left by one part of the attacking band had trailed off to the north toward the Pecos.[3]

On April 15 Col. William R. Shafter, commanding officer at Fort Clark, announced to his officer staff that there would have to be a step up in scouting activity into the lower Pecos River area. All roads, trails, springs, and water crossings between Fort Clark and Fort Stockton would have to be kept under constant surveillance to prevent hostile Indian transit across the region. This surveillance would commence the next day and Lt. John L. Bullis was given the orders to commence the activity with a scouting patrol into the area.[4] Bullis, commanding

233

the Seminole-Negro Indian scout detachment, was told that he could take as many scouts as he felt necessary. Bullis astounded Shafter and Col. Edward Hatch when he announced that he would take only three scouts. A small detachment would leave a smaller trail and wouldn't alarm any roving bands of Indians as would a larger body of troops. Bullis's logic carried the discussion and he announced he would take Sgt. John Ward, Pvt. Pompey Factor, and Trumpeter Isaac Payne. Ward and Factor were five-year veterans of the scout detachment and were excellent trailers. Both had been with Colonel Mackenzie's column during his punitive raid into Mexico in 1873 and during the campaign of 1874. Payne was a newcomer with only two months of service with the scout detachment.[5]

At noon on April 16 the four-man scout detachment left Fort Clark accompanied by a supply wagon train bound for Fort Stockton and escorted by Company A, Twenty-fifth U.S. Infantry.[6] Bullis and the three scouts remained with the wagon train for six days. On the morning of April 22 they remained with the wagon train for one hour during the train's northward trek from the campsite at Beaver Lake. Bullis then led the scouts west toward the Pecos River. Two hours after leaving Beaver Lake the scouts discovered signs of a small Indian band. The trail led up Johnson's Run, a dry arroyo that drained into the Devils River from the west. Since the trail was old and apparently made by only four or five unshod ponies, Bullis decided to ignore it and he and the scouts continued their trek to the west. At sundown the detachment went into camp about twenty-five miles west of Beaver Lake. By 6 A.M. on April 23 the four were winding their way down Howard Canyon, stopping occasionally to reconnoiter those arroyos feeding into the canyon. Throughout the next two days they continually moved westward, reconnoitering first the Fielder Draw ford of the Pecos and later the springs at the head of Big Fielder Creek. On April 24 they turned south and at sundown camped in Thurston Canyon. Bullis decided to turn southeast to reconnoiter the most frequented ford of the Rio Grande in the area. At first light they were in the saddle and by noon on April 25 they were at the ford opposite Eagle Nest Creek. Short scouting forays failed to turn up any fresh trails, so they moved downstream for twenty-two miles and camped in a cave overlooking the Rio Grande.[7]

At sunrise on April 26 Payne left early on a solo scout and returned shortly before noon with news of many old trails but no recent tracks. After dinner the group broke camp and began moving east toward Fort Clark. Shortly before 2 P.M., some three miles east of their camp the previous night, they struck a freshly-made trail. The trail was quite large, came from the direction of the nearest settlement, and led off to the northwest in the direction of the Eagle Nest Crossing of the Pecos. They now knew they were on to something for most of the tracks, at

Pompey Factor, circa 1910. His discharge papers were destroyed in a fire, leaving only his Medal of Honor as proof of his military service. He reluctantly submitted it to the Pension Bureau in 1926 and was granted his pension. *Photograph courtesy the William Loren Katz Collection.*

least fifty, were ringed by at least twenty unshod ponies. The detachment began following the trail at a gallop. At a little after 3 P.M. they neared the eastern incline to the Eagle Nest Crossing. Some two hundred yards below them was a party of twenty-five or thirty Indians preparing to ford the river with a herd of around fifty horses. The Indians were so intent on their crossing preparations that they were not aware of the scouts. After securing their horses, the four crept up to some bushes about a hundred yards down and along the edge of the incline above the Indians. All of the Indians were dismounted except for one woman. Lying prone behind the covering bush, they began to formulate a plan to separate the Indians from the herd and, if possible, capture the dismounted Indians.[8]

The plan was for Factor and Payne to move down among the rocks on both sides of the Indians and get as close as possible to the Indian herd. They would then commence firing and in the process stampede the horses up the incline and away from the Indians. Bullis and Ward would commence firing on the Indians once the herd had passed beyond their position. After about five minutes Factor and Payne were in position and when both began firing pandemonium broke out. The horses scattered back up the incline just as planned, with Factor and Payne close on their backsides. One of the Indians had managed to get mounted and sped up the incline, trying desperately to check the stampede. Just as he reached the edge of the incline a volley from Bullis and Ward killed him. Factor and Payne now rejoined Bullis and Ward among the rocks. Their first tactical objective in separating the Indians from their horses had been accomplished. The second objective was now much in doubt as the Indians had recovered from their surprise and were seen hurrying up among the rocks, firing as they

235

advanced. The scouts were working their Sharps carbines as fast as they could, but the Indian firing was becoming more menacing by the minute. Most of the Indians were pinned down by their firing, but a few had gained cover behind rock ledges along the rim of the incline and were within yards of some of the milling horses.[9]

The firing between the two groups continued almost unabated for fifteen minutes. Bullis then realized the severity of the situation. Not only were they outnumbered nearly five to one, but the Indians appeared to be armed with Winchester lever-action repeating rifles, far superior to the soldiers' Sharps carbines in rapid-fire situations.[10] During a brief lull several Indians worked themselves beyond the mass of milling horses, where they began firing and yelling until the horses were stampeded back toward the incline to the river bank. Factor and Payne desperately tried to turn the herd back but their efforts were quickly foiled by rapid fire from the Indian snipers hidden among the nearby rocks. As soon as the horses had passed the scouts' position, one of the scouts noticed four Indians running toward their tethered horses. All four scouts poured rapid fire on the four Indians and two went down. The other Indians fled for cover, one limping from a leg wound. Bullis realized they were in an untenable position and urged the others to get to their horses. Firing and retreating, they quickly made their way to the horses. Just as they began to mount, several Indians sprang up from the rocks on two sides and unleashed a furious fire upon them. Factor and Payne were the first to get mounted. Ward was the next to reach his horse and mount. Just as he reared about and put the spurs to his mount he turned to see Bullis grab his saddle horn and prepare to swing into the saddle. One bullet ricocheted from a rock, spooking Bullis's horse, which bolted wildly. Bullis lost his grip on the saddle horn and he fell violently to the ground. Factor and Payne put the spurs to their mounts and bolted for the open ground to the east until Ward yelled frantically, "We can't leave the Lieutenant, boys!" Factor and Payne reined up and within seconds had unsheathed their carbines. They charged into the fray, drawing up between the Indians and Ward and Bullis. Ward had drawn up at Bullis's side and hoisted him up behind him amid a withering fire. As soon as Bullis swung up behind Ward, a shot cut through Ward's carbine sling and as Ward put the spurs to his horse another shot shattered his carbine stock. Factor and Payne held the Indians at bay briefly by firing into the Indian herd, prompting the herd to scatter. Amid this confusion the four scouts beat a hasty retreat to the east. They did not stop until they got to Painted Cave on the Devils River some twelve miles from the fight. They camped there for the night and Bullis had no trouble expressing his gratitude to the scouts for what they had done. The foursome left for Fort Clark the next morning at sunrise and covered the forty-three miles to Fort Clark by late that afternoon. Bullis reported to Shafter immediately. During the eleven-day patrol they had covered 326 miles and they would now be able to fill in a few blank spaces on maps of the area. The areas of good grass, water sources and suitable river fords Bullis had plotted proved to be invaluable later in the year when Colonel Shafter led a large expedition into the area. Most importantly they had intercepted and punished a marauding band of Indians, killing three and wounding a fourth.[11]

Later in the evening, during officers' call, Bullis related the particulars of the scout to the assembled officers and closed with the request that with Colonel Shafter's approval, he would like to recommend that the three scouts be awarded Medals of Honor for their deeds. Shafter concurred and requested that Bullis make out a complete and detailed report of the incident.[12] Bullis did so and the report was forwarded along with Shafter's endorsement to Gen. Edward O. C. Ord, commander of the Department of Texas. Ord incorporated the report into General Order no. 10, dated May 12, 1875. Ord then forwarded Bullis's report to the adjutant general's office in Washington, D.C. Ord's endorsement praised the scouts for their "courageous and soldierly conduct" and made the formal recommendation for them to be awarded Medals of Honor. Gen. W. T. Sherman approved the award and the secretary of war ordered the medals to be engraved on May 22, 1875. The medals for the three scouts were received at Fort Clark on July 1, 1875. Two of them were again in the field, this time guiding Shafter's expedition onto the Staked Plains. A courier carrying mail and dispatches to Shafter delivered the medals to his camp on the South Concho River, where he acknowledged their receipt on the morning of July 8, 1875.[13] In a simple dress ceremony that evening, Sgt. John Ward and Trumpeter Isaac Payne were presented this nation's highest award for gallantry in action. Pvt. Pompey Factor had been transferred to Fort Duncan, but Shafter eventually presented the Medal of Honor to him on March 15, 1876. Pompey Factor, like John Ward and Isaac Payne, could only make an "X" to acknowledge the receipt of his Medal of Honor. This, however, did not lessen the men's pride in the medals, as all three would cherish them until their deaths.[14]

John L. Bullis, whose life was saved that day near the Pecos River, went on to a long and distinguished military career. A sub-post to Fort Sam Houston, north of San Antonio, was named in his honor. Camp Bullis has become a part of the psyche of the tens of thousands of soldiers and airmen who have trained there, thanks to the intrepid gallantry of three brave Seminole-Negro Indian scouts who refused to abandon their lieutenant.

Allen Walker. His fluency in the Spanish language would serve him well as a soldier and officer in the Philippine Scouts and later as a U.S. Marshal in the Texas
Rio Grande borderlands. *Courtesy Albino Walker, Laredo, Texas.*

CHAPTER 19

Gallantry among the Chaparral

December 30, 1891

Pvt. Allen Walker

For more than three decades between 1877 and 1911 Mexico was dominated by a single president, Porfirio Diaz.[1] While Diaz, a dictator, did have the support of a majority of the Mexican citizenry he also had many vocal detractors, primarily liberal journalists. After Diaz's hotly contested reelection in 1888 his opponents became increasingly militant. Liberal journalists openly called for his forcible overthrow, which incited his supporters into more violent responses. Among those liberal journalists forced to flee the wrath of Diaz's supporters was a tight-knit triad comprised of former general Francisco R. Sandoval, Ignacio Martinez, and Catarino E. Garza. The three fled into South Texas, each eventually settling in various communities along the Rio Grande from Laredo to Brownsville. Their plan was to organize an opposition movement within the lower Rio Grande Valley borderlands of South Texas, clearly cognizant that this would be in violation of U.S. neutrality laws. By late 1889 Sandoval was in a U.S. federal prison for actively recruiting U.S. citizens for his liberation army. Ignacio Martinez lay dead at the hands of assassins at Laredo, after publishing scathing anti-Diaz editorials in his newspaper, *El Mundo*. Catarino Garza, on the other hand, had successfully evaded the pro-Diaz agents as well as Texas and U.S. officials and continued with his plans to raise a northern army to liberate Mexico from Diaz.[2]

Garza successfully increased his support throughout early and mid-1890. Money from undisclosed sources gave increasing impetus to the movement.[3] President Diaz was so alarmed that he dispatched three thousand additional troops to patrol the Mexican side of the lower Rio Grande border. By September Garza had outfitted and organized a force of around forty men.[4] On September 16 Garza, the self-proclaimed chief of the Liberation Army of the North, led his men across the Rio Grande for their first strike against the Diaz regime. The attack upon the customs house at Camargo was mildly successful, but a Mexican cavalry force quickly drove Garza's force back and they fled back across the Rio Grande. This and later attacks upon customs houses prompted Mexican diplomatic demands to the U.S. State Department for more stringent enforcement of U.S. neutrality laws.[5]

On December 2, 1891, the U.S. attorney general wrote to Paul Fricke, U.S. marshal for the Western District of Texas, urging him to do everything in his power to prevent any violation of neutrality laws by Catarino Garza and his followers. A number of suspected Garza sympathizers were already in jail in Rio Grande City and Brownsville, but the cases against them were weak, based upon questionable informants and hearsay testimony without any hard proof or evidence. The U.S. marshal's office for the Southern District of Texas was grossly undermanned and the problem was apparently beyond the control of a few federal marshals, so it was decided that the U.S. Army would support and complement federal authorities. In addition, the new governor of Texas, James S. Hogg, dispatched an additional company of Texas Rangers to help the federal and local authorities enforce state laws. The series of clashes, pursuits, and guerrilla warfare that lasted in its most active stages for the next two years was referred to as the "Tin Horn War." It was a supreme test for some of America's earliest practitioners of counterinsurgent operations. Men like Capt. John G. Bourke, Capt. Henry M. Wesells, and Capt. J. H. McNeil of the Texas Rangers faced a wily enemy whose movements were spasmodic and secretive. The Garza revolutionaries, either through threats and intimidation or through genuine support, had the cooperation of the general American populace in the lower Rio Grande Valley, which made it incredibly difficult to gather intelligence about the revolutionaries and even more difficult to keep secret their own movements against the revolutionaries. The revolutionaries could easily scatter into the dense chaparral brushlands and reassemble in designated points at the first sign of trouble. They wore no uniforms and easily melded into the populace, often posing as ranch hands in search of "las vacas pierdas." By spreading rumors and false information to unsuspecting, well-intentioned journalists and informants they confounded and confused intelligence data and exhausted the authorities with unnecessary movements. When pressed closely by government authorities on either side of the Rio Grande, they easily escaped by crossing to the opposite side. These were just a few of the problems and tactical disadvantages that the U.S. Justice, State and War Departments and Texas state authorities faced as they began to intensify their efforts in countering insurgency along the border.[6]

By December 22, 1891, the entire Third U.S. Cavalry garrisons from Forts Brown, Clark, Ringgold, and McIntosh were involved in active field operations against the revolutionaries. With a vast array of federal troops, Texas Rangers, federal marshals, local sheriffs and deputies in the field, it was just a question of time before they made contact with the revolutionaries. Those Mexican Americans in the settlements and ranches along the Rio Grande who were sympathetic to the Garza movement became vehemently resentful of searches of their ranches and premises. Deputy marshals were assigned to accompany each scouting party in order to prevent any breaches of constitutional law and to counter any subsequent claims of civil rights violations. Despite the many hindrances, patrols and spies were kept in the field constantly. Roads, river crossings, and suspected collaborators were kept under almost constant surveillance.[7]

The first major breakthrough in information gathering came on the morning of December 21, 1891, when U.S. Deputy Marshal Manuel Bañados of Edinburg, Texas, appeared at Fort Ringgold post headquarters to meet with Capt. John G. Bourke. Bañados, a very energetic and intelligent man, had succeeded in passing himself off as a dispatch courier for Catarino Garza and had elicited much information about Garza and his followers, including the report that one hundred of Garza's men were at that very moment gathering near La Grulla and were planning to cross into Mexico that night when the moon rose. He also indicated to Captain Bourke that there was reason to suspect that Deputy Marshal Tomás Garza was in full collusion with the revolutionaries.[8]

The garrison at Fort Ringgold was already threadbare, with only two understrength companies available for service. Not wanting to leave the post totally unprotected, Captain Bourke decided to select only the nineteen men from Troop C, Third Cavalry, and Company E, Eighteenth Infantry, who volunteered for the duty. At four o'clock that evening, Bourke, Bañados and Lt. Charles Hays, along with nineteen enlisted troopers and a six-mule wagon, an escort wagon, and one buckboard, started out for La Grulla, nineteen miles southeast of the post. The small command arrived at La Grulla shortly after sundown and Deputy Marshal Garza was immediately arrested and placed in irons. Bourke and Bañados began to interrogate Garza about the movements of Catarino Garza's men. Bourke was explicit about the seriousness of the activity that, Garza, a federal official, was suspected of being involved in. Tomás Garza, trusting in Bourke's confidence, told them that Catarino Garza used an isolated point near the Texas–Mexican

241

Catarino E. Garza, 1894. His scheme to use the Rio Grande borderlands of Texas as a base for his planned overthrow of Mexican President Porforio Diaz was thwarted by Pvt. Allen Walker's attack on a band of couriers and the resulting capture of documents detailing his command structure. *Photograph courtesy the Western History Collections, University of Oklahoma.*

Railroad between present-day Los Angeles, Texas, and the Frio River, some one hundred and fifty miles to the north, as his staging area. According to Tomás Garza, the presence of the Garzaites near Los Angeles would be purposely made public in the hopes of drawing the soldiers from Forts McIntosh and Ringgold into that area. In the meantime, Garza planned to divide his forces into three groups. One group was to march southwestward into Mexico, crossing the Rio Grande several miles above Laredo. This group was to attract all the attention possible, but was only supposed to meet other groups of Garza's men in the mountains of the state of Coahuila. The rest of the Garza forces were to be split into two other groups. One group would cross the Rio Grande near Guerrero, Mexico, and make a bold bluff against that town, which, it was hoped, would draw out all the Mexican army troops from Camargo. The third band was a force that was supposed to stage at nearby Retamal that very night and was to move across the Rio Grande to strike at the unprotected city of Camargo.[9]

Tomás Garza agreed to show Bourke the staging area at Retamal, but told him that his nineteen men would be outmatched by the one hundred revolutionaries he expected to be there. Bourke decided to go ahead and make a night attack at least to disperse Garza's men and prevent the sacking of Camargo. The small command would have to move quickly if the mission was to succeed, so it was decided to leave the wagons at La Grulla and the command started out through the chaparral to the northeast with two men on each horse. After about a mile or so the command crossed the Corpus Christi Road and within an hour the command had advanced to within a mile of Retamal. Upon Tomás Garza's suggestion, they dismounted and left their horses with a two-man guard. The remainder of the men crawled through the chaparral in search of the Garza camp. Before they had gone one thousand yards they noticed a small lake on their right with one or more campfires burning briskly along its banks. They advanced around the small lake toward the nearest fire. The men had been given explicit orders not to talk, whisper, laugh, cough, spit, or light any matches and they were not to answer any challenges. When the command was about one hundred yards from the nearest campfire the soldiers were challenged by one of the pickets, "Quien Vive?" They gave no reply but remained still and within a few seconds they heard a second challenge of, "Quien Vive?" Shortly afterward two shots rang out from the Garza pickets. The soldiers returned fire, which sent the revolutionaries scattering into the dense brush. When the first shots rang out, Tomás Garza made a break for freedom and also disappeared into the brush. Pursuit was impossible because of the dense foliage and darkness. The soldiers searched the campground but all they found was a complete saddle outfit along with 120 rounds of Winchester carbine ammunition. The men and horses were exhausted and the men decided to camp nearby for the night.[10]

Early the next morning, Tuesday, December 22, 1891, the command returned to La Grulla to get their wagons and ascertain whether or not the revolutionaries had made their planned crossing. After the command arrived at the La Grulla crossing, they found two men hiding in a nearby thicket and took them into custody for interrogation. If the revolutionaries had crossed the river they had done it somewhere else, for there was no evidence that a large number of horses had passed over the crossing. The command started back for the post via Retamal in the hopes that they might make contact with small groups or individual revolutionaries. The command arrived at Retamal around noon and began to set up a campsite while two small parties were sent to search the surrounding area. One party, Deputy Marshal Bañados and two enlisted troopers, headed southwest. The second party comprised of Deputy Marshal Manuel Perez, Cpl. Charles Edstrom, and Pvt. David Loyd, moved northeastward. The latter party had been gone only about fifteen minutes and had advanced about half a mile into a huisache and mesquite thicket when they ran headlong into a band of revolutionaries, who immediately opened fire at close range. Perez turned about and managed to escape from the hail of fire, Corporal Edstrom was knocked from his horse by a bullet wound to the left leg, and Private Loyd faltered from a grazing bullet wound in the right knee and found himself surrounded at gunpoint. As the revolutionaries advanced closer, one of them fired another shot at Edstrom and struck him in the head. One revolutionary dismounted to remove Edstrom's pistol and cartridge belt but found the young cavalryman still gasping for life. The revolutionary then fired another shot into Edstrom's head at such close range that the young corporal's face was horribly powder burned. In the meantime, Perez had galloped back to alert the main command. Bourke mounted up the available men and ordered the advance at double time with Sgt. Sam Shling, Sgt. Gustav Gilb, and Cpl. Robert Honeyman in the advance. The lead cavalry troopers, followed closely by the sprinting infantrymen, had to move across a flat, open area while under fire from the revolutionaries, who were hidden in the hillside's dense chaparral. As the troops advanced the revolutionaries shouted "Kill the damned Gringos!" Lieutenant Hays, mounted on a young wild mare, bolted straight toward the revolutionaries' positions and quickly fell with a bullet wound to his right side. Sergeants Shling and Gilb and Corporal Honeyman pushed through and engaged the revolutionaries in hand-to-hand fighting. After about five minutes the Garzaites broke and scattered into the cactus before they could be encircled. Cpl. Arthur D. Dougherty kneeled and with a steady aim fired his Springfield rifle, hitting one of the Garza leaders, who reeled in his saddle and was caught by a comrade, who led him and his mount out of sight into the chaparral. Bourke then ordered "Cease Fire" and the wounded men, along with Corporal Edstrom's body, were quickly loaded into the wagons. The soldiers started a rapid march for Fort Ringgold, where they arrived shortly before sunset.[11]

Bourke immediately telegraphed word of the engagement to Department of Texas headquarters at San Antonio. Edstrom's killing added a new dimension to the Garza affair. The Garzaites had not only committed murder, but those who were American citizens had also implicated themselves in an act of treason. Newspapers in New York City, Chicago, New Orleans, and San Antonio carried major stories about Corporal Edstrom's death. The frenzy of newspaper articles about the engagement with Sioux Indians at Wounded Knee, South Dakota, in December 1890 had receded and stories about the army's pursuit of revolutionaries in the South Texas brushlands were new and sensational. While reporters for the *New York Herald, New York Times*, and *Harper's Weekly* were boarding southbound trains, the lonely notes of taps echoed across the Rio Grande as Corporal Edstrom was laid to rest in the post cemetery at Fort Ringgold on the evening of December 23.[12]

Shortly after Bourke and his command had arrived back at Fort Ringgold on the evening of December 22, Lt. G. T. Langhorne was ordered to take to the field with a command of twenty-three men from Troop C, Third Cavalry, and two deputy marshals. This command was also to scout the area around La Grulla for any signs of straggling revolutionaries. Among those twenty-six men was twenty-five-year-old Pvt. Allen Walker from Patriot, Indiana. For the past several months Walker had served as a teamster for the Quartermaster Department driving supply wagons between Fort Ringgold and Hebbronville. An excellent teamster, Walker had become fluent in Spanish during his five years of service in the southwest. After learning of Corporal Edstrom's death Walker requested to be released from teamster duty so he could participate in scouting duty. While in the post headquarters building to request his release from teamster duty, Walker listened intently to an embittered Captain Bourke as he issued verbal orders to Lieutenant Langhorne "to kill on sight any of Garza's men found prowling over the country with arms in hand, but to be careful not to harass innocent people." Langhorne led his small command to La Grulla and then to Havana. Along the river road between La Grulla and Havana they took three suspected revolutionaries into custody. Langhorne returned to the post on the evening of December 23 to report that he had found the ranches around Havana totally devoid of adult males.[13]

During the next several days the momentum of the movements and policies intended to suppress the Garza revolution increased. On December 23, 1891, the commanding officer at Eagle Pass agreed to send out his patrols in unison with Mexican troops on the opposite bank. On that same day Gen. David S. Stanley announced that he was dispatching two additional troops of the Third Cavalry from Fort Clark to Fort Ringgold and Capt. F. S. Hardie, while on a scout to the east and southeast of Fort Duncan into the area around Los Angeles and Carrizo Springs, trailed a band of ninety-one suspected revolutionaries to the Rio Grande near El Indio.[14]

On December 24 Captain Bourke attended the late evening Christmas Eve Mass at Del Gallo Catholic Church in Rio Grande City.[15] Rumors were rampant among the milling crowds that Mexicans sympathetic to Garza might cross the Rio Grande and attempt to rescue the Garzaites then in the guardhouse at Fort Ringgold. Upon his return to the post, Bourke placed half of the garrison on special guard and placed Gatling guns in commanding positions around the guardhouse. Later that same evening Bourke went to the office of U.S. Commissioner Walter Downs in Rio Grande City, where he made a formal charge against Catarino Garza, Cayetano Garza, Sixto Longoria, Julian Flores, and Eustorgio Ramón, charging the five men with high treason. According to evidence gathered from informants these individuals were the leading figures in the revolutionary movement and had been present at the engagement at Retamal on December 22 when U.S. troops were fired upon. When Bourke returned to the post that night he found that Texas Gov. James S. Hogg had telegraphed to express his regrets over Corporal Edstrom's death and assured his cooperation in all respects in the protection of federal authorities and property on the state's border. Governor Hogg also announced that he was sending a company of Texas Rangers to assist United States authorities. General Stanley also had telegraphed reporting the transfer of Troops A and I of the Third Cavalry from Fort Sam Houston to Forts McIntosh and Ringgold. Additional wagons and supplies necessary to support these men were to be dispatched from Fort Clark. Stanley also informed Captain Bourke that the U.S. district attorney and his staffs at San Antonio and Brownsville were prepared to proceed against violators of the neutrality laws as soon as they had sufficient evidence.[16]

On Christmas Day the garrison at Fort Ringgold remained at readiness and, except for an opossum drinking a punch bowl of eggnog and running amok through the dining hall, the morning passed in relative reverence. Shortly after noon Langhorne sent in two suspected Garzaites as prisoners to be detained in the guardhouse.[17]

Early on Saturday morning, December 26, Señor P. Ornelas, consul general of Mexico at San Antonio, met with General Stanley in his office at Fort Sam

Houston. Señor Ornelas had received communications from Gen. Lorenzo Garcia, commander of the Mexican troops at Mier, about specific American citizens suspected of being involved in Garza's revolutionary affairs in some way. General Stanley turned the names and addresses over to U.S. District Attorney A. J. Evans for such action as he might deem necessary. The information was then sent to Bourke as intelligence data for field investigation. Late that evening Bourke called a staff meeting with all available commissioned officers, Deputy Marshal Bañados, and Starr County Sheriff W. W. Sheely in attendance. After several hours of deliberations over the data General Garcia had provided it was decided to move early the next morning against the suspected ranches. At sunrise on December 27 Langhorne and twenty hand-picked men accompanied by Marshal Banados and Sheriff Sheely were in the saddle and headed south. Their first objective was to investigate the area north of Havana Ranch, twenty-two miles southeast of Rio Grande City. While Langhorne and his men moved south and east, Captain Hardie's troops moved south along the Rio Grande from Fort McIntosh.[18]

At 9 A.M. on December 28 Bourke received further intelligence from General Garcia, whose urgent and reliable reports placed Catarino Garza and his men on the Casa Blanca Ranch, some thirty miles north of Roma. Bourke, Captain Mackey, and a force of fifteen Texas Rangers under the command of Capt. J. A. Brooks immediately took to the field. Captain Hardie and the thirty men of Troop G, Third Cavalry, advanced downriver to Salineno by sundown on December 28 and were joined later that evening by Bourke's contingent. At midnight a messenger sent by Carrizo Sheriff Robert Haynes brought word that the Garzaites were concentrating at a point twelve miles north of Lopeño in an area called the Charco Redondo. After a brief conference it was decided to send couriers to the various commands and order a converging movement on certain ranches in the Charco Redondo area suspected of harboring the Garzaites. At 2:45 that morning Captain Hardie and the joint civil-military command struck out to the northwest along the Rio Grande. Lieutenants Beach and Short and thirty-four troopers were camped at Pineño, where they were notified by courier at sunrise on December 29 that they were to hold their position. Another courier arrived at Fort Ringgold just after sunrise and reported to Captain Wheeler, who was temporarily in command of the post. Wheeler immediately sent word to Langhorne to have his men mount up and move to unite with Captain Hardie's command. As the first sergeant passed down the rows of beds, waking the troopers in Troop C quarters, the troopers growled at the orders to again take to the bush. For Pvt. Allen Walker, for example, the order placed him on scouting patrol for the third time within the past thirty-six hours. By 9 A.M. Langhorne and twenty-six troopers were on the road to Roma.[19]

In the meantime, Captain Hardie's command joined Lieutenant Beach's command at Pineño a little after sunrise. After a brief stop for breakfast the joint command headed northwest along the Rio Grande. As the command moved up the river road, several suspected revolutionaries were taken into custody. By noon the command had reached the Soledad Ranch, where they encamped to wait for Captain Mackey's troops and the posse from Carrizo under Sheriff Haynes, which arrived within an hour. After the men were treated to dinner the entire command, except for the wagons, prisoners, and a small guard detail, struck out through the chaparral to the northeast. The civilian contingent, including the Texas Rangers under Captain Brooks, the posse under Sheriff Haynes, U.S. Deputy Marshal Van Riper and two Mexican guides sent by General Garcia, were in the lead. Fifteen miles out of the Soledad Ranch the column closed in on the La Purisima Ranch. The Texas Rangers ran in at a gallop amid fluttering chickens, barking dogs, and screaming women and children running around with their hands in the air. One of the rangers rode up to the women and told them in Spanish not to be afraid as they did not want to hurt anybody. None of Garza's men were found, but the soldiers discovered an unusually large quantity of blankets and jerked beef. The command's suspicions were further aroused when several women from the ranch were found burning brush in some nearby woods. It may have been innocent labor, but it could have been a signal fire. The command decided to push on to the José M. Garcia Ranch some six miles to the north and hoped to reach there before sunset. When the command arrived at the Garcia Ranch the occupants refused to give any information whatsoever. There were a great many horses on the ranch and the tracks of at least two hundred shod horses were discovered leading back into the nearby chaparral. The command followed the tracks at a gallop and at sunset the two Mexican trailers were challenged by the Garza pickets. Shots were fired by both sides but the Garzaites dashed off into the dense chaparral where pursuit was impossible in the darkness. The command then withdrew a short distance and went into camp. Langhorne and his troop were that same evening going into camp near El Sauz, some thirty miles to the south.[20]

The command at the Garcia Ranch rose at sunrise and was startled by several distant gunshots, which they suspected were signal shots fired by the Garza spies. Captains Bourke and Mackey and two enlisted troopers left the camp after breakfast and started southward for the Pineño Ranch. Captain Hardie's troops, along with a newly arrived posse from Zapata County, the marshals, and the Texas Rangers, continued northward. By noon this command had moved more than ten miles and had searched the Una de Gato, Penta, and Villa Ranches. Hardie was now convinced that the revolutionaries were close at hand and he decided to continue northward at least as far as Rendado. Tracks of large numbers of shod horses were evident along the road. The pace was quickened and at the Colorado Ranch Hardie's hunch paid off. The Garzaites had been pressed so hard that they had been forced to abandon a badly wounded comrade, Sixto Longoria. Hardie took him prisoner and, aware of the seriousness of Longoria's wound, left several of his men to escort him back to Fort Ringgold where he could receive medical attention. Hardie persistently pushed the command on toward Rendado, leaving the Colorado Ranch at 3 P.M. on December 30.[21]

Langhorne was also driving his men hard and shortly before sundown on December 30 he drew his detachment up at the Colorado Ranch just an hour behind Captain Hardie's command. At the ranch he found the two enlisted men who had been left behind with the wounded prisoner, Sixto Longoria. Langhorne's men and their mounts needed a rest and with darkness almost upon them Langhorne decided to camp there and establish contact with Hardie's command the next morning.[22] At 7 A.M. on December 31 Langhorne dispatched Private Walker to move up Hardie's trail and overtake him as soon as possible. Walker was also to deliver a pouch full of orders and dispatches to Captain Hardie's command. Walker followed the trail through the heavy sand and mesquite brakes at a moderate gait. After six miles, around 8:30 A.M., he approached one of the eastern branches of Fandango Creek. Just as he came to a clearing in the chaparral that stretched several hundred yards to the north, Walker thought he heard faint voices coming from the mesquite to his rear. Walker quickly secreted himself in some brush near the road and waited. After several minutes, three well-armed Latin American men approached, conversing in Spanish. Intelligence reports had noted that on occasion the Garza revolutionaries could be identified by white hatbands worn around their wide-brimmed sombreros. Walker, noting this identifying feature on the three approaching riders, concluded that they were Garzaites, drew his Springfield carbine, and waited. When the three men were opposite him about twenty yards away, he challenged them and they quickly went for their guns. Walker opened fire on them and shot one of the revolutionaries from his horse. The revolutionaries returned fire and Walker retaliated with rapid fire on them, reloading quickly with cartridges he held in his mouth. The two mounted revolutionaries had problems controlling their startled mounts and turned to retreat.

Walker then found himself under severe fire from several other revolutionaries in the brush and mesquite thickets around him. The firing intensified and the young soldier turned to retreat. Just as he turned about, he fired a parting shot and hit one of the revolutionaries' horses, killing it instantly and throwing the rider to the ground. Unable to oppose the odds against him and remembering the treatment of Corporal Edstrom at the hands of the Garzaites, Walker stowed his rifle and made a run for the command with about twenty revolutionaries in pursuit.[23]

Langhorne's detachment had saddled up about thirty minutes after Walker left the camp and were about three miles behind him. Upon hearing the firing they advanced at a gallop. The revolutionaries chased Walker for almost a mile but were held at bay by his accurate pistol fire. When Langhorne's detachment arrived, the Garzaites scattered in all directions. They had been so intent upon getting Private Walker that they did not stop to recover the saddlebags, saddle, and coat belonging to one of the two Garzaites Walker had attacked, which proved to be a serious mistake. Walker led the command back to the scene of the fight and began a thorough search of the abandoned items. Inside the rolled coat on the abandoned saddle, Walker found a commission paper for a lieutenant in Garza's revolutionary army. Inside the saddlebags were several documents, one a proclamation inciting those of Mexican blood to rebel against Diaz. Other documents were receipts for property the revolutionary army planned to seize. These documents proved to be the beginning of the end for the Garza revolutionary army movement in South Texas. Langhorne continued to drive his command to the southeast toward Las Cuevitas Ranch, where, according to spies sent out the night before, several of Garza's important officers were supposed to be in hiding. No suspects were found there upon the troops' arrival, however, and the command camped nearby for the night.[24]

Early on New Year's Day the command resumed a rapid march southeast toward the Prieto Ranch about five miles away. Sheriff W. W. Sheely, who was familiar with the locale, rode in the lead. Several miles into the march Sheely observed a mounted Latin American man hiding in a wooded area along the road. The man bolted upon his discovery but he was quickly overtaken and arrested. A number of documents were found in his possession, which identified him as Pablo Muñoz, one of Garza's colonels. Langhorne led the command forward along Muñoz's tracks. After less than a mile a body of men was discovered camped at the foot of a slight elevation off to their left about a quarter of a mile in the distance. Langhorne dismounted most of his troops and led them in a spirited charge into the Garzaites' camp. Private Walker assumed the advance across a two hundred-yard clearing and into the revolutionaries' camp, all the while under severe fire. The revolutionaries, blocked from mounted escape by a fence line, fled pell-mell into the dense mesquite and chaparral. Walker again seized the opportunity and began a thorough search of the abandoned equipment. Among the documents Walker found were enlistment and commission papers listing many names and a general order showing the overall organization of the Garza revolutionary army.[25]

The band of revolutionaries Langhorne's command struck at Prieto Ranch on New Year's Day had been engaged on December 30 by Captain Hardie's command near Charco Redondo. Minor clashes between military and civil officials and Garzaites continued throughout the year but for the most part the Garza revolutionary movement in South Texas was broken. The capture of the documents by Private Walker, Sheriff Sheely, and Lt. G. T. Langhorne's command assured its demise. Catarino Garza himself did not stop running until he reached Costa Rica.[26]

Pvt. Allen Walker, who had enforced his nation's neutrality laws with gallantry and disregard for his own personal safety, received high praise from his company commander, Lt. G. T. Langhorne. On March 2, 1892, Capt. John G. Bourke wrote a letter to the Department of Texas commander, Gen. David S. Stanley, recommending Private Walker for the Medal of Honor. Bourke wrote, "Private Walker exhibited so much courage, efficiency, coolness and self reliance when away from his command that I feel constrained to recommend that he be granted a Medal of Honor." General Stanley endorsed the recommendation on March 9, 1892, and forwarded it to Washington, D.C., where Gen. J. M. Schofield formally approved the award on April 14, 1892.[27] This formal approval came just as Private Walker was detailed to appear before the U.S. Circuit Court in San Antonio as a witness. Private Walker's appearance as a prosecution witness before the court may be the only time in which a Medal of Honor recipient was called upon in a court of law to give testimony concerning his deed of gallantry.[28] Pvt. Allen Walker's Medal of Honor was sent from Washington, D.C., on April 25, 1892, to his duty station at Fort Ringgold. It is unknown exactly when and under what circumstances he actually received his medal.[29]

Six months after Private Walker captured the documents, approximately 340 men faced charges of conspiracy to violate United States neutrality laws. The trials of the accused took place in the federal courthouse at San Antonio. Even though many of the accused were acquitted or received minor fines and jail terms, some of the major actors such as Pablo Muñoz received as much as eighteen months in federal prison. Most of those sentenced to prison terms were incarcerated at the federal houses of corrections at Baltimore or Detroit.[30] The issue of Americans in South Texas violating U.S. neutrality laws became an issue again during and after the Mexican Revolution of 1910 to 1917. The less-populated border areas of West Texas and New Mexico suffered more during this period, in terms of the loss of life and property, than did the more populous South Texas border areas. One reason for this may have been a more pronounced awareness in South Texas of the penalties for violating neutrality laws. If that was the reason for a more tranquil situation, then much credit belongs to Pvt. Allen Walker and the others like him who fought gallantly in the brief and obscure "Tin Horn War" of 1891 to 1893 in the chaparral brushlands of deep South Texas.

Biographies

—— ✯ ——

The biographies compiled herein for each recipient, with a few exceptions, were extracted from a variety of public documents. Biographies for the officer recipients were compiled from their Appointment, Commission and Promotion (ACP), "Personnel files," in Records Group 94, various officer military histories found within their respective regiments recorded within Records Group 391, and pension file records within Records Group 15.

Biographical information on the enlisted recipients came initially from the "Enlistment registers," and "Enlistment papers," within Records Group 94 and pension files in Records Group 15. Further data was obtained from pertinent census records in Records Group 29 and individual documents-received files in Records Group 94, and supplemented with various other secondary sources, all deliniated to the individual, in the "Biographies Sources" section.

George E. Albee
Lieutenant, Twenty-fourth U.S. Infantry

George Emerson Albee was born at Lisbon, New Hampshire, on January 27, 1845, the only son of Otis A. and Maria Gould Albee. The family relocated to Baraboo, Wisconsin, in 1852 and George received his education in the public schools there.

On June 25, 1862, George Albee enlisted as a private in Company G, First Wisconsin Regiment of Berdan Sharpshooters. He was wounded at the second battle of Bull Run on August 30, 1862, and was granted convalescent leave to Wisconsin. On December 22, 1863, he reenlisted in the Third Battery, Wisconsin Light Artillery, and was discharged from this unit on March 7, 1864, in order to accept an appointment as a second lieutenant in Company F, Thirty-sixth Wisconsin Infantry. He participated in the engagements at Spotsylvania, May 8–12, 1864; Cold Harbor, May 31–June 5, 1864; and at Ream's Station on August 25, 1864, where he was captured by Confederate forces. He was confined at Libby Prison in Richmond, but on September 27, 1864, was paroled from the parolee camp near Annapolis, Maryland, and was formally exchanged on December 16, 1864. He was mustered out at Madison, Wisconsin, on July 25, 1865.

Albee received a regular army commission as a second lieutenant on September 18, 1865, with the Thirty-sixth U. S. Infantry (Colored), and was reappointed on January 3, 1867, with the Forty-first U.S. Infantry (Colored). On November 11, 1869, he was promoted to first lieutenant with the newly organized Twenty-fourth U.S. Infantry. Between September and November 1869 he temporarily commanded Ninth U.S. Cavalry detachments in the Carroll and Bacon expeditions onto the northwestern high plains region of Texas. During these two expeditions he performed continuing and conspicuous acts of gallantry that merited his being awarded the Medal of Honor. During 1870 Albee served with his company at Fort Brown and on recruit escort duty at Nashville, Tennessee. In April 1871 he returned to Texas and was instrumental in quelling civil disturbances in Limestone County.

On July 11, 1872, he married Fredericka Hawes at Baraboo, Wisconsin. After returning to duty at Fort Brown, Texas, he was plagued with colds, pneumonia, and severe pulmonary conditions and was granted a one-year convalescent leave effective May 1873. In August 1874 he volunteered his services for the R. S. Mackenzie Staked Plains campaign and served as temporary commander of the Seminole-Negro scout detachment during the campaign He was involved in engagements near Red Hill, Tule, and Palo Duro Canyons on September 26–28, 1874. During the campaign he also served as a special correspondent for the *New York Herald* newspaper and provided the first printed accounts of the Mackenzie engagement at Palo Duro Canyon.

During 1875–1876 Albee designed an improvement in cavalry girths and saddles and submitted it to the army for field trials. During 1877–1878 he purchased and resided upon a ranch near Boerne, Texas. On June 27, 1878, a U. S. Army Retiring Board formally declared him retired due to the disability of phthisis pulmonalis he had incurred in the line of duty. In 1882 Albee became inspector of artillery ammunition for the Winchester Repeating Arms Company of New Haven, Connecticut, and continued in this capacity until his retirement in 1911. From 1892 to 1897 he served as brigade inspector, instructor, and ordnance officer for the Connecticut National Guard with the rank of major. He was breveted captain on February 27, 1900, for "gallant services in the actions against hostile Indians on the Brazos River, Texas, September 16, 1869 and October 28–29, 1869" and was commissioned a captain on the retired list effective June 11, 1900.

Albee was a member of the Connecticut Society of the Sons of the American Revolution and a companion of the Order of the Congressional Medal of Honor Legion of the United States. After retiring from the Winchester company he resided at Chesterton and Laurel, Maryland, between 1911 and 1918. He died on March 24, 1918, at Laurel, Maryland, and was interred at Arlington National Cemetery. He was survived by two daughters, Mab Corbin Albee and Maria Hawes Albee.

Frank D. Baldwin
Lieutenant, Fifth U.S. Infantry

Frank Dwight Baldwin was born on June 26, 1842, near Manchester, Michigan, to Francis L. and Betsey Ann Baldwin. In his youth he spent a great deal of time in the outdoors hunting and trapping along the St. Joseph River in southwestern Michigan. He attended the public schools of Constantine and in the fall of 1861 entered Hillsdale College.

At the outset of the Civil War Baldwin left school to accept a commission as a first lieutenant with the Nineteenth Michigan Infantry, effective September 5, 1862. In his first major action near Brentwood, Tennessee, he was captured by Confederate troops commanded by Gen. Nathan B. Forrest and was imprisoned for seven months before he was exchanged and released on September 19, 1863. Several weeks later Baldwin was ordered to defend a railroad bridge over the Stones River near Murfreesboro, Tennessee. His position was overwhelmed by Confederate troops commanded by Gen. Joseph Wheeler and Baldwin found himself a prisoner once again. During the winter of 1863–1864 Baldwin commanded various scouting detachments in actions against Confederate guerrilla units in the area around McMinnville, Tennessee. On January 23, 1864, he was promoted to captain. During 1864 Baldwin was very active in engagements in Georgia at Resaca, May 14–15, 1864; Cassville, May 19, 1864; Dallas Hills, May 25, 1864; Golgotha, June 1, 1864; Culp's Farm, June 22, 1864; Peachtree Creek, July 20, 1864; and the capture of Atlanta on September 2, 1864. On December 22, 1864, he was involved in the final capture of Savannah, Georgia. During the Carolinas campaign he fought in actions at Averasboro, North Carolina, on March 16, 1865, and at Bentonville, North Carolina, on March 21, 1865. On June 26, 1865, he was mustered out of the volunteer service at Detroit at the rank of lieutenant colonel.

Baldwin actively pursued a regular army commission, which was granted on February 23, 1866, with the rank of second lieutenant. Initially with the Nineteenth U.S. Infantry, this unit was consolidated to become the Thirty-seventh U.S. Infantry and Baldwin was assigned to Fort Ellsworth, Kansas.

On January 10, 1867, Baldwin married Alice Blackwood at Northville, Michigan. During 1868 he served at Fort Wingate, New Mexico, as commissary officer for the post and the adjoining Bosque Redondo Navajo Reservation.

In early 1869 reorganization dissolved the Thirty-seventh U.S. Infantry and Baldwin was assigned to Company E, Fifth U.S. Infantry, and over the next several years he was stationed at Forts Hays and Larned in Kansas. During 1873 and early 1874 he was assigned to recruiting duty in Michigan and Kentucky. In June 1874 Baldwin was assigned to the logistics for the scouting and courier detachments of the Nelson A. Miles Indian Territory expedition. During this campaign he commanded the cavalry detachment that relieved the Indian siege on the buffalo hunter camp at Adobe Walls on June 27, 1874. Baldwin was extremely active in engagements at Battle Creek on August 30, 1874; at White Fish Creek, September 7, 1874; and on November 8, 1874, on the North Fork of McClellan Creek. At the conclusion of the Indian Territory campaign Baldwin served in various capacities at Camp Supply, Fort Sill, and Newport Barracks, Kentucky.

On July 12, 1876, his unit left Fort Leavenworth, Kansas, to take part in the Sioux campaign. On December 6, 1876, Baldwin learned the location of Sitting Bull's command from scouts. In order to block Sitting Bull's escape route Baldwin marched his troops for forty-eight hours through a snowstorm during which temperatures dipped to forty degrees below zero. On December 18, 1876, Baldwin's troops struck Sitting Bull on the Red Water River, soundly beating Sitting Bull's warrior force. This seventy-three-mile march in forty-eight hours in bitterly cold temperatures remains one of the greatest infantry feats of the entire Indian War era. News of the victory was transmitted across the nation and Baldwin was heralded as "Custer's Avenger." He was again cited for gallantry in the engagement at Wolf Mountains on January 8, 1877, when Crazy Horse's warriors were routed. After a year of continuous field duty and in poor health Baldwin was granted a convalescent leave to Florida during the winter of 1878–1879. Baldwin's last action against Indians was a minor clash at Big Porcupine Creek, Montana, on March 8, 1880.

Inflicted with severe paroxysm, Baldwin again was sent to Florida for rehabilitation and afterward was granted a six-month leave of absence to study the military structure and installations of Europe. In October 1881 he was assigned to duty as acting judge advocate of the military Department of Columbia. In this capacity he was able to continue his study and practice of law. One of his most adept briefs in 1885 was entitled, "Opinion on Incorporating in a Specification Under a Charge, Instances of Previous Trials and Convictions." During 1883–1884 he settled Indian dissatisfaction on the Moses and Colville reservations in Washington Territory. In 1885 he personally conducted the negotiations that returned the Nez Perce tribe to their native lands in the Northwest.

When Baldwin returned to field duty with his regiment he was stationed at Fort Ellis, Montana, through 1886. In 1887 he served at Fort Pembina and Fort Buford in North Dakota. During 1888–1890 he was posted to Texas and served at Fort Bliss, Fort Davis, Camp Peña Colorado, and Fort Clark. On February 27, 1890, Baldwin received the brevet rank of captain, "for his continued exhibition of gallantry during the Indian Territory Expedition in Texas in 1874."

In late 1890, upon the personal request of Gen. N. A. Miles, Baldwin was assigned to duty as assistant inspector general and was ordered to the scene of disturbances on the Pine Ridge Sioux Indian Agency in South Dakota. He remained in the field as an aide to General Miles throughout the disturbances and the subsequent surrender of hostile Sioux on January 16, 1891. He was afterward part of the inspector general's staff, which investigated the conduct of Col. James W. Forsyth's Seventh Cavalry troops at the battle of Wounded Knee.

In June 1891 Baldwin was assigned to duty as inspector of small arms at Chicago, Illinois. On December 3, 1891, through the efforts of General Miles and former comrades in arms, he was granted his first Medal of Honor for his distinguished gallantry in action at Peachtree Creek, Georgia, on July 20, 1864. On October 29, 1894, he was assigned to duty as acting Indian Agent for the Kiowa Agency at Anadarko, Oklahoma. During his tenure in that capacity he was cited for excellent administration in improving conditions on behalf of the Kiowa tribe. On November 28, 1894, he was granted his second Medal of Honor for his rescue of Julia and Adelaide German on November 8, 1874, on the North Fork of McClellan Creek, Texas. He was promoted to major in April 1898.

At the outset of the Spanish-American War Baldwin sought a combat command in Cuba but was instead posted to Chickamauga, Tennessee, in a training capacity as acting inspector general with the Third Army Corps. After the surrender of Spanish troops in Cuba Baldwin served as inspector general for occupation troops at Matanzas, Cuba.

In December 1899 Baldwin was promoted to lieutenant colonel and assigned with the Fourth U.S. Infantry to Cavite Province, Philippine Islands, where in March 1901 he was instrumental in the capture of Mariano Trias, vice president of the Filipino insurrectionist government and two thousand of his followers. He was promoted to colonel effective July 26, 1901, and given command of the Twenty-seventh U.S. Infantry. He commanded the Lake Lanao Expedition on Mindanao Island and personally led his troops in the attack at Bayan on May 2, 1902. He was promoted to brigadier general effective June 9, 1902, and was specially cited by President Theodore Roosevelt in General Order no. 90, dated May 5, 1902. He later served as the commander of the military Department of the Viscayas, Philippine Islands, where he remained until February 22, 1903.

Baldwin assumed command of the military Department of Colorado at Denver in April 1903. On June 15, 1904, Hillsdale College conferred an honorary doctorate of law degree upon General Baldwin in recognition of his many military accomplishments. In April 1905 he was assigned as commander of the Southwest Military Division at Oklahoma City, Oklahoma, and remained in that position until his retirement on June 26, 1906.

Baldwin retired to Denver, Colorado. At age seventy-five he served as the adjutant general of the state of Colorado during 1917–1919. He died in his home at Denver on April 22, 1923, and was buried at Arlington National Cemetery at Washington, D.C. He was survived by his wife, Alice; a daughter, Juanita Williams-Foote; son-in-law, Carlos Williams-Foote; and two grandsons, Baldwin and Gloster Williams-Foote.

George H. Bell
Coxswain, USS *Santee*

George H. Bell was born at Sunderland, County of Durham, in England on March 12, 1839. Sometime during the mid-1840s his family moved to Newcastle-on-Tyne and at age fourteen he went to sea for the first time. By the age of twenty-one he had sailed across the Atlantic and Indian Oceans and the Black, Mediterranean, Baltic, and Caribbean Seas. During a docking at New York City Bell enlisted in the United States Navy on May 12, 1861, and was assigned as an able seaman to the West Gulf squadron. In July he shipped out on board the USS *Santee*, commanded by Capt. Henry Eagle. Bell was quickly appointed to coxswain because of his experience and superior seamanship skills.

On November 7, 1861, as pilot of the second launch from the *Santee* on a two-launch raiding party sent into Galveston Bay, Texas, Bell performed the deed for which he was awarded the Navy Medal of Honor. During this raid he incurred a serious wound to his throat. After a brief convalescent stay at the Brooklyn Navy Yard Hospital, Bell was assigned to the USS *Western World*.

Later he served on the *Ohio*, *Brooklyn*, and *Mohican*. Bell was active in engagements at Fort Polaski, Georgia, on April 11, 1862; the battle of Mobile Bay on August 5, 1864; and was a member of the storming party that captured Fort Pickens. He reenlisted on April 15, 1864. His final action of the Civil War was as a member of the storming party that assaulted Fort Fisher, North Carolina, on January 15, 1865.

After the decommissioning of the USS *Brooklyn* at the Brooklyn Navy Yard Bell was assigned to the receiving ship USS *North Carolina*. In early April 1865, while on shore leave in New York City, he was "shanghaied" aboard a commercial sailing vessel by unsavory recruiting agents for a voyage to Cuba. It was there that he learned of the war's end. He returned to New York City to confront the desertion charges he knew had been filed against him because of his unauthorized absence. He named the commercial agents, their tactic of buying him numerous drinks, and his waking up only after the ship was far at sea. The story was all too familiar to naval authorities and, upon Bell's promise to work off his missed time, the desertion charge was expunged from his record.

In June 1866 Bell returned to Newcastle and married a longtime girlfriend. He continued in the merchant marine service until 1887, when recurrent infections from his old throat wound forced his retirement. He worked as a carpenter and bricklayer in Newcastle until his absolute retirement in 1903. He applied for and was granted a U.S. Civil War disability pension. By 1916 he was severely crippled by lumbago and rheumatism. He died on September 26, 1917, and was buried in Elswick Cemetery at Newcastle. He was survived by a niece, Elizabeth Halleday.

Hjalmar Fredrik Bergendahl
Private, Fourth U.S. Cavalry

Hjalmar Fredrik Bergendahl was born at Gothenborg (Goteborg), Sweden, on October 11, 1851. His education included training in music and woodworking. He first came to the United States in 1870 and resided at Boston, Massachusetts. He enlisted in the United States Army on November 17, 1871. At the time of his enlistment he listed his occupation as a wood carver.

After recruit training at Carlisle Barracks he was assigned to Company D, Fourth U.S. Cavalry, then garrisoned at Fort Richardson, Texas. He would later be stationed at Forts Griffin, Concho, and Clark. During his service in Texas he took part in engagements at the North Fork of the Red River on September 29, 1872, and at Remolino, Mexico on April 23, 1873. During the 1874 Staked

Plains campaign, he volunteered for field duty despite the fact that he was a member of the regimental band at the time. During this campaign he was cited for "gallantry in a long chase after Indians" and was awarded the Medal of Honor. On February 20, 1876, at Fort Sill, Indian Territory, Bergendahl was promoted to corporal conductor of the Fourth Cavalry regimental band. He was discharged from the army on November 17, 1876, at Fort Robinson, Nebraska.

After his discharge Bergendahl returned to Sweden and continued his music studies for two years. In 1878 he returned to the United States and again enlisted in the Fourth U.S. Cavalry on August 28, 1878, at Boston. During his second enlistment he served at various posts in Colorado, New Mexico, and Arizona during campaigns against hostile Ute and Apaches. On January 20, 1880, Bergendahl accepted an early discharge in order to accept a position in the Swedish army.

On June 1, 1882, Bergendahl was accepted as an extra field musician in the Royal Bohusian Regiment of the Swedish army. In 1884 he attended the Corporal School at Carlsborg and upon graduation was promoted to field musician. During Swedish army maneuvers at Skane, Sweden, in 1884, Bergendahl demonstrated such outstanding horsemanship and marksmanship that he was promptly promoted to staff musician with the rank of sergeant in the Royal Supply Battalion. On July 28, 1885, he was promoted to warrant officer. He retired from the Swedish army on June 22, 1910, and resided at Goteborg, Sweden, until his death on January 31, 1924. He is buried at Ostra Kyrkcogardeu (The Cast Cemetery) at Goteborg.

Samuel Bowden
Private, Sixth U.S. Cavalry

Samuel Bowden was born circa 1846 at Salem, Massachusetts. He enlisted in the U.S. Army on October 18, 1867, at Boston and listed his occupation as a teamster. After basic training at the U.S. Cavalry Recruit Depot at Carlisle Barracks, Pennsylvania, he was assigned to duty at Austin, Texas, as a clerk in the Department of Texas quartermaster's office. He was promoted to corporal on March 1, 1870.

In early September 1870, while stationed at Fort Richardson, Texas, Bowden volunteered for field duty. On October 5, 1870, he was cited for "gallantry in action" near Bluff Creek in Archer County, Texas, and was awarded the Medal of Honor. During the winter of 1870 he was treated at the post hospital at Fort Richardson for remittent fever and severe dysentery.

On February 1, 1871, Samuel Bowden received an early discharge under Special Order no. 45 from the adjutant general's office in Washington, D.C.

Edward Branagan
Private, Company F, Fourth U.S. Cavalry

Edward Branagan was born at Louth, Ireland, circa 1846. It is not known when he came to the United States, but he did enlist in the U.S. Army at New York City on January 23, 1871, stating his occupation as a soldier. After basic cavalry training at Carlisle Barracks, Pennsylvania, he was assigned to Company F, Fourth U.S. Cavalry, and posted to Fort Richardson, Texas. During his single enlistment with the Fourth United States Cavalry he participated in engagements against Indians at Blanco Canyon, October 11, 1871; Clear Fork of the Brazos River, October 19, 1871; North Fork of the Red River, September 29, 1872; Tule Canyon, September 27, 1874; and Palo Duro Canyon, September 28, 1874. In December 1872 he was promoted to corporal. Branagan was a member of the detachment that, from June 8–12, 1871, brought Kiowa chiefs Satanta and Big Tree from the Fort Sill Reservation to Jacksboro, Texas, for criminal trial in the district court. This delivery by federal military authorities of admitted Indian criminals to Texas civil authorities remains one of the epochal events of the trans–Mississippi Indian Wars.

Edward Branagan was discharged as a sergeant at Fort Sill, Oklahoma, on January 23, 1876.

Robert G. Carter
Lieutenant, Company E, Fourth U.S. Cavalry

Robert Goldwaite Carter was born on October 29, 1845, at Bridgton, Maine, to Henry and Elizabeth Carter. He was the youngest of four sons. In 1848 the family moved from Bridgton to Portland when Henry Carter was elected to the Maine Legislature. Robert Carter spent most of his early youth in Portland and was educated there and later in Haverhill, Massachusetts, where the family resided after 1858.

In 1862 Robert Carter enlisted in the Twenty-second Massachusetts Infantry, despite being offered a commission by his father, then chairman of the military committee of the Massachusetts Senate. Assigned to Company H, Carter took part in the following engagements: Bull Run on August 29, 1862; the battle of Antietam on September 17, 1862; the battle of Fredericksburg on December 13,

1862; the battle of Chancellorsville on May 1, 1863; the battle of Gettysburg on July 1, 1863; and the battle of the Wilderness on May 5, 1864. From August 1863 until May 1864 he conveyed new recruits for the Fifth Army Corps of the Army of the Potomac. In this capacity he captured five deserters and broke up the most lucrative bounty fraud ring in existence. He was mustered out upon the expiration of his term of service on October 4, 1864.

On July 1, 1865, Carter was appointed as a cadet at the U.S. Military Academy. During his senior year, while on a weekend outing on August 4, 1869, he swam to the rescue of a young girl in the middle of the Hudson River after the boat in which she had been riding capsized.

Shortly after graduation on June 15, 1870, Carter wed Mary M. Smith. His first duty assignment was to Company E, Fourth U.S. Cavalry, at Fort Concho, Texas. Between 1870 and 1873 he served also in Texas at Forts Richardson, Griffin, and Clark. Shortly after his transfer to Fort Richardson on April 9, 1871, he was appointed the post adjutant. One of his first successful duties was to defuse a riot situation between the local Jacksboro citizens and Fort Richardson soldiers. Sent alone into Jacksboro, he confronted the citizen mob. Through his sound argument and determined manner he convinced the citizen mob to disperse.

From August 2, 1871, until November 18, 1871, Carter participated in two field campaigns into the Indian Territory and the Staked Plains of West Texas. He was specially cited during the campaign for his actions on the night of October 6, when he prevented a dangerous stampede of the command's horses by massive thirst-crazed buffalo herds. He was also cited for personal bravery and gallantry against Indians near Blanco Canyon in Crosby County on October 10–12, 16, and 19, 1871. During the engagement of October 10, while performing the deed for which he was later awarded the Medal of Honor, he suffered a serious compound fracture of his left leg. Carter was again cited for a two-week-long pursuit and capture of ten armed deserters during a sub-zero snowstorm from November 29 to December 9, 1871. Between May 7–19, 1872, he was active in engagements with hostile Indians and bandits near Whaley's Ranch, Texas. From September 4–28, 1872, he was in command of a detachment escorting Kiowa chiefs Satanta and Big Tree from Huntsville, Texas, to Atoka, Indian Territory. He was officially lauded for his good judgment in transporting these Indians to Atoka rather than to the undermanned post of Fort Sill, where a large assembly of Indians had created a very volatile situation. Carter was again especially cited in reports and general orders for his conduct at the battle of Remolino, Mexico, on May 19, 1873.

Biographies

In October 1873 Carter sought surgical relief for his injured leg but was advised against the surgery and was given a certificate of disability and placed on convalescent leave. He resided at Bradford and Newtonville, Massachusetts, from December 1873 until March 30, 1876. He was promoted to first lieutenant on February 21, 1875, and on June 28, 1876, was formally retired from active military service.

From 1875 until 1876 Carter served as general manager of Jordan, Marsh & Company department stores in Massachusetts. From 1877 to 1881 he was a visiting special instructor of military science and hygiene at Newton High School in Newton, Massachusetts. During the academic year of 1879–1880 he served as professor of military science and tactics at Massachusetts Institute of Technology. In 1881–1882 he served as principal of the faculty school at the U.S. Military Academy at West Point.

Between 1884 and 1935 Carter pursued a literary career and based many of his writings about his Civil War and Indian War experiences on his personal diary and accounts of fellow officers and enlisted men. In 1886 he began writing a series of Texas-oriented short stories, the most notable among them being "The Cowboy's Verdict and Jackrabbits Victory" in *Youth's Companion Magazine* and "Buffalo vs. Bulldog," "The Mackenzie Raid into Mexico," "Tragedies of Canyon Blanco," "On the Trail of Deserters," and "Pursuit of Kicking Bird" in *Outing Magazine*. In 1895 he began to research and publish genealogical and historical monographs for the Maine Historical Society and the Maine Commandery of the Loyal Legion including "Colonel Thomas Goldwaite—Was He a Tory?" "Joseph Goldwaite, A Colonial Soldier at Louisburg," "Colonel Benjamin Goldwaite in the Acadian and Louisburg Expeditions," "General Knox and the Loyalist," "Joseph Goldwaite, the Barrackmaster of Boston," "Philip Goldwaite, the Tory of Witchcastle," "History of an Old Uniform," "A Yankee Sailor on a British Battleship," and "The Clerk of Fort Pownal." Between July 1896 and October 1898 he serialized his personal Civil War diary accounts in *The Maine Bugle* newspaper. After 1900 his stories became more Civil War-oriented in "Reminiscences of the Campaign and Battle of Gettysburg," "The Princess' Son, A Romance of the Civil War," "John Morrison, or a Farmerboy's Presentiment at Gettysburg," and "Life in a Conscript Camp, or Stirring Events Among the Bounty Jumpers."

On January 30, 1903, after having corrective surgery for his 1871 leg injuries, Carter was restored to active duty with the rank of colonel of cavalry and permanently retired as a captain of cavalry on April 23, 1904. He remained on general recruiting duty until August 7, 1906. He resumed his literary career by assisting in the compilation and editing of *Wilson's Regiment, A History of the Twenty-Second Massachusetts Volunteer Infantry*, *Familiar History*, *General Records* (2 vols.), *War letters from the Battle Front, or Lights and Shadows of the War* (2 vols.) and *Wearing the Cadet Gray or Memories of West Point Days* (2 vols.) During 1911–1912 he prepared for the Maine Historical Society, "The Record of the Military Service of Colonel Benjamin Goldwaite, A Provincial Soldier," and "The Record of the Military Service of Captain Joseph Goldwaite, Adjutant of Pepperal's Regiment at the Siege of Louisburg."

In 1913 Carter's book, *Four Brothers in Blue* (Washington, D.C.: Gibson Brothers), was awarded the *Leslie's Magazine* Literary Award for the best story on the Civil War. In 1919 he began to publish a series of monographs about his Fourth U.S. Cavalry experiences on the Texas frontier, including "The Mackenzie Raid into Mexico," "Massacre of Salt Creek Prairie and the Cowboys Verdict," "Tragedies of Canon Blanco, A Story of the Texas Panhandle," "On the Trail of Deserters, A Phenomenal Capture," and "Pursuit of Kicking Bird, A Campaign in the Texas Bad Lands." He also authored the following books: *The Old Sergeant's Story: Winning the West from the Indians and Bad Men in 1870–1876*, *The Art and Science of War Versus the Art of Fighting*, and *On the Border with Mackenzie: or Winning West Texas From the Comanches.*

He was a member of the Military Order of the Loyal Legion, Massachusetts, New York, and District of Columbia Commanderies from 1878 to 1906; companion of the Order of the Congressional Medal of Honor Legion of the United States (1902–1903); charter companion, Military Order of the Medal of Honor Society (1909); life member, Maine Historical Society; member, Army and Navy Club, New York City and Washington, D.C. (1888–1935); companion (1913), commander (1921), vice commander (1925), Order of the Indian Wars; junior vice commander (1925), senior vice commander (1926), commander (1927), D.C. Commandery, Military Order of the Loyal Legion; and member, Legion of Valor of the United States (1928). During his tenure as commander of the Order of Indian Wars in 1921 he successfully won revision of the War Department's official listing of Indian Wars campaigns which, through gross negligence, had omitted the 1871–1874 campaigns in Texas and the Indian Territory against hostile Kiowa, Comanche, and affiliated tribes.

Between 1914 and 1916 Carter was an early advocate of a national war preparedness system designed along the lines of the Swiss system of reserve officer training in the public schools.

He was granted a brevet to first lieutenant for "Specially gallant conduct in action against Indians on the Fresh Water Fork of the Brazos River, Texas on

October 10, 1871" and a brevet to captain for "Gallant services in action against Kickapoo, Lipan, and Mescalero Apache Indians at Remolino, Mexico. May 18, 1873." In addition to the Medal of Honor, Carter also was awarded the Civil War and Indian Wars campaign medals.

Carter died on January 4, 1936, at Washington, D.C., and was buried at Arlington National Cemetery. He was survived by a daughter, Natalie C. Hilgarde of St. Louis, Missouri; a grandson, Carter Hilgarde; and two grand-daughters, Helen C. Johnson of Washington, D.C., and Dorothy B. Eynon of Chevy Chase, Maryland.

Amos Chapman
Scout, U.S. Army Quartermaster Department

It appears from available records that Amos Chapman was born on March 15, 1837, near Kalamazoo, Michigan, to John and Betsy Chapman. Amos was the eldest of seven brothers and four sisters. Around 1856 the family moved to Charriton County, Missouri. In 1864 Amos left home to work as a teamster for a freighting company that transported supplies to frontier army posts between Fort Leavenworth, Kansas, and Santa Fe, New Mexico. During his two years with the freighting company he acquired a great deal of knowledge about the geography of the southern Great Plains and its Indian inhabitants.

In June 1866 he was hired by the U.S. Army Quartermaster Department as a courier. He served out of Fort Lyon, Colorado, and made many dangerous rides between frontier posts and commands patrolling against raiding Indians. During early 1867 he served under Gen. W. H. Penrose and was assigned to Capt. Nicolas Nolan's Company A, Tenth U.S. Cavalry. During an engagement near Sheridan Roost, Colorado, he incurred minor gunshot wounds in the jaw and in both hands.

In mid-1867 Chapman returned briefly to his home near Chillicothe, Missouri. He hired on with Charley Biggers, a noted wagonmaster, who managed numerous westbound immigrant wagon trains. Biggers hired Chapman as his head scout because he felt Chapman was one of the most able scouts on the frontier, with knowledge about Indians second only to Kit Carson. During the two-month journey from Leavenworth, Kansas, to Trinidad, Colorado, Amos proved his ability by saving the life of a young boy bitten by a rattlesnake, killing a drunken bully in self defense, and rescuing twelve train members from being captured by Indians. In the latter incident he led the rescue party in a sharp skirmish against chief Bull Hump's Osage warriors. In this skirmish near Pawnee Rock, Kansas, on June 16,

1867, he sustained two minor gunshot wounds in the right arm. Later in the train's journey he personally negotiated safe passage for the train by striking a bargain with the Cheyenne chief Roman Nose.

In 1868 Chapman was personally selected by Gen. George A. Custer to serve as scout and guide for his Washita campaign. Amos participated in the attack on Black Kettle's Cheyenne village at the battle of the Washita on November 27, 1868. Shortly afterward Chapman served as a scout for the command under Maj. A. W. Evans of the Third U.S. Cavalry. Chapman demonstrated his superior marksmanship at the battle of Soldier Spring on December 25–27, 1868. He continued to serve as an army scout until 1873.

During most of 1873 Chapman was among many of the small hunting parties that hunted, skinned, and transported the buffalo hides from the hunting grounds south of Fort Dodge, Kansas. In 1874, when the Kiowas, Comanches, Arapaho, and Southern Cheyenne went on the warpath, Chapman again signed up with the U.S. Army Quartermaster Department. During the 1874–1875 Indian Territory campaign he served as a courier, scout, and interpreter for Col. J. W. Davidson's column out of Fort Sill. He participated gallantly in the buffalo wallow fight on September 9–12, 1874, and was awarded the Medal of Honor for his actions. As a result of the wounds incurred in this battle his right foot was amputated. Despite his disability he remained quite active and was retained by the Quartermaster Department until 1883.

On March 18, 1876, Chapman married Mary Bunhio (Onehiou), a Cheyenne Indian woman, in a brief civil ceremony at Camp Supply, Indian Territory. Between then and 1879 he served as the post interpreter at Forts Reno and Cobb in Indian Territory and at Fort Elliott in Texas. During his tenure in this position in 1878 he was instrumental in disarming a band of 250 Northern Cheyenne and bringing them into the Cheyenne Agency. When bands under chiefs Dull Knife and Little Wolf attempted to escape northward to their homelands in Montana and Wyoming. Chapman guided the Fourth U.S. Cavalry's pursuit of the runaways and participated in the engagement at White Woman's Creek, Kansas, on September 27, 1878. The series of skirmishes and maneuverings of this chase later became immortalized in the motion picture *Cheyenne Autumn*.

Between 1879 and 1882 Chapman served on several occasions as Gen. Phillip Sheridan's personal interpreter and advisor in his negotiations with the Cheyenne and Arapaho tribes. In 1882, through the efforts of Gen. Nelson A. Miles and four other officers, Chapman was granted a disability pension. Eventually settling on his wife's allotted land on the Cheyenne Agency near Seiling, Oklahoma, he developed one of the earliest successful cattle ranches in western Oklahoma. During this time he also worked as a teamster and hauled freight from Guthrie to Seiling.

In 1884 Chapman guided and suggested routes to teams surveying and building overland freight routes from the Southern Kansas Railroad terminus at New Kiowa, Oklahoma. During part of 1887 and 1888 Chapman obtained and successfully carried out a survey and grading of right-of-way contract for the Denver, Enid and Gulf Railroad.

In 1890 Chapman served as a deputy United States marshal and in August 1891 he shot and killed two cowboys who resisted arrest after being caught transporting cattle illegally into the Cherokee Outlet. Because of the furor about this incident Chapman resigned from the marshal service in 1892 and retired to his ranch near Seiling. Throughout the years Chapman befriended many of his former Cheyenne adversaries and became a trusted friend and advisor to them. After 1896 he made several annual trips to Washington, D.C., and was a guest of Nelson A. Miles, then commanding general of the army. Miles never restrained his admiration for Chapman and in his memoirs referred to him as one of the bravest of the brave men he had ever known. In 1917, upon the death of William F. "Buffalo Bill" Cody, Chapman was elevated to honorary chief of scouts of the U.S. Army.

Amos Chapman died on July 18, 1925, at Seiling, Oklahoma. He was survived by a daughter, Ida Chapman Toller, and two sons, Temple and Samuel. Originally interred in a family plot on their ranch, the remains of Amos and Mary Chapman were reinterred at the Brumfield Cemetery near Seiling in 1979.

John W. Comfort
Private, Company A, Fourth U.S. Cavalry

John W. Comfort was born in 1845 at Philadelphia, Pennsylvania, to Cyrus and Sarah Comfort. He was educated in the public schools and was a resident of the Twelfth Ward. Prior to the Civil War he worked as a molder, carpenter, and clerk.

At the outset of the Civil War Comfort enlisted in Company I of the Twenty-ninth Pennsylvania Infantry at Philadelphia. By the time of his first major action of the war at the battle of Chancellorsville on May 2–3, 1863, he held the rank of corporal. At the battle of Gettysburg his unit was positioned near Rock Creek and withheld several assaults by Jeb Stuart's brigade. During the East Tennessee campaign, Comfort was especially active at the battle of Chickamauga on September 19–20, 1863. During the battle of Chattanooga on November 23–25, 1863, Comfort led his squad in scaling the cliffs of Lookout

Mountain and was part of one of the first Union units to reach the summit amid bitter hand-to-hand fighting. During the drive toward Atlanta, as a sergeant, he was especially prominent at the battles of Resaca on May 14–15, 1864, and at Pine Log Creek on May 18, 1864. On September 2, 1864, he participated in the final assault upon Atlanta. The Twenty-ninth Pennsylvania spearheaded the "march to the sea," and afterward the capture of Savannah. Comfort took part in several minor skirmishes during the Carolinas campaign, and on April 26 Comfort participated in the surrender ceremony between General Sherman and Confederate Gen. Joseph E. Johnston. One month after the Grand Review at Washington, D.C., he was discharged from the Union army on July 17, 1865, at Alexandria, Virginia.

On November 28, 1865, Comfort enlisted in Battery K, First U.S. Artillery. During his service in this unit he was stationed at Fort Brown, Texas, and at New Orleans and Greenville, Louisiana. He was discharged on November 28, 1868, and returned to Philadelphia. He reenlisted on April 18, 1870, this time in the Fourth U.S. Cavalry. He participated in engagements at the Big Bend of the Brazos River on May 18, 1871; at Red Hill on September 25, 1874; at Palo Duro Canyon on September 28, 1874; and at Laguna Tahoka on November 6, 1874. On November 5, 1874, several miles southeast of Laguna Tahoka, he was specially cited for gallantry, "in running down and killing an Indian at a long distance from his command," for which he was awarded the Medal of Honor. He was discharged on April 18, 1875, and immediately reenlisted. On June 1, 1878, he was issued a certificate of disability for chronic alcoholism not consequent on military service and was formally discharged from the army on June 26, 1878, at Fort Clark, Texas. From 1878 until 1882 he was employed as a civilian mule packer by the Quartermaster Department at Fort Clark.

Between 1883 and 1885 he resided in California, where he worked as a clerk. He reenlisted on July 3, 1885, in Battery E, First U.S. Artillery (L), and during this enlistment he was stationed at the Presidio, San Francisco; Fort Riley, Kansas; and Fort Douglas, Utah. He reenlisted in the same unit on July 3, 1890. On December 29, 1890, he was involved in the actions on the Wounded Knee Reservation near Drexel Mission, South Dakota. He was cited for honorable mention for gallantry in general orders. As a member of Battery E, First U.S. Artillery, he moved an artillery piece to the relief of a companion battery that had been incapacitated by a severe fire from Indians hidden in a nearby ravine. Comfort took charge during a highly confused period and delivered a withering fire into the Indian positions.

On Dcember 6, 1892, Comfort received his final discharge from the U.S. Army and returned to Philadelphia. On November 29, 1893, he died from pneumonia and was buried at Mount Peace Cemetery. At the time of his death he was a member of Winfield Scott Post no. 114 of the Grand Army of the Republic.

John Connor
Corporal, Company H, Sixth U.S. Cavalry

John Connor was born at Galway, Ireland, circa 1845. His first known enlistment in the U.S. Army was at Jefferson, Texas, on July 19, 1869. After several months on Reconstruction duty in East Texas he was transferred to Fort Richardson, Texas, then on the northern frontier. He was promoted to corporal on May 1, 1870. On July 12, 1870, he suffered a severe head wound in action against Kiowa and Comanche Indians at the battle of the Little Wichita River. It was during this engagement that he performed the deeds for which he was awarded the Medal of Honor. Connor was promoted to the rank of sergeant on December 15, 1870, and was discharged on July 18, 1874.

Connor reenlisted in Battery B, Second U.S. Artillery, on January 22, 1875, at Fort McHenry, Maryland. During his fifteen-year period of service in the Second Artillery he served at Fort McHenry until 1877; Washington, D.C., Arsenal, 1878–1885; Camp Hancock, Georgia, 1886–1887; Huntsville, Alabama, 1888; Fort Barrancas, Florida, 1889; and Fort Warren, Massachusetts, 1890.

Connor received his final discharge from the army on December 5, 1890. On December 12, 1890, he became a resident of the U.S. Soldier's Home at Washington, D.C. On December 7, 1896, he married Cora G. Hoover of Pittsburgh, Pennsylvania, and they resided in Alexandria, Virginia.

Connor was admitted to the hospital at the U.S. Soldier's Home in 1905 and he died on February 5, 1907, of intestinal nephritis. A Catholic, Connor was buried at the U.S. Soldier's Home National Cemetery. He was survived by his wife, Cora G. Connor. An inventory of his effects listed a trunk of sundries with one sole valuable, a Medal of Honor. His wife was last known to be living in Pittsburgh in 1910.

William DeArmond
Sergeant, Company I, Fifth U.S. Infantry

William DeArmond was born circa February 1842 to King and Esther DeArmond near Okeana in Butler County, Ohio. He was educated in the public schools but upon the death of his father he was forced to work the family farm full time until his late teens.

On July 29, 1863, DeArmond left home and traveled to nearby Cincinnati, where he enlisted in Company C, Second Ohio Heavy Artillery Regiment. As part of the Fifth Division, Twenty-third Army Corps, he participated in the campaigns for Eastern Kentucky, Eastern Tennessee, and Atlanta. He was promoted to corporal on April 5, 1864, and to sergeant in September 1864. He actively participated in engagements at Mumfordville, Kentucky, on October 23, 1863; Cleveland, Tennessee, on August 17, 1864; and Charleston, Tennessee, on August 19, 1864. He was mustered out of the volunteer service on April 3, 1865.

On April 3, 1866, DeArmond enlisted in the regular army with the Eighteenth U.S. Infantry at New York City. He served at Forts Casper, Reno, and Fetterman in Wyoming Territory during the 1867–1868 Sioux disturbances. He was involved in several minor skirmishes near Sweetwater Bridge, Wyoming, during the winter of 1867–1868. He worked on construction of the wagon road between Fort Fetterman and the Black Hills, South Dakota, and finished his enlistment guarding railroad construction crews near North Platte Station in Nebraska. After his discharge on April 3, 1869, he returned to St. Joseph, Missouri, where on June 3, 1869, he wed Julia A. Carpenter.

On July 2, 1869, DeArmond reenlisted in Company I, Fifth U.S. Infantry, at Fort Leavenworth, Kansas. During this enlistment DeArmond was stationed at various posts in Kansas. He was involved in several minor clashes with Indians while protecting railroad and telegraph construction crews. On July 2, 1874, he again reenlisted at Fort Dodge, Kansas. During the 1874–1875 Indian Territory expedition he was killed in action on September 9, 1874, while repulsing an attack on a supply train by hostile Kiowa and Comanche warriors. His body was interred in a solemn ceremony where he fell in what is now Hemphill County, Texas. He was survived by his wife, Julia A. DeArmond, of Fort Leavenworth, Kansas, and a brother, James DeArmond, of Indiana.

William Dixon
Scout, U.S. Army Quartermaster Department

William Dixon was born on September 25, 1850, at Wheeling in Ohio County, Virginia, in what is now West Virginia and was an orphan by the age of twelve. An uncle, Thomas M. Dixon, took William and a sister to his home in Ray County, Missouri. His sister died of typhoid fever in 1864 and shortly afterward Billy ran away from home. He cut and provided firewood to several

Missouri River steamboat companies and hunted and trapped in the areas around Westport, Missouri, and Wyandotte, Kansas.

In April 1865 Dixon was hired by the Army Quartermaster Department as a teamster. He drove supply wagons out of Fort Leavenworth to Fort Harker, Kansas, and Fort Collins, Colorado, and returned via Fort Kearney, Nebraska. During 1866 he worked briefly as a farm laborer but in 1867 he returned to working as a teamster for the Quartermaster Department. During the fall of 1867 he accompanied the peace commission that negotiated treaties with several Southern Plains tribes at Medicine Lodge, Kansas, on October 28, 1867. Dixon served as a teamster with the Custer column in the Washita campaign during the winter of 1868–1869.

In the spring of 1869 Dixon began hunting buffalo full time in the Saline River Valley of Kansas. The lucrative nature of buffalo hunting allowed him to build a way station near Hays City, Kansas. By 1872 the railroad's westward extension put him out of business. During most of 1872 Dixon resumed buffalo hunting on a full-time basis and eventually drifted south into the Texas Panhandle. By the summer of 1874 he was a member of the hunting contingent based at Adobe Walls, Texas. This buffalo hunter camp, manned by twenty-nine hunters, was attacked and besieged by a force of several hundred Kiowa, Comanche, Arapaho, and Cheyenne warriors on June 27, 1874. Dixon is given credit for breaking the will of the attacking Indians when he reportedly wounded the inciting medicine man with a spectacular rifle shot of more than half a mile in distance.

On September 6, 1874, Dixon signed up with the U.S. Army Quartermaster Department as a scout and courier. On September 12, 1874, he participated in the buffalo wallow fight, for which he was awarded the Medal of Honor. He remained as a scout for the army at Fort Elliott, Texas, until 1883. After the organization of Hutchinson County, Texas, he became its first postmaster and a notary public at Adobe Walls while at the same time maintaining a two thousand-acre ranch nearby. On October 18, 1894, he married Olive King near Parnell in Hall County, Texas. From this union seven children were born: Dora (December 29, 1895), Bobbie (September 6, 1897), Drew (September 13, 1899), Edna (June 11, 1903), Archie (June 22, 1906), Olive (October 9, 1908), and Hugh (November 18, 1910).

In April 1901 Dixon was elected as the first sheriff and tax collector for Hutchinson County. He resigned the position within a month to work full time at his ranching operations. During the winter of 1903–1904 his herds were devastated and he was forced to sell his holdings to the larger Turkey Track Ranch. He moved to Plemons and later Delfin, Oklahoma, where he established a

271

boarding house and hotel. After two years he returned to Dallam County, Texas, and filed a preemption claim on 160 acres near Texline. During the years from 1906 to 1910 he worked feverishly to develop and improve his ranch. He enjoyed his hobbies of raising pointer bird dogs and gardening before his health began to decline in 1911. In 1912, working closely with his wife, he began to compile notes for an autobiography. In early 1913 he contracted pneumonia and died on March 9, 1913. After a Masonic funeral he was laid to rest at Texline, Texas, but in 1929 his remains were exhumed and reinterred at Adobe Walls.

In 1917 William "Billy" Dixon was stripped of his Medal of Honor and removed from the Medal of Honor Roll. On June 12, 1989, he and four other former scouts were reinstated to the Medal of Honor Roll by an Army Board on Correction of Military Records. Billy Dixon's Medal of Honor is on display in the Panhandle-Plains Historical Museum at Canyon, Texas.

James B. Dosher
Post Guide, U.S. Army Quartermaster Department

James Belle Dosher was born on May 2, 1826, in Warren County, Tennessee, to John and Rachel Speers Dosher. As an infant and throughout his formative youth his family moved steadily westward. At age one he lived in a stockade enclosure constructed for protection from Indians in Lincoln County, Kentucky. After the death of his maternal grandfather at the hands of Indians, the family moved to Indiana and lived there for three years. In 1831 the family again moved west to Williamson County, Illinois, where the area around Crab Apple Lake was Dosher's home for the next eight years. It was here that he learned the woodcraft, hunting, and trailing skills that served him throughout his lifetime. A Delaware Indian the family had befriended and retained as a handyman instructed James and his younger brothers, Harrison and Joseph, in the Indian style of tracking and surviving in the wild. Along with the marksmanship training from his father and the rudimentary grammar skills taught by his mother, this was the only education Dosher had.

In 1840 the family again moved west, this time to Missouri, first to Wright County, and later to their permanent home in Laclede County. At the outset of the Mexican-American War in the summer of 1846, James left home for Texas, intent upon enlisting in the volunteer army. By the time he arrived in San Antonio in the fall of 1847 the volunteer army had left to invade Mexico.

Capt. J. J. Cureton, head of one of the Texas Ranger recruiting parties, happened to be in San Antonio at the same time as Dosher and on October 22, 1847,

Dosher enlisted in Cureton's company of Texas Rangers. During his one year of service this company ranged along the frontier from the San Saba River to the mesquite chaparral below Corpus Christi. During one pursuit Dosher trailed bandits as far as Camargo, Mexico. During that first term of service he served alongside such ranger notables as R. A. Gillespie and Buck Beary. After his discharge in April 1848 he returned to Missouri and in 1849 he married Viola M. Eddings. Shortly after the birth of their first son, John, in January 1851, the couple moved to Texas. They settled for two years in Grayson County and in 1853 moved to Parker County, where they resided for almost two years before settling permanently in Jack County in early 1855. The couple's second child, a daughter, Perneta, was born in early 1855 just prior to their move to Jack County.

On February 1, 1855, Dosher filed on a preemption claim of several hundred acres fifteen miles south of present-day Jacksboro. He is said to have built the second house in Jack County at Salt Hill, one mile west of Barton Chapel. Over the next several years he spent a great deal of time developing his farm. In January 1858 he was summoned to serve on the first grand jury formed in Jack County. At various times he also worked as a laborer on county road construction crews and, during Indian hostilities, served as a private in Capt. M. D. Tackett's company of Texas Rangers. During this service he acquired an excellent knowledge of the North Texas frontier. As part of Col. L. S. Ross's frontier regiment he participated in the battle of the Pease River on December 18, 1860. Between 1856 and 1860 two daughters, California and Fredonia, were born to the family.

After Texas seceded from the Union, Dosher served in the Jack City Rangers, a company of troops recruited for local protection against marauding Indians. The unit took part in the removal of Federal troops from Camp Cooper and Fort Chadbourne and provided relay riders between Austin and the northwestern frontier areas. On March 11, 1862, Dosher enlisted in the Stephens County frontier regiment of Texas State Troops commanded by Col. J. M. Norris. During this enlistment, while on courier duty, Dosher and six others were attacked by a war party of Indians between Lost Valley and Fort Belknap. Dosher's accurate rifle marksmanship was credited with repulsing the attack. On December 27, 1862, he reenlisted in the Clay County frontier regiment at Camp Brunson, a unit commanded by Col. J. E. McCord.

On March 1, 1864, the frontier regiment was mustered into the Confederate Army and became known as the Forty-sixth Texas Cavalry regiment. This unit was at various times stationed at Fort Belknap, Camp Cooper, Camp Brunson, and the Shackelford Salt Works. After the close of the Civil War, Dosher returned his attention to his ranch and farming interests.

In May 1868 Dosher responded to the U.S. Army's plea for civilian guide positions at nearby Fort Richardson. He was immediately accepted and was employed as the post guide at Fort Richardson. During his tenure in this capacity he became known as "Jim" to the soldiers. He was involved in numerous scouting patrols and minor engagements, but was especially active in engagements at the Little Wichita River, July 12, 1870; Bluff Creek, October 5, 1870; South Fork, Little Wichita River, November 17, 1870; and Brazos and Wichita Rivers divide, May 20, 1871. During July to November 1871 he served as the guide for R. S. Mackenzie's Staked Plains campaign. Dosher terminated his service as the post guide at Fort Richardson on January 5, 1872.

During much of 1873 Dosher served as the guide for surveying crews for the Mattix Surveying Company, which did much of the original land surveying in Northwest Texas, especially along the Red River and along the one hundredth west meridian. He not only guided the surveyors, but also built their temporary quarters and provided fresh deer, antelope, and buffalo meat with his excellent marksmanship. During the major Indian outbreaks of 1874 Dosher served briefly with the Texas Ranger frontier battalion commanded by John B. Jones, and participated in the second battle of Lost Valley on July 12, 1874.

After 1878 Dosher spent most of his time developing his farming and ranching interests and became one of the earliest members of the Northwest Texas Cattle Raisers Association. He married a second time to Martha J. Roebuck on July 29, 1880. He was married a third time to Catherine McNealy on October 13, 1881.

Dosher's health began to decline severely after 1898. He died circa February 1901 and was interred in the Bottoms Family Cemetery, one mile west of Barton Chapel in southwest Jack County. He was survived by his wife, Catherine; one son, William J., and William's wife, Nancy Dosher; five daughters, California, Edney Jane Bottoms, Perneta Bomer, Fredonia Bottoms, and Mary Wood; two grandsons, Edward E. Dosher and William E. Bottoms; and two granddaughters, Rose Bottoms and Pearl Putnam.

The greatest testament to James B. Dosher's character can be gleaned from the writings of H. H. McConnell, a former sergeant of the Sixth U.S. Cavalry who served with Dosher in the 1870s. In his 1889 book, *Five Years a Cavalryman*, McConnell wrote of Dosher:

> His coolness and bravery and woodcraft were the admiration of the troops. Another generation or two and this class of men will only live in song or story. Resident for long years on this frontier, he knew every landmark of its pathless woods, or still more difficult prairie. Cool, self reliant, modest, sober, tireless,

he was a thorough and competent guide and a brave and intelligent man. Many of the fellows that I have known, in fact the majority of them, who hang around frontier posts and call themselves "guides," are frauds who have no more knowledge of the country or the habits of the Indians than could be picked up by any one who hunts cattle for a year or two. "Jim" Doshier (sic) was not one of this kind—he was a guide in fact.

In 1917 Dosher was one of five former U.S. Army scouts or guides formally stricken from the official Army Medal of Honor Roll. On June 12, 1989, an Army Board for Correction of Military Records reinstated him and the four other former scouts to the Medal of Honor Roll. On December 4, 1991, Lt. Gen. Horace G. Taylor presented a new-design Army Medal of Honor to Velma B. Reed, Dosher's great-granddaughter, in a ceremony at the University of North Texas at Denton. Reed immediately transferred custody of the medal to the Texas Parks and Wildlife Department and the 1944-style medal and ribbon are now on permanent display at Fort Richardson State Historical Park.

George H. Eldridge
Sergeant, Company C, Sixth U.S. Cavalry

George H. Eldridge was born at Sackett Harbor, New York, on May 12, 1846, to Harrington and Caroline Smedley Eldridge. Harrington Eldridge had served in the Mexican-American War and was pensioned for wounds incurred during the war. Shortly after moving to Redford (Wayne County), Michigan, circa 1855, both of his parents died, leaving George orphaned at the age of nine. George was raised by an uncle, Nelson Finney, who trained him as an apprentice mechanic. At the outset of the Civil War, Finney refused to allow Eldridge to enlist because of his age and the non-completion of his apprenticeship. Upon learning of the death of his half-brother, Horace Smedley, at the battle of Malvern Hill, Eldridge became determined to enlist and successfully joined Company A, Twenty-fourth Michigan Infantry, at Detroit on August 15, 1862.

During May 1863 at the Chancellorsville campaign, Eldridge was detailed for duty with the ambulance corps. Later, while on temporary duty in Battery B, Fourth U.S. Artillery, he was badly wounded by shrapnel and narrowly escaped being taken prisoner. After several months of treatment and rehabilitation at Philadelphia he was again assigned to the ambulance corps, and he continued in that capacity until the end of the war. He was mustered out on April 25, 1865, and returned to Redford, Michigan, to resume his apprenticeship training.

Upon completion of his training Eldridge enlisted in the Sixth U.S. Cavalry at Detroit on May 23, 1867. During this enlistment he served four years on the Texas frontier at Forts Richardson and Griffin. He was active in engagements on May 30, 1870, at Holliday Creek, Texas, and at the battle of the Little Wichita River on July 12, 1870. His actions on the Little Wichita River in singularly attacking a band of Indians attempting to capture a pack mule supply contingent merited his Medal of Honor award. He was discharged at Fort Hays, Kansas, on May 23, 1872, and two days later he married Mary M. Bachstein. He farmed near Fort Hays until November 8, 1874, when he reenlisted in the Sixth U.S. Cavalry. During his second enlistment he served at various posts in Colorado and Arizona in campaigns against hostile Ute and Apaches. He was discharged on November 8, 1879, at Fort Grant, Arizona.

After his discharge from the army Eldridge was employed as a civilian mechanic at Fort Grant, where he continued in that capacity until 1884. During this time he resided at Apache Pass and Dos Cabezas, Arizona. In 1885 he purchased a ranch near Safford, Arizona. From 1888 until 1892 he served as justice of the peace judge for Precinct 8 in Graham County, Arizona. His ranching interests were decimated by severe droughts in 1893 and 1894. He returned to his position as mechanic at Fort Grant and also obtained appointment as a notary public. In declining health he moved to Westgate, California, in 1905 to be near the hospital of the Pacific Branch of the U.S. Soldier's Home. He applied for enrollment on the Army Medal of Honor Roll on May 20, 1916, and was granted certificate no. 155, effective September 27, 1916. George Eldridge died of influenza on November 18, 1918, and was buried at the Los Angeles National Cemetery. He was survived by his children, Elsie, George, Charles, Mary, Preston, Maud, Hattie, Josephine, Albert, Alice, Elizabeth, and Donald.

Pompey Factor
Private, Seminole-Negro Indian Scouts

Pompey Factor was born circa 1845 near Fort Smith, Arkansas. According to scant sources it appears he was the eldest of two sons and three daughters born to Hardy and Esther Factor. Pompey was a member of the Seminole-Creek Negro tribe, which evolved as a result of the intermingling of Seminole and Creek Indians with kidnapped and runaway slaves. Dispossessed from their tribal homelands in Florida as a result of the Second Seminole War they were temporarily exiled to Fort Smith, Arkansas, to await assignment to their assigned lands in the Indian Territory. A number of the able-bodied members of the tribe apparently accompanied the U.S. Army as scouts, cooks, and servants during their march into Mexico during the Mexican-American War. At the war's end and upon their return many were disenchanted with the assigned lands and with certain treaty provisions. Aware of the absence of slavery in Mexico, several Seminole and Negro bands joined with chiefs Wild Cat and John Horse. This assemblage immigrated to Mexico sometime between 1849 and 1852. The Seminole Negroes were eventually granted a nine-square-mile tract of land along the Sabinas River near the village of Nacimiento in exchange for military services against the Indians who constantly preyed upon Mexican ranches.

In 1869 the U.S. government enticed the Seminole factions to return to their reservation lands. No provisions were made for members of the tribe of African ancestry. Capt. F. W. Perry and Maj. Zenas Bliss queried the Department of Texas commander, Gen. J. J. Reynolds, as to the feasibility of enlisting them as U.S. Army scouts. Permission was granted and Pompey Factor was among the second group enrolled at Fort Duncan, Texas, on August 16, 1870. From 1870 to 1874 Factor served at Fort Duncan. In May 1873 Factor was one of the several reconnoitering spies sent in advance of Col. R. S. Mackenzie's Fourth U.S. Cavalry troops during the punitive raid on Remolino, Mexico. He was an active participant in engagements at Kickapoo Springs on December 10, 1873, and at Eagle Nest Crossing of the Pecos River on April 25, 1875. At the latter action he and two other scouts held off a numerically superior band of Indians, which enabled one of the other scouts to rescue and carry to safety their commanding officer, Capt. John L. Bullis, for which the scouts earned the Medal of Honor. On July 30, 1876, Factor was especially mentioned for gallantry in a bitterly intense engagement at Zaragosa, Mexico.

On January 1, 1877, Factor deserted from Fort Clark, Texas, and fled to Musquiz, Mexico. On November 30, 1878, he requested a pardon and was reinstated on May 25, 1879. He was discharged from the scouts on November 19, 1880, after making up his lost time. He resided at Brackettville with his wife, Annie, and daughter, Adelia, until 1882, when he moved to Rio Grande City, Texas, and worked as a farm laborer. In 1897 he returned to Musquiz, Mexico, where he resided for the next twenty years. Around 1917 he returned to Brackettville. On May 24, 1926, an attorney, Edgar Gaddis of Brackettville, initiated Factor's application for a disability pension. His discharge papers had been destroyed in a fire, leaving only his Medal of Honor as proof of his service. Reluctantly, Factor allowed Gaddis to submit the medal to the pension bureau. He was granted a pension. Factor died on March 28, 1928, and was buried at the Seminole-Negro Indian Scout Cemetery at Brackettville. He was survived by a niece, Ida Griner.

William Foster
Sergeant, Company F, Fourth U.S. Cavalry

William Foster was born at Somersetshire, England, circa 1832. Nothing is known of his family or early background other than that he served in a British artillery unit during the Crimean War. In October 1861 he immigrated to the United States and on November 14, 1861, he enlisted in Company I, Second New York Heavy Artillery, at Camp Arthur on Staten Island. Because of his expertise he was promoted to sergeant on January 3, 1862. He was serving as an instructor at Bethesda Station, Maryland, on March 22, 1862, when he was detached to Battery D (Platt's), Second U.S. Artillery, by order of Gen. George McClellan. During his service in this unit Foster compiled an outstanding war record. He was active in engagements at Yorktown, Virginia, in April–May 1862; West Point, Virginia, on May 2, 1862; Gaines Mill, Virginia, on June 27, 1862; Golding's Farm, Virginia, on June 28, 1862; Savage Station, Virginia, on June 29, 1862; Manassas, Virginia, on August 30, 1862; Antietam, Maryland, on September 14, 1862; Fredericksburg, Virginia, on December 13, 1862; Chancellorsville, Virginia, on May 4, 1863; Marye's Height, Virginia, on May 2–3, 1863; Salem Height, Virginia, on May 8, 1863; Brandy Station, Virginia, on June 9, 1863; Gettysburg, Pennsylvania, on July 1–3, 1863; Culpepper Courthouse, Virginia, on September 24, 1863; Auburn, Virginia, on October 14, 1863; Buckland Mills, Virginia, on October 19, 1863; Mine Run, Virginia, on November 26, 1863; Wilderness, Virginia, on May 5–6, 1864; Todd's Tavern, Virginia, on May 7, 1864; Spottsylvania, Virginia, on May 8, 1864; Drewery's Bluff, Virginia, on May 16, 1864; Cold Harbor, Virginia, on May 31, 1864; Trevillian Station, Virginia, on June 11, 1864; Staunton River Bridge, Virginia, on June 25, 1864; Petersburg, Virginia, on July 30, 1864; Charlestown, West Virginia, on August 23, 1864; Winchester, Virginia, on September 19, 1864; Fisher's Hill, Virginia, on September 22, 1864; Luray Valley, Virginia, on September 24, 1864; and Cedar Creek, Virginia, on October 19, 1864. Having enlisted formally in the regular U.S. Army on October 26, 1862, Foster was transferred at the war's end to San Jose, California, where he was discharged on February 6, 1867.

On March 6, 1867, Foster reenlisted in Battery F, Fifth U.S. Artillery, at Richmond, Virginia. He spent this entire enlistment at Sedgwick Barracks at Washington, D.C., where he was discharged on March 6, 1870. On March 18, 1870, he enlisted in the Fourth U.S. Cavalry at Carlisle, Pennsylvania. During his five-year enlistment in the Fourth Cavalry he was involved in engagements against Indians at Mount Paso, Texas, on July 14, 1870; Fresh Water Fork of the

Brazos River on October 19, 1871; North Fork of the Red River on September 29, 1872; Palo Duro Canyon on September 28, 1874; and Laguna Quatro on November 3, 1874. At the battle of the North Fork of the Red River Sergeant Foster led an advance rank into the main resistance and secured the main point of resistance amid bitter and often hand-to-hand combat, thus earning the Medal of Honor. After the battle he was placed in charge of more than one hundred Indian prisoners. So humane was his treatment that Cohaya and Mumsukawa, two Comanche prisoners, still spoke glowingly of their treatment by the army sixty years later in 1933. Foster was discharged from the Fourth Cavalry on March 18, 1875, at Fort Richardson, Texas.

On April 5, 1875, Foster enlisted in the Third U.S. Artillery at Fort Hamilton, New York, and was stationed there until his discharge on April 4, 1880. He immediately journeyed west to Point San Jose, California, where he enlisted in Battery F, Fourth U.S. Artillery, and was stationed at the Presidio of San Francisco. On July 4 Foster was part of the ceremonial crews that fired artillery salutes to begin Independence Day activities. On the morning of July 5 he was admitted to the post hospital complaining of severe chest pains and he was found dead in his hospital bed early in the morning of July 6, 1880. This valiant warrior left behind seven discharge statements signed by company and battery commanders all citing his high character of faithfulness, energy, intelligence, and bravery. He was buried in the Presidio of San Francisco post cemetery at sunset on July 7, 1880.

John J. Given
Corporal, Company K, Sixth U.S. Cavalry

John J. Given was born circa 1840 near Owensboro (Daviess County), Kentucky. During the Civil War he served in Company G, Second Kentucky (Union) Cavalry. He took part in the battle of Perryville, Kentucky, on October 8, 1862. Throughout most of the Civil War he served in the field against Confederate guerrillas operating in northern Kentucky.

Given enlisted in the regular U.S. Army at Cincinnati, Ohio, on April 2, 1866. During 1866–1867 Given served at Greenville, Texas, on Reconstruction duty. In early 1868 he was transferred to Fort Griffin on the northwest Texas frontier. On March 6, 1868, he was involved in his first action against Indians at Paint Creek. He was discharged on April 2, 1869, and reenlisted immediately. He was promoted to corporal on September 1, 1869. In January 1870 he was transferred to Fort Richardson, Texas. He was killed in action during the battle of the Little Wichita River on July 12, 1870. His valiant attempt to recover a fallen trooper resulted in his death and merited him one of the earliest Indian Wars posthumous Medal of Honor awards. His remains were never recovered from the battlefield in Archer County. A Medal of Honor headstone in his honor has been installed at San Antonio National Cemetery.

John Harrington
Private, Company H, Sixth U.S. Cavalry

John Harrington was born at Detroit, Michigan, circa March 1848. Nothing is known of his family or his early years. He was a sailor aboard grain and ore ships on the Great Lakes for a time. He enlisted in the U.S. Army at Cleveland, Ohio, on December 19, 1870. He was sent to Carlisle Barracks, Pennsylvania, for basic training at the Cavalry Recruit Depot. Assigned to Company H, Sixth U.S. Cavalry, he arrived at Fort Richardson, Texas, on January 9, 1871. In March 1871 he was transferred to Kansas where for the next two years he served at Forts Hays, Riley, and Dodge. In 1874, while stationed at Fort Lyon, Colorado, he served as part of the Nelson A. Miles column in the 1874–1875 Indian Territory campaign, during which he was involved in engagements at the Red River on August 30, 1874, and at the buffalo wallow fight on September 12–14, 1874. In the latter engagement Harrington, three other soldiers, and two scouts, were carrying dispatches to an incoming supply train when they were attacked by more than one hundred Kiowa, Comanche, and Cheyenne warriors. Despite being wounded, Harrington continued to aid in the defense of the party's position and to aid and comfort the other wounded, actions for which he was awarded the Medal of Honor. After treatment and rehabilitation for his wounds at Camp Supply, Indian Territory, he returned to Fort Lyon, Colorado. He was promoted to corporal on September 14, 1875, and was discharged from the Sixth U.S. Cavalry on December 19, 1875, at Fort Bowie, Arizona.

Harrington returned to Kansas and reenlisted in the Fifth U.S. Cavalry and in this regiment he participated in campaigns against the Sioux, Cheyenne, and Ute. He was active in engagements at Hat Creek, Wyoming, on July 17, 1876; Slim Buttes, Dakota Territory, on September 9, 1876; Owl Creek, Dakota Territory, on September 14, 1876; Chadron Creek, Nebraska, on October 23, 1876; Powder River, Wyoming, on November 25–26, 1876; and Clark's Fort, Montana, on September 4, 1878. During the 1879 White River Ute expedition he was in the engagement at Milk River, Colorado, on October 5, 1879. He was discharged from the Fifth Cavalry in December 1885 and reenlisted in Troop B, Third U.S. Cavalry on January 20, 1886. Between 1886 and 1890 he served at various posts in Arizona. In 1891 he served at Forts Sam Houston, Clark, Ringgold, and Brown in Texas in operations against revolutionaries who were violating U.S. neutrality laws. Having transferred to the Twenty-third United States Infantry he was discharged on January 20, 1896, at Fort Brown but immediately reenlisted. In July 1898 Harrington transferred to the Fifth U.S. Infantry and served briefly in Puerto Rico during the Spanish-American War. As a cook in Company K, Fifth U.S. Infantry, he was transferred to the Philippine Islands and served in the Batac sector for eight months.

Harrington was formally retired from the army on February 21, 1901, and returned to San Antonio, Texas, to live. He died there from acute alcoholism on January 4, 1905, and was buried in San Antonio National Cemetery.

Francis Snow Hesseltine
Colonel, Thirteenth Maine Infantry

Francis Snow Hesseltine was born on October 10, 1833, at Bangor, Maine, to Peter and Sarah Hesseltine. He was reared and educated the greater part of his youth in Bangor. He began his study of law at age seventeen and worked as a court clerk in Bangor and later in Portland. On October 2, 1853, he married Carrie W. Curtis. Carrie Hesseltine died on June 11, 1856, just as Francis began his first year of law studies at Waterville College.

At the outset of the Civil War, Hesseltine volunteered for the Third Maine Infantry. On May 31, 1861, he was appointed a captain commanding Company G, a unit comprised of present and former Waterville College students. The Third Maine Infantry was rushed to Washington, D.C., to complement the defensive perimeter. In early July his unit was told to prepare for action and begin movement toward Manassas, Virginia. His company was one of the units that delayed the victorious Confederate forces at the Centreville Bridge, preventing an even greater disaster for the Union.

On November 14, 1861, Hesseltine was transferred to the Thirteenth Maine Infantry and promoted to the rank of major. He participated in the campaign for New Orleans and on April 28, 1862, he was promoted to lieutenant colonel and made commander of the regiment. From May 1862 until September 1862 he served as commanding officer of the prisoner-of-war facility on Ship Island, Mississippi. From October 21, 1862, until August 31, 1863, he commanded Fort Macomb, Louisiana. The Thirteenth Maine Infantry became a part of the Thirteenth Army Corps under Brig. Gen. Napoleon Dana effective September 1, 1863. In this capacity, Hesseltine and his troops were actively involved in intrusions onto the Texas Gulf Coast at Brownsville, Aransas Pass, and Fort Esperanza. On the morning of November 17, 1863, when Hesseltine waded ashore at Aransas Pass, he planted the U.S. flag on Texas soil for the first time since the surrender of Federal forces in April 1861.

During the period of December 28–31, 1863, Hesseltine led a one hundred-man reconnaissance patrol onto Matagorda Peninsula. Despite attacks by a large Confederate cavalry force and severe weather conditions, he and his troops successfully repelled the enemy cavalry force and also drove a small Confederate picket detachment from the peninsula, earning Hesseltine the Medal of Honor.

From April to June 1864 Hesseltine served on a general court martial board at New Orleans. During the summer and fall of 1864 he served under Gen. Phillip H. Sheridan in the Shenandoah Valley campaign.

Hesseltine was discharged from the volunteer Union military service at Augusta, Maine, on January 6, 1865. In May 1865 he successfully passed the bar exam and was admitted to practice in Maine. In July 1865 he married Rebecca M. Stark. He became registrar of bankruptcy at Savannah, Georgia, and continued in that capacity until 1870.

In November 1871 Hesseltine entered into private law practice at Melrose, Massachusetts. He became active in civic and veteran affairs. He was a member of the Grand Army of the Republic, U.S. Grant Post at Melrose; the Loyal Legion; and was one of the early supporters of the Military Order of the Congressional Medal of Honor Legion in Boston. His second wife died in 1893 and he was married for a third time in 1900 to Caroline G. Thomas. He retired in 1912 because of failing health and resided at Newton, Massachusetts, where he died on February 17, 1916. He was buried in Wyoming Cemetery at Melrose and was survived by his wife, Caroline G. Hesseltine; a sister, Sarah Neally of Penobscot, Maine; and three children from his second marriage, Norman, Gertrude, and Marion.

John James
Corporal, Company I, Fifth U.S. Infantry

John James was born circa 1838 at Manchester, England. It is not known when he immigrated to the United States, but he first enlisted in the U.S. Army on June 6, 1872, at Albany, New York. At the time of his enlistment he listed his occupation as a bookkeeper. His first assignment was with the Fifth U.S. Infantry in New Mexico. In 1873 he was transferred to Fort Leavenworth, Kansas. In May 1874 he was assigned to Fort Dodge, Kansas, and in July of that year he marched southward as part of the Nelson A. Miles column of the Indian Territory expedition. On August 30, 1874, he participated in the battle of the Red River near the mouth of Tule Canyon, Texas. On September 9–12, 1874, he was active in the battle of the Upper Washita River, sometimes referred to as the Lyman Train battle. During this action in present-day Hemphill County, Texas, James performed continuing acts of gallantry during the Indian siege on the train and earned the award of the Medal of Honor.

During much of 1876 James was involved in campaigns against the Cheyenne and Sioux. He participated in engagements at Cedar Creek, Montana, on October 21, 1876; Bark Creek, Montana, on December 7, 1876; and Red Water Creek, Montana Territory, on December 18, 1876. In the Nez Perce campaign James was cited for gallant conduct at the engagement on Snake Creek in the Bear Paw Mountains, Montana, on September 30, 1877. From October 8, 1877, until 1882 he served with Company H, Ninth U.S. Infantry. He received an early discharge from that unit in order to be enrolled as a provost guard at the Fort Leavenworth Federal Penitentiary. He served in that position until November 1885, when he was permanently discharged from the U.S. Army by reason of general disability.

On December 8, 1885, James was enrolled as a resident of the U.S. Soldier's Home in Washington, D.C. In 1891 he was pensioned for failing vision, nervous disability, heart disease, and partial paralysis of the left leg. On May 23, 1902, he died of pulmonary tuberculosis. He was buried in the Soldier's Home National Cemetery at Washington, D.C., and was survived by a sister, Isabella James, of Manchester, England.

Daniel Keating

Corporal, Company M, Sixth U.S. Cavalry

Daniel Keating was born in Cork County, Ireland, in 1852 to Michael and Catherine Keating. At age three Daniel was brought to the United States with his family and they settled in East Boston. Daniel was educated in the public schools and in his early teens was apprenticed as a bootmaker. On October 24, 1867, he left home and enlisted in the U.S. Army at Carlisle Barracks, Pennsylvania. After several months of basic cavalry training he was assigned to Company M, Sixth Cavalry, then stationed at Austin, Texas. In September 1869 Keating was transferred to Jefferson, Texas, where he contracted dysentery and malarial fever. By November he was rehabilitated and was assigned to Athens, Texas, monitoring elections and suppressing civil disturbances. Keating was promoted to corporal on February 8, 1870, and was once again stationed at Jefferson. Shortly after his arrival there he contracted pneumonia and was saved from death only by the diligent efforts of the post surgeon.

In March 1870 Keating and his company were assigned to Fort Richardson, Texas, where the Sixth Cavalry was ordered to take offensive scouting patrol actions against hostile Indian bands. On October 5, 1870, at Bluff Creek in Archer County, Texas, his gallantry in action merited him the award of the Medal of Honor. On November 1, 1870, he was promoted to sergeant. In March 1871 he was transferred to Fort Lyon, Colorado, where he contracted smallpox in the summer of 1872 and suffered terribly from congestion of the brain. On October 24, 1872, he was honorably discharged from the military service.

Keating returned to his home at Boston, Massachusetts, and became a shipping agent for a furniture company, where he worked for twenty-five years. He married Mary A. Keefe at the Church of Assumption in Boston on October 26, 1874. In 1897 he was pensioned as a result of service-incurred infirmities. Keating died on June 20, 1912, and was buried in the Holy Cross Cemetery at Malden, Massachusetts. He was survived by his children, Michael, Laura, Esther, Daniel, Ada, and Hilary, and two brothers, Henry and Cornelius F. Keating.

John J. H. Kelly
Sergeant, Company I, Fifth U.S. Infantry

John J. H. Kelly was born near Rushville in Schuyler County, Illinois, on December 27, 1850, to William O. and Martha Ann Kelly. About 1857 the family relocated to a farm near Springfield, where John was educated in the public schools. He enlisted in the U.S. Army at Springfield on August 19, 1872, was assigned to Company I, Fifth U.S. Infantry, and served at various posts in Kansas over the next two years. In July 1874 he was posted to Fort Dodge, Kansas, to be part of the Nelson A. Miles column of the Indian Territory expedition. On August 30, 1874, Kelly was involved in the battle of the Red River near the junctures of Tule and Palo Duro Canyons in present-day Briscoe County, Texas. During September 9–14, 1874, his gallant conduct against Comanche, Kiowa, Cheyenne, and Arapaho Indians earned him the Medal of Honor.

During the 1876 Sioux campaign Kelly participated in several engagements: Cedar Creek, Montana, on October 21, 1876; Bark Creek, Montana, on December 7, 1876; and at Red Water Creek, Montana, on December 18, 1876. During the Nez Perce campaign and later Sioux and Crow disturbances he was also active in engagements at: Bear Paw Mountains, Montana, on September 30, 1877; Clark's

Fork, Montana, on September 4, 1878; Milk River, Montana, on July 17, 1879; Poplar Creek, Montana, on August 10, 1879; Porcupine Creek, Montana, on March 8, 1880; and the Crow Agency, Montana, on November 5, 1887.

On September 14, 1884, he married Thilda Johnson at Fort Keough, Montana. Between 1888 and 1892 Kelly was assigned to Forts Bliss, Davis, Clark, and Ringgold in Texas. In 1893 he was assigned to Jackson Barracks, Louisiana, where he was appointed an ordnance sergeant. During the Spanish-American War Kelly served in Puerto Rico. On September 22, 1902, he was formally retired from the army at Fort McPherson, Georgia. He returned to his home at Springfield, Illinois, and became a construction worker. He was a devout member of the United Brethren Church. He died of heart failure on February 4, 1907, and was buried in Oak Ridge Cemetery in Springfield on a grassy knoll overlooking the Lincoln tomb. His former employer, J. S. Culver, said of him, "Sergeant Kelly was with us from the time he retired to the date of his death and a better, truer man never lived." He was survived by his wife, Thilda; a son, John E.; and five daughters, Virginia, Doris, Josephine, Evelyn, and Bertha, all of Springfield. He was also survived by three brothers, Jasper M. Kelly of Edinburg, Illinois; Benjamin F. Kelly and W. D. Kelly, both of Oklahoma; and a sister, Bertha E. Dunn, of Springfield.

Thomas Kelly
Private, Company I, Fifth U.S. Infantry

Thomas Kelly was born in Mayo County, Ireland, circa May 1836. It is not known exactly when he immigrated to the United States but he did enlist in the U.S. Army at New York City on April 8, 1858, listing his occupation as laborer. He was assigned to Company E, First U.S. Cavalry, and was posted in the Pacific Northwest along the Oregon Trail at such posts as Fort Dallas, Fort Randolph, and Camp Salmon Falls. He deserted on March 14, 1859, but was apprehended near Fort Laramie, Wyoming, on April 3, 1859. He was tried, convicted, and eventually restored to duty. He was transferred to Company H, First U.S. Cavalry, on February 29, 1860, and was discharged at Fort Laramie, Wyoming, on April 8, 1863.

Kelly remained out of the army for more than a year before reenlisting on May 1, 1864, in Company I, Fifth U.S. Infantry, at Los Piñón, New Mexico. He was discharged on May 1, 1867, at Fort Union, New Mexico. Kelly chose to remain out of the army for more than two years before he reenlisted on August 5, 1869, at Fort Wallace, Kansas. He was discharged on August 5, 1874, at Fort

Dodge, Kansas. He immediately reenlisted and left with his unit as part of the Nelson A. Miles column that marched southward into the panhandle regions of Oklahoma and Texas during the Indian Territory expedition. On August 30, 1874, he participated in the battle of the Red River. During September 9–12, 1874, he was involved in the defense of the Lyman wagon train that was besieged by several hundred Kiowa, Comanche, and Cheyenne near the Upper Washita River in Hemphill County, Texas. His continuous acts of gallantry during this engagement earned him the Medal of Honor.

After his return to Fort Leavenworth in April 1875 he married Rose Mehan, a twice-widowed mother of four. Kelly served during the 1876–1879 campaigns against the Sioux, Nez Perce, and Crow in Montana and the Dakota Territory. He was discharged on August 4, 1879, at Fort Keough, Montana, and returned to Leavenworth, Kansas, where he resided permanently. He was employed as a teamster and laborer at the Fort Leavenworth Federal Prison until various illnesses forced his retirement in 1905. In 1907 he was pensioned for his Civil War service. He was admitted to the hospital of the Western Branch, National Home for Disabled Volunteer Soldiers, at Leavenworth on March 21, 1919. He died on March 25, 1919, and was buried at Mount Calvary Cemetery at Leavenworth. He was survived by his wife, Rose Kelly, and two daughters, Ellen O'Connor and Mary Forge.

On April 4, 1995, Berenice O'Connor, Thomas Kelly's granddaughter, donated his Medal of Honor to the Frontier Army Museum at Fort Leavenworth, Kansas.

Thomas Kerrigan
Sergeant, Company H, Sixth U.S. Cavalry

Thomas Kerrigan was born at Tipperary, Ireland, circa 1845. He enlisted in the U.S. Army on October 1, 1866, at New York City. At the time of his enlistment he listed his occupation as that of a machinist. He was assigned to Company H, Sixth U.S. Cavalry, and was assigned to Reconstruction duty in East Texas. He served two years in the towns of Greenville, Jefferson, and Athens before he was transferred to Fort Richardson on the West Texas frontier in the latter part of 1869. On July 12, 1870, the small command of which he was a member was attacked by more than two hundred Kiowa and Comanche Indians in what became known as the battle of the Little Wichita River. For his gallantry in action during this engagement he was awarded the Medal of Honor. In March 1871 his unit was transferred to Fort Hays, Kansas, and he was discharged there on October 1, 1871.

John Kirk
Sergeant, Company L, Sixth U.S. Cavalry

Born on November 15, 1848, in Fairview Township, York County, Pennsylvania, John Kirk was the son of James and Elizabeth H. Kirk. He was reared and educated in York County. At age fourteen he ran away to Harrisburg, where he succeeded in enlisting in Company B, Twentieth Pennsylvania Cavalry. In his first major action of the war he was captured on September 7, 1863, near Bath, West Virginia, during a surprise Confederate cavalry attack. He was incarcerated as a prisoner of war at Belle Island, South Carolina, and was paroled and exchanged on March 6, 1864. Less than two months later he was in the attack on Savannah, Georgia, as part of Company L, Ninth Pennsylvania Cavalry. At the war's end he was near Lexington, North Carolina.

On July 21, 1868, Kirk enlisted in the regular army at Carlisle, Pennsylvania, and was assigned to Company L, Sixth U.S. Cavalry. For much of 1868–1869 he served on Reconstruction duty in such East Texas towns as Jefferson, Greenville, Athens, and Canton. On September 1, 1869, he was promoted to corporal and was stationed to Fort Richardson on the West Texas frontier. On November 1, 1869, he was promoted to first sergeant. On July 12, 1870, the fifty-man command of which he was a member was attacked by a numerically superior force of Kiowas and Comanches. In this engagement Sergeant Kirk kept the many new recruits from becoming panic-stricken and separating. He kept them formed into squads and ran among intense fire for fifty yards to rescue Sgt. William Winterbottom. After he returned to the main command he kept the troops in rank formation and maintained them in proper distance all the while under fire from the attacking Indians. He remained at the head of his company for nine hours performing his duties. He was presented his Medal of Honor for these actions on August 25, 1870.

In April 1871 Kirk was transferred to Fort Hays, Kansas. On December 18, 1872, he was promoted to sergeant major on the Sixth U.S. Cavalry's headquarters staff. He was discharged on July 21, 1873, upon expiration of his service and he returned to his home at New Cumberland, Pennsylvania. After working at a local steel mill for a number of years he eventually became a local grocery storekeeper. Throughout the community he was referred to as "Major Kirk." For a number of years he was active as the superintendent of the children's department at Baughman Methodist Church in New Cumberland. Kirk was noted as being an immaculate dresser, often attired in white ducks, black derby hat, and sporting an ornate cane. He was an active member of the International Order of Odd Fellows,

Lodge no. 160, and Perservance Lodge no. 21 of Free & Accepted Masons. He was a staunch Republican and was unabashedly patriotic, turning out for every Memorial Day parade until his health no longer permitted his participation. He was active in Grand Army of the Republic activities, especially during the national encampment at Portland, Oregon, in 1913. He was recognized there as one of the few surviving Civil War ex-prisoners of war. He retired in 1907 due to failing health and was eventually pensioned for the Civil War and as a Medal of Honor recipient.

Kirk was admitted to the U.S. Soldier's Home at Washington, D.C., in 1908 and remained there as a resident until 1918. He applied for and was granted the 1904-style Medal of Honor on April 15, 1907. On May 4, 1916, he submitted the application and documentation for his enrollment upon the Army and Navy Medal of Honor Roll. His application was the first submitted from an Indian Wars veteran. He was issued Medal of Honor Roll Certificate no. 81, approved May 27, 1916. Kirk died on March 2, 1920, at New Cumberland, Pennsylvania, of complications from diabetes. He was survived by a niece, Grace Rosenberger, and was buried at Mount Olivet Cemetery at New Cumberland, Pennsylvania.

George K. Kitchen
Sergeant, Company H, Sixth U.S. Cavalry

George K. Kitchen was born on October 5, 1849, near Pottsville in Lebanon County, Pennsylvania. He first enlisted in the U.S. Army at Harrisburg, Pennsylvania, on July 20, 1870. After basic cavalry training at Carlisle Barracks, Pennsylvania, and Jefferson Barracks, Missouri, he was assigned to Company H, Sixth U.S. Cavalry, then posted at Fort Richardson, Texas. In April 1871 he was transferred to Fort Wallace, Kansas. On January 15, 1872, Kitchen was promoted to corporal, and four months later, on May 2, he was promoted to sergeant. At the battle of the Upper Washita River on September 9–12, 1874, Kitchen was cited for gallantry in action and awarded the Medal of Honor. On April 23, 1875, he was again cited for gallantry in action at Sappa Creek, Kansas. On July 20, 1875, he reenlisted in Company I, Fifth U.S. Cavalry. During his service in this unit he participated in engagements at Hat Creek, Wyoming, on July 17, 1876; Slim Buttes, Dakota Territory, on September 9, 1876; Owl Creek, Dakota Territory, on September 14, 1876; and White River, Colorado, on October 10, 1879. On July 21, 1875, he married Annie L. Allen at Cheyenne, Wyoming. He remained as a sergeant with Company I, Fifth U.S. Cavalry, for fifteen continuous years and became a first sergeant in 1881. One of his first duties at that rank was to command the escort detail for Gen. P. H. Sheridan on his survey and inspection tour of Yellowstone National Park in 1881. Kitchen served continuously until his retirement on October 10, 1900, while on active duty in the Philippine Islands.

After retirement Kitchen and his family resided at Safford, Arizona, until 1908. He spent two years at Los Angeles, California, before moving to San Antonio, Texas, in 1910. He was employed by the Army Quartermaster Department at Fort Sam Houston as a foragemaster. While in that position he was implicated in a fraud conspiracy for aiding in the making of false claims and of making false entries in official records. For his part he was fired from his position and was sentenced to three years in confinement by a general court martial board on June 1, 1914. Kitchen, already saddened by the recent death of his wife, faced a three-year jail sentence. A granddaughter, Hazel Wright, rose to his defense by submitting a recommendation for clemency to the army's judge advocate general. Her plea was based on the long, honorable, and distinguished service of the accused, his excellent character during his connection of more than forty years with the government, and his desire to make reparation by testifying against his co-conspirator. The judge advocate general, Zenas R. Bliss, agreed, and that portion of the sentence imposing confinement was remitted.

Over the next two years Kitchen worked as a grain-purchasing agent residing at Denver, Colorado, and St. Paul, Minnesota. Upon his return to San Antonio in 1917 he was successful in obtaining an Indian War and Medal of Honor pension. On August 29, 1917, he was granted Medal of Honor Certificate no. 337. He was also issued Indian Wars Campaign Medal no. 947. He died on November 22, 1922, of heart failure and was buried in St. Mary's Cemetery at San Antonio. He was survived by a son, George R. Kitchen, and a daughter, Laura K. Platt of San Diego, California. In March 1965 Laura Platt donated her father's 1897- and 1904-style Medals of Honor to the Freedom Foundation at Valley Forge, Pennsylvania.

John W. Knox
Corporal, Company I, Fifth U.S. Infantry

According to scant sources he was born circa 1849 to William A. and Mary Knox of Des Moines County, Iowa. He left home and enlisted in the U.S. Army on May 13, 1873, at Fort Leavenworth, Kansas. He was assigned to Company I, Fifth U.S. Infantry. In August 1874 he was promoted to corporal and transferred to Fort Dodge, Kansas. He was a member of the Nelson A. Miles column of the 1874–1875 Indian Territory expedition. During this expedition he participated in the battle of the Red River on August 30, 1874, and at the battle of the Upper

Washita River during September 9–12, 1874. His gallant acts during the latter engagement earned him the Medal of Honor.

During the Yellowstone Campaign in 1876 he participated in several more engagements: Cedar Creek, Montana, on October 21, 1876; Bark Creek, Montana, on December 7, 1876; and at Redwater Creek, Montana, on December 18, 1876. During the 1877 Nez Perce campaign he participated in the final action of the campaign at Bear Paw Mountains on September 30, 1877. In the brief campaign against the Bannock tribe he was in action at the battle of Clark's Fork, Montana, on September 4, 1878. On July 17, 1879, he took part in the engagement at Milk River, Montana, against Sitting Bull's Sioux warriors, his final action against Indians. After three years at Fort Leavenworth he was transferred to Fort Keough, Montana, where he remained until 1888. Between 1888 and 1892 Knox was stationed at Forts Bliss, Clark, Ringgold, and Brown in Texas. During his service in Texas he participated in field duty in the Lower Rio Grande River Valley against Garza revolutionaries.

After his transfer to Jackson Barracks at New Orleans, Louisiana, Knox began to suffer seriously from a myriad of health problems. On June 21, 1893, he was discharged on a medical disability certificate. On July 15, 1893, he was pensioned for his disabilities and was admitted to the U.S. Soldier's Home at Washington, D.C., where he remained as a resident until he was dismissed per Special Order no. 23, dated July 2, 1895. He was dropped from the pension rolls on November 11, 1898, because of failure to claim his pension. After he left the U.S. Soldier's Home he disappeared into obscurity and was never heard from again.

William Koelpin
Sergeant, Company I, Fifth U.S. Infantry

William Koelpin was born at Stebbin, Prussia (Germany) on October 6, 1848. Nothing is known of his life prior to his first enlistment in the U.S. Army. When he enlisted at Brooklyn, New York, on December 1, 1870, he listed his occupation as locksmith. He was assigned to Company I, Fifth U.S. Infantry, and was stationed at Fort Leavenworth, Kansas. By 1873 he had been promoted to corporal and in April 1874 he was promoted to sergeant.

On May 28, 1874, Koelpin was transferred to Fort Dodge, Kansas. Over the next two months he served as head of maintenance for the wagons used on the Nelson A. Miles column for the Indian Territory expedition. During this expedition he participated in the battle of the Red River on August 30, 1874, and the battle of the Upper Washita River on September 9–12, 1874. During the latter engagement Koelpin was cited for gallantry in action against Indians who had laid siege to the supply train of which he was a member. He was awarded the Medal of Honor for his deeds and received it in a ceremony at Fort Leavenworth, Kansas, on July 28, 1875. Koelpin was discharged from the army on December 1, 1875. He remained out of the army for two years before again enlisting on April 17, 1877, in Battery I, Fifth U.S. Artillery, at New York City. He served six consecutive enlistments in this unit. During his twenty-three years in the unit he was assigned to: Fort Niagara, New York, from 1877 to 1882; Fort Hamilton, New York, from 1883 to 1887; Alcatraz Island, California, from 1893 to 1897; Cuba and Puerto Rico from 1898 through 1899; and Fort Hancock, New Jersey, from 1900 until his retirement. During his artillery service Koelpin was instrumental in improving and refining fixed and mobile artillery equipment and became an expert instructor in artillery operations and tactics. In April 1900 reorganization plans converted the Fifth U.S. Artillery into the Fifty-fifth Coast Artillery. Koelpin was formally retired from that unit on May 29, 1902. Koelpin died of heart failure on January 2, 1912, at Brooklyn, New York. He was buried in the Lutheran Cemetery in the Middle Village section of Brooklyn.

David Larkin
Farrier, Company F, Fourth U.S. Cavalry

David Larkin was born in December 1840 at Cork, Ireland, to Daniel and Ellen Connell Larkin. He enlisted in the U.S. Army at Boston, Massachusetts, on November 25, 1865, shortly after immigrating to the United States. After two months of basic training at Carlisle Barracks, Pennsylvania, he was assigned to Company F, Fourth U.S. Cavalry, then posted at San Antonio, Texas. Between 1866 and 1868 he served primarily on Reconstruction duty in north central Texas, and for a time escorted surveying crews and mail coaches. Shortly after his three-year enlistment expired he reenlisted on November 25, 1868, at Chambers Creek near Corsicana, Texas. After transfer to Fort Griffin, Texas, on the northwest Texas frontier in May 1870 he began to take part in field operations against Indian bands. He was an active participant in engagements against Kiowas and Comanches at Crawfish Creek on October 29, 1869; North Hubbard Creek on April 3, 1870; Mountain Pass on July 14, 1870; Fresh Water Fork of the Brazos River on October 11, 1871; North Fork of the Red River on September 29, 1872; Kickapoo Springs on December 7, 1873; and Palo Duro Canyon on September 28, 1874. During the engagement on the North Fork of the

Red River, Larkin was a part of the charging rank that encountered the main Indian resistance. Despite murderous fire that felled three troopers near him and wounded his mount, Larkin charged down the head of a ravine and prevented the Indians from breaking out of the perimeter and gaining a nearby milling herd of horses. His Medal of Honor award was for these actions.

During the 1876 campaigns against the Sioux and Northern Cheyenne in Nebraska, Wyoming, and Montana, Larkin was involved in engagements at Chadron Creek, Nebraska, on October 23, 1876, and Bates Creek, Montana, on November 25, 1876. During 1877 and 1878 he was involved in escorting Indian prisoners to reservations in the Indian Territory and in preventing Southern Cheyenne from uniting with the Northern Cheyenne. During this service he was involved in minor actions at Sand Creek, Kansas, on September 21, 1878, and at Punished Woman's Creek, Kansas, on September 27, 1878. Larkin was discharged on July 21, 1881, at Fort Sill, Oklahoma.

Larkin returned to Boston, Massachusetts, and married circa 1883. He was employed as a shipping agent for a furniture retailer in Cambridge. In 1892 he obtained an invalid pension for injuries received during a stampede of horses at Fort Griffin, Texas, in February 1870. Larkin was a charter member of the Medal of Honor Legion formed at Boston in 1891. He died of heart failure on May 8, 1905, and was buried in Arlington, Massachusetts, at St. Paul's Cemetery. He was survived by a son, Benjamin D. Larkin.

Gregory P. Mahoney
Private, Company E, Fourth U.S. Cavalry

Gregory Patrick Mahoney was born on May 2, 1850, to Patrick and Joanna Mahoney at Pontypool, South Wales, Great Britain. It is believed that he came to the United States in mid-1871 and resided at Boston, Massachusetts, where on November 8, 1871, he enlisted in the U.S. Army, listing his occupation as a laborer. After basic cavalry training at Carlisle Barracks, Pennsylvania, he was assigned to Company E, Fourth U.S. Cavalry. He joined his company at Fort Richardson, Texas, on February 19, 1872. In this unit Mahoney was active in engagements at North Fork of the Red River, September 29, 1872; Remolino, Mexico, May 19, 1873; Tule Canyon, September 27, 1874; Palo Duro Canyon, September 28, 1874; Double Lakes, November 3, 1874; and Chadron Creek, Nebraska, October 23, 1876. In the engagement near Tule Canyon, Mahoney and two fellow troopers were in the advance of an attack on a large body of Kiowa, Cheyenne, and Comanche Indians who were attempting to stampede the main command's horses in order to divert the command away from the main Indian encampment. For this brazen attack on a numerically superior Indian band, Mahoney was awarded the Medal of Honor. He was discharged as a private at Fort Robinson, Nebraska, on November 8, 1876.

John May
Sergeant, Company L, Sixth U.S. Cavalry

John May was born at Wurtemburg, Germany, circa 1837. It is not known when he immigrated to the United States. He enlisted in the U.S. Army at Camden, New Jersey, on September 29, 1866. He was assigned to Company L, Sixth U.S. Cavalry, and was assigned to Reconstruction duty in East Texas, where he served at such towns as Greenville, Athens, and Corsicana. He was promoted to corporal on May 20, 1867, and to sergeant on April 8, 1868. On Christmas Eve, 1869, at Greenville, Texas, May found a young soldier drunk on guard duty. The soldier pulled his pistol and fired a shot that narrowly missed May's head. May quickly wrestled the gun from the soldier's grasp and subdued him. Seven months later May demonstrated acts of gallantry over a seven-hour period during the battle of the Little Wichita River on July 12, 1870, which earned him the award of the Medal of Honor.

In April 1871 the Sixth Cavalry was transferred to various posts in Kansas. May's company was posted to Fort Hays and he was discharged there on September 29, 1871. He immediately reenlisted. During the 1874 Indian Territory expedition he was transferred to Fort Dodge, Kansas, and was assigned to a farrier detachment preparing the expedition's horses. On July 10, 1874, May was seriously injured from the kick of a horse while attempting to shoe it. He remained in the post hospital for more than a month, during which he had surgery to reset his broken nose. Shortly after his transfer back to Fort Hays he married Annette Gregory on March 15, 1875. In early 1876 the Sixth Cavalry was transferred to various posts in Arizona. May served at Camp Grant and Fort Bowie during operations against Chiricahua Apaches and was discharged on September 30, 1876. May and his family returned to Junction City, Kansas, and applied for a homestead, where he farmed for three years. In 1879 he worked for the railroad near Las Animas, Colorado. In 1881 May was forced to move back to Junction City, Kansas, because of health problems. Recurring infections from an imperfectly set lachrymal duct from his right eye impaired his vision.

May applied for and was granted an invalid disability pension in 1881. He died on March 19, 1886, at La Junta, Colorado, as a result of another kick in the face by a horse, which he was grooming at the time. He was buried at Fairview Cemetery at La Junta. He was survived by his wife, Annette May, and three daughters, Minnie, Daisey, and Maggie. Annette May remarried several months after John's death to E. E. Deabenport and they resided in La Junta.

William McCabe
Private, Company E, Fourth U.S. Cavalry

William McCabe was born circa 1845 at Belfast, Northern Ireland. Exactly when he immigrated to America is unknown, but he resided in Mexico for some time prior to the American Civil War. From 1863 to 1867 he served as a scout for Gen. Ignacio Zaragosa's loyalist army fighting against the French occupation. Whether he was among the early Irish immigrants to Mexico or whether he was an American who volunteered to help Mexico is not known.

As of early 1871 McCabe was employed as a civilian scout and guide at Fort Duncan, Texas. During 1872 Col. W. A. Shafter used him as a spy operating within the northern Mexican states of Coahuila, Tamaulipas, and Nuevo Leon. Because of his fluency in Spanish, his connections with the Mexican populace, and his knowledge of the terrain McCabe gathered much valuable information on trans-border cattle thefts, movements of Indian and bandit groups, and data on revolutionary activities.

McCabe enlisted in the U.S. Army on February 3, 1874, at Fort Duncan, Texas. At the time of his enlistment he stated his occupation as a miner. During his service in Company E, Fourth U.S. Cavalry, he was a member of the contingent of enlisted scouts used by Col. R. S. Mackenzie. This detachment was comprised of enlisted troopers Mackenzie selected personally for their linguistic skills, horsemanship, marksmanship, general intelligence, and stamina. McCabe, as part of this contingent, was given credit in reports for operating at long distances from the main command in a reconnoitering capacity during the 1874 Staked Plains campaign. He was active in engagements at Red Hill on September 25, 1874, and at Tule and Palo Duro Canyons on September 26–28, 1874. His gallant attack upon a large body of Cheyenne Indians near Tule Canyon on September 27 merited him the award of the Medal of Honor. He was promoted to corporal in November 1874. On May 30, 1875, he was discharged from the army at Fort Sill, Indian Territory, on a surgeon's certificate of disability for a severe hernial rupture.

Upon the recommendation of Col. R. S. Mackenzie, McCabe was employed with the U.S. Quartermaster Department at Fort Brown, Texas, as a scout and guide, effective November 1, 1875. He served in that position until August 31, 1876, when he moved to Brackettville, Texas, where he was employed at Fort Clark as a special packer from March 1, 1877, to April 10, 1877. This position was a cover, for he was actually working as a spy for Col. W. R. Shafter and submitted numerous intelligence dispatches from Piedras Negras, Mexico, during that period. As of March 1878 he was a deputy sheriff for Kinney County at Eagle Pass, Texas. By May 1880 he was again operating as an operative inside Mexico. He was last known to be living at Eagle Pass as of December 1881.

Franklin M. McDonnold
Private, Company G, Eleventh U.S. Infantry

Franklin M. McDonnold purportedly was born at Bowling Green, Kentucky, circa 1850. He enlisted at Fort Griffin, Texas, on June 7, 1871, and at that time he stated his occupation as a teamster.

During the first year of his enlistment his assigned duty was that of a guard or escort for stagecoaches carrying the U.S. Mail. He was detailed most frequently on the very dangerous segment between Fort Richardson and Fort Griffin in north central Texas. On August 3, 1872, McDonnold's successful defense of a mail coach attacked by a band of Indians merited him the award of the Medal of Honor. On September 7, 1872, he was promoted to corporal. On December 4, 1873, McDonnold deserted from Fort Griffin. Records indicate that he was never apprehended nor did he later apply for a pardon. Franklin M. McDonnold, if that indeed was his true name and not an alias, simply disappeared into obscurity and was never heard from again.

Henry A. McMaster
Corporal, Fourth U.S. Cavalry

Henry A. McMaster was born in 1847 to John and Mira A. McMaster at Augusta, Maine. He was the second eldest of five children and was educated in the public schools of Kennebec County.

When the Civil War began he attempted to enlist but was rejected because of his age. On December 5, 1863, he stated his age as eighteen and successfully enlisted in the Twenty-ninth Maine Infantry, which participated in the capture of New Orleans and afterward in the Red River campaign in northwestern Louisiana. At the battle of Sabine Cross Roads on April 8, 1864, McMaster rendered gallant service with a small force of fellow soldiers by holding back the

Confederate advance along the Mansfield Road. After being transferred to Washington, D.C., he served briefly as an orderly at army headquarters. He rejoined his unit for the Shenandoah Valley campaign, and participated in the battle of Opequan on September 19, 1864, and at Fisher's Hill on September 22. At the battle of Cedar Creek on October 19, 1864, he survived the brutal carnage of the infamous peach orchard and was cited on the regimental roll of honor. At the war's end he was posted to Washington, D.C., where he served as part of the guard detail over the Lincoln assassins during May 4–6, 1865. He was mustered out of the Twenty-ninth Maine Infantry as a corporal on June 21, 1866, at Hilton Head, South Carolina.

On June 10, 1871, McMaster enlisted in the Fourth U.S. Cavalry at Memphis, Tennessee, and was assigned to Company A at Fort Richardson, Texas. He was promoted to corporal on July 2, 1872. He was wounded in action on September 29, 1872, at the battle of the North Fork of the Red River. During this action he singularly engaged and repulsed a large body of Indians attempting a breakout through a narrow ravine. His actions merited him the award of the Medal of Honor. He died of a severe chest wound at the post hospital at Fort Griffin on November 11, 1872. He was originally buried in the Fort Griffin post cemetery on November 12, 1872, but his remains were later reinterred at the San Antonio National Cemetery at San Antonio, Texas.

William McNamara Jr.
Sergeant, Company F, Fourth U.S. Cavalry

William McNamara Jr. was born in Mayo County, Ireland, in 1837 to William and Mary McAlister McNamara. He immigrated alone to the United States about 1850. He first enlisted in the U.S. Army at New York City on December 3, 1856, and was assigned to Company F, First U.S. Cavalry, and sent to the western frontier.

Throughout 1857 and 1858 McNamara served at various posts along the Santa Fe and Oregon Trails. In 1858 he participated in actions to quell Mormon War disturbances near Salt Lake City, Utah. During 1859 he was assigned to various posts in Kansas and Nebraska and he escorted immigrant trains along the Cimmaron Crossing Cut of the Santa Fe Trail. In September 1859 he campaigned against the Kiowas and Comanches in the Smoky Hill River area of Kansas. In 1860 he was posted near Bent's Fort, Colorado Territory, and campaigned against Setank's band of Kiowas along the Purgatory River. On July 11, 1860, he was active in the engagement at Blackwater Springs, Nebraska.

At the outset of the Civil War McNamara was helping to construct the original Fort Lyon in southeastern Colorado Territory when his unit was ordered east to bolster the defense perimeter for Washington, D.C. In his first action of the Civil War during July 1861, McNamara and his fellow troopers covered the rear of the retreating Union forces after the disaster at Bull Run. On August 3, 1861, the First Cavalry was formally redesignated the Fourth Cavalry. Throughout most of late 1861 and early 1862 McNamara served as escort and provost guard at the Army of the Potomac headquarters at Washington, D.C. His first offensive battle action of the war occurred during the Middle Tennessee campaign. He was involved in actions at Sparta, Tennessee, on August 17, 1863, and Nashville, Tennessee, on December 15–16 1864. In one of the ironies of the war, McNamara's company initiated the firing at the battle of Shiloh, which killed their former commanding officer, Confederate Gen. Albert Sidney Johnston. As a sergeant, McNamara was active in engagements at Corinth, Pontotoc, West Point, Okolona, and Columbus, Mississippi. During late 1864 and early 1865 he was part of G. P. Buell's cavalry thrust through Alabama and rendered outstanding service at Blue Pond and Selma, Alabama.

After promotion to first sergeant on January 1, 1866, McNamara served a brief stint of Reconstruction duty in Georgia, Texas, and Louisiana. In early 1867 the Fourth Cavalry was transferred to various posts on the West Texas frontier. During his decade-long service in Texas McNamara participated in engagements against Kiowa, Comanche, Cheyenne, Kickapoo, and Lipan Apache tribes. He was especially active in engagements at Blanco Canyon, October 29, 1869; North Hubbard Creek, April 3, 1870; Mountain Pass, July 14, 1870; Fresh Water Fork of the Brazos River, October 11, 1871; North Fork of the Red River, September 29, 1872; Kickapoo Springs on the Nueces River, December 10, 1873; Palo Duro Canyon, September 28, 1874; and the Salt Fork of the Red River on October 9, 1874. He was awarded the Medal of Honor for his gallantry in charging into the main point of Indian resistance, and forcing their retreat at the North Fork of the Red River on September 29, 1872.

During the Fourth Cavalry's brief participation in the Powder River campaign against the Sioux and Northern Cheyenne, McNamara was in action at Chadron Creek, Nebraska, on October 23, 1876, and at Bates Creek, Wyoming, on November 25, 1876. In 1877 and 1878 McNamara was involved in escorting Indian prisoners to reservations in the Indian Territory, and in preventing Southern Cheyenne bands from uniting with Northern Cheyenne tribes. During this assignment he was engaged in action at Sand Creek, Kansas, on September 21, 1878, and Punished Woman's Creek, Kansas, on September 27, 1878.

On January 24, 1879, McNamara was reduced to the rank of private, and reassigned to Company A. By March 26, 1880, he had risen again to the rank of sergeant. During the period from 1881 until mid-1887 McNamara was assigned to various posts in New Mexico and Arizona. He participated in active field operations against Apaches led by Geronimo, Chihuahua, and Nana. He was especially active in the engagement at Devil's Creek, Mogollon Mountains, New Mexico, on May 22, 1885.

On August 8, 1887, while stationed at Fort Lowell, Arizona, McNamara was formally retired from the army after almost thirty-one years of continuous service. After his retirement he resided briefly at New York City. Between 1888 and 1892 he resided in Ireland. He returned from Ireland and resided in Manhattan, New York City, with his son until his death from kidney failure on March 16, 1912. He was buried in Calvary Cemetery in the Woodside section of Manhattan, New York City. He was survived by one son, William H. McNamara; daughter-in-law, Catherine; two granddaughters, Mary and Evelyn; and a grandson, William McNamara III.

John Mitchell
Sergeant, Company I, Fifth U.S. Infantry

John Mitchell was born at Dublin, Ireland, circa May 1846. It is believed that he immigrated to the United States with his family circa 1852, and they eventually settled near Peoria, Illinois. At the outset of the Civil War John Mitchell enlisted in the Fourteenth Illinois Cavalry. In his first major action of the war near Jamestown, Kentucky, on April 25, 1863, he was instrumental in the capture of twenty-three Confederate soldiers. During the period from May to July 1863 Mitchell was part of the Union forces sent to pursue and capture Confederate Gen. John H. Morgan's guerrilla force. Mitchell was active in a brief engagement against Morgan's forces near Morristown, Tennessee, on June 2, 1863. He was again active in action when Union forces caught up to Morgan's command near New Lisbon, Ohio, on July 21, 1863. During much of 1864 Mitchell was part of the Union command sent in pursuit of the Confederate Cherokee raiders through western North Carolina and eastern Tennessee. At the war's end he was mustered out on August 31, 1865, returned to Peoria, and again worked on the family farm.

On August 19, 1867, Mitchell enlisted in the regular U.S. Army at Peoria. He was assigned to the Eighteenth Infantry and spent the next three years on Reconstruction duty primarily near Atlanta, Georgia. He was discharged at

Atlanta on August 19, 1870, and on August 24 he was at Fort Leavenworth, Kansas, where he enlisted in the Fifth U.S. Infantry. During his first three years he served at various posts in Kansas and was primarily involved in railroad and stagecoach escort duties. In 1874 he was posted to Fort Dodge, Kansas, and became a part of the Nelson A. Miles column of the 1874–1875 Indian Territory expedition into Oklahoma and the Texas Panhandle. On August 30, 1874, he participated in the engagement near Palo Duro Canyon on the Prairie Dog Fork of the Red River. Two weeks later during September 9–14, 1874, he was involved in the battle of the Upper Washita River. During the siege upon a government supply train by several hundred Kiowa, Comanche, and Cheyenne warriors, Mitchell, as a member of the train escort, was cited by Capt. Wyllys Lyman for conspicuous acts of gallantry and was subsequently awarded the Medal of Honor.

In 1876, during his second enlistment with the Fifth U.S. Infantry, Mitchell performed outstanding and gallant services in the campaigns against Sioux and Northern Cheyenne tribes. During this campaign he was active in engagements at Cedar Creek, Montana, October 21, 1876; Bark Creek, Montana, December 7, 1876; and Red Water Creek, Montana, December 18, 1876. During the 1877 campaign against the Nez Perce and later Crow and Sioux disturbances he was again active in engagements at Bear Paw Mountains, Montana, September 30, 1877; Clark's Fork, Montana, September 4, 1878; Milk River, Montana, August 10, 1879; and Porcupine Creek, Montana, on March 8, 1880. In August 1876 Mitchell was again recommended for the Medal of Honor. He was cited by General Miles for single-handedly conveying very important dispatches and mail in an open boat through Indian-infested country from the mouth of the Powder River in Montana to Fort Buford, North Dakota, a distance of more than one hundred and ten miles. Some of the messages and mail he conveyed included some of the first accounts verifying and detailing the destruction of Gen. G. A. Custer's command on the Little Big Horn River. The recommendation was disallowed on the grounds that he already possessed a Medal of Honor. He was later cited for "Honorable Mention" for this deed. On March 1, 1881, Mitchell was appointed to ordnance sergeant and served in that capacity at Fort Assinniboine, Montana, and later at Fort Sherman, Idaho, where he was formally retired on September 17, 1894.

During retirement Mitchell resided at the International Hotel at San Francisco, California. He died of heart failure on May 1, 1904, at the Presidio of San Francisco U.S. General Hospital and was buried on May 3, 1904, at the San Francisco National Cemetery. He never married and had no known survivors.

William W. Morris
Corporal, Company H, Sixth U.S. Cavalry

William W. Morris was born in 1846 at Dover, Tennessee. He was raised and educated at Dover and was trained as a bookkeeper. He was working in that capacity when the Civil War began. He left his job on October 18, 1862, and enlisted in Company M, Twelfth Tennessee Cavalry, which was part of Confederate Gen. E. Kirby Smith's West Tennessee Command. In that unit Morris saw severe action at the battle of Murfreesborough on December 31, 1862, and at Stone River on January 2, 1863. During 1863 Morris took part in the Middle Tennessee campaign and was involved in action at Albany, Kentucky, on April 25, 1863. He was promoted to second lieutenant on October 1, 1863. During the latter part of 1863 and for the most part of 1864 he served with Gen. John H. Morgan's raiders and participated in cavalry raids as far north as Ohio and Indiana. During the latter part of 1864 in the East Tennessee campaign he was involved in actions at Rogersville, Thorn Hill, and Bull's Gap, Tennessee. On September 4, 1864, during an engagement near Greeneville, Tennessee, he was riding near General Morgan when Morgan was killed in action. During that campaign Morris was wounded twice and captured. He was paroled as a prisoner of war at Memphis, Tennessee, on May 25, 1865.

After the war Morris returned to his bookkeeping job. He remained in commercial business for seven years before he enlisted in the U.S. Army on June 1, 1872, at Louisville, Kentucky. He was assigned to Company K, Sixth U.S. Cavalry, and was stationed at Fort Wallace, Kansas. For most of 1872 Morris served as the regiment's quartermaster orderly. During 1873 he served as a teamster for the quartermaster department, and in April 1874 was transferred to Company H and promoted to corporal.

During the 1874–1875 Indian Territory expedition he was active in the battle of the Upper Washita River, September 9–12, 1874. In this engagement he was cited for gallantry in action, which merited his award of the Medal of Honor. On April 23, 1875, Morris performed outstanding brave service in an engagement against Cheyenne Indians on Sappa Creek in northwestern Kansas. In that engagement he was cited for gallantry and recommended for the Medal of Honor a second time by Lt. Austin Henely. Under Henely's orders, Morris had led a decoy detachment up the crest of a hill under severe fire to allow other detachments to flank the Indian positions. Morris's name was stricken from the list of names submitted to the War Department on November 16, 1876, for the reason that he had received a Medal of Honor for former service.

In early 1876 Morris was transferred to Camp Bowie, Arizona. On April 10, 1876, he participated in an engagement against Apache Indians in the San Jose Mountains. Morris was promoted to quartermaster sergeant on August 1, 1876. On June 1, 1877, he received a discharge at the expiration of his enlistment.

As of 1898 Morris was employed with the U.S. Postal Service at Italy, Texas. After he moved from Italy, circa 1902, his whereabouts are unknown.

Solon D. Neal
Private, Company L, Sixth U.S. Cavalry

Solon D. Neal was born in 1846 at Hanover, New Hampshire, to Eli and May Neal. Solon had an older brother, Joseph; a younger brother, Frank; and a sister, Mary. Solon Neal was educated in the public schools of Hanover. At the outbreak of the Civil War he attempted to enlist but his father prohibited it. Solon continued with his schooling and apprenticeship as a carpenter, but on March 1, 1866, he left home and enlisted in the army. After basic cavalry training at Carlisle Barracks, Pennsylvania, he was assigned to Company L, Sixth U.S. Cavalry.

During 1866 to 1869 he served on Reconstruction duty in East Texas at Bonham, McKinney, Jefferson, and Greenville. During this duty he trailed outlaw bands such as the Bob Lee gang, assisted civil authorities in law enforcement, patrolled against vigilante groups, and monitored elections. He was promoted to sergeant on February 20, 1867. He was discharged on March 1, 1869, and immediately reenlisted. In early 1870 he was transferred to Fort Richardson for field duty against raiding bands of Kiowa and Comanche Indians. During this duty he was cited for gallantry in action near the Little Wichita River on July 12, 1870, for which he was awarded the Medal of Honor. He was transferred to Fort Harker, Kansas, in early 1871 and was discharged there on May 29, 1871.

Neal remained out of the army for almost a year before he reenlisted in Company K, Eleventh U.S. Infantry, at Fort Richardson, Texas. After escorting railroad-surveying crews, mail coaches, and supply trains during that enlistment he was discharged on April 15, 1877. He reenlisted in the Tenth U.S. Infantry on January 8, 1878, at Fort Clark, Texas, but soon obtained a transfer to Company C, Eighth U.S. Cavalry. Between 1878 and 1883 he served in the field against Mexican bandits and trans-border Indian raiders.

On February 20, 1883, Neal reenlisted in Company B, Nineteenth U.S. Infantry, and followed that enlistment with another from 1888 to 1893 in Company G, Sixteenth U.S. Infantry. In 1893 he was accepted for appointment as an ordnance sergeant and served in that capacity at Indianapolis Arsenal until he retired on August 20, 1897.

After his retirement Neal resided in San Antonio, Texas. The night he arrived in San Antonio the suitcase containing his original Medal of Honor was stolen. He applied for and obtained a replacement but the replacement medal was not of the original 1862 design but of the then-new 1897 design. He lived a quiet, sedate life in San Antonio for more than twenty years. He died of old age at the station hospital at Fort Sam Houston on November 1, 1920, and was buried at the San Antonio National Cemetery. His stature as a patriotic American was evidenced by his will, which left his entire estate of $5,000 to the American Red Cross.

Frederick S. Neilon
Sergeant, Company H, Sixth U.S. Cavalry

Frederick S. Neilon was born on June 22, 1846, at Boston, Massachusetts. He was raised and educated in Boston and was pushed by his mother toward a career in business. He completed his business training in 1864 and, despite his mother's pleas, enlisted in the army as a second-class private in the ordnance corps at the Watertown Arsenal on March 31, 1864. After three years of work on ordnance development and logistics he was discharged as a first-class private on March 31, 1867.

From 1867 to 1872 Neilon was employed by the W. E. Jarvis Company of Boston as a machinist and clerk. In the summer of 1872 he became disgruntled with his position and, unable to cope with his mother's expectations, he went west to try and better his condition. Unable to find a better position in Chicago he became discouraged and enlisted in the U.S. Army on August 11, 1872, under the alias Frank Singleton.

Neilon was stationed initially at Fort Riley, Kansas, and later at Forts Wallace and Dodge in Kansas. In July 1874 he was posted to Fort Dodge as a part of the Nelson A. Miles column of the Indian Territory expedition against Kiowa, Comanche, and Southern Cheyenne Indians. During this expedition into the northwestern part of Texas and the Indian Territory he participated in the engagements at Palo Duro Canyon on August 30, 1874, and at the Upper Washita River on September 9–12, 1874. During the latter engagement he was wounded in the leg while conveying ammunition under fire to outlying defensive positions. He was awarded the Medal of Honor for this deed. Because of the severity of the wound Neilon was discharged on a certificate of disability on May 6, 1875.

Neilon returned home to Boston and, at his mother's urging, continued with his business education. Afterward he entered the stock brokerage business, a vocation he pursued for eighteen years. On February 6, 1889, he married Elizabeth P. Regal and from this union were born two daughters. On August 14, 1890, Neilon was present at a planning meeting at the Latin School in Boston in which the New England Medal of Honor Legion was first formally formed. After its formation he continued to be a member of the Medal of Honor Legion for almost a quarter of a century. On December 4, 1893, he applied for a new Medal of Honor engraved in his real name. After a complete explanation of the circumstances by which he came to enlist under a fictitious name, he was granted a new medal on February 1, 1894.

After the Panic of 1893, Neilon's fortunes in the brokerage business began to fail. In 1895 he acquired the position of assistant inspector of customs with the U.S. Customs Service at Boston. The death of his wife in 1897 left him to care for his two young daughters. He moved to Somerville, Massachusetts, where his sister helped him care for the girls. He died on September 13, 1916, and was buried at St. Paul's Cemetery at Arlington, Massachusetts. He was survived by his daughters, Elinor Neilon and Louise Kenney, and two sisters, Mrs. Thomas J. Hannon of Cambridge and Mrs. P. H. Rafferty of Somerville.

William O'Neill
Corporal, Company I, Fourth U.S. Cavalry

William O'Neill was born circa 1848 at Tarriffville, Connecticut. Nothing is known of his family or early life. He enlisted in the U.S. Army at New York City on March 21, 1870. At that time he listed his occupation as that of a cabinetmaker. After basic cavalry training at Carlisle Barracks, Pennsylvania, he was assigned to Company I, Fourth U.S. Cavalry, and was posted to Fort Concho, Texas. He began to participate in active field operations against Indian bands and bandits in May 1870. During his service in Texas he participated in engagements at Beals Creek, March 28, 1872; North Fork of Red River, September 29, 1872; Remolino, Mexico, May 19, 1873; Kickapoo Springs, December 10, 1873; and Palo Duro Canyon, September 28, 1874. At the engagement on the North Fork of the Red River in September 1872, he performed continuing acts of gallantry for which he was awarded the Medal of Honor. He was discharged as a corporal upon expiration of service at Denison, Texas, on March 21, 1875.

John F. O'Sullivan
Private, Company I, Fourth U.S. Cavalry

John Francis O'Sullivan was born in Kerry County, Ireland, in 1856 to John and Anna Sealy O'Sullivan. Exactly when the O'Sullivan family came to the United States is not known, but by 1869 John F. O'Sullivan was a thirteen-year-old tired and hungry orphan roaming the streets and back alleys of New York City. He was befriended by Smith E. Lane, a New York City businessman and former Union officer, who took O'Sullivan off the streets and assumed legal guardianship for him. Lane also obtained O'Sullivan a job at the exclusive Union Club and tutored him into a refined expert waiter. In early 1870 O'Sullivan expressed a desire to set out on his own and join the army to see the West. Lane, aware that O'Sullivan's age would be a barrier to enlistment, sought the help of an old friend, Arthur MacArthur, an army recruiting officer. In order to get O'Sullivan enlisted as a minor they had to search the regulations and approach even higher-level officials. On March 16, 1870, Captain MacArthur wrote to Maj. John P. Hatch, the recruiting depot commander at Carlisle Barracks, Pennsylvania, requesting instructions for O'Sullivan's possible enlistment. MacArthur remarked in his letter that despite the fact that the young man was an orphan and a minor, he appeared to be smart and intelligent. Hatch replied that O'Sullivan could be enlisted with the consent of his guardian if he had the capacity to learn the trumpet or if he stood five feet, five inches high as a soldier. John O'Sullivan must certainly have developed a rapid musical talent as his height was two inches below the required minimum.

On March 22, 1870, John O'Sullivan stood before Captain MacArthur and took the oath of allegiance to formally enlist in the mounted service of the United States. After five weeks of basic cavalry training at Carlisle Barracks, Pennsylvania, he was assigned to Company I, Fourth U.S. Cavalry, and posted to Fort Concho, Texas. During his five-year enlistment he served exclusively at various posts in Texas. He was active in engagements with Indians at Blanco Canyon, October 11, 1871; North Fork of Red River, September 29, 1872; Remolino, Mexico, May 19, 1873; Kickapoo Springs, December 10, 1873; Palo Duro Canyon, September 28, 1874; and Muchaque Canyon, December 8, 1874. In the engagement near Muchaque Canyon his gallantry during a long pursuit and engagement against a band of Indians resulted in his award of the Medal of Honor. O'Sullivan was discharged at Denison, Texas, on March 22, 1875.

O'Sullivan returned to New York City and resumed his job as a waiter at the Union Club in New York City, where he remained for more than thirty-two years.

In 1897 and 1904 he obtained new design Medals of Honor and rosettes. He died on May 19, 1907, of heart failure at his residence at 317 East Forty-sixth Street in Manhattan, New York City, and was buried at Calvary Cemetery in Manhattan.

Adam Payne (Paine)
Private, Seminole-Negro Indian Scouts

Adam Payne was born circa 1842 near Alachua, Florida. His parents likely were descendants of slaves belonging originally to the Seminole chief King Payne. After King Payne's death circa 1812 his slaves reverted to the chief Micanopy. After the end of the Second Seminole War in Florida in August 1842, Micanopy and the black chief John Horse led the remaining expatriated Seminoles and blacks to reserved lands in the Indian Territory. Adam Payne spent his infancy and early childhood in the area of present-day Wewoka, Oklahoma. After Micanopy's death in 1848 his slaves reverted to Billy Bowlegs, a leader of the Seminole-Creek alliance. Likely displeased over the land allotments and ruling policies of the dominant Creeks, many of the Seminole, Kickapoo, and their related black bands decided around 1849 to emigrate to Mexico. These three groups were eventually awarded tracts of land in return for their military services against Kiowa, Comanche, and Apache bands, which constantly ravaged the many ranches of Mexico's northeastern frontier. The band to which Payne belonged was first settled near Nacimiento, and later to Las Parras, places where Payne grew into manhood and acquired his expert tracking and fighting skills.

In 1869 the Seminole and Kickapoo bands in Mexico were persuaded to reenter the United States for resettlement upon their tribal lands in Kansas and the Indian Territory. These bands were also allotted liberal monthly annuities, but the treaty made no allocations for those members of black ancestry, so beginning in July 1870 a number of the Seminole-allied blacks were allowed to enlist as scouts for the U.S. Army.

Payne first enlisted at Fort Duncan, Texas, on November 12, 1873. During his two-year stint with the Seminole-Negro Indian scout detachment Payne participated in engagements against Indians at Kickapoo Springs, December 10, 1873; Quitaque Peak, September 20, 1874; Tule Canyon, September 27, 1874; Palo Duro Canyon, September 28, 1874; Double Lakes, November 3, 1874; and Laguna Tahoka, November 6, 1874. During the engagement at Quitaque Peak, Payne boldly engaged a numerically superior band of attacking Indians and enabled four other scouts to evade the Indians. For this deed of gallantry Payne was awarded the Medal of Honor. Col. R. S. Mackenzie later referred to Adam

Payne as a scout of great courage who possessed more cool daring than any scout he had ever known.

After his final discharge at Fort Clark on February 19, 1875, Payne moved to Brownsville, Texas, where he was employed as a civilian teamster for the army Quartermaster Department at Fort Brown. During a night of revelry in Brownsville on Christmas Eve, 1875, Payne became embroiled in a dispute with a young cavalry trooper. Payne's temper erupted and he stabbed the young soldier in the heart, mortally wounding him. Payne fled across the Rio Grande with a murder charge hanging over his head. He sought temporary refuge among the small Seminole-Creek Negro community in Matamoras before Mexican authorities detained him. Because of jail overcrowding he purportedly was incarcerated with a number of others in the municipal bullfighting stadium. A tropical storm damaged the stadium a short time later and Payne escaped. He fled north along the Rio Grande and at some point fell into the company of Frank Enoch, another fugitive. By December 1876 the two were taking refuge in the Seminole-Negro Indian scout village near Brackettville. Ironically, the members of the Brackettville Seminole-Negro village were embroiled with the local authorities over the issue of harboring other fugitive felons. An unknown village resident informed Kinney County authorities about Payne and Enoch's presence. Acting upon a felony arrest warrant from Cameron County, Kinney County Sheriff L. C. Crowell, with only two men assisting him, devised a plan to carry out the arrests. Along with Deputy Sheriff Claron A. Windus and a deputized citizen teamster, James Thomas, the trio surrounded the main clearing in the center of the village. Shortly before midnight on December 31, 1876, they entered the clearing with guns leveled and announced themselves. As a number of the fugitive felons were being assembled for shackling, Payne and Enoch began to resist. Deputy Windus discharged his shotgun and struck both. Adam Payne was killed instantly and Enoch was mortally wounded. Payne was buried on January 1, 1877, in the small clearing, which became the Seminole-Negro Indian scout cemetery. His death at the hand of Deputy Sheriff Claron A. Windus marks the only known instance of a Medal of Honor recipient dying at the hand of another recipient.

Isaac Payne
Trumpeter, Seminole-Negro Indian Scouts

Isaac Payne was born circa 1854 near Musquiz, Coahuila, Mexico, to Caesar and Abbie Payne. He and his family immigrated to the United States in May

1870 as part of a group headed by John Kibbetts. Isaac Payne first enlisted in the Seminole-Negro scout detachment at Fort Duncan, Texas, on October 7, 1871.

Payne served at Fort Duncan until April 1873, when he was transferred to Fort Clark. During his service with the Seminole-Negro scout detachment he participated in engagements at Remolino, Mexico, May 19, 1873; Palo Duro Canyon, September 28, 1874; Eagle Nest Crossing of Pecos River, April 26, 1875; Devils River, April 1, 1877; Lake Quemado, May 4, 1877; Zaragosa, Mexico, September 26, 1877; Big Bend of the Rio Grande River, November 1, 1877; Sierra Carmel Ranch, Mexico, November 29–30, 1877; and Burros Mountains, Mexico, May 3, 1881. During the engagement at Eagle Nest Crossing in 1875, while in action against a numerically superior band of Indians, he aided fellow scouts in saving the life of his commanding officer, the act that merited his being awarded the Medal of Honor.

On April 29, 1874, he married Julia Shields and they had three children, Charles (1876), Robert (1877), and Ellen (1880). In June 1880 Payne was one of six leaders of the Seminole-Negro community at Brackettville who unsuccessfully attempted to get the federal government to support their return to the Seminole Reservation in the Indian Territory.

During 1891–1894 Payne performed active field service during the Catarino Garza revolutionary activities. These activities by violators of United States neutrality laws occurred in the lower Rio Grande River Valley border areas of South Texas. During field operations against these bandits and revolutionaries he participated in engagements on December 24, 1892, in Starr County, Texas, and was especially gallant in the last engagement of the campaign at Las Mulas Ranch on February 23, 1893.

Isaac Payne was discharged from the army on January 21, 1901, at Fort Ringgold, Texas. After discharge he resided briefly at Rio Grande City, Texas, before moving to his old home at Musquiz, Mexico, where he died on January 12, 1904. He was buried at Musquiz in the Bacune Btimi Cemetery. He was survived by a brother, Adam; three sisters, Effie, Elsie and Eve; two sons, Charles and Robert; and a daughter, Ellen.

Josiah J. Pennsyl
Sergeant, Company M, Sixth U.S. Cavalry

Josiah Joseph Pennsyl was born on September 22, 1852, near Rainsburg, Pennsylvania, to Charles and Margaret Pennsyl. He was educated in the public schools of Bedford County and during his youth he worked or was trained in farming, blacksmithing, and shoemaking. In January 1871 he ran away from home in hopes of becoming a success in the West. He first made his way east to Carlisle, Pennsylvania, where he enlisted in the U.S. Army on January 17, 1871. After cavalry recruit training at Carlisle Barracks he was assigned to duty with Company M, Sixth U.S. Cavalry, then posted at Fort Richardson, Texas. On December 1, 1872, he was promoted to sergeant. He was cited for outstanding service in leading a detachment along the Arkansas River in successful pursuit of a band of deserters on March 17–20, 1873. During the 1874–1875 Indian Territory expedition, Pennsyl was a part of the Nelson A. Miles column operating out of Fort Dodge, Kansas. He was involved in the battle of the Upper Washita River on September 9–12, 1874. During this engagement he was cited for continuing acts of gallantry for which he was awarded the Medal of Honor.

In April 1875 Pennsyl was transferred to Fort Grant, Arizona, where he was discharged on January 17, 1876. Because of the warm, arid climate that alleviated his mild asthmatic condition he chose to settle in the area. He first worked as a teamster but later worked as both a mining carpenter and shoemaker. In the early 1880s he filed for a 160-acre tract under the Homestead Act. The tract was adjacent to and just west of the Fort Grant Military Reservation boundaries at Pima. For many years Pennsyl sold hay and horses to the army. He became one of the primary financial investors in the Gila Valley Cooperative Creamery Company at Pima, Arizona. His humble, frugal nature was surmounted only by his fervent patriotism. In 1914 he approached Mrs. Thomas F. Preston, the superintendent of schools in Pima, concerned that the school did not have a flagpole nor a flag. After he paid for the flag and flagpole and its installation, "Joe," as he was called by local residents, walked to the school every Monday morning and joined the students in reciting the Pledge of Allegiance.

In 1917 Pennsyl was pensioned for his Indian War service. After 1918 he experienced heart disease and hardening of the arteries that rendered him an invalid. He died on January 22, 1920, and was buried in the Pima City Cemetery. He was survived by a brother, Benjamin Pennsyl of Bedford, Pennsylvania, and sisters, Etta Bratton of Altoona, Pennsylvania, Emma Poole, also of Altoona, and Lottie Bayhour of Troy, Ohio.

Edwin Phoenix
Corporal, Company E, Fourth U.S. Cavalry

Edwin Phoenix was born on May 15, 1844, at St. Louis, Missouri. He first enlisted in the U.S. Army there on January 5, 1867. He was assigned to Company

F, Thirty-fourth U.S. Infantry, but effective March 28, 1869, was transferred to Company F, Sixteenth U.S. Infantry under army reorganization plans. During his first enlistment he served on Reconstruction duty in Georgia and Mississippi. After his discharge from the Sixteenth Infantry on January 5, 1870, at Vicksburg, Mississippi, he reenlisted in the Fourth U.S. Cavalry at Jefferson Barracks, Missouri, on January 20, 1870.

During the R. S. Mackenzie punitive raid on Remolino, Mexico, on May 18–19, 1873, Phoenix was cited for "praiseworthy conduct" during the engagement. On September 27, 1874, near Tule Canyon, Texas, Phoenix, along with several fellow troopers, attacked and drove off a numerically superior band of Cheyenne, Kiowa, and Comanche Indians. For this deed Phoenix was awarded the Medal of Honor. He was discharged from the Fourth U.S. Cavalry at Fort Concho, Texas, on December 20, 1875.

Phoenix returned home to St. Louis but reenlisted in Company H, Third U.S. Infantry, at Jefferson Barracks, Missouri, on February 19, 1876. During most of 1876 he was involved in quelling Reconstruction disturbances in Holly Springs, Mississippi, and at Pineville, Natchitoches, and New Orleans, Louisiana. In 1877 he was dispatched to Scranton, Pennsylvania, to quell labor disturbances in the coalfields of central Pennsylvania. In 1878 he participated in the campaign against Nez Perce Indians in Montana and Idaho. On July 21, 1878, at the battle of Clearwater, Idaho, while serving as first sergeant of Company H, Third U.S. Infantry, he was again cited for conspicuous brave conduct in action. He received his final discharge from the army on February 18, 1880.

In civilian life Phoenix resided and worked in Montana, Colorado, Arizona, and California as a mining carpenter. He never married and settled eventually around 1925 at Los Angeles, California, where he resided at the Pacific Branch, Soldier's Home. On August 20, 1931, he was formally entered on the Army and Navy Medal of Honor Roll and was issued Medal of Honor Certificate no. 370.

Edwin Phoenix died of heart failure at the Pacific Branch, Soldier's Home at Los Angeles, California, on September 5, 1932. He was buried at the U.S. Veteran's Administration Cemetery at Los Angeles.

Samuel Porter
Farrier, Company L, Sixth U.S. Cavalry

Samuel Porter was born in 1844 at Cracklin Township of Montgomery County, Maryland, to William M. and Margaret Lizeas Porter, the fifth of six children born to that union. He worked on the family farm and received little formal education. In 1862 he took a job as a teamster hauling goods between New York City and Washington, D.C. On a whim on August 13, 1862, he enlisted in Company K, Eleventh New York Cavalry (Scott's 900) at Washington, D.C. During much of 1863 he was assigned as an orderly on Gen. John G. Barnard's staff at the light artillery camp of instruction at Washington, D.C. During his field service he was involved in engagements at Fairfax Station, Virginia, June 27, 1863, and Edward's Ferry, Virginia, on August 27, 1863. During a part of 1864 Porter participated in the Red River campaign in Louisiana. At the war's end he was at Memphis, Tennessee, where he was discharged on May 8, 1865.

On March 15, 1866, Porter enlisted in the regular army at Cincinnati, Ohio, was assigned to Company L, Sixth U.S. Cavalry, and was posted to Greenwood, Louisiana. He was later assigned to Wilkinson Plantation, Louisiana, and during most of 1869 was stationed at Jefferson, Texas. In early 1870 he was transferred to Fort Richardson, Texas, where he was engaged in active field operations against raiding Indians. He was cited for conspicuous acts of gallantry during the battle of the Little Wichita River on July 12, 1870, and was awarded the Medal of Honor. He also participated in an engagement on October 5, 1870, at Bluff Creek. He was promoted to corporal on September 24, 1871.

From 1872 to 1874 Porter was assigned to various posts in Kansas and Colorado. On January 30, 1872, he was promoted to sergeant. He was mentioned for exceptional good conduct for his service in pursuing a dangerous band of deserters along the Arkansas River during March 17–20, 1873. Porter was part of the Nelson A. Miles column of the 1874–1875 Indian Territory expedition. During that campaign he participated in the battle of the Red River on August 30, 1874. He was discharged at Fort Bayard, New Mexico, on January 29, 1876. After his discharge he worked at various places in the West and settled in Silver City, New Mexico, until 1902, when failing health forced him to move to Los Angeles, California. He resided at the Pacific Branch, U.S. Soldier's Home at Los Angeles until his death on April 17, 1920.

James N. Pratt

Blacksmith, Company I, Fourth U.S. Cavalry

James N. Pratt was born on September 12, 1851, at Bellefontaine, Ohio, to Frank and Maria Wilson Pratt, the sixth of seven children. He was educated in the public schools of Logan County and was apprenticed as a blacksmith. At the outbreak of the Civil War he attempted to enlist but was rejected because of his age.

310

In February 1870 Pratt traveled to Cincinnati and enlisted in the U.S. Army. He was assigned to Company I, Fourth U.S. Cavalry, then posted to Fort Concho, Texas. On September 29, 1872, Pratt participated in the battle of the North Fork of the Red River. During this engagement against Kiowa and Comanches, Pratt went to the aid of his commanding officer, Lt. Charles L. Hudson, whose horse had been disabled, leaving the officer in a dangerous situation. Pratt's successful rescue of that officer earned him the award of the Medal of Honor. In May 1873 Pratt participated in the R. S. Mackenzie punitive raid on Remolino, Mexico. This raid against Kickapoo and Mescalero Apache bands involved a 160-mile ride for thirty-two hours into the interior of Mexico. Pratt rendered outstanding service in caring for the command's horses during the ride and at the commencement of the attack led one of the ranks that made the first assault into the Indians' village. This action of May 18–19, 1873, contributed greatly to the suppression of raids by Indian bands harbored within Mexico.

While encamped on the Nueces River in August 1873, Pratt incurred a severe hernia while shoeing a horse and was recommended for a disability discharge on November 11, 1873. Pratt returned to his home at Bellefontaine, Ohio, where he was employed as a teamster, mechanic, and blacksmith. On July 2, 1885, he married Alice V. Carter of Leesburg, Virginia. The couple moved to Lima, Ohio, where they resided for seven years. In 1893 the couple moved to West Duluth, Minnesota, where on September 22, 1894, they adopted an infant girl whom they named Maria Wilson Pratt. Pratt began to suffer from debilitating illnesses in 1900 and the family returned to Bellefontaine. On October 13, 1903, Pratt died of kidney disease. His obituary in the *Bellefontaine Examiner* characterized him as an honorable man in all his dealings and charitable almost to a fault. No one who ever asked him for aid was refused and where help was needed, he was always ready to help. He was buried in his family's plot in the Bellefontaine City Cemetery. He was survived by his wife, Alice; daughter, Maria; two brothers, Frank, of Terre Haute, Indiana, and Edward, of Indianapolis, Indiana; and a sister, Mary, of Bellefontaine.

William Rankin
Sergeant, Company F, Fourth U.S. Cavalry

William Rankin was born in February 1838 in Lewistown, Pennsylvania. By the age of seventeen he was working as a molder at a factory in Harrisburg, Pennsylvania. On September 14, 1855, he enlisted in the U.S. Army. He was sent to Fort Leavenworth, Kansas, for basic training and was assigned to Company F, First U.S. Cavalry. Rankin spent his first year escorting freight and immigrant wagon trains along the Oregon Trail between Fort Kearney, Nebraska, and Fort Leavenworth. During 1857 he escorted freight trains and surveying crews along the Santa Fe Trail between the Cimarron Crossing of the Arkansas River and Santa Fe, New Mexico. During 1858, under the command of Albert Sidney Johnston, he helped quell the Mormon disturbances around Salt Lake City, Utah. By mid-1859 Rankin was on duty along the Santa Fe Trail. In May he participated in John Sedgwick's campaign against Kiowa and Comanche Indians in the Smokey Hill River area of central Kansas. In September 1859 he accompanied a small delegation led by Capt. William D. Saussure, which met with Tahousan, Big Pawnee, and Buffalo, chiefs in the Kiowa and Comanche tribes, in an attempt to pacify Indian complaints. During this experience and subsequent contacts with the Southern Plains tribes, Rankin became familiar with their language, habits, and their leadership. During the late spring of 1860 he served in the field in the Purgatory River area of southeastern Colorado. On July 11, 1860, he was active in the engagement at Blackwater Springs, Colorado.

In 1861 Rankin was in Colorado assisting in the construction of the original Fort Lyon. On May 29, 1861, he received orders to report to Fort Leavenworth. Once the scattered units of the First Cavalry were congregated at Leavenworth they were immediately ordered east to form part of the perimeter defenses of Washington, D.C. Rankin saw his first action of the war at the first battle of Bull Run on July 21, 1861. He was promoted to sergeant in September 1861 and he served gallantly throughout the war, actively participating in thirty-four engagements. In one of the great ironies of the war, Rankin and his fellow company members unleashed the volley of firing on April 6, 1862, at the battle of Shiloh, which killed their former commanding officer, Albert Sidney Johnston. On June 27, 1863, Rankin was cited for gallantry in action near Salem, Tennessee. During the Chickamauga campaign he was involved in actions at Chickamauga Ridge, Sparta, and Missionary Ridge. In 1864 he participated in the Meridian campaign in Mississippi, participating in actions at Corinth, Pontotoc, West Point, Okalona, and Columbus. Rankin led many of his company's lightning movements in actions at Selma and Blue Pond, Alabama.

After the war's end Rankin served on Reconstruction duty in Georgia, Louisiana, and in 1867 was posted to Texas. On July 31, 1867, he was at Fort Mason, Texas, where he reenlisted for the fourth time. Throughout his service in Texas he repeatedly led pathfinder groups comprised of civilian guides, Indian scouts, and enlisted trailers, which operated in advance of and at long distances from the main columns of troops during campaigns against Indians in 1869, 1871, 1872, and 1874. These groups measured distances, mapped the terrain, and provided estimates of Indian strength and directions of movements. During this service Rankin participated in engagements at Catfish Creek, October 28–29, 1869; North Hubbard Creek, April 3, 1870; Mountain Pass, July 14, 1870; Fresh Water Fork of the Brazos, October 11, 1871; North Fork of the Red River, September 29, 1872; and Palo Duro Canyon on September 28, 1874. At the engagement on the North Fork of the Red River in 1872, he had led the advanced ranks into the main point of Indian resistance, incurring a serious stomach wound. He was awarded the Medal of Honor for his deeds in this action. During 1875 Rankin was assigned to Forts Sill and Reno in the Indian Territory. During this time he was quite active in organizing and administering Indian affairs on the Kiowa–Comanche and Cheyenne Reservations. During 1876 the Fourth U.S. Cavalry served briefly in the Powder River campaign in northeastern Wyoming against hostile Sioux and Northern Cheyenne. Rankin rendered outstanding service in this campaign at Bates Creek, Wyoming, on November 25, 1876, when Dull Knife's village was destroyed. After his return to Texas in 1877 he was stationed at Fort Elliott, Texas, where he remained until 1879.

Between 1881 and 1887 Rankin was actively engaged in field operations and actions against Apache Indians in New Mexico, Arizona, and Mexico. During the Apache campaigns he especially distinguished himself in action at Horseshoe Canyon, New Mexico, on April 23, 1882. He rendered outstanding services as a trailer and packer against Geronimo's band of Chiricahuas in operations in the Sierra Madre and Terres Mountains of north central Mexico between July and November 1885. His last engagement against the Apaches was at Lang's Ranch, New Mexico, on October 10, 1885.

Rankin's military career ended on April 11, 1890, at Fort Huachuca, Arizona, when he was formally placed on the U.S. Army retired list. He returned to Lewistown, Pennsylvania, where he resided until he died on February 2, 1916. At the time of his death he possessed the 1862, 1897, and 1904 versions of the Medal of Honor; a medal awarded to him by the governor of Texas; and a gold medal awarded to him by the Mexican President Porfirio Diaz, which Rankin had earned for rescuing the daughter of a prominent Mexican rancher from Apaches. Rankin had tracked the Apaches for more than four hundred miles through the mountains of north central Mexico and alone secured the girl from the Apaches. He was buried in St. Mark's Episcopal Community Cemetery at Lewistown. He was survived by a sister, Mrs. Angeline Deering of Lewistown.

Peter P. Roth

Private, Company A, Sixth U.S. Cavalry

Peter Paul Roth was born on June 5, 1850, at Beffendorf, Germany, to Philipp and Maria A. Roth. It is unknown when he immigrated to the United States but he first enlisted in the U.S. Army at Brooklyn, New York, on April 8, 1870. He was first assigned to Company G, Tenth U.S. Infantry, and was eventually posted to Fort Brown, Texas; he deserted from there on July 27, 1871. While a deserter-at-large, he enlisted again under the name of Peter Rolls on March 25, 1873, was assigned to Company A, Sixth Cavalry, and was posted to Fort Hays, Kansas. On December 24, 1873, while stationed at Fort Wallace, Kansas, he surrendered himself as a deserter under the provisions of an 1873 presidential proclamation and was restored to duty without trial on the condition that he serve out the lost time.

On May 11, 1874, Roth was transferred to Fort Dodge, Kansas. During the fall of 1874 he participated in the Nelson A. Miles Indian Territory expedition against Southern Plains tribes. He was involved in the battle of the Red River on August 30, 1874, and later during the expedition, while serving as a courier escort, was cited for gallantry in action in the battle of the buffalo wallow on September 12, 1874. He was awarded the Medal of Honor for his acts during this engagement.

During mid-1875 Roth's regiment was transferred to Fort Wingate, New Mexico, and later to Fort Apache, Arizona, to quell outbreaks of hostilities by assorted bands of Apaches. On January 9, 1876, Roth participated in an engagement near Fort Apache. He was discharged on June 10, 1879, at Camp Verde, Arizona.

Roth reenlisted on June 19 and was assigned to Company G, Eleventh U.S. Infantry, and was posted to Fort Bennett and later to Forts Sully and Pierce in the Dakota Territory. He completed this enlistment at Fort Leavenworth, Kansas, where he was discharged as a sergeant on account of expiration of service on June 18, 1884. Roth remained out of the army for almost a year before reenlisting on July 12, 1885, in the Eleventh U.S. Infantry. He was posted to Fort Leavenworth, Kansas; Fort Abraham Lincoln, Dakota Territory; and lastly to Madison Barracks, New York. During the latter part of this enlistment he began to suffer from rheumatism, neuralgia, and heart problems resulting from exposure in extremely cold weather. On June 30, 1888, he was sent to the Army and Navy Hospital at Hot Springs, Arkansas, for rehabilitative treatment. He was discharged there on a disability on April 30, 1889. He resided at the U.S. Soldier's Home in Washington, D.C., until December 11, 1890, when he returned to his home in Beffendorf, Germany.

On August 14, 1893, he married Margaretha Seuffert Merz. Wilhelm, the only child from their union, was born on December 30, 1896. Peter Roth was involved in the wood products business in Rottenmunster. He died of heart disease on January 18, 1907, and was buried in the Rottenmunster City Cemetery. He was survived by his wife, Margaretha; son, Wilhelm; and three grandchildren, Luise, Franz, and Rosa Merz. Wilhelm Roth enlisted in the German army in 1912 and was killed in action against Allied forces in 1917.

Frederick H. Schwabe
Sergeant, Company I, Fifth U.S. Infantry

Frederick H. Schwabe was born circa 1850 at Stirlingshire, Scotland, where he received a business- and music-oriented education. At age eighteen he immigrated alone to America, at the urging of his mother, in the hope of becoming a success in business. His early hopes for success in a commercial career were dashed by the post–Civil War recession that culminated in the panic of 1873. He finally decided to enlist in the army at Fort Leavenworth, Kansas, on April 6, 1873, under the assumed name of Fred S. Hay in an attempt to hide his failure in business from his mother. Schwabe was assigned to Company I of the Fifth U.S. Infantry and was posted to Fort Leavenworth. Due to his outstanding soldierly qualities and education he rose rapidly through the ranks and attained the rank of sergeant in just over one year.

Schwabe's first major field service against Indians occurred in the Indian Territory expedition of 1874–1875. He was active in engagements against hostile Southern Cheyenne and Arapaho at the Red River on August 30, 1874. During the September 9–12, 1874, battle of the Upper Washita River he was actively engaged against Kiowa and Comanche bands and his conspicuous acts of gallantry in this engagement earned him the Medal of Honor. Schwabe next served in the 1876 campaign against the Sioux and Northern Cheyenne. He was active in engagements at Cedar Creek, Montana, October 21, 1876; Bark Creek, Montana, December 7, 1876; and Red Water Creek, Dakota Territory, December 18, 1876. During the 1877–1878 campaign against the Nez Perce he was especially active in the last major engagement of the campaign at Eagle Creek in the Bear Paw Mountains of Montana on September 30, 1877. Schwabe was discharged from the army on April 6, 1878, at the rank of sergeant major.

Schwabe did not reenlist but gained employment as a civilian clerk with the U.S. Army paymaster's office. When he did reenlist on September 15, 1880, he attempted to do so under his true name but was told that he would not get credit for a continuous record so he enlisted under his alias in the Second U.S. Cavalry. During his twenty-two years of continuous service with that regiment he was assigned to Fort Spokane, Washington, 1885–1889; Fort Lowell, Arizona, 1890–1894; Fort Wingate, New Mexico, 1895–1896; Huntsville, Alabama, 1897–1898; Cuba, 1899–1902; and Fort Ethan Allen, Vermont, and Fort Myer, Virginia, 1902. While stationed at Fort Huachuca, Arizona, on October 8, 1894, he filed the naturalization papers for his U.S. citizenship with the U.S. District Court at Albuquerque, New Mexico. As a result of his continuing efforts, Special Order no. 276, dated November 23, 1894, was issued from the adjutant general's office in Washington, D.C., stating that he be borne on regimental records under his true name. While stationed at Fort Wingate, New Mexico, Schwabe's original Medal of Honor was destroyed in a fire. Four years later, while stationed at Huntsville, Alabama, he was serving as the regimental flag bearer during a review and parade of troops when he lost his replacement Medal of Honor on the parade ground.

On February 16, 1899, Schwabe shipped out to Cuba as a member of the non-commissioned officer's staff. He participated in the Santiago campaign and remained in Cuba as part of the occupation forces until April 14, 1902. He was sent to Fort Ethan Allen, Vermont, for rehabilitation briefly before he was assigned to his new duty station at Fort Myer, Virginia. He was appointed drum major, Second U.S. Cavalry Band, on October 28, 1902. On November 7, 1902, he was formally retired from the U.S. Army. During retirement he resided at Newark and Highlands, New Jersey. On October 2, 1908, Schwabe was granted Indian Wars Campaign Medal no. 904. He died on January 14, 1914, at Highlands, New Jersey, and was buried in Bayview Cemetery at Leonardo, New Jersey. Schwabe's 1904-style Medal of Honor is on permanent display at the post museum at Schofield Barracks, Hawaii.

Edward C. Sharpless
Corporal, Company H, Sixth U.S. Cavalry

Edward Clay Sharpless was born at Chicago Junction in Marion County, Ohio, on August 20, 1853, to Benjamin and Isabella Sharpless, the first of three sons born to the couple. Along with his brothers, Charles and George, Edward was raised and educated in the public schools of Marion County, Ohio, and Jones County, Iowa. Along with his father and two brothers he farmed until he ran away from home in the fall of 1872. He made his way to Columbus, Ohio, where he enlisted in the U.S. Army on November 17, 1872. After basic cavalry training at Carlisle Barracks, Pennsylvania, he was assigned to Company H of the Sixth U.S. Cavalry and was posted to Fort Riley, Kansas. He was promoted to corporal on May 1, 1874. Sharpless' six-feet-tall stature and weight of 190 pounds was exceptional for a cavalry trooper. During the 1874–1875 Indian Territory expedition he served as part of the N. A. Miles column operating out of Fort Dodge, Kansas. During the campaign Sharpless volunteered for the hazardous duty of courier and dispatch rider and it was in this capacity during the battle of the Upper Washita River that he was cited for gallantry in action and awarded the Medal of Honor.

On April 23, 1875, while in action against Cheyenne and Arapaho Indians along Sappa Creek in Kansas, Sharpless was again cited for gallant and meritorious service in action. On September 14, 1875, he was promoted to sergeant. During 1876 he was transferred to various posts in New Mexico and Arizona to quell hostile Apache Indians. Sharpless was present at the Warm Springs Reservation near Winston, New Mexico, when Geronimo and his Apache band surrendered and agreed to go onto the San Carlos Reservation in Arizona. Sharpless was discharged at Fort Bowie, Arizona, on November 19, 1877.

Sharpless returned to his home in Ohio and resumed farming with his family. On December 24, 1878, he married Hannah Motson at Chicago Junction, Ohio. Six children—three sons, Harry, Edward, and Irwin, and three daughters, Mae, Lulu, and Princess—were born to them between 1880 and 1896. The Sharpless family resided at Chicago Junction until 1889, then moved to Marion, Ohio, until 1901. Between 1902 and 1909 the family again farmed the original family homestead near present-day Willard, Ohio. In 1909 Sharpless's original Medal of Honor and certificate were destroyed in a fire at the family's residence. Shortly afterward Sharpless moved his family to a homestead tract near Mountainair in Torrance County, New Mexico. In 1917 Sharpless returned to Willard, Ohio, leaving his Mountainair homestead to the care of his daughter and son-in-law, Princess and John Bixler. He retired from farming in 1925 and in 1926 applied for a new Medal of Honor certificate. He was granted an Indian War and Medal of Honor pension in 1926, and was entered upon the official Army and Navy Medal of Honor Roll as of November 14, 1927. After his wife's death in 1931 Sharpless was sent to live at the Soldier and Sailor's Home at Sandusky, Ohio. On October 6, 1931, while on a short home leave, Sharpless, age seventy-eight, again ran away from home. Instead of returning to the Soldier's Home he boarded a New Mexico-bound train. Edward C. Sharpless lived out his remaining years at Mountainair. He died there on January 12, 1934, from complications of an enlarged spleen incurred while attempting to tame a troublesome horse. He was survived by his three sons, Edward F. Sharpless of Willard, Ohio; Irwin B. Sharpless; and Harry D. Sharpless, and his three daughters, Princess Bixler of Mountainair, New Mexico; Mae B. Simpson of Flagstaff, Arizona; and Lulu Sharpless of Mountainair.

Charles E. Smith
Corporal, Company H, Sixth U.S. Cavalry

Charles E. Smith was born circa 1844 at Auburn, New York. He enlisted in the U.S. Army at St. Louis, Missouri, on February 13, 1869. After basic cavalry training at Carlisle Barracks, Pennsylvania, he was assigned to Company H, Sixth U.S. Cavalry. He was initially assigned to Reconstruction duties in East Texas at Jefferson. Smith was promoted to corporal on October 1, 1869. During late 1869 he performed various civil actions at Carthage and Mount Pleasant in implementing Reconstruction policies. In January 1870 he was transferred to Fort Richardson, Texas, to participate in active field operations against raiding bands of Kiowa and Comanche Indians. On July 12, 1870, during an engagement on the Little Wichita River in present-day Archer County, Texas, Smith was cited for gallantry in action and awarded the Medal of Honor. On August 31, 1870, he was promoted to quartermaster sergeant. In April 1871 he was transferred to Fort Lyon, Colorado, and was discharged there upon expiration of service on February 13, 1874.

George W. Smith
Private, Company M, Sixth U.S. Cavalry

George W. Smith was born in 1848 at Greenpoint, New York, to Charles G. and Elizabeth Smith. He was educated in the public schools there and afterward became employed as a drugstore clerk. On January 31, 1870, he left home to enlist in the U.S. Army. After basic cavalry training at Carlisle Barracks, Pennsylvania, he was assigned to Company M of the Sixth U.S. Cavalry. He was first posted to Tyler, Texas, where he was assigned to various Reconstruction duties. In May 1870 Smith was transferred to Fort Richardson, Texas, and was immediately sent into the field in active patrols against Kiowa and Comanche Indians. During one of his earliest patrols he was prominent in a skirmish with Indians at Bluff Creek in present-day Archer County, Texas, on October 5, 1870.

In April 1871 he was transferred to Fort Lyon, Colorado. On March 28, 1873, Smith and Cpl. Fred March rode into Pueblo, Colorado, trailing a stolen government horse. Despite a hostile town populace, Smith recovered the stolen horse and intimidated the mob in the process. On January 25–28, 1874, he was part of a small party of selected troopers sent in pursuit of a dangerous band of army deserters who had vowed not to be taken alive. Smith assisted in tracking them for forty-five miles during a blinding snowstorm to Granada, Colorado, and was instrumental in arresting the deserters.

During the 1874 Indian Territory expedition Smith was part of the N. A. Miles column, which operated southward into the Texas Panhandle from Fort Dodge, Kansas. On August 30, 1874, Smith participated in the battle of the Red River near Palo Duro Canyon in present-day Armstrong County, Texas. He was awarded the Medal of Honor for gallant actions in the engagement known as the battle of the buffalo wallow on September 12, 1874. During this engagement against a numerically superior force Smith was wounded twice and died of those wounds. He was buried by a relief party the next morning in the buffalo wallow he had defended.

Despite a plea in December 1874 from his father, Charles G. Smith, his remains were never recovered for removal to New York City because of the remoteness of the battle site. George W. Smith's Medal of Honor was forwarded to his father by registered mail on September 8, 1875.

James Smythe
Private, Company M, Sixth U.S. Cavalry

James Smythe was born on May 28, 1849, in eastern Canada. His parentage and early background are not known. He lived and worked as a molder at St. Louis, Missouri, for an unknown period prior to enlisting in the U.S. Army. On November 1, 1867, he enlisted under the alias of James Anderson and was borne as such on all government records. After basic cavalry training at Carlisle Barracks, Pennsylvania, he was assigned to Company M of the Sixth U.S. Cavalry and was posted to Fort Richardson, Texas. In May he was detailed to support civil authorities at Canton, Texas. On July 14, 1869, he was transferred to Tyler, Texas, where he remained until December 31, 1869.

Indian depredations in north central Texas had increased to alarming rates and Smythe's company was transferred back to Fort Richardson. On October 5, 1870, he was active in an engagement at Bluff Creek near present-day Scotland, Texas. For his conspicuous gallantry during this engagement he was awarded the Medal of Honor. On November 8, 1870, Smythe was promoted to corporal.

In April 1871 Smythe was transferred to Fort Lyon, Colorado. He participated in the 1874–1875 Indian Territory expedition under Col. N. A. Miles. During this campaign he was active in the engagement on the Red River near Palo Duro Canyon, Texas, on August 30, 1874, and at Cheyenne Agency, Indian Territory, on April 6, 1875. During the period from 1876 to 1879 Smythe was assigned to various posts in New Mexico and Arizona. On September 8–10, 1877, he participated in his last engagement against Apache Indians on the San Francisco River in the Mogollon Mountains, Arizona. Smythe was discharged on April 3, 1879.

Smythe returned to St. Louis, Missouri, where he resided and worked as a stationery engineer for thirty-seven years. On November 14, 1880, he married Nellie E. Hanlon. They had no children. Smythe's health began to decline in 1917 and he died on May 31, 1918, of pneumonia. He was buried at St. Peter and Paul's Cemetery at St. Louis and was survived by his wife, Nellie E. Smythe.

Emanuel Stance
Sergeant, Company F, Ninth U.S. Cavalry

Emanuel Stance was born circa 1847 near the northeastern Louisiana town of Lake Providence. On October 2, 1866, he enlisted in the U.S. Army. He was assigned to the Ninth U.S. Cavalry, one of two all-black cavalry regiments being formed at the time. After five months in outfitting and training he was posted to San Antonio, Texas. On April 1, 1867, he was promoted to corporal, assigned to "F" Company, and was transferred to Fort Davis.

Stance saw his first action against Mescalero Apaches on December 5, 1867, near Eagle Spring Station near present-day Van Horn, Texas. An Apache attack on the eastbound stage had already cost the life of one Ninth Cavalry trooper serving as escort when a charge by Corporal Stance's detachment drove the Apaches away, saving the life of the stage driver. Shortly after this encounter Stance was promoted to sergeant.

Throughout Stance's entire army career his aggressive nature and quick temperament led him into a variety of conflicts with fellow soldiers. Beginning on December 14, 1868, and later on December 26, 1872, these conflicts resulted in general court martials. In the field he compiled an outstanding record, being cited for gallantry and good conduct in action at Salt Fork of the Brazos River, September 16, 1869; headwaters of Fresh Water Fork of the Brazos River, October 28–29, 1869; headwaters of Llano River, November 24, 1869; near Kickapoo Springs, May 19–20, 1870; headwaters of Concho River, July 22, 1871; and near Good Spring Creek on May 17, 1872. His gallant actions near Kickapoo Springs on May 19–20, 1870, earned for him the first Army Medal of Honor awarded to an African American during the Indian Wars. Stance's actions near Good Spring Creek on May 17, 1872, resulted in the capture of a Comanchero agent from New Mexico and assisted in the dismantling of the Comanchero trade in stolen Texas livestock.

After participating in the 1874–1875 Indian Territory expedition with the G. P. Buell column from Fort Griffin, Texas, Stance also took part in Col. W. R. Shafter's 1875 trans–Pecos expedition. In July 1876 the Ninth U.S. Cavalry was assigned to posts in New Mexico to quell outbreaks by Apaches and Southern Utes. During these campaigns Stance participated in engagements at Florida Mountains, September 15, 1876; Dog Canyon, August 5, 1878; Rio Puerco, January 12, 1880; San Mateo Mountains, January 17, 1880; San Andreas Mountains, February 3, 1880; Miembrillo Canyon, April 6–9, 1880; and Dragoon Mountains, October 4, 1881.

From December 1877 until April 1878, Stance was part of a composite detachment sent to suppress disturbances during the West Texas "Salt War" near San Elizario, Texas. During the period from 1882 to 1884 Stance was assigned to Fort Sill, Indian Territory, where he was involved in arresting and repelling "Sooner" intruders upon Indian lands. In 1883, while commanding a detachment from his company, he rendered exceptional service in arresting Creek Indian trespassers on the Kiowa–Comanche Reservation. His actions quelled a possible outbreak of violence between the three tribes.

In 1884 Stance, as part of the regimental rifle team, participated in the U.S. Army competition rifle meet at Fort Leavenworth, Kansas. On August 16, 1885, he was assigned to Fort Robinson, Nebraska. On December 26, 1886, he reenlisted for the final time. After twenty years of arduous field duty he suffered from arthritic pain and recurring bouts of pleurisy. For unknown reasons his regiment became involved in a myriad of internal conflicts. Within three months of their arrival at Fort Robinson there were at least three homicides within the regiment and numerous troopers had been treated for knife wounds and abrasions incurred in brawls. On December 25, 1887, Lt. Joseph Garrard, while returning to Fort Robinson from the nearby town of Crawford, Nebraska, discovered the body of another homicide victim. The body of Sgt. Emanuel Stance lay in the snow several feet off the side of the road. According to the report of army Surgeon A. W. Taylor, Stance had died as the result of four gunshot wounds fired at close range.

On December 27, 1887, Maj. Andrew Burt issued a special order setting aside a period of mourning and outlining a fitting burial ceremony for Stance in the Fort Robinson post cemetery. A sixteen-man firing squad sounded a final tribute as Stance's remains were lowered into the frozen Nebraska soil. He was survived by a son, Emanuel Stance Jr., of San Antonio, Texas. When the Post Cemetery at Fort Robinson was discontinued in 1947, Sergeant Stance's remains were transferred to the Fort McPherson National Cemetery at Maxwell, Nebraska.

Alonzo Stokes

Sergeant, Company H, Sixth U.S. Cavalry

Alonzo Stokes was born on July 10, 1836, at Zanesfield in Logan County, Ohio. His father, Joseph, was a storekeeper and farmer and a War of 1812 veteran.

Joseph's first wife died in 1829 and he then married Mary A. Austin, the mother of Alonzo and Deborah Stokes.

Alonzo was educated in the public schools of Logan County and was apprenticed as a carpenter. At the outset of the Civil War he enlisted in the Thirteenth Independent Ohio Light Artillery. During the battle of Shiloh on April 6, 1862, a direct hit on a caisson by Confederate artillery caused a severe panic and the total abandonment of the battery's position, which caused the unit to be disbanded. Stokes was reassigned to Battery S of the Tenth Ohio Light Artillery. On April 26, 1862, at the battle of Pittsburg Landing, Tennessee, he was wounded by shrapnel from Confederate artillery fire. After being hospitalized for several weeks he was furloughed to his home for recuperation.

After the Civil War ended Stokes decided to enlist in the regular army. He traveled to Cincinnati, Ohio, where he enlisted in the Sixth U.S. Cavalry on May 9, 1869. After basic cavalry training at Carlisle Barracks, Pennsylvania, he was assigned to Company A and posted at Jefferson, Texas. During this three-year enlistment he served on Reconstruction duty in Louisiana and East Texas. Stokes was involved in several minor clashes in East Texas with the Bob Lee gang, a guerrilla band of ex-Confederates intent upon disrupting Union-enforced Reconstruction policies. Stokes was discharged on May 9, 1868, at Fort Richardson, Texas.

Alonzo Stokes returned to his home in Ohio but on December 1, 1868, he decided to reenlist. He was again assigned to Company H, Sixth U.S. Cavalry, and was posted to Fort Richardson, Texas, where he participated in field operations against Kiowa and Comanche Indian raiders. On July 21, 1869, he was promoted to sergeant. On July 12, 1870, he was part of a command attacked by a numerically superior force of Kiowas and Comanches near the Little Wichita River in present-day Archer County, Texas. In the ensuing eight-hour battle that followed, Stokes performed continuous acts of gallantry in action for which he was awarded the Medal of Honor.

In April 1871 Stokes was transferred to Fort Riley, Kansas, and on March 20, 1872, was transferred to the Sixth U.S. Cavalry Regimental Band. He was discharged at Fort Lyon, Colorado, on December 1, 1873, and eight days later reenlisted at Jefferson Barracks, Missouri. He remained at Jefferson Barracks in a training capacity. On July 4, 1876, he volunteered for Independence Day ceremonial duties at the nearby St. Louis Arsenal. As a former artilleryman he volunteered to be part of one of the gun crews that were to fire several light artillery pieces to mark the culmination of the day's activities. He was the third man of a five-man gun crew on the second artillery piece in the line. After the number one cannon had fired its first charge, Stokes's cannon quickly followed with a thunderous roar and a cloud of smoke. The number one man had vented the breach and the second man on the crew had sponged the barrel to remove residual materials from the earlier firing. Stokes's job was to push the powder charge down the barrel with a long ramming rod. As he reached the breach end of the barrel with the ramming rod, the powder charge ignited prematurely. The subsequent explosion drove the ramming rod out with a tremendous force. The rod struck Stokes in the head, killing him instantly.

Stokes was buried with full military honors on July 5, 1876, at the Jefferson Barracks National Cemetery at St. Louis, Missouri. He was survived by two sisters, Deborah Green and Mary Inskeep, both of Union County, Ohio; one brother, Joseph Stokes Jr. of Logan County, Ohio; a brother-in-law, Joel Inskeep of Urban, Ohio; and a sister-in-law, Harriet Stokes of Bellefontaine, Ohio.

Ernest Veuve
Farrier, Company A, Fourth U.S. Cavalry

Ernest Veuve was born on March 19, 1843, at Cernier, in the canton of Neucastle in western Switzerland. He was raised and educated at Cernier and became fluent in both French and English. He immigrated alone to the United States in 1862 at the age of eighteen. Nothing is known of his movements over the next seven years, other than that he enlisted in the U.S. Army at Jackson Barracks, Louisiana, on December 17, 1869. After basic cavalry training at Carlisle Barracks, Pennsylvania, he was assigned to Company A, Fourth U.S. Cavalry, and was posted to Fort Concho, Texas.

During his service in Texas Veuve participated in engagements with Indians at North Fork of the Red River, September 29, 1872; Remolino, Mexico, May 19, 1873; Tule Canyon, September 27, 1874; Palo Duro Canyon, September 28, 1874; and Double Lakes on November 3, 1874. During the engagement near Double Lakes on November 3, 1874, he performed the act of conspicuous gallantry for which he was awarded the Medal of Honor. For most of the time during the 1874 Staked Plains campaign he served as a volunteer enlisted scout. As a member of the enlisted scout detachment he ranged on long-distance scouting patrols far from the main command. In this capacity he served in conjunction with Indian scouts and citizen guide contingents. Veuve was discharged as a corporal on December 17, 1874, at Fort Griffin, Texas.

Veuve reenlisted in Company H, Third U.S. Infantry, at New Orleans, Louisiana, on January 16, 1875. During most of 1875 and 1876 he served on

Reconstruction duty at New Orleans, Pineville, and Natchitoches in Louisiana helping to suppress civil disturbances. After a short stint of similar duty at Holly Springs, Mississippi, he was sent to Scranton, Pennsylvania, in 1877 to help quell labor unrest. In 1878 Veuve was transferred to Fort Missoula, Montana. He was active in the engagement at Clearwater River, Montana, on July 21, 1878, and on January 15, 1880, was discharged at Fort Missoula.

On January 22, 1880, Veuve married Annie McCauley at St. Francis Xavier Church in Missoula. He settled permanently in Missoula and worked as a lumberman, woodcutter, carpenter, and gardener. Elena, the couple's only surviving daughter, became an accomplished musician and the first telephone operator in Missoula. Ernest Veuve died on June 17, 1916, and was buried in the Missoula City Cemetery. In 1972 the U.S. Army Reserve Training Center at Missoula was named in his honor.

Allen Walker
Private, Company C, Third U.S. Cavalry

Samuel Allen Walker was born on January 19, 1866, at Patriot, Indiana, to William and Eveline Walker. Allen was the eldest of four children in the family. He was raised on a farm near Vevay and was educated in the public schools of Switzerland County.

On August 20, 1884, Walker enlisted in the army at Indianapolis. He was assigned to Company H, Nineteenth U.S. Infantry, and was posted to various posts along the Mexican border in South Texas. He was discharged at San Antonio, Texas, on August 19, 1889, and reenlisted three days later in Company C, Third U.S. Cavalry. During this enlistment he participated in active field operations during the "Tin Horn War" of 1890–1893 against Mexican revolutionaries in South Texas. Walker was active in engagements against C. E. Garza's band of revolutionaries in South Texas at Retamal, December 21–22, 1891; Charco Rendado, December 29, 1891; Rendado, December 31, 1891; and Rancho Prieto, January 1, 1892. During the encounter near Rendado on December 31, 1891, Walker attacked a band of revolutionaries. As a result of his attack one revolutionary was wounded and another's horse was killed. Documents Walker recovered from an abandoned coat and saddlebags enabled federal authorities to prosecute the revolutionaries and contributed in great measure to the end of the Garza rebellion in South Texas. For this deed Walker was awarded the Medal of Honor.

While stationed at Fort Ringgold Walker married Alvina Fuentes, the daughter of a wealthy local Mexican American ranching family. Walker was discharged from the Third Cavalry as a farrier on August 22, 1894. He reenlisted on August 23, 1894, with Company E, Fifth United States Cavalry, and was discharged on August 23, 1897, upon expiration of service. His wife died on July 22, 1898, shortly before Walker was granted a transfer to Company G, Eighteenth U.S. Infantry. After his discharge from this unit he remained out of the army for a brief time before he reenlisted on January 10, 1900. On June 30, 1901, he was discharged as a sergeant in order to accept a commission with the newly organized Philippine Scouts. He was formally commissioned a first lieutenant in the scouts, effective July 1, 1901, and was reappointed as a commissioned officer on July 1, 1905. During his service with the Philippine Scouts he served with distinction on the islands of Samar and Mindanao. He was especially prominent in engagements against insurgent revolutionaries at Loquilon, Samar Island, February 8, 1902, and near Cuartel, Samar Island, on February 9–10, 1902. From 1904 to 1911 Walker was stationed on the island of Mindanao in administrative occupation duties. He was promoted to captain of the Forty-third Company, Philippine Scouts, on August 14, 1908. Upon the disbandment of the Philippine Scouts in 1911 he reverted back to his previous rank in the regular army. He was assigned to the Twenty-third U.S. Infantry and was promoted to sergeant major on September 1, 1911, and was formally retired on September 19, 1911.

After a brief stay at his home in Indiana, Walker moved to his permanent residence at Laredo, Texas, and successfully obtained appointment as a deputy U.S. marshal for the Southern District of Texas effective January 1, 1914. As of June 24, 1916, he was formally placed on the list of retired U.S. Army officers as a captain, Philippine Scouts. He eventually rose to the position of U.S. marshal for the Southern District of Texas and served in that capacity until April 24, 1924. In 1926 he married Enriqueta Peña at Laredo.

Samuel Allen Walker died on September 10, 1953, at Brooke Army Medical Center at San Antonio. He was buried with full military honors in the Catholic Cemetery at Laredo. He was survived by his wife, Enriqueta Walker; three daughters, Paula Walker, Enriqueta Newsome, and Eva Ortegon; four sons, Albino, Servando, Ceasar, and Pete; and a brother, Dr. William H. Walker of Portland, Indiana.

John Ward
Sergeant, Seminole-Negro Indian Scouts

John Ward was born circa 1847 near El Moral, Mexico. There is no definitive information on his parents available from public records. He was likely one of the earliest Seminole-Negroes born in Mexico as he was born several years before the major groups were known to have immigrated to Mexico. His family was likely part of the bands led by chiefs Wild Cat and Caocahootchie, whose complement of Seminole, Kickapoo, Creek, and black volunteers had accompanied Gen. John E. Wool's column during the Mexican-American War. They purportedly served as scouts, teamsters, cooks, foragers, and laundresses. During their service in Mexico they apparently were contacted by prominent ranchers from the north Mexican state of Coahuila with the view of hiring them as herders and fighters against Apache and Comanche cattle thieves. After the end of the war most of the Seminole and Seminole-Negroes returned to their temporary lands in Arkansas and eastern Indian Territory, where they remained for almost two years before deciding to emigrate to Mexico. Those of black ancestry were granted land near El Moral, but were later moved farther into the interior near Musquiz. John Ward likely lived most of his formative youth at Musquiz, for he was living there in 1870 when the United States negotiated a treaty for the return of the Kickapoo and Seminole to their reservations in Kansas and Indian Territory. These groups moved to the border at Eagle Pass, Texas. All went well until the U.S. commissioners informed them that the treaty made no accommodation for those of black ancestry. Capt. F. W. Perry and Maj. Zenas R. Bliss sought and obtained permission to recruit them as Indian scouts. On July 4, 1870, near the Mexican village of Piedras Negras, Job Bruner, the Seminole-Negro band's chief religious man, married John Ward and Juda Julia Wilson under Seminole law.

By August 16, 1870, most of the able-bodied males of the Seminole-Negro tribe were camped on Elm Creek near Fort Duncan, Texas. On that date John Ward was formally enlisted as a scout for the U.S. Army. It has been speculated in several sources that the surname Ward was an incorrect interpretation by the enlistment officer of his true name, Warrior. Dolly, the second daughter born to Juda and John, was born on July 4, 1871. Their first daughter, Laura, was born in 1866. Ward remained at Fort Duncan until January 1872, when part of the detachment was transferred to Fort Clark. Ward and his family spent the next twenty years residing on the Fort Clark Military Reservation. During that time four other children were born to the Wards. Abby, their third daughter, was born in 1872, Nancy in 1873, and Carolina in 1875. Toney, their first son, was born in 1879 and Philip in 1881. On November 16, 1876, Juda and John legally confirmed their union under Texas civil law in a marriage ceremony officiated by Capt. John L. Bullis.

During his twenty-four years of service in the scouting detachment Ward participated in numerous scouting patrols and pursuits of raiding Indian bands and bandits. He was a member of the pathfinder detachment that led Col. Ranald Mackenzie's troops deep into Mexican territory and struck the hostile Kickapoo and Mescalero Apache villages near Remolino, Mexico, on May 18–19, 1873. Ward became one of Mackenzie's most trusted and reliable scouts and was given credit by him as being one of the first scouts to discover the large Indian encampment in Palo Duro Canyon on September 27, 1874. He was promoted to sergeant on December 31, 1874. Ward was especially proficient during Col. W. R. Shafter's trans–Pecos expedition in 1875 in locating critical water sources in the barren mountain and basin region of West Texas. Ward received positive mention by all of his commanding officers and was generally looked upon as being among the most reliable and trustworthy of the scout detachment's members. During the highly emotional friction between the Seminole-Negro community and civil authorities at Brackettville in January 1877, Ward was one of the few scouts who did not desert or threaten mutiny. On April 26, 1875, Ward's rescue of Capt. John L. Bullis while under fire from Indians merited him the award of the Medal of Honor. During his many years of service Ward participated in engagements against Indians at the mouth of the Devils River, April 1, 1877; Lake Quemado, May 4, 1877; Zaragosa, Mexico, September 26, 1877; Big Bend of Rio Grande River, November 1, 1877; Sierra Carmel Ranch, Mexico, November 29–30, 1877; and Sierra Burros Mountains, Mexico on May 3, 1881.

During the period from 1884 until 1894 Ward served against smugglers, bandits, and Mexican revolutionaries in the lower Rio Grande Valley region of South Texas. In late 1891 when violators of federal neutrality laws participated in the Garza rebellion, Ward served with the Third U.S. Cavalry in conjunction with Texas Rangers and U.S. marshals. At age forty-seven he rendered active and gallant service in action against Mexican revolutionaries at Las Mulas Ranch in Starr County, Texas, on February 23, 1893. This was his last action and brought an end to the brief conflict known as the "Tin Horn War." Ward was discharged from the service of the United States on October 5, 1894.

After his discharge Ward resided at Rio Grande City, Texas, and worked as a farm laborer. In March 1896 after his health began to decline and hamper his ability to work he applied for a disability pension. His success in obtaining the pension was due in great part to the efforts of Maj. John L. Bullis, Ward's former commanding officer, and the man whose life he had saved twenty-one years earlier. Ward returned to the Seminole-Negro village at Fort Clark and became one of the most prosperous Seminole-Negroes. He raised and marketed vegetables in Brackettville, which he cultivated on a four-acre tract almost up to the day he died. In 1909 he began to suffer severely from rheumatism and heart disease. On

March 24, 1911, he died peacefully in his sleep. He was buried the next day in the Seminole-Negro Indian Scout Cemetery. He was survived by his wife, Juda; daughters, Dolly July, Carolina July, and Phyllis Ward; a son, Toney Ward; and grandchildren, John July, Harry Miller, Lucy July, William Miller, Nellie Ward, and Phyllis Ward, all of Brackettville, Texas.

Lewis Warrington III
First Lieutenant, Fourth U.S. Cavalry

Lewis Warrington was born on November 12, 1847, at Washington, D.C. He was the only child born to Lewis and Mary Warrington. His father was a United States Navy Paymaster and his grandfather was Commodore Lewis Warrington, the American naval hero of the War of 1812. Lewis spent the majority of his youth in Washington, D.C., but on occasion lived on his mother's Maryland estate. During these visits to Maryland he became an avid sportsman and developed exceptional equestrian skills. Most of his education was in the exclusive Georgetown section of Washington, D.C., where he attended school with the children of many prominent government officials.

In late 1858 Warrington's father was assigned to duty at the Pensacola Navy Yard in Florida. At the outbreak of the Civil War Warrington and his mother were evacuated back to Washington, D.C. In January 1861 Warrington enrolled at Georgetown University and completed almost two years of study before the college was taken over by the army. Lewis attempted at that time to enlist but his mother refused to sign the consent papers. Warrington eventually acquired a civilian clerk position with the U.S. Army Quartermaster Department at the Watertown Arsenal near Boston and remained in this position throughout the Civil War.

During the remainder of 1865 and into early 1866 Warrington worked as a sales associate for National Union Life Insurance Company. When he resigned that position he returned to his clerk position with the Quartermaster Department and began to actively pursue appointment for a regular army commission. Desirous of a cavalry appointment on the frontier he submitted his application directly to President Andrew Johnson on April 21, 1866. Along with his application were letters of recommendation from old family friends: Gens. Christopher C. Augur, William Maynadier, E. D. Townsend, and Ulysses S. Grant, and Adms. Joseph Smith and S. P. Lee. E. D. Townsend, who later became the adjutant general of the army, referred to Lewis as one of the finest horsemen he had ever seen. Warrington was notified of his appointment as a second lieutenant of cavalry on February 18, 1867. After passing the required physical and written exams, he was commissioned a second lieutenant with the Fourth U.S. Cavalry. He was assigned as the junior officer of Company L and was posted to Fort McKavett, Texas. Over the next four years he served for varying periods at Fort Griffin, Fort Richardson, Fort Concho, and Fort Clark.

On January 10, 1872, Warrington was assigned to the signal corps at Washington, D.C., for training in field operations communication techniques. In late February 1872 he was recalled to assume command of Company L upon the retirement of its senior officer. On September 29, 1872, he led his company in the engagement on the North Fork of the Red River and on November 19, 1872, he was cited for gallant conduct in that engagement in General Order no. 99.

Warrington spent much of 1873 on recruiting duty along the East Coast. In the early months of 1874 he organized the Fourth Cavalry's field communication system. He served with distinction throughout the 1874 Indian Territory expedition, being especially active in the engagements at Palo Duro Canyon on September 28; Laguna Tahoka, November 3; and Muchaque Valley on December 8. In the latter engagement his dogged pursuit of a band of Indians and the subsequent skirmish with that band resulted in his being awarded the Medal of Honor. Warrington's award was the only non-ex post facto award to an officer during the Indian Wars.

During most of 1876 and 1877 Warrington was posted to various duty stations in Oklahoma. On July 28, 1876, he commanded a detachment that confronted and elicited the surrender of a large band of recalcitrant Southern Cheyenne under White Antelope and Sand Hill near Fort Reno. During his subsequent service at Fort Reno drinking, gambling, and increasing indebtedness began to seriously jeopardize his career. On August 28, 1877, while at Fort Reno, he was court-martialed for public drunkenness and conduct unbecoming an officer and was sentenced to be dismissed from the service of the United States but was granted clemency by President Rutherford B. Hayes. He was instead suspended in rank and command, sentenced to serve on one-half pay, and confined to the limits of his duty station for one year. He was transferred to Company C, effective March 28, 1878, at Fort Clark, Texas. In August 1878 he was charged with violating the orders of his previous court martial by leaving the post on at least six occasions between May 25 and July 5, 1878. In August 1878 he was acquitted of these charges.

On October 12, 1878, Warrington was granted a three-month leave of absence and he returned to Washington, D.C. On December 18, 1878, he was ordered to rejoin his company, which was then stationed at Fort Sill, Oklahoma.

He traveled via Galveston and San Antonio and was at San Antonio registered in the Menger Hotel on New Year's Eve. That evening he attended a gala ball and party, which lasted until the early morning hours of January 1, 1879. During the late afternoon army Assistant Surgeon M. K. Taylor was summoned to Warrington's room, where Warrington complained of fever, chills, and severe throat congestion. Despite Taylor's efforts, Lewis Warrington III succumbed to double pneumonia at 11:45 p.m. on January 4, 1879. He was buried at the San Antonio National Cemetery and was survived only by an aunt, Rebecca Scott Henriques of Washington, D.C.

James C. Watson
Corporal, Company L, Sixth U.S. Cavalry

James Curtic Watson was born circa 1846 at Cochecton, New York, to John and Mary Watson, the third of the couple's four children. There were two older sisters, Lusandra and Emily, and a younger brother, Robert. James spent his entire youth at Cochecton and was educated there in the public schools. At age twelve he was entered into a carpentry apprenticeship under his father's tutelage. When the Civil War broke out he attempted to enlist but was rejected because of his age. In October 1863 he ran away from home and made his way to Philadelphia, where on October 9, 1863, he enlisted in Company D, 183rd Pennsylvania Infantry. During March and April 1864 he was assigned to recruiting duty in Philadelphia. While at nearby Carlisle Barracks he met and married Alice Adella. In late May 1864 he was transferred to Cold Harbor, Virginia. The 183rd Pennsylvania sustained a 50 percent casualty rate when it made fourteen consecutive frontal assaults against the Confederate breastworks at Cold Harbor. Watson survived those assaults only to be wounded in the head in a minor clash with the Fifty-third Georgia Infantry on June 4, 1864. Watson was promoted to corporal on June 1, 1865, and was mustered out of the volunteer army at Washington, D.C., on July 13, 1865.

On July 17, 1867, Watson enlisted in the regular U.S. Army, was assigned to Company K, Sixth U.S. Cavalry, and was first posted to Greenville, Texas. He served at Greenville and Jefferson on Reconstruction duty, but by February 1870 had been transferred to Fort Richardson on the Texas frontier. On April 1, 1870, he was transferred to Company L and promoted to corporal. He was cited for gallantry in action against Kiowa and Comanche Indians at the battle of the Little Wichita River on July 12, 1870, and was awarded the Medal of Honor. On October 15, 1870, he was promoted to sergeant and in January 1872 he was appointed as provost sergeant. On April 20, 1872, he was divorced from Alice Adella at Cumberland County, Pennsylvania.

For the next eleven years Watson was posted to various posts in Kansas, Colorado, and New Mexico during campaigns against the Cheyenne, Arapaho, Ute, and Apache tribes. He was active in engagements at Red River, Texas, August 30, 1874; Leitendorf Mountains, New Mexico, January 9, 1877; Ralston Flat, New Mexico, December 13, 1877; Las Animas Mountains, Mexico, December 18, 1877; Ojo Caliente, New Mexico, September 26–30, 1879; and Dog Canyon, New Mexico, on April 17, 1880. Watson received his final discharge at Jefferson Barracks, Missouri, on April 8, 1882.

On August 1, 1882, Watson married Matilda A. Fink at St. Louis, Missouri. In November 1882 the couple moved to Chicago, Illinois, where he became employed as a hotel keeper. Irene, their only child, was born on March 4, 1883. In 1888 Watson began to have severe, recurring headaches. This illness coupled with a declining general body disability steadily worsened. After several severe seizures in October 1889 he was admitted to the Cook County Insane Asylum, having been diagnosed as suffering from epileptic insanity. He died there on January 7, 1890, and was buried at Rosehill Cemetery. He was survived by his wife, Matilda, and daughter, Irene.

Michael Welch
Sergeant, Company M, Sixth U.S. Cavalry

Michael Welch was born in 1844 at Poughkeepsie, New York. He grew up in Poughkeepsie and worked as a miller in a flour mill.

He enlisted in the U.S. Army at New York City on October 2, 1866. After two months of basic cavalry training at Carlisle Barracks, Pennsylvania, he was initially assigned to Company M, Sixth U.S. Cavalry. He was assigned to Reconstruction duties in East Texas, serving primarily at Greenville, Tyler, and Athens. On February 21, 1867, he was promoted to corporal. During election difficulties in November 1869, Welch was appointed to provost sergeant. In early 1870 he was transferred to Fort Richardson on the Indian-plagued northwestern Texas frontier. On October 5, 1870, his gallantry in action at Bluff Creek in present-day Archer County, Texas, earned him the Medal of Honor. On April 20, 1871, he was promoted to quartermaster sergeant and shortly afterward he was transferred to Fort Supply, Indian Territory, where he was discharged upon expiration of service on October 2, 1871.

Benjamin Wilson
Private, Company M, Sixth U.S. Cavalry

Benjamin Wilson was born at Pittsburgh, Pennsylvania, circa November 1844. Nothing is known of his family or early life. He enlisted in the U.S. Army at Cincinnati, Ohio, on June 11, 1869. Upon enlistment he listed his civilian occupation as a clerk. After several months in training at Carlisle Barracks, Pennsylvania, he was assigned to Company M, Sixth U.S. Cavalry. He joined his company at Tyler, Texas, on September 11, 1869. During much of 1869 and the early part of 1870 Wilson divided his time on Reconstruction duty at Tyler and Greenville, Texas. By August 1870 he had been transferred to Fort Richardson, Texas, on the northwestern frontier. After two months as company clerk he began to take part in active field scouting duties against raiding Kiowa and Comanche bands. During an engagement at Bluff Creek in present-day Archer County, Texas, on October 5, 1870, he was cited for gallantry in action and was awarded the Medal of Honor. On January 20, 1871, Wilson was promoted to corporal. After the Sixth U.S. Cavalry's transfer to Kansas he was posted to Fort Hays and was promoted to sergeant on February 16, 1872. He was discharged there on June 11, 1874.

Wilson resided at St. Louis, Missouri, until January 16, 1875, when he reenlisted in the army. During this enlistment Wilson served in Company F of the Second U.S. Infantry. His service in this unit was at various posts in the Pacific Northwest, primarily Fort Harney, Oregon, where he was discharged on January 15, 1880.

William Wilson
Sergeant, Company I, Fourth U.S. Cavalry

William Wilson stated in his Navy enlistment records that he was born in 1844 at Palmyra, New Jersey. He left home in 1862 and resided in nearby Philadelphia, Pennsylvania.

On August 15, 1862, he enlisted in the U.S. Navy at Philadelphia. He was assigned to the USS *Water Witch* of the South Atlantic Squadron. On September 6, 1862, the vessel set out for its second combat cruise off Port Royal, South Carolina. On October 2, 1862, Wilson experienced his first action of the war at St. John's Bluff, Florida. In conjunction with the USS *Cimarron* and USS *Uncas*, the *Water Witch* shelled the Confederate fort at St. John's Bluff and forced the fort to be abandoned, enabling the Union to control the St. John's River up to

Jacksonville. On June 3, 1864, at 2 a.m. while anchored off Ossabaw Sound, Georgia, the *Water Witch* was captured by a surprise attack of Confederate boarding launches. William Wilson was a prisoner of war until the end of the war.

Upon his return to Philadelphia, Wilson enlisted in the U.S. Army on October 30, 1865. Most of his first enlistment with Company I, Fourth U.S. Cavalry, was spent on Reconstruction duty at Brownsville, Texas, and in New Orleans and Grand Ecore, Louisiana. After his discharge at Grand Ecore on October 30, 1868, Wilson returned to Philadelphia. On May 5, 1869, he reenlisted in the Fourth U.S. Cavalry, listing his occupation as a soldier. During his first major action, while pursuing a band of cattle thieves near Beals Creek, Texas, he captured one of the bandits and killed two others. The capture of this bandit enabled military and civil authorities to end the destructive Comanchero trade that had stifled the western expansion of the Texas frontier ranching industry. Wilson was awarded the Medal of Honor for the deeds he performed on March 28, 1872. Six months later he assumed command of a disorganized company, whose commanding officer had been disabled. He reorganized the company and led them under fire against Indians who were entrenched in a ravine and whose resistance had prevented the closing off of escape routes through which large numbers of the Indians were escaping. Wilson continued to lead the company against the Indians' entrenched positions until he was relieved by the company commander. For these actions of September 29, 1872, he was awarded a second Medal of Honor.

During his remaining service in Texas Wilson was involved in engagements against Indians at Kickapoo Springs, December 10, 1873; Tule Canyon, September 26–27, 1874; Palo Duro Canyon, September 28, 1874; Laguna Quatro, November 3, 1874; and Muchaque Valley, December 8, 1874. In the 1876 Powder River campaign in Wyoming, Wilson was active in the engagement near Bates Creek on the North Fork of the Powder River on November 26, 1876. During the attempted Cheyenne outbreak from Indian Territory, he was involved in several minor clashes at Bluff Creek, Kansas, September 18, 1878; Sand Creek, Kansas, September 21, 1878; and Punished Woman's Creek, Kansas, on September 27, 1878.

From 1879 to 1884 Wilson resided in Philadelphia. He reenlisted there on April 26, 1884. During this enlistment he served in Troop B, Fourth U.S. Cavalry. He was posted to Fort Myer, Virginia; Gilroy's Ranch, California; and to several posts in Arizona. On June 6, 1886, he participated in his final action against the remnants of Geronimo's Chiracauhua Apaches in the Patagonia Mountains of Arizona.

During much of the time Wilson spent at Fort Myer, Virginia, and Gilroy's Ranch, California, he participated in numerous equestrian events. He was able to demonstrate his outstanding riding and swordsmanship skills in numerous exhibitions and competitions.

On April 26, 1894, Wilson enlisted for the final time at Gilroy's Ranch, California, and shortly afterward was transferred to the Presidio of San Francisco. He began to seek medical treatment for severe pain in his lower extremities upon his arrival at San Francisco and was found to have cancerous growths. On December 22, 1895, after surgery to remove those growths, he succumbed to the weakening effects of the cancer and died in his sleep. He was survived by his wife, Sadie Wilson, formerly of Philadelphia.

William "Billy" Wilson earned two Medals of Honor and a Certificate of Merit. He was a member of the California Chapter 101 of the Grand Army of the Republic, the Congressional Medal of Honor Legion, the Army and Navy Union and the Knights of Templar. He was interred with full military honors at the San Francisco National Cemetery at the Presidio of San Francisco.

Claron A. Windus
Bugler, Company L, Sixth U.S. Cavalry

Claron Augustus Windus was born in 1851 at Janesville, Wisconsin, to George and Mary Windus, the youngest of seven children. Claron was educated in the public schools of Rock County and received musical training from his father.

At the outset of the Civil War, Windus attempted to follow his three older brothers off to war but his mother prevented him from doing so. In September 1864 he ran away from home and made his way to Camp Randall at Madison, where he convinced the recruiting officer for the Fifth Wisconsin Volunteer Infantry to enlist him as a drummer. During his brief service he was active in actions at Petersburg, Virginia, March 25–April 2, 1864, and Sailor's Creek, Virginia, April 5, 1865. His last Civil War duty was to drum cadence for the Fifth Wisconsin Infantry as it participated in the Grand Review through Washington, D.C. By the first week of July he was back in Madison, once again a civilian.

Unwilling to face the wrath of his parents, fourteen-year-old Claron Windus decided to strike out on his own. He made his way to Indianapolis, Indiana, and obtained employment as a cigar maker. On October 12, 1866, he left that endeavor and enlisted in the army. Whatever words he used on the recruiting officer must have been very convincing, for he was barely fifteen years old. After basic cavalry training at Carlisle Barracks, Pennsylvania, Windus was assigned to Company L,

Sixth U.S. Cavalry, and was stationed at Fort Richardson, Texas. In April 1867 his company was assigned to garrison the sub-post of Fort Belknap. On July 7, 1867, he, along with Pvt. Charles Williams, stole four army horses and deserted into the night. He was apprehended on his thirteenth day of freedom near Fort Gates. On February 10, 1868. Windus was found guilty on both court martial charges of desertion and theft of government property. He was sentenced to be confined at hard labor and to forfeit all pay for one year. Despite pleas of clemency from army Surgeon Henry McElderry, Lt. Col. S. D. Sturges, Lt. Charles H. Campbell, and Sgt. George W. Dixon his sentence was not reduced. During late 1868 and for most of 1869 Windus served on various Reconstruction duties in East Texas. He was instrumental in helping to quell the activities of the Bob Lee gang, a band of former Confederate guerrillas who actively opposed federal Reconstruction policies. During this time Windus served in various East Texas towns such as Pilot Grove, Jefferson, and Bonham. During the 1870 elections he was cited for his outstanding service as an election monitor at McKinney, Texas.

In May 1870 Windus was transferred back to Fort Richardson to contend with mounting depredations by Indian bands. On the morning of July 7, 1870, Windus was part of a fifty-man detachment sent in pursuit of a band of Indian raiders who had attacked a stagecoach west of Fort Richardson. On July 12, more than two hundred Indians ambushed the detachment near the Little Wichita River. Windus served as a bugler and orderly during the engagement and assisted the wounded medical officer, George W. Hatch, in caring for the wounded troopers. As orderly he was sent constantly under fire to deliver verbal orders to the various company commanders. He also assisted in clearing Indian snipers from prominent elevations along the command's path of retreat and on the morning of July 13 he volunteered, along with two other men, to ride to Fort Richardson to bring reinforcements to the beleaguered command. For these conspicuous acts of bravery he was awarded the Medal of Honor.

During most of November–December 1870 Windus was detailed as an orderly for general court martials held at Fort Richardson. On April 21, 1871, he was transferred to Fort Hays, Kansas. Shortly afterward he was sent on detached duty as an orderly to Department of Missouri headquarters at Fort Leavenworth. Shortly after his return to Fort Hays he was discharged effective October 12, 1871.

After his discharge Windus returned to Jacksboro, Texas. Between the latter months of 1871 and early 1875 he was employed as a teamster and mail agent. During this time he resided for brief periods at Dallas and San Angelo. By July 1875 he was residing at Brackettville, Texas, where he was appointed a deputy sheriff under Sheriff L. C. Crowell. Brackettville, at the time, was perhaps the wildest town on the Texas frontier and provided many dangerous situations for Windus, who became known to the local populace as "Deputy Gus." One such incident involved Col. Edward Hatch, commander of the Ninth U.S. Cavalry regiment at nearby Fort Clark. Hatch, angered over the frequent arrests and heavy fines levied on some of his troops, had refused to cooperate with the local civil authorities. Hatch ridiculed the local authorities and went so far as threatening to burn the town and arrest Crowell and Windus and place them in irons in the post stockade. On two previous genteel attempts by Crowell and Windus, Hatch had rebuffed their attempts to respond to their warrants and post the incumbent bond. On the third attempt on January 13, 1876, Windus, the former Civil War drummer boy, heavily armed and purportedly wearing his Medal of Honor, elicited from the Civil War general a meek agreement to accompany him to the courthouse to respond to the warrant and post the required bond. On December 31, 1876, Windus became embroiled in the most serious incident during his tenure as a deputy. Informants from the Seminole-Negro Indian scout community had informed Sheriff Crowell of the presence of four fugitive felons in their village. Crowell formulated a plan whereby Deputy Windus, himself, and a local teamster, James Thomas, would, in the darkness, encircle the open area in the center of the village. At exactly midnight, when the revelers would be in the central open area preoccupied with celebrating the New Year, the lawmen would announce themselves and hopefully make the arrests without resistance. At midnight the three entered the central clearing and loudly announced their presence and intent. All went according to plan until the suspects were isolated and Crowell began to shackle them. Two of the wanted felons, Adam Payne and Frank Enoch, began to resist and attempted to flee. Windus, who was the closest, fired his shotgun at the fleeing felons. Payne was killed instantly and Enoch was mortally wounded. Windus was immediately jumped during the confusion by the tribal headman, Robert Kibbet, and order was restored only by Crowell and Thomas firing warning shots. This incident is noteworthy because the death of Adam Payne at the hands of Claron Windus marks the only known instance of one Medal of Honor recipient dying at the hands of another recipient.

On January 22, 1877, Gus Windus tendered his resignation as constable and deputy sheriff at a special term meeting of the county commissioner's court. He was promptly appointed to the office of Kinney County assessor of taxes. On February 3, 1877, he married Agnes Ballantyne. Between 1877 and 1878, he and his wife purchased more than five thousand acres of land sold at public delinquent tax sales. At age twenty-six, Windus became one of the largest landowners in Kinney County, Texas.

In 1879 Windus was hired by the U.S. Treasury Department as a mounted customs inspector. During his five years as a customs inspector he served at Eagle Pass, Corpus Christi, and Laredo. He resigned his position at the end of his term and returned home to Brackettville. Windus financed and managed the Coffin Stage Line, which transported freight, mail, and passengers between Brackettville and the railroad depot at Spofford. During the time in Brackettville he expended much time and money in further developing his vast land holdings.

In 1887 Windus was approached by his old friend, L. C. Crowell, who was a U.S. marshal at the time. The violations of the U.S. neutrality laws by P. A. Valdez and Catarino Garza and their followers required the attentions of a larger complement of deputy U.S. marshals. Crowell, knowing that Windus was fluent in Spanish and familiar with federal customs laws, quickly obtained Windus an appointment. Windus served as a deputy U.S. marshal until 1896, when most of the violators of U.S. neutrality laws were in federal prisons.

On July 6, 1897, Windus obtained a license to lay a pipeline from Las Moras Creek to his house in Brackettville. He formed his own construction company, then designed and supervised the layout for a water pipeline and pumping facilities, which made his home the first in Brackettville to have running water. Windus tendered his services to the War Department on July 6, 1898, and was appointed to the rank of captain with the Ninth Volunteer Infantry of Immunes. He was assigned to Camp Corbin near New Orleans as an instructor and later participated in the Santiago Campaign in Cuba as a mounted cavalry officer. His unit secured supply lines between depots and the frontlines. He also secured and interrogated prisoners and supervised their removal to the rear for processing and incarceration. In March 1899 he contracted malaria and was sent to Camp Meade, Pennsylvania, for convalescence and was discharged on May 21, 1899.

On April 5, 1900, Windus again applied to the Treasury Department for a position as a special customs agent. He obtained the position and was assigned to the office at Rio Grande City, where he remained for six years. On February 5, 1907, he was transferred to Langtry, Texas, and later to Lajitas, near what is now the Big Bend National Park. In 1915 he became the deputy customs inspector at Presidio, an especially dangerous assignment due to the revolutionary activities of Colomba and Pancho Villa. After several armed encounters with Villa's men in 1916, a detachment of troops was dispatched to guard the strategic crossing at Presidio and the customs house. When a flu epidemic broke out among the troops during the winter of 1916–1917 Claron and Agnes Windus almost single-handedly suppressed it. Both went for days without sleep while they cooked, bathed, and nursed more than ninety stricken soldiers. When the dangers had subsided the soldiers were withdrawn and Windus was transferred to the more secure office at Marathon, where he remained until his retirement from the U.S. Customs Service on August 31, 1920. He obtained an Indian Wars and Medal of Honor pension after his enrollment on the Medal of Honor Roll. After his return to his home at Brackettville he began to suffer a decline in health. In 1921 Windus received an invitation from the Secretary of War to come to Washington, D.C., to participate in the ceremonial escort for the World War I unknown soldier, but was forced to decline on account of his ill health. Claron A. Windus died on October 18, 1927, at the post hospital at Fort Sam Houston at San Antonio. He was laid to rest in the Masonic Cemetery at Brackettville and was survived by his wife, Agnes, and two daughters, Lucie Welch and Cora Windus.

William Winterbottom
Sergeant, Company A, Sixth U.S. Cavalry

William Winterbottom was born on October 9, 1846, at Manchester, England. Nothing is known of his family or early life. He likely came to the United States circa 1862. He enlisted in Company G, Third Rhode Island Cavalry, at Providence on February 16, 1864. This unit was immediately dispatched to Louisiana to participate in the Red River campaign under the command of Gen. Nathan Banks. On April 19, 1864, he was part of a command that was being ferried up the Red River aboard the USS *Superior*. Near Campti, Louisiana, Confederate guerrillas on shore attacked the vessel. Winterbottom sustained a leg wound during the encounter and was discharged at New Orleans on November 29, 1865, after declining to return with the unit to its muster-out site at Providence, Rhode Island.

It is believed that Winterbottom returned briefly to England. He next appeared at Boston, Massachusetts, where he enlisted in the regular U.S. Army on October 16, 1866. After five weeks of basic cavalry training at Carlisle Barracks, Pennsylvania, he was assigned to Company A, Sixth Cavalry. He was first stationed at Austin, Texas, where he arrived on December 10, 1866. Between 1867 and late 1869 he served on Reconstruction duty at various towns in East Texas. In the latter part of 1869 the increasing number of Indian raids necessitated his transfer to the northwestern frontier. He was assigned to Fort Richardson and began to participate in scouting duty against raiding Indian bands. On July 12, 1870, his gallantry in action at the battle of the Little Wichita River in present-day Archer County, Texas, merited for him the award of the Medal of Honor. In April 1871 his regiment was transferred to various posts in

Kansas. While at Camp Limestone, Kansas, he was discharged upon expiration of service on October 16, 1871.

After leaving the army, Winterbottom resided at St. Louis, Missouri, where he met and married Martha Mellon. After only a few years of marriage, Martha Winterbottom died of tuberculosis on September 29, 1883. Winterbottom moved shortly afterward to Boston, Massachusetts, where in 1886 he married Catherine Fant. The couple eventually resided at Bayonne, New Jersey, where Winterbottom was employed as a teamster and dockworker. William and Catherine Winterbottom had four children, Albert, George, Ellen, and Kate. In 1924, through the efforts of the Grand Army of the Republic, William Winterbottom was formally enrolled upon the Army and Navy Medal of Honor Roll. After his retirement he moved to Jersey City, New Jersey, and died there on April 4, 1932, of a cerebral apoplexy. He was buried at Bay View Cemetery at Jersey City, New Jersey.

Zachariah T. Woodall
Sergeant, Company I, Sixth U.S. Cavalry

Zachariah Taylor Woodall was born circa September 1849 at Alexandria, Virginia, to George and Elizabeth Woodall. He was the youngest of four children, preceded by one sister, Virginia, and two brothers, Andrew and Ralph. The Woodalls lived in a modest neighborhood in Alexandria, where the elder Woodall worked as a machinist. Zachariah was reared and educated in Alexandria. Although he was only twelve when the Civil War began there are some indications that he may have served with the U.S. Navy during the war.

Six years after the end of the Civil War, Woodall was at Carlisle, Pennsylvania, where he enlisted in the U.S. Army on January 24, 1871. After cavalry basic training he was assigned to Company I, Sixth U.S. Cavalry, and was posted to Fort Richardson, Texas. On April 15, 1872, he was sent on detached duty for Reconstruction service to Chocktaw County, Mississippi, where as a newly promoted corporal he began his lifelong service under Adna R. Chaffee. During much of 1873 Woodall served on detached service at Fort Sill, Indian Territory, and Fort McKavett, Texas. By the time he arrived at his duty station of Fort Harker, Kansas, he had risen to the rank of sergeant. In August 1874 he took to the field against Kiowa, Comanche, Cheyenne, and Arapaho bands as part of the N. A. Miles column in the Indian Territory expedition. On August 30, 1874, he participated in the battle of the Red River in Palo Duro Canyon. On September 12, 1874, Woodall, while serving as a courier escort, was involved in the fight at the buffalo wallow in present-day Hemphill County, Texas. Despite a severe hip wound early in the engagement, Woodall continued to assist in the defense of his comrades, three of whom had also been wounded. For his gallantry in this incident he was awarded the Medal of Honor. After his release from the hospital at Camp Supply, Indian Territory, Woodall rejoined his company at Fort Dodge, Kansas.

In the fall of 1875 Woodall was transferred to the Department of Arizona and posted to Fort Verde, Arizona. During his service against Warm Springs and Chiracahua Apaches he was active in engagements at Smith's Mill, Arizona, on May 20, 1878; Big Dry Wash, Arizona, July 17, 1882, and Babispe Mountains, Mexico, on June 23, 1885.

Woodall was a member of the regimental rifle team that competed at Creedmore, New York, on September 30, 1879. In October 1880 Woodall was appointed the non-commissioned officer in charge of a select military escort that accompanied President Rutherford B. Hayes during his tour of the Pima Indian Agency. Sergeant Woodall continued his field duty against Geronimo's band of Apaches and was present when Geronimo first surrendered at Seymour's Creek, Mexico, on March 15, 1883.

In 1891 Woodall participated in his last engagement against Indians during the Wounded Knee campaign at Little Grass Creek, South Dakota, on January 1, 1891. Shortly afterward he transferred to the non-commissioned officer staff as first sergeant. In late 1892 he was appointed an ordnance sergeant and was assigned to the Rock Island Arsenal in Illinois. In December 1893 he was transferred to the St. Louis Arsenal at Jefferson Barracks, Missouri, where he remained until 1898. On June 12, 1898, he reported for duty at the Cabana Fortress Ordnance Depot at Havana, Cuba. He served briefly in field operations near El Caney, Cuba. During this field service he contracted yellow fever in June 1899. After his transfer back to the Cabana Fortress Depot at Havana he suffered a relapse and was hospitalized at Las Animas Hospital. Late in the night of September 11, he entered into a coma and died in the early morning hours of September 12, 1899. He was initially interred at the Camp Columbia post cemetery near Havana, Cuba. After the war's end his remains were re-interred in the Spanish-American War section of Arlington National Cemetery at Washington, D.C. He was never married and there were no known survivors. In addition to the Medal of Honor, Woodall also possessed a Certificate of Merit.

Biographies Sources

GEORGE E. ALBEE: Pension file certificate XC-2659057, RG 15 (National Archives); "G. E. Albee Personnel file," file 1318, Appointment, Commission, and Promotion–1872, RG 94 (National Archives); and S. A. Mulholland, *Military Order: Congressional Medal of Honor Legion of the United States* (Philadelphia: Town Printing, 1905), 613–616.

FRANK D. BALDWIN: F. D. Baldwin, Personnel file, file 3365, Appointment, Commission, and Promotion–1875, RG 94; Frank D. Baldwin," *National Cyclopedia* (New York: J. T. White Co., 1917), xiv, 339–340; and A. B. Baldwin, *Memoirs of the Late Frank D. Baldwin, Major-General, U.S. Army* (Los Angeles: Wetzel Publishing Co., 1929).

GEORGE H. BELL: Pension file certificate 35894, RG 15.

FREDERICK H. BERGENDAHL: Enlistment papers, Nov. 17, 1871, and Aug. 28, 1878; W. C. Lott to Office of the Adjutant General, June 2, 1897, Adjutant General's Office–Documents Received, file 53290, Adjutant General's Office–1897; "Personnel file Hjalmar Fredrik Bergendahl," Official Records of the Royal Support Battalion, Staff Musician, Swedish Army of Military Retirees, Stockholm, Sweden.

SAMUEL BOWDEN: Enlistment papers, Oct. 18, 1867; and U.S. Army, Special Order no. 45, Feb. 1, 1871, RG 94.

EDWARD BRANAGAN: Enlistment papers, Jan. 23, 1871, RG 94.

ROBERT G. CARTER: R. G. Carter, Personnel file, file 3679, Appointment, Commission, and Promotion–1873, RG 94; G. W. Cullum, *Biographical Register of U.S. Military Academy Graduates, 1802–1890*, Class of 1870, entry 2349, 101–102; Mulholland, *Military Order: Congressional Medal of Honor Legion of the United States*, 617–620; "Obituary," *Washington 'Post*, Jan. 5, 1936, p. 6, col. 3.

AMOS CHAPMAN: Pension file certificate 221433, RG 15; Wayne Montgomery, "Amos Chapman, Scout," *Frontier Times* (May, 1972), 26–28; 44–47; and Glenn Shirley, *Buckskin and Spurs: A Gallery of Frontier Rogues and Heroes* (New York: Hastings House Publishers, 1958), 145–152; and I. C. Toller to C. M. Neal Jr., Oct. 10, 1972, letter.

JOHN W. COMFORT: Pension file, application 1143421, RG 15; Compiled Service Record, Company I, Twenty-ninth Pennsylvania Infantry, RG 94; Merle C.

Olmsted, "John W. Comfort; Portrait of a U.S. Regular, 1865–1892," *Military Collector and Historian*, 20 (Winter, 1968), 126; and "Obituaries," *Philadephia Public Ledger*, Dec. 2, 1893.

JOHN CONNOR: Pension file, application 965594, certificate 670338, RG 15.

WILLIAM DIXON: Pension file, application 1296132, certificate 1056765, RG 15; F. S. Bard, *Life and Adventures of "Billy" Dixon of Adobe Walls, Panhandle, Texas*; Pat Nobles, "Billy Dixon, Boy Scout," *Real West* (Feb., 1987), 26–29.

JAMES B. DOSHER: Pension file, Mexican War, certificate 16814, Apr. 7, 1887 and wc-13340, Mar. 19, 1901, RG 15; and H. H. McConnell, *Five Years a Cavalryman; or Sketches of Regular Army Life on the Texas Frontier, Twenty Odd Years Ago* (Jacksboro, Texas: J. N. Rogers & Co., 1889), 218–219.

WILLIAM DEARMOND: Pension file, Julia A. DeArmond, application 218810, certificate 171172, RG 15; Compiled Service Record, Second Ohio Heavy Artilery, Company C, RG 94.

GEORGE H. ELDRIDGE: Compiled Service Record, Twenty-fourth Michigan Infantry, Company A, RG 94; and Pension file application 1051738, certificate 86008, RG 15.

POMPEY FACTOR: Pension file, application 20180, certificate 13093, RG 15; and Art Leatherwood, "Pompey Factor," in Ron Tyler, Douglas E. Barnett, Roy R. Barkley, Penelope C. Anderson, and Mark F. Odintz (eds.), *The New Handbook of Texas* (6 vols.; Austin: Texas State Historical Association, 1996), II, 933.

WILLIAM FOSTER: Enlistment papers, 1862–1875, RG 94; and "Death of a Warrior with a Notable Record," *San Francisco Evening Bulletin*, July 16, 1880, p. 1.

JOHN J. GIVEN: Compiled Service Record, Second Kentucky Cavalry (Union), Company G, RG 94; and Art Leatherwood, "John J. Given," in Tyler, et al. (eds.), *The New Handbook of Texas*, III, 176.

JOHN HARRINGTON: File 962768, Adjutant General's Office–Documents Received, 1901 (filed with file 360765, Adjutant General's Office–Documents Received, 1905), RG 94.

FRANCIS S. HESSELTINE: Pension file, application 358124, certificate 1078739, RG 15; and Mulholland, *Military Order: Congressional Medal of Honor Legion of the United States*, 346–357.

JOHN JAMES: Pension file, application 557816, certificate 334304, RG 15.

DANIEL KEATING: Pension file, application 1185991, RG 94.

Biographies

JOHN J. H. KELLY: Pension file, application 14549, certificate 9172, RG 94.

THOMAS KELLY: Pension file, application 787751, certificate 521680; and file 1306245, Adjutant General's Office–Documents Received, 1907, RG 94.

THOMAS KERRIGAN: Enlistment papers, Oct. 1, 1866, RG 94.

JOHN KIRK: Compiled Service Record, Twentieth Pennsylvania Cavalry, Companies B, F, and L, RG 94; pension file, C-2536673, RG 15.

GEORGE K. KITCHEN: Pension file, application 11997, certificate 7724, RG 15; and Art Leatherwood, "George K. Kitchen," in Tyler, et al. (eds.), *The New Handbook of Texas*, III, 1133.

JOHN W. KNOX: Pension file, application 1152526, certificate 874350, RG 15.

WILLIAM KOELPIN: File 1865583, Adjutant General's Office–Documents Received, 1912, RG 94.

DAVID LARKIN: Pension file, application 1014587, certificate 801890, RG 15; and Mulholland, *Military Order: Congressional Medal of Honor Legion of the United States*, 630.

GREGORY P. MAHONEY: National Library of Wales, *Index to Births in England and Wales, Registrar's District of Pontypool* (London: General Register Office, 1986), XXVI, 165.

JOHN MAY: Pension file, application 435604, certificate 380140, RG 15.

WILLIAM MCCABE: Enlistment papers, Feb. 3, 1874, RG 94; Mackenzie to Assistant Adjutant General, Department of Texas, Oct. 5, 1875, Fourth U.S. Cavalry Letters Sent Book, 1874–1889, entry 259, 140, RG 391 (National Archives).

FRANKLIN M. MCDONNOLD: Enlistment papers, June 7, 1871, RG 94.

HENRY A. MCMASTER: U.S. Census (1860), Kennebec County (Augusta), Maine, 181, RG 29 (National Archives); Compiled Service Record, Twenty-ninth Maine Infantry, Company F, RG 94; Enlistment papers, June 10, 1871, RG 94; and Final Statement papers, Fourth U.S. Cavalry, RG 94.

WILLIAM MCNAMARA: R. H. Hibberd to Adjutant General's Office, Mar. 19, 1912, file 1892352, Adjutant General's Office–1912, RG 94; and U.S. Census (1900), New York (Brooklyn), vol. 91, e.d. 441, sheet 6, line 98, RG 29 (National Archives).

JOHN MITCHELL: U.S. Census (1860), Peoria, Ill., Second Ward, 176, RG 29; Compiled Service Record, Fourteenth Illinois Cavalry, RG 94; Enlistment papers, Aug. 19, 1867, RG 94; and file 790052, Record and Pension Office–Letters Received, May 13, 1904, RG 94.

WILLIAM W. MORRIS: Compiled Service Record, Companies C and M, Twelfth Tennessee Cavalry (Confederate), RG 94; file 92710, Adjutant General's Office–Documents Received, 1898, RG 94; and U.S. Census (1900), Ellis County (Italy), Texas, vol. 34, e.d. 33, sheet 13, line 14, RG 29.

SOLON D. NEAL: U.S. Census (1860), Grafton County (Hanover), New Hampshire, 12, RG 29; Enlistment papers, Mar. 6, 1866–Mar. 6, 1893, RG 94; and Office of the County Clerk, Bexar County, Texas, probate file 11103, Jan. 24, 1921.

FREDERICK S. NEILON: Enlistment papers, Aug. 11, 1872, RG 94; Pension file, application 206350, certificate 136726, RG 15; file 19768, Adjutant General's Office–Documents Received, 1893, RG 94; and "Obituaries," *Boston Evening Transcript*, Sept. 13, 1916.

WILLIAM O'NEILL: Enlistment papers, Mar. 21, 1870, RG 94.

JOHN F. O'SULLIVAN: A. McArthur to J. P. Hatch, Mar. 16, 1870, Letters Received Book, Endorsements and Memorandum, 20, Carlisle Barracks, Pennsylvania, RG 393; Enlistment papers, Mar. 22, 1870, RG 94; and New York City, Department of Health, Certificates and Records of Deaths, certificate 17049, filed May 19, 1907.

ADAM PAYNE: Special enlistment registers, Nov. 12, 1873, RG 94; Strong, *My Frontier Days*, 26; and Donald A. Swanson, *Enlistment Records of Indian Scouts—Fort Clark, Texas* (Bronte, Texas: Ames-American Printing Co., circa 1990), 32.

ISAAC PAYNE: U.S. Census (1860), Kinney County (Brackettville), Texas, 36, RG 29; and Art Leatherwood, "Isaac Payne," in Tyler, et al. (eds.), *The New Handbook of Texas*, V, 102.

JOSIAH J. PENNSYL: U.S. Census (1860), Bedford County (Rainsburg), Pennsylvania, 11, RG 29; T. F. Preston to C. M. Neal Jr., Mar. 3, 1973, interview; and Pension file, application 10905, certificate 7097, RG 15.

EDWIN PHOENIX: Enlistment papers, Jan. 5, 1867–Feb. 19, 1875, RG 94; and Pension file C-2,606,884, RG 15.

SAMUEL PORTER: U.S. Census (1850), Montgomery County (Macklin Township), Maryland, family 288, RG 29; Compiled Service Record, Eleventh New York Cavalry, Companies K and P, RG 94; Enlistment papers, Mar. 15, 1866, RG 94; and Pension file C-22361751, RG 15.

JAMES N. PRATT: U.S. Census (1860), Logan County (Bellefontaine), Ohio, 1, RG 29; Pension file, application 199666, certificate 138900, RG 15; and "Obituaries, James N. Pratt," *Bellefontaine Examiner*, Oct. 14, 1903.

Biographies

WILLIAM RANKIN: File 2376984, Adjutant General's Office–Documents Received, 1916, RG 94; and "A Famous Soldier Dies," *Democrat and Sentinel (Lewistown, Pa.)*, Feb. 10, 1916, 8, 1.

PETER P. ROTH: Pension file, XC-871664, RG 15; and D. P. Perrine to C. M. Neal Jr., Oct. 10, 1973, letter.

EDWARD C. SHARPLESS: Pension file XC-871664, RG 15.

FREDERICK H. SCHWABE: File 461543, Adjutant General's Office–Documents Received, 1916, RG 94.

CHARLES E. SMITH: Enlistment papers, Feb. 13, 1869, RG 94.

GEORGE W. SMITH: Enlistment papers, Jan. 31, 1870, RG 94; Final Statement papers, "Pvt. George W. Smith, Sixth U.S. Cavalry," RG 94; and N. Miles to C. Smith, Dec. 25, 1874, file 5519, Letters Received, 1874, RG 94.

JAMES SMYTHE: Pension file, application 15265, RG 15; and "Deaths," *St. Louis Post Dispatch*, June 2, 1918.

EMANUEL STANCE: Enlistment papers, Oct. 2, 1866–Dec. 26, 1886, RG 94; and Frank N. Schubert, "The Violent World of Emanuel Stance, Fort Robinson, 1887," *Nebraska History*, 55, no. 2 (1974), 203–219.

ALONZO STOKES: Logan County Geneological Society, *Thomas Garwood Family History*, 327; Compiled Service Record, Tenth Ohio Artillery (L), RG 94; "The Accident at the Arsenal," *St. Louis Republican*, July 6, 1876, 8, 3; and "Accident," *St. Louis Times*, July 5, 1876, 8, 4.

ERNEST VEUVE: Pension file, application 13833, certificate 9044, RG 15; and Agnes McDonald to Rex E. Neal, Jan. 7, 1975, Eugene, Ore., interview.

ALLEN WALKER: Pension file C-17806263, RG 15.

JOHN WARD: Pension file, application 1175862, certificate 961935, RG 15.

LEWIS WARRINGTON III: Personnel file, file 180, Appointment, Commission, and Promotion–1879, RG 94.

JAMES C. WATSON: Pension file application 434050, certificate 312142, RG 15.

MICHAEL WELCH: Enlistment papers, Oct. 2, 1866, RG 94.

BENJAMIN WILSON: Enlistment papers, June 11, 1869–Jan. 16, 1875, RG 94.

WILLIAM WILSON: File 30964, Documents Received, Adjutant General's Office, 1896, RG 94; Fred A. Hunt, "American Orders of Knighthood," *Overland Monthly*, 57 (June, 1911), 589; and "Died," *San Francisco Examiner*, Dec. 24, 1895.

Claron A. Windus: Pension file, application 12427, certificate 1425535, RG 94.

William Winterbottom: Pension file XC-2650965, RG 15.

Zachariah T. Woodall: U.S. Census (1850), Alexandria, Virginia, family 262, 643, RG 29; W. H. Carter, *The Life of Lt.-General Adna R. Chaffee*, 73–75; and files 283547F, 291407, Adjutant General's Office–Documents Received, 1899, RG 94.

Notes

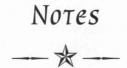

Chapter 1
Attack on the CSS Royal Yacht

1. Brig. Gen. P. O. Hebert to Secretary of War, Sept. 27, 1861, U.S. War Department, *The Official Compiled Records of the Union and Confederate Armies in the War of the Rebellion* (Washington, D.C.: Government Printing Office, 1890–1921), Series I, vol. 4, 112; hereafter cited as *CRWR-Armies* for Union or Confederate Army documents with appropriate series, volume, and page numbers following. Hebert, Confederate commander of the Department of Texas, was not impressed with Texas coastal fortifications. He wrote, "I find this coast in almost a defenseless state . . . The port of Galveston is partially defended by a few open sand works, mounted with guns of calibres ranging from 18-pounders to 32-pounders, and of course totally inadequate to resist a bombardment with heavy guns." For orders and the command structure of the Military District of Galveston, see Hebert, Oct. 4, 1861, Orders 19 and 20, *CRWR-Armies*, I, 4, 113. For the assignment of Cmdr. W. W. Hunter, Confederate Navy, to command naval defenses and vessels in the port of Galveston see Hebert, Nov. 4, 1861, Special Order 87, U.S. War Department, *The Official Compiled Records of the Union and Confederate Navies in the War of the Rebellion* (Washington, D.C.: Government Printing Office, 1890–1921), Series I, vol. 16, 848–849; hereafter cited as *CRWR-Navies*, for Union or Confederate Navy documents with appropriate series, volume and page numbers following. For gun placements see *CRWR-Armies*, I, 4, 117. See also Calvin C. Cowles (comp.), *The Official Military Atlas of the Civil War* (New York: Fairfax Press, 1983), plate no. 38, for a map of Galveston Bay and fortifications.

At age forty-three, P. O. Hebert was already a former governor of Louisiana. A brilliant engineering student, he ranked first in his class at West Point in 1840. George W. Cullum (ed.), *Biographical Register of the Officers and Graduates of the U.S. Military Academy at West Point, 1802–1867* (2 vols.; New York: D. Van Nostrand, 1868), I, 592; hereafter cited as Cullum, *Biographical Register.*

William W. Hunter was born in Pennsylvania but lived most of his life in Louisiana. He resigned his position as a commander, U.S. Navy, on April 2, 1861. He was given the rank of captain in the Confederate Navy. He commanded naval defenses along the coast of Texas from 1861 to 1863. U.S. Navy, *Register of the Officers of the Confederate Navy, 1861–1865* (Washington, D.C.: Government Printing Office, 1931), 95.

2. William Mervine to Secretary of the Navy, Sept. 13, 1861, *CRWR-Navies*, I, 16, 667.

Henry Eagle was a sixty-year-old New Yorker who had entered the Navy in 1818 and retired in 1863. Edward W. Callahan, *List of Officers of the Navy of the United States and of the Marine Corps from 1775 to 1900* (New York: Haskell House Publishers, 1969), 95; hereafter cited as Callahan, *List of U.S. Navy Officers.*

James E. Jouett was born near Lexington, Kentucky, on February 7, 1826. He was the grandson of Jack Jouett, the famed, "Paul Revere of the South," whose warnings had prevented the British from capturing Thomas Jefferson and the Virginia Legislature in 1781. As an ensign at the outset of the Mexican War, Jouett had commanded a detachment of sailors and marines sent to reinforce Gen. Zachary Taylor's positions during a critical stage of the battle of Palo Alto on May 8, 1846, near Brownsville, Texas. He eventually rose to the rank of rear admiral and retired in 1891. He died on September 30, 1902, at Sandy Spring, Maryland. Callahan, *List of U.S. Navy Officers*, 304. "James E. Jouett," *The National Cyclopedia of American Biography* (59 vols.; Clifton, N.J.: J. T. White, 1893), IV, 501–502.

The USS *Santee*, a 1,726-ton sailing frigate launched in 1855 at Portsmouth, New Hampshire, was 205 feet in length and its armament included a total of forty-four guns. An early victim of the evolving steam-powered navy, the *Santee* was decommissioned in 1862 and served as a school ship at the Newport Naval Training Base until 1865. From 1865 until 1912 the *Santee* served as a training ship for midshipmen at the U.S. Naval Academy. U.S. Navy Department, *Dictionary of American Naval Fighting Ships.* (8 vols.; Washington, D.C.: Government Printing Office, 1959), VI, 325; hereafter cited as *American Fighting Ships.*

3. Master P. F. Appel, commanding CSS *Bayou City*, "Abstract of the logbook of CSS *Bayou City*," CRWR-Navies, I, 16, 859–865. The CSS *General Rusk*, a 750-ton side-wheel steamship, more than two hundred feet long, was built at Wilmington, Delaware, in 1857. The state of Texas seized it from the Southern Steamship Company in early 1861. On April 17, 1861, she captured the Union transport USS *Star of the West*, whose attempt to re-supply Fort Sumter led to the first shots of the Civil War. In 1862 the *Rusk* was renamed the *Blanche* and, while flying the British flag, was destroyed near Marianao, Cuba, by the pursuing USS *Montgomery*. Her destruction in Spanish territorial waters while flying the British flag prompted international protests against the U.S. Navy; see *American Fighting Ships,* II, 525.

The CSS *Royal Yacht*, a forty-ton, four-masted schooner, was chartered for Confederate naval service from the Charles Chubb family. See *CRWR-Navies*, I, 16, 844. Thomas Chubb to W. W. Hunter, Oct. 9, 1861. On April 15, 1863, while running the blockade to Cuba, the *Royal Yacht* was captured by the USS *William G. Anderson*; see *American Fighting Ships*, II, 563.

4. Eagle to Jouett and J. G. Mitchell, Nov. 7, 1861, *CRWR-Navies*, I, 16, 756.

5. No mention is made of the purpose or presence of the third launch in the expedition in either Eagle's order, Nov. 7, 1861, CRWR-Navies, I, 16, 756, nor in Jouett's delayed report, Jouett to Thompson, May 13, 1879, Letters Received by the Secretary of Navy from Squadron Commanders, 1841–1886, Records of the Office of Naval Records, RG 45 (National Archives); hereafter cited as Jouett Report. The only mention of the third launch and its function in the expedition is found in Capt. H. Eagle, commanding, "Abstract of Logbook, USS *Santee*," *CRWR-Navies*, I, 16, 759. The entry for November 7, 1861, states, "At 11:40 p.m. the third cutter, commanded by Mr. Lambert, Master's Mate, also left to be stationed at the beacon to be a guide to answer signals."

6. Capt. H. Eagle, commanding, Logbook of U.S. Navy ship, USS *Santee*, November 1861, Records of the Office of Naval Records, RG 45. Daily events described between November 5 and November 11, 1861, were extracted from this logbook. It contains data about daily on-board activities and ancillary information such as tides, winds, temperature, water depth, ship's location, and observations of other ships.

7. There seemed to be minor confusion between Jouett and Eagle in regard to the primary target and sequence of events for the expedition. According to Eagle's order as cited, Eagle to Jouett and Mitchell, *CRWR-Navies*, I, 16, 756, the primary objective was to first capture the schooner (the *Royal Yacht*), then make an attempt to capture the *General Rusk*. In Jouett to Eagle, Nov. 14, 1861, *CRWR-Navies*, I, 16, 757, Jouett states, "if we could pass the armed schooner guarding the channel and the Bolivar and (Fort) Point forts, to try to surprise and burn the man-of-war steamer *General Rusk*, lying under Pelican Island Fort (Jackson)." In Jouett Report, 4, Jouett states, "Our plan was to surprise the *General Rusk* under cover of the darkness, that being the larger craft, and afterwards to capture the *Royal Yacht*. In case we were discovered, our orders were not to attempt to capture the *General Rusk*, that vessel being too strong to warrant an attack by our small force unless we could surprise her." In W. W. Carter to Jouett, May 9, 1879 (filed with Jouett Report; hereafter cited as Carter to Jouett, May 9, 1879), Carter wrote, "We set off under your command with the purpose of destroying the *Rusk*."

8. Master P. F. Appel, C.S.N., commanding, "Logbook of CSS *Bayou City*," *CRWR-Navies*, I, 16, 864. The *Colonel Stell* was chartered for Confederate service on September 29, 1861, by the Texas Marine Department. A paddle-wheel steamship with a draft of only two and a half feet and 175 feet in length, she was armed with a variety of field artillery pieces and was protected by cotton bales; *American Fighting Ships*, II, 510.

9. Jouett to Eagle, Nov. 14, 1861, *CRWR-Navies*, I, 16, 757–758. In this, his first report, Jouett wrote, "In attempting to avoid the sentinels on Pelican fort, we grounded on [sic] Bolivar (Pelican) Spit. At this juncture we were discovered." Jouett makes no mention of the second launch ramming into the first launch, shattering several oars. In his delayed report, Jouett Report, 4–5, Jouett wrote, "Got abeam of the *General Rusk* when my boat grounded on a shoal or spit. The second launch ran into my boat breaking my oars and making a noise."

10. P. F. Appel, Logbook of CSS *Bayou City*, *CRWR-Navies*, I, 16, 864.

11. Jouett Report, 5.

12. Ibid, 6.

13. There is some confusion as to whether all of the wounded were in the first launch or whether some Union casualties were crew members on the second launch. In Eagle to William McKean, Nov. 12, 1861, *CRWR-Navies*, I, 16, 755, Eagle listed the wounded but does not state to which launch they had been assigned. John L. Emmerson, coxswain, died of his wounds on November 10. It would have been unusual for two coxswains to be assigned to the same launch, but as this was a volunteer composite command, normal manning may not have been followed. Bell was certainly the coxswain on the first launch, as per Jouett Report, 6–7. Seaman Charles Hawkins, one of the wounded on the first launch, was later awarded the Navy Medal of Honor for his gallantry in the attack on Fort Fisher, North Carolina, on December 23, 1864. See U.S. Senate, Committee on Veterans Affairs, "Medal of Honor Recipients, 1863–1973," 93rd Cong., 1st sess., 1973, Committee Print no. 15, p. 114; hereafter cited as Senate Committee, "Medal of Honor Recipients."

14. Jouett Report, 6–7. The central controversy of the expedition remains the supposed failure of the second launch to board the *Royal Yacht* on the starboard bow as ordered and its purported firing upon the first launch. In Hunter to Hebert, Nov. 11, 1861, *CRWR-Navies*, I, 16, 760, Hunter described the damage done to the *Royal Yacht*, "The Yacht was pierced with 19 musket balls on the port side; starboard side, 8, foremast, 5, in her cabin 5." This would clearly indicate that the second launch had boarded or attempted to board on the port beam. It is the author's contention that the second launch originally had attempted to board near the foremast on the starboard side, which would account for the five balls found in that area. Most likely Coxswain John L. Emmerson was standing at the tiller and was the first to fall from the sentry's firing, thus causing temporary loss of control of the launch, which likely veered to the right. After the other Confederate crew members began to fire, there simply was not enough time or opportunity to regain the starboard side. In all fairness to the second launch, the first launch was also out of position. In Jouett Report, 6, Jouett wrote, "The recoil of the gun sent the boat astern and frustrated the attempt to board." The first launch thus veered to the left toward the stern of the schooner and the boarding was nearer to the stern than the beam as intended.

15. Jouett Report, 7. Jouett may have had reason to fear the possibility of friendly fire. He was likely aware of launch expeditions from the USS *Niagara* and USS *Colorado* into Pensacola Bay on August 3, 1861, when fifteen Union sailors were wounded and three were killed. One of the dead sailors, Charles H. Lamphere, apparently was shot in the heart by friendly fire. See also Theodore Bailey to W. W. Mervine, Aug. 7, 1861, *CRWR-Navies*, I, 16, 610, and John H. Russel to W. W. Mervine, Sept. 14, 1861, *CRWR-Navies*, I, 16, 670–673.

16. Jouett Report, 8. In his second report on the attack on the *Royal Yacht*, Hunter wrote, "There was found on board of her (*Royal Yacht*), a midshipman's uniform cap, one United States cutlass, and one navy revolver, one boat's grapnel, one 12-pounder shrapnel shell, loaded, fuzed, and marked, 'U.S.N., Ordnance Department, Washington, 1861,' placed by the wooden chest used as a magazine . . . and a bloody sheet pierced with ball

holes, and one broken boarding pike." Hunter to Hebert, Nov. 11, 1861, *CRWR-Navies*, I, 16, 760.

17. Jouett to Secretary of the Navy, May 13, 1879, 10–11. Carter to Jouett, May 9, 1879, 3.

18. Jouett Report, 11, Jouett wrote, "All this time I had seen or heard nothing from the second launch since she poured a murderous fire into us just before we boarded. In fact I had ceased to count her in the fight and never knew what had become of her till I reached the Santee." In Carter to Jouett, May 9, 1879, 3, Carter wrote, "I remained engaged with the schooner's crew forward until you boarded, but shortly the cry of Santee was heard and our crew retired to their boats."

The fact that Carter used the plural "boats" indicates that, at least temporarily, the members of the second launch may have participated on board the schooner. In Hunter to Hebert, Nov. 11, 1861, *CRWR-Navies*, I, 16, 760–761, Hunter concludes after a verbal report from Capt. Leon Smith, commanding the *General Rusk*, that the *Yacht* "was surprised and attacked and boarded simultaneously on both sides by an overwhelming force of two or more launches." Most of the myriad of questions about the raid could be reconciled had Lt. John G. Mitchell filed a report on the activities of the second launch, but no such report was filed. The passed midshipman's uniform cap found on the *Royal Yacht* indicates that Mitchell at least briefly participated in the actions.

19. Jouett Report, 12. See also Mitchell S. Goldberg, "A Federal Naval Raid into Galveston Harbor, November 7–8, 1861: What Really Happened?" *Southwestern Historical Quarterly*, 76 (July, 1972), 66.

20. Jouett Report, 12. Thomas Chubb to W. W. Hunter, Oct. 9, 1861, *CRWR-Navies*, I, 16, 844. Chubb submits an agreement regarding the charter and services of the *Royal Yacht* and includes the names of the crew. They were: John E. Davidson, Thomas C. Saunders, John Greenough, Ambrose Snow, Robert Readman, Jacob Franzes, Henry N. Duble, Michael D. Connell, Peter McGenity, John Kelly, George Baker, Ira G. Rogers, M. Webb, and I. E. Davidson. See also John A. Dix and Edward Pierrepont to Lt. Col. Martin Burke, Apr. 10, 1862, *CRWR-Armies*, II, 2, 1313–1314. This report of the Commission Relating to State Prisoners says that Thomas Chubb was released on February 4, 1862, and Ira G. Rogers on February 6, 1862. The other men were incarcerated as prisoners of war at Fort Lafayette in New York Harbor.

21. Eagle stated, "Thirteen prisoners were taken, three of whom are wounded," in Eagle to McKean, Nov. 12, 1861, *CRWR-Navies*, I, 16, 755. In Eagle to Gideon Welles, Nov. 15, 1861, *CRWR-Navies*, I, 16, 757, Eagle wrote, "He was three hours in the launch pulling for the ship, and had the care of 12 prisoners and 6 of his wounded men."

22. Jouett Report, 13.

23. Upon the surrender of the Pensacola Navy Yard on January 12, 1861, Jouett was taken prisoner along with the rest of the garrison. See V. M. Randolph to Jouett, Jan. 16, 1861, *CRWR-Navies*, I, 4, 59. See also Isaac Toucey, Jan. 16, 1861, and Feb. 4, 1861, *CRWR-Navies*, I, 27, 350–351.

24. Eagle reported, "At 6:15 a.m. the first launch returned . . . At 7:30 took the launches in. From 6 to 8 hoisted up the third cutter," Eagle, Abstract of Logbook of USS *Santee*, Nov. 8, 1861, *CRWR-Navies*, I, 16, 759. Eagle's logbook entries make no extra or special mention of the second launch, only intimating "took the launches in." Both Jouett and Eagle's reports omit any mention of the second launch's part in the conflict at the *Royal Yacht*. Only in Confederate reports do we gain any insight into the second launch's part in the fight and that part seems to have been more intense than Jouett would have led one to believe. In Hunter to Hebert, Nov. 11, 1861, *CRWR-Navies*, I, 16, 760, Hunter reported that nineteen musket balls pierced the port side and eight balls pierced the starboard side, thus indicating that the second launch poured forth, at the minimum, almost two and a half times the musket and pistol fire of the first launch. See also P. F. Appel, Logbook, CSS *Bayou City*, Nov. 8, 1861, in *CRWR-Navies*, I, 16, 865. Appel reported, "Seven oars belonging to the U.S. frigate *Santee* were found on Bolivar Point." The oars were muffled and several bullet holes could be seen on the upper end, showing plainly that the schooner's crew discovered and fired into the *Santee's* boats before the crew boarded the schooner. Lights and rockets Eagle had promised to help Jouett find the *Santee* had not been displayed, which apparently created a minor tiff between the two. In Jouett Report, 14–15, Jouett explains Eagle's reason for the failure to do so because, "He (Eagle) was afraid of calling me from my work." Eagle may have believed the fire aboard the *Royal Yacht* was instead the *General Rusk*, which he knew was the first objective of the raid, with the capture of the *Royal Yacht* to follow.

25. Thomas M. Potter, ship doctor, Logbook/Medical Journal, USS *Santee*, Nov. 8, 1861, Records of the Office of Naval Records and Library, RG 24 (National Archives). See also Eagle to McKean, Nov. 12, 1861, *CRWR-Navies*, I, 16, 755.

26. Potter, Logbook/Medical Journal, USS *Santee*, Nov. 8, 1861, states "Bell, George H., Coxswain. Admitted November 8, 1861, for gunshot wound in back between scapula and vertebra, also severe contusion over thyroid cartilage. Coughed up some blood, was in near state of collapse. Ball found lodged in throat during operation, November 16."

27. Secretary of the Navy, *General Orders and Circulars Issued by the Secretary of Navy, 1863* (Washington, D.C.: U.S. Navy, 1863), 9.

28. G. H. Bell to Commissioner of Pensions, Pension file, application no. 49372, certificate no. 35894, Records of the U.S. Veterans Administration, RG 15 (National Archives). On his application form Bell wrote, "I was presented a Medal of Honor by Admiral David Porter at Hampton Roads, Virginia prior to the capture of Fort Fisher." He made no mention of the exact date nor of the vessel or circumstance of the award ceremony. In George H. Bell to Secretary of the Navy, Nov. 26, 1864, Register of Letters of Acknowledgment for Medals of Honor, January 1, 1862–December 31, 1866, Records of the Bureau of Naval Personnel, RG 24, he acknowledges receipt of his medal on November 26, 1864, from aboard the USS *Mohican*.

29. Senate Committee, "Medal of Honor Recipients"; Secretary of the Navy, General Order no. 17, July 10, 1863, 29. In W. F. Beyer and O. F. Keydel, *Deeds of Valor: How America's Heroes Won the Medal of Honor* (2 vols.; Detroit: Perrien-Keydel Co., 1903),

II, 8–10, page 9 features a pictorial depiction of the raid entitled, "The Destruction of the Royal Yacht," by " –Henderson, 1901." The picture erroneously shows a steam launch.

Only four Navy Medal of Honor deeds were chronologically earlier than George H. Bell's. These were John Williams (June 26, 1861), Benjamin Swearer (August 29, 1861), William Thompson (November 7, 1861), and John Williams (November 7, 1861).

CHAPTER 2
A Wild Reconnaissance on Matagorda Peninsula

1. John Y. Simon (ed.), *The Papers of Ulysses S. Grant* (22 vols.; Carbondale, Ill.: Northern Illinois University Press, 1982), IX, 195–197. See also Francis S. Hesseltine, "Amusing the Enemy," Civil War Papers, Boston Commandery, Loyal Legion of the United States (Library of Congress, Washington, D.C.), 32; hereafter cited as Hesseltine, "Amusing the Enemy"; and F. S. Hesseltine to W. F. Beyer and O. F. Keydel, June 8, 1899, Beyer-Keydel Papers, Burton Collections (Detroit Public Library, Detroit, Michigan).

2. F. S. Hesseltine to T. G. Ransom, Jan. 1, 1864, *CRWR-Navies*, I, 20, 746–748. C. C. Washburn to N. P. Banks, Jan. 1, 1864, *CRWR-Navies*, I, 20, 746.

3. E. S. Rugeley to J. P. Bryan, Jan. 4, 1864, *CRWR-Navies*, I, 21, 857–858; and E. P. Turner to W. Alston, Dec. 30, 1863, *CRWR-Navies,* I, 21, 748–749.

4. Hesseltine, "Amusing the Enemy," 34. Although very detailed, Hesseltine's account transposes incidents of another reconnaissance of Matagorda on January 21–24, 1864, into his account of the December 28–31, 1863, reconnaissance. This makes conciliation of locations during the first reconnaissance extremely difficult. See T. G. Ransom to H. G. Brown, Jan. 24, 1864, *CRWR-Navies*, I, 21, 50–51; and Strong to Bell, Jan. 1, 1864, *CRWR-Navies*, I, 20, 742–743.

5. The USS *Granite City* was a 106-feet-long side-wheel steam gunboat armed with seven guns. Previously a Confederate blockade runner with a thirty-inch draft, it had been captured and re-outfitted by the U.S. Navy; see *American Fighting Ships*, II, 530. The USS *Sciota* was a 507-ton, 158-feet-long screw gunboat carrying four heavy caliber guns. See *American Fighting Ships*, VI, 382–383. See also Hesseltine, "Amusing the Enemy," 37.

6. Though unnamed in Hesseltine's accounts, his description of a German family with two sons involved in the war best fits one of the few families who resided at times on that part of the peninsula. John and Catherine Zipprian, German immigrants, maintained several lime kilns on the peninsula for making cement from oyster shells. One of these kilns was near Brown Cedar Cut, the approximate landing site for Hesseltine's detachment. United States Eighth Census (1860), Matagorda County, Texas, Population Schedule, Town of Matagorda, p. 4; Matagorda County Historical Commission, *Historic Matagorda County*, ed. Frances Parker (2 vols.; Houston: D. Armstrong, 1986), I, 106–107. See also Hesseltine, "Amusing the Enemy," 34.

7. The USS *Hatteras*, a huge 210-feet-long iron side-wheel steamer, was sunk by the CSS *Alabama* near Galveston on January 11, 1863. See *American Fighting Ships*, III, 270–271.

8. E. P. Turner to H. Bee, Dec. 30, 1863 [7:30 a.m.], and E. P. Turner to W. A. Alston, Dec. 30, 1863 [5 p.m.], *CRWR-Armies*, I, 26, 484–485. See also E. P. Turner to W. A. Alston, Dec. 31, 1863, *CRWR-Navies*, I, 20, 748–749.

9. Hesseltine to Ransom, Jan. 1, 1864, *CRWR-Navies*, I, 20, 747. C. W. Lamson may have filed a report on the *Granite City's* actions, but the logbook was lost either during the *Granite City's* capture by Confederates near Calcasieu, Louisiana, in April 1864 or its destruction by Union vessels on January 21, 1865, near Velasco, Texas. Turner to Walston, Dec. 30, 1863, *CRWR-Armies*, I, 26, 484; and Washburn to Banks, Jan. 2, 1864, *CRWR-Armies*, I, 26, 480–483.

10. A. Buchel to L. G. Aldrich, Dec. 31, 1863, *CRWR-Armies*, 1, 26, 485–486.

11. Carl L. Duaine, *The Dead Men Wore Boots* (Austin: San Felipe Press, 1966), 32; M. J. Wright, *Texas in the War* (Hillsboro, Texas: Hill Junior College Press, 1965), 100. For a biography of Buchel see Robert W. Stephens, *August Buchel: Texas Soldier of Fortune* (Dallas: s.p., circa 1973). See also Hesseltine to Ransom, Jan. 1, 1864, *CRWR-Navies*, I, 20, 746–748, and Hesseltine, "Amusing the Enemy," 36–37.

12. A small number of Buchel's scouts had flanked the breastworks earlier and joined several scouts already on the peninsula. The actions late in the evening of December 29 were the result of these men attempting to rejoin Buchel. See Buchel to L. G. Aldrich, Dec. 31, 1863, *CRWR-Navies*, I, 21, 750.

13. E. P. Turner to T. D. Woodward, Dec. 6, 1863, *CRWR-Armies*, I, 26, 487.

14. L. Smith to J. Magruder, Dec. 1, 1863, *CRWR-Armies*, I, 26, 465. Smith expressed a great deal of concern over the quality of the men assigned to man the guns on the *Carr*, stating, "they cannot speak a word of English and cannot tell their nostrils from a double barrel shotgun." They apparently became quite proficient with the guns after four weeks of training.

15. G. H. Perkins, in "Abstract of Log of U.S.S. Sciota," *CRWR-Navies*, I, 20, 747, states the initial landing site variously as twelve miles below the peninsula at Smith's Landing; Confederate officer E. P. Turner in *CRWR-Armies*, I, 26, 484, says seven miles from the mouth of Caney Creek; and Hesseltine in *CRWR-Armies*, I, 26, 482 states seven miles from the head of the peninsula, which all best approximate the landing site as Brown Cedar Cut. Eight miles down the peninsula equates to Edelbach Flats.

16. Hesseltine, "Amusing the Enemy," 39; Hesseltine to Ransom, Jan. 1, 1864, *CRWR-Armies*, I, 26, 482.

17. This is an approximation as none of the reports on the affair provide place names. This appears to be an appropriate rendezvous point for the *Carr* and *Cora* as E. S. Rugeley's report states their plan was to "land our force on the peninsula and move up to within a safe distance, reconnoiter and if prudent make the attack." See Rugeley to Turner, *CRWR-Navies*, I, 21, 857–858.

18. G. H. Perkins, "Abstract Log of the U.S.S. Sciota," Jan. 3, 1864, *CRWR-Navies*, I, 20, 745–746. Perkins to J. P. Gillis, Jan. 3, 1864, *CRWR-Navies*, I, 20, 743–744; and Carroll S. Alden, *George H. Perkins, Commodore U.S.N.: His Life and Letters* (Boston: Houghton-Mifflin Co., 1914), 166–168. Twenty-two of the younger men in the small boats were later drowned or died of exposure when their boats were swamped in the heavy swells, which was the worst home-front disaster of the war for Matagorda County. For accounts of this matter see Rugeley to Bryan, Jan. 4, 1864, *CRWR-Navies*, I, 21, 857–858; Matagorda County Historical Commission, *Historic Matagorda County*, I, 165–167; and Lorraine B. Jeter, *Matagorda, Early History* (Baltimore: Gateway Press, 1974), 88–89.

19. Hesseltine, "Amusing the Enemy," 40.

20. Ibid.

21. J. H. Strong to H. H. Bell, Jan. 1, 1864, *CRWR-Navies*, I, 20, 742–743; G. H. Perkins, "Abstract Log of U.S.S. Sciota," *CRWR-Navies*, I, 20, 745–746; and G. H. Perkins to J. P. Gillis, Jan. 3, 1864, *CRWR-Navies*, I, 20, 743–744. Confederate correspondence does not indicate the destruction of either the *Carr* or *Cora*. The vessel driven ashore was likely the *Alamo*, a smaller vessel similar in profile to the *Carr*. See also Washburn to Banks, Jan. 2, 1864, *CRWR-Armies*, I, 26, 480–481.

22. Hesseltine to Ransom, Jan. 1, 1864, *CRWR-Armies*, I, 26, 483.

23. Ibid.

24. Turner to Bee, Dec. 30, 1863, *CRWR-Armies*, I, 26, 484; Buchel to Aldrich, Dec. 31, 1863, *CRWR-Armies*, I, 26, 485.

25. T. G. Ransom to C. C. Washburn, Jan. 3, 1864 (enclosure), Beyer-Keydel Papers.

26. Ibid.

27. C. C. Washburn to C. P. Stone (chief of staff), Jan. 6, 1864, *CRWR-Armies*, I, 26, 481.

28. Hesseltine, "Amusing the Enemy," 32.

29. Hesseltine to W. F. Beyer and O. F. Keydel, June 8, 1899, Beyer-Keydel Papers. U.S. Congress, Senate, "General Staff Corps and Medals of Honor," 66th Cong., 1st sess., 1919, Sen. Exec. Doc. 58 (Serial 7609), case no. 1516, p. 347; hereafter cited as Senate, "Medal of Honor Review Board," with case number and page; and Hesseltine to Adjutant General's Office, Feb. 13, 1895, Adjutant Generals Office–Documents Received, file 408201, Office of the Adjutant General–1894 (filed with file 232745, Office of the Adjutant General–1895), RG 94 (National Archives).

CHAPTER 3

Repulsing the Tribes in Comancheria

1. N. D. Badger to Commissioner Elderken, Nov. 30, 1869, "List of Indians . . ." Kiowa–Comanche Indian Archives, Military Relations File (Oklahoma Historical Society Archives, Oklahoma City). Only 558 of the 2,458 registered Comanches were not at the

reservation. On the other hand 1,808 Kiowas, 322 Kiowa–Apaches and 400 Shawnees remained absent from the monthly registration. The Quohadas, or runaways from all tribes, who had never registered upon the reservation, were estimated at 1,960. Altogether 5,048 remained away from the reservation.

2. Ulysses S. Grant, *Personal Memoirs of U. S. Grant* (7 vols.; New York: Charles L. Webster & Co., 1886), II, 541.

3. W. C. Notson, Post Medical Record, Fort Concho, Oct. 13, 1869, Records of the Office of the Adjutant General, RG 94. Neither Notson nor Carroll mentioned the name of this Mexican informant. This was a practice Mackenzie greatly emphasized to protect the identity of spies and informants even from the eyes of clerks and adjutants. See also H. Carroll to Assistant Adjutant General, Sub-District of the Pecos, Oct. 14, 1869, 1 (filed with file 1646M–1647M, Adjutant General's Office–Letters Received, 1870), RG 94; hereafter cited as Carroll Report, Oct. 14, 1869. See M-619, roll 730, exp. 215–220. See also C. C. Rister, "Harmful Practices of Indian Traders of the Southwest, 1865–1876," *New Mexico Historical Review*, 6 (July, 1931), 240–241.

4. Most U.S. Army maps and correspondence of the period label this 2,862 feet conical-shaped peak in what is now central Borden County as Muchaque Peak. It was likely named so by the New Mexican Comancheros or Indians who came there to trade, as "mucha que" in Spanish means much of what (ever). Somehow the spelling was corrupted into its present-day name, Mushaway Peak. See "Mushaway Peak," in Ron Tyler, Douglas E. Barnett, Roy R. Barkley, Penelope C. Anderson, and Mark F. Odintz (eds.), *The New Handbook of Texas* (6 vols.; Austin: Texas State Historical Association, 1996), IV, 906.

5. H. Carroll to Assistant Adjutant General, Sub-District of the Pecos, Oct. 14, 1869, Fifth Military District, file 1646M– Fifth Military District, 1869 (copy filed with Adjutant General's Office–Documents Received, file 13892, Office of the Adjutant General, Principal Records Division, 1893), RG 94.

6. Carroll's report makes no mention of points of reference during the scout, other than the Colorado and Brazos Rivers. The points mentioned previous to Saleh Lake, and those successive points are the author's approximation of Carroll's locations as estimated from mileages and directions provided in his report.

7. Carroll Report, Oct. 14, 1869, 2–3; and G. E. Albee, Appointment, Commission, and Promotion "Personnel file," 1318, Appointment, Commission, and Promotion–1872, Records of the Adjutant General's Office, RG 94.

8. Carroll Report, Oct. 14, 1869, 4; and G. E. Albee to H. W. Lawton, July 26, 1893, Adjutant General's Office–Documents Received, file 13892, Principal Records Division–1893, RG 94; hereafter cited as Albee to Lawton, file 13892.

9. Albee to Lawton, file 13892.

10. W. C. Notson, Post Medical Record, Fort Concho, Oct. 13, 1869, RG 94. Only Notson mentions Ira J. Culver's presence in the Carroll command. Culver later became an army assistant surgeon so he may have accompanied the expedition as an acting medical officer.

11. S. A. Mulholland, *Military Order: Congressional Medal of Honor Legion of the United States* (2 vols.; Philadelphia: Town Printing, 1905), 613; and Hatch, "Record of Events," Co. L, Ninth U.S. Cavalry Regimental Returns, RG 94.

12. Carroll Report, Oct. 14, 1869; Notson, Post Medical Record, Fort Concho, Oct. 13, 1869, RG 94; and Hatch, "Record of Events," Ninth U.S. Cavalry Regimental Returns, September–October, 1869, RG 94.

13. P. M. Boehm to Assistant Adjutant General, Sub-District of the Brazos, Nov. 4, 1869, Adjutant General's Office–Documents Received, file 8059, Office of the Adjutant General–1894 (filed with Adjutant General's Office–Documents Received, file 6663, Principal Records Division–1894), RG 94; hereafter cited as Boehm Report, Nov. 4, 1869.

14. Ibid.

15. Estimates of Indian casualties may be found in Col. Edward Hatch, "Tabular Statement of Expeditions and Scouts of the Ninth United States Cavalry, for Quarter ending December 31, 1869," Department of Texas–Letters Received, box 1, RG 393 (National Archives). J. J. Reynolds to Office of the Adjutant General, General Order no. 225, Dec. 6, 1869, Adjutant General's Office–Letters Received, file 1835M, Office of the Adjutant General–1869, RG 94. The Indians, Quohadas, and Apaches later claimed that none of their members were killed during the October 28 fighting, according to an interview in B. H. Grierson to Office of the Adjutant General, Feb. 8, 1870, Adjutant General's Office–Letters Received, file 1794M, Office of the Adjutant General–1869, RG 94. See also Albee to Lawton, file 13892, and Boehm Report, Nov. 4, 1869.

16. Boehm Report, Nov. 4, 1869; and Albee to Lawton, file 13892.

17. J. W. Clous to Assistant Adjutant General, Sub-District of the Brazos, Nov. 7, 1869, Adjutant General's Office–Documents Received, file 8059, Office of the Adjutant General–1894 (filed with file 6663, Principal Records Division, Office of the Adjutant General–1894); P. M. Boehm to Assistant Adjutant General, Sub-District of the Brazos, Nov. 4, 1869 (also filed with file 6663, Principal Records Division, Office of the Adjutant General–1894), RG 94; J. W. Clous to Assistant Adjutant General, Sub-District of the Brazos, Nov. 22, 1869, Adjutant General's Office–Letters Received, file 1835M, Office of the Adjutant General–1869, RG 94; and W. C. Notson, Post Medical Record, Fort Concho, November 1869, RG 94. Albee brought one of the captives with him to Fort Concho. The fifteen-year-old Comanche girl was severely debilitated from disease and according to Notson, "his Samaritan views are probably frustrated." She was eventually returned to her tribe on the reservation near Fort Sill. In Clous's report of November 22, 1869, he reported on the interrogation of the Indian prisoners by the Tonkawa, Castile. According to Castile, two Tonkawa women and two Tonkawa boys were being held by Toshaway (Silver Knife) of the Penneteka Comanches, and Millie Jane Durgan, a white captive, was being held by the Kiowa woman, O-Mah.

18. J. Oakes to Assistant Adjutant General, Fifth Military District, Nov. 13, 1869, Department of Texas–Letters Received, file 285M; J. Clous to Assistant Adjutant General, Sub-District of the Brazos, Nov. 22, 1869, Adjutant General's Office–Letters

Received, file 1835M (filed with file 1794M, Office of the Adjutant General–1869); and B. Grierson to Office of the Adjutant General, Feb. 8, 1870, Adjutant General's Office–Letters Received, file 285, Office of the Adjutant General–1870 (filed with file 1794M, 1869), all filed with Adjutant General's Office–Documents Received, file 6663, Principal Records Division–1894, RG 94.

19. Arthur MacArthur, "Board on Distinguished and Meritorious Service," Adjutant General's Office–Documents Received, file 5461, Office of the Adjutant General–1889; G. E. Albee, Adjutant General's Office–Documents Received, file 13892, Office of the Adjutant General–1893, RG 94; and H. W. Lawton to J. M. Bacon, July 27, 1893, Adjutant General's Office–Documents Received, file 465, Office of the Adjutant General–1894, (filed with Adjutant General's Office–Documents Received, file 13892, Principal Records Division–1893), RG 94. See also Mulholland, *Military Order: Congressional Medal of Honor Legion of the United States*, II, 613–616.

20. W. Shafter to Office of the Adjutant General, Aug. 10, 1893, Adjutant General's Office–Documents Received, file 13892, Office of the Adjutant General–1893, RG 94.

21. J. M. Bacon to Office of the Adjutant General, Aug. 2, 1893; Bacon to Office of the Adjutant General, Dec. 15, 1893; and W. R. Shafter to Office of the Adjutant General, Aug. 10, 1893. All the preceding filed in Adjutant General's Office–Documents Received, file 13892, Office of the Adjutant General–1893, RG 94.

22. H. Corbin to Albee, Jan. 30, 1894, Adjutant General's Office–Documents Received, file 13892, Office of the Adjutant General–1893, RG 94; and Senate, "Medal of Honor Review Board," case no. 2206, p. 422. Apparently, due to confusion or clerical error in 1893, Albee's original citation was wrong about the deed and the date. Albee became aware of the error upon reading the War Department's updated listing of October 31, 1897. His award should have been based upon Bacon's eyewitness account in stating:

> At the onset of the engagement my camp was charged by Indians in numbers largely superior to my own, when Lieutenant Albee promptly moved out with a small detachment, and by his good management and example held the Indians in check until the command could saddle up and re-inforce him.

This statement referred to the actions of October 28, 1869. Despite Albee's September 13, 1907, and June 1, 1916, correspondence to the adjutant general, the errors were never corrected. The deed portrayed in his Medal of Honor citation was the September 16, 1869, action for "attacking with three men a force of eleven Indians and reconnoitering the country beyond." This action was also the basis for his eventual brevet to captain in 1900.

CHAPTER 4
Sergeant Stance to the Rescue

1. Fort McKavett is in Menard County, forty-five miles southeast of San Angelo. The post was named in honor of Capt. Henry McKavett, Eighth U.S. Infantry, who was killed at the battle of Monterrey during the Mexican-American War. It now is a state historical

park administered by the Texas Parks and Wildlife Department. See Vivian Smyrl, "Fort McKavett," in Tyler, et al. (eds.), *The New Handbook of Texas*, II, 111.

2. W. Steele, adjutant general, state of Texas, "Abstract (partial) of depredations by Indians, previous to and since 1870 . . .," *Transcripts from the Office of the Adjutant General of Texas, 1870–1876,* (Austin: Texas Adjutant General's Office, 1876), 154, 166–167, RG 401 (Texas State Archives, Austin); hereafter cited as "Abstract of Indian depredations." Assistant Adjutant General, Department of the Missouri, January 1870, "Tabular Statement of Murders, Outrages, Robberies and Depredations Committed by Indians in the Department of Missouri and Northern Texas in 1868 and 1869," Department of the Missouri–Letters Received, file 102R, Department of the Missouri–1870, RG 393.

3. These engagements in 1869 and early 1870 were quite destructive to the Mescalero Apaches, Comanches, and Kiowas. Their significance in the pacification of West Texas has largely been ignored. See Gen. J. J. Reynolds, "General Reynolds on Successful Combats," *Army and Navy Journal*, 6 (Oct. 9, 1869), 110. A compilation of documents on these engagements are in Adjutant General's Office, Principal Records Division, file 8059, Adjutant General's Office–Documents Received, 1894; and includes, F. S. Dodge to Assistant Adjutant General, Department of Texas, Feb. 7, 1870, Adjutant General's Office–Letters Received, file 493M, Office of the Adjutant General–1870; and J. M. Bacon to Assistant Adjutant General, Department of Texas, Feb. 7, 1870, Adjutant General's Office–Letters Received, file 494M, Office of the Adjutant General–1870, RG 94.

4. Steele, "Abstract of Indian depredations," 14–15.

5. H. Lehmann, "Nine Years Among the Indians, 1870–1879," *Frontier Times*, 40 (Feb.–Mar., 1963), 6. Herman Lehmann did not disclose the specific Apache affiliation of this raiding band but they were likely Mimbres Apaches. Phillip Buchmeier stated in an affidavit that some of the Indians spoke English, wore parts of army uniforms, wore their hair plaited, and were armed with pistols. Mimbres Apaches served briefly as U.S. Army scouts and wore plaited hair. See P. Buchmeier to Lawrie Tatum, July 2, 1870, Captives File, Comanche–Kiowa Archives, Depredations Division, Records of the Bureau of Indian Affairs, RG 75 (Oklahoma Historical Society Archives, Oklahoma City, Oklahoma).

6. United States Ninth Census (1870), Mason County, Texas, Population Schedule, 460, RG 29 (National Archives). See also Mason County Historical Commission, *Mason County Historical Book* (Mason: Mason County Historical Society, 1976), 34–35. Phillip Buchmeier married Auguste Lehmann on June 5, 1863, less than a year after her first husband, Moritz Lehmann, died. Herman and Willie were Phillip Buchmeier's stepsons.

7. Lehmann, "Nine Years Among the Indians," 7–8.

8. H. Carroll to J. L. Bullis and E. Stance, May 19, 1870, Special Order no. 73, paragraphs II and III, Special Orders Book, Post Records, Fort McKavett, Texas, p. 165, RG 94.

9. W. A. Austerman, *Sharps Rifles and Spanish Mules: The San Antonio–El Paso Mail, 1851–1881* (College Station: Texas A&M University Press), 320–321.

10. Lehmann, "Nine Years Among the Indians," 8–9; and E. Stance to Post Adjutant, Fort McKavett, May 26, 1870, Adjutant General's Office–Letters Received, file 720S, AGO–1870, RG 94; hereafter cited as Stance Report.

11. Lehmann, "Nine Years Among the Indians," 9. Lehmann was mistaken when he stated, "we ran into a party of Rangers (they were dismounted at a waterhole, preparing to camp)." He also erroneously stated that the engagement occurred near Lipan Creek.

12. Stance Report; Lehmann, "Nine Years Among the Indians," 8–9. The first clash occurred about five miles north of the Nine-Mile Waterhole in extreme northwest Menard County near the Del Vanado Ranch.

13. W. Lehmann, "Loyal Valley," *San Antonio Herald*, June 2, 1870; Stance Report; E. Maczen, "House Mountain, Llano County," *San Antonio Herald,* May 23, 1870; and Lehmann, "Nine Years Among the Indians," 9.

14. Stance Report; Hugh D. Corwin, *Comanche and Kiowa Captives in Oklahoma* (Guthrie, Okla.: Cooperative Publishing Company, 1959), 113–115.

15. Stance Report.

16. Ibid.

17. W. Lehmann, "Loyal Valley," *San Antonio Herald,* June 2, 1870. See also Post Adjutant, Fort McKavett, "Tabular Statements of Expeditions and Scouts Against Indians in the Vicinity of Fort McKavett, Texas, Second Quarter, 1870," Records of the Fifth Military District, Records of U.S. Army Continental Commands, RG 393.

18. H. Carroll to Headquarters, Sub-District of the Pecos, June 1, 1870, Adjutant General's Office–Letters Received, file 720S, Office of the Adjutant General–1870, RG 94. Stance was mentioned for meritorious service at Eagle Springs Station, December 5, 1867; Salt Fork of the Brazos River, September 16, 1869; headwaters of the Fresh Water Fork of the Brazos River, October 28–29, 1869; and headwaters of the Llano River on November 24, 1869.

19. T. M. Vincent to J. Potts, July 5, 1870, Adjutant General's Office–Letters Received, file 428EB21, Office of the Adjutant General–1870, RG 94.

20. Despite mention of a formal award ceremony in F. D. Downey, *The Buffalo Soldiers in the Indian Wars* (New York: McGraw-Hill Publishing Company, 1969), 44, the author could find no mention of a ceremony in post returns, regimental returns, post medical records, nor in Stance's letter acknowledging receipt of his medal.

21. E. Stance to Office of the Adjutant General, July 24, 1870, Adjutant General's Office–Letters Received, file 892S, Office of the Adjutant General–1870, RG 94.

CHAPTER 5
Surrounded at the Little Wichita

1. W. S. Nye, *Carbine and Lance: The Story of Old Fort Sill* (Norman: University of Oklahoma Press, 1937), 144.

2. W. R. Baker to J. Oakes, July 15, 1870, "Report of a Montague County Citizens Committee on area depredations," Department of Texas, Letters Received Book, vol. 3,

letter no. 579, pp. 173–181, RG 393; and J. Oakes to Assistant Adjutant General, Department of Texas, "Report of Persons Killed by Indians near the Post of Fort Richardson, 1st & 2nd Quarter, 1870," Department of Texas, 1870–1876, "Indian files," item 4875, box 1 RG 393; hereafter cited as "Indian files," RG 393. See also Adjutant General's Office–Letters Received, files 167 (filed with file 161M), 397T, 398T, 435T, 936, and 937, all in Adjutant General's Office–Letters Received, 1870, RG 94; I. N. Walter to Post Adjutant, Fort Richardson, June 4, 1870, Department of Texas–Letters Received, file R94, Department of Texas–1870, "Indian files," RG 393. See also Oakes to Assistant Adjutant General, Department of Texas, Sept. 12, 1870, Department of Texas–Letters Received, file R233, Department of Texas–1871, "Indian files," RG 393.

3. L. Tatum to B. Grierson, June 15, 1870, Adjutant General's Office–Letters Received, file 1075M, Office of the Adjutant General–1870, RG 94.

4. J. Oakes to Assistant Adjutant General, Department of Texas, June 2, 1870, Department of Texas, Letters Received, file R91, Department of Texas–1870, box 1, "Indian files," RG 393. Oakes to Assistant Adjutant General, Department of Texas, "Report of Persons Killed by Indians near the Post of Fort Richardson, 3rd Quarter, 1870," RG 393. See also "Dispatch from Weatherford Times," *Galveston Tri-Weekly News*, July 15, 1870, p. 1, col. 1; "Capture of U.S. Mail by Indians," *Galveston Tri-Weekly News*, July 27, 1870, p. 1, col. 4; and "Great Indian Raid," *Dallas Herald*, July 9, 1870, p. 2, col. 5.

5. Sands was passing through Fort Richardson on his way from Shreveport, Louisiana, to his assignment at Fort Griffin. He and his detachment were preparing to leave just as the three mail coach survivors appeared at the post. Post Adjutant, Post Returns, Fort Richardson, Texas, July 1870, "Casually at Post," July 5, Returns from U.S. Army Military Posts, 1800–1916, RG 94; and G. W. Hatch, Post Medical Record, Fort Richardson, Texas, July 1870, 177, RG 94.

6. C. B. McLellan to Assistant Adjutant General, Department of Texas, July 16, 1870, Department of Texas–Letters Received, file R149, Department of Texas–1870, pp. 1–10, RG 393. This is McLellan's original report of the scouting expedition. All mention of movements, times, and locations are extracted from this report. See also Adjutant General's Office–Letters Received, file 456T, Office of the Adjutant General–1870 (filed with file 2765, Office of the Adjutant General–1889), RG 94; military biographies of J. Kirk, W. Winterbottom, A. Stokes, and C. Watson are in the "Biographies" section of this book; and J. Oakes, Sixth U.S. Cavalry Regimental Returns, July 1870, "Detached Enlisted Men–Company L," RG 94.

7. James B. Dosher, "Autobiography of James B. Dosher." This unpaginated, unpublished handwritten autobiography composed from diary entries was generously provided to the author by C. H. (Buster) Bottoms of Brownfield, Texas, a great-grandson of James B. Dosher; hereafter cited as Dosher, "Autobiography," and entry date.

8. J. Oakes to Assistant Adjutant General, Department of Texas, July 17, 1870, Adjutant General's Office–Letters Received, file 456T, Office of the Adjutant General–1870 (filed with file 2765, Office of the Adjutant General–1889), RG 94; and B. Grierson to Post

Commander, Fort Richardson, Aug. 23, 1870, Department of Texas–Letters Received, files S523 and R213(5), Department of Texas–1870, "Indian files," RG 393.

9. Dosher, "Autobiography," July 12, 1870; George H. Eldridge to Office of the Adjutant General, July 27, 1916, "Application for Army Medal of Honor Roll," Adjutant General's Office–Documents Received, file 2403823, Office of the Adjutant General–1916, RG 94; and McLellan to Post Adjutant, Fort Richardson, file R149, 4–5, RG 393.

10. Dosher, "Autobiography," July 12, 1870.

11. McLellan was expecting a joint Fourth and Sixth Cavalry scouting patrol from Fort Griffin to meet him. Upon meeting Sands at the scene of the stage attack on the morning of July 6, he gave Sands a special order from Colonel Oakes that he was to deliver to Maj. G. A. Gordon, commander of Fort Griffin, which requested that Gordon immediately dispatch a force into the area of the headwaters of the Little Wichita River. The heavy rains early on the morning on July 10 prevented Sands from arriving before Gordon had already dispatched his available cavalry manpower to the northwest and southwest. Post Adjutant, Post Returns, Fort Griffin, Texas, July 1870, "Record of Events," RG 94; Post Surgeon, Post Medical Record, Fort Griffin, Texas, p. 178, RG 94; Dosher, "Autobiography," July 12, 1870; G. Eldridge, "Application for Army Medal of Honor Roll," file 2403823, Office of the Adjutant General–1916, RG 94; and J. T. Patzki, Post Medical Record, Fort Richardson, July 1870, 177–180, RG 94. See also [dispatch, *Waco Register*], "The Indian Fight in Texas," *Army and Navy Journal*, 7 (Sept. 17, 1870), 70–71; "Fight with Indians," *Dallas Herald,* Aug. 6, 1870, 1, 8; and "List of Wounded," *Dallas Herald,* Aug. 20, 1870, 2, 3.

12. G. Eldridge, "Application for Army Medal of Honor Roll," file 2403823, Office of the Adjutant General–1916, RG 94.

13. McLellan to Post Adjutant, Fort Richardson, file R149, 4–5, RG 393; and Dosher, "Autobiography," July 12, 1870.

14. Dosher, "Autobiography," July 12, 1870; McLellan to Post Adjutant, Fort Richardson, file R149, 4–5, RG 393; and J. Oakes, Sixth U.S. Cavalry Regimental Returns, July 1870, "Record of Events," RG 94.

15. John Kirk to Office of the Adjutant General, May 18, 1916, "Application for Army Medal of Honor Roll," Adjutant General's Office–Documents Received, file 2398190, Office of the Adjutant General–1916 (filed with file 1231769, Office of the Adjutant General–1916), RG 94; McLellan to Post Adjutant, Fort Richardson, file R149, 4–5, RG 393; and Dosher, "Autobiography," July 12, 1870.

16. Kirk to Office of the Adjutant General, May 18, 1916, "Application for Army Medal of Honor Roll," Adjutant General's Office–Documents Received, file 2398190, Office of the Adjutant General–1916 (filed with file 1231769, Office of the Adjutant General–1916), RG 94; Dosher, "Autobiography," July 12, 1870; and Patzki, Post Medical Record, Fort Richardson, July 1870, 177–178, RG 94.

17. A. C. Taylor to Office of the Adjutant General, Nov. 15, 1889, Adjutant General's Office, Documents Received, file 515, Office of the Adjutant General–1889 (filed with file 5461, Office of the Adjutant General, Principal Records Division–1889), RG 94.

18. Dosher, "Autobiography," July 12, 1870.

19. Ibid.

20. Ibid.

21. Patzki, Post Medical Record, Fort Richardson, July 1870, 179, RG 94. Patzki wrote that "The systemic strategy displayed by the savages exhibited an almost civilized mode of skirmish fighting, struck the officers and men engaged." See also Dosher, "Autobiography," July 12, 1870.

22. Dosher, "Autobiography," July 12, 1870; Nye, *Carbine and Lance*, 145; and Kirk to Office of the Adjutant General, May 18, 1916, Adjutant General's Office–Documents Received, file 1231769, Office of the Adjutant General–1916, RG 94.

23. McLellan to Post Adjutant, Fort Richardson, July 16, 1870, file R149, 5, RG 393.

24. Dosher, "Autobiography," July 12, 1870.

25. Patzki, Post Medical Record, Fort Richardson, July 1870, 180, RG 94; and McLellan to Post Adjutant, Fort Richardson, July 16, 1870, file R149, 10, RG 393.

26. Dosher, "Autobiography," July 12, 1870; Patzki, Post Medical Record, Fort Richardson, July 1870, 180, RG 94; and McLellan to Post Adjutant, Fort Richardson, July 16, 1870, file R149, 10, RG 393. From among all of the wounds Patzki described in detail, only Gustav Smith's corresponds to Dosher's account.

27. Dosher, "Autobiography," July 12, 1870; and McLellan to Post Adjutant, Fort Richardson, July 16, 1870, file R149, 10, RG 393.

28. Dosher, "Autobiography," July 12, 1870; McLellan to Post Adjutant, Fort Richardson, July 16, 1870, file R149, 5, RG 393; and J. Oakes, Sixth U.S. Cavalry Regimental Returns, July 1870, "Record of Events," RG 94.

29. Dosher, "Autobiography," July 12, 1870.

30. Dosher, "Autobiography," July 12, 1870; McLellan to Post Adjutant, Fort Richardson, July 16, 1870, file R149, 8–9, RG 393; and Post Commander, Fort Richardson, Post Returns–Fort Richardson, July 1870, "Record of Events," RG 94.

31. McLellan to Post Adjutant, Fort Richardson, July 16, 1870, file R149, 9, RG 393.

32. Ibid., 10.

33. J. Oakes to H. C. Wood, July 17, 1870, Department of Texas–Letters Received, file R150, Department of Texas–1870, "Indian files," RG 393. See also McLellan to Post Adjutant, Fort Richardson, July 16, 1870, file R149 [Endorsement] J. Oakes to Department of Texas, Commanding Officer, July 17, 1870, cover page, RG 393.

34. E. D. Townsend to J. J. Reynolds, Sept. 7, 1870, Adjutant General's Office, file A138, Office of the Adjutant General–1870, RG 94.

35. McLellan to Post Adjutant, Fort Richardson, July 16, 1870, Adjutant General's Office–Letters Received, file 456T, Office of the Adjutant General–1870 (filed with file 2765, Office of the Adjutant General–1889), RG 94. This file contains the letters from each recipient acknowledging receipt of their Medals of Honor.

36. Ibid. Only the letter from John Connor, dated October 23, 1870, mentions a ceremony.

37. Upon the death of a soldier a board of officers was appointed as a Council of Administration (a *pro tempore* probate court) to determine pay due, assets, debts, next of kin, and compile an inventory of personal effects. This compilation was forwarded to the second auditor's office of the Treasury Department for proper disbursal. For Given, see Lt. Adam Kramer to Office of the Adjutant General, July 19, 1870, Final statement papers, John J. Given, RG 94; "Inventory of Effects, John J. Given," Department of Texas–Letters Received, file 592, Department of Texas–1870, RG 393; and U.S. Department of the Treasury, Office of the Second Auditor, "Effects Books," ledger entry no. 589877, July 27, 1870, RG 217 (National Archives).

CHAPTER 6
Skirmish at Bluff Creek

1. G. W. Schofield to P. H. Sheridan, Feb. 5, 1870, Department of the Missouri–Letters Received, file 161M, Department of the Missouri–1870, RG 393.

2. Nye, *Carbine and Lance*, 142–143.

3. L. Tatum to J. Oakes, June 18, 1870, Department of Texas–Letters Received, file S139, Department of Texas–1870, "Indian Files," RG 393. See also Adjutant General's Office–Letters Received, file 1075M, Office of the Adjutant General–1870, RG 94.

4. A. D. Nelson to Assistant Adjutant General, Department of Missouri, Sept. 23, 1870 (filed with Adjutant General's Office–Letters Received, file 1253M, Office of the Adjutant General–1870), RG 94; and E. S. Parker to L. Tatum, May 27, 1870, Kiowa Depredations File, Indian Archives Division (Oklahoma Historical Society, Oklahoma City, Okla.).

5. Dosher, "Autobiography," circa Oct. 10, 1870; and D. Madden to Post Adjutant, Fort Richardson, Oct. 10, 1870, Adjutant General's Office–Letters Received, file 486T, Office of the Adjutant General–1870, RG 94.

6. J. Oakes to Post Adjutant, Fort Richardson, Sept. 25, 1870, Post Orders Book, RG 94. See also T. C. Tupper to Post Adjutant, Fort Richardson, Oct. 14, 1870, Sixth U.S. Cavalry Regimental History, item 835, RG 391 (National Archives).

7. D. Madden to Post Adjutant, Fort Richardson, Oct. 10, 1870, Adjutant General's Office–Letters Received, file 486T, Office of the Adjutant General–1870, RG 94.

8. J. Oakes to Post Adjutant, Fort Richardson, Special Order no. 197, Sept. 25, 1870, Special Orders Issued, 1870, Post Orders Book, RG 94.

9. W. A. Rafferty to Post Adjutant, Fort Richardson, Oct. 15, 1870, Adjutant General's Office–Letters Received, file 454T, Office of the Adjutant General–1870, RG 94; hereafter cited as Rafferty Report. All subsequent mileage and points of location were extracted from Rafferty's official report of the scout and engagement.

10. Dosher, "Autobiography," Oct. 4, 1870.

11. Ibid., Oct. 5, 1870.

12. Dosher, "Autobiography," Oct. 5, 1870; and Rafferty Report.

13. Dosher, "Autobiography," Oct. 5, 1870. The specific action of individual troopers is based partly upon Philip S. Cooke, *Cavalry Tactics or Regulations for the Instruction, Formations and Movements of the Cavalry* (Washington, D.C.: Government Printing Office, 1862), 68–71; and supplemented with Adjutant General's Office–Documents Received, files 6014–(1889), files 2113, 2261, 2367, 3228–(1890), and Maj. W. A. Rafferty, "Brevet letter, no. 18," filed with Adjutant General's Office–Documents Received, file 4352; all filed with Adjutant General's Office–Documents Received, file 5461, Office of the Adjutant General, Principal Records Division–1889, "The MacArthur Board," RG 94.

14. Dosher, "Autobiography," Oct. 5, 1870; J. Oakes, Sixth U.S. Cavalry Regimental Returns, October 1870, "Record of Events," RG 94; and Post Adjutant, Fort Richardson, to Department of Texas, "Tabular Report of Scouts and Expeditions from Fort Richardson, Texas, Fourth Quarter–1870," filed with "Indian files," RG 393.

15. Dosher, "Autobiography," Oct. 7, 1870. Private Anderson's (Smythe's) aggressive dive into the bushes in pursuit of the fleeing Indian resulted in a severe case of poison ivy exposure. See J. Patzki, "Sick Report of U.S. Troops," Post Medical Record, Fort Richardson, Oct. 10, 1870, RG 94; and J. Patzki, Post Medical Record, Fort Richardson, October 1870, 189, RG 94.

16. Rafferty Report.

17. Ibid.

18. Rafferty Report; and J. Oakes to J. Reynolds, Oct. 12, 1870, Adjutant General's Office–Letters Received, file 454T, Office of the Adjutant General–1870, RG 94.

19. J. Reynolds to W. T. Sherman, Oct. 24, 1870, Adjutant General's Office–Letters Received, fiie 454T, Office of the Adjutant General–1870, RG 94.

20. W. T. Sherman to E. D. Townsend, Nov. 9, 1870, Adjutant General's Office–Letters Received, file 454T, Office of the Adjutant General–1870, RG 94.

21. Cpl. Daniel Keating acknowledged receipt of his medal on January 1, 1871, but returned it with a request that the erroneous engraving of his first name be corrected. Letters from all but Dosher acknowledging receipt of their medals are in Adjutant General's Office–Letters Received, files 366, 369, 426, 683, and 796, Office of the Adjutant General–1871 (filed with file 454T, Office of the Adjutant General–1870 in M-619, roll 821, exposures, 0675-0682), RG 94.

22. Senate, "Medal of Honor Review Board," case no. 995 (Dosher), 114; and case no. 2476 (Anderson, Bowden, Keating, Welch, and Wilson), 435–436.

23. U.S. Army, Board for Correction of Military Records, June 12, 1989, docket no. AC88-10374, in the case of William F. Cody (deceased), Department of the Army, Washington, D. C.

24. "Ceremony Honoring Texas Medal of Honor Recipients and Restoration of the Medal of Honor to James B. Dosher," Dec. 4, 1991, *1941: Texas Goes to War* conference, University of North Texas, Denton, Texas. See also Nita Thurman, "Frontier-era Texan regains Medal of Honor; World War II heroes also lauded," *Dallas Morning News*, Dec. 5, 1991, sec. A, pp. 33, 35, and 49.

Notes to pages 85-88

CHAPTER 7
Ambushed in Congrejo Canyon

1. U.S. House, Committee on Military Affairs, "Reduction of the Military Establish-ment," Hearings on House Report 384 (W. T. Sherman testimony, Jan. 30–31, 1874), 43rd Cong., 1st sess., 1874 (Serial 1615), 270–275. See also Adjutant General's Office–Letters Received, file 1305, Office of the Adjutant General–1871, for transcripts and correspondence dealing with the inspection tour at the time of the Warren train mas-sacre. See National Archives Microcopy no. 666, roll 10, exposures 118–303. The best rendering of the army's dilemma of instituting Reconstruction policies and moving troops to the frontier appears in William L. Richter, *The Army in Texas During Reconstruction, 1865–1870* (College Station: Texas A&M University Press, 1987), 66–71. See also Robert G. Carter, *On the Border with Mackenzie: or Winning West Texas from the Comanches* (Washington, D.C.: Eynon Printing Co., 1935), 82, for Carter's personal experience with General Sherman.

2. House Committee, "Reduction of the Military Establishment," 273–274. See also Nye, *Carbine and Lance,* 159–184; and C. C. Rister, *Border Captives,* 166.

3. The best rendering of this incident, considered the worst Indian depredation in North Texas, is in Benjamin Capps, *The Warren Wagontrain Raid* (New York: The Dial Press, 1974). The trial of the Indian chiefs involved appears in C. C. Rister, "The Significance of the Jacksboro Indian Affair of 1871," *Southwestern Historical Quarterly,* 29 (Jan., 1926), 181–200.

4. The best day-to-day account of the 1871 joint Grierson–Mackenzie Expedition can be found in Robert G. Carter, "Itenerary of March to Indian Territory, etc. 1871," Robert G. Carter Diary, Aug. 2, 1871–Sept. 7, 1871, item no. 89, Earl Vandale Collection (Center for American History, University of Texas at Austin; hereafter cited as CAH). For preparations for the second expedition see Mackenzie correspondence, Sept. 6, 1871–Oct. 2, 1871, Letters Sent, 1871, Fourth U.S. Cavalry Expedition Letterbook, Expedition Records, Records of U.S. Army Mobile Commands, RG 391; hereafter cited as Fourth U.S. Cavalry Expedition Letterbook. See also Mackenzie, Fourth U.S. Cavalry Regimental Returns, Sept.–Oct. 1871, "Record of Events," Records of Regular U. S. Army Cavalry Regiments, 1833–1916, RG 94; hereafter cited as Fourth U.S. Cavalry Returns; and C. C. Rister, *Fort Griffin on the Texas Frontier* (Norman: University of Oklahoma Press, 1956), 87. An excellent map delineating Mackenzie's 1871–1872 route through Shackelford, Throckmorton, and Haskell Counties may be found in G. P. Buell to C. C. Augur, May 6, 1873, Department of Texas–Letters Received, file 1906, Department of Texas–1873, "Indian files," RG 393.

5. H. M. Smith to Secretary of War W. W. Belknap, Oct. 1, 1871, Department of Texas–Letters Received, file 1791, Department of Texas–1871, "Indian files," RG 393; Mackenzie to Assistant Adjutant General, Department of Texas, Nov. 16, 1871, Department of Texas–Letters Received, file 2120, Department of Texas–1871, "Indian files," RG 393; and Carter, *On the Border with Mackenzie,* 167–168.

366

6. Carter, *On the Border with Mackenzie,* 161–164. Edward M. Heyl had transferred to the Fourth Cavalry on January 1, 1871. During the Civil War he had compiled an outstanding combat record as a sergeant and lieutenant with the Third Pennsylvania Volunteer Cavalry. During his 1867–1870 service with the Ninth Cavalry, he incurred no less than six wounds and participated with distinction in actions against Indians on at least five occasions. "Personnel file, Edward M. Heyl," file 4143, Appointment, Commission and Promotion file–1873, Records of the Adjutant General, RG 94. Francis B. Heitman, *Historical Register and Dictionary of the U.S. Army, 1789–1903.* (Washington, D.C.: Government Printing Office, 1903), 527. See Mackenzie to Office of the Adjutant General, Dec. 3, 1869, Adjutant General's Office–Letters Received, file 1835M, Office of the Adjutant General–1869 (filed with Adjutant General's Office–Documents Received, file 13892, Principal Records Division, 1893), RG 94, for Mackenzie's praise and citation of Heyl's gallantry. See also Adjutant General's Office–Documents Received, file 6663, Principal Records Division, Office of the Adjutant General–1894, RG 94. For Mackenzie's response to Tatum's request to recover the two Smith boys, see Mackenzie to Assistant Adjutant General, Department of Texas, Nov. 16, 1871, Department of Texas–Letters Received, file 2120, Department of Texas–1871, "Indian files," RG 393.

7. Carter, *On the Border with Mackenzie,* 165–168. The author believes the location of this campsite to be a sub-canyon on the east side of the White River, approximately 3.6 miles southeast, below the State Highway 193 bridge over the White River. The site is delineated upon U.S. Geological Survey, Mount Blanco, 1966 series, quadrangle map at Latitude, 33°45′30″ North and Longitude, 101°11′30″ West. In Mackenzie to Assistant Adjutant General, Department of Texas, Nov. 15, 1871, Department of Texas–Letters Received, file 521, Department of Texas–1871, RG 393, he reported that sixty-six horses were lost. See also Robert G. Carter, "The Midnight Alarm and Attack," typescript, Panhandle-Plains Historical Historical Museum Archives (Panhandle-Plains Historical Museum, Canyon, Texas), 5–7.

8. Carter, *On the Border with Mackenzie,* 167–168.

9. "Crawfish Creek," in Tyler, et al. (eds.), *The New Handbook of Texas,* II, 394. The author believes that the initial contact with the Quohadas occurred approximately 2.5 miles west of the confluence of Crawfish Creek with the White River. The site is approximately 1.4 miles south on State Highway 651 from its intersection with State Highway 193 and is on the present-day J. Bridwell Ranch. A rough sketch of the area Carter drew circa 1920 entitled, "Battle of Blanco Canyon," is part of the Ernest Wallace Collection at Texas Tech University at Lubbock. A copy may also be found in the Crosby County Pioneer Memorial Museum Archives at Crosbyton in *Crosby County Historical Survey Committee Newsletter,* 6, no. 4 (1971), 1. The author believes the deep ravine mentioned and depicted in the sketch was Crawfish Creek. Lt. W. A. Hoffman's map labeled the sub-canyon through which Crawfish Creek flows as Canyon Congrejo. See W. A. Hoffman, "Map of Portions of Young and Bexar Counties, Texas," 3Y23, map 70, folder 1189/3, M. L. Crimmins Collection, CAH.

10. Carter, *On the Border with Mackenzie,* 171. See also Carter, "The Midnight Alarm and Attack," 8.

11. Carter, "The Midnight Alarm and Attack," 8.

12. Each Indian tribe had distinctive markings on its arrows, but by 1871 most Southern Plains tribes had acquired firearms, making identification of Indian tribes at battle or crime scenes difficult. See House Committee, "Reduction of the Military Establishment," Gen. W. T. Sherman testimony, 275; and J. T. Patzki, Annual Report–1869, Post Surgeon, Fort Richardson, Texas, 192 (copy in box 2D15, M. L. Crimmins Collection, CAH) for comments on Indian use of firearms. Carter, *On the Border with Mackenzie*, 182, credits Comanches under Chief Quanah Parker as the opposing Indians. The author chose to affix the deeds to the Quohada Comanches under the Chief Para-o-coom, as per an actual Indian participant, the Comanche Cohaya, in Nye, *Carbine and Lance*, 195.

13. Carter, "The Midnight Alarm and Attack," 9.

14. Carter, *On the Border with Mackenzie,* 175. Carter never exposed or addressed a reason or excuse for Heyl's sudden retreat, saying only in *On the Border with Mackenzie*, 186, that, "Heyl later in 1888 admitted to Henry W. Lawton that, 'it was the bluest moment of his military life.'" The author believes the retreat occurred because Heyl's men simply could not maintain sufficient fire to effectively retard the Indians' advance in their front. Heyl's Company K was the only company in the regiment equipped with multiple varieties of carbines in a field test experiment. The seventy-five members of the company were armed variously with Springfield, Remington, and Sharps .50-caliber breech-loading carbines. All other companies in the regiment were armed with .50-caliber rifled Spencer carbines. The Spencer had a tubular magazine inserted into the butt plate of the stock and could be fired in a rapid seven-shot mode or as a single-shot breech-loader. Carter's squad was thus able to deliver a more intense fire. See Ordnance-General, "Summary Statement of Ordnance and Ordnance Stores on Hand in Regular and Volunteer Army Organizations, 1862–1876, Fourth U.S. Cavalry, During the Fourth Quarter, 1871," vol. 9, Records of the Office of the Ordnance General, RG 156 (National Archives).

15. Carter, "The Midnight Alarm and Attack," 10; Carter, *On the Border with Mackenzie*, 175.

16. Carter, "The Midnight Alarm and Attack," 10. See also Nye, *Carbine and Lance*, 195, for the Indian version of the affair.

17. Carter, "The Midnight Alarm and Attack," 11. Mackenzie much preferred the Spencer carbine with its tubular magazine for cavalry use in field campaigns. His only reservation, possibly referring to the Gregg affair, was that the spiral spring in the tubular magazine weakened when carried loaded on long scouts and would fail to chamber a round in desperate situations. See Mackenzie to Chief of Ordnance, Feb. 10, 1873, Fourth U.S. Cavalry Letterbook, Letters Sent, item 14, RG 391.

18. Carter, "The Midnight Alarm and Attack," 12–13.

19. Ibid., 12.

20. Carter, *On the Border with Mackenzie*, 181–182.

21. Carter, *On the Border with Mackenzie*, 182. Some sources state Gregg's first name as Seander, but the Register of Enlistments lists him as Leander, as do the Fourth U.S.

Cavalry Regimental Returns from October 1871. See U.S. Army, Office of the Adjutant General, Register of Enlistments in the U.S. Army, 1798–1914, National Archives Microcopy no. 233, roll 36, p. 343, entry 708, RG 94; and R. S. Mackenzie, Returns from Fourth U.S. Cavalry, October, 1871, Returns from Regular Army Cavalry Regiments, 1833–1916, National Archives Microcopy no. 744, roll 41, RG 94; hereafter cited as Regimental Returns. See also United States Eighth Census (1860), Belmont County, Ohio, Population Schedule, Goshen Township, 153, National Archives Micropcopy no. 653, roll 937, RG 29. Carter, "The Midnight Attack and Alarm," 14, describes Gregg's burial site as under the shadow of the butte (Mount Blanco) at its southeast foot. In Carter's sketch, "Battle of Blanco Canyon," at the Crosby County Pioneer Museum Archives, he clearly indicates the site to be on the west side of the White River. The canyon's most prominent feature, Mount Blanco, is a 280-feet high, bulbous rim of the escarpment, dissected by State Highway 193 on the canyon's eastern rim. Several prominent twin-faced extensions of the escarpment, or buttes, as Carter designated them, may be found along the northwest rim of Crawfish Creek sub-canyon (Congrejo Canyon). The site in the author's estimation appears on USGS, Floydada, SE, quadrangle map, series 1966 at Latitude, 33°47' North and Longitude, 101°16' West.

22. Carter, *On the Border with Mackenzie*, 185.

23. Carter, *On the Border with Mackenzie,* 198. In his initial report, Mackenzie to Assistant Adjutant General, Department of Texas, Nov. 15, 1871, Department of Texas–Letters Received, file 521, Department of Texas–1871, RG 393, he omits mention of his arrow wound of October 15, stating only the reason for his early return as, "on account of sickness." The Fourth Cavalry Regimental Return for October 1871 states, "the two Comanches were killed, after wounding Colonel Mackenzie in the thigh." Mackenzie likely omitted mentioning the wound to circumvent a move within the War Department at the time, which referred all active-duty officers with multiple service-incurred wounds before retirement boards for examination.

24. Carter's non-presence during the 1874 Indian Territory–Staked Plains campaign is clearly demonstrated in entries in Returns from Regular U.S. Army Cavalry Regiments, 1833–1916, Fourth U.S. Cavalry, September–December, 1874, National Archives Microcopy no. 744, roll 42, which lists him as, "Absent on sick leave"; and R. G. Carter to Assistant Adjutant General, Department of Texas, Nov. 28, 1874, "Certificates of Disability," filed variously from Bradford and Newtonville, Massachusetts, during the time of the campaign in "Personnel file, Robert G. Carter," Appointment, Commission and Promotion file 3679, Office of the Adjutant General–1873, RG 94. See also Carter to Assistant Adjutant General, Department of Texas, Register of Letters Received, Department of Texas, 1873–1874, 33, 300, 499, RG 393. For a critical examination of the non-presence and en absentia literary work on the book, *On the Border with Mackenzie*, see W. G. Tudor, "Was Carter with Mackenzie at the Palo Duro in 1874?" paper presented at West Texas Historical Association annual meeting, Mar. 30, 1992, Alpine, Texas (copy in author's possession).

25. R. G. Carter to Office of the Adjutant General, Mar. 22, 1875, Adjutant General's Office–Letters Received, file 1524, Office of the Adjutant General–1875, RG 94.

26. Carter to Office of the Adjutant General, Nov. 6, 1897, Adjutant General's Office–Documents Received, file 65174, Office of the Adjutant General–1897; Carter to Office of the Adjutant General, Dec. 22, 1898, Adjutant General's Office–Documents Received, file 178520, Office of the Adjutant General–1898; and Carter to Office of the Adjutant General, Feb. 28, 1900, Adjutant General's Office–Documents Received, file 312711, Office of the Adjutant General–1900, all of the preceding filed with, "Personnel file, Robert G. Carter," Appointment, Commission and Promotion file 3679, Office of the Adjutant General–1873, RG 94. See also Carter, "Medal of Honor papers," Adjutant General's Office–Documents Received, file 65174, Principal Records Division–1897, RG 94; and Carter, *On the Border with Mackenzie,* 210–212.

27. J. M. Wainwright, "Book Reviews," *Journal of the U.S. Cavalry Association,* 44 (Nov.–Dec., 1935), 72–73.

CHAPTER 8

Striking the Comancheros on Beals Creek

1. Pursuit of marauding Indians or bandits across the border into Mexico was not allowed until a formal agreement between the two nations was signed on July 29, 1882. See U.S. Army, Office of the Adjutant General, "Compiled papers relating to the Frelinghuysen-Romero Agreement of July 29, 1882," Adjutant General's Office–Letters Received, file 663, Office of the Adjutant General–1883, National Archives Microcopy no. 689, roll 81, RG 94. Pursuit of depredating Indians by the U.S. Army onto Indian reservations in the Indian Territory was not allowed until July 21, 1874. See Robert M. Utley, *Frontier Regulars: The U.S. Army and the Indians, 1866–1891* (New York: Macmillan, 1973), 195–216.

2. F. L. Britton, Annual Report for the year of 1872, Exhibit F, "Statement of Depredations by Indians in the State of Texas, Previous to 1872," 229, Records of the Adjutant General of the State of Texas, RG 401.

3. Ibid.

4. D. R. Clendenin to J. W. Pullman, May 13, 1871, District of New Mexico–Letters Received, file U48, District of New Mexico–1871, RG 393; and Clendenin to J. I. Gregg, May 31, 1871, District of New Mexico–Letters Received, file U60, District of New Mexico–1871, RG 393, as cited in C. L. Kenner, *A History of New Mexican–Plains Indian Relations* (Norman: University of Oklahoma Press, 1969), 167, 184, 186–187. The Comancheros' infrastructure could have been broken by these captures but for the manner in which they were prosecuted. See Kenner, *History of New Mexican–Plains Indian Relations,* 189–190.

5. For in-depth coverage of the Comanchero trade system see C. C. Rister, "Harmful Practices of Indian Traders of the Southwest, 1865–1876," *New Mexico Historical Review,* 6 (July, 1931), 231–248; J. E. Haley, "The Comanchero Trade," *Southwestern Historical Quarterly,* 38 (Jan., 1935), 157–176; C. L. Kenner, *History of New Mexican–Plains Indian Relations,* 155–200; and Texas Historical Commission, "Archaeology of Mackenzie Reservoir," *Archaeological Survey Report,* 24 (1978), 36–38.

6. Kenner, *History of New Mexican–Plains Indian Relations*, 158–159.

7. H. Carroll to Assistant Adjutant General, Sub-District of the Pecos, Oct. 14, 1869, Fifth Military District–Letters Received, file 1646M, Fifth Military District–1869 (filed with Adjutant General's Office–Documents Received, file 13892, Office of the Adjutant General, Principal Records Division–1893), RG 94.

8. J. M. Hunter, *The Bloody Trail in Texas* (Bandera, Tex.: Hunter Publishing, 1931), 120, 124. Hunter's account contains several errors and omissions on significant aspects of the Cato affair. Among those is his failure to completely identify Cato and the time frame of his activities. Marshall Cato may have been Hunter's subject. See United States Ninth Census (1870), Bexar County, Texas, Population Schedule, Fort Concho and vicinity, 12 for Marshall Cato, 14 for James R. Cloud, and 17 for Cato Mitchell, the domestic servant for Lt. George G. Lott of the Eleventh U.S. Infantry. As of 1872, Cato was seventeen years old and Marshall was twenty-five. Possibly brothers, both were listed as being from Oakland (Yalobusha County), Mississippi.

9. Some, like D. H. Biggers, *Shackelford County Sketches* (Albany, Tex.: The Clear Fork Press, 1974), 101–102, give the date as March 6, 1868. The author believes the date was December 5, 1873; see Fort Griffin Post Returns, "Record of Events," December 1873, RG 94.

10. Carter, *On the Border with Mackenzie*, 388–389.

11. Although, as cited previously, Lawrie Tatum, the Kiowa–Comanche Reservation agent, and a devout Quaker, cooperated with military officials by sending out written warnings of impending raids, most other Quakers involved in Indian Bureau affairs refused to admit the guilt of their charges. See J. M. Haworth to C. Beede, May 8, 1873, in D. H. Winfrey and J. M. Day (eds.), *The Indian Papers of Texas* (5 vols.; Austin: Pemberton Press, 1966), IV, item 216, 333–335; and T. Battey, *Life and Adventures of a Quaker Among the Indians* (Boston: Lee and Shephard, 1891; reprint, Williamstown, Mass.: Cornerhouse Publishers, 1972), 238–240.

12. W. Wilson to Assistant Adjutant General–Department of Texas, Mar. 29, 1872, Tabular Statements of Expeditions and Scouts Against Indians in Adjacent Territory, Post of Fort Concho, During the First Quarter, 1872, RG 393; and Sgt. William Wilson to Post Adjutant, Fort Concho, Mar. 29, 1872, Adjutant General's Office–Letters Received, file 1582, Office of the Adjutant General–1872, RG 94; hereafter cited as Wilson Report. All directions, duration of travel, and events of Wilson's detachment were extracted from these two documents, which Sergeant Wilson wrote.

13. Wilson Report and United States Tenth Census (1880), Tom Green County, Texas, Population Schedule, Town of San Angelo, dwelling 206, family 206, p. 381. As of 1872 Gabriel Monroe was twenty-five years old. He was originally from near Santa Fe, New Mexico, and served as one of the guides at Fort Concho for more than a decade.

14. Wilson Report.

15. Wilson Report. The only detailed map of the area found was drawn by Lt. John Conline, Ninth U.S. Cavalry, circa May 1872. The map was likely constructed from Lt. William Hoffman's field notes. Hoffman had accompanied Capt. N. B. McLaughlin's

April 27–May 13, 1872 reconnaissance expedition. Apalonio Ortiz accompanied the expedition and directed its movements. The purpose of the expedition was to gauge the veracity of Ortiz's disclosures to Maj. J. P. Hatch. The author used the streams, prominent points, directions, and distances from this map to correlate with Wilson's report to arrive at a battle site estimate. Ortiz later stated to Hatch that his place of capture was "a fork of the Colorado, fifty miles from Fort Concho," which equates to present-day Beals Creek, designated as Point of Rocks Creek on Conline's map. This map was drawn up in May 1872 but was not submitted to Department of Texas Headquarters until 1874. See John Conline, Department of Texas–Letters Received, file 3404, Department of Texas–1874, RG 393; and N. B. McLaughlin to J. P. Hatch, May 5, 1872, Department of Texas–Letters Received, file 1385, Department of Texas–1872, RG 393.

16. Wilson Report. The Secretary of War, upon examining Wilson's report, requested a more specific report as to whether the people involved were American citizens or Mexican trans-border raiders. See E. D. Townsend to Augur, May 20, 1872, Department of Texas–Letters Received, file 1494, Department of Texas–1872, RG 393.

17. Wilson Report.

18. W. C. Notson, Post Medical Record, Fort Concho, March 1872, vol. 205, 58–59, RG 94.

19. United States Ninth Census (1870), San Miguel County, New Mexico Territory, Population Schedule, Town of La Cuesta, dwelling 19, family 16, 66, RG 29. At the time of his capture, Ortiz was a married twenty-nine-year-old farm laborer with a four-year-old daughter.

20. J. P. Hatch to G. Granger, Mar. 31, 1872, District of New Mexico–Letters Received, file C.31, District of New Mexico–1872, District of New Mexico, Military Division of the Missouri, RG 393; J. P Hatch to Assistant Adjutant General, Department of Texas, Apr. 15, 1872, Department of Texas–Letters Received, file 73, Department of Texas–1872, RG 393; J. P Hatch to G. Granger, Apr. 16, 1872, District of New Mexico–Letters Received, file C-36, District of New Mexico–1872, RG 393; A. Ortiz to J. Hatch, May 21, 1872, Department of Texas–Letters Received, file 1478, Department of Texas–1872, RG 393. See also E. Wallace, *Ranald S. Mackenzie's Official Correspondence Relating to Texas, 1871–1873* (Lubbock: West Texas Museum Association, 1967), 45–51, 69–71; and J. W. Clous to Office of the Adjutant General, Adjutant General's Office–Letters Received, files 2346, 2566, Office of the Adjutant Genral–1874, RG 94. During his original interrogation on March 31, 1872, Ortiz intentionally misstated the names of his comrades and their addresses. He disclosed the correct names and addresses on April 14, 1872, when informed of the seriousness of his crime, and when promised a possible recommendation of a pardon for his continued cooperation.

21. J. P. Hatch to Assistant Adjutant General, Department of Texas, Mar. 30, 1872, Adjutant General's Office–Letters Received, file 1582, Office of the Adjutant General–1872, RG 94.

22. C. C. Augur to P. H. Sheridan, Apr. 17, 1872, Adjutant General's Office–Letters Received, file 1582, [first endorsement] Office of the Adjutant General–1872, RG 94.

23. Ibid., third endorsement.

24. C. C. Augur to Expedition Adjutant, June 13, 1872, Fourth U.S. Cavalry Expedition Letterbook, Letters Received, 1872, p. 5, RG 391.

25. W. Wilson to Expedition Adjutant, July 21, 1872, Fourth U.S. Cavalry Expedition Letterbook, Letters Received, 1872, p. 6, item 14, RG 391.

CHAPTER 9
Ambush at Salt Creek

1. Austerman, *Sharps Rifles and Spanish Mules*, 200–204, 320.

2. Ibid., 320–321. See also War Department of the United States, *Indian Hostilities in Texas, 1871–1872* (Washington, D.C.: War Department, 1894), 26–27; and W. Steele, "Abstract (partial) of depredations by Indians previous to and since 1873 so far as reported to the Adjutant General's Office, State of Texas," in *Transcripts from the Office of the Adjutant-General of Texas, 1870–1876* (Austin: Adjutant General's Office, 1876), 14–15, RG 401.

3. W. Merritt to Assistant Adjutant General, Department of Texas, Apr. 29, 1872, Adjutant General's Office–Letters Received, file 1850, Office of the Adjutant General–1872, RG 94. See also Z. R. Bliss, "Reminiscences of Zenas R. Bliss, Major General, U.S. Army, 1854–1876," vol. 5, box 2Q441, Zenas R. Bliss Reminiscences, 1854–1894 (CAH); hereafter cited as Bliss, "Reminiscences, 1854–1876"; and Marcella Lera to P. Cusack, June 20, 1872, Adjutant General's Office–Letters Received, file 1850, Office of the Adjutant General–1872, RG 94. Gen. C. C. Augur, commanding the Department of Texas, clearly attempted to conceal the negligence of not sending an escort with an arms shipment. In Merritt's April 29 report he stated, "A number of arms and supply of ammunition was taken from the train by the band before burning it, how many arms I cannot say. It was the supply which was lately sent from the arsenal at San Antonio to Fort Stockton." In Augur to J. B. Fry, May 3, 1872, Adjutant General's Office–Letters Received, file 1850, Office of the Adjutant General–1872, RG 94, Augur wrote, "Merritt is mistaken in saying there were arms and ammunition on the train. The only ordnance stores on the train belonging to the Army were some bridles and saddles and horse equipment." All army correspondence on this affair is in Adjutant General's Office–Letters Received, 1872, file 1850, Office of the Adjutant General–1872, RG 94. In Nye, *Carbine and Lance*, 203, he cites a letter from C. Beede to E. Hoag, June 21, 1872, in which Beede, critical of the army's role in Indian affairs, referred to the Howards Well affair and stated, "it furnished the Indians with an ample supply of the latest and most approved style of arms and plenty of ammunition."

4. Austerman, *Sharps Rifles and Spanish Mules*, 215, 236, 249–250.

5. Steele, "Abstract (partial) of depredations," 14–15; and War Department, *Indian Hostilities in Texas*, 27.

6. G. P. Buell, Eleventh U.S. Infantry Returns, "Record of Events," July 1872, RG 94; and Austerman, *Sharps Rifles and Spanish Mules*, 321–322.

7. Jack County Genealogical Society, *The History of Jack County, Texas* (Dallas: Curtis Media Corporation, 1985), 16; Ida L. Huckaby, *Ninety-Four Years in Jack County, 1854–1948* (Waco: Texian Press, 1974), 28–34; and J. Creaton, "John Creaton, An Autobiography, 1856–1932," box 2Q490, vol. 5, p. 8, John Creaton Autobiography and Reminiscences, 1856–1932 (CAH); hereafter cited as Creaton, "Autobiography."

8. U.S. Army, Office of the Adjutant General, Register of U.S. Army Enlistments, 1866, entry 2032, National Archives Microcopy no. 233, roll 31, RG 94; United States Seventh Census (1850), Westchester County, New York, Population Schedule, Town of Cortlandt, 250, RG 29; United States Ninth Census (1870), Shackelford County, Texas, Population Schedule, Fort Griffin, 124, RG 29; and United States Eleventh Census (1890), Lincoln County, New Mexico, Special Schedule, Veteran Census, Town of Ruidoso, 1, RG 29.

9. U.S. Army, Office of the Adjutant General, Register of Enlistments, 1871, June 7, 1871, entry 476, RG 94. The spelling of his surname in the register is McDonnold. In other official records, except for his letter acknowledging receipt of his medal, it is spelled McDonald. The author uses the spelling of the recipient and the recruiting officer, rather than a variety of clerks' assumed spelling of the more common form of the name.

10. Frank Taylor was killed near Salt Creek, eight miles east of Fort Belknap, on May 31, 1870. The Rock Creek Station, sometimes referred to as Murphy's Station, was attacked on July 6, 1870. The driver and two passengers on an arriving coach narrowly escaped. J. Oakes to Assistant Adjutant General, Department of Texas, June 2, 1870, Department of Texas–Letters Received, file R91, Department of Texas–1870, "Indian files," RG 393. For the reports of mid-1872 Indian attacks in the immediate area of Salt Creek and the stage station at Belknap, see J. Whitney to Post Adjutant, Fort Griffin, June 27, 1872, Adjutant General's Office–Letters Received, file 3016, Office of the Adjutant General–1872 (filed with file 1582, Office of the Adjutant General–1872) on Luckett's surveying party; and D. P. Taylor to Post Adjutant, Fort Griffin, July 9, 1872, Adjutant General's Office–Letters Received, file 3367, Office of the Adjutant General–1872, on the B. Peebles killing. All of these reports are in RG 94.

11. See the U.S. Army compiled papers on the affair in Adjutant General's Office–Letters Received, file 1305, Office of the Adjutant General–1871, RG 94. See also Carter, *On the Border with Mackenzie*, 81; Nye, *Carbine and Lance*, 126–131; and H. Strong, *My Frontier Days and Indian Fights on the Plains of Texas* (Wichita Falls, Texas: n.p., circa 1925), 21.

12. C. C. Augur, Aug. 20, 1872, General Order no. 17, General Orders and Circulars Issued, 1871–1872, RG 393 (copy in Frank Kell Collection, CAH); hereafter cited as General Order no. 17, Aug. 20, 1872. The author estimates the attack to have occurred between eight and nine miles east of Fort Belknap, at the point where present-day U.S. Highway 380 crosses Salt Creek at the northernmost extent of Lake Graham. The only map of the area for 1872

was found in T. A. Baldwin to Post Adjutant, Fort Richardson, March 1873, Department of Texas–Letters Received, file 2343, Department of Texas–1873, "Indian files," RG 393. W. H. Wood, "Summary of Ordnance and Ordnance Stores in the Hands of Troops in the Service of the U.S., Eleventh U.S. Infantry, third quarter, 1872," RG 156.

13. Creaton, "Autobiography," 8.

14. Ibid., 9. Creaton incorrectly states that the attack occurred near Fort Phantom Hill, but does mention the killing of the lead horse and the overturning of the coach.

15. Creaton, "Autobiography," 9; and Augur in General Order no. 17, Aug. 20, 1872. This order by Augur was a condensed extract from Col. W. H. Wood's Fort Griffin Post Order of Aug. 5, 1872, and made no mention of the overturning of the coach.

16. Creaton, "Autobiography," 8.

17. C. C. Augur, Aug. 20, 1872, General Order no. 17, (filed with Adjutant General's Office–Letters Received, file 3474, Office of the Adjutant General–1872), RG 94.

18. Extensive research in post, regimental, department and adjutant general's office records failed to find Wood's report about the incident as McDonnold and Collins related.

19. The U.S. Army, given the responsibility for protection of overland mail transport in western frontier areas, lost twenty-seven troopers killed and twenty-two wounded between May 1867 and July 1872 in Indian attacks upon mail coaches and way stations. These figures were extracted from George W. Webb (ed.), *Chronological List of Engagements Between Regular Army of the U.S. and Various Tribes of Hostile Indians Especially During 1838 to 1898 Inclusive, As Reported by Department Commanders to the Adjutant General of the Army* (St. Joseph, Mo.: Wing Printing and Publishing Co., 1939), serialized for 1867–1872 in G. W. Webb, *Winners of the West*, Official Bulletin, National Indian War Veterans, March–May 1937 editions, microfilm (Perry–Castañeda Library, University of Texas at Austin). In the two July 1872 incidents in which Eleventh U.S. Infantry mail escorts had repulsed Indian attacks, they were significantly different from the McDonnold affair in that in those instances the Indians had been able to obtain the mail bags. See W. H. Wood, Eleventh U. S. Infantry Regimental Returns, "Record of Events," July 1872, RG 94.

20. Augur, General Order no. 17, Aug. 20, 1872, RG 94.

21. C. Augur to Office of the Adjutant General, Aug. 20, 1872, Adjutant General's Office–Letters Received, file 3474, Office of the Adjutant General–1872, National Archives Microcopy no. M-666, roll 81, exp. 0158-0159, RG 94.

22. F. M. McDonnold to Office of the Adjutant General, Nov. 7, 1872, Adjutant General's Office–Letters Received, file 4651, Office of the Adjutant General–1872, National Archives Microcopy no. M-666, roll 91, exp. 0162, RG 94.

23. Nye, *Carbine and Lance,* 200–202.

24. U.S. Congress, House, "Reduction of the Military Establishment," 43rd Cong., 1st sess., House report 384, 1874, (1624), 37; and Don Rickey, *Forty Miles a Day on Beans and Hay: The Enlisted Soldier Fighting the Indian Wars* (Norman: University of Oklahoma Press, 1963), 145–155.

25. U.S. Army, Office of the Adjutant General, Register of U.S. Army Enlistments, 1866, entry 2032, National Archives Microcopy no. 233, roll 31, RG 94; United States Seventh Census (1850), Westchester County, New York, Population Schedule, Town of Cortlandt, 250, RG 29; United States Ninth Census (1870), Shackelford County, Texas, Population Schedule, Fort Griffin, 124, RG 29; and United States Eleventh Census (1890), Lincoln County, New Mexico, Special Schedule, Veteran Census, Town of Ruidoso, 1, RG 29.

26. James L. Fenton, "Walter James (a.k.a. Frank) Collinson," in Tyler, et al. (eds.), *The New Handbook of Texas*, II, 219.

27. Creaton, "Autobiography," 8.

28. U.S. Senate, "Medal of Honor Review Board," case no. 2356, 409.

29. C. C. Augur to Office of the Adjutant General, Aug. 20, 1872, Adjutant General's Office–Letters Received, file 3474, Office of the Adjutant General–1872, RG 94.

30. Lloyd M. Raymer, certified professional geneologist, Bowling Green, Kentucky, "Warren County, Kentucky, McDonald (McDonnold) families," March 4, 1991, found no mention of a Franklin M. McDonald (McDonnold), ever being born in or residing in Warren County, Kentucky. An extensive search of all 1860 and 1870 U.S. Census population schedules indicated but one McDonald (McDonnold) family with a son named Franklin that had ties to Kentucky. That Franklin McDonald was born circa 1856 in Missouri, and curiously at the time of Franklin M. McDonnold's enlistment was a resident of Gainesville (Cooke County), Texas. The father was listed as being a native of Kentucky. See United States Eighth Census (1860), Cooke County, Texas, Population Schedule, Town of Gainesville, 54; and United States Ninth Census (1870), Cooke County, Texas, Population Schedule, Town of Gainesville, 196, RG 29.

CHAPTER 10

The Battle of the North Fork of the Red River

1. R. S. Mackenzie to Assistant Adjutant General, Aug. 4, 1874, Letters Sent Book, 1874–1884, 43–46, Fourth U.S. Cavalry Regimental Records, Records of U.S. Army Mobile Commands, 1821–1942, RG 391. According to a notation preceeding the entry, this memorandum was written in 1872 but was not entered into the letterbook until 1874.

2. Mackenzie to C. C. Augur, June 4, 1872, Department of Texas–Letters Received, file 1670, Department of Texas–1872, RG 393.

3. W. Merritt to Assistant Adjutant General, Department of Texas, July 6, 1872, in "Reports of Persons Killed or Captured by Indians, 1872–1888," other records, item no. 4907, Records of U.S. Army Continental Commands, Military Department of Texas, RG 393. Merritt's command arrived on the scene less than half an hour after the raiders left. He dispatched a detachment to pursue the raiders and they encountered them after a ten-mile chase. Despite being outgunned and outmanned, the Ninth Cavalry troopers repeatedly attacked the raiders' positions until forced to withdraw when they ran out of ammunition. See Bliss, "Reminiscences of Zenas R. Bliss, 1854–1876," 177–184; U.S. War Department,

Indian Hostilities in Texas, 8–11, 26; and the compiled army report on the incident in Adjutant General's Office–Letters Received, file 1850, Office of the Adjutant General–1872, RG 94. See also Lieutenant Cooney's report on Lieutenant Vincent's death in Department of Texas–Letters Received, files 1147, 1184 and 1279, Department of Texas–1872, RG 393.

4. Mackenzie's insistence upon the accurate mapping of the area of operations can be seen in his correspondence on the subject. See Mackenzie to Chief Engineer, U.S. Army, June 20, 1872, p. 11; Mackenzie to Assistant Adjutant General, Department of Texas, Oct. 8, 1872, p. 60; and Mackenzie to Commanding Officer, Fort Concho, Oct. 13, 1872, p. 61, all in Fourth U.S. Cavalry Expedition Letterbook, Letters Sent, RG 391. See also Mackenzie, Special Order no. 43, Sept. 21, 1872, Fourth U.S. Cavalry Expedition Letterbook, 130, RG 391; and J. W. Clous, "Map of Colonel R. S. Mackenzie's Scouts across the Staked Plains to New Mexico and return to the West Fork of Red River in the months of July, August, September and October 1872," Office of the Chief Engineer of the Department of Texas, Nov. 23, 1875, U.S. Army Signal Corps, photograph no. 111-SC-8873P, Still Photo Division, RG 77.

5. Mackenzie, Special Order no. 41, Sept. 19, 1872, Fourth U.S. Cavalry Expedition Letterbook, Special Orders Issued, 128, RG 391.

6. Mackenzie to G. Chilson, Sept. 7, 1872, Fourth U.S. Cavalry Expedition Letterbook, entry 46, 41, RG 391; Special Order no. 47, paragraph I, 135, Oct. 12, 1872, Special Orders Issued, Fourth U.S. Cavalry Expedition Letterbook, RG 391.

7. As of 1872 the Tonkawa Indian scout detachment was comprised of fifteen members. See Register of U.S. Army Enlistments, Indian Scouts, 1866–1877, vol. 150–151, National Archives Microcopy no. 233, roll 70, RG 94.

8. R. G. Carter, *The Old Sergeant's Story: Winning the West from the Indians and Bad Men in 1870–1876* (New York: F. B. Hitchcock Co., 1926), 82–83; Nye, *Carbine and Lance*, 209.

9. Carter, *On the Border with Mackenzie*, 376. Carter, *The Old Sergeant's Story*, 82–83. See also C. C. Augur," Department of Texas, Mackenzie's Battles," *Army and Navy Journal*, 9 (Nov. 16, 1872), 212–213.

10. Mackenzie's insistence upon each man having one hundred rounds of ammunition on his person during tactical operations can be seen in Special Order no. 6, July 2, 1872, and Circular no. 2, June 28, 1872, both in Fourth U.S. Cavalry Expedition Letterbook, 100, RG 391.

11. W. A. Thompson, "Scouting with Mackenzie." *Journal of U.S. Cavalry Association*, 10 (Dec., 1897), 430–431. According to Thompson, the Indians believed the command to be a herd of buffalo being driven by their own people, which allowed the soldiers to approach within half a mile of the village before they were discovered.

12. Ibid. See also Company Commander reports to Expedition Adjutant, Oct. 10–11, 1872, Fourth U.S. Cavalry Expedition Letterbook, 40–49; and J. W. Clous to Office of the Adjutant General, June 28, 1898, Adjutant General's Office–Letters Received, file 98045,

Office of the Adjutant General–1898 (filed with "Personnel file, John W. Clous," Appointment, Commission and Promotion file 247, Appointment, Commission and Promotion–1874), RG 94. Clous conducted a nine-year effort to obtain a brevet and a Medal of Honor for his actions during the engagement, but the Secretary of War ruled adversely on his Medal of Honor application on April 13, 1899.

13. Mackenzie to Assistant Adjutant General, Department of Texas, Oct. 12, 1872, Letters Sent, Fourth U.S. Cavalry Expedition Letterbook, 55–58, RG 391.

14. Carter, *The Old Sergeant's Story*, 85.

15. W. Davis to Adjutant for the Scouting Expedition, Oct. 10, 1872, Letters Received, Fourth U.S. Cavalry Expedition Letterbook, 41, RG 391. The main body of the village was situated along the banks of present-day Cabin Creek, approximately three miles northeast of the town of Lefors in Gray County. The village, in scattered clusters of lodges, extended three miles along Cabin Creek upon lands occupied by the J. Haynes and R. Sawyer ranches. There were also at least three small detached camps. One was in the woods just northwest of Lefors and a second was just east of the mouth of Cabin Creek on the river's north bank. A third camp for the herders was south of the river, along either Turkey or Grapevine Creek. See Gunnar Brune, *Springs of Texas* (Fort Worth: Branch-Smith, Inc., 1981), 196–197. C. L. Hudson to Adjutant for the Scouting Expedition, Oct. 10, 1872, Letters Received, 1872, Fourth U.S Cavalry Expedition Letterbook, 42–43, RG 391.

16. One of the other objectives for the Fourth Cavalry during the campaign was to field test, evaluate, and conclude on the adoption of a new metallic cartridge pistol for the regiment. As of September 1872 the companies within the regiment used an assorted variety of pistols, expressing in most cases the personal preference of the company commander. During the battle only one squad from Company L was equipped with the Colt .44 metallic cartridge pistol. Companies A and I used the Colt .44 with percussion caps, while Company D and the majority of L Company used the Remington .44 with percussion caps. Captain Davis's Company F used the Smith & Wesson .44 metallic cartridge pistol. The use of the metallic cartridge pistols in this action may have been their first use in a major Indian Wars engagement. See Mackenzie to Comley, Sept. 19, 1872, Fourth U.S. Cavalry Expedition Letterbook, 49, RG 391. See also Department of Texas–Letters Received, file 2757, Department of Texas–1872, RG 393; and Ordnance General, "Summary of Ordnance and Ordnance Stores in the hands of Troops in the service of the U. S., during 4th quarter, 1872, 4th US Cavalry," Records of the U.S. Army Ordnance General, RG 156.

17. Thompson, "Scouting with Mackenzie," 420.

18. Carter, *The Old Sergeant's Story*, 85. See also W. Davis to Office of the Adjutant General, Oct. 12, 1872, Final statement papers, John Dorcas, Fourth U.S. Cavalry, RG 94. Dorcas was a twenty-seven-year-old native of Longford, Ireland. In Special Order no. 44 on October 1, 1872, Mackenzie decreed that the creek upon which the command was then encamped would be named in Dorcas's honor. Pvt. John Kelly, a twenty-three-year-old native of Waterford, Ireland, who died of his wounds on October 11, was accorded a like honor in Special Order no. 47 with a creek in Blanco Canyon. Mackenzie to Adjutant for

the Scouting Expedition, Oct. 1, 1872, Orders and Circulars Issued, 1872, Special Order no. 47, paragraph VII, 136, Fourth U.S. Cavalry Expedition Letterbook, RG 391.

19. Beyer and Keydel, *Deeds of Valor*, II, 167; and W. Davis to J. A. McKinney, Oct. 10, 1872, Letters Received, Fourth U.S. Cavalry Expedition Letterbook, 41, RG 391.

20. L. Warrington to Adjutant for the Scouting Expedition, Oct. 10, 1872, Fourth U.S. Cavalry Expedition Letterbook, 44–47, RG 391.

21. W. Thompson to Adjutant for the Scouting Expedition, Oct. 10, 1872, Fourth U.S. Cavalry Expedition Letterbook, 47–48, RG 391.

22. C. Hudson to Adjutant for the Scouting Expedition, Oct. 10, 1872, Fourth U.S. Cavalry Expedition Letterbook, 42–43. Hudson had been elevated to command of Company I under Special Order no. 14, July 21, 1872, as a result of McLaughlin's illness.

23. "James N. Pratt obituary," *Bellefontaine Examiner*, Oct. 14, 1903. Hudson's report does not mention Pratt or Wilson's actions during the battle and only mentions one horse that was lost accidentally. The specifics of Pratt's deed were gleaned from a congratulatory letter from Hudson or Mackenzie to Pratt, which was a part of his estate upon his death. His family provided the contents of the letter to the newspaper for the obituary.

24. Beyer and Keydel, *Deeds of Valor*, II, 167–168.

25. Hudson to Adjutant for the Scouting Expedition, Oct. 10, 1872, Letters Received, 1872, Fourth U.S. Cavalry Expedition Letterbook, 43, RG 391.

26. Mackenzie to Assistant Adjutant General, Department of Texas, Oct. 12, 1872, Letters Received, 1872, Fourth U.S. Cavalry Expedition Letterbook, 55–58. Thompson, "Scouting with Mackenzie," 431, stated that the Comanches later admitted to him that "they lost fifty-two warriors." In his report Warrington mentioned the discovery of a white woman's body among those found in and along the ravine where the most severe fighting occurred. Warrington to Adjutant for the Scouting Expedition, Oct. 10, 1872, Letters Received, 1872, Expedition Letterbook, 44–47, RG 391.

27. H. Strong, *My Frontier Days*, 39.

28. Mackenzie to Assistant Adjutant General, Department of Texas, Oct. 12, 1872, Adjutant General's Office–Letters Received, file 4546 (filed with file 4148, Office of the Adjutant General–1872), RG 94. Mackenzie stated that the number of prisoners reported was 124, of whom 8 died on the return march. Francisco Nieto was counted as an Indian but was later separated from the Indians. This accounts for the Fort Concho post surgeon's entry of October 21, which states, "Companies 'D' and 'I', 4th Cavalry with Company 'E', 11th Infantry along with AAS. I. J. Culver arrived back on post with 115 Indian squaws." Post Surgeon, Fort Concho, Post Medical Record, Oct. 21, 1872 entry, RG 94.

As regimental quartermaster, Lt. Henry Lawton was responsible for recording and maintaining prisoners and captured property and was quite adept in the universal Indian sign language. Lieutenant Leiper was a former interpreter at the Kiowa Agency. Foster and Osmer were specially detailed by Mackenzie to care for the prisoners. See Circular no. 12, July 9, 1872, Fourth U.S. Cavalry Expedition Letterbook, 105, and Special Order no. 12, paragraph II, July 8, 1872, Fourth U.S. Cavalry Expedition Letterbook, 106. Osmer had resided near

Puerto de Luna, New Mexico, and likely was used as a spy or guide. United States Ninth Census (1870), Mora County, New Mexico Territory, Population Schedule, Town of La Junta, precinct 11, 15, RG 29. For Lawton see J. Parker, *The Old Army Memories, 1872–1918* (Philadelphia: Dorrance & Co, 1929), 33. For Leiper, see Mackenzie to Assistant Adjutant General, Department of Texas, June 22, 1872, Letters Sent, 1872, Fourth U.S. Cavalry Expedition Letterbook, 12, RG 391; and Nye, *Carbine and Lance,* 149. See also Mackenzie to J. P. Hatch, July 6, 1872, Letters Sent, 1872, Fourth U.S. Cavalry Expedition Letterbook, 15–16, RG 391.

29. Mackenzie to Assistant Adjutant General, Department of Texas, Oct. 12, 1872, Letters Sent, 1872, Fourth U.S. Cavalry Expedition Letterbook, 55–58; R. G. Carter Diary, box 2B181, Robert Goldwaithe Carter Papers, 1870–1930 (CAH); United States Ninth Census (1870), Maverick County, Texas, Population Schedule, Town of Eagle Pass, family 51, p. 515; and U.S. Congress, House, "Depredations on the Frontiers of Texas," 43rd Cong., 1st sess., 1872, H. Exec. Doc. 257 (1615), deposition 54, Francisco S. Nieto, 19–20.

30. J. P. Hatch to Assistant Adjutant General, Department of Texas, July 15, 1872, Adjutant General's Office–Letters Received, file 3113, Office of the Adjutant General–1872, RG 94. U.S. Congress, Senate, "The Relief of D. G. & D. A. Sanford," May 13, 1874, 43rd Cong., 1st sess., Sen. Rpt. 345, (1587), (to accompany Senate Bill 735); and U.S. Congress, House, "Comanche depredations in Texas, D. G. & D. A. Sanford," 45th Cong., 2nd sess., 1877, H. Rpt. 465, (1823), vol. 2, 6 pages. Evidence gathered from several lodges after the battle proved, among other things, complicity in the July 14 attack on the El Paso Overland Mail thirty-three miles west of Fort Concho.

31. Mackenzie to Assistant Adjutant General, Department of Texas, Oct. 12, 1872, file 4148, Office of the Adjutant General–1872, RG 94.

32. Carter, *The Old Sergeant's Story,* 86; and L. Charleton, "John B. Charleton in Forgotten Indian Fights of Texas," *Houston Post,* Apr. 28, 1936, p. 4, col. 4.

33. Mackenzie to Company Commanders, Oct. 9, 1872, paragraph III, Circulars issued, June–October 1872, Fourth U.S. Cavalry Expedition Letterbook, 115–116, RG 391. The report Davis filed caused severe dissension among several officers. Mackenzie, in commenting to Davis about the report, asserted "where there is so much that is creditable, official care should be taken not absent that which works injustice to others." See J. McKinney to W. Davis, Oct. 12, 1872, Letters Sent, June–December, 1872, Fourth U.S. Cavalry Expedition Letterbook, 52–55, RG 391. This conflict had unfortunate repercussions, for Mackenzie never issued another circular requesting reports from company commanders on engagements. The result is the scant documentation on such actions as Remolino, Tule Canyon, Palo Duro Canyon, and Laguna Tahoka.

34. Mackenzie to Assistant Adjutant General, Department of Texas, Oct. 12, 1872, Adjutant General's Office–Letters Received, file 4546 1/2 (filed with file 4148, Office of the Adjutant General–1872, in National Archives Microcopy no. 666, roll 86, exposures 0216-0258), RG 94. See also Company Commanders to Adjutant for the Scouting Expedition, Letters Received, June–December 1872, Fourth U.S. Cavalry Expedition

Letterbook, 40–48. The total list of enlisted men mentioned for gallantry in the various reports totaled eighteen. W. Davis to Adjutant for the Scouting Expedition, Oct. 10, Fourth U.S. Cavalry Expedition Letterbook, 40–42, mentioned W. McNamara, W. Foster, J. Lane, J. Kelly, J. B. Charleton, J. Erwing, H. A. Moore, W. Miller, J. A. Brooks, D. Larkin, E. Branagan, W. Rankin, J. Kelly, H. Hennier, and T. C. Poland. C. L. Hudson to Adjutant for the Scouting Expedition, Oct. 10, 1872, Fourth U.S. Cavalry Expedition Letterbook, 42–43, mentions W. O'Neill and J. Pratt. L. Warrington to Adjutant for the Scouting Expedition, Oct. 10, 1872, Fourth U.S. Cavalry Expedition Letterbook, 44–47, mentions Wilson; and W. Thompson to Adjutant for the Scouting Expedition, Oct. 10, 1872, Fourth U.S. Cavalry Expedition Letterbook, 47–48, mentions H. McMaster. One can only assume what criteria Mackenzie used in narrowing the list down to nine in his report. Whether he based his decisions upon conversations with the various commanders is pure speculation. The author, after reviewing the Judge Advocate General's, "Index to Court Martials," National Archives Microcopy no. 1105, RG 153 (National Archives), believes that recent indiscretions by some of those mentioned, most notably Sgt. John B. Charleton for his release of deserters in February 1874, resulted in their omission. See John B. Charleton, General Court Martial Order no. 16, March 19, 1874, RG 153.

35. E. D. Townsend to C. C. Augur, Nov. 21, 1872, Adjutant General's Office–Letters Received, 1872, file 4546 1/2, Office of the Adjutant General–1872, (filed with file 4148, Office of the Adjutant General–1872); Townsend to Augur, Department of Texas–Letters Received, file 2867, Department of Texas–1872, RG 393; and Letters Sent Register, 1872, Department of Texas, entry no. 941, RG 393.

36. G. P. Buell to Assistant Adjutant General, Department of Texas, Dec. 28, 1872, Department of Texas–Letters Received, file 116, Department of Texas–1873, RG 393. Buell incorrectly identifies David Larkin as William Larkin. See also recipients (McNamara, Foster, Larkin, Branagan, and Rankin) to Office of the Adjutant General, Dec. 27, 1872, Adjutant General's Office–Letters Received, file 399, Office of the Adjutant General–1873, RG 94.

37. W. A. Thompson to Office of the Adjutant General, Nov. 11, 1872, final statement papers, Cpl. Henry A. McMaster, Fourth U.S. Cavalry, 1872, RG 94; and "Effects Books," Second Auditor's Office, Records of the Department of Treasury, RG 217.

38. C. C. Augur, "Department of Texas, Fourth Cavalry," *Army and Navy Journal*, 10 (Jan., 1873), n.p. This account from an unnamed correspondent at Fort Concho was only a small part of the article that Augur submitted to the *Army and Navy Journal*. The unnamed correspondent erred when he identified Pratt as a corporal and Branagan as a blacksmith. He also erred when he mentioned Edward Branagan instead of Cpl. William O'Neill. See also O'Neill, Pratt, and Wilson to Office of the Adjutant General, Dec. 29, 1872, Adjutant General's Office–Letters Received, file 398, Office of the Adjutant General–1873, RG 94.

39. C. C. Augur to P. H. Sheridan, Oct. 28, 1872, Adjutant General's Office–Letters Received, file 4365, Office of the Adjutant General–1872; Secretary of War to Secretary of Interior, Oct. 31, 1872, Adjutant General's Office–Letters Received, file 4785, Office of the

Adjutant General–1872 (both filed with Adjutant General's Office–Letters Received, file 4148, Office of the Adjutant General–1872), RG 94; L. Tatum to C. Augur, Jan. 16, 1873, Department of Texas–Letters Received, file 408, Department of Texas–1873, "Indian files," RG 393; and C. C. Rister, *Border Captives: The Traffic in Prisoners by Southern Plains Indians, 1835–1875* (Norman: University of Oklahoma Press, 1940), 174–179.

40. A. J. Fountain, Texas state senator and J. H. Brown, Texas state representative, Senate Bill no. 34, January 16, 1873, enacted May 26, 1873, Records of the Thirteenth Texas Legislature, Senate Journal, 91–93. For a rendering on this joint resolution, see Richard A. Thompson, *Crossing the Border with the Fourth Cavalry* (Waco: Texian Press, 1986), 74–75. This remains the only known joint resolution passed by a state legislature in special session to praise a military unit and its commander for specific military actions. See also C. C. Augur to Office of the Adjutant General, circa June 1873, Adjutant General's Office–Letters Received, file 2366, Office of the Adjutant General–1873, RG 94. For Indian reactions to army acts of kindness see Nye, *Carbine and Lance*, 209, 213–214.

CHAPTER 11

Besieged on the Upper Washita

1. For the various reports and accounts of this battle see Miles to Assistant Adjutant General, Department of the Missouri, Sept. 1, 1874, Adjutant General's Office–Letters Received, file 3852 (filed with file 2815, Office of the Adjutant General–1874); N. A. Miles, "Record of Events," August 1874, Fifth U.S. Infantry Returns; and J. Oakes, "Record of Events," August 1874, Sixth U.S. Cavalry Returns, RG 94. See also Joe Taylor (ed.), *Indian Campaign on the Staked Plains, 1874–1875; Military Correspondence from the War Department, Adjutant General's Office, File 2815–1874* (Canyon: Panhandle-Plains Historical Society, 1962), 21–28, 197–199; N. A. Miles, *Personal Recollections and Observations* (Chicago: The Werner Co., 1896), 164–168; Robert C. Carriker (ed.), "Thompson McFadden's Diary of an Indian Campaign, 1874," *Southwestern Historical Quarterly*, 75 (Oct., 1971), 202–205; and Lonnie J. White, "The First Battle of the Palo Duro Canyon," *Texas Military History*, 6 (Fall, 1967), 222–235. It was during this battle that Capt. Adna R. Chaffee reportedly shouted his famous command, "Forward! If any man is killed, I will make him a Corporal!" See Virginia W. Johnson, *The Unregimented General: A Biography of Nelson A. Miles* (Boston: Houghton Mifflin, 1962), 53.

2. W. H. Carter, *The Life of Lieutenant General Adna R. Chaffee* (Chicago: University of Chicago Press, 1917), 72; Miles to Assistant Adjutant General, Department of the Missouri, Sept. 1, 1874; and Miles to Pope, Sept. 5, 1874, Adjutant General's Office–Letters Received, file 3857 (both filed with file 2815, Office of the Adjutant General–1874), RG 94. Most of the surface water sources in this area are highly brackish, alkaline, and gypsum-saturated and, especially during a severe drought, would be unfit for human consumption.

3. Miles, "Record of Events," September 1874, Fifth U.S. Infantry Returns, RG 94; and Lyman to Assistant Adjutant General (G. W. Baird), Sept. 25, 1874 (filed with file 2815,

Office of the Adjutant General–1874), RG 94; and W. Lyman, "A Fight with the Comanches and Kiowas," *Army and Navy Journal*, 12, (Oct. 31, 1874), 186. The base camp was located near several lagunas near present-day Clarendon.

4. John Long, "A Panhandle Pioneer," *Frontier Times Monthly*, 4 (Nov., 1926), 45. Long was a teamster with the Lyman train and was an eyewitness to the incident. See also J. T. Marshall, *The Miles Expedition of 1874–1875: An Eyewitness Account of the Red River War*, ed. Lonnie J. White (Austin: The Encino Press, 1971), 19.

5. F. D. Baldwin to Assistant Adjutant General, Indian Territory Expedition, Sept. 10, 1874, Adjutant General's Office–Letters Received, file 3912, Office of the Adjutant General–1874 (filed with file 2815, Office of the Adjutant General–1874), RG 94. After Baldwin and his scouts captured the boy, named Tehan, the Indians began looking for him. They followed Baldwin's trail and in the process discovered the Lyman train.

6. W. H. Lewis to Assistant Adjutant General, Department of the Missouri, Sept. 12, 1874, Adjutant General's Office–Letters Received, file 3942, Office of the Adjutant General–1874 (filed with file 2815, Office of the Adjutant General–1874), RG 94. The Lyman wagon train consisted of thirty-six wagons. The personnel of the train consisted of thirty-six teamsters, thirty-eight infantrymen, twenty cavalry troopers (only thirteen had serviceable horses), three officers, one civilian scout, and seven soldiers traveling casually to join the Miles column. Of the 105 men, only 26 of the teamsters were not armed.

This engagement was referred to by the U.S. Army as the battle of the Upper Washita (River). The location of the engagement is delineated by a map in W. Lyman to Assistant Adjutant General, Department of the Missouri, Sept. 25, 1874, Adjutant General's Office–Letters Received, file 4623, Office of the Adjutant General–1874 (filed with file 2815, Office of the Adjutant General–1874), RG 94. The site in Hemphill County is generally located at Latitude, 35°45′ North and Longitude, 100°12′ West and in 1999 was excavated by J. Brett Cruse of the Texas Historical Commission. See J. Brett Cruse, "The Texas Red River War Battlesites Project," paper presented at Order of the Indian Wars, Annual Assembly, Amarillo, Texas, Sept. 18, 1999 (copy in author's possession).

Artistic renditions of the battle by Frederic Remington appear in F. Downey, *Indian Fighting Army* (New York: C. Scribner & Sons, 1941), 187, titled "Protecting A Wagon Train." The original, titled "Indian Warfare," may be seen at the Gilcrease Institute in Tulsa, Oklahoma.

7. Davis S. Wilde, "His Dad was a Hero Fighting the Indians," *Willard Times-Writer* (Ohio), circa May 1972. Edward F. Sharpless, son of Cpl. Edward C. Sharpless, to Charles M. Neal Jr., June 8, 1973, interview (notes in author's possession).

8. Estimates of the number of Indians involved varied from two hundred to nine hundred from among the various accounts. Lyman, in his dispatch to W. H. Lewis in file 3942, stated that there were several hundred. In file 3909 Miles stated that there were from three to four hundred. Scout J. T. Marshall in *The Miles Expedition* estimated seven to nine hundred. Sgt. George K. Kitchen in T. F. Rodenbough, *Sabre and Bayonet* (New York: Dillingham Co.,1897), 300, says between seven and eight hundred, yet in Keydel and Beyer, *Deeds of Valor*, II, 188, he states four hundred. The most common figure participants estimated is the

figure used in this chapter. Variances likely resulted when at least a hundred Indians left the Lyman fight to take part in the attack on the couriers at the buffalo wallow fight. See also Nye, *Carbine and Lance*, 281–282.

9. E. F. Sharpless to C. M. Neal Jr., June 8, 1973, interview.

10. The events described hereafter are a compendium of cited accounts from Sgt. George K. Kitchen in T. F. Rodenbough, *Sabre and Bayonet*, 300–304; Beyer and Keydel, *Deeds of Valor*, II, 186–189; Carriker (ed.), "Thompson McFadden's Diary of an Indian Campaign," 211–212; W. Lyman, "A Fight with the Comanches and Kiowas," 186–187. Granville Lewis, "Proceedings of a board to retire disabled officers," Fort Leavenworth, Kans., Jan. 29, 1879, case no. 13, Records of the Office of the Surgeon General, RG 112 (National Archives), (copy filed with "Personnel file, Granville Lewis," file 1015, Appointment, Commission and Promotion–1871), RG 94. Teamster John J. Long, "A Panhandle Pioneer," *Frontier Times*, 4 (Nov., 1926), 45; Teamster J. W. McKinley, "J. W. McKinley's Narrative," *Panhandle-Plains Historical Review*, 36 (1936), 67–68; Marshall, *The Miles Expedition of 1874–1875: An Eyewitness Account of the Red River War*, 15–26; Lemuel T. Wilson, "Memoirs of His Service with Lieutenant Baldwin's Scouts in Texas, I.T., and Kansas in 1874," files Q-17 and Z-12, Order of Indian Wars Collection (U.S. Army Military History Research Center, Carlisle Barracks, Pennsylvania; hereafter cited as USAMHRC); "Personnel file, Wyllys Lyman," file 1368, Appointment, Commission and Promotion–1891, RG 94; and E. R. Archambeau (ed.), "The Battle of Lyman Wagon Train," *Panhandle-Plains Historical Review*, 36 (1963), 89–101.

11. G. K. Kitchen to Office of the Adjutant General, July 31, 1917, "Application for Enrollment on the Army Medal of Honor Roll," George K. Kitchen Pension file certificate no. 7724, RG 15 (National Archives).

12. Long, "A Panhandle Pioneer," 45. The Indians by this time had disabled so many mules that the train was becoming disjointed. Long mentions the difficulty of having to stop and cut loose the disabled mules and then restart with the remainder. The cavalry troopers were busy preventing the stampede of their horses and the beef herd and could render no assistance to the teamsters.

13. Lyman to Assistant Adjutant General, Department of the Missouri, Sept. 25, 1874, Adjutant General's Office–Letters Received, file 2815, Office of the Adjutant General–1874, RG 94. Lyman said of Sergeant Mitchell, "He was now very active and his pluck and skill were conspicuous. He is a pattern skirmisher. The latter part of the day he had charge here." Mitchell's skirmish lines were firing so rapidly that one of the cavalry horses ran wildly into the line of fire and was killed instantly. See J. Oakes, "Record of Events," Sixth U.S. Cavalry Regimental Returns, September 1874, RG 94.

14. Lyman, "A Fight with the Comanches and Kiowas," 186; and George W. Fox to J. W. Davidson, April 2, 1874, Adjutant General's Office–Letters Received, file 1615, Office of the Adjutant General–1874, RG 94. In this letter Fox alludes to the fact that the civilian traders at the Anadarko–Wichita Agency had openly traded arms and ammunition not only to the Cheyenne and Wichita but also to Kiowas and Comanches. Otterbelt, a

Quohada Comanche, and Tabanonica, a Kiowa, both boasted of their newly obtained arms and ammunition to Fox. Kicking Bird, a Kiowa chief, later substantiated Fox's information. Otterbelt even boasted to Fox that, "back of the lodge (his) he had a mule loaded with ammunition."

15. G. Lewis to retirement board, Fort Leavenworth, Kansas, Jan. 29, 1879, 6 (copy filed with "Personnel file, Granville Lewis," file 1015, Appointment, Commission and Promotion–1871), RG 94.

16. Lyman, "A Fight with the Comanches and Kiowas," 186. In an affidavit Lewis submitted to the retirement board he states, "with the aid of private soldiers, I had extracted the ball myself with a knife and a razor." After his left leg was amputated as a result of the wound he served as the assistant quartermaster at the Fort Leavenworth Federal Penitentiary until his disability retirement. Pvt. P. M. Canna was designated as his caretaker in Fifth U.S. Infantry Returns for September 1874. See also Post Surgeon, Post Medical Record, Camp Supply, Indian Territory, September 1874, RG 94.

17. Lyman, "A Fight with the Comanches and Kiowas," 186, reported, "This mortar like firing by the Indians caused a great deal of consternation and panic among some of the troops and Lieutenant West had to be active to preserve composure."

18. Lyman to Commanding Officer, Camp Supply, Sept. 10, 1874, Adjutant General's Office–Letters Received, file 3942, (filed with file 2815, Office of the Adjutant General–1874), RG 94. Some confusion exists about the given name of this teamster. Lyman states, "The Assistant Wagoner McCoy is mortally wounded, I fear." Carriker (ed.), "Thompson McFadden's Diary of an Indian Campaign," 211, states, "one soldier and one Teamster [Wagoner McCoy] killed." The author believes this was James McCoy, a former soldier at Fort Dodge. The term "wagoner" was an army designation for a teamster.

19. Rodenbough, *Sabre and Bayonet*, 303. Beyer and Keydel, *Deeds of Valor*, II, 187, features a painting by __ Bacon, 1901, depicting Sergeant Neilon (Singleton) performing his Medal of Honor deed entitled "Sergeant Neilon Carrying Ammunition to the Besieged Troopers."

20. Lyman to Assistant Adjutant General, Sept. 25, 1874, file 2815, Office of the Adjutant General–1874, RG 94.

21. For a biographical sketch of Schmalsle see Montana Historical Society, *Illustrated History of Yellowstone Valley* (Helena: Montana Historical Society, 1907), 434–435.

22. Rodenbough, *Sabre and Bayonet*, 301–302. According to Sergeant Kitchen, on one of these night forays for water on September 10, Tehan, the boy captive Baldwin turned over to Lyman on September 9, escaped. In Lyman to Assistant Adjutant General, Sept. 25, 1874, file 2815, Office of the Adjutant General–1874, Lyman reports that after the battle, "thirty rifle pits covering this water hole were afterwards counted."

23. J. Long, "A Panhandle Pioneer," 45. For a somewhat different version of Schmalsle's escape see Lemuel T. Wilson, "Desperate Indian Fighting Near Fort Elliott Site is Delineated by Noted Scout," *Pampa Daily News*, [n.d.], Order of Indian Wars Collection (USAMHRC).

24. Peter J. S. Cleary, Army Assistant Surgeon, Oct. 21, 1874, "Special Reports on Individual Soldiers," file SSD 636, item 631, box 1, Records subdivision of Surgeon General, RG 94. Cleary also addresses the death of James L. Stanford, the assistant wagonmaster, in Post Medical Record, Fort (Camp) Supply, I.T., August–September 1874, 28–29, RG 94, in which he writes, "An Assistant Wagonmaster was also badly wounded and afterwards died of his wounds in Post Hospital."

25. Long, "A Panhandle Pioneer," 45.

26. Rodenbough, *Sabre and Bayonet,* 302–303.

27. Ibid., 304–305.

28. Lyman to Assistant Adjutant General, Department of the Missouri, Sept. 25, 1874, file 2815, Office of the Adjutant General–1874, RG 94.

29. These were the survivors of the buffalo wallow fight.

30. Lyman, "A Fight with the Comanches and Kiowas," 187; and Post Commander, Camp Supply, I.T., Camp Supply Post Returns, "Record of Events," Sept. 12–18, 1874, entries, RG 94.

31. Edward F. Sharpless to Charles M. Neal Jr., June 8, 1973, interview (notes in author's possession). See also Wilde, "His Dad Was a Hero Fighting the Indians." The official citation for Sharpless states: "While carrying dispatches was attacked by 125 hostile Indians, whom he and a comrade fought throughout the day." All other citations for Lyman train recipients read either as "Gallantry in action," or "Gallantry in action with Indians," so the question arises as to who was his comrade? Only Morris and Sharpless were designated as Company H couriers in Sixth Cavalry Regimental Returns for September 1874, and the presence of the other cavalry recipients at the train is verified from several sources. One can easily write the omission of the comrade's name and proper citation off to a monumental clerical error as the inaccuracies were already in place by 1882. See P. H. Sheridan, *Record of Engagements with Hostile Indians within the Military Division of the Missouri* (Washington, D.C.: Government Printing Office, 1882), 41. This source names John Harrington, a buffalo wallow recipient, as Sharpless's comrade. In 1888 a board that compiled documentation on gallant deeds performed by soldiers since the end of the Civil War failed to correct the error. See "Proceedings of Distinguished and Meritorious Service Board," Adjutant General's Office–Letters Received, file 5461, Office of the Adjutant General–1889, National Archives Microcopy no. 689, roll 717, exp. 19, RG 94. It must also be considered that no documentation was ever submitted and that the recommendation was verbal. A closer examination of the relationships between those involved, however, raises the specter of severe interpersonal conflicts, which may have affected the process. Strangely, Lt. Frank West filed no report on the activities of the cavalrymen during the battle, which illustrates Miles's insistence upon infantry omnipotence, especially during joint field operations, which may have caused friction between Lyman and West. Lyman's erratic behavior during the campaign may have made West more reluctant to consult with Lyman, who had already complained to his superiors that his men were talking about him behind his back. He was

referred to by his men as "Old Whoopla" because he tended to make trivial matters into explosive issues. After the siege of the train was lifted, he went so far as to suggest that, "if his men had only been equipped with Rice trowel bayonets we could have beaten them off sooner." See Lyman, "Staving Fight with Indians—Utility of Rifle Pits," *New York Times*, Sept. 30, 1874, p. 1. Lyman's condition worsened and by May 1875 he was furloughed in charge of his family. In August 1875 the Cincinnati, Ohio, chief of police billed the army for services rendered in searching for him. See E. C. Mason to the Adjutant General's Office, Adjutant General's Office–Letters Received, file 4285, Office of the Adjutant General–1875 (filed with file 2687, Office of the Adjutant General–1875). In light of Lyman's problems, West, likely in a dispute with Lyman, independently dispatched Sharpless and his comrade at the same time as Schmalse, or before, except in the opposite direction. It must be considered that their location was sev-enty-eight miles from Camp Supply, while Compton's cavalry encampment on Sweetwater Creek was only fifty-five miles away. Frank West and his relationship with Corporal Morris must also be considered as a part of the puzzle. West's older brother had been killed by Confederates in the East Tennessee campaign, where Morris had served as a Confederate cavalry officer, which may have affected West's attitude toward Morris. Curiously, Morris was cited for a second Medal of Honor for a deed performed at Sappa Creek, Kansas, on April 23, 1875. In the report citing Morris, an uninitialed entry stated, "This man's name stricken out as he received a Medal for former services." See file 1821 Office of the Adjutant General–1875 (filed with file 2815, Office of the Adjutant General–1874). For whatever reasons or causes, the absence of documentation for Sharpless and his comrade and the exact circumstances of their deed remain a myste-rious part of Medal of Honor history.

32. Miles to Office of the Adjutant General, Mar. 21, 1875, Adjutant General's Office–Letters Received, file 1821, Office of the Adjutant General–1875 (for Lyman train recipients), and Miles to Assistant Adjutant General, Sept. 24, 1874, Adjutant General's Office–Letters Received, file 4278 (for buffalo wallow recipients), both filed with file 2815, Office of the Adjutant General–1874, RG 94; and N. A. Miles, Medal of Honor Review Board, 1916–1917, "File of 2,625 Cases Showing Synopsis and Basis of Award in Each Case," cases 2185, 2200 and 2204, p. 254, Adjutant General's Office–Documents Received, file 1462171, Office of the Adjutant General–1917, RG 94, for extracts of administrative chronology and documentation inventory for each Medal of Honor awarded up to that time In addition to Sgt. Frederick S. Neilon, another recipient from the Lyman train battle, Sgt. Fred S. Hay was also serving under an alias. "Hay's" name was actually Frederick H. Schwabe. His reason for enlisting under an alias, to hide his failure in business from his family, was the same as Neilon's. Schwabe was not borne on regimental records under his true name until November 23, 1894. See Adjutant General's Office–Documents Received, file 8399, Office of the Adjutant General–1894 (filed with file 1821, Office of the Adjutant General–1875, thence file 2815, Office of the Adjutant General–1874). See also F. H. Schwabe to Office of the Adjutant General, Adjutant General's Office–Documents Received, file 461543, Office of the Adjutant General–1907, RG 94.

33. See Adjutant General's Office–Letters Received, files 4030–4035, Office of the Adjutant General–1875 (filed with file 2815, Office of the Adjutant General–1874 on National Archives Microcopy no. 666, roll 162, exp. 259–270, 282–283) for letters acknowledging receipt of medals from the Fifth U.S. Infantrymen (Hay, James, J. Kelly, T. Kelly, Koelpin, and Mitchell). For the Sixth Cavalry recipients see Adjutant General's Office–Letters Received, file 2815, Office of the Adjutant General–1874, which includes file 5710, Office of the Adjutant General–1875 (Pennsyl); file 5976, Office of the Adjutant General–1875 (Kitchen); and file 4302, Office of the Adjutant General–1875 (Morris), National Archives Microcopy no. 666, roll 162, exp. 0331–2, 0449, 0459–60, RG 94. Letters from Singleton and Sharpless could not be found. None of the letters from cavalry recipients mention a formal ceremony.

34. N. A. Miles, General Order no. 20, July 28, 1875, General, Special and Field Orders Issued–1875, Headquarters, Fort Leavenworth, Kansas, RG 393. See also Miles to Koelpin, July 28, 1875, Adjutant General's Office–Documents Received, file 28500, Principal Records Division–1892, RG 94.

35. On May 18, 1875, the War Department forwarded Sergeant DeArmond's medal to the Second Auditor's Office of the Treasury Department for delivery to his legal representative. See E. D. Townsend to Second Auditor, May 18, 1875, Adjutant General's Office–Letters Received, file 1821, Office of the Adjutant General–1875 (filed with file 2815, Office of the Adjutant General–1874), RG 94. On or around July 22, 1875, the Second Auditor's Office forwarded the medal to Mrs. Julia A. DeArmond, whose listed address was Headquarters, Fifth U.S. Infantry, Fort Leavenworth, Kansas. See Julia A. DeArmond, Widow's Pension, cert. 171.172, RG 15; William DeArmond, Fifth U.S. Infantry, Final Statement Papers, RG 94; and "Effects Book," Office of the Second Auditor, Department of the Treasury, RG 217. Frederick S. Neilon (Frank Singleton) received his medal on or around May 18, 1875. See F. S. Neilon to Office of the Adjutant General, Nov. 27, 1893, Adjutant General's Office–Documents Received, file 19768, Principal Records Division–1893, RG 94. Neilon's 1893 request to return his original for a new Medal of Honor engraved under his true name was the first such request received and granted. His original Medal of Honor, as of June 1972, was in the aforementioned Adjutant General's Office–Documents Received file from 1893.

CHAPTER 12

The Buffalo Wallow Fight

1. Each of the five columns also sent many small scouting detachments to fan out to the sides in advance of the main body of troops. These small reconnaissance detachments were highly important, for their job was to locate the Indian camps, track the Indians' movements, and communicate with the other columns and supply points. They prevented unnecessary movements by the main columns, thus preserving the condition of the command's horses. Each of the five columns used a unique mix of Indian and white scouts. For an examination of these groups, see Robert C. Carriker, "Mercenary Heroes: The Scouting

Detachments of the Indian Territory Expedition, 1874–1875," *Chronicles of Oklahoma*, 51 (Fall, 1973), 309–324.

2. Col. John W. Davidson's column was supposed to have left Fort Sill on or around August 24, 1874, but was detained because of disturbances on the Wichita–Anadarko Reservation. The disturbances resulted from hostile tribes attempting to register after the deadline and balking at the suggestion that they surrender their arms. Severe fighting broke out as a result of their attempts to incite the friendly reservation tribes. J. W. Davidson to Assistant Adjutant General, Department of Texas, August 27, 1874, Department of Texas–Letters Received, file 3490 (filed with file 2815, Office of the Adjutant General–1874), RG 94.

3. The location of this engagement, often referred to either as the battle of the Red River or the first battle of Palo Duro Canyon, was along the main north prong of present-day Battle Creek in southeast Armstrong County. See the sources on this engagement in note 1 of Chapter 11.

4. Rodenbough, *Sabre and Bayonet*, 285–286; and T. E. Way, *Sergeant Fred Platten's Ten Years on the Trail* (William, Ariz.: Williams News Press, 1939), 8–9. Sergeant Platten also witnessed Pettyjohn's death and his version differs somewhat from that of Lt. J. S. Payne. Platten says Pettyjohn's horse fell and he was lanced while lying on the ground, while Payne states that Pettyjohn was shot in the arm and lanced while he was mounted. For additional comments on the incident see G. W. Baird, "Position of Indian Territory Expedition Commands," 4, in Papers of Maj. George W. Baird, 1874–1891, Manuscripts Division, Archives (Kansas State Historical Society, Topeka, Kans.); here-after cited as Baird, "Indian Territory Expedition." In this source Baird reported, "Private Jas. H. Pettyjohn, Co. M, Sixth Cavalry, while going with the First Sergeant Whust for morning report book lost from a wagon was surrounded by Indians, killed and scalped." Pvt. Smith E. Foster, a former Eighth Cavalry trooper with Price's command, further clouds the incident by stating, "The Sergeant's horse was killed and the Private (Pettyjohn) was killed. This happened just as we were pulling out, and we heard the fir-ing." See Smith E. Foster to W. W. Camp, circa Nov. 1921, in Walter W. Camp Papers, box 5, file 7, notes 368–380, Manuscripts Department (Lilly Library, Indiana University, Bloomington, Ind.). Mumsukawa, a Quohada Comanche witness, related, "We chased after them. The man who was riding the white horse was thrown to the ground. Big Bow and the other Kiowa were on foot too, but Black Horse, being mounted, caught up rapid-ly. Big Bow shot the soldier who was on the sorrel horse. As he fell slowly from his horse, Big Bow caught him in his arms and scalped him. The other man ran into the brush along the branch and disappeared." See W. S. Nye, *Bad Medicine and Good: Tales of the Kiowas* (Norman: University of Oklahoma Press, 1962), 217–218.

5. O. K. Dixon, *The Life of "Billy" Dixon, Plainsman, Scout and Pioneer.* (Dallas: P. L. Turner, 1927), 199–200. See also Marie Sandoz, *The Buffalo Hunters: Story of the Hide Men* (New York: Hastings House Publishers, 1954), 213.

6. Nye, *Carbine and Lance*, 281–282. According to Indians Nye interviewed in the 1930s, those the couriers encountered were mostly Kiowas with a few Comanches, who

had left the siege on the Lyman wagon train. There were about one hundred Indians involved, belonging to bands led by the chiefs Big Bow, Poor Buffalo, Yellow Wolf, and Tohausen. See W. S. Nye, "Excitement on the Sweetwater," *Chronicles of Oklahoma*, 16 (June, 1938), 241–242.

7. Dixon, *The Life of "Billy" Dixon*, 199–200. Rodenbough, *Sabre and Bayonet*, 290. Pvt. John Harrington's version was likely a verbal account to J. S. Payne circa 1885, when both were in the Fifth U.S. Cavalry. Harrington was apparently illiterate in April 1875, when he acknowledged receipt of his Medal of Honor by making his mark. According to later army correspondence he had acquired literacy prior to 1898. See also Beyer and Keydel, *Deeds of Valor*, II, 189–192. There was no Harrington correspondence among the Beyer-Keydel Collection in the Detroit Public Library, so apparently Beyer and Keydel obtained their account from Rodenbough.

8. Rodenbough, *Sabre and Bayonet*, 290.

9. Ibid., 291. This was likely the Kiowa medicine man Eagle Chief.

10. Ibid., 291–292.

11. O. K. Dixon, "The Buffalo Wallow Fight," an extract booklet from Dixon, *The Life of "Billy" Dixon*, 6. In Rodenbough, *Sabre and Bayonet*, 293–294, and Beyer and Keydel, *Deeds of Valor*, II, 191, Amos Chapman claimed credit for carrying Smith into the wallow. See Sgt. Z. T. Woodall to William Dixon, Jan. 4, 1889, Olive K. Dixon Papers (Panhandle-Plains Historical Archives, Canyon, Tex.). In this letter Woodall wrote, "did you read the account (in our Wild Indians) were [sic] Amos carried Smith on his back and not know that his left leg was shot off until he got to the wallow do you ever hear tell of such a dam [sic] lie when he knows very well that you carried both of them there yourself." Chapman's wounds were far too serious to have enabled him to have performed the feat. See the account in question in R. I. Dodge, *Our Wild Indians* (Hartford, Conn.: A. D. Worthington & Co., 1890), 631–632, the first major literary account of the incident. Chapman's account from *Our Wild Indians* appears verbatim in Rodenbough, *Sabre and Bayonet*, 293–294, and Beyer and Keydel, *Deeds of Valor*, II, 191. Dixon admitted fault in the matter as he had failed to respond to Dodge's request for his account. This also led to a number of erroneous artistic renditions of the buffalo wallow fight.

The earliest artistic rendition of the incident was by noted western artist Frederic Remington. It first accompanied a literary account of the incident titled, "Twenty-five to One" in Miles, *Personal Recollections and Observations of Nelson A. Miles*, 177. The same Remington drawing appears in Fairfax Downey, *Indian Fighting Army*, 211, and is titled, "Stand of the Couriers." Another Remington drawing, "The Circle of Death," has often been identified in error as portraying the buffalo wallow battle. See C. C. Smith, "From Colonel C. C. Smith," *Frontier Times*, 10 (Dec., 1932), 103. "The Circle of Death" portrayed an event in Arizona, circa 1896, and involved soldiers of the Sixth U.S. Cavalry. It first accompanied a literary account in Frank Norris, "A Memorandum of Sudden Death," *Collier's Weekly* (Jan. 11, 1902), 11.

12. Dixon, "The Buffalo Wallow Fight," 6.

13. Ibid.

14. Ibid., 7; and Miles, "General Order No. 18," *Army and Navy Journal*, 12 (Oct. 17, 1874), 148.

15. Dixon, "The Buffalo Wallow Fight," 7. No mention is made of the location of the wallow relative to the Miles trail. If the site of the present-day buffalo wallow monument is accurate, then the Miles trail would have been from 1.5 to 2.5 miles west-northwest of the wallow.

16. Rodenbough, *Sabre and Bayonet*, 296.

17. Dixon, "The Buffalo Wallow Fight," 7–8.

18. Dixon, *The Life of Billy Dixon*, 200; Dixon, "The Buffalo Wallow Fight," 7–8; and Rodenbough, *Sabre and Bayonet*, 296.

19. W. R. Price to Assistant Adjutant General, Department of the Missouri, Sept. 23, 1874, Headquarters, Wingate Battalion, Eighth U.S. Cavalry, camp on the Canadian River, ten miles west of Antelope Hills, Adjutant General's Office–Letters Received, file 4258, Office of the Adjutant General–1874 (filed with file 2815, Office of the Adjutant General–1874 on National Archives Microcopy no. 666, roll 159, exp. 281–298), RG 94. This was the first U.S. Army correspondence about the buffalo wallow engagement and Price's description of the battle scene is very explicit, even to the depth (one and a half feet) and width (six feet) of the wallow. In S. E. Foster to W. W. Camp, circa November 1921, W. W. Camp Papers, Foster stated, "When we left the men at the wallow, Price told Lieutenant Rogers of L Company to take the men at the wallow back to the Sweetwater where Dixon thought they would find the Miles command. Price gave Rogers a detail to do this. They did take them back toward the Sweetwater until they met the Sixth Cavalry who had an ambulance that took them to Camp Supply." Was Foster mistaken or did Rogers disobey Price's orders, thus further promulgating the conflict between Price and Miles? For the particulars of the conflict between Price and Miles, see Records of the Judge Advocate General, General Court Martial file no. PP-4678, Maj. William R. Price, July 1875, Fort Lyon, Colo., RG 156.

20. Smith E. Foster to W. W. Camp, circa November 1921, field notes 368–380, W. W. Camp Papers. The scenario of Chapman firing on his advancing rescuers can be understood more fully in light of Foster's account of the events of those few minutes: "While Dixon was giving directions to Surgeon McLain on how to get to the wallow, one of the soldiers found a note attached to a stick. The stick was stuck into the ground on the side of the trail, near where the trail crossed the Washita River. The note was wet and the writing severely faded. Major Price wanting better light in which to try and make out the writing, walked up onto a nearby knoll and sat down. At the time Major Price had a red blanket draped over his shoulder. The men in the wallow could see him, but not Dixon or the others, and they thought he was an Indian." In Dixon, "The Buffalo Wallow Fight," 8, Billy stated, "I was describing in detail all that had happened when I looked up and saw that the relief party was bearing too far north. I fired my gun to attract their attention, and

then waived it in the direction which they were to go." In light of these concurrent events, the reaction of the men in the wallow become more understandable.

21. Ibid.

22. Miles was so angry about this situation that his appeal to Gen. P. H. Sheridan resulted in a Department of the Missouri circular on October 13, 1874, that mandated the arming of the Eighth U.S. Cavalry with .45-caliber Springfield carbines.

23. Carter, *The Life of Lieutenant General Adna R. Chaffee*, 75.

24. P. S. Cleary, Post Medical Record, Camp Supply, I.T., September–October 1874, 26–30, RG 94; Lewis to Office of the Adjutant General, Nov. 9, 1874, Adjutant General's Office–Letters Received, file 4681, Office of the Adjutant General–1874, RG 94; and Post Adjutant, Camp Supply, "Casually at Post," Post Returns, Camp Supply, I.T., September–October, 1874, RG 94, NA.

25. Miles to Assistant Adjutant General, Sept. 24, 1874, Adjutant General's Office–Letters Received, file 4278, Office of the Adjutant General–1874 (filed with Office of the Adjutant General, file 2815, Office of the Adjutant General–1874), RG 94. See also Miles, "General Order No. 18," *Army and Navy Journal*, 12 (Oct., 17, 1874), 148, and Miles, *Personal Recollections*, 173–174.

26. Miles to Adjutant General, Oct. 9, 1874, Adjutant General's Office–Letters Received, file 4278, Office of the Adjutant General–1874 (filed with file 2815, Office of the Adjutant General–1874), RG 94.

27. Miles to William Dixon, Dec. 24, 1874, in Olive K. Dixon Papers. An interesting sidelight is that in 1884 Billy Dixon established a home site on the very site where he received his Medal of Honor from Miles. Dixon to Office of the Adjutant General, Dec. 26, 1874, Adjutant General's Office–Letters Received, file 5603, Office of the Adjutant General–1874, RG 94.

28. Dixon, "The Buffalo Wallow Fight," 10.

29. Miles, General, Special and Field Orders Issued, 1874–1875, Military Division of the Missouri, General Order no. 28, Jan. 24, 1875, Fort Sill, I.T. Baird, "Indian Territory Expedition Commands," 15, verifies the presence of Miles and the two recipients at Fort Sill. The award ceremony apparently took place as the Miles command marched out of Fort Sill on its return to Fort Dodge.

30. Amos Chapman to Office of the Adjutant General, Feb. 19, 1875, Adjutant General's Office–Letters Received, file 1064, Office of the Adjutant General–1875, RG 94. This is Amos Chapman's letter acknowledging receipt of his Medal of Honor "at the hands of General Nelson A. Miles" from Camp Supply, Indian Territory. According to the "Record of Events," Camp Supply Post Returns, February 1875, Miles arrived on February 8 and left the post on February 9, so the actual presentation took place on either of these dates.

31. John Harrington to Office of the Adjutant General, Mar. 29, 1875, Adjutant General's Office–Letters Received, file 1835, Office of the Adjutant General–1875 (filed with file 1750, Office of the Adjutant General–1875), RG 94. This is Harrington's letter

acknowledging receipt of his Medal of Honor. The letter apparently was written and witnessed by his company commander, Lt. W. W. Wallace, at Fort Lyon, Colorado.

32. H. P. Perrine to Office of the Adjutant General, June 10, 1875, "Inventory of effects for Pvt. George W. Smith, Sixth U.S. Cavalry," Final statement papers, RG 94; and Miles to Charles G. Smith, Dec. 31, 1874, Adjutant General's Office–Letters Received, file 5519, Office of the Adjutant General–1874 (filed with file 2815, Office of the Adjutant General–1874), RG 94.

33. Dixon, "The Buffalo Wallow Fight," 11.

34. Miles to Charles G. Smith, Dec. 25, 1874, Adjutant General's Office–Letters Received, file 5519, Office of the Adjutant General–1874 (filed with file 2815, Office of the Adjutant General–1874 [textual]). Also in Office of the Adjutant General, Register of Letters Received, 1874, entry no. 5519, p. 1112, RG 94.

35. J. L. McCarthy, *Adobe Walls Bride* (San Antonio: Naylor Press, 1955), 254–255. The site was located through the efforts of John J. Long, a longtime resident of Mobeetie, Texas, and a teamster for the Miles column in 1874. Western movie star William S. Hart was the major donor to the monument fund.

36. Ibid., 256. Julia Lockett, a longtime friend of Olive Dixon, wrote and suggested the inscription for the monument.

37. Senate, "Medal of Honor Review Board," case no. 1000–1003, 477.

38. Department of the Army, Board For Correction of Military Records, Washington, D.C., docket no. AC88-10374, June 12, 1989, in the case of William F. ("Buffalo Bill") Cody. U.S. Army scouts and guides were enrolled by and paid by the Quartermaster Department, an integral part of the army. The duties of a scout or guide were determined to be as much as or more military in nature than a contract surgeon serving in the army. Army contract surgeon John O. Skinner, retroactively awarded a Medal of Honor in 1915 for a deed performed in 1873, was not removed by the review board in 1917. Mary A. Walker, a Civil War contract surgeon, was restored to the U.S. Army Medal of Honor Roll in 1977. Her original removal in 1917 had been based primarily upon the question of her service, "not appearing to have been distinguished in action or otherwise." Volumes of documents validated the deeds Cody and the four other scouts performed. In view of these points the board acted affirmatively upon William G. Cody's petition on June 12, 1989, and restored his grandfather, William F. Cody, to the U.S. Army Medal of Honor Roll. The board also extended its decision to the four other army scouts affected, and Amos Chapman, William (Billy) Dixon, James B. Dosher, and W. W. Woodall were also restored to the Medal of Honor Roll.

CHAPTER 13
For Habitual Courage Near Quitaque Peak

1. For the findings of Boehm's scouting forays and Mackenzie's intentions, see Mackenzie to Assistant Adjutant General, Department of Texas, Sept. 19, 1874, Department of Texas–Letters Received, files 3838 and 3926, Department of Texas–1874,

"Indian files." RG 393, NA. The most comprehensive sources on the history of the Seminole-Negroes may be found in Kevin Mulroy, *Freedom on the Border* (Lubbock: Texas Tech University Press, 1993), and Kenneth W. Porter, *The Black Seminoles*, eds. Thomas P. Senter and Alcione M. Amos (Gainesville: University Press of Florida, 1996). See also J. W. Hunter, "A Negro Trooper of the Ninth Cavalry," *Frontier Times*, 4 (Apr., 1927), 11; and E. Hatch to Assistant Adjutant General, Department of Texas, Aug. 9, 1875, Department of Texas–Letters Received, file 4489, Department of Texas–1875 (filed with Adjutant General's Office–Letters Received, file 488M, Office of the Adjutant General–1870), RG 94. All file 488M documents in National Archives Microcopy no. 619, rolls 799–800.

2. G. E. Albee, "Mackenzie's Expedition," *Galveston News*, Oct. 22, 1874, p. 2, cols. 2–3, mentions only four scouts on this scouting foray as does Strong, *My Frontier Days*, 49. The author chose to use the figure of five as stated by C. Hatfield, "Campaign of Colonel R. S. McKenzie [sic] in 1874," file X–25, Charles A. P. Hatfield Papers, Order of Indian Wars Collection (USAMHRC); hereafter cited as "Campaign of Colonel R. S. McKenzie." Hatfield was a junior officer assigned to the Seminole-Negro scout detachment. He kept a very detailed diary during the campaign and mentioned two of the scouts by name.

3. Upon his initial enlistment on November 12, 1873, he was entered in the 1873 Register of Enlistments, Special enlistments (Indian Scouts), entry no. 152, by Lt. J. L. Bullis as Adam Payne. Upon his second enlistment on June 1, 1874, he was entered in the register, entry no. 178, by Lt. L. O. Parker as Adam Paine, which has caused a great deal of confusion about the correct spelling of his name. On the same day as his second enlistment, another scout, Isaac Payne, also reenlisted. It is the author's contention that in an effort to differentiate between two non-sibling enlistees with the same-sounding surname that Parker entered the surname Paine for Adam. Bullis was the commander of the Seminole-Negro scout detachment and was familiar with the names. The error has been perpetuated since Adam was cited for the Medal of Honor during the enlistment in which he was carried in the register as Paine. Among all known sources consulted no reference could be found to a Seminole-Negro family with the surname Paine. Reference to the surname Payne, however, may be found in the following official sources: United States Tenth Census (1880), Kinney County, Texas, Population Schedule, Town of Brackett, pp. 298, 301, 306, 309; Lt. P. Kelliher to Post Adjutant, Fort Duncan, Texas, Oct. 6, 1871, "List of Seminole-Negro Indians lately arrived at the Camp of the Seminole-Negro Scouts at Fort Duncan, Texas, from the Nueces River," Department of Texas–Letters Received, file 1762, Department of Texas–1871, "Indian files," box 7, RG 393; Minutes of County Commissioner's Court, 1877, Kinney County, "W. W. Arnett's claim of remuneration for performance of inquest on Adam Payne," book 1, 150 (Kinney County Courthouse Archives, Brackettville, Texas); and Lt. H. L. Ripley, "Survey of Fort Clark, Texas, Military Reservation, Map Blueprint No. 14," June 1893, Records of the Office of the Quartermaster General, RG 92.

4. Strong, *My Frontier Days*, 53.

5. The cavalry camp was located at Silver Falls Lake on the White River in Crosby County, nineteen miles northwest from the main supply camp. The main supply camp,

often referred to as Anderson's Fort, at various times was located near Soldier Mound on Duck Creek near present-day Spur in Dickens County, and on the White River at the mouth of Blanco Canyon. Evidence from loose papers inside the Fourth U.S. Cavalry Expedition Letterbook indicates that there was semaphore communication between the two sites. One sheet indicates that the possible inaugural message was, "Send me up a cigar." For an archeological survey of the main supply camp see Wayne Parker, "Mackenzie's Supply Camp," *Grain Producer's News*, 30 (July, 1979), 4–7.

6. The location cited is the author's interpretation from the following sources: R. S. Mackenzie, Company A, "Record of Events," in Fourth U.S. Cavalry Regimental Returns, Sept. 20, 1874, RG 94; J. H. Dorst, "Scouting on the Staked Plains with Mackenzie in 1874," *The United Service*, 13 (Sept.–Oct., 1885), 405; and C. A. Hatfield, "Campaign of Colonel R. S. McKenzie," 4. The author believes the initial clash with the Indians occurred near the springs at Latitude, 34°11.688′ North and Longitude, 101°2.112′. See "Quitaque Creek," in Tyler, et al. (eds.), *The New Handbook of Texas*, V, 395.

7. Some disparity exists about the number of Indians involved in the attack upon the scouts. Strong, *My Frontier Days*, 49, stated, "There proved to be only seven Indians." Dorst, "Scouting with Mackenzie," 405, stated, "the scouts reported they had been attacked by some twenty Indians." G. E. Albee, "Mackenzie's Expedition," *Galveston News*, Oct. 22, 1874, p. 2, reported that the scouts "were discovered and attacked by about twenty-five Comanches." Hatfield, "Campaign of Colonel R. S. McKenzie," 4, states the scouts found themselves surrounded "by about forty Kiowas." The author contends there were seven Indians who pursued the scouts as their tracks would have been distinct upon the flat plains.

8. Hatfield, "Campaign of Colonel R. S. McKenzie, 4; and Albee, "Mackenzie's Expedition," *Galveston News*, Oct. 22, 1874, p. 2.

9. Albee, "The Battle of Palo Duro Canyon," *New York Herald*, Oct. 16, 1874, 2. See also J. M. Hunter (ed.), "The Battle of Palo Duro Canyon," *Frontier Times*, 21 (Jan., 1944), 179. Among the Southern Plains tribes, especially the Kiowa, the Spencer carbine and the Lehman rifle had virtually replaced the bow and arrow as the dominant weapons. See Capt. G. K. Sanderson to Assistant Adjutant General, Department of Texas, Sept. 25, 1874, Adjutant General's Office–Letters Received, file 4035, Office of the Adjutant General–1874 (filed with file 3490, Office of the Adjutant General–1874), RG 94.

10. The four miles from the site of the initial clash with the Indians to the edge of the escarpment encompassed a roughly 550 feet rise in elevation, the last quarter of a mile to the cliffline an ascent of 250 feet. Payne likely ascended onto the plains just south of where State Highway 97 intersects the escarpment, nine miles west of Flomot. The Seminole-Negro scout detachment at the time was armed with the 1867 metallic cartridge converted 1864 Sharps .50–.70 caliber, rim-fire, breach-loading, single-shot, single-trigger carbines with the twenty-inch barrel. See Lt. J. L. Bullis, Twenty-fourth U.S. Infantry, "Summary of Ordnance and Ordnance Stores in the hands of troops in the Service of the United States during the Third Quarter, ending September, 1874," RG 156.

11. Strong, *My Frontier Days*, 49. The location of the main column's dinner campsite is best approximated by Hatfield, "Campaign of R. S. McKenzie," 4, which states it was "fifteen miles back to our camp," from the attack and Mackenzie, Company A, "Record of Events," in Fourth U.S. Cavalry Regimental Returns, September 1874, which stated, "marched 18 miles and halted at water hole on Staked Plains." These figures place the noon campsite as being near present-day Dougherty in Floyd County.

12. Captain Albee and the Seminole-Negro scouts pursued the Indians back to Quitaque as per Mackenzie to Assistant Adjutant General, Department of Texas, Sept. 29, 1874, "Memorandum of march of the First Column from Camp on Fresh Fork of the Brazos," Sept. 20, 1874, Department of Texas–Letters Received, file 3926, Department of Texas–1874 (filed with file 4050, Department of Texas–1874, "Indian files," box 2, RG 393; hereafter cited as "Memorandum of march." See also Strong, *My Frontier Days*, 49–50; Hunter (ed.), "The Battle of Palo Duro Canyon," 179; and Hatfield, "Campaign of Colonel R. S. McKenzie," 5, for discussion of N. B. McLaughlin's pursuit of the southbound Indians.

13. Mackenzie to Adjutant for the Scouting Expedition, Dec. 2, 1874, Special Order no. 36, paragraph III, Special Orders and Circulars Issued, Fourth U.S. Cavalry Expedition Letterbook, 275, RG 391.

14. Mackenzie to Assistant Adjutant General, Department of Texas, Jan. 7, 1875, Department of Texas–Letters Received, file 100, Department of Texas–1875, RG 393; and Mackenzie to Office of the Adjutant General, Jan. 7, 1875, Adjutant General's Office–Letters Received, file 255, Office of the Adjutant General–1875, RG 94. The above cited documents and subsequent ones dealing with Mackenzie's recommendations for medals for men of his command, and the War Department's ruling that particular acts of gallantry be stated in each case may be found in National Archives Microcopy no. 666, roll 160, exposures 0387–0395, RG 94.

15. E. D. Townsend to C. C. Augur, Feb. 2, 1875, Adjutant General's Office–Letters Received, file 4917, Office of the Adjutant General–1875 (filed with file 2815, Office of the Adjutant General–1874), RG 94.

16. Mackenzie to E. D. Townsend, Aug. 31, 1875, Adjutant General's Office–Letters Received, file 4917, Office of the Adjutant General–1875 (filed with file 2815, Office of the Adjutant General–1874), RG 94.

17. Mackenzie to Commanding Officer, Fort Clark, Nov. 7, 1875, entry no. 289, Letters Sent, Fourth U.S. Cavalry Expedition Letterbook," 149, RG 391.

CHAPTER 14

Repulsing the Cheyenne at Tule Canyon

1. Mackenzie to H. W. Lawton, Aug. 23, 1874, Special Order no. 6, paragraph VI, Fourth United States Cavalry Expedition Letterbook, 256, RG 391; and Mackenzie to P. H. Sheridan, April 7, 1875, R. S. Mackenzie Personal Letterbook, 1873–1878, typescript,

34 (Gilcrease Institute, Tulsa, Okla.) See also Hatfield, "Campaign of Colonel R. S. McKenzie," 6. It is the author's contention that Francisco Tefoys(a), also known as Johnson, was a twenty-nine-year-old resident of Puerto de Luna, New Mexico. See United States Ninth Census (1870), New Mexico Territory, County of San Miguel, Population Schedule, Town of Puerto de Luna, p. 179, RG 29 (National Archives Microcopy no. 593, roll 895). He was probably part of a band of Comanchero traders that was broken up by Mackenzie's sweep through the area in August 1872. Under some nineteenth-century form of plea bargain he was enlisted under the name Francisco as a scout by Maj. William R. Price at Fort Wingate, New Mexico, on May 18, 1874. See "Special and Miscellaneous Enlistments, Indian Scouts, 1866–1877," Register of United States Army Enlistments, vol. 150–151, in M-233, roll 70, entry no. 87, RG 94. As per telegraphic instructions of July 23, 1874, from the Military Department of the Missouri, Francisco was expeditiously mustered out on August 8, less than three months into his six-month enlistment. Arrangements were made for his travel to Fort Concho, where he was hired by Lt. Henry W. Lawton. The name Johnson was likely supplanted by the secretive Mackenzie to hide Francisco Tefoys(a)'s true identity, even from his subordinate officer corps. Likely by Mackenzie's design, Tefoys(a) has been confused by some with the Tonkawa scout, Johnson (Opay-yet-tah), who was still under his April 1, 1874, one-year enlistment. As of August 23, 1874, Johnson was present at Fort Griffin as sergeant of the Tonkawa Indian scout detachment. See also Mackenzie to T. M. Vincent, May 9, 1878, R. S. Mackenzie Personal Letterbook, 1873–1878, typescript, entry no. 273, p. 76 (Gilcrease Institute, Tulsa, Okla.); and Mackenzie to Expedition Adjutant, Special Order no. 37, paragraph IX, Dec. 19, 1874, Circulars and Orders Issued, Fourth U.S. Cavalry Expedition Letterbook, 277, RG 391.

2. Albee, "Mackenzie's Expedition," *Galveston News*, Oct. 22, 1874, p. 2; Charleton, "The Battle of Palo Duro Canyon," *Winners of the West*, 19 (Apr. 28, 1942), 1; and Strong, *My Frontier Days*, 50–51. In Mackenzie to Expedition Adjutant, Aug. 30, 1874, Special Order no. 8, Circulars and Orders Issued, Fourth U.S. Cavalry Expedition Letterbook, 257, Mackenzie indicated that all but eight Tonkawas were to be assigned to the G. P. Buell column. Mackenzie in Special Orders no. 23 and no. 37, Fourth U.S. Cavalry Expedition Letterbook, 265–266, 277, listed seven enlisted men by name as assigned to scouting duty. The Register of Enlistments for Indian Scouts indicates fifteen Tonkawas enlisted at the time of the campaign; therefore, seven served with the Mackenzie column. One Lipan–Apache, Tinarte, was brought from Fort Sill to serve as a spy. Along with the twenty-one Seminole-Negro scouts and the two civilian guides, Henry Strong and Francisco Tefoys(a), the total scouting contingent numbered thirty-eight.

3. Charleton, "The Battle of Palo Duro Canyon," 2; and Carter, *The Old Sergeant's Story*, 104–105. Former Sgt. John B. Charleton, from among all of those who provided accounts about the campaign, was the only one to have mentioned this engagement. Former Lt. William A. Thompson, "Scouting with Mackenzie," *Journal of the U.S. Cavalry Association*, 10 (Dec., 1897), 431, makes no mention of this engagement. Albee alluded to this engagement when in referring to his service during the 1874 campaign he

wrote: "Later I was for a time in command of the Tonkawa, Lipan, and Seminole Scouts, and one day, when about twelve miles in advance of the main command, the hostiles delivered an attack on my party while we were grazing our horses and lunching at noon. We repulsed the attack and chased them several miles." See G. E. Albee to H. W. Lawton, July 26, 1893, Adjutant General's Office–Documents Received, file 13892, Principal Records Division–1893, RG 94.

Physical evidence of this engagement, near the present-day community of Vigo in western Swisher County, is found in Bruce Gerdes to Frank Collinson, Jan. 12, 1938, Earl Vandale Papers, 1819–1947 (CAH). Gerdes indicates the finding of numerous Springfield .45–70 caliber cartridges at the Vigo location. Indian confirmation of the engagement of September 25, 1874, was made by the Kiowa sub-chief White Horse. In "Talk with White Horse," Oct. 21, 1874, Military Division of the Missouri–Letters Received, file 4511, Military Division of the Missouri–1874, Special File, Indian Territory Expedition, box 7, RG 393; hereafter cited as "Talk with White Horse," White Horse stated, "The Indians had out eight scouts who had a fight with Mackenzie's scouts and that night the Indians went and fired on General Mackenzie." The evidence of the engagement is indisputable, but Mackenzie's reasons for failing to mention this brief engagement are left to specula-tion. The author contends that at the outset of the engagement there was a verbal dispute between Lt. George E. Albee, the detachment's temporary commander, and Sgt. John B. Charleton as Charleton alluded to in Carter, *The Old Sergeant's Story*, 92, and in Carter, *On The Border with Mackenzie*, 383–384. The author further contends that Lt. William A. Thompson was given command of the scouting detachment as a result of this conflict. Thompson became scouting detachment commander on September 26 by Mackenzie's verbal order. See Special Order no. 22, Headquarters, Southern Column, Oct. 22, 1874, Special Orders and Circulars Issued, Fourth U.S. Cavalry Expedition Letterbook, 265, RG 391. The author believes that R. G. Carter attempted to cover the matter; for example, in Carter, *The Old Sergeant's Story*, 92, he omits the name of the officer involved. He fur-ther attempts to cloud the issue by alluding that this incident occurred during the 1872 campaign when he wrote, "One more incident occurred on this same scout." In alluding to this conflict he mentioned enlisted scout William McCabe, who did not enlist in the U.S. Army until February 3, 1874.

4. Mackenzie, "Memorandum of march of the Column from Camp on Freshwater Fork of the Brazos, September 20–29, 1874," Sept. 29, 1874, Department of Texas–Letters Received, file 4050, Department of Texas–1874, "Indian files," RG 393; hereafter cited as, "Memorandum of march, Sept. 20–29, 1874," with page number. In the entry for September 26 Mackenzie credits Lieutenant Thompson with the discovery of this herd. See also Albee to Lawton, July 26, 1893, Adjutant General's Office–Documents Received, file 13892, RG 94.

5. Strong, *My Frontier Days*, 55–56; and Dorst, "Scouting with Mackenzie," 407.

6. Dorst, "Scouting with Mackenzie," 407.

7. Mackenzie, "Record of Events," Company A, in Fourth U.S. Cavalry Regimental Returns, September 1874, RG 94; Mackenzie, "Memorandum of march, Sept. 20–29,

1874," 3; Hatfield, "Campaign of Colonel R. S. McKenzie," 5–6; Strong, *My Frontier Days*, 56; Dorst, "Scouting with Mackenzie," 407–408; Carter, *On the Border with Mackenzie*, 484–486; Bruce Gerdes to Earl Vandale, Jan. 25, 1940, "Briscoe County, Texas," Earl Vandale Papers (CAH); and U.S. Department of the Interior, Geological Survey, "Rock Creek Quadrangle Map." The sketch Bruce Gerdes drew on January 25, 1940, pinpoints the exact location of the September 25–27 campsites from evidence such as cartridges and other artifacts found at the location.

8. Mackenzie, "Memorandum of march, Sept. 20–29, 1874," 5; and Nye, *Bad Medicine and Good*, 218–219.

9. Carter, *On the Border with Mackenzie*, 485.

10. Albee, "Mackenzie's Expedition," *Galveston News*, Oct. 22, 1874, 2; Dorst, "Scouting with Mackenzie," 407–408; and Carter, *On the Border with Mackenzie*, 484.

11. Dorst, "Scouting with Mackenzie," 408.

12. Mackenzie, Company A, "Record of Events," in Fourth U.S. Cavalry Regimental Returns, September 1874; Dorst, "Scouting with Mackenzie," 409; Strong, *My Frontier Days*, 52; and Carter, *On the Border with Mackenzie*, 486. The regimental returns composed from company commander reports clearly indicate that Pvt. E. Veuve initiated the firing that night from the Second Battalion. Since Carter was not there and the source of his information about Pvt. Moses Goodwin is not cited the author chose to give more credence to the report of an actual participant.

13. Mackenzie, "Memorandum of march, Sept. 20–29, 1874," 5; and Strong, *My Frontier Days*, 56.

14. Mackenzie, "Memorandum of march, Sept. 20–29, 1874," 5–7; and Carter, *The Old Sergeant's Story*, 105.

15. E. Phoenix to Office of the Adjutant General, Aug. 20, 1931, "Application for Medal of Honor Certificate" (filed with Edwin Phoenix Pension file no. C-2606884), RG 15; Mackenzie, "Memorandum of march, Sept. 20–29, 1874," 5–6; and Strong, *My Frontier Days*, 57.

16. Hatfield, "Campaign of R. S. McKenzie," 8; Hunter (ed.), "The Battle of Palo Duro Canyon," 179.

17. Albee, "Mackenzie's Expedition," *Galveston News*, Oct. 22, 1874, p. 2; and Hunter (ed.), "The Battle of Palo Duro Canyon," 179.

18. Charleton, "The Battle of Palo Duro Canyon," 2; and Carter, *The Old Sergeant's Story*, 105–106.

19. Carter, *The Old Sergeant's Story*, 93–94; and Strong, *My Frontier Days*, 57.

20. Strong, *My Frontier Days*, 57–58.

21. Hatfield, "Campaign of Col. R. S. McKenzie," 9.

22. Mackenzie, Companies E and L, "Record of Events," Fourth U.S. Cavalry Regimental Returns, September 1874; Albee, "Mackenzie's Expedition," *Galveston News*, Oct. 22, 1874, p. 2; Hunter, "The Battle of Palo Duro Canyon," 180; Carter, *On the Border with Mackenzie*,

490; Hatfield, "Campaign of Col. R. S. McKenzie," 5–6; Dorst, "Scouting With Mackenzie," 411; and Col. E. Z. Steever, Regimental History, Fourth U.S. Cavalry, 1855–1906, item 734, 6–7, RG 391.

23. Mackenzie to Assistant Adjutant General, Department of Texas, Oct. 26, 1874, Special Order no. 23, paragraph I, Oct. 26, Circulars and Orders Issued, 1874, Fourth U.S. Cavalry Expedition Letterbook, 265, RG 391. This special order stated: "The verbal order of September 29, 1874 directing Captain Parke, 10th Infantry to shoot ponies captured from hostile Indians is confirmed and Captain Parke is authorized to expend for said purpose, twelve hundred and forty (1240) rounds of ammunition." See also Mackenzie to Acting Assistant Adjutant General, Headquarters Southern Column, Nov. 21, 1874, Special Order no. 34, paragraph II, Circulars and Orders Issued, 1874, Fourth United States Cavalry Expedition Letterbook, 274, RG 391. The disposition of the captured stock is delineated in Mackenzie to Assistant Adjutant General, Department of Texas, Oct. 1, 1874, Department of Texas–Letters Received, files 3973 and 4310, Department of Texas–1874, RG 393. In this source Mackenzie reported that 1,424 ponies, mules, and colts were captured, and 184 animals were distributed as rewards for the spies and scouts and as replacements for lost or unserviceable animals within the command. See also Mackenzie to Assistant Adjutant General, Department of Texas, Oct. 26, 1874, Letters Sent, 1874, Fourth U.S. Cavalry Expedition Letterbook, 27–28, RG 391.

24. Mackenzie to Assistant Adjutant General, Department of Texas, Department of Texas–Letters Received, file 100, Department of Texas–1875, "Indian files," RG 393.

25. E. D. Townsend to C. C. Augur, Feb. 2, 1875, Adjutant General's Office–Letters Received, file 4917, Office of the Adjutant General–1875 (filed with Adjutant General's Office–Letters Received, file 2815, Office of the Adjutant General–1874), RG 94.

26. Mackenzie to Office of the Adjutant General, Aug. 31, 1875, Adjutant General's Office–Letters Received, file 4917, Office of the Adjutant General–1875 (filed with Adjutant General's Office–Letters Received, file 2815, Office of the Adjutant General–1874), RG 94.

27. Secretary of War to Office of the Adjutant General, Oct. 13, 1875, Adjutant General's Office–Letters Received, file 4917, Office of the Adjutant General–1875 (filed with Adjutant General's Office–Letters Received, file 2815, Office of the Adjutant General–1874), RG 94.

28. Office of the Adjutant General to Chief Clerk, War Department, Oct. 19, 1875, Adjutant General's Office–Letters Received, file 4917, Office of the Adjutant General–1875 (filed with Adjutant General's Office–Letters Received, file 2815, Office of the Adjutant General–1874), RG 94.

29. Edwin Phoenix to Office of the Adjutant General, Nov. 5, 1875, Adjutant General's Office–Letters Received, file 5703, Office of the Adjutant General–1875 (filed with Adjutant General's Office–Letters Received, file 2815, Office of the Adjutant General–1874), RG 94.

30. Gregory Mahoney to Office of the Adjutant General, Jan. 28, 1876, Adjutant General's Office–Letters Received, file 681, Office of the Adjutant General–1876 (filed

with Adjutant General's Office–Letters Received, file 2815, Office of the Adjutant General–1874), RG 94.

31. William McCabe to Office of the Adjutant General, Jan. 28, 1876, Adjutant General's Office–Letters Received, file 837, Office of the Adjutant General–1876 (filed with Adjutant General's Office–Letters Received, file 2815, Office of the Adjutant General–1874), RG 94.

CHAPTER 15
Gallantry on the High Plains

1. Miles to Gen. John Pope, Oct. 14, 1874, Adjutant General's Office–Letters Received, file 2815, Office of the Adjutant General–1874, RG 94.

2. White Horse to unnamed interviewer, "Talk with White Horse," Oct. 21, 1874, Special File–Indian Territory Expedition, 1874–1875, Military Division of the Missouri, RG 393. This is the first known Indian account of the various tribes following Mackenzie's attack on Palo Duro Canyon. See also G. K. Anderson to Assistant Adjutant General, Department of Texas, Sept. 25, 1874, Adjutant General's Office–Letters Received, file 4035, Office of the Adjutant General–1874 (filed with file 3490, Office of the Adjutant General–1874), RG 94; and Nye, *Carbine and Lance*, 290.

3. Davidson to Assistant Adjutant General, Department of Texas, Dec. 22, 1874, Adjutant General's Office–Letters Received, files 180 and 183, Office of the Adjutant General–1875 (all filed with file 2815, Office of the Adjutant General–1874), RG 94.

4. Neill to Assistant Adjutant General, Department of the Missouri, Nov. 11, 1874, Adjutant General's Office–Letters Received, file 4708, Office of the Adjutant General–1874; and Davidson to Assistant Adjutant General, Department of Texas, Jan. 26, 1875, file 769, Office of the Adjutant General–1874, both filed with file 2815, Office of the Adjutant General–1874, RG 94.

5. Nye, *Carbine and Lance*, 297. During the early part of the campaign these bands had been on a raid into North Central Texas and were outside the area converged upon by the various army columns.

6. Mackenzie to Assistant Adjutant General, Department of Texas, Nov. 8, 1874, Department of Texas–Letters Received, files 4262, 4310, 4530, 4549, 4883, and 4986 (filed with file 4050, Department of Texas–1874, "Continuation of itenerary of the march of First Southern Column, September 29–November 8, 1874"), "Indian files," RG 393; hereafter cited as "Continuation of Itenerary."

7. Mackenzie in Mackenzie to Assistant Adjutant General, Department of Texas, Oct. 26, 1874, file 4310, Department of Texas–1874, RG 393, reported that the carts were loaded with dried meat. Thompson, "Scouting with Mackenzie," 431–432, stated that the ox teams were loaded with supplies and ammunition. Strong, *My Frontier Days*, 63, stated that they had some lances in the wagons. Dorst, in "Scouting with Mackenzie," 535, made no mention of the wagon contents. Mackenzie alluded to the capture of Tafoya

and Valdez in Mackenzie to Assistant Adjutant General, Department of Texas, Nov. 9, 1874, Letters Sent, 1874, Fourth U.S. Cavalry Expedition Letterbook, 32, in which he stated, "The captured horses have been given principally to two Mexicans induced to go with us."

8. José P. Tafoya was a thirty-eight-year-old farm laborer from La Cuesta, New Mexico. He was likely related to Francisco and was a Comanchero cohort to Theodore Valdez and the La Cuesta, Puerto de Luna, and Gallinas Springs bands of Comancheros. He served as a spy operative for Mackenzie until 1878 and then served with the Seminole-Negro scouts until May 1880. He afterward served as a guide for Col. Adna R. Chaffee at Fort Stanton, New Mexico, until 1884, and farmed near Chaperito, New Mexico, until his death at Park Springs on June 24, 1913. See José P. Tafoya to Commissioner of Pensions, May 20, 1902, Indian War Invalid Pension Application no. 1285904, Records of the U. S. Veterans Administration, RG 15.

9. Thompson, "Scouting with Mackenzie," 431–432, mentioned that a wagon was burned and that two of those captured agreed to pilot the command in exchange for the release of the others. Dorst, "Scouting with Mackenzie," 535, described the events of October 7 and mentioned only coming upon six ox-drawn Mexican wagons and that those with the wagons claimed to be buffalo hunters. José P. Tafoya and Theodore Valdez were already under Mackenzie's employment effective October 7 by Special Order no. 29, in Fourth U.S. Cavalry Expedition Letterbook, 270, so they definitely were not among those encountered on October 8.

10. Mackenzie to Adjutant for the Scouting Expedition, Nov. 13, 1874, Special Order no. 29, Fourth U.S. Cavalry Expedition Letterbook, 270, RG 391; Mackenzie to Assistant Adjutant General, Department of Texas, Oct. 26, 1874, Letters Sent, 1874, Fourth U.S. Cavalry Expedition Letterbook, 27–28, RG 391; and Mackenzie to Assistant Adjutant General, Department of Texas, Nov. 9, 1874, Department of Texas–Letters Received, file 4986, Department of Texas–1874, RG 393. In Mackenzie to Augur, Oct. 21, 1874, Letters Sent, 1874, Fourth U.S. Cavalry Expedition Letterbook, 24–25, RG 391, he expresses his intent to reward the Lipan Indian spies and New Mexican guides with promises of large rewards of horses, "should we succeed through them" (in finding Indian camps). He hoped that the news of these rewards would make allies of all "the rascally cow thieves and buffalo hunters of the upper Canadian and Pecos and between hope and fear break up for a time their leading, and have them as allies." See Mackenzie to P. H. Sheridan, June 12, 1874, R. S. Mackenzie Personal Letterbook, typescript, 34 (Gilcrease Institute, Tulsa, Okla.). See also Special Order no. 37, paragraph IX, Dec. 19, 1874, Fourth U.S. Cavalry Expedition Letterbook, 276–277, RG 391. This order to H. W. Lawton to pay the guides up to date specifically mentions Francisco Tafoya, José P. Tafoya, and Theodore Valdez.

11. Strong, *My Frontier Days*, 62–63.

12. Mackenzie to Expedition Adjutant, Oct. 26, 1874, Special Order no. 23, Fourth U.S. Cavalry Expedition Letterbook, 265–266, RG 391; and W. Rankin, Adjutant General's Office–Documents Received, files 704887, Office of the Adjutant General–1898, and

312988, Office of the Adjutant General–1900, "Statement of Service," and "Retirement papers," RG 94.

13. Mackenzie to Assistant Adjutant General, Department of Texas, Oct. 5, 1875, Letters Sent, item 259, Fourth U.S. Cavalry Expedition Letterbook, 140, RG 391; Enlistment papers, Richard M. Mansfield, May 8, 1871, RG 94; and Enlistment papers, William McCabe, Feb. 3, 1874, RG 94.

14. Strong, *My Frontier Days,* 50, 75; and Enlistment papers, Robert Shiels, Dec. 3, 1869, RG 94.

15. Strong, *My Frontier Days*, 50–53, 57, 75–77; and Comfort to Office of the Adjutant General, Nov. 14, 1892, Adjutant General's Office–Documents Received, file 41621, Principal Records Division, Office of the Adjutant General–1892, RG 94.

16. Strong, *My Frontier Days*, 36, 38, 50–53, 74–77; Enlistment papers, Frank Fitzgerald, April 21, 1871, RG 94; and Enlistment papers, Edward J. O'Brien, Sept. 24, 1874, RG 94.

17. Carter, *The Old Sergeant's Story*, 68, n. 1, 166; and Strong, *My Frontier Days*, 50–53, 75–76.

18. Mackenzie to Assistant Adjutant General, Department of Texas, Oct. 29, 1874, Letters Sent, 1874, Fourth U.S. Cavalry Expedition Letterbook, 28–30, RG 391.

19. Ibid. Mackenzie's decision to relieve Captain Boehm's Company E from further field service and to retain certain officers at the supply camp greatly affected the information available to historians about the second sweep of the campaign. Lts. C. A. P. Hatfield and Joseph H. Dorst, who kept very detailed diary accounts of the campaign, were thus absent from the second sweep operations. Mackenzie's very brief generalized report and Charleton and Strong's scant remembrances after forty years are the only firsthand accounts of the command's actions during early November.

20. All distances and directions of movement for the main command are extracted from Mackenzie, "Continuation of itenerary." See also Mackenzie, "Record of Events," November 1874, Fourth U.S. Cavalry Regimental Returns, RG 94.

21. The name provided for this arroyo is the author's estimation of the command's location using Mackenzie, "Continuation of itenerary." Plum Creek arroyo in southwest Crosby County best coincides with the entry "moved southwest three miles and struck the head of a large canyon" (Rescate–Yellow House). See also Strong, *My Frontier Days*, 64.

22. Mileage and direction of travel provided in Mackenzie, "Continuation of itenerary," indicates that this campsite was likely at the present-day Buffalo Springs Lake, three miles east of the Lubbock city limits.

23. Strong, *My Frontier Days*, 64–65, mentions this action. According to Strong, Thompson was present, but Thompson made no mention of the incident in "Scouting with Mackenzie," 432–433. Interestingly the sub-canyon where the Indians abandoned their camp was afterward labeled Thompson's Canyon on post-1874 U.S. Army maps. The location is now Mackenzie State Park.

24. Mackenzie, "Continuation of itenerary."

25. Mackenzie, "Record of Events," November 1874, Fourth U.S. Cavalry Regimental Returns, RG 94.

26. Mackenzie, "Continuation of itenerary." Extrapolation of movements from Laguna Rica by direction, east, and mileage, nine miles, places the command at Laguna Sombiga (Mound Lake) shortly after noon on November 3. For a description of this lake see "Mound Lake," in Tyler, et al. (eds.), *The New Handbook of Texas*, IV, 860.

27. "Double Lakes," in Tyler, et al., (eds.), *The New Handbook of Texas*, II, 685. Twelve miles east from Laguna Sombiga (Mound Lake) is Double Lakes, not Laguna Quatro (also known as Twin Lakes and French's Lake).

28. Strong, *My Frontier Days*, 65. The Indians commonly cached their vast herds away from their camps for safety reasons. The valley-like depression and the freshwater springs at the northern tip of Double Lakes, which is now the T–Bar Ranch headquarters, would have been the only logical and viable location. See Brune, *Springs of Texas*, 300.

29. Strong, *My Frontier Days*, 65, states "I shot two and Verve (sic) of A Company killed one." Mackenzie to Office of the Adjutant General, Aug. 31, 1875, Adjutant General's Office–Letters Received, file 4917, Office of the Adjutant General–1875 (filed with file 2815, Office of the Adjutant General–1874) described Veuve's actions as "the gallant manner in which he faced a desperate Indian." Mrs. Agnes MacDonald of Eugene, Oregon, a neighbor to Ernest Veuve in Missoula, Montana, during the early 1900s, recalled one story about him "jumping on an Indian in Texas"; see Agnes MacDonald to Rex E. Neal, January 7, 1975, interview (letters about the interview in author's possession). Beyer and Keydel, *Deeds of Valor*, II, 193, described Veuve's deed as "a brief hand-to-hand fight with a hostile Indian when separated from his comrades." See also Mackenzie to Acting Assistant Adjutant General, Nov. 15, 1874, Special Order no. 31, Fourth U.S. Cavalry Expedition Letterbook, 272, RG 391. Mackenzie to Assistant Adjutant General, Department of Texas, Nov. 8, 1874, Letters Sent, Fourth U.S. Cavalry Expedition Letterbook, 30, RG 391. Thompson, "Scouting with Mackenzie," 432.

30. Mackenzie to Assistant Adjutant General, Department of Texas, Nov. 8, 1874, Fourth U.S. Cavalry Expedition Letterbook, 31, RG 391. The village was likely that of the Quohada Comanche chiefs Patchaquire and Horseshoe. Patchaquire is translated either as Otterbelt or Beaver. He was the second chief under Mow-wi and often roamed and raided with the Cheyenne and Mescalero Apaches. See also Mackenzie to Assistant Adjutant General, Department of Texas, Nov.16, 1874, Department of Texas–Letters Received, file 4262, Department of Texas–1874, "Indian files," RG 393.

31. Nye, *Carbine and Lance*, 209; and Strong, *My Frontier Days*, 40, 56.

32. Mackenzie, "Continuation of itenerary," Nov. 8, 1874, Department of Texas–Letters Received, file 4986, Department of Texas–1874, "Indian files," RG 393. This report forwarded with Mackenzie, "Continuation of itenerary," includes Mackenzie's very brief report on the Nov. 3–5, 1874, actions.

33. Strong, *My Frontier Days*, 65.

34. The location of this brief skirmish was likely near the largest of the three freshwater springs at the north end of Tahoka Lake on the May estate, three miles south of Wilson in Lynn County. See Brune, *Springs of Texas*, 300.

35. Carter, *The Old Sergeant's Story*, 68.

36. Mackenzie, "Record of Events," November 1874, Fourth U.S. Cavalry Regimental Returns, RG 94; Strong, *My Frontier Days*, 65–66; Mackenzie to Assistant Adjutant General, Department of Texas, Nov. 9, 1874, Department of Texas–Letters Received, file 4530, Department of Texas–1874, "Indian files," RG 393; Thompson, "Scouting with Mackenzie," 432; Dorst, "Scouting with Mackenzie," 540; Allyn Capron to Post Adjutant, Presidio of San Francisco, Nov. 20, 1889, Adjutant General's Office–Letters Received, file 6122, Office of the Adjutant General–1889 (filed with file 5461, Office of the Adjutant General–1889), RG 94.

37. "Report of Indian Depredations," Nov. 1, 1875, item no. 235, in Winfrey and Day (eds.), *The Indian Papers of Texas*, IV, 374, 381, 383. The time frame, proximity, number of Indians involved and quantity of stock stolen from Coleman, Callahan and Tom Green Counties in October, correlates closely to the number of Indians encountered and the number of horses recovered from the Indians.

38. Mackenzie to Assistant Adjutant General, Department of Texas, Jan. 7, 1875, Department of Texas–Letters Received, file 100, Department of Texas–1875, RG 393. See also Adjutant General's Office–Letters Received, file 255, Office of the Adjutant General–1875 (filed with file 2815, Office of the Adjutant General–1874), RG 94.

39. E. D. Townsend to C. C. Augur, Feb. 2, 1875, Adjutant General's Office–Letters Received, file 4917, Office of the Adjutant General–1875 (filed with file 2815, Office of the Adjutant General–1874), RG 94.

40. Mackenzie to Office of the Adjutant General, Aug. 31, 1875, Adjutant General's Office–Letters Received, file 4917, Office of the Adjutant General–1875 (filed with file 2815, Office of the Adjutant General–1874), RG 94.

41. Secretary of War to Office of the Adjutant General, Oct. 13, 1875, Adjutant General's Office–Letters Received, file 4917, Office of the Adjutant General–1875 (filed with file 2815, Office of the Adjutant General–1874), RG 94.

42. Office of the Adjutant General to Chief Clerk, War Department, Oct. 19, 1875, Adjutant General's Office–Letters Received, file 4917, Office of the Adjutant General–1875 (filed with file 2815, Office of the Adjutant General–1874), RG 94.

43. E. Veuve to Office of the Adjutant General, Nov. 5, 1875, Adjutant General's Office–Letters Received, file 5703, Office of the Adjutant General–1875 (filed with file 2815, Office of the Adjutant General–1874), RG 94.

44. The letter from John Comfort acknowledging receipt of his medal could not be found. In Mackenzie, Returns of U.S. Army Regular Cavalry Regiments, Fourth U.S. Cavalry, January 1876, Comfort is listed as "on detached duty at Cantonment on the Sweetwater (Fort Elliott) under Lt. W. A. Thompson." The Returns from U.S. Army

Military Posts, 1800–1916, Cantonment on the Sweetwater (Fort Elliott), indicates Comfort was "in the field until January 28."

CHAPTER 16
Baldwin's Battlewagons to the Rescue

1. Grace E. Meredith, *Girl Captives of the Cheyennes: A True Story of the Capture and Rescue of Four Pioneer Girls* (Los Angeles: Gem Publishing Co., 1927), 1; Frances R. Kestler (comp.), *The Indian Captivity Narratives* (New York: Garland Publishing Co., 1990), 491.

2. Meredith, *Girl Captives of the Cheyennes*, 159–160; and Kestler (comp.), *The Indian Captivity Narratives*, 497–498.

3. At least seven different sources mention seven different Cheyenne chiefs as being in command or responsible for the attack on the German family. The most accurate indictment comes from Catherine German in Meredith, *Girl Captives of the Cheyennes*, 108–109, when she personally identified sixteen males and two females of the nineteen Indians involved in the attack. The prime perpetrator, Kicking Horse, fearing identification, fled but purportedly was later killed by troops at Sappa Creek, Kansas, on April 23, 1875. See also T. H. Neill to Assistant Adjutant General, Department of the Missouri, Mar. 2, 1875, file 1547M, Department of the Missouri–Letters Received, 1875 (filed with file 2815, Office of the Adjutant General–1874), RG 94; and G. D. West, "The Battle of Sappa Creek," *Kansas Historical Quarterly*, 34, no. 2 (1968), 150–178.

4. Meredith, *Girl Captives of the Cheyennes*, 18.

5. Ibid., 17–19; and C. C. Hewitt to Post Adjutant, Fort Wallace, Oct. 2, 1874, Adjutant General's Office–Letters Received, file 1547M, Office of the Adjutant General–1874 (filed with file 2815, Office of the Adjutant General–1874), RG 94.

6. Johnson, *The Unregimented General*, 59, 66. After the 1876 Custer disaster an investigation was launched into the source of arms for the Sioux and other plains tribes. See "Correspondence relating to the proposed prohibition on the sale of arms and ammunition by Indian traders to Indians, 1876–1878," Adjutant General's Office–Letters Received, file 4408, Office of the Adjutant General–1876, in National Archives Microcopy no. 666, roll 294, RG 94.

7. Davidson to Assistant Adjutant General, Department of Texas, Dec. 22, 1874, Adjutant General's Office–Letters Received, file 180, 1874; and Davidson to Augur, Jan. 9, 1875, Adjutant General's Office–Letters Received, file 277, Office of the Adjutant General–1875 (both filed with file 2815, Office of the Adjutant General–1874), RG 94; and Nye, *Carbine and Lance*, 291.

8. Baird, "Indian Territory Expedition," 12. According to Miles, Fifth U.S. Infantry Regimental Returns, October 1874, RG 94, Lt. Henry B. Bristol, commanding Company D, was taken ill as of October 28, which elevated Lt. Hobart K. Bailey to temporary command of the company.

9. Although not identified completely in any account of the expedition, this surgeon was Junius L. Powell. He apparently was serving as a civilian contract surgeon during the

campaign, but gained appointment as an army assistant surgeon in 1878. See F. B. Heitman, *Historical Register and Dictionary of the United States Army, 1789–1903* (Washington, D.C.: Government Printing Office, 1903), 803.

10. F. D. Baldwin, "Baldwin Diary," Nov. 6, 1874, 3. The portion of Baldwin's personal diary, which deals with the Indian Territory Expedition, 1874–1875, is an integral part of the Papers of Maj. George W. Baird, 1874–1891 (Manuscripts Division, Archives of the Kansas Historical Society, Topeka, Kans.); hereafter cited as Baldwin Diary, date of entry, and page. See also Johnson, *The Unregimented General*, 55.

11. H. Farnsworth to Field Adjutant, Eighth U.S. Cavalry, Nov. 7, 1874, Adjutant General's Office–Letters Received, file 4955, Office of the Adjutant General–1874; and Miles to Assistant Adjutant General, Department of the Missouri, Nov. 9, 1874, Adjutant General's Office–Letters Received, file 5057, Office of the Adjutant General–1874 (both filed with file 2815, Office of the Adjutant General–1874), RG 94.

12. Baldwin Diary, Nov. 7, 1874, 4–5. Baldwin's campsite this night was at a series of springs one mile upstream from present-day Lake McClellan. These springs are situated in a dense grove of cottonwood trees as described in Alice B. Baldwin, *Memoirs of the Late Frank D. Baldwin, Major-General, U.S. Army* (Los Angeles: Wetzel Publishing Co., 1929), 72; hereafter cited as Baldwin, *Baldwin Memoirs*. These springs are located on the W. A. Bralley ranch on the south boundary of the National Guard's Panhandle training area. See Brune, *Springs of Texas*, 198.

13. Baldwin Diary, Nov. 8, 1874, 6; and Baldwin, *Baldwin Memoirs*, 73.

14. See Nye, *Carbine and Lance*, 91; P. I. Wellman, *The Indian Wars of the West* (Garden City: Doubleday, 1954), 91–97; and P. H. Sheridan, *Record of Engagements with Hostile Indians within Department of the Missouri, 1868–1882* (Washington, D.C.: Government Printing Office, 1882), 22, for examples of Indian atrocities upon prisoners at the outset of army attacks.

15. Baldwin, *Baldwin Memoirs*, 71–76; Meredith, *Girl Captives of the Cheyennes*, 102; Miles, "Company D, Detached duty," Fifth U.S. Infantry Regimental Returns, November 1874, which lists Sgt. Charles Reinstine and Pvts. G. Burke, T. Butler, F. Klusman, C. Bush, B. Gaines, and R. Hogan as being members of the artillery detachment under command of Lieutenant Baldwin to Camp Supply.

16. Baldwin, *Baldwin Memoirs*, 76. Long Back, a Cheyenne sub-chief, was the one who held Sophia and Catherine. He had been in the village until minutes before the attack.

17. Baldwin Diary, Nov. 8, 1874, 9, 15; and Baldwin, *Baldwin Memoirs*, 76.

18. Baldwin Diary, Nov. 8, 1874, 10–15; Miles, *Personal Recollections*, 174–176; and Robert H. Steinbach, *A Long March: The Lives of Frank and Alice Baldwin* (Austin: University of Texas Press, 1989), 92.

19. Baldwin Diary, Nov. 8, 1874, 11–12; and Miles to Assistant Adjutant General, Department of the Missouri, Nov. 9, 1874, Adjutant General's Office–Letters Received, files 4884, 5057, Adjutant General's Office–Letters Received, 1874 (filed with file 2815, Office of the Adjutant General–1874), RG 94. This large playa lake (Deep Lake) is on the

west side of State Highway 70, four and a half miles north of Panhandle Community and two miles south of the intersection with Ranch Road 749.

20. Baldwin Diary, Nov. 8, 1874, 10 mentions two Indians killed and several wounded in the assault on the village. The Indian dropped from his saddle by Overton's charge raised the total to three, which corresponds to N. A. Miles, Company D, "Record of Events," Fifth U.S. Infantry Returns, November 1874, RG 94, which states "3 or 4 killed and about same number wounded."

21. Baldwin Diary, Nov. 8, 1874, 12.

22. Miles, Company D, entry no. 13, Fifth U.S. Infantry Returns, November 1874, RG 94. See also Miles, *Personal Recollections*, 175.

23. Kestler (comp.), *The Indian Captivity Narratives*, 494.

24. Meredith, *Girl Captives of the Cheyennes*, 108–109; and T. H. Neill to Assistant Adjutant General, Department of the Missouri, Mar. 2, 1875, Adjutant General's Office–Letters Received, file 1547M, Office of the Adjutant General–1875 (filed with file 2815, Office of the Adjutant General–1874), RG 94.

25. N. A. Miles to Assistant Adjutant General, Department of the Missouri, Nov. 9, 1874, Adjutant General's Office–Letters Received, file 5057, Office of the Adjutant General–1874 (filed with file 2815, Office of the Adjutant General–1874), RG 94.

26. U.S. Congress, House, "Catharine and Sophia L. German," 44th Cong., 1st sess., 1877, H. Exec. Doc. 59 (1687), 3.

27. Miles to Office of the Adjutant General, Jan. 17, 1890, Adjutant General's Office–Documents Received, file 2367, Office of the Adjutant General–1890 (filed with file 5461, Office of the Adjutant General–1889), RG 94.

28. J. Coburn to F. D. Baldwin, Nov. 6, 1891, Miscellaneous letters, box 5, Frank Dwight Baldwin Papers, Western Historical Manuscripts (H. E. Huntington Library, San Marino, Calif.).

29. Ibid.

30. J. Coburn to F. D. Baldwin, Dec. 31, 1891 (excerpted from F. E. Warren to Secretary of War John W. Weeks, May 21, 1921), Miscellaneous letters, box 5, Baldwin Papers. As late as 1921 Baldwin was still attempting to gain recognition for his Stones River deed. His efforts in obtaining a Distinguished Service Medal for that deed were ruled upon adversely by an Army Decorations Board on December 8, 1921. See John W. Weeks to Francis E. Warren, Dec. 8, 1921, Miscellaneous letters, box 5, Baldwin Papers; and Senate, "Medal of Honor Review Board," case 2496, p. 384.

31. W. Schmalsle to F. D. Baldwin, Feb. 18, 1892, Miscellaneous letters, box 5, Baldwin Papers.

32. A. Baldwin to F. Baldwin, Aug. 31, 1892, Letters, Alice B. to Frank D. Baldwin, box 11, Baldwin Papers. See also Steinbach, *A Long March: The Lives of Frank and Alice Baldwin*, 161.

33. Miles to Office of the Adjutant General, Mar. 26 and Nov. 1, 1894, Adjutant General's Office–Documents Received, files 4914, 4946, and 9264, Principal Records

Division, Office of the Adjutant General–1894 (filed with file 5461, Office of the Adjutant General–1889), RG 94. See also "Personnel file, Frank D. Baldwin," file 3365, Appointment, Commission and Promotion file, 1875, RG 94.

34. U.S. Senate, "Medal of Honor Review Board," case 1755, p. 456–457.

35. Baldwin to Office of the Adjutant General, June 1, 1905, Miscellaneous letters, box 5, Baldwin Papers, and Baldwin to Office of the Adjutant General, Jan. 23, 1909, Adjutant General's Office–Documents Received, file 1029601, Principal Records Division, Office of the Adjutant General–1909, RG 94. Baldwin, in applying for the new 1904-design medal, requested that he be allowed to retain the originals. In pleading the value of the originals Baldwin claimed, "they were pinned on my coat by my Commanding General with conspicuous ceremony." If there was an award ceremony for his second Medal of Honor, it may have occurred circa December 1896 in Washington, D.C., when Baldwin rejoined Miles as part of his staff.

CHAPTER 17
Pursuit and Close Combat on the High Plains

1. P. H. Sheridan to W. T. Sherman, Oct. 29, 1874, telegram, Adjutant General's Office–Letters Received, file 2815, Office of the Adjutant General–1874, RG 94.

2. Due to Mackenzie's stringent policy of preserving the identity of his spies, it is probable that only white members of the command participated in the interrogations. Matthew Leiper had been a Comanche sub-agent and spoke Comanche fluently. "Personnel file, Matthew Leiper, Jr.," file 2396, Appointment, Commission and Promotion file, 1880, RG 94. Henry W. Lawton was expertly adept in the universal Indian sign language as mentioned in Parker, *The Old Army Memoirs*, 33. William Rankin and William Foster had more than two decades of experience among the Southern Plains Indians and likely had at least rudimentary Indian language skills. Foster had been designated in a special order by Mackenzie in 1872 as caretaker for prisoners, some of whom were now prisoners for a second time. To expose Francisco Tafoya, José P. Tafoya, Theodore Valdez, or Tinarte and Castile to the prisoners would have endangered them should any of the prisoners escape and rejoin their bands. Though most of Mackenzie's public reports identify them as scouts or guides, some of his private correspondence indicates they were also to be used as spies. See Mackenzie to Adjutant for the Scouting Expedition, Oct. 1, 1872, Special Order no. 47, paragraph IV, Circulars and Special Orders Issued, 1872, Fourth U.S. Cavalry Expedition Letterbook, 136, RG 391; and Mackenzie to T. Schwan, Nov. 11, 1874, Letters Sent, 1874, Fourth U.S. Cavalry Expedition Letterbook, 32–33, RG 391.

3. Mackenzie to T. Schwan, Nov. 11, 1874; and Mackenzie to Assistant Adjutant General, Department of Texas, Nov. 11, 1874, 35, both in Fourth U.S. Cavalry Expedition Letterbook, 32–33, 35, RG 391.

4. Dorst, "Scouting with Mackenzie," 541.

5. Strong, *My Frontier Days*, 68. According to Mackenzie, "Record of Events," December 1874, Fourth U.S. Cavalry Regimental Returns, eighteen animals were lost to the elements between the December 3 and 14.

6. Dorst, "Scouting with Mackenzie," 541.

7. Mackenzie to Assistant Adjutant General, Department of Texas, Jan. 7, 1875, "Continuation of itenerary of First Southern Column, Dec. 3–19, 1874," Department of Texas–Letters Received, file 104, Department of Texas–1875, RG 393, hereafter cited as "Continuation of itenerary, Dec. 3–19, 1874"; and Strong, *My Frontier Days*, 66. Casa Maria is likely a misinterpretation by either Mackenzie, Thompson, or McKinney of the Spanish "casa amarilla," or "yellow house." The upper Yellow House Draw area in the northwest corner of Hockley County near Silver Lake was an important rendezvous point for various tribes. Small rooms excavated into the yellow clay banks gave the area, drainage basin, and canyon its name. See Charles G. Davis, "Yellow House Draw (Canyon)," in Tyler, et al. (eds.), *The New Handbook of Texas*, VI, 1117.

8. Mackenzie, "Continuation of itenerary, Dec. 3–19, 1874"; and Strong, *My Frontier Days*, 67.

9. Mackenzie, Fourth U.S. Cavalry Regimental Returns, December 1874, listed W. T. Duggan of the Tenth U.S. Infantry as "temporarily assigned to Company L." See Mackenzie to Adjutant for the Scouting Expedition, Dec. 19, 1874, Special Order no. 37, paragraph V, Special Orders Issued, 1874, Fourth U.S. Cavalry Expedition Letterbook, 276–278, RG 391; and Strong, *My Frontier Days*, 67. Lewis Warrington III grew up in the affluent Georgetown section of Washington, D.C., the only son of Lewis Warrington Jr., a U.S. Navy paymaster, and grandson to one of the earliest American naval heroes, Lewis Warrington. The elder Warrington's successes against the Tripolian pirates and the British in the War of 1812 were instrumental in establishing the U.S. Navy as a world sea power. See "Personnel file, Lewis Warrington, III," file 180, Appointment, Commission and Promotion file, 1879, RG 94.

10. Warrington to Acting Assistant Adjutant General, Scouting Expedition, Dec. 19, 1874, Department of Texas–Letters Received, file 100, Department of Texas–1875, "Indian files," RG 393; hereafter cited as Warrington Report, Dec. 19, 1874. See also Carter, *On the Border with Mackenzie*, 516–517.

11. The location stated is an estimation based upon Mackenzie's "Continuation of itenerary, Dec. 3–19, 1874," and William Hoffman's map, "Portions of Young and Bexar Counties, Texas," C. L. Crimmins Collection, map 70, 3Y23, folder 1189/3, C. L. Crimmins Collection (CAH), which delineates present-day Wet Tobacco Creek as Warrington Creek.

12. Strong, *My Frontier Days*, 68, claims credit for the capture of the Indian boy, while Warrington Report, Dec. 19, 1874, describes in detail his capture of the Indian. Strong did not date his purported capture, but in *My Frontier Days*, 68–69, he states that on December 8 he made a day-long ride with Lt. W. A. Thompson to McLaughlin's camp near Flat Top Mountain so he could not have been in the two distant locations at once.

13. Warrington Report, Dec. 19, 1874. Warrington wrote, "the Indian was overtaken by myself and Pvt. Bergendahl . . . who shot and mortally wounding him, Pvt. O'Sullivan . . . shooting him a second time."

14. Warrington Report, Dec. 19, 1874, in mentioning this occurrence, states only, "his bow being broken by one of two men." The author credits Bergendahl with the deed, based on the Company I, "Record of Events," December 1874, Fourth U.S. Cavalry Returns, which states, "the two Indians were killed by Private Bergendahl."

15. Warrington Report, Dec. 19, 1874. See also C. C. Augur, "Tabular Statement of Expeditions and Scouts Against Indians, made in the Department of Texas, During the Year, ending August 31, 1875," Adjutant General's Office–Letters Received, file 5689, Office of the Adjutant General–1875, RG 94.

16. Warrington Report, Dec. 19, 1874.

17. Mackenzie, "Continuation of itenerary, Dec. 19, 1874."

18. Ibid. Laguna Sabinas was renamed Shafter Lake after Col. William R. Shafter, who conducted a mapping survey of the region in 1875. It is located seven miles northwest of the present-day town of Andrews. See "Shafter Lake," in Tyler, et al. (eds.) *The New Handbook of Texas*, V, 988–989.

19. Strong, *My Frontier Days*, 68.

20. Mackenzie, "Continuation of itenerary, Dec. 3–19, 1874"; Dorst, "Scouting with Mackenzie," 542; and Strong, *My Frontier Days*, 69.

21. Mackenzie, Special Order no. 37, Dec. 19, 1874, Special Orders Issued, Fourth U.S. Cavalry Expedition Letterbook, 276–278, RG 391.

22. Mackenzie to Assistant Adjutant General, Department of Texas, Dec. 24, 1874, Department of Texas–Letters Received, file 4986, Department of Texas–1874, "Indian files," RG 393.

23. Mackenzie to Assistant Adjutant General, Department of Texas, Jan. 7, 1874, Department of Texas–Letters Received, file 100, Department of Texas–1875, "Indian files," RG 393.

24. Ibid.

25. Ibid.

26. E. D. Townsend to Commanding General, Department of Texas, Feb. 2, 1875, Adjutant General's Office–Letters Received, file 4917, Office of the Adjutant General–1875 (filed with file 2815, Office of the Adjutant General–1874), RG 94.

27. Senate, "Medal of Honor Review Board," case 2470, 410.

28. Mackenzie to Office of the Adjutant General, Aug. 31, 1875, Adjutant General's Office–Letters Received, file 4917, Office of the Adjutant General–1875 (filed with file 2815, Office of the Adjutant General–1874), RG 94.

29. John O'Sullivan to Office of the Adjutant General, Nov. 18, 1875, Adjutant General's Office–Letters Received, file 5898, Office of the Adjutant General–1875 (filed with file 2815, Office of the Adjutant General–1874), RG 94. The letter from Frederick

H. Bergendahl acknowledging receipt of his Medal of Honor could not be found. His medal was sent via registered mail on October 19, 1875, as per Office of the Adjutant General, file 4917, Office of the Adjutant General–1875. The average time from sending to receipt was seven days. In Mackenzie, October 1875, Fourth U.S. Cavalry Regimental Returns, RG 94, Bergendahl's presence at Fort Sill on October 26, 1875, is ascertained.

30. E. Wallace, *Ranald S. Mackenzie on the Texas Frontier* (Lubbock: West Texas Museum Association, 1964), 166.

CHAPTER 18
Outgunned at Eagle Nest Crossing

1. J. M. Hayworth to Commissioner of Indian Affairs, Sept. 20, 1875, Annual Report of the Commissioner to the Secretary of the Interior, 1875 (Washington, D.C.: Government Printing Office, 1875), 272, RG 75 (National Archives). The Essaqueta Apaches Hayworth referred to were also known as the Kiowa–Apaches. They numbered around three hundred and were headed by a chief named Pacer. In the early nineteenth century they had left the western Apaches and adopted the Kiowa plains culture. As of April 27, 1875, the Quohada Comanches under Black Beard and Quanah were camped three hundred miles north of the Rio Grande. See E. Wallace, "The Journal of R. S. Mackenzie's Messenger to the Kwahadi," *Red River Valley Historical Review*, 3, no. 2 (1978), 227–246.

2. William Steele, adjutant general, state of Texas, to Committee on the Frontier, 1875 Constitutional Convention, Oct. 7, 1875, "Abstract (partial) of depredations by Indians, previous to and since 1873, as reported to the Adjutant General's Office, Texas," 14–15, RG 401.

3. J. W. French to Assistant Adjutant General, Department of Texas, Mar. 29, 1875, Adjutant General's Office–Letters Received, file 1817, Office of the Adjutant General–1875 (filed with files 1879 and 2241, Office of the Adjutant General–1875), RG 94.

4. John Lapham Bullis was born at Farrington, New York, on April 17, 1841. After compiling a distinguished Civil War record he obtained a regular army appointment as a second lieutenant on September 3, 1867. He went on to serve twenty-eight years with the Twenty-fourth U.S. Infantry, eight of those as commander of the Seminole-Negro Indian scout detachment. He earned the nicknames "Whirlwind" and "Thunderbolt" participating in no less than fourteen engagements against Indians in Texas, Mexico, and New Mexico. The Texas Legislature honored him for his service to the Texas frontier in a special resolution in 1882. Bullis died at San Antonio, Texas, on May 26, 1911, and is buried at San Antonio National Cemetery. See Michael Tate, "John L. Bullis," in Tyler, et al. (eds.), *The New Handbook of Texas*, I, 823–824.

5. Judge Advocate General of the U.S. Army to Pvt. Dindie Factor, Apr. 9, 1875, court martial case file no. PP-4519, Pvt. Dindie Factor, Seminole-Negro Indian scout, Records of the Judge Advocate General, RG 153. The court martial of Pvt. Dindie Factor for inciting mutiny severely split the Seminole-Negro Indian scout detachment. Various scouts

had opposed one another as defense and prosecution witnesses in the trial that found Factor guilty. The severe sentence of dishonorable discharge, forfeiture of all pay, and confinement for six months only created more severe tensions between the groups of scouts. Bullis's selection of only three scouts for the patrol was likely a move to prevent any further friction from developing on the patrol. It is also believed that the three scouts Bullis selected were his most trusted and dependable scouts and he may have wanted to remove them from the turbulence of the scout encampment. Various sources incorrectly mention Dindie Factor as being either the son or father of Pompey Factor. The Dindie Factor court martialed in April 1875 was one of Pompey Factor's elder brothers. Pompey Factor and his wife, Annie, had a son they named Dindie, but that was years later when they lived in Mexico. The Dindie Factor mentioned by K. W. Porter, "The Seminole-Negro Indian Scouts, 1870–1888," *Southwestern Historical Quarterly*, 55 (Jan., 1952), 367, who lived in Nacimiento, Mexico, and possessed his father's Medal of Honor in 1943 was not the scout Dindie Factor. Dindie Factor, the scout who was court-martialed in 1875, was born circa 1842 according to the U.S. Army Register of Enlistments and as of 1943 he would have been more than one hundred years old.

6. J. L. Bullis to Assistant Adjutant General, Department of Texas, Apr. 27, 1875, Adjutant General's Office–Letters Received (series 2649-2813), file 2696, Office of the Adjutant General–1875, RG 94; hereafter cited as Bullis Report, file 2696. This is Bullis's written report of the scout and fight. Most of the mileages, directions, times, locations, and events are taken from this report. See also Post Adjutant, "Tabular Statements of Expeditions and Scouts against Hostile Indians from Fort Clark, Texas, Second Quarter, 1875," box 1, RG 393.

7. Bullis Report, file 2696. Bullis errs when he states, "Found signs of Indians on Johnson's Run, a dry arroyo that runs into the Pecos from the east." The arroyo he alluded to, Johnson's Run, drains from the west into the Devils River.

8. Ibid.

9. Porter, "The Seminole-Negro Indian Scouts, 1870–1881," 366.

10. Bullis to the Office of the Ordnance General, Apr. 17, 1875, "Summary of Ordnance and Ordnance Stores in the hands of troops in the service of the U.S. during the first quarter ending March 31, 1875," RG 156. The Winchesters Bullis referred to as the weapons the Indians used were likely the Model 1873, black iron frame, .44-caliber lever-action repeaters, which were very common in Mexico, and commonly referred to as "las carbinas negras."

11. Confusion exists as to the tribal affiliation of the band the detachment encountered. The last of the off-reservation Comanches, the Quohadas, were negotiating their surrender as of April 19 on the White River, some 350 miles north of the mouth of the Pecos River. See Nye, *Carbine and Lance*, 302–303. In W. R. Shafter to Office of the Adjutant General, Oct. 26, 1875, Adjutant General's Office–Letters Received, file 5675, Office of the Adjutant General–1875 (filed with file 6124, Office of the Adjutant General–1875), RG 94, Shafter expresses the belief that most recent area depredations

were likely perpetrated by Mescalero Apaches from the Bosque Redondo Reservation in New Mexico.

12. Bullis Report, file 2696.

· 13. Commanding Officer, Fort Clark to Assistant Adjutant General, Department of Texas, July 1, 1875, Department of Texas–Letters Received, file 2783, Department of Texas–1875, RG 393; Shafter to Assistant Adjutant General, Department of Texas, July 8, 1875, from camp on South Concho River, Department of Texas–Letters Received, file 3042, Department of Texas–1875, RG 393. See also Department of Texas, Register of Letters Received Book, 1875, entries no. 2783 and no. 3042, RG 393.

14. P. Factor to Office of the Adjutant General, Mar. 15, 1876, Adjutant General's Office–Letters Received, file 2815, Office of the Adjutant General–1874, box 9, RG 94.

CHAPTER 19
Gallantry among the Chaparral

1. Porfirio Diaz did not serve as the president of Mexico from 1880 to 1884.

2. J. M. Hunter (ed.), "The Garza Revolution in 1890," [extracted from the *Uvalde Leader News*], *Frontier Times*, 19 (Jan., 1942), 135–136.

3. See G. M. Cuthbertson, "C. E. Garza and the Garza War," *Texana*, 12 (Fall, 1974), 335–348, for a general overview of the conflict. It was never proved for certain from what sources Garza received his financial support but Cuthbertson cites several possible sources within the Mexican government in "C. E. Garza and the Garza War," 341. Sixto Longorio, a captured Garzaite, maintained that certain Garza family members and sympathetic storekeepers in Laredo, Rendado, and Rio Grande City provided ammunition. See John G. Bourke to Assistant Adjutant General, Department of Texas, Jan. 6, 1892, Department of Texas–Letters Received, file 150, Department of Texas–1892, "Synopsis of conversation with prisoner, Sixto Longorio at Brownsville, Texas on Jan. 6, 1892," Letters Received, Department of Texas, Special Indian–Mexican Files, 1891–1892, Records of U.S. Army Continental Commands, 1821–1920, RG 393; hereafter cited as "Synopsis of conversation with Sixto Longorio."

4. John G. Bourke Diary, vol. 107, Jan. 1–2, 1892, 159–171, Special Collections, United States Military Academy Library, West Point, New York; hereafter cited as Bourke Diary, volume, entry date, and page. Bourke obtained details of Garza's exact movements during the period from September to December 1891 during the interrogation of Sixto Longorio on January 1, 1892.

5. "Synopsis of conversation with Sixto Longorio."

6. A large map of the various 1891–1893 operations against these violators of U.S. neutrality laws may be seen in Department of Texas–Letters Received, file 16329, Special Indian–Mexican Files, Letters Received Relating to the Garza Revolution, 1891–1893, item no. 4877, RG 393. The spelling of place names used in this work were extracted from this map and do not always concur with the contemporary spellings of the same locations.

7. D. S. Stanley, General, Commanding Military Department of Texas, to Office of the Adjutant General, Jan. 22, 1892, Adjutant General's Office–Documents Received, file 24002, Principal Records Division–1892, "Brief in Case of Mexican Revolutionists from September 16, 1891 to January 4, 1892," p. 10, RG 94; cited hereafter as "Brief in Case of Mexican Revolutionists." This is the single most valuable source on military operations against the Garzaites. It includes chronologically ordered extracts of all military and diplomatic correspondence on the Garza Revolution. The emphasis of protecting civil rights is a dominant theme throughout the correspondence. D. S. Stanley to Office of the Adjutant General, Jan. 22, 1892, Adjutant General's Office–Documents Received, file 16239, Principal Records Division–1892, includes extracts of both U.S. and Mexican army officer's reports of operations, and correspondence from diplomatic officials. For a compiled file of Mexican documents, see Gabriel Saldivar (comp.), *Documentos de La Rebelion de Catarino E. Garza en La Frontera de Tamaulipas y Sur de Texas, 1891–1892* (Mexico City: La Presa del Congresa Mejicana, 1943). Copy in N. E. Benson Latin American Collection, University of Texas at Austin.

8. Bourke Diary, vol. 107, Dec. 21, 1891, 134–140.

9. Ibid., vol. 107, Dec. 22, 1891, 141–145. Bourke's diary provides much more detail of the day's events than does his official report submitted to Department of Texas Headquarters on December 23, 1891.

10. Bourke Diary, vol. 107, Dec. 21, 1891, 137; and "Brief in case of Mexican Revolutionists," 13–15.

11. "Brief in case of Mexican Revolutionists," 13–15.

12. "Corporal Edstrom's Funeral," *San Antonio Express*, Jan. 1, 1892, p. 2, col. 3. See also Bourke Diary, vol. 107, Dec. 23, 1891, 146, for a very detailed, colorful, and moving account of the ceremony. When the post cemetery at Fort Ringgold was discontinued in 1947, Corporal Edstrom's remains were reinterred at Alexandria National Cemetery at Pineville, Louisiana.

13. Bourke Diary, vol. 107, Dec. 22, 1891, 142–143.

14. Bourke Diary, vol. 107, Dec. 25, 1891, 145–146; and "Brief in case of Mexican Revolutionists," 13–16.

15. Bourke Diary, vol. 107, Dec. 24, 1891, 148.

16. "Brief in Case of Mexican Revolutionists," 16–17.

17. Bourke Diary, vol. 107, Dec. 25, 1891, 148. Several diplomatic documents in D. S. Stanley to Office of the Adjutant General, Jan. 22, 1892, Adjutant General's Office–Documents Received, file 16239, Principal Records Division–1891 mention the use of intelligence data from Mexican spies provided by Mexican diplomatic and military officials. These spies apparently had infiltrated some of Garza's contingents. Spies on the Texas side of the Rio Grande constantly monitored major trail and road intersections to report on the movements of large bodies of mounted men.

18. "Brief in Case of Mexican Revolutionists," 17–18.

19. Bourke Diary, vol. 107, Dec. 28–30, 1891, 151–154, includes a more detailed account of Hardie's command for December 28–30, 1891, than Hardie's official report.

20. Ibid.

21. Ibid.

22. Ibid. Some confusion existed about the name of the wounded man Hardie's command captured at Colorado Ranch on December 30. According to Bourke Diary, vol. 107, Jan. 1–2, 159–171, relating to his January 1, 1892, talk with Sixto Longorio, he had given Captain Hardie the fictitious name of Juan Garza for fear that they might have killed him had he given them his true name. Sheely, who was with Langhorne's command, knew Longorio personally and he then acknowledged his true name.

23. Langhorne to Post Adjutant, Fort Ringgold, Jan. 2, 1892, Department of Texas–Documents Received, file 115, Department of Texas–1892, Letters and Reports Received, Garza Revolution, 1891–1892, RG 393; hereafter cited as Langhorne Report, Jan. 2, 1892. Bourke Diary, vol. 107, Dec. 31, 1891, 157. See also Adjutant General's Office–Documents Received, file 16239, Principal Records Division–1891, and Adjutant General's Office–Documents Received, file 24002, Principal Records Division–1892, RG 94. The report on Langhorne's patrol of December 28, 1891, to January 1, 1892, includes Private Walker's account of his encounter with the revolutionaries.

24. The documents Walker captured were taken immediately to U.S. District Court Clerk G. G. Duval at Brownsville. After indictment all of the cases were transferred to the U.S. Circuit Court at San Antonio for the May 1892 term.

25. Langhorne Report, Jan. 2, 1892; Stanley to Schofield, Jan. 3, 1892, Adjutant General's Office–Documents Received, file 22831, Principal Records Division–1892; and Stanley to Schofield, Jan. 23, 1892, Adjutant General's Office–Documents Received, file 24731, Principal Records Division–1892 (both filed with file 16239, Principal Records Division–1891), RG 94. This latter file includes certified copies of the documents Private Walker, Sheriff Sheely, and Langhorne's command captured. The originals were retained by Commissioner Walter Downs and submitted to the District Court. See also "Work of the Troops," *San Antonio Express*, Jan. 4, 1892, p. 1, col. 1; and "Rest Their Case," *San Antonio Express*, May 24, 1892, p. 6, col. 1.

26. Cuthbertson, "C. E. Garza and the Garza War," 346. Garza is believed to have first fled to New Orleans in December 1893. In early 1894 he was in San José, Costa Rica, where he published a thirty-two-page booklet entitled, *The Era of Tuxtepec in Mexico or To Be in Russia in America* (San José, Costa Rica: n.p., 1894). He became embroiled in a coup attempt in Colombia and is said to have been killed in the storming of the jail at Bocas del Toro, Colombia, on March 8, 1895.

27. Bourke to Assistant Adjutant General, Department of Texas, Mar. 2, 1892, Adjutant General's Office–Documents Received, file 27642, Principal Records Division–1892, RG 94. See also Office of the Adjutant General of the U.S. Army, General Order no. 33, May 16, 1892, General Orders Issued–1892 (filed with Adjutant General's Office–Documents Received, file 5461, Office of the Adjutant General–1889), RG 94. J. M. Schofield, "Army Officials Commended," *San Antonio Daily Express*, May 19, 1892, p. 1, col. 3.

28. According to Third U.S. Cavalry Regimental Returns, Enlisted men on detached duty, April 1892, Pvt. Allen Walker is listed as being "detailed as a witness before the U.S. Court in San Antonio as of April 11, 1892." An exhaustive search in U.S. District and Circuit Court records and the available San Antonio newspapers for the period failed to locate mention of Walker's testimony or appearance before the court.

29. U.S. Senate, "Medal of Honor Review Board," case no. 2510, 397.

30. U.S. Department of Justice, Records of U.S. Circuit Courts, Western District of Texas, San Antonio, criminal case files 112–452, RG 21 (Federal Records Center, Fort Worth, Texas). See also B. G. Duval to P. Fricke, Aug. 29, 1892, "Final Commitment in Circuit Court, U.S. vs. Pablo Munos," criminal case no. 115, Records of U.S. Circuit Courts, Western District of Texas, San Antonio, May term, 1892, RG 21 (Federal Records Center, Fort Worth, Texas).

Bibliography

BOOKS

Allen, Jeremiah C., comp. and ed. *Subject Index to the General Orders and Circulars of the War Department and the Headquarters of the Army, Adjutant General's Office, 1861–1880.* Washington: Government Printing Office, 1882.

Allred, Dykes, ed. *Great Western Indian Fights.* Garden City, N.Y.: Doubleday and Co., Inc., 1960.

Amchan, Arthur J. *The Most Famous Soldier in America: Nelson A. Miles, 1839–1925.* Alexandria, Va.: Amchan Publications, 1990.

Amos, Preston E. *Above and Beyond in the West: Black Medal of Honor Winners, 1870–1890.* Falls Church, Va.: Pioneer America Society Press, 1974.

Andrist, Ralph K. *The Long Death: The Last Days of the Plains Indian.* New York: Macmillan, 1964.

Ashburn, P. M. *A History of the Medical Department of the United States Army.* Boston: Houghton-Mifflin Co., 1929.

Association of the Graduates of the U.S. Military Academy. *Annual Reunion of the Association of the Graduates of the U.S. Military Academy at West Point, N.Y., 1870–1940.* Newburgh, N.Y.: Association of Graduates, annually.

Athearn, Arthur J. *William Tecumseh Sherman and the Settlement of the West.* Norman: University of Oklahoma Press, 1956.

Atkinson, Mary J. *Indians of the Southwest.* San Antonio: The Naylor Company, 1935.

———. *The Texas Indians.* San Antonio: The Naylor Company, 1935.

Austerman, Wayne R. *Sharps Rifles and Spanish Mules: The San Antonio–El Paso Mail, 1851–1881.* College Station: Texas A&M University Press, 1985.

Babb, T. A. *In the Bosom of the Comanches.* Dallas: Hargreaves Printing Co., 1912.

Bailey, John W. *Pacifying the Plains.* Westport, Conn.: Greenwood Press, 1979.

Bailey, Ralph E. *Indian Fighter: The Story of Nelson A. Miles.* New York: William Morrow and Co., Inc., 1965.

Bibliography

Bailey, Seth T. *The Comanche Wars*. Derby, Conn.: Monarch Books, 1963.

Baldwin, Alice B., ed. *Memoirs of the Late Frank D. Baldwin, Major-General, U.S. Army*. Los Angeles: Wetzel Publishing Co., 1929.

Bard, Frederick S. *Life and Adventures of "Billy" Dixon of Adobe Walls, Panhandle, Texas*. Guthrie, Okla.: Cooperative Publishing Co., 1914.

Battey, Thomas C. *The Life and Adventures of a Quaker Among the Indians*. Boston: Lee and Shephard, 1891. Reprint, Williamstown, Mass.: Cornerhouse Publishers, 1972.

Bedford, Hilary G. *Texas Indian Troubles*. Dallas: Hargreaves Printing Co., Inc., 1905.

Berthong, Donald J. *The Southern Cheyennes*. Norman: University of Oklahoma Press, 1963.

Beyer, W. F. and O. F. Keydel. *Deeds of Valor: How America's Heroes Won the Medal of Honor*. 2 vols. Detroit: Perrien-Keydel Co., 1903.

Bierschwale, Margaret. *Fort McKavett, Texas: Post on the San Saba*. Salado, Texas: Anson Jones Press, 1966.

Biever, Ralph. *Frontier Life in the Army*. Glendale, Calif.: Arthur H. Clark Co., 1932.

Biggers, Don H. *Shackelford County Sketches*. Albany, Texas: The Clear Fork Press, 1974.

Bowden, J. J. *The Exodus of Federal Forces from Texas*. Austin: Eakin Press, 1986.

Boyd, James P. *Recent Indian Wars*. Philadelphia: Publishers Union, 1892.

Brady, Cyrus T. *The Conquest of the Southwest: The Story of a Great Spoilation*. New York: D. Appleton & Co., 1905.

Branch, E. Douglas. *The Hunting of the Buffalo*. New York: D. Appleton & Co., 1929.

Brandes, Raymond. *Troopers West: Military and Indian Affairs on the American Frontier*. San Diego: Frontier Heritage Press, 1970.

Brill, Charles J. *Conquest of the Southwestern Plains*. Oklahoma City: Golden Saga Publishers, 1938.

Brown, Dee. *Bury My Heart at Wounded Knee: An Indian History of the American West*. New York: Holt Publishing Co., 1970.

Brown, John H. *Indian Wars and Pioneers of Texas*. Austin: Bun C. Jones & Co., 1895.

Brune, Gunnar. *Springs of Texas*. Fort Worth: Branch-Smith, Inc., 1981

Buel, James W. *Hero Tales of the American Soldier and Sailor as told by the Heroes and their Comrades*. Philadelphia: Century Manufacturing Co., 1899.

———. *Behind the Guns with American Heroes*. Chicago: International Pub. Co., 1899.

———. *Heroes of the Plains*. Philadelphia: West Pub. Co., 1891.

Burton, Harley T. *A History of the J. A. Ranch*. Austin: Von Boechman-Jones Co., 1928.

Byrne, Patrick E. *Soldiers of the Plains*. New York: Minton, Balch & Co., 1926.

Cagle, Elden. *Quadrangle: The History of Fort Sam Houston*. Austin: Eakin Press, 1985.

Callahan, Edward W., ed. *List of Officers of the United States Navy and of the Marine Corp from 1775 to 1900*. New York: Haskell House Publishers, 1969.

Capps, Benjamin. *The Warren Wagontrain Raid*. New York: The Dial Press, 1974.

Carriker, Robert C. *Fort Supply, Indian Territory: Frontier Outpost on the Plains.* Norman: University of Oklahoma Press, 1970.

——— and E. R. Carriker (eds.). *An Army Wife on the Frontier: The Memoirs of Alice Blackwood Baldwin, 1867–1877.* Salt Lake City: University of Utah Library, 1975.

Carroll, John M. *Buffalo Soldiers West.* Fort Collins, Colo.: The Old Army Press, 1971.

———. *The Black Military Experience in the American West.* New York: Livewright Publishing Co., 1972.

———, ed. *The Papers of the Order of Indian Wars.* Fort Collins, Colo.: The Old Army Press, 1975.

———. *The Medal of Honor; Its History and Recipients for the Indian Wars.* Bryan, Texas: s.p., 1979.

Carter, Robert G. *The Old Sergeant's Story: Winning the West from the Indians and Bad Men in 1870–1876.* New York: F. B. Hitchcock Co., 1926.

———. *On the Border with Mackenzie: or Winning West Texas from the Comanches.* Washington, D.C.: Eynon Printing Co., 1935.

Carter, William H. *From Yorktown to Santiago with the Sixth U.S. Cavalry.* Baltimore: The Friedenwalk Co., 1900.

———. *The Life of Lieutenant-General Chaffee.* Chicago: University of Chicago Press, 1917.

Centennial Committee of U.S. Military Academy. *Graduates of West Point Who Have Been Presented with Medals of Honor.* Washington, D.C.: Government Printing Office, 1904.

Chalfant, William Y. *Cheyennes and Horse Soldiers.* Norman: University of Oklahoma Press, 1989.

Chappell, Gordon. *The Search for the Well-Dressed Soldier, 1865–1880: Development and Innovations in U.S. Army Uniforms on the Western Frontier.* Tucson: Arizona Pioneers Historical Society, 1966.

Chariton, Wallace C., *100 Days in Texas, The Alamo Letters.* Plano: Wordware Publishing Co., 1990.

Clendenen, Clarence C. *Blood on the Border: U.S. Army and Mexican Irregulars.* New York: Macmillan, 1969.

Conger, Roger N. *Frontier Forts of Texas.* Waco: Texian Press, 1966.

Conover, George W. *Sixty Years in Southwest Oklahoma.* Anadarko, Okla.: N. T. Plummer, 1927.

Cook, John R. *The Border and the Buffalo.* Topeka: Crane & Co., 1907.

Cooke, Donald E. *For Conspicuous Gallantry: Winners of the Medal of Honor.* Maplewood, N.J.: C. S. Hammond, 1966.

Cooke, Philip S. *Cavalry Tactics or Regulations for the Instruction, Formations and Movements of the Cavalry.* Washington, D.C.: Government Printing Office, 1862.

Corwin, Hugh D. *Comanche and Kiowa Captives in Oklahoma and Texas.* Guthrie, Okla.: Cooperative Publishing Co., 1959.

Bibliography

Crouch, Carrie J. *A History of Young County, Texas*. Austin: Texas State Historical Association, 1956.

Cullum, George W. *Biographical Register of the Officers and Graduates of the U.S. Military Academy at West Point, New York from its Establishment in 1802 to 1890*. Boston: Houghton-Mifflin, 1891.

Dale, Edward E. *The Indians of the Southwest*. Norman: University of Oklahoma Press, 1949.

———. *Frontier Ways: Sketches of Life in the Old West*. Austin: University of Texas Press, 1959.

———. *Frontier Trails: The Autobiography of Frank M. Canton*. Norman: University of Oklahoma Press, 1966.

Deaton, E. L. *Indian Fights on the Texas Frontier*. Fort Worth: Pioneer Publishing Co., 1927.

Deubler, Mellie. *Pioneer Life in Oklahoma*. Coffeyville, Kans.: n.p., circa 1970.

Dines, Glen. *Long Knife*. New York: Macmillan Co., 1961.

Dixon, Olive K. *The Life of Billy Dixon*. Dallas: P. L. Turner, 1927.

Dixon, William (Billy). *The Life and Adventures of Billy Dixon of Adobe Walls*. Guthrie, Okla.: Cooperative Publishing Co., 1914.

Dodge, Richard I. *Our Wild Indians*. Hartford: A. D. Worthington & Co., 1890.

Donovan, Frank. *The Medal: The Story of the Medal of Honor*. New York: Dodd, Mead & Co., 1962.

Downey, Fairfax. *The Buffalo Soldiers in the Indian Wars*. New York: McGraw-Hill Publishing Co., 1969.

———. *Indian Fighting Army*. New York: C. Scribners & Sons, 1941.

Duaine, Carl L. *The Dead Men Wore Boots, An Account of the Thirty-Second Texas Volunteer Cavalry, CSA, 1862–1865*. Austin: San Felipe Press, 1966.

Dunlay, Thomas W. *Wolves for the Blue Soldiers*. Lincoln: University of Nebraska Press, 1982.

DuPuy, William A. and Jenkins, John W. *World War and Historic Deeds of Valor*. Chicago: National Historic Publications Association, 1919.

Dykes, J. C. *Great Western Indian Fights*. Garden City, N.Y.: Doubleday and Co., 1960.

Ellis, Richard N. *General Pope and the United States Indian Policy*. Albuquerque: University of New Mexico Press, 1970.

Fassig, O. L., comp. *Report on the Publications of the U.S. Signal Service, 1861–1891*. Washington, D.C.: Government Printing Office, 1913.

Fay, George F., ed. *Military Engagements between United States Troops and Plains Indians; documentary inquiry by the U.S. Congress*. Greeley, Colo.: University of Northern Colorado Press, 1973.

Fehrenbach, T. R. *Comanches: The Destruction of a People*. New York: Alfred A. Knopf, Inc., 1974.

Ferris, Robert G., ed. *Soldier and Brave*. Washington, D.C.: Government Printing Office, 1971.

Flanagan, Mike. *The Old West: Day by Day.* New York: Facts on File, Inc., 1995.

Foner, Jack D. *The United States Soldier between Two Wars: Army Life and Reforms, 1865–1898.* New York: Humanities Press, 1970.

Forsyth, George A. *The Story of the Soldier.* New York: The Brampton Society, 1908.

Fort Wayne Public Library. *Major-General Henry W. Lawton of Fort Wayne, Indiana.* Fort Wayne: Fort Wayne Public Library, 1954.

Fowler, Arlen. *The Black Infantry in the West, 1869–1891.* Westport, Conn.: Greenwood Pub. Corp., 1971.

Friederich, Rudolf J. *Medal of Honor Citation Supplements*, ed. Philip M. Weber. Chicago: Orders and Medals Society, 1968.

Gardner, Raymond H. *The Old Wild West.* San Antonio: Naylor Co., 1944.

Glass, L. N. *The History of the Tenth Cavalry, 1866–1920.* Fort Collins, Colo.: The Old Army Press, 1972.

Grace, J. S. and R. B. Jones. *A New History of Parker County.* Weatherford, Texas: Democrat Publishing Co., 1906.

Grant, Ulysses S. *Personal Memoirs of Ulysses S. Grant.* 7 vols. New York: Charles L. Webster's Company, 1886.

Gregg, Robert D. *The Influence of Border Troubles between the U.S. and Mexico, 1876–1910.* Baltimore: Johns Hopkins Press, 1937.

Gregg, Rosalie, ed. *A History of Wise County, A Link with the Past.* Burnet, Texas: Nortex Press, 1977.

Haley, J. Evetts. *Fort Concho and the Texas Frontier.* San Angelo, Texas: San Angelo Standard Times, 1952.

Haley, James L. *Buffalo War: The History of the Red River Indian Uprising of 1874.* Garden City, N.Y.: Doubleday Co., 1976.

Hamilton, Allen L. *Sentinel of the Southern Plains: Fort Richardson and the Northwest Texas Frontier, 1866–1878.* Fort Worth: Texas Christian University Press, 1988.

Hammer, Kenneth M. *The Springfield Carbine on the Western Frontier.* Bellevue, Nebr.: Old Army Press, 1970.

Hammersley, L. R. *Records of Living Officers of the United States Army.* Philadelphia: L. R. Hammersley and Company, 1884.

Heitman, Francis B. *Historical Register and Dictionary of the United States Army from its Organization, September 29, 1789 to March 2, 1903.* Washington, D.C.: Government Printing Office, 1903.

Herr, John K. and Edward S. Wallace. *The Story of the U.S. Cavalry, 1775–1942.* Boston: Little, Brown & Co., 1953.

Holden, William C. *Alkali Trails.* Dallas: The Southwest Press, 1930.

Hoig, Stan. *The Peace Chiefs of the Cheyennes.* Norman: University of Oklahoma Press, 1980.

Hopper, James. *Medal of Honor.* New York: The John Day Co., 1929.

Horton, Thomas F. *History of Jack County.* Jacksboro, Texas: Gazette Printing, circa 1930.

Huckaby, Ida L. *Ninety-four Years in Jack County*. Austin: Stock Co., 1949.

Hunt, Elvid. *History of Fort Leavenworth, 1827–1927*. Fort Leavenworth: General Service School's Press, 1926.

Hunter, John M. *The Bloody Trail in Texas: Sketches and Narratives of Indian Raids and Atrocities on our Frontier*. Bandera, Texas: J. M. Hunter, 1931.

Hyde, George E. *Indians of the High Plains*. Norman: University of Oklahoma Press, 1959.

Jacobs, Bruce. *Heroes of the Army: The Medal of Honor and its Winners*. New York: W. W. Norton, 1956.

Jennings, N. A. *A Texas Ranger*. Dallas: Turner Co., 1930.

Jessup, John E. and Louise B. Ketz. *Encyclopedia of the American Military*. 3 vols. New York: Charles Scribner's Sons, 1994.

Johnson, R. V. and C. C. Buel. *Battles and Leaders of the Civil War*. New York: Century Co., 1888.

Johnson, Virginia W. *The Unregimented General: A Biography of Nelson A. Miles*. Boston: Houghton-Mifflin, 1962.

Jones, C. N., comp. *Early Days in Cooke County, 1848–1873*. Gainesville: Cooke County Heritage Society, 1977.

Jones, Douglas C. *The Treaty of Medicine Lodge*. Norman: University of Oklahoma Press, 1966.

Jouett, James E. *Statement of Service, James E. Jouett*. Washington, D.C.: Judd & Detweiler Printer, 1879.

Katz, William L. *Black Indians: A Hidden Heritage*. New York: Atheneum, 1986.

Kenner, Charles L. *A History of New Mexican–Plains Indian Relations*. Norman: University of Oklahoma Press, 1969.

Kerrigan, Evans E. *American War Medals and Decorations*. New York: Viking Press, 1971.

Kestler, Frances R. *The Indian Captivity Narrative, A Woman's View*. New York: Garland Publishing, 1990.

Knight, Oliver. *Following the Indian Wars: The Story of the Newspaper Correspondents among the Indian Campaigns*. Norman: University of Oklahoma Press, 1960.

Lambert, Joseph L. *One Hundred Years with the 2nd Cavalry*. Topeka, Kans.: Copper Printing Co., 1939.

Lang, George C., Raymond L. Collins, and Gerard F. White, comps. *Medal of Honor Recipients, 1863–1994, Vol. I, Civil War to Second Nicaraguan Campaign*. New York: Facts On File, Inc., 1995.

Latorre, Felipe A. and Doris L. *The Mexican Kickapoos*. Austin: University of Texas Press, 1976.

Leckie, William H. *The Buffalo Soldiers: A Narrative of Negro Cavalry in the West*. Norman: University of Oklahoma Press, 1967.

————. *The Military Conquest of the South Plains*. Norman: University of Oklahoma Press, 1963.

————, ed. *Indian Wars of the Red River Valley*. Sacramento: Sierra Oaks Publishing Co., 1986.

Lee, Irwin H. *Negro Medal of Honor Men*. New York: Dodd, Mead and Co., 1969.

Lehman, Lloyd. *Sherman: Fighting Prophet*. New York: Harcourt, 1932.

Lehmann, Herman. *Nine Years Among the Indians, 1870–1879*. Austin: J. M. Hunter, 1927.

Loftin, Jack. *Trails through Archer County, Texas*. Austin: Eakin Press, 1979.

Longstreet, Stephen. *War Cries on Horseback: The Story of the Indian Wars of the Great Plains*. New York: Doubleday and Co., 1970.

Lott, Virgil N. *Wars in the Chaparral*. San Antonio: Naylor Press, 1934.

Marshall, J. T. *The Miles Expedition of 1874–1875: An Eyewitness Account of the Red River War*, ed. Lonnie J. White. Austin: Encino Press, 1971.

Marshall, S. L. A. *Crimsoned Prairie: The Wars between the United States and the Plains Indians during the Winning of the West*. New York: Scribner's, 1972.

Matagorda County Historical Commission. *Historic Matagorda County, Volume I*. Houston: D. Armstrong Co., 1986.

Mayhall, Mildred P. *The Kiowas*. Norman: University of Oklahoma Press, 1962.

————. *The Indian Wars of Texas*. Waco: Texian Press, 1965.

McCarthy, John L. *Adobe Walls Bride: The Story of Billy and Olive Dixon*. San Antonio: Naylor Press, 1955.

McConnell, H. H. *Five Years a Cavalryman: Or Sketches of Regular Army Life on the Texas Frontier Twenty Odd Years Ago*. Jacksboro, Texas: J. N. Rogers & Co., 1889.

McConnell, Joseph C. *The West Texas Frontier*. Palo Pinto, Texas: Texas Legal Bank & Book Co., 1939.

Meredith, Grace E., ed. *Girl Captives of the Cheyennes: A True Story of the Capture and Rescue of Four Pioneer Girls*. Los Angeles: Gem Publishing Co., 1927.

Merrill, James M. *Spurs to Glory*. Chicago: Rand McNally & Co., 1966.

Miles, Nelson A. *Personal Recollections and Observations of Nelson A. Miles*. Chicago: The Werner Co., 1896.

————. *Serving the Republic*. New York: Harper, 1911.

Miller, Robert. *Buffalo Soldiers: The Story of Emanuel Stance*. Morristown, N.J.: Silver Press, 1995.

Mishkin, Bernard. *Rank and Warfare among the Plains Indians*. New York: J. J. Augustin, 1940.

Moody, Ralph. *Stagecoach West*. New York: Thomas Y. Crowell Co., 1967.

Mooney, James. *Seventeenth Annual Report of the Bureau of American Ethnology, 1865–1896 (Calendar History of the Kiowa Indians)*. Washington, D.C.: Government Printing Office, 1898.

Mulholland, St. Claire A. *Military Order: Congressional Medal of Honor Legion of the United States*. 2 vols. Philadelphia: Town Printing, 1905.

Muller, William G. *The Twenty-Fourth Infantry, Past and Present*. Fort Collins, Colo.: The Old Army Press, 1972.

Bibliography

Mulroy, Kevin. *Freedom on the Border: The Seminole Maroons in Florida, the Indian Territory, Coahuila and Texas.* Lubbock: Texas Tech University Press, 1993.

Nankivell, John H. *The History of the Twenty-Fifth Regiment United States Infantry, 1869–1926.* Fort Collins, Colo.: The Old Army Press, 1972.

Nelson, John Y. *Fifty Years on the Trail.* London: Chatto & Windus, 1889.

Notson, William M. *Fort Concho Medical History, January 1869–July 1872.* San Angelo, Texas: Fort Concho Museum, 1974.

Nye, Wilbur S. *Carbine and Lance: The Story of Old Fort Sill.* Norman: University of Oklahoma Press, 1937, 1942, 1969.

———. *Bad Medicine and Good: Tales of the Kiowas.* Norman: University of Oklahoma Press, 1962.

———. *Plains Indian Raiders.* Norman: University of Oklahoma Press, 1968.

O'Neal, Bill. *Fighting Men of the Indian Wars.* Stillwater, Okla.: Barbed Wire Press, 1991.

Parker, James. *The Old Army: Memories, 1872–1918.* Philadelphia: Dorrance & Co., 1929.

Peters, Joseph P. *Indian Battles and Skirmishes on the American Frontier, 1790–1898.* New York: Argonaut Press, Ltd., 1966.

Phillips, Edwin D. *Texas and its Late Military Occupation.* New York: Van Nostrand, 1862.

Pierce, Michael D. *The Most Promising Young Officer: A Life of Ranald Slidell Mackenzie.* Norman: University of Oklahoma Press, 1993.

Pirtle, Caleb III and Michael F. Cusack. *The Lonely Sentinel, Fort Clark: On Texas' Western Frontier.* Austin: Eakin Press, 1985.

Pohanka, Brian C. *Nelson A. Miles, A Documentary Biography of His Military Career, 1861–1903.* Glendale, Calif.: The Arthur H. Clark Co., 1985.

Porter, Joseph C. *Paper Medicine Man: John G. Bourke.* Norman: University of Oklahoma Press, 1986.

Porter, Kenneth W. *The Black Seminoles: History of a Freedom-Seeking People.* Revised and edited by Alcione M. Amos and Thomas P. Senter. Gainesville: University Press of Florida, 1996.

Potomac Corral of the Westerners. *Great Western Indian Fights.* Omaha: University of Nebraska Press, 1960.

Potter, W. R. *History of Montague County, Texas,* 3rd ed. Saint Jo, Texas: S. J. T. Printing Co., 1975.

Powell, W. F. *Cooke County History.* Dallas: Curtis Media Corp., 1992.

Price, George F. *Across the Continent with the 5th Cavalry.* New York: Van Nostrand Publishers, 1883.

Prucha, Francis P. *The Sword of the Republic.* New York: The Macmillan Co., 1969.

Reeder, Russell P. *The Mackenzie Raid.* New York: Ballantine Books, 1935.

———. *Medal of Honor Heroes.* New York: Random House, 1965.

Richardson, Rupert N. *The Comanche Barrier to South Plains Settlement.* Glendale, Calif.: Arthur H. Clark Co., 1933.

————. *The Frontier of Northwest Texas, 1846–1876.* Glendale, Calif.: Arthur H. Clark Co., 1963.

Richter, William L. *The U.S. Army in Texas during Reconstruction, 1865–1870.* College Station: Texas A&M University Press, 1987.

Rickey, Don Jr. *Forty Miles a Day on Beans and Hay: The Enlisted Soldier Fighting the Indian Wars.* Norman: University of Oklahoma Press, 1963.

————. *War in the West: The Indian Campaigns.* Fort Collins, Colo.: The Old Army Press, 1956.

Ridings, Sam P. *The Chisholm Trail.* Guthrie, Okla.: Cooperative Pub. Co., 1936.

Rister, Carl C. *The Southwestern Frontier, 1865–1881.* Glendale, Calif.: Arthur H. Clark Co., 1928.

————. *Southern Plainsmen.* Norman: University of Oklahoma Press, 1938.

————. *Border Captives: The Traffic in Prisoners by Southern Plains Indians, 1835–1875.* Norman: University of Oklahoma Press, 1940.

————. *Border Command: General Phil Sheridan in the West.* Norman: University of Oklahoma Press, 1944.

————. *Fort Griffin on the Texas Frontier.* Norman: University of Oklahoma Press, 1956.

Robinson, Charles M. III. *Bad Hand: A Biography of General Ranald S. Mackenzie.* Austin: State House Press, 1993.

Rodenbough, Theopolis F. *Fighting for Honor.* New York: G. W. Dillingham Co., 1893.

————. *Sabre and Bayonet: Stories of Heroism and Military Adventure.* New York: G. W. Dillingham Co., 1897.

Saldivar, Gabriel. *Documentation de la Rebellion de Catarino Garza en la Frontera de Tamaulipas y Sur de Tejas, 1891–1892.* Mexico City: La Presa del Congreso Mejicana, 1943.

Sandoz, Mari. *The Buffalo Hunters, Story of the Hidemen.* New York: Hastings House, 1954.

————. *Hostiles and Friendlies.* Lincoln: University of Nebraska Press, 1959.

Schofield, J. M. *Forty-six Years in the Army.* New York: Century Co., 1916.

Schott, Joseph L. *Above and Beyond: The Story of the Congressional Medal of Honor.* New York: G. P. Putnams' Sons, 1963.

Schubert, Frank N., comp. and ed. *On the Trail of the Buffalo Soldier, Biographies of African Americans in the U.S. Army, 1866–1917.* 2 vols. Wilmington, Del.: Scholarly Resources Inc., 1995.

————. *Black Valor: Buffalo Soldiers and the Medal of Honor, 1870–1898.* Wilmington, Del.: Scholarly Resources Inc., 1997.

Sheridan, Phillip H. *Records of Engagements with Hostile Indians.* Washington, D.C.: Government Printing Office, 1882.

————. *Personal Memoirs.* New York: Charles L. Webster & Co., 1888.

Sherman, William T. *Memoirs of General W. T. Sherman.* New York: Charles L. Webster & Co., 1892.

Bibliography

Shirley, Glenn. *Buckskin and Spurs*. New York: Hastings House Publishers, 1958.

Sigerfoos, Ed. *Historical Sketch of the 5th U.S. Infantry*. New York: Fifth Infantry Regimental Press, 1902.

Smith, A. Morton. *The First One Hundred Years in Cooke County*. San Antonio: The Naylor Co., 1976.

Smith, C. L. and J. D. Smith. *The Boy Captives*. Bandera, Texas: J. M. Hunter, 1927.

Smythe, H. *Historical Sketch of Parker County and Weatherford, Texas*. St. Louis: Louis C. Lavat Printers, 1877.

Stanley, David S. *Personal Memoirs of Major-General D. S. Stanley*. Cambridge: Harvard University Press, 1917.

Stephens, Robert W. *August Buchel, Texas Soldier of Fortune*. Dallas: s.p., 1974.

Stevens, Phillip H. *Search Out the Land: A History of American Military Scouts*. Chicago: Rand McNally, 1969.

Strong, Henry W. *My Frontier Days and Indian Fights on the Plains of Texas*. Wichita Falls, Texas: n.p., circa 1925.

Stroud, Harry A. *Conquest of the Prairies*. Waco: The Texian Press, 1968.

Swanson, Donald A. *Enlistment Records of Indian Scouts—Fort Clark, Texas*. Bronte, Texas: Ames-American Printing Co., circa 1990.

Tassin, R. *Double Winners of the Medal of Honor*. Canton, Ohio: Daring Books, 1987.

Tatum, Lawrie. *Our Red Brothers and the Peace Policy of President Ulysses S. Grant*. Philadelphia: J. C. Winston & Co., 1899.

Taylor, Joe F., ed. *The Indian Campaign on the Staked Plains, 1874–1875: Military Correspondence from the War Department Adjutant General's Office, File 2815–1874*. Canyon, Texas: Panhandle-Plains Historical Society, 1962.

Tetterington, Bill. *Broken Promises*. Phoenix, Ariz.: Golden West Press, 1973.

Thompson, Richard A. *Crossing the Border with the 4th Cavalry, Mackenzie's Raid into Mexico—1873*. Waco: The Texian Press, 1986.

Time-Life Books. *The Soldiers*, ed. David Nevin. New York: Time Life Books, 1973.

Tinkel, Lon. *13 Days to Glory*. College Station: Texas A&M University Press, 1985.

Tolman, Newton F. *The Search for General Miles*. New York: G. P. Putnam's Sons, 1968.

Trenholm, Virginia C. *The Arapahoes: Our People*. Norman: University of Oklahoma Press, 1970.

U.S. Army, Military Division of the Missouri. *Communications of Philip H. Sheridan while attached to the Military Division of the Missouri, September 26, 1868–November 1, 1882*. Washington, D.C.: Government Printing Office, 1883.

U.S. Army, Office of the Chief of Ordnance. *Index to Reports of Chief of Ordnance, 1864–1912*. Washington, D.C.: Government Printing Office, 1913.

U.S. Navy Department. *Record of Medals of Honor Issued to the Blue-Jackets and Marines of the U.S. Navy, 1862–1910*. Washington, D.C.: Government Printing Office, 1910.

U.S. Navy Department. *Register of Officers of the Confederate States Navy, 1861–1865*. Washington, D.C.: Office of Naval Records and Library, 1931.

U.S. Navy Department. *Above and Beyond the Call of Duty, The Navy Medal of Honor, 1861–1949*. Washington, D.C.: Government Printing Office, 1950.

U.S. Navy Department. *Dictionary of American Naval Fighting Ships*. 8 vols. Washington, D.C.: Government Printing Office, 1959.

U.S. War Department. *Indian Hostilities in Texas, 1871–1872*. Washington, D.C.: Government Printing Office, 1872.

U.S. War Department. *Circular, U.S. Army Medals of Honor*. Washington, D.C.: Government Printing Office, 1897.

Utley, Robert M. *Frontier Regulars: The U.S. Army and the Indians, 1866–1891*. New York: Macmillan, 1973.

Vestal, Stanley. *Warpath and Council Fire: The Plains Indian's Struggle for Survival in War and in Diplomacy, 1851–1891*. New York: Random House, 1948.

Wallace, Ernest and E. A. Hoebel. *The Comanches: Lords of the South Plans*. Norman: University of Oklahoma Press, 1952.

Wallace, Ernest. *Ranald S. Mackenzie on the Texas Frontier*. Lubbock: West Texas Museum Association, 1964.

———, ed. *Ranald S. Mackenzie's Official Correspondence Relating to Texas, 1871–1873*. Lubbock: West Texas Museum Association, 1967.

———, ed. *Ranald S. Mackenzie's Official Correspondence Relating to Texas, 1873–1879*. Lubbock: West Texas Museum Association, 1968.

Walton, George. *Sentinel of the Plains: Fort Leavenworth and the American West*. Englewood Cliffs, N.J.: Prentice-Hall, 1973.

Way, Thomas E. *Sergeant Fred Platten's Ten Years on the Trail of the Redskins*. Williams, Ariz.: Williams News Press, 1939.

Webb, George W. *Chronological List of Engagements between the Regular Army of the United States and Various Indian Tribes*. St. Joseph, Mo.: Wing Printing and Publishing Co., 1939.

Weigley, Russell F. *History of the United States Army*. New York: The Macmillan Co., 1967.

Wellman, Paul I. *Death on the Prairie*. New York: Macmillan Co., 1934.

———. *The Indian Wars of the West*. Garden City: Doubleday, 1954.

Wharton, Clarence. *Satanta: The Great Chief of the Kiowa and His People*. Dallas: Banks, Upshaw & Co., 1935.

Wheeler, Homer. *Buffalo Days: Forty Years in the Old West*. Indianapolis: The Bobbs-Merril Co., 1925.

Whisenhunt, Donald. *Fort Richardson: Outpost on the Texas Frontier*. El Paso: Texas Western Press, 1968.

White, Lonnie J. *The Battles of Adobe Walls and Lyman's Wagon Train*. Canyon, Texas: Panhandle-Plains Historical Society, 1964.

————, ed. *The Miles Expedition of 1874–1875: An Eyewitness Account of the Red River War*. Austin: The Encino Press, 1971.

————. *Hostiles and Horse Soldiers: Indian Battles and Campaigns in the West*. Boulder, Colo.: Pruett Publishing Co., 1972.

White, Virgil D., ed. *Index to Medal of Honor Recipients, 1863–1978*. Waynesboro, Tenn.: The National Historical Publishing Company, 2000.

Whitman, Sidney E. *The Troopers: An Informal History of the Plains Cavalry, 1865–1890*. New York: Hastings House, 1962.

Wilbarger, J. W. *Indian Depredations in Texas*. Austin: Hutchings Printing House, 1889.

Williams, J. W. *Old Texas Trails*. Burnet, Texas: Eakin Press, 1979.

Winfrey, Dorman H. and James M. Day, eds. 5 vols. *The Indian Papers of Texas*. Austin: Pemberton Press, 1966.

Wood, H. Clay. *Instructions, the Result of Actual Experience for our Frontier Service*. San Antonio: Army Hand Press, 1870.

Wormser, Richard C. *The Yellowlegs: The Story of the United States Cavalry*. Garden City, N.Y.: Doubleday, 1966.

Wooster, Robert. *Nelson A. Miles and the Twilight of the Frontier Army*. Lincoln: University of Nebraska Press, 1993.

————. *The Military and United States Indian Policy, 1865–1903*. New Haven: Yale University Press, 1988.

————. *Soldiers, Sutlers, and Settlers: Garrison Life on the Texas Frontier*. College Station: Texas A&M University Press, 1987.

ARTICLES

Anderson, John Q. "Fort Elliott, Texas, Last Guard of the Plains Indians." *Texas Military History*, 2 (Nov., 1962), 243–254.

Archambeau, Ernest R., ed. "The Battle of Lyman's Wagon Train." *Panhandle-Plains Historical Review*, 36 (1963), 89–101.

————, ed. "Monthly Reports of the 4th Cavalry, 1872–1874." *Panhandle-Plains Historical Review*, 38 (1965), 95–153.

Ashcraft, Allan C. "Corporal Hesse's Medal of Honor." *Military Review*, 41 (May, 1961), 77–81.

Aston, B. W. "Federal Military Occupation of the Texas Southwestern Frontier, 1865–1871." *Texas Military History*, 8, no. 3 (1970), 123–134.

Athearn, Robert G. "War Paint Against Brass: The Army and the Plains Indians." *Merchant's Magazine*, 6 (May, 1956), 11–22.

Baird, G. W. "General Miles' Indian Campaigns." *Century Magazine*, 42 (July, 1891), 351–370.

Beaumont, E. B. "Over the Border with Mackenzie." *United Service*, 12 (Mar., 1885), 281–288.

Benedict, J. W. "Diary of a Campaign against the Comanches." *Southwestern Historical Quarterly*, 32 (Apr., 1929), 300–310.

Brown, W. C. "The Charge of the Wagon Train." *The Quartermaster Review*, 1 (Nov.–Dec., 1921), 17–19.

Caperton, Thomas J. and LoRheda Fry. "U.S. Army Food and its Preparation during the Indian Wars, 1865–1890." *Palacio*, 80, no. 4 (1974), 29–45.

Carriker, Robert C., ed. "Thompson McFadden's Diary of an Indian Campaign, 1874." *Southwestern Historical Quarterly*, 75 (Oct., 1971), 198–232.

———. "Mercenary Heroes: The Scouting Detachments of the Indian Territory Expedition, 1874–1875." *Chronicles of Oklahoma*, 51 (Fall, 1973), 309–324.

Chamberlain, Orville T. "The American Star of Valor." *Bellman Magazine*, 24 (Jan.–Feb., 1918), 70–72.

Crane, R. C. "The Settlement in 1874–1875 of Indian Troubles in West Texas." *West Texas Historical Association Yearbook*, 1 (1925), 3–14.

Crimmins, Martin L. "General Mackenzie and Fort Concho." *West Texas Historical Association Yearbook*, 10 (1934), 16–31.

———. "Notes on the Establishment of Fort Elliott and the Buffalo Wallow Fight." *Panhandle-Plains Historical Review*, 25 (1952), 45–69.

Cuthbertson, Gilbert M. "C. E. Garza and the Garza War." *Texana*, 12, no. 4 (1974), 335–348.

Dorst, Joseph H. "One Who Was There, Scouting on the Staked Plains with Mackenzie in 1874." *United Service Magazine*, 13 (Oct., 1885), 400–414, 532–543.

———. "Ranald Slidell Mackenzie." *Register of 20th Annual Reunion of the Association of U.S.M.A. Graduates* (1889), 72–75.

———. "Ranald Slidell Mackenzie." *Journal of the U.S. Cavalry Association*, 10 (Dec., 1897), 367–382.

Essin, Emmett M. III. "Mules, Packs and Packtrains." *Southwestern Historical Quarterly*, 74 (July, 1970), 52–63.

Fisher, O. Clark. "The Life and Times of King Fisher." *Southwestern Historical Quarterly*, 64 (Oct., 1960), 232–247.

Fitzhugh, Lester N. "Saluria, Fort Esperanza, and Military Operations on the Texas Coast, 1861–1864." *Southwestern Historical Quarterly*, 61 (July, 1957), 66–100.

Frisbie, F. S. "The Medal of Honor Legion." *American Historical Register and Monthly Gazette of the Historical and Patriotic Hereditary Societies of the United States*, 1 (Sept., 1894), 66–70.

Greer, James K., ed. "The Diary of James Buckner Barry, 1860–1862." *Southwestern Historical Quarterly*, 36 (Oct., 1932), 144–162.

Griffis, Joseph K. (Tehan). "The Battle of the Washita." *Chronicles of Oklahoma*, 8 (Sept., 1930), 272–281.

Haley, J. Evetts. "The Comanchero Trade." *Southwestern Historical Quarterly*, 38 (Jan., 1935), 157–176.

Bibliography

Harrison, Lowell H. "Damage Suits for Indian Depredations in the Adobe Walls Area, 1874." *Panhandle-Plains Historical Review*, 36 (1963), 37–60.

Hatfield, Charles A. P. "The Comanche, Kiowa and Cheyenne Campaign in Northwest Texas and Mackenzie's Fight in the Palo Duro Canyon, September 26, 1874." *West Texas Historical Association Yearbook*, 5 (June, 1929), 118–123.

Hunt, Fred A. "American Orders of Knighthood." *Overland Monthly*, 57 (June, 1911), 582–591.

Hunter, J. M. "The Garza Revolution in 1890." *Frontier Times*, 19 (Jan., 1942), 135–136.

———, ed. "The Battle of Palo Duro Canyon." *Frontier Times*, 21 (Jan., 1944), 177–181.

Johnson, John A. "The Medal of Honor, Sgt. John Ward and Private Pompey Factor." *The Arkansas Historical Quarterly*, 29 (Winter, 1970), 361–375.

Leach, John A. "Search and Destroy on the American Plains." *Military History of Texas and the Southwest*, 9, no. 1 (1971), 55–60.

Leckie, William H. "The Red River War of 1874–1875." *Panhandle-Plains Historical Review*, 29 (1956), 78–100.

Long, John. "A Panhandle Pioneer," *Frontier Times Monthly*, 4 (Nov., 1926), 44–45.

Montgomery, F. C. "U.S. Surveyors Massacred." *Kansas Historical Quarterly*, 1 (May, 1931), 266–272.

Montgomery, Wayne. "Amos Chapman, Scout." *Frontier Times*, 46 (Apr., 1972), 26–28, 44, 46–47.

Neal, Charles M. Jr. "Incident at Las Moras Creek." *Annals of the Medal of Honor Historical Society*, 13, no. 1 (1990), 16–19.

Neighbors, Kenneth. "Tonkawa Scouts and Guides." *West Texas Historical Association Yearbook*, 49 (1973), 90–113.

Nobles, Pat. "Billy Dixon—Boy Scout." *Real West*, (Feb., 1987), 26–29.

Nye, Wilbur S. "Excitement on the Sweetwater." *Chronicles of Oklahoma*, 16 (June, 1938), 241–242.

Olch, Peter D. "Medicine in the Indian Fighting Army." *Journal of the West*, 21, no. 3 (1982), 32–41.

Olmsted, Merle C. "John W. Comfort: Portrait of a U.S. Regular, 1865–1892." *Military Collector and Historian*, 20 (Winter, 1968), 126.

Parker, Wayne. "Mackenzie's Supply Camp." *Grain Producer's News*, 30 (July, 1979), 4–7.

Pate, J'Nell. "The Red River War of 1874—An Enlisted Man's Contribution." *Chronicles of Oklahoma*, 54 (Summer, 1976), 263–275.

Peery, Dan W. "The Kiowa's Defiance." *Chronicles of Oklahoma*, 13 (Mar., 1935), 30–36.

Porter, Kenneth W. "Wild Cat's Death and Burial." *Chronicles of Oklahoma*, 21 (Mar., 1943), 41–43.

———. "The Seminole-Negro Indian Scouts, 1870–1881." *Southwestern Historical Quarterly*, 55 (Jan., 1952), 358–377.

———— and Edward S. Wallace. "Thunderbolt of the Frontier." *New York Westerners Brand Book*, 8 (1961), 73–75, 82–86.

Richardson, Rupert N. "The Comanche Indians at the Adobe Walls Fight." *Panhandle-Plains Historical Review*, 4 (1931), 24–38.

Rister, Carl C. "The Significance of the Jacksboro Indian Affair of 1871." *Southwestern Historical Quarterly*, 29 (Jan., 1926), 181–200.

Rogers, Jerry L. "The Indian Territory Expedition's Winter Campaign, 1874–1875." *Texas Military History*, 8, no. 4 (1970), 233–250.

Schubert, Frank N. "The Violent World of Emanuel Stance, Fort Robinson, 1887." *Nebraska History*, 55, no. 2 (1974), 203–219.

Smith, C. C. "Colonel C. C. Smith Writes About the Germaine Sisters." *Frontier Times*, 10 (Dec., 1932), 103.

Stout, Joseph A. Jr. "Davidson's Campaign." *Red River Valley Historical Review*, 3, no. 2 (1978), 194–201.

Tate, Michael L. "Indian Scouting Detachments in the Red River War, 1874–1875." *Red River Valley Historical Review*, 3, no. 2 (1978), 202–226.

Taylor, Joe F., ed. "The Indian Campaign on the Staked Plains, 1874–1875: Military Correspondence from the War Department Adjutant General's Office, File 2815." *Panhandle-Plains Historical Review*, 35 (1962), 315–368.

Thoburn, Joseph B. "Horace P. Jones, Scout and Interpreter." *Chronicles of Oklahoma*, 2 (Dec., 1924), 11, 12, 380, 391.

Thompson, William A. "Scouting with Mackenzie." *Journal of the U.S. Cavalry Association*, 10 (Dec., 1897), 429–433.

Wallace, Edward S. "General Ranald Slidell Mackenzie, Indian Fighting Cavalryman." *Southwestern Historical Quarterly*, 56 (Jan., 1953), 378–396.

Wallace, Ernest. "Prompt in the Saddle: The Military Career of Ranald S. Mackenzie." *Military History of Texas and the Southwest*, 9, no. 3 (1971), 161–189.

———— and Adrian S. Anderson. "R. S. Mackenzie and the Kickapoos: The Raid into Mexico in 1873." *Arizona and the West*, 7 (Summer, 1965), 105–126.

White, Lonnie J., ed. "Kansas Newspaper Items Relating to the Red River War of 1874–1875." *Panhandle-Plains Historical Review*, 36 (1963), 71–88.

————. "Indian Battles in the Texas Panhandle, 1874." *Journal of the West*, 6 (Apr., 1967), 278–309.

————. "The First Battle of the Palo Duro Canyon." *Texas Military History*, 6 (Fall, 1967), 222–235.

Wolfe, George D. "The Indians Named Him Bad Hand." *True West*, 9 (Aug., 1961), 16–18.

Zimmerman, Jean L. "Colonel Ranald S. Mackenzie at Fort Sill." *Chronicles of Oklahoma*, 44 (Spring, 1966), 12–21.

Bibliography

CONGRESSIONAL DOCUMENTS

39-2 Sen. Report 156 (1279), Doolittle Commission on Decline in Indian Population.

39-2 House Exec. Doc. 23 (1288), Protection of immigrant routes from Indians.

39-2 House Misc. Doc. 40 (1302), Grant on Issuance of Arms to Indians.

39-2 House Misc. Doc. 41 (1302), Issue of arms to Kiowas and other Indians.

40-1 Sen. Exec. Doc 2 (1308), General Sherman on protection of trains.

40-1 Sen. Exec. Doc. 13 (1308), Indian hostilities.

40-2 Sen. Exec. Doc. 60 (1317), Raids on Texas by Kiowas and Comanches.

40-2 House Exec. Doc. 97 (1337), Peace Commission.

40-2 House Exec. Doc. 340 (1346), Kickapoos raiding Texas from Mexico.

40-2 Sen. Misc. Doc. 150 (1408), Texas Legislature on Indians harbored in Mexico.

40-2 House Exec. Doc. 1 (1414), Annual Report, Commissioner of Indian Affairs, 1869.

40-2 House Exec. Doc. 125 (1417), Indian agents on Kiowas and Comanches.

40-2 House Exec. Doc. 158 (1418), Number of Indians in tribes in Texas.

40-2 House Exec. Doc. 240 (1418), Difficulties with Indians.

40-2 House Misc. Doc. 137, 139 (1433), Outrages committed by Indians.

40-2 House Misc. Doc. 142 (1433), Indian depredations (captures) in Texas.

40-3 House Exec. Doc. 1 (1446), Annual Report, Secretary of War, 1870.

40-3 House Exec. Doc. 1 (1449), Annual Report, Commissioner of Indian Affairs, 1870.

40-3 House Exec. Doc. 123 (1460), Appropriations for depredations by Kiowas.

41-2 House Misc. Doc. 139 (1433), Outrages by Indians.

42-1 Sen. Misc. Doc. 37 (1467), Investigation of Indian outrages in Texas by Mexican Indians.

42-2 House Exec. Doc. 1 (1503), Annual Report, Secretary of War, 1871.

42-2 House Exec. Doc. 1 (1505), Annual Report, Commissioner of Indian Affairs, 1871.

42-2 House Exec. Doc. 216 (1515), Indian raids into Texas from Mexico.

42-3 House Exec. Doc. 1 (1558), Annual Report, Secretary of War, 1872.

42-3 House Exec. Doc. 1 (1560), Annual Report, Commissioner of Indian Affairs, 1872.

42-3 House Exec. Doc. 13 (1563), Depredations on Texas Rio Grande frontier.

42-3 House Exec. Doc. 39 (1565), Report of Commissioners on Texas frontier outrages by Mexicans.

42-3 House Exec. Doc. 62 (1565), Depredations claims against Kiowas and Comanches from Kansas wagon train attack.

43-1 House Exec. Doc. 1 (1597), Annual Report, Secretary of War, 1873.

43-1 House Exec. Doc. 1 (1601), Annual Report, Commissioner of Indian Affairs, 1873.

43-1 House Exec. Doc. 90 (1607), Appropriations for removal of Kickapoo.

43-1 House Exec. Doc. 222 (1614), Protection of the Texas frontier, Telegraph lines for.

43-1 House Exec. Doc. 236 (1614), Appropriations for Kickapoo removal.

43-1 House Exec. Doc. 257 (1615), Report on Texas frontier.

43-1 House Report 282 (1615), Board on Texas military sites.

43-1 House Report 384 (1615), Reduction of the U.S. Army.

43-1 House Misc. Doc. 289 (1621), Depredations on Mexican border.

43-1 House Report 395 (1624), Depredations on Texas frontier.

43-2 Sen. Exec. Doc. 22 (1629), Indians and whites killed in 1873.

43-2 House Exec. Doc. 1 (1635), Annual Report, Secretary of War, 1874.

43-2 House Exec. Doc. 1 (1639), Annual Report, Commissioner of Indian Affairs, 1874.

43-2 House Exec. Doc. 65 (1645), Depredation claims, 1864–1874.

43-2 House Exec. Doc. 141 (1648), Appropriations for Kickapoos.

44-1 Sen. Report 118 (1667), Relief for Amos Chapman.

44-1 House Exec. Doc. 1 (1674), Annual Report, Secretary of War, 1875.

44-1 House Exec. Doc. 1 (1680), Annual Report, Commissioner of Indian Affairs, 1875.

44-1 House Exec. Doc. 59 (1687), Germain girls.

44-1 House Exec. Doc. 102 (1689), Tonkawa Indian Scouts.

44-1 House Misc. Doc. 37 (1698), Compensation for losses.

44-1 House Report 343 (1709), Indian depredations on Texas Rio Grande frontier.

44-1 House Report 645 (1712), Kiowa depredations, 1871–1872, Shackelford County.

45-1 House Exec. Doc. 4 (1773), Condition of German girls.

45-1 House Exec. Doc. 13 (1773), Mexican border troubles.

45-2 Sen. Exec. Doc. 62 (1781), Certificate of Merit.

45-2 Sen. Misc. Doc. 23 (1785), Removal of Kickapoos.

45-2 House Report 378 (1823), Captive children from Texas (Susanna Lee Marble).

45-2 House Report 465 (1823), Comanche depredations in Texas, 1872 (Sanford claims).

45-2 House Report 701 (1824), U.S. and Mexican Indian difficulties.

45-2 Sen. Exec. Doc. 19 (1870), Indian invasions of Texas, 1854–1877.

45-2 House Misc. Doc. 64 (1920), Indian raids from Mexico.

46-2 Sen. Report 40 (1893), Problems on Rio Grande frontier.

46-2 Sen. Report 551 (1897), Warren wagon train claims.

46-2 Sen. Res. 691 (1899), Relief for Amos Chapman.

46-2 House Report 256 (1935), Warren wagon train claims.

47-1 Sen. Res. 691 (2007), Relief for Amos Chapman.

48-1 House Report 1135 (2256), Depredation claims against Kiowas and Comanches.

49-1 House Exec. Doc. 125 (2399), Compiled depredation claims.

49-2 House Report 4108 (2501), Wearing of military decorations.

50-1 Sen. Report 1530 (2524), Wearing of badges of certain American orders.

50-1 House Report 1696 (2602), Adjudication of Indian depredation claims.

51-1 Sen. Report 124 (2703), Permission to wear badges of certain orders.

51-1 House Report 1522 (2811), Permission to wear badges of certain orders.

53-2 House Report 1276 (3272), Medal of Honor to volunteers in 1863.

53-3 Sen. Report 928 (3289), Resolution on Medal of Honor.

54-1 Sen. Report 378 (3363), Issue of duplicates for lost or destroyed medals.

54-1 Sen. Report 587 (3364), Ribbons and rosettes for Medal of Honor.

54-1 House Report 379 (3458), Ribbons and rosettes for Medal of Honor.

54-1 House Report 1742 (3463), Medals to Gettysburg volunteers.

54-1 House Report 1747 (3463), Extend Medal of Honor eligibility to civilians attached to Army.

54-2 House Report 2586 (3555), Recognize officer Medal of Honor recipients.

55-2 House Report 68 (3717), Rosettes for Navy Medal of Honor.

56-2 House Exec. Doc. 538, Digest of decisions on Indian affairs.

57-1 Sen. Report 179 (4257), Issue of duplicate medals.

58-2 Sen. Report 27 (4570), Issue of duplicate medals.

58-2 House Report 1886 (4581), Issue of duplicate medals.

58-2 House Doc. 83 (4671), Legislation relevant to issue of Medal of Honor.

59-2 Sen. Report 7250 (5061), Recipients to retain old design Medals of Honor.

59-2 House Report 7086 (5064), Recipients to retain old design Medals of Honor.

63-2 Sen. Report 639 (6553), Army and Navy Medal of Honor Roll.

63-2 House Report 512 (6559), Army and Navy Medal of Honor Roll.

64-1 Sen. Report 240 (6897), Army and Navy Medal of Honor Roll.

64-1 House Report 113 (6903), Army and Navy Medal of Honor Roll.

65-1 Sen. Report 114 (7249), Permit Americans to wear foreign medals.

65-1 House Report 173 (7252), Permit Americans to wear foreign medals.

66-1 Sen. Exec. Doc. 58 (7609), General Staff Corps and the Medal of Honor.

93-1 Sen. Com. Print 15, Senate Committee on Veteran's Affairs, Medal of Honor Recipients, 1863–1973.

FEDERAL RECORDS GROUPS

These are records of executive branch agencies, most of which are on deposit at the National Archives in Washington, D.C., or at various federal records centers. Some records groups are available on microfilm and where this is existent, the microcopy and roll numbers have been indicated in parentheses. The one exception herein is for Records Group 29, Bureau of the Census, whose microfilm inventory is too extensive for listing. Pamphlets detailing the microfilm inventory for each Records Group are available by requesting the pamphlet describing the microcopy number.

Records Group 15: Records of the U.S. Veteran's Administration

General Index to Pension Files, 1861–1934 (T-288).

Index to Indian War Pensions, 1892–1926 (T-318).

Pension Records. These are the single most valuable source of biographical information on a veteran. The application, certificate, and file number are necessary to locate the pension file.

	Application no.	Certificate no.	File no.
Albee, George E.			XC-2659057
Bell, George H.		35894	
Chapman, Amos		221433	
Comfort, John W.	1143421		
Connor, John	965594	670338	
DeArmond, Julia A.		171172	
Dixon, William	1296132	1056765	
Eldridge, George H.	1051738	86008	
Factor, Pompey	20180	13093	
Hesseltine, Francis S.	358124	1078739	358124
James, John	557816	334304	
Keating, Daniel	1185991		
Kelly, John J. H.	14549	9172	
Kelly, Thomas	787751	521680	
Kirk, John	1272421	1045223	C-2536673
Kitchen, George K.	11997	7724	
Knox, John	1152526	874350	
Larkin, David	1014587	801890	
May, John	435604	380140	
Neilon, Fred. S. (Singleton)	206350	136726	
Pennsyl(e), Josiah	10905	7097	
Phoenix, Edwin			C-2606884
Porter, Samuel	1190797	1047283	C-22361751
Pratt, James N.	199666	138900	
Roth, Peter P.	693956	441067	
Sharpless, Edward C.	12120		XC-871664
Smythe, James (Anderson)	15265		
Veuve, Ernest	13833	9044	
Walker, Allen			C-17806263
Ward, John	1175862	961935	
Watson, James C.	434050	312142	
Windus, Claron A.	12427	1425535	
Winterbottom, William			XC-2650965

Records Group 21: Records of the District Courts of the United States (Fort Worth Federal Records Center)

> U.S. District Courts: Southern District of Texas
>> Brownsville: Court Dockets, 1853–1945.
>> Laredo: U.S. Commissioner's Reports, 1889–1916.
> U.S. District Courts: Western District of Texas
>> San Antonio: Criminal Records, 1892–1956.
>> Law (Circuit Court), 1879–1912.

Bibliography

Records Group 24: Records of the Bureau of Naval Personnel

Abstracts of Service of Naval Officers, "Records of Officers," 1798–1893 (M-330).

Register of Medals of Honor, 1861–1924. This register of the letters sent to the Navy Department by recipients acknowledging receipt of their Medal of Honor offers a wealth of information. A recipient's deportment, literacy, and the circumstance of the receipt of the Medal of Honor may be found therein.

Records Group 29: Records of the Bureau of the Census

Sixth (1840) through Fourteenth (1920) Population Schedules of the Census of the United States.

Records Group 45: Records of the Office of Naval Records

Logbooks of U.S. Navy Ships
USS *Santee*, 1861
USS *Seminole*, 1863–1864

Records Group 56: Records of the Department of Treasury

Office of the Second Auditor. Accounts of pay due and personal effects of deceased soldiers were forwarded to the Second Auditor's Office for disbursal to the next of kin and claimants.

Records Group 59: Records of the Department of State

Dispatches from U.S. Consuls in Matamoras, Mexico, 1826–1906 (M-281).
Dispatches from U.S. Consuls in Nuevo Laredo, Mexico (M-280).
Dispatches from U.S. Consuls in Piedras Negras, Mexico, 1868–1906 (M-299).

Records Group 75: Records of the Bureau of Indian Affairs

Records of the Depredations Division, 1835–1896.

Records Group 77: Records of the Office of the Chief of Engineers

Cartographic Records Division, 1836–1942.

Records Group 92: Records of the Office of the U.S. Army Quartermaster General

Reports of Persons and Articles Hired (scouts, guides, packers, interpreters, teamsters, wagons, and etc.)
Correspondence Relating to Decorations and Awards, 1905–1926 (Campaign Badges, Certificates of Merit, Distinguished Service Cross, and Silver Star).
Records of Burials at U.S. Military Installations

Records Group 94: Records of the Office of the Adjutant General

Official Records of the War of the Rebellion
Records of the Union and Confederate Armies, 1861–1865 (M-262).
Records of the Union and Confederate Navies, 1861–1865 (M-275).
The above records are also found in bound, indexed volumes in most large libraries.

Register of U.S. Army Enlistments, 1798–1914 (M-233).
> "Enlistment Papers." These are the actual enlistment forms that relate additional information not found in enlistment registers. Information on the enlistee, such as literacy, conjugal status, previous wounds, and identifying marks, is provided. These are not on microfilm.

> "Final Statement Papers." Upon the death of a soldier the company commander completed these. They include location and circumstances of the death, location of burial, an inventory of personal effects, and pay due to the soldier. These were forwarded to the Second Auditor's Office of the Treasury Department for disbursal to the next of kin.

Index to Letters Received by the Adjutant General's Office, 1861–1889 (M-725).

Registers of Letters Received by the Adjutant General's Office, 1812–1889 (M-711). These contain a brief description of each letter received by the Adjutant General's Office.

> Letters Received by the Adjutant General's Office, 1861–1870 (M-619). Subjects included in this listing are limited to Medal of Honor history, Indian affairs in Texas, compilations of documents that relate to engagements, Medal of Honor history, and awards that occurred in Texas.

1863

File 699273: Early Medal of Honor ceremony.

File 92467-S, slip 489258: Consolidated papers on Medal of Honor.

1868

File 1275M: Papers relating to Kickapoo, Lipan, and Mescalero Apaches inhabiting Mexico adjacent to the U.S., 1868–1869.

File 42I: Medicine Lodge Treaty implementation (roll 629).

1869

File 534 (EB): Request for list of Medal of Honor recipients.

File 703M: Policy on Indians refusing to go onto reservation (roll 722).

1870

File 104: General Wheaton recommends Eighth U.S. Cavalry men for Medal of Honor.

File 293T: Papers on July 12, 1870, engagement on Little Wichita River (filed with 2765-AGO, 1889).

File 325T, 454T, 456T: Sixth Cavalrymen awarded Medal of Honor (filed with 2765-AGO, 1889).

File 720S: Sgt. E. Stance report of scout.

File 786: Indian depredations, Military Division of Missouri.

File 892S: Stance receipt of Medal of Honor.

File 488M: Papers relating to the return of Kickapoo and Seminole-Negro Indians from Mexico to the U.S., 1870–1875 (M-666, rolls 799-800).

Bibliography

Letters Received by the Adjutant General's Office, 1871–1880 (M-666):

1871

File 366, 369, 426: Sixth Cavalry recipients acknowledge receipt of medals.

1872

File 867: Scout G. W. Woodall (includes file 5579-AGO, 1875).

File 1582: William Wilson report (M-666, roll 60).

File 3474: F. M. McDonald (McDonnold) Medal of Honor deed.

File 4099: Department of Texas, Annual Report.

File 4148 (includes file 4546-1/2): Report of engagement on North Fork, Red River, on September 29, 1872 (roll 86).

File 5176 (includes file 3970, AGO, 1974): Medal of Honor laws.

1873

File 398: Branagan receipt of Medal of Honor.

File 399: Foster, Larkin, and others acknowledge receipt of Medals of Honor.

File 3269: Medal of Honor laws and regulations (filed with file 5176, AGO, 1872).

1874

File 2686: Indian War criterion for Medal of Honor.

File 2815: Papers on 1874–1875 Red River War (M-666, rolls 159-164).

File 2694: General Order on Second Cavalrymen and Medal of Honor (includes file 3963).

File 3970: (filed with 5176-AGO, 1872) Laws on Medal of Honor.

File 4278: Medal of Honor for Buffalo Wallow fight (filed with file 2815, AGO, 1874).

File 4623: Lyman train battle map (filed with file 2815, AGO,1874).

File 4681: Amos Chapman and Medal of Honor (filed with file 2815, AGO, 1874).

File 5057: Baldwin rescue of German girls (filed with file 2815, AGO, 1874).

File 5519: Request for return of G. W. Smith's remains to New York (filed with file 2815, AGO, 1874).

1875

File 252: Warrington report of Medal of Honor deed (filed with file 2815, AGO, 1874).

File 255: Mackenzie on gallant acts (filed with file 2815, AGO, 1874).

File 785: E. Miller for duplicate Medal of Honor.

File 1064: Amos Chapman receipt of medal.

File 1420: General Crook on Medal of Honor (filed with file 5176, AGO, 1872).

File 1653: Affairs on Rio Grande–Texas frontier (M-666, rolls 195-211).

File 1750, 1835: J. Harrington receipt of Medal of Honor (filed with file 2815, AGO, 1874).

File 1821: Lyman Wagon Train and Sappa Creek engagements and Medals of Honor (filed with file 2815, AGO, 1874).

File 1846: Anderson request for duplicate Medal of Honor.

File 2686: Indian War criterion for Medal of Honor.

File 2696: Bullis report of scout.

File 4030-36: Hay, James, T. Kelly, J. J. H. Kelly, Koelpin, and Mitchell receipt of Medals of Honor (filed with file 2815, AGO, 1874).

File 4069: J. Knox receipt of Medal of Honor (filed with file 2815, AGO, 1874).

File 4302: W. W. Morris receipt of Medal of Honor (filed with file 2815, AGO, 1874).

File 4783: Medal of Honor for Sappa Creek, Kansas (filed with file 2815, AGO, 1874).

File 4917: Mackenzie on specific acts of gallantry (filed with file 2815, AGO, 1874).

File 5261: Sheerin receipt of Medal of Honor.

File 5384: Lytle receipt of Medal of Honor.

File 5579: G. W. Woodall service as scout (filed with file 867, AGO, 1872).

File 5703: Veuve and Phoenix receipt of Medals of Honor (filed with file 2815, AGO, 1874).

File 5710: Pennsyl receipt of Medal of Honor (filed with file 2815, AGO, 1874).

File 5898: O'Sullivan receipt of Medal of Honor (filed with file 2815, AGO, 1874).

File 5976: Kitchen receipt of Medal of Honor (filed with file 2815, AGO, 1874).

File 6153 and 3036: W. W. Morris disallowed second Medal of Honor (filed with file 2815, AGO, 1874).

1876

File 2134: Seminole-Negro Indian Scouts Medal of Honor deed.

File 681: Mahoney receipt of Medal of Honor (filed with file 2815, AGO, 1874).

File 837: McCabe receipt of Medal of Honor (filed with file 2815, AGO, 1874).

File 4408: Sale of arms to Indians (roll 294).

1878

File 10818-A(EB): Medal of Honor history—Little Big Horn battle.

File 771: Civil War Medal of Honor.

1879

File 3313-A (EB): Medal of Honor history—Mitchell Raiders.

Letters Received by the Office of the Adjutant General, Main Series, 1881–1889 (M-689):

1881

File 2466: Hesse.

1882

File 8847-A (EB): Compiled papers on Medal of Honor history.

1884

File 817: Medal of Honor for "Forlorn Hope Party" in 1863.

1888

File 1369C (EB): E. Stance personal effects.

1889

File 2765: Medals of Honor to Cavalrymen in Texas (filed with file 5461, AGO, 1889).

Files 1674, 4468: Amos Chapman.

File 5461: Compiled records pertaining to U.S. Army personnel who have distinguished themselves since the Civil War "The MacArthur Board" (M-689, rolls 717–722).

Index to General Correspondence of the Adjutant General's Office, 1890–1917 (M-698).

Roll 763: Subject of Medal of Honor. The documents indexed alphabetically herein are classified as "Medal of Honor Papers," and are a source of information on addresses of recipients, applications for new medals and rosettes, applications for the Medal of Honor Roll and pension, legal issues involving the medal, and Medal of Honor organizations.

Documents Received by the Adjutant General's Office, 1890–1917. Most of the files listed hereafter are from the Index-Subject cards on roll 763 on the subject of the Medal of Honor. Some files, however, relate to personnel matters such as transfers, retirement, death notices, and etc., and were obtained from the Index to General Correspondence of the Adjutant General's Office, 1890–1917.

1890

File 3684, Principal Records Division (PRD): William McNamara retirement.

File 8440, PRD: Recommendation for second Medal of Honor for John Mitchell (filed with file 5461, AGO, 1889).

1891

File 11192, PRD: Amos Chapman.

File 11358, PRD: Denis Ryan.

File 12213, PRD: Z. T. Woodall to Ordnance Sergeant.

File 20181, PRD: John W. Comfort cited at Wounded Knee (filed with file 5461, AGO, 1889).

File 15082, PRD: Amos Chapman.

1892

File 24002, PRD: Compiled papers on Garza rebellion.

File 24731, PRD: Allen Walker.

File 27624, PRD: Allen Walker Medal of Honor deed.

File 27807, PRD: John O'Sullivan.

File 28500, PRD: William Koelpin.

File 31566, PRD: William Wilson.

File 31604, PRD: Amos Chapman.

File 41621, PRD: J. W. Comfort retirement.

File 42604, PRD: Z. T. Woodall.

File 43010, PRD: Amos Chapman.

1893

File 3742, PRD: Medal of Honor list for Medal of Honor legion.

File 5895, PRD: Medal of Honor recipient listing.

File 13892, PRD: Albee application.

File 18320, PRD: Medal of Honor recipient list with addresses.

File 18952, PRD: L. S. Lytle loss of Medal of Honor at San Antonio.

File 19768, PRD: Singleton (Neilon) explains assumed name.

File 20488, PRD: Singleton (Neilon) explains assumed name.

File 355121, PRD: Hesseltine request for Medal of Honor application.

File 408201, PRD: Submission of Hesseltine application.

1894

File 150, PRD: Neilon.

File 465, PRD: G. E. Albee and Medal of Honor.

File 1886, PRD: Neilon.

File 2264, PRD: McNamara retirement.

File 4914, PRD: F. D. Baldwin Medal of Honor.

File 4946, PRD: F. D. Baldwin Medal of Honor.

File 6489, PRD: John Mitchell retirement.

File 9264, PRD: F. D. Baldwin Medal of Honor.

File 9542, PRD: Isaac Payne.

1895

File 17953A, PRD: John James.

File 25335, PRD: E. Stance Jr., inquiry about father.

File 29695, PRD: Isaac Payne.

Bibliography

1896

File 30964, PRD: William Wilson's death.

File 47545, PRD: G. E. Albee.

1897

File 52211, PRD: D. Larkin requests rosette.

File 53290, PRD: F. Bergendahl requests rosette.

File 59730, PRD: S. Neal on loss of Medal of Honor.

File 60221A, PRD: G. Kitchen.

File 65174, PRD: Carter Medal of Honor.

1898

File 283547F, PRD: Death of Z. T. Woodall.

File 68439, PRD: Isaac Payne.

File 70487, PRD: William Rankin.

File 70852, PRD: John Harrington.

File 97210, PRD: W. W. Morris.

File 97744, PRD: John Harrington.

1899

File 283547F, PRD: Administration of Woodall estate.

File 291407, PRD: Disposition of Woodall effects.

File 293145, PRD: C. Windus.

1900

File 312988, PRD: William Rankin retirement.

File 360765, PRD: John Harrington retirement.

1901

File 382440, PRD: Samuel Porter.

File 389940, PRD: J. Harrington.

File 407038, PRD: C. Windus.

File 412663, PRD: Allen Walker.

1902

File 433568, PRD: William Koelpin.

File 433817, PRD: Samuel Porter.

File 461998, PRD: Compiled papers on new Medal of Honor design.

1903

File 468167, PRD: Medal of Honor pension.

File 92467-R-1, PRD: Change in Medal of Honor design.

1904

File 522970, PRD: J. J. H. Kelly on loss of original Medal of Honor.

File 527025, PRD: John Mitchell death.

File 905693, PRD: Listing of Medal of Honor recipients.

File 922296, PRD: G. K. Kitchen.

File 92467-R-2, PRD: Consolidated file on Medal of Honor.

File 932204, PRD: Carter new Medal of Honor.

File 933356, PRD: O'Sullivan new Medal of Honor.

File 933914, PRD: Hesseltine request for new Medal of Honor.

File 934143, PRD: Carter Medal of Honor inscription.

File 936825, PRD: Hesseltine request for new Medal of Honor.

File 937625, PRD: Neilon new Medal of Honor.

File 938536, PRD: Medal of Honor Legion.

File 942205, PRD: Roster of living Medal of Honor recipients.

File 957736, PRD: Roster of living Medal of Honor recipients with addresses.

1905

File 961968, PRD: List of Philadelphia, Pa., recipients.

File 962768, PRD: John Harrington death.

File 965560, PRD: O'Sullivan old Medal of Honor.

File 981628, PRD: Hesseltine new Medal of Honor.

File 1000265, PRD: Solon D. Neal.

File 1007497, PRD: Hesseltine—Medal of Honor Legion on old for new Medal of Honor.

File 1014488, PRD: Escorts for Medal of Honor recipient's funerals.

File 1029601, PRD: F. D. Baldwin.

File 1032151, PRD: List of Ohio Medal of Honor recipients.

1906

File 1112435, PRD: Walker on replacement of lost Medal of Honor.

1907

File 917860A, PRD: John O'Sullivan.

File 1218341, PRD: List of recipients exchanging old Medal of Honor for new design.

File 1225484, PRD: F. Schwabe request for new Medal of Honor.

File 1306245, PRD: Thomas Kelly.

1910

File 1623081, PRD: Addresses of Medal of Honor recipients.

1912

File 28500, PRD: William Koelpin.

File 1865583, PRD: William Koelpin.

File 1892353, PRD: William McNamara's death.

File 1938630, PRD: List of New York Medal of Honor recipients.

File 1971824, PRD: New York City Medal of Honor Legion.

File 1973491, PRD: Medal of Honor confiscated for debt.

1913

File 2027721, PRD: Medal of Honor Association of New England.

File 2108237, PRD: Two Medals of Honor to Baldwin.

1914

File 2191969, PRD: Army and Navy Medal of Honor Legion.

1915

File 2302547, PRD: Medal of Honor Legion members and addresses.

File 2349009, PRD: Medal of Honor Legion.

File 2495888, PRD: Medal of Honor Legion.

1916

File 29695, PRD: Isaac Payne.

File 461543, PRD: F. S. Schwabe (Hay).

File 1231769, PRD: Interpretation of Indian Wars "in action" (John Kirk).

File 2376984, PRD: William Rankin's death.

File 2397979, PRD: Interpretation of "in action."

File 2398190, PRD: John Kirk application for Medal of Honor Roll.

File 2399050, PRD: Eligibility for retirees.

File 2399750, PRD: Application for Medal of Honor Roll guidelines.

File 2403427, PRD: F. D. Baldwin application for Medal of Honor Roll.

File 2403698, PRD: G. E. Albee on eligibility for Medal of Honor Roll.

File 2403823, PRD: G. H. Eldridge application for Medal of Honor Roll.

File 2407254, PRD: R. G. Carter application for Medal of Honor Roll.

File 2411162F, PRD: Medal of Honor Board and living recipient list.

File 2480230, PRD: Medal of Honor Board.

File 2480855, PRD: E. C. Sharpless, Medal of Honor Roll.

File 2495888, PRD: Ohio Medal of Honor Legion.

File 2575925, PRD: Amos Chapman.

File 2581570, PRD: Medal of Honor Board.

1917

File 1462171, PRD: Medal of Honor Board Report on 2,625 cases (includes file 249162-1916).

File 2411162, PRD: Medal of Honor Board—Chapman.

Records of the General Correspondence of the Record and Pension Office
Index to General Correspondence of the Record and Pension Office (M-686).
RPO File 699273 (1902); Compiled papers on Medal of Honor.

Returns from U.S. Army Military Posts, 1800–1916 (M-617).
Fort Brown, 1866–1886 (roll 152).
Fort Concho, 1867–1878 (roll 241).

Fort Clark, 1866-1881 (roll 214).
Fort Dodge, Kans., 1866–1882 (roll 319).
Fort Duncan, 1868–1883 (roll 336).
Fort Griffin, 1867–1881 (roll 429).
Fort McIntosh, 1881–1902 (rolls 683, 684).
Fort McKavett, 1852–1883 (rolls 687, 688).
Fort Richardson, 1866–1878 (roll 1008).
Fort Ringgold, 1885–1894 (roll 1022).
Fort Sill, I.T., 1869–1875 (roll 1173).
Fort (Camp) Supply, I.T., 1868–1879 (roll 1243).

In addition to monthly accounting of manpower assigned to the post, the Post
Returns include a "Record of Events" section that describes the day-to-day
military events, i.e., arrival and departure of scouting and escort detachments. More detailed information about events can be found in:

Post Medical Record-History: Written by the post surgeons, these records
provide the most detailed account of daily activities on the post even to
the point of providing meteorological data. The surgeon's entries often
add precise details of a battle, especially if a surgeon was present.

Fort Clark, 1875, vol. 907.
Fort Concho, 1869–1874, vols. 401–407.
Fort Griffin, 1870, vol. 102.
Fort Richardson, 1870–1875, vols. 235–238.
Fort Supply, I.T., 1874, vol. 166.

Register of Patients: These records, also written by the post surgeon, provide information such as the treatment of wounds, autopsy reports,
and description of circumstances of wounds.

Fort Brown, 1875, vol. 256.
Fort Griffin, 1872, vols. 145–146.
Fort Richardson, 1870–1871, vols. 95–96.
Fort Supply, I.T., 1874, vol. 39.

Returns of U.S. Army Regular Cavalry Regiments, 1821–1916 (M-744).
Fourth U.S. Cavalry, 1864–1876 (rolls 41, 42).
Sixth U.S. Cavalry, 1868–1874 (roll 62).
Ninth U.S. Cavalry, 1866–1872 (roll 87).

These are monthly manpower accounting returns of a regiment. Information
provided includes the number of sick men in the regiment in any given
month. The names of men detailed on a particular patrol or detached
duty or those men on leave are also provided. The "Record of Events"
section provides a detailed account of the regiment's activities for that
month.

Bibliography

Returns of U.S. Army Regular Infantry Regiments, 1833–1916 (M-665).
Fifth U.S. Infantry, 1870–1879 (roll 58).
Eighth U.S. Infantry, 1858–1865 (roll 92).
Tenth U.S. Infantry, 1871–1879 (roll 115).
Eleventh U.S. Infantry, 1866–1872 (roll 125).
Twenty-fourth U.S. Infantry, 1866–1880 (rolls 245, 246).

Compilation of Documents relating to the Military and Naval Service of Blacks awarded the Congressional Medal of Honor from the Civil War to the Spanish-American War (Microcopy Publication M-929). This compilation of documents is comprised of documents from several federal records groups, but primarily from Records Group 94. Roll 2: Indians Campaigns; Target 4: Pompey Factor; Target 10: Adam Paine; Target 11: Isaac Payne; Target 13: Emanuel Stance; and Target 15: John Ward.

Appointments, Commission, and Promotion Papers (ACP Files). These are officer "personnel files." They include character references, qualification tests, and other documents relating to promotions and other personnel matters. Medal of Honor documents are often included.

Albee, George E., 1318, ACP–1872.
Baldwin, Frank D., 3365, ACP–1875.
Bourke, John G., 6291, ACP–1883.
Carter, Robert G., 3679, ACP–1873.
Davis, Wirt, 4360, ACP–1878.
Leiper, Mathew, 2396, ACP–1880.
Lewis, Granville, 1015, ACP–1871.
Lyman, Wyllys, 1073, ACP–1875.
Mackenzie, Ranald S., 3877, ACP–1873.
Thompson, William A., T46B, ACP–1868.
Warrington, Lewis, 180, ACP–1879.

Records Group 112: Records of the Office of the Surgeon General (Army)

Records of the U.S. Army Medical Examining Boards, 1862–1896. Officers disabled in the line of duty were required to appear before a board comprised of army surgeons. Affidavits and testimony pertaining to the circumstance of wounds or injury are very detailed and add very specific details to a battle or incident that may not be available from other sources.

Case no. 13, Lt. Granville Lewis, Jan. 29, 1879, Fort Leavenworth, Kans.

Records Group 125: Records of the Office of the Judge Advocate General (Navy)

Records of General Courts Martial and Courts of Inquiry of the Navy Department, 1799–1867.

Records Group 153: Records of the Office of the Judge Advocate General (Army)

Bureau of Military Justice, 1869–1876.

Register of General Courts Martial (M-1105).
File PP1100, Anderson, James, March 1870.
File PP2797, Comfort, John W., Sept. 1872.
File PP4519, Factor, Dindie, April 1875.
File PP1946, Kerrigan, Thomas, July 1871.
File PP2974, Neal, Solon D., Nov. 1874.
File PP3610, Phoenix, Edwin, Nov. 1873.
File PP4985, Porter, Samuel, Jan. 1875.
File PP265, Stance, Emanuel, Jan. 1869.
File PP2955, Stance, Emanuel, Jan. 1873.
File PP44, Windus, Claron A., Feb. 1868.
File PP2365, Welch, Michael, Dec. 1871.
File PP3107, Wilson, William, March 1873.
File PP3726, Wilson, Benjamin, Oct. 1873.
File PP3728, Wilson, Benjamin, Jan. 1874.

Records Group 156: Records of the Office of the Chief of Ordnance (Army) (M-1281)

Summary Statements of Quarterly Returns of Ordnance and Ordnance Stores on Hand in Regular and Volunteer Army Organizations, 1862–1876.
Fourth, Sixth, and Ninth U.S. Cavalries: Vol. 9, 1866–1871 (roll 3).
Fifth and Eleventh U.S. Infantries: Vol. 1, 1872–1876 (roll 8).
Volumes 1 and 2 on roll 8 include all regiments for 1872–1876.

Records Group 159: Records of the Office of the Inspector General, 1814–1939

Index to Letters Sent, 1863–1889.
Letters Sent, 1863–1889.
Index to Letters Received, 1863–1891.
Register of Letters Received, 1863–1889.
Letters Received, 1863–1894.
See also the Inspector General's Annual Reports filed with the Secretary of War's Annual Report to Congress. These give a good overall view of the military efficiency of a particular military unit.

Records Group 217: Records of the U.S. General Accounting Office

General Records of the Department of Treasury, Second Auditor's Office.
"Effects Books." These bound registers with their alphabetical and chronological entries denote the final disposition of a deceased soldier's personal effects and estate.

Bibliography

Records Group 231: Records of the United States Soldier's Home
Registers of Inmates.
Records of Inmates, 1803–1943.
    Statements of Service and Descriptions of Deceased Inmates, 1880–1940.

Records Group 391: Records of Regular U.S. Army Mobile Units, 1821–1942
Records of the Fourth U.S. Cavalry.
    Name Index to Regimental Letters Sent, 1870, 1874–1882.
        Regimental Letters Sent, 1856–1906.
    Name Index to Letters Received, 1874–1913.
        Registers of Letters Received, 1867–1907.
    Orders, General Orders, and Circulars Issued, 1860–1890.
    Special Orders Issued, 1866–1881.
    Military Histories of Officers, 1873–1903.
    Regimental Histories, 1855–1926.
    Regimental Returns, 1860–1918.
    Regimental Descriptive Books, 1855–1907.
    Expedition Records (Letterbooks):
        Scouting Expedition: July–October, 1871.
        Scouting Expedition: June–December, 1872.
        Southern Column–Indian Territory Expedition: August–November, 1874.
        Letters and Endorsements Sent and Orders Issued, 1871, 1872, 1874.
        Register of Letters Received, 1872.
        Orders and Circulars Issued, 1872.
Records of the Sixth U.S. Cavalry.
    Regimental Letters Sent, 1867–1882.
    Endorsements Sent, 1862–1885.
    Registers of Letters Received, 1867–1870 and 1872–1906.
    Orders, General Orders, Special Orders, and Circulars Issued, 1873–1884.
    General and Special Orders Issued, 1871–1875.
    Military Histories of Officers, 1861–1912.
    Histories of the Sixth Cavalry and Related Records, 1867–1915.
    Monthly Returns, 1866–1910.
    Reports and Tabular Statements of Scouting Expeditions, 1867–1891.
    Journal of Events and Routes of Scouting Expeditions, 1871–1873.
    Proceedings of General, Regimental, and Summary Courts Martial, 1865–1912.
Records of the Ninth U.S. Cavalry.
    Name and Subject Index to Letters Sent, 1886–1887.
    Regimental Orders and Circulars Issued, 1875–1891.
    Letters, Orders, and Reports Received from and Relating to Members of the Ninth Cavalry, 1867–1898.

Records Group 393: Records of U.S. Army Continental Commands, 1821–1920

Records of Geographical Divisions and Departments and Military Reconstruction Districts.

Records of the Division of the Missouri.

"Special Files" of Headquarters, Division of the Missouri, Relating to Military Operations and Administration, 1863–1885 (M-1495).

Indian Territory Expedition (Red River War), May 1874–April 1875 (rolls 8–9).

Indian Prisoners, October 1874–August 1875 (roll 9).

Rio Grande Disturbances, March 1872–January 1879 (rolls 11–13).

Seminole Negro Indian Scouts, August 1872–June 1876 (roll 13).

Department of Texas and the Fifth Military District.

Office of Civil Affairs.

Letters Received Relating to Indian Depredations and Crimes, 1868–1870.

Department of Texas, 1870–1913.

Name and Subject Indexes to Letters Received.

Registers of Letters Received, April 1870–1898.

Letters Received, April 1870–1898.

Letters Received Relating to Difficulties with Indians ("Indian Files"), 1870–1876 (item 4875).

Letters and Reports Received Relating to the Garza Revolution, 1891–1893 (item 4877).

Record Cards and Correspondence Relating to Various Subjects.

No. 28985: Seminole-Negro Indian Scouts.

No. 35506: Mexican Border Troubles.

General Orders and General Court Martial Orders, 1871–1875.

Tabular Statements of Expeditions and Scouts, 1869–1890.

Military Histories of Officers in the Department, 1869–1899.

Reports of Persons Killed or Captured by Indians, 1872–1888.

Cartographic Records, 1837–1920. Maps of some scouting patrols and expeditions are deposited here, along with engineer blueprints of some military posts within the department.

Records of the Sub-District of the Rio Grande, 1873–1881.

Reports of Scouting Expeditions.

Records of the Sub-District of the Upper Red River, 1874–1876.

Letters Sent: October 1874–January 1876.

Registers of Letters Received and Endorsements Sent.

General Orders Issued: October 1874–July 1875.

Special Orders Issued: November 1874–December 1875.

Bibliography

Department of Missouri, 1868–1913.
    Indian Territory Expedition, 1874–1875.
        Letters Sent, 1874–1875 (item 2927).
        Endorsements, 1874–1875 (item 1928).
        Special Orders, 1874–1875 (item 2929).

NEWSPAPERS

Army and Navy Journal (volumes 6–13 deal with the 1869–1875 period).
    Vol. 6, p. 97, "War Coming to the Plains."
    Vol. 6, p. 110, "General Reynold's on Successful Combats."
    Vol. 6, p. 707, "Indian Troubles."
    Vol. 6, p. 360, "The Indian Campaign of 1869."
    Vol. 6, p. 744, 792, "The Indian Problem."
    Vol. 6, p. 231, "Army Record for the Years, 1868–1869."
    Vol. 7, pp. 70–71, "Indian Fight in Texas."
    Vol. 7, p. 214, "Indian Fight in Texas October 5, 1870."
    Vol. 7, p. 502, "The Indian Difficulties."
    Vol. 7, p. 721, "Frontier Defense."
    Vol. 8, p. 391, "The Army on the Frontier."
    Vol. 8, p. 767, "Scout of the Fourth Cavalry."
    Vol. 9, p. 609, "Indian Atrocities."
    Vol. 9, pp. 212, 213, "Department of Texas, Mackenzie's Battles."
    Vol. 10, n.p. January 1873, "Medal of Honor Award Ceremony at Fort Concho."
    Vol. 10, p. 330, "Indian Fights."
    Vol. 10, p. 668, "Mackenzie's Raid."
    Vol. 10, p. 728, "Mackenzie's Raid."
    Vol. 11, pp. 21, 155, "Indian Atrocities."
    Vol. 11, pp. 485–493, "Hostile Indians."
    Vol. 11, pp. 165, 180–181, "Department of Texas."
    Vol. 12, p. 186, "A Fight with Comanches and Kiowas."
    Vol. 12, pp. 227–228, "Military Division of the Missouri."
    Vol. 12, p. 101, "Colonel Miles Expedition."
    Vol. 12, p. 275, "Miles Expedition at Washita River, Texas."
    Vol. 12, pp. 148, 164, "General Order No. 18" and "Colonel Miles Expedition."
    Vol. 12, p. 388, "Colonel Mackenzie's Expedition."
    Vol. 12, pp. 453–456, "Colonel Miles' Expedition."
    Vol. 12, p. 505, "Indian Campaigns, Summer 1874."
    Vol. 12, pp. 565–566, "Colonel Miles Expedition."
    Vol. 13, p. 101, "Expeditions Against Hostile Indians."
    Vol. 13, p. 823, "Indian Fighting."
    Vol. 32, p. 347, "Stars and Garters for Indian Wars."
    Vol. 51, p. 1433, "Pension Plan for Medal of Honor Winners."

Vol. 52, p. 944, "Statistical Analysis of Army Medals of Honor."
Vol. 53, p. 1420, "Letter to the Editor about the Medal of Honor."
Vol. 53, pp. 1357, 1368, "Analysis of Medal of Honor Laws."
Vol. 53, p. 1434, "The Medal of Honor Question."
Vol. 53, p. 1293, "The Medal of Honor Roll."

Bellefontaine (Ohio) Examiner
"Obituary Notices–James N. Pratt," Oct. 14, 1903.

Canadian (Texas) Record
"Interesting Facts about Buffalo Wallow," Mar. 18, 1920.
"Hemphill County has Historic Spot," June 25, 1936.

Dallas Herald
"Great Indian Raid," July 9, 1870; p. 2, col. 5.
"Fight with Indians," Aug. 20, 1870; p. 1, col. 8.
"List of Wounded," Aug. 20, 1870; p. 2, col. 3.

Galveston News
"Palo Duro Canyon," Oct. 22, 1874.

Galveston Tri-Weekly News
"Capture of U.S. Mail by Indians," July 15, 1870, p. 1, col. 1.

Harper's Weekly
Vol. 36, "Hunt for Garza," Jan. 30, 1892, pp. 103, 113.
Vol. 37, "Garza Rebellion," Dec. 30, 1893, pp. 1247, 1249.

Houston Post
"John B. Charleton in Forgotten Indian Fights of Texas," Apr. 28, 1936, p. 4.

Lewistown (Pa.) Democrat & Sentinel
"A Famous Soldier Dead, Funeral was Friday," Feb. 10, 1916, p. 8, col. 1 (William Rankin).

New York Times
"Sherman on the Indians," Jan. 27, 1874, p. 1, col. 7; and Feb. 15, 1874, p. 4, col. 2.
"Staving Fight with Indians—Utility of Rifle Pits," Sept. 30, 1874, p. 1, col. 4.

San Antonio Express
"Told by Convicts," July 6, 1892, p. 8, cols. 2, 3.
"Carmen Ybanez's Case," July 7, 1892, p. 8, col. 2.
"More about Garza," July 8, 1892, p. 8, col. 2.
"Testimony All In," July 9, 1892, p. 8, col. 2.
"Ybanez Goes Free," July 10, 1892, p. 3, col. 4.

San Antonio Herald
"Dispatch from House Mountain, Llano County," May 23, 1870.
"Dispatch from Loyal Valley," June 2, 1870.

San Francisco Evening Bulletin
"Death of a Warrior with a Notable Record," July 16, 1880 (William Foster).

Bibliography

San Francisco Examiner
"Deaths–Comrade William Wilson," Dec. 24, 1896.

St. Louis Republican
"Celebrating the Fourth," July 6, 1876, p. 8, col. 3 (Alonzo Stokes).
"The Accident at the Arsenal," July 6, 1876, p. 8, col. 5.

St. Louis Times
"Accidents," July 5, 1876, p. 8, col. 4 (Alonzo Stokes).

Willard (Ohio) Times-Writer
Davis S.Wilde, "His Dad was a Hero, Fighting the Indians," circa May 1972
(Edward C. Sharpless).

Winners of the West
"A Mackenzie Fight," Mar. 30, 1928.
"Colonel C. C. Smith on Sergeant Woodall," Jan. 30, 1930.
"Sketch of Old Fourth Cavalry," Aug. 30, 1930.
"The Battle of Palo Duro Canyon," Apr. 28, 1942.

PERSONAL COLLECTIONS

Detroit Public Library, Detroit, Michigan
Burton Special Collections
Oscar F. Keydel Papers, 1898–1902 (collection no. 1213)

Gilcrease Institute Archives, Tulsa, Oklahoma
R. S. Mackenzie Letterbook, 1875–1883

Huntington Library, San Marino, California
Frank D. Baldwin Papers, 1861–1921
Edwin D. Phillips Typescript

Indiana University, Bloomington, Indiana
Lilly Library
Walter M. Camp Papers

Kansas State Historical Society, Topeka, Kansas
George W. Baird Papers, 1874–1891

Nebraska Historical Society, Lincoln, Nebraska
John G. Bourke Papers, 1873–1898

Oklahoma Historical Society, Oklahoma City, Oklahoma
Indian Archives
Military–Indian Relations and Captives
Arapahoe, Cheyenne, Comanche, and Kiowa Files

Panhandle-Plains Historical Museum and Archives, Canyon, Texas
Olive K. and William (Billy) Dixon Papers
Charles A. P. Hatfield Transcript
Frank Collinson Papers on Jim Greathouse

453

Bruce Gerdes Collection

John J. Long Transcript

J. W. McKinley Narrative

San Francisco Public Library

United Indian War Veterans Collection

Stanford University Library, Palo Alto, California

William R. Shafter Papers, 1862–1938

Folders 1–10, 66–79

Texas State Library and Archives Division, Austin, Texas

Map Collection

No. 916, Rio Grande frontier (1878)

No. 953, Shafter map of Mexican borderlands

No. 954, Route of G. P. Buell's 1874 column

No. 1301, Rio Grande borderlands

No. 1591, Military map of Rio Grande frontier

No. 1904, Fort Clark military reservation

Records Group 401: Records of the Office of the Adjutant General of the State of Texas

Texas Technological University, Lubbock, Texas

The Southwest Collection

Map Collection (M-157)

M-4.5 Trails and Routes of Fourth U. S. Cavalry

M-12.5 Mackenzie Expedition of 1872

M-4 Rio Grande Frontier, 1881

Ernest Wallace Collection

United States Army Military History Research Center, Carlisle Barracks, Pennsylvania

Order of Indian Wars Collection

Lemuel Wilson Memoirs–Reminiscences

Charles A. P. Hatfield Diary

Edward A. Brininstool Collection

William C. Brown Collection

Joseph H. Dorst Papers

R. S. Mackenzie Letterbook, 1873–1874

United States Military Academy Library and Archives, West Point, New York

George F. Hamilton Papers

Joseph H. Dorst Papers

University of Texas at Austin

Center for American History

Zenas R. Bliss Reminiscences, 1854–1894

Robert Goldwaite Carter Papers, 1870–1930

Robert G. Carter Diary, June 15, 1870–Dec. 14, 1876, item 89

John Creaton Autobiography and Reminiscences, 1856–1932

Bibliography

Martin L. Crimmins Collections, 1813–1954
Frank Kell Collections
Ben C. Stuart Papers
Jesse Sumpter Reminiscences
Earl Vandale Collections, 1819–1947

INTERVIEWS AND CORRESPONDENCE

C. H. "Buster" Bottoms to Charles M. Neal Jr., Brownfield, Texas, Nov. 28, 1973, interview (Subject: James B. Dosher diary, audio cassette and notes in author's possession).

Robert G. Crisp to Charles M. Neal Jr., Sept. 28 and Oct. 28, 1973 (Subject: John Kirk, letters in author's possession).

Col. S. Geijer, Office of the Swedish Army Attache, Washington, D.C., to Charles M. Neal Jr., Feb. 8, 1973 (Subject: Frederick Bergendahl, letter in author's possession).

Emma Goldman to Charles M. Neal Jr., Aug. 11, 1978, interview (Subject: Claron A. Windus, audio cassette in author's possession).

Agnes MacDonald to Mrs. C. L. Pillows, Apr. 18, 1971 (Subject: Ernest Veuve, letter in author's possession).

Agnes MacDonald to Charles M. Neal Jr., May 5, 1971; Feb. 24, 1972; Apr. 26, 1972; Nov. 22, 1974; and Dec. 26, 1974 (Subject: Ernest Veuve, letters in author's possession).

Agnes MacDonald to Rex E. Neal, Eugene, Ore., Jan. 8, 1975, interview (Subject: Ernest Veuve, notes in author's possession).

Wayne Montgomery to Charles M. Neal Jr., Sept. 21 and Oct. 3, 1972 (Subject: Amos Chapman, letters in author's possession).

Rex E. Neal to Charles M. Neal Jr., Jan. 10, 1975, telephone conversation (Subject: Ernest Veuve, notes in author's possession).

Lt. Col. David P. Perrine to Charles M. Neal Jr., Oct. 10, 1973 (Subject: Peter Roth, letter in author's possession).

T. F. Preston to Charles M. Neal Jr., Mar. 3, 1973 (Subject: Josiah Pennsyl, letter in author's possession).

Edward F. Sharpless to Charles M. Neal Jr., Willard, Ohio, June 12, 1973, interview (Subject: Edward C. Sharpless, notes in author's possession).

Claus R. Simpson to Charles M. Neal Jr., Sept. 1, 1975 (Subject: Edward C. Sharpless, letter in author's possession).

Roy Simpson to Charles M. Neal Jr., May 16, 1973 (Subject: Edward C. Sharpless, letter in author's possession).

Ida Chapman Toller to Charles M. Neal Jr., Oct. 7, 1972 (Subject: Amos Chapman, letter in author's possession).

Albino Walker to Charles M. Neal Jr., Mar. 12, 1991 (Subject: Allen Walker, letter in author's possession).

PAPERS READ AT MEETINGS

Cruse, J. Brett, Texas Historical Commission, "The Texas Red River War Battlesites Project." Paper presented at Order of Indian Wars annual assembly, Sept. 18, 1999, Panhandle-Plains Museum, Canyon, Texas. Copy in author's possession.

Tudor, W. G. 1992, "Was Robert G. Carter with Mackenzie at the Palo Duro in 1874?" Paper presented at West Texas Historical Association annual meeting, Mar. 30, 1992, Alpine, Texas. Copy in author's possession.

Appendix A

Chronological Listing of Congressional Medal of Honor Awards within the State of Texas

Cpl. John C. Hesse[1]	San Antonio (Bexar)	Apr. 23, 1861
Sgt. Joseph K. Wilson	San Antonio (Bexar)	Apr. 23, 1861
Coxswain George H. Bell	Galveston Bay (Galveston)	Nov. 7–8, 1861
Col. Francis S. Hesseltine	Matagorda Peninsula (Matagorda)	Dec. 29, 1863
Lt. George E. Albee[2]	Yellow House Canyon (Lubbock)	Sept. 16, 1869
Sgt. Emanuel Stance	Kickapoo Springs (Concho-Menard)	May 20–21, 1870
Cpl. John Connor	Little Wichita River (Archer)	July 12, 1870
Sgt. George H. Eldridge	Little Wichita River (Archer)	July 12, 1870
Cpl. John J. Given*	Little Wichita River (Archer)	July 12, 1870
Sgt. Thomas Kerrigan	Little Wichita River (Archer)	July 12, 1870
Sgt. John Kirk	Little Wichita River (Archer)	July 12, 1870
Sgt. John May	Little Wichita River (Archer)	July 12, 1870
Pvt. Solon D. Neal	Little Wichita River (Archer)	July 12, 1870
Farrier Samuel Porter	Little Wichita River (Archer)	July 12, 1870
Cpl. Charles E. Smith	Little Wichita River (Archer)	July 12, 1870
Sgt. Alonzo Stokes	Little Wichita River (Archer)	July 12, 1870
Cpl. James C. Watson	Little Wichita River (Archer)	July 12, 1870
Bugler Claron A. Windus	Little Wichita River (Archer)	July 12, 1870
Sgt. William Winterbottom	Little Wichita River (Archer)	July 12, 1870

Pvt. James Smythe[3]	Bluff Creek (Archer)	Oct. 5, 1870
Cpl. Samuel Bowden	Bluff Creek (Archer)	Oct. 5, 1870
Scout James B. Dosher[4]	Bluff Creek (Archer)	Oct. 5, 1870
Cpl. Daniel Keating	Bluff Creek (Archer)	Oct. 5, 1870
Sgt. Michael Welch	Bluff Creek (Archer)	Oct. 5, 1870
Pvt. Benjamin Wilson	Bluff Creek (Archer)	Oct. 5, 1870
Lt. Robert G. Carter	Blanco Canyon (Crosby)	Oct. 10, 1871
Sgt. William Wilson	Beals Creek (Mitchell)	Mar. 28, 1872
Pvt. Franklin M. McDonnold	Salt Creek (Young)	Aug. 3, 1872
Pvt. Edward Branagan	North Fork, Red River (Gray)	Sept. 29, 1872
Sgt. William Foster	North Fork, Red River (Gray)	Sept. 29, 1872
Farrier David Larkin	North Fork, Red River (Gray)	Sept. 29, 1872
Cpl. Henry A. McMaster*	North Fork, Red River (Gray)	Sept. 29, 1872
Sgt. William McNamara	North Fork, Red River (Gray)	Sept. 29, 1872
Cpl. William O'Neill	North Fork, Red River (Gray)	Sept. 29, 1872
Blacksmith James N. Pratt	North Fork, Red River (Gray)	Sept. 29, 1872
Pvt. William Rankin	North Fork, Red River (Gray)	Sept. 29, 1872
Sgt. William Wilson[5]	North Fork, Red River (Gray)	Sept. 29, 1872
Sgt. William DeArmond*	Upper Washita River (Hemphill)	Sept. 9, 1874
Sgt. Frederick H. Schwabe[6]	Upper Washita River (Hemphill)	Sept. 9–12, 1874
Cpl. John James	Upper Washita River (Hemphill)	Sept. 9–12, 1874
Cpl. John J. H. Kelly	Upper Washita River (Hemphill)	Sept. 9–12, 1874
Pvt. Thomas Kelly	Upper Washita River (Hemphill)	Sept. 9–12, 1874
Sgt. George K. Kitchen	Upper Washita River (Hemphill)	Sept. 9–12, 1874
Cpl. John W. Knox	Upper Washita River (Hemphill)	Sept. 9–12, 1874
Sgt. William Koelpin	Upper Washita River (Hemphill)	Sept. 9–12, 1874
Sgt. John Mitchell	Upper Washita River (Hemphill)	Sept. 9–12, 1874

Cpl. William W. Morris	Upper Washita River (Hemphill)	Sept. 9–12, 1874
Sgt. Frederick S. Neilon[7]	Upper Washita River (Hemphill)	Sept. 9–12, 1874
Cpl. Edward C. Sharpless	Upper Washita River (Hemphill)	Sept. 9–12, 1874
Sgt. Josiah J. Pennsyl	Upper Washita River (Hemphill)	Sept. 9–12, 1874
Scout Amos Chapman[8]	Buffalo Wallow (Hemphill)	Sept. 12, 1874
Scout William Dixon[9]	Buffalo Wallow (Hemphill)	Sept. 12, 1874
Pvt. John Harrington	Buffalo Wallow (Hemphill)	Sept. 12, 1874
Pvt. Peter P. Roth	Buffalo Wallow (Hemphill)	Sept. 12, 1874
Pvt. George W. Smith*	Buffalo Wallow (Hemphill)	Sept. 12, 1874
Sgt. Zachariah T. Woodall	Buffalo Wallow (Hemphill)	Sept. 12, 1874
Pvt. Adam Payne	Quitaque Peak (Floyd)	Sept. 20 1874
Pvt. Gregory P. Mahoney	Tule Canyon (Briscoe)	Sept. 27, 1874
Pvt. William McCabe	Tule Canyon (Briscoe)	Sept. 27, 1874
Cpl. Edwin Phoenix	Tule Canyon (Briscoe)	Sept. 27, 1874
Farrier Ernest Veuve	Double Lakes (Lynn)	Nov. 3, 1874
Cpl. John W. Comfort	Tahoka Lake (Lynn)	Nov. 5, 1874
Lt. Frank D. Baldwin[10]	North Fork, McClellan Creek (Gray)	Nov. 8, 1874
Pvt. Frederick H. Bergendahl[11]	Muchaque Valley (Dawson)	Dec. 8, 1874
Pvt. John F. O'Sullivan	Muchaque Valley (Dawson)	Dec. 8, 1874
Lt. Lewis Warrington III[12]	Muchaque Valley (Dawson)	Dec. 8, 1874
Pvt. Pompey Factor	Eagle Nest Crossing (Val Verde)	Apr. 25, 1875
Trumpeter Isaac Payne	Eagle Nest Crossing (Val Verde)	Apr. 25, 1875
Sgt. John Ward	Eagle Nest Crossing (Val Verde)	Apr. 25, 1875
Pvt. Allen Walker	East Fork, Fandango Creek (Jim Hogg)	Dec. 30, 1891

---

* Denotes posthumous award.

[1] John C. Hesse and Joseph K. Wilson were removed from the Army Medal of Honor Roll in 1917 as their deeds had not been performed in actual combat with an armed enemy.

[2] Albee was also cited for gallant actions on October 28, 1869, and those actions likely carried over into surrounding counties.

[3] James Anderson enlisted and was awarded his Medal of Honor under this alias. His real name was James Smythe.

[4] James B. Dosher was removed from the Army Medal of Honor Roll in 1917. He was reinstated by the Department of the Army Board for Correction of Military Records on June 12, 1989.

[5] William Wilson is one of five men to have been awarded two Army Medals of Honor.

[6] Fred S. Hay enlisted and was awarded his Medal of Honor under this alias. His true name was Frederick H. Schwabe.

[7] Frederick S. Neilon was this man's true name. He enlisted and was awarded the Medal of Honor under the alias Frank Singleton.

[8] Amos Chapman was removed from the Army Medal of Honor Roll in 1917, but he was reinstated by the Department of the U.S. Army on June 12, 1989.

[9] William Dixon was removed from the Army Medal of Honor Roll in 1917, but his Medal of Honor was reinstated by the U.S. Army on June 12, 1989.

[10] Frank D. Baldwin became one of five men to be granted two Army Medals of Honor. On December 3, 1891, he was granted his first for a deed performed at the battle of Peachtree Creek, Georgia, on July 20, 1864. The Medal of Honor awarded for his gallantry near McClellan Creek, Texas, was not granted until November 28, 1894.

[11] Mushaway Valley is the canyon directly west of Mushaway Peak. On army maps and correspondence it is referred to as Muchaque.

[12] Warrington's Medal of Honor was issued on April 12, 1875, thus making his the only one issued to an officer at the time of his deed and not retroactively awarded as were all other awards to officers during the Indian Wars.

Appendix B

——— ★ ———

General and Physical Statistics for Recipients[1]

Place of Birth

United States	43			Foreign Born	23
Arkansas	1	Michigan	3	Canada	1
Connecticut	1	Missouri	1	England	5
District of Columbia	1	New Hampshire	2	Germany	3
Florida	1	New Jersey	1	Ireland	9
Illinois	1	New York	5	Mexico	2
Iowa	1	Ohio	4	Scotland	1
Kentucky	2	Pennsylvania	6	Sweden	1
Louisiana	1	Tennessee	2	Switerland	1
Maine	3	Virginia	1		
Maryland	1	West Virginia	1		
Massachusetts	3	Wisconsin	1		

Age at Time of Deed

Mean (average)
26.2 years

Youngest 18
(John O'Sullivan)

Oldest 44
(James B. Dosher)

Lifespan[2]

Mean (average)
60.4 years

Last (oldest) surviving
recipient to die 91
(Robert G. Carter)

First (youngest) recipient
to die 32
(Lewis Warrington)

Height

Mean (average)
5'8"

Shortest 5'4"
(John O'Sullivan)

Tallest 6'1"
(George Kitchen)

Race

White	62
Black	5

Literacy[3]

Literate	61 (91%)
Illiterate	6 (9%)

461

[1] Statistics on recipient physical characteristics do not include those for recipients Albee, Hesseltine, Warrington, Baldwin, and Dosher, which were not available. The weight of those men who enlisted in the U.S. Army was rarely recorded in the enlistment registers and thus weight information was unavailable.

[2] Life span is based upon the known life span of fifty-four recipients and does not include the longevity of the four posthumous awardees.

[3] Statistics about literacy were compiled from enlistment papers, pension files, and from correspondence with the Adjutant General's Office.

Appendix C

—— ☆ ——

LOCATIONS OF INTERMENT OF MEDAL OF HONOR RECIPIENTS
WHO EARNED THEIR MEDALS IN THE STATE OF TEXAS

ARIZONA

Pima City Cemetery
Pennsyl, Josiah J.

CALIFORNIA

Los Angeles–Los Angeles National Cemetery
Eldridge, George H.
Phoenix, Edwin
Porter, Samuel

San Francisco–San Francisco National Cemetery
Foster, William
Mitchell, John
Wilson, William

COLORADO

La Junta–City Cemetery
May, John

DISTRICT OF COLUMBIA

Arlington National Cemetery
Albee, George E.
Baldwin, Frank D.
Carter, Robert G.
Woodall, Zachariah T.

Soldiers' Home National Cemetery
Connor, John
James, John

Congressional Cemetery
    Hesse, John C.[1]

ILLINOIS

Chicago–Rosehill Cemetery
    Watson, James C.

Springfield–Oak Ridge Cemetery
    Kelly, John J. H.

KANSAS

Leavenworth–Mt. Calvary Cemetery
    Kelly, Thomas

MASSACHUSETTS

Arlington–St. Paul's Cemetery
    Larkin, David
    Neilon, Frederick S.

Malden–Holy Cross Cemetery
    Keating, Daniel

Melrose–Wyoming Cemetery
    Hesseltine, Francis S.

MISSOURI

St. Louis–Jefferson Barracks National Cemetery
    Stokes, Alonzo

St. Louis–St. Peter's Cemetery
    Smythe, James[2]

MONTANA

Missoula–City Cemetery
    Veuve, Ernest

NEBRASKA

Maxwell–Fort McPherson National Cemetery
    Stance, Emanuel

NEW JERSEY

Bayonne–New York Bay Cemetery
    Winterbottom, William

Leonardo–Bayview Cemetery
    Schwabe, Frederick H.

NEW MEXICO

Mountainair–City Cemetery
    Sharpless, Edward C.

NEW YORK

New York City (Queens)–Lutheran Cemetery
    Koelpin, William
New York City (Manhattan)–Calvary Cemetery
    O'Sullivan, John F.
New York City (Queens)–Calvary Cemetery
    McNamara, William

OHIO

Bellefontaine–City Cemetery
    Pratt, James N.

OKLAHOMA

Seiling–Brumfield Cemetery
    Chapman, Amos

PENNSYLVANIA

Lewistown–St. Mark's Episcopal Cemetery
    Rankin, William

New Cumberland–Mt. Olivet Cemetery
    Kirk, John

Philadelphia (Rockledge)–Mt. Peace Cemetery
    Comfort, John W.

SOUTH CAROLINA

Columbia–Columbia National Cemetery
    Wilson, Joseph K.[3]

TEXAS

Adobe Walls
    Dixon, William

Barton's Chapel–Bottoms Family Cemetery
    Dosher, James B.

Brackettville–Masonic Cemetery
  Windus, Claron A.

Brackettville–Seminole-Negro Indian Scout Cemetery
  Factor, Pompey
  Payne, Adam
  Payne, Isaac[4]
  Ward, John

Buffalo Wallow Battleground
  Smith, George W.[5]

Laredo–Catholic Cemetery
  Walker, Allen

San Antonio–San Antonio National Cemetery
  DeArmond, William[6]
  Given, John J.[7]
  Harrington, John
  McMaster, Henry A.
  Neal, Solon D.
  Smith, George W.
  Warrington, Lewis

San Antonio–St. Mary's Cemetery
  Kitchen, George K.

GREAT BRITAIN
  Newcastle on Tyne–Elswick Cemetery
    Bell, George H.

GERMANY
  Rottenmunster–City Cemetery
    Roth, Peter P.

MEXICO
  Musquiz/Nacimiento–Bacune Btimi Cemetery
    Payne, Isaac[8]

SWEDEN
  Goteberg–Ostra Kyrkcogardeu, The Cast Cemetery
    Bergendahl, Frederick H.

UNKNOWN

Bowden, Samuel
Branagan, Edward
Kerrigan, Thomas
Knox, John W.
Mahoney, Gregory P.
McCabe, William
McDonnold, Franklin M. (McDonald)
Morris, William W.
Smith, Charles E.
Welch, Michael
Wilson, Benjamin

---

[1] John C. Hesse was removed from the official Army Medal of Honor Roll in 1917 as his deed had not been performed in actual armed conflict with the enemy.

[2] This man served and was awarded his Army Medal of Honor under the alias of James Anderson. His headstone denotes his true name.

[3] Removed from the official Army Medal of Honor Roll in 1917.

[4] "In Memoriam" headstone. He is believed to be buried in Musquiz, Mexico.

[5] Buried on the field of battle. Remains were never recovered. The headstone at San Antonio National Cemetery is "In Memoriam."

[6] Buried on the field of battle. Remains were never recovered. The headstone at San Antonio National Cemetery is "In Memoriam."

[7] Remains were never recovered from the field of battle. The headstone at San Antonio National Cemetery is "In Memoriam."

[8] Thought to have died near Musquez/Nacimiento, Mexico. The headstone at the Seminole-Negro Indian Scout Cemetery at Brackettville is "In Memoriam."

Appendix D

——— ✯ ———

CONGRESSIONAL MEDAL OF HONOR RECIPIENTS: TEXAN

1. ADAMS, Lucian. Sgt., USA. (B-Port Arthur), WWII.

*2. AUSTIN, Oscar P. PFC, USMC. (B-Nacogdoches; LD-Arizona), VN.

3. AUSTIN, William G. Sgt., USA. (B-Galveston), IW.

*4. ANDERSON, Richard A. L/Cpl., USMC. (B-Washington D.C; E, LD-Houston), VN.

*5. BARKLEY, David B. Pvt., USA. (B-Laredo), WWI.

6. BENAVIDEZ, Roy P. SSgt., USA. (B-Cuero), VN.

*7. BENNETT, Steven L. Capt., USAF. (B-Palestine; LD-Lousiana), VN.

8. BOLTON, Cecil H. 1st Lt., USA. (B-Florida; LD-San Antonio), WWII.

*9. BORDELON, William J. SSgt., USMC. (B-San Antonio), WWII.

*10. CARSWELL, Horace S. Jr. Major, USAF. (B-Fort Worth), WWII.

11. COLE, Robert G. Lt. Col., USA. (B-San Antonio), WWII.

*12. CREEK, Thomas E. L/Cpl., USMC. (B-Missouri; LD-Amarillo), VN.

13. DAVILA, Rudolph B. Sgt., USA. (B-El Paso; E, LD-California), WWII.

*14. DAVIS, George A. Jr. Major, USAF. (B-Dublin), Korea.

15. DEALEY, Samuel D. Commander, USN. (B-Dallas), WWII.

16. DEETLINE, Frederick. Pvt., USA. (B-Germany; LD-San Antonio), IW.

17. DIXON, William. Scout, USA. (B-West Virginia; E, LD-Texas), IW.

18. DOSHER, James B. Post Guide, USA (B-Tennessee; E, LD-Jacksboro), IW.

19. EDWARDS, Daniel R. PFC, USA. (B-Mooreville; LD-Arkansas), WWI.

20. FACTOR, Pompey. Pvt., Seminole-Negro Scouts. (B-Arkansas; LD-Brackettville), IW.

21. FIELDS, James H. 1st Lt., USA. (B-Caddo), WWII.

*22. FOWLER, Thomas W. 2nd Lt., USA. (B-Wichita Falls), WWII.

23. FERGUSON, Frederick E. CWO, USA. (B-Pilot Grove; LD-Arizona), VN.

24. FREEMAN, Archibald. Pvt., USA. (B-New York; LD-Groesbeck), CW.

25. GALER, Robert E. Major, USMC. (B-Washington; LD-Dallas), WWII.

26. GARCIA, Marcario. SSgt., USA. (B-Mexico; LD-Alief), WWII.

*27. GONZALES, Alfredo. Sgt., USMC. (B-Edinburg), VN.

*28. GRAVES, Terrence C. 2nd Lt., USA. (B-Corpus Christi; LD-New York), VN.

*29. GUILLEN, Ambrosio. Sgt., USMC. (B-Colorado; E, LD-El Paso), Korea.

30. HARRELL, William G. Sgt, USMC. (B-Rio Grande City), WWII.

31. HARRINGTON, John. Pvt., USA. (B-Michigan; LD-San Antonio), IW.

*32. HARRIS, James L. 2nd Lt., USA. (B-Hillsboro), WWII.

33. HARRISON, William K. Commander, USN. (B-Waco), MD.

*34. HAWKINS, William D. 1st.Lt., USMC (B-Kansas; E, LD-El Paso), WWII.

35. HAYDEN, David E. HA/lc., USN. (B-Florence), WWI.

36. HERRERA, Silvestre S. PFC., USA. (B-El Paso), WWII.

37. HOLLAND, Milton M. Sgt/Major, USA. (B-Austin; LD-Maryland), CW.

38. HOWZE, Robert L. 2nd Lt., USA. (B-Overton), IW.

*39. HUGHES, Lloyd H. 2nd Lt., USAF. (B-Louisana; LD-San Antonio), WW II.

*40. HUTCHINS, Johnnie D. SFC., USN. (B-Weimar), WWII.

41. KANE, John R. Colonel, USAF. (B-McGregor), WWII.

42. KEARBY, Neel E. Colonel, USAF. (B-Wichita Falls), WWII.

*43. KEATHLEY, George D. SSgt., USA. (B-Olney), WWII.

*44. KEITH, Miguel. L/Cpl., USMC. (B-San Antonio; LD-Nebraska), VN.

*45. KILMER, John E. Hospitalman, USN. (B-Illinois; LD-San Antonio), Korea.

*46. KIMBRO, Truman. T/4g., USA. (B-Madisonville), WWII.

47. KITCHEN, George K. Sgt., USA. (B-Pennsylvania; LD-San Antonio), IW.

*48. KNIGHT, Jack L. 1st Lt., USA. (B-Garner), WWII.

49. KNIGHT, Joseph F. Sgt., USA. (B-Illinois; LD-Lubbock), IW.

*50. KNIGHT, Raymond L. lst Lt., USAF. (B-Katy), WWII.

*51. LAW, Robert D. Spc/4c., USA. (B-Fort Worth), VN.

*52. LEE, Milton A. PFC., USA. (B-Louisiana; LD-San Antonio), VN.

*53. LEONARD, Turney W. 1st Lt., USA. (B-Dallas), WWII.

54. LOGAN, James M. Sgt., USA. (B-McNeil), WWII.

55. LOPEZ, Jose M. Sgt., USA. (B-Mission), WWII.

*56. LUMMUS, Jack. 1st Lt., USMC. (B-Ennis), WWII.

*57. MARTINEZ, Benito. Cpl., USA. (B-Fort Hancock), Korea.

*58. MATHIS, Jack W. 1st Lt., USAF. (B-San Angelo), WWII.

59. McCABE, William Pvt., USA. (B-N. Ireland; E. LD-Eagle Pass), IW.

60. McCLEERY, Finnis D. PSgt., USA. (B-Stephenville), VN.

61. McLENNON, John. Musician, USA. (B-Fort Belknap), IW.

62. McNERNEY, David H. 1st Sgt., USA. (B-Massachusetts; LD-Crosby), VN.

*63. MITCHELL, Frank N. lst Lt, USMC. (B-Indian Gap), Korea.

64. MOORE, William. Boatswain, USN. (B-Massachusetts; LD-Austin), CW.

*65. MORELAND, Whitt L. PFC., USMC. (B-Waco: LD-Arkansas), Korea.

66. MORGAN, John C. 2nd Lt., USAF. (B-Vernon; LD-Nebraska), WWII.

67. MURPHY, Audie L. 1st Lt., USA. (B-Farmersville), WWII.

68. NASH, James J. Pvt., USA. (B-Kentucky; LD-San Antonio), SAW.

69. NEAL, Solon D. Pvt., USA. (B-New Hampshire; LD-San Antonio), IW.

70. O'BRIEN, George H., Jr. 2nd Lt., USMC. (B-Fort Worth), Korea.

71. PAYNE, Adam. Pvt. USA. (B-Florida; LD-Brackettville), IW.

72. PAYNE, Isaac. Pvt., Seminole Negro Scouts. (B-Mexico; LD-Brackettville), IW.

73. PENDLETON, Charles F. Cpl., USA. (B-Tennessee; LD-Fort Worth). Korea.

*74. ROAN, Charles H. PFC., USMC. (B-Claude), WWII.

75. ROBIE, George F. 1st Lt., USA. (B-New Hampshire; LD-Galveston), CW.

*76. ROBINSON, James E. 1st Lt., USA. (B-Ohio; E, LD-Texas), WWII.

77. RODRIGUEZ Cleto. PFC., USA. (B-San Marcos), WWII.

78. SAMPLER, Samuel M. Cpl., USA. (B-Decatur; LD-Florida), WWI.

79. SASSER, Clarence E. Spc/5c., USA. (B-Chenango), VN.

80. SHELTON, George M. Pvt., USA. (B-Brownwood; LD-California), PI.

*81. STEINDAM, Russell A. lst Lt, USA. (B-Austin), VN.

82. STONE, James L. lstLt., USA. (B-Arkansas; E. LD-Texas), Korea.

83. TURNER, George B. PFC., USA. (B-Longview), WWII.

84. WALKER, Allen. Pvt., USA. (B-Indiana; LD-Laredo), Garza Rebellion-MD.

*85. WALLACE, Herman C. PFC., USA. (B-Oklahoma; E, LD-Lubbock), WWII.

86. WARD, John. Sgt., Seminole-Negro Scouts. (B-Arkansas; LD-Brackettville), IW.

*87. WATKINS, Travis E. M/Sgt., USA. (B-Arkansas; E, LD-Gladewater), Korea.

88. WELD, Seth L. Cpl., USA. (B-Maryland; LD-San Antonio), PI.

89. WHEELER, George H. S/1c., USN. (B-San Antonio), Chile.

90. WHITELEY, Eli L. 1st Lt., USA. (B-Florence), WWII.

*91. WILSON, Alfred M. PFC., USMC. (B-Illinois; LD)-Odessa), VN.

 92. WINDUS, Claron A. Pvt., USA. (B-Wisconsin: LD-Brackettville), IW.

*93. YOUNG, Marvin R. SSgt., USA. (B-Alpine), VN.

*Posthumous

Abbreviations:

USA	United States Army
USAF	United States Air Force (Army Air Corp)
USMC	United States Marine Corps
USN	United States Navy
B	Birthplace
E	Recipient resided in Texas prior to enlistment in military service for an unknown period of time
LD	Legal Domicile (criterion used for this classification would be that the recipient maintained a residence, was gainfully employed and paid local taxes in Texas; recipient also lived most of his life in Texas and is buried therein)
CW	Civil War
IW	Indian Wars
SAW	Spanish-American War
PI	Philippine Insurrection
MD	Mexican Disturbances
WWI	World War I
WWII	World War II
VN	Vietnam

Posthumous award ceremonies to next of kin, known to have taken place in Texas, are as follows:

Johnnie D. Hutchins: Sam Houston Colisum (Houston), September 1944.

Jack L. Knight: Camp Walters (Weatherford), June 15, 1945.

Raymond L. Knight: J. H. Reagan High School Auditorium (Houston), October 22, 1945.

George A. Davis: Reese AFB (Lubbock), May 14, 1954.

Appendix E

——— ✪ ———

MEDAL OF HONOR RECIPIENTS INTERRED IN TEXAS

1. ANDERSON, Richard A. Forest Park Lawndale Cemetery, Houston
2. BARKLEY, David B. San Antonio National Cemetery, San Antonio
3. BARNES, William H.[1] San Antonio National Cemetery, San Antonio
4. BOLTON, Cecil H. Fort Sam Houston National Cemetery, San Antonio
5. BORDELON, William J. Fort Sam Houston National Cemetery, San Antonio
6. BOWEN, Chester B. Greenwood Cemetery, Weatherford
7. BRATLING, Frank[2] Fort Bliss National Cemetery, El Paso
8. CARSWELL, Horace S. Jr. Oakwood Cemetery, Fort Worth
9. CREEK, Thomas E. Llano Cemetery, Amarillo
10. DAVIS, George A. Jr.[3] Lubbock City Cemetery, Lubbock
11. DeARMOND, William[4] San Antonio National Cemetery, San Antonio
12. DEETLINE, Frederick San Antonio National Cemetery, San Antonio
13. DIXON, William Adobe Walls Memorial, south of Spearman
14. DOSHER, James B. Bottoms Family Cemetery, Barton Chapel
15. FACTOR, Pompey Seminole-Negro Indian Scout Cemetery, Brackettville
16. FALCOTT, Henry San Antonio National Cemetery, San Antonio
17. FIELDS, James H. Houston National Cemetery, Houston
18. FOWLER, Thomas W. Crestview Memorial Park, Wichita Falls
19. FREEMAN, Archibald Bethel Cemetery, Groesbeck
20. GARCIA, Marcario Houston National Cemetery, Houston
21. GIVEN, John J.[5] San Antonio National Cemetery, San Antonio
22. GONZALES, Alfredo Hillcrest Cemetery, Edinburg
23. GUILLEN, Ambrosio Fort Bliss National Cemetery, El Paso
24. HARRELL, William G. Fort Sam Houston National Cemetery, San Antonio
25. HARRINGTON, John San Antonio National Cemetery, San Antonio

26. HARRIS, James L.   Ridge Park Cemetery, Hillsboro
27. HOOKER, George[6]   Fort Bliss National Cemetery, El Paso
28. HUGHES, Lloyd H.   Fort Sam Houston National Cemetery, San Antonio
29. HUTCHINS, Johnnie D.   Lakeside Cemetery, Eagle Lake
30. KEARBY, Neel E.   Hillcrest Memorial Park, Dallas
31. KILMER, John E.   San Jose Burial Park, San Antonio
32. KITCHEN, George K.   St. Mary's Cemetery, San Antonio
33. KNIGHT, Jack L.   Holder's Memorial Chapel Cemetery, Cool
34. KNIGHT, Joseph F.   Lubbock City Cemetery, Lubbock
35. KNIGHT, Raymond L.   Houston National Cemtery, Houston
36. LAW, Robert D.   Mt. Olive Cemetery, Fort Worth
37. LEE, Milton A.   Fort Sam Houston National Cemetery, San Antonio
38. LEONARD, Turney W.   Grove Hill Memorial Park, Dallas
39. LUMMUS, Jack   Myrtle Cemetery, Ennis
40. MARTINEZ, Benito[7]   Fort Bliss National Cemetery, El Paso
41. MATHIS, Jack W.   Fairmount Cemetery, San Angelo
42. McMASTER, Henry A.   San Antonio National Cemetery, San Antonio
43. MITCHELL, Frank N.[8]   City Park, Roaring Springs
44. MOORE, William   Oakwood Cemetery, Austin
45. MURPHY, Daniel J.   Oakwood Cemetery, Jefferson
46. NASH, James J.   San Antonio National Cemetery, San Antonio
47. NEAL, Solon D.   San Antonio National Cemetery, San Antonio
48. PAYNE, Adam   Seminole-Negro Indian Scout Cemetery, Brackettville
49. PAYNE, Isaac   Seminole-Negro Indian Scout Cemetery, Brackettville
50. PENDLETON, Charles F.   Laurel Land Memorial Cemetery, Fort Worth
51. ROBIE, George F.   New City Cemetery, Galveston
52. ROBINSON, James E. Jr.   Fort Sam Houston National Cemetery, San Antonio
53. RODRIGUEZ, Cleto   Fort Sam Houston National Cemetery, San Antonio
54. SUHLER, Simon[9]   San Antonio National Cemetery, San Antonio
55. SMITH, George W.[10]   San Antonio National Cemetery, San Antonio
56. STEINDAM, Russell A.   Restland Memorial Park, Dallas
57. WALKER, Allen   Catholic Cemetery, Laredo
58. WALLACE, Herman C.   Lubbock City Cemetery, Lubbock

59. WARD, John	Seminole-Negro Indian Scout Cemetery, Brackettville
60. WARRINGTON, Lewis	San Antonio National Cemetery, San Antonio
61. WATKINS, Travis E.	Gladewater Memorial Park, Gladewater
62. WELD, Seth L.	Fort Sam Houston National Cemetery, San Antonio
63. WHITELEY, Eli L.	College Station City Cemetery, College Station
64. WILSON, Alfred M.	Sunset Memorial Cemetery, Odessa
65. WINDUS, Claron A.	Masonic Cemetery, Brackettville
66. WOODALL, William H.[11]	San Antonio National Cemetery, San Antonio
67. YOUNG, Marvin R.	Sunset Memorial Cemetery, Odessa

---

[1] Reinterred at San Antonio in 1867 from Indianola, Texas, as an unknown.

[2] Reinterred at Fort Bliss from Fort McRae, New Mexico.

[3] Headstone is "In Memoriam." Remains were never recovered from crash site near Sinnuiju, North Korea.

[4] Headstone is "In Memoriam." Sergeant DeArmond's remains were interred in an unmarked grave near the Washita River in Hemphill County, Texas.

[5] Headstone is "In Memoriam" as Corporal Given's body was never recovered from battlefield in Archer County, Texas.

[6] Headstone is "In Memoriam." Killed in action near Tonto Creek, Arizona, and his remains were never recovered.

[7] Originally interred at Fort Hancock Cemetery and reinterred at Fort Bliss in 1987.

[8] Memorialized in city park. His remains were never recovered from battlefield near Hansan-ni, South Korea.

[9] This man received his medal under the alias of Charles Gardner. He is the only known Jewish recipient during the Indian Wars.

[10] Headstone is "In Memoriam." Remains were buried where he fell and were never recovered from the location in Hemphill County, Texas, known as the Buffalo Wallow Battleground.

[11] Headstone is "In Memoriam." After his death in Mexico, he was buried in an inaccessible locale and his remains have never been recovered.

Additional note: Pvt. Charles C. Roan, a World War II U.S. Marine Corps recipient, is interred at the American Battlefield Memorial Commission Cemetery in Manilla, Philipine Islands. An "In Memoriam" marker to him has been erected in the City Cemetery at Claude, Texas.

Appendix F

—— ✭ ——

CONGRESSIONAL MEDAL OF HONOR: LOCATION OF DEEDS

UNITED STATES   1,990

Alabama	122	Nebraska	13
Alaska	1	Nevada	1
Arizona	164	New Mexico	18
Arkansas	11	New York	9
California	15	North Carolina	109
Colorado	12	Oklahoma	1
Connecticut	1	Oregon	1
District of Columbia	4	Pennsylvania	65
Florida	12	Rhode Island	7
Georgia	87	South Carolina	35
Hawaii	19	South Dakota	30
Idaho	4	Tennessee	103
Kansas	13	Texas	68
Kentucky	3	Utah	1
Louisiana	59	Virginia	707
Maine	3	West Virginia	4
Maryland	29	Wyoming	5
Massachusetts	1		
Minnesota	1		
Mississippi	155		
Missouri	8		
Montana	89		

FOREIGN	1,310		
Belgium	20	Morocco	3
Brazil	3	Nicaragua	10
Burma	1	North Pole	2
Canada	1	Pacific Islands	138
Chile	3	Peru	4
China	63	Philippine Islands	141
Cuba	104	Portugal	2
Dominican Republic	6	Romania	7
Egypt	2	Sicily	5
France	187	Somalia	2
Germany	50	Tunisia	3
Haiti	8	Uruguay	2
Holland	3	Vietnam	260
Italy	64		
Japan	5	UNSPECIFIED GEOGRAPHICAL	
Korea	146	LOCATIONS	
Liberia	2	On board ships	121
Luxembourg	2	Air combat	5
Mexico	61	Other	32

NOTES

Whenever locations for U.S. Navy Medal of Honor line of profession awards were given, the location was accredited to the state or nation in whichever port the ship was located rather than as an unspecified on-board ship award.

Nine Civil War awards were given for gallantry during the various actions of a vessel and specific locations were virtually impossible to pinpoint.

Several Indian War and Civil War deeds crossed over several political boundaries and were classified as unspecified locations rather than deal with fractional credits.

Other unspecified location awards would include awards to Lindbergh, Walker, and the nine unknown.

The above figures include retroactive awards for the Civil War, Spanish-American War, World Wars I and II, and Vietnam through July 12, 2002, including the J. Okubo special waiver award.

Index

---★---

477

Soldier Mound (Dickens County), 43, 87

Spencer carbines, 55, 62, 66, 88, 368 nn.14, 17

Springfield rifles, 115, 144, 146, 182, 186, 244, 249, 368 n.14, 392 n.22

Staked Plains (a.k.a. Llano Estacado) [*See* High Plains]

Stance, Emanuel, Sgt.: 360 n.18; MoH deed, 54–56; letter acknowledging receipt of MoH, 50, 57; biography, 320–321

Stanford, J. L., 149

Stanley, D. S., Gen., 246–247, 251

Stanton, Edward, xii

Star of the West, USS, 12, 348 n.3

Steiger, _____, Sgt., 165

Steward, R., Pvt. , 70

Stokes, Alonzo, Sgt.: 61, 65, 74 ; MoH deed, 67, 69; biography, 321–323

Stone Calf (Cheyenne chief), 191, 216

Strong, Henry, Guide, 136, 180, 184, 186, 196–199

Strupp, Otto, Sgt., 3–4

Supply Camp, R. S. Mackenzie's, 394–395 n.5

Sweetwater Creek (Wheeler County), 144, 151, 158, 166; couriers (Sharpless and Morris) besieged near, 150–151, 387 n.31

— T —

Tabananica (Comanche chief), 191, 208

Tafoya, Francisco (a.k.a. Johnson), 179–181, 396–397, n.1

Tafoya, José P.: 193, 196, 223, 402 n.8

Tahoka Lake (*See* Laguna Tahoka)

Tatum, Lawrie, 60, 77, 78, 80, 82, 86, 87, 139

Taylor, J. H., Col., 223

Taylor, Zachary, Gen., lost gold medal at San Antonio in 1848, 5

Tenth U.S. Cavalry, 77

Tenth U.S. Infantry, 187

Terrell, H. J., AAS, 79–81

Texans, list of MoH awards accredited to, 468–471 App. D

Texas A&M University, 4–6

Texas frontier: 36, 78, 85, 101, 112, 233; raids upon by Indians, Comancheros and Mexicans, 36, 51–52, 59–60, 78, 86, 98, 101–105, 111, 125–126, 240; R. S. Mackenzie placed in charge of affairs on, 36

Texas Legislature, commends R. S. Mackenzie and his troops, 382 n.40

Texas, Military Department of, 83, 245, 251

Texas Rangers, 101, 240–241, 247–249

Texas (Tonkawa Indian woman), 94

Third U.S. Cavalry, 241, 245–247

Thirteenth Maine Volunteer Infantry, 22–31

Thompson, W. A., Lt., 133, 184, 194, 197, 222

Thompson's Canyon (sub-canyon of Yellowhouse–Rescate Canyon in Lubbock County), 403 n.23

Threemile Creek (Hemphill County), 166

Tinarte (Lipan–Apache), 397 n.2

To-hausen (Kiowa chief), 192, 221

Tongue River (a.k.a. South Fork of Pease River), 171

Tonkawa Indian Scouts (*See* Scouts)

Townsend, E. D., Adj. Gen., 74, 117, 177, 187, 228–229

Treasury, Department of, 138, 168, 364 n.37, 388 n.35

Treaty of Medicine Lodge Creek, Kansas (1867), 35–36, 60, 120

Trinity River, West Fork of, 72, 79, 119

Tule Canyon, 156, 180–181, 185–187

Tupper, T. C., Capt., 78–79

Twenty-fourth U.S. Infantry, 124, 127–128

Twenty-fifth U.S. Infantry, 234

— U —

Upper Washita River, action near on September 9–14, 1874, 140–153

U.S. Air Force (also Army Air Corp): MoH recipients, accredited to Texans, 468–471 App. D; Texans as a percentage of all Army Air Corp, WWII awards, 6; MoH presentation ceremonies in Texas

About the Author

Charles M. Neal Jr. taught Texas and American history in the Aldine Independent School District in Houston, Texas, for twenty-five years. His interest in the frontier U.S. Army was fostered by his father, a mounted rifleman in the First Cavalry Division of the 1930s at Fort Clark, Texas. Neal holds degrees in history from Southwest Texas and Sam Houston State Universities and is a thirty-year member of the Medal of Honor Historical Society. He currently resides in Porter, Texas.

Colophon

This book is set in Times, which was designed by Stanley Morison for use in *The Times* of London. It was adopted for its legibility and suitability for modern printing and first appeared in *The Times* on October 3, 1932. The display faces are Oxford and Palatino. The book was printed by Edwards Brothers on 55# Gladfelter in Lillington, North Carolina.